The Annals of Bristol in the Nineteenth Century - Primary Source Edition

John Latimer

THE

ANNALS OF BRISTOL

IN THE NINETEENTH CENTURY.

BY

JOHN LATIMER,

EDITOR OF THE BRISTOL MERCURY, 1858-83.

Bristol:

W. & F. MORGAN, CLARE STREET.

1887.

Butler & Tanner,
The Selwood Printing Works,
Frome, and London.

TO

MR. CHARLES SOMERTON,

AND

MR. GEORGE SOMERTON,

WHOSE UNFAILING KINDNESS AND CONSTANT COURTESY

DURING A LITERARY CONNECTION

EXTENDING OVER UPWARDS OF A QUARTER OF A CENTURY

HAVE BEEN AMONGST THE

PLEASANTEST INCIDENTS OF MY LIFE,

AND HAVE

ILLUSTRATED THOSE GENTLER AMENITIES OF LETTERS

WHICH IT IS

GOOD TO REMEMBER AND RECORD.

PREFACE.

The collection of materials with a view to a continuation of Evans's Chronological History of Bristol was begun upwards of twenty years ago by the compiler of this work. The pressure of other literary pursuits, however, caused the project to be deferred from time to time; and it eventually became a question whether, if a supplementary record were to be produced at all, the story of so eventful a century was not deserving of a worthier memorial than the bald epitome of facts and dates which had been originally contemplated. As is not unusual in such labours, the introduction of details in connection with topics of prominent importance threw into relief the meagreness of the rest of the narrative; and it at length seemed desirable—whilst retaining the chronological form adopted at the outset—to attempt a comprehensive sketch of the political, municipal, commercial, and social life of the community during a period which has been hitherto imperfectly treated by local writers.

To what extent the task has been satisfactorily performed must be left to the judgment of the reader. Some may possibly complain that events which they deem important have been inadequately treated, or even omitted. Others may object that incidents in their eyes trivial have received an attention they did not deserve. A third class of critics, again, may disapprove of the expressions of personal opinion which are sometimes, though rarely, introduced. To those who do not find all their conceptions realised, it can only be pleaded, that the work of selecting and narrating historical facts, either in a national or a local point of view, is seldom accomplished so as to satisfy all tastes. Disclaiming any pretension to complete success where faultlessness was perhaps unattainable, the compiler trusts that few occurrences of permanent interest have wholly escaped notice, that his criticisms, where he has ventured to express an opinion, are untinctured by party or sectarian spirit, and that the volume presents as broad and faithful a picture of the period under review as space and materials would allow.

Though the "annals" have been for the most part compiled from the local newspapers—of which many thousand copies have been examined—much new and valuable matter has been derived from official documents, notably from the records and account books of the Corporation, a perusal of which was kindly permitted by Mr. Daniel Travers Burges, the Town Clerk, and Mr. John Tremayne Lane, the City Treasurer. Both gentlemen were also so obliging as to render personal assistance in clearing up points of difficulty, and the former has also contributed some interesting anecdotes of bygone celebrities. A friend who passed away whilst the closing sheets of the work were in the hands of the printer, the late Mr. Edward Greenfield Doggett, Clerk to the Incorporation of the Poor, allowed extracts to be taken from the minute books of that ancient body. Mr. John Taylor, the City Librarian, offered essential service by throwing open the large and curious store of local literature under his charge, and by supplementing it from his private collection. Amongst others to whom the compiler owes grateful thanks may be mentioned the Rev. Canon Norris, Archdeacon of Bristol, the Rev. S. W. Wayte, Mr. F. W. Newton, Secretary to the Charity Trustees, the late Mr. Leonard Bruton, Secretary to the Chamber of Commerce, the Rev. J. M. Wilson, headmaster of Clifton College, the Rev. Talbot Greaves, vicar of Clifton, Mr. Edward C. Sampson, Postmaster of Bristol, Mr. C. H. Hunt, Clerk to the Barton Regis Board of Guardians, Mr. Alderman Naish, Mr. W. Edwards George, Mr. S. H. Swayne, Mr. Josiah Thomas, and Mr. John Lavars. Finally, an especial acknowledgment is due to Mr. William George, an indefatigable antiquary whose knowledge of local history and vast accumulation of rarities rendered his unwearied assistance of peculiar value.

TRELAWNY PLACE,
March, 1887.

THE ANNALS OF BRISTOL

IN THE

NINETEENTH CENTURY.

Before entering upon the chronological record to which the following pages are devoted, a faint attempt to sketch the state of Bristol and its inhabitants at the commencement of the century may not be uninteresting. The great commercial prosperity of the city down to the revolt of the American colonies is a matter of history; and though the subsequent war was disastrous to some distinguished local firms, the vast wealth that continued to flow in from the West India Islands, and the lucrative Spanish wool and wine trades, contributed largely to the well-being of the community, and were advantages on which the merchants of other ports looked with envious admiration. It is true that Bristol had lost its long-cherished title to rank as second city of the kingdom. The marvellous growth of the cotton trade in Lancashire after 1785 had caused a corresponding increase in the exports and imports of Liverpool; and no adequate efforts were made to compete with the upstart rival, either by the introduction of new industries, the reduction of the exorbitant duties levied upon shipping by the Corporation, or the removal of those difficulties in the navigation of the Avon which had tempted commerce to forsake the Bristol Channel for the more commodious Mersey. As is not unfrequently the case in ancient and solidly-founded communities, Bristol was too wealthy to be enterprising, and many of her influential sons, having become rich in the beaten paths of commerce, were opposed through selfishness or indolence to the striking out of new ones. In despite, for example, of the local cheapness of labour and fuel, only one feeble effort was made to introduce cotton spinning. The competition of Yorkshire in cheap woollen goods, which must have been an uphill task against the reputation and skill of the West of England, was contemptuously ignored until men suddenly awoke to the fact that the bulk of the trade was irrevocably lost through northern enterprise. With equally disastrous consequences, the Avon, which from tidal peculiarities could not be entered in safety except by ships specially built for lying on its muddy shores at low water, was left with all its natural defects, as if to deter strangers from venturing in to jostle the old magnates of the Exchange.

The government of the city was conducted on the same narrow-minded principles. Many men of capital, paying large rentals, employing many workmen, and being in every sense entitled to rank as leading citizens, were not "freemen" according to corporate technology; they had consequently no votes at parliamentary elections, and their influence in local government could not have been less if they had been Hottentots. Having wrested their birthright from the inhabitants, the Corporation, self-elected, and repudiating all control, spent a large proportion of the city revenues in the maintenance of ostentatious "state," and in luxurious entertainments to the select circle which found favour in its sight. On the other hand, the duties of civic government were for the most part either evaded or loftily ignored. The paving, lighting, and watching of the city were miserably imperfect. The footways, where they existed, were so narrow that, even a quarter of a century later, the newspapers occasionally congratulated their readers when a week passed away without an accident to pedestrians. These casualties were largely due to what a writer in the *Monthly Magazine* for May, 1799, termed "the barbarous custom of using sledges in the public streets for the conveyance of goods," which appears to have been almost universal. The drivers in descending a slope dragged their sledges against the edge of the pavement; and, as the packages overhung the vehicles, the peril of foot-passengers may be imagined.

The cleansing of all but the leading thoroughfares was generally left to the elements. One of the local newspapers of Nov. 9th, 1799, complained:—"Pigs, goats, and other animals are suffered to wander about the streets with impunity; at the same time the lives of the inhabitants are nightly endangered by heaps of mortar, ashes, and rubbish." The sprinkling of feeble lamps, lighted by the parochial authorities, often became extinct about midnight through lack of oil. From occasional broad insinuations in the public press, the watchmen—frequently decrepit old drunkards, and sometimes worn-out servants of members of the Corporation—were not merely inefficient, but were suspected of conniving at nocturnal offences. Beyond the city boundaries, in Clifton, Cotham, Redland, and the populous eastern suburbs, there was not a single public lamp or a single night-constable. As was natural under such circumstances, burglaries and highway robberies were of constant occurrence, and a vast majority of the criminals escaped detection.

The prevalence of crime, however, contributed to delay that complete separation of the upper and lower classes of citizens which is one of the most striking phenomena of later times. In 1801, with comparatively few exceptions, the merchant dwelt near his warehouses, as the trader lived over his shop; and many narrow and sombre-looking streets, now lined with stores and offices or given up to labouring families, then contained the dwellings of the rich as well as the poor. Though the sanitary conditions of old-fashioned town life, especially in a city which had no public water supply, left much to be desired, they were accompanied by some compensating advantages. There was not that gulf between master and workman which has been deepened if not created by the isolation of the capitalist from the labourer, and disputes between the two classes were arranged without those terrible social conflicts which are amongst the greatest calamities of modern industry. A neighbourly feeling and habit of association also existed amongst the citizens to an extent unknown in our day. "Perhaps there is no place in England," observed the writer in the *Monthly Magazine* already quoted, "where public and social amusements are so little attended to as here." Such pleasures, in fact, were limited to a short theatrical season and to the rare dissipation of a ball or concert. Travelling for purposes of health, relaxation, or amusement was never dreamt of by the trading classes—a fact not very surprising when it is remembered that the speed of stage-coaches averaged only five miles an hour, that the fares were high, that the traveller was almost shaken to pieces through the execrable state of the roads, and that highway robberies formed an inevitable item of each week's news. A holiday sojourn at the seaside was practicable only to the wealthy. The population of the parish of Weston-super-Mare in 1801 numbered 138, only twelve of whom (probably three families) were not dependent on agriculture; and the lodging-house keeper was still in the future. The summer recreation of prosperous tradesmen therefore chiefly consisted in an evening stroll on the Grove or in Queen Square, where the noisy rooks added a rural attraction to the stately mansions of the merchants and to the masts of the sturdy old vessels moored in the river. College Green had also its votaries, for there the youth of Bristol, enrolled as volunteers, trooped to drill after the labours of the day. But the most cherished amusement of middle-aged citizens was an occasional visit to the suburban bowling-greens kept at the Ostrich Inn, over Durdham Down, Stapleton, Totterdown, Brislington, Henbury, and other villages, to which parties of friends resorted to enjoy their grog and tobacco in the country air, and afforded each other mutual protection from footpads on their return. In the long nights of winter, after the dismal tallow candles in the shop windows* had been extinguished, and warerooms had been carefully secured, the parlours of the principal taverns were filled by neighbours eager to exchange the gossip of the day. Almost every citizen had his habitual evening resort; and when a charitable or patriotic subscription was on foot, "the gentlemen frequenting" the Bush, the White Lion, the Rummer, or the Mulberry Tree, would sometimes club upwards of fifty guineas in token of their sympathy.

Conviviality, as may be supposed, was often carried to excess. In fact, entire sobriety was commonly regarded as more contemptible than drunkenness, and there is abundant evidence that a "three-bottle man" had fewer censors than admirers. At the dinner of the Parent Colston Society in 1865, an old member, whose father had also belonged to the society, described the manner in which the anniversary was celebrated about the beginning of the century. The party assembled for dinner at four o'clock (an unusually late hour in those days), had oysters at nine, and grilled bones at four in the morning. Drinking was then resumed until the time came for breakfast, which was always hot and sumptuous, being made out of the presentable remains of the previous day's banquet. The example of the richer classes was followed, as far as their means would allow, by the poor, and in spite of the multitudinous public-houses few trades were so prosperous as that of the innkeeper. Schools, on the other hand, were few in number and bad in quality — facts which appear to have been regarded with great equanimity, for the general committee of the

* By a common understanding, the number of candles in each window was limited to two. According to a tradition preserved by Mr. Leech, an old trader who had been alarmed by the competition of a new rival, was relieved of apprehension when the latter took to lighting up an additional dip: such reckless extravagance could end only in ruin. "Open" shops—that is, shops with unglazed windows—were rapidly disappearing at the beginning of the century, but there was one in High Street until 1824; and another, at 23, Castle Street, kept by a brushmaker, lingered until 1827, if not later.

local Sunday-schools reported in 1786 that "the instruction to be obtained at a Sunday-school is fully adequate to all the purposes of the lower classes of people." Three-fourths of the labouring community thus attained mature age wholly illiterate, and many of the remainder gradually became so owing to the literary destitution in which they lived. Books were so dear that few were purchased by the trading class. And when the paltry little newspapers of the time cost sixpence each, while the average wages of working men did not reach 16*s.* a week, it is not difficult to imagine the scantiness of political knowledge amongst the masses.

As if the mental deprivation of the people was not sufficiently degrading in its tendency, the legislature lent its aid to make matters worse. It was at that time a capital felony to pick a pocket or to steal a pewter pot; and constant executions took place of men, women, and even boys and girls, for crimes now deemed deserving of only a few months' imprisonment. Persons merely suspected of offences were treated whilst awaiting their trial with abominable cruelty; ruffianly press gangs, trampling upon the liberty of the subject, seized upon unhappy sailors as they reached homo after long voyages, and dragged them from their families for lifelong servitude in the navy; public whippings and the punishment of the pillory took place in the principal streets after almost every quarter session.

Brutalized by scenes to which the law lent its sanction, the poor plunged in so-called amusements of a congenial character. Bull-baiting, dog-fighting, badger-baiting, cock-fighting, had their devoted admirers; but pugilism was the especial delight of Bristolians, some of whom attained national fame for their tenacity and "science." It must be added that these inhuman sports, so far from being disapproved, were lauded and patronized by distinguished politicians and men of fashion. Members of the Royal Family were not ashamed to be present at a prize-fight, while the services of a practised "bruiser" were in request by political agents at every contested election. One more social fact of the period is worthy of record. Down to 1800, nearly one-tenth of all the deaths in the kingdom were due to small-pox, and a large proportion of the population, in Bristol as elsewhere, had their faces disfigured by that terrible disease. The beneficent discovery of vaccination by a Gloucestershire worthy began, however, to be largely recognised in 1801, and in a few years the ravages of the malady sank to insignificance.

The nineteenth century opened gloomily. The war with France during the previous seven years had doubled the national debt and imposed a constantly increasing burden of taxation on the people, whilst the extensive conquests of the French on the Continent, coupled with the armed neutrality organized by Russia against England, had caused great embarrassment to commerce and deprived the consumer of foreign supplies of corn. The latter circumstance was the more calamitous inasmuch as the domestic crops, which had been deficient for four successive years, produced scarcely half of their average yield in 1800. In January, 1801, the official price of wheat in Gloucestershire stood at 169*s.* 6*d.* per quarter. Various measures were adopted by Parliament to avert the effects of the famine. Bounties were offered upon imports of grain and fish. The distillation of corn was forbidden. The manufacture of starch was suspended for a twelvemonth. Millers were subjected to supervision by the Excise and to a legal standard of profits, and they were prohibited from manufacturing fine flour. Bakers were allowed to make brown bread only, and penalties were imposed on those who sold bread less than twenty-four hours old, or who heated stale bread for the purpose of stimulating the consumer's appetite. [One Bristol baker was mulcted in a fine of £19 10*s.*, and a large quantity of his bread was confiscated, for infringing the stale bread laws.]

Private ingenuity was racked to assist the efforts of the legislature. The mayor of Bristol, following the example of many of the nobility, announced that the Mansion-house dinners would be restricted to a single course; the serving of bread at "afternoon tea" was given up; pastry of every kind was tabooed from the tables of the rich; wearers of hair-powder, an article which had been almost universally used by the upper classes of both sexes, adopted various substitutes for flour, or dropped the practice altogether; poultices at public institutions were ordered to be made of linseed or turnips; persons in receipt of relief from the poor laws were forbidden to keep dogs. The Corporation of Bristol, which had voted £500 in the previous year for purchasing corn, offered premiums for importations of potatoes, and promised loans without interest to fishermen for fitting out additional boats. [Between 1800 and 1803 inclusive, the bounties paid for fish by the Corporation amounted to over £970.] In spite of every exertion the official average price of wheat in Gloucestershire for the month of March reached the astonishing sum of 184*s.* 4*d.* per quarter. The wages of unskilled labourers in Bristol being only about 8*s*. or 9*s*. per week, it is needless to say that when coarse bread advanced to 1*s*. 10*d*. the quartern loaf it was beyond the reach of great numbers of the inhabitants. The flour of rice, oats, barley, rye, and peas was largely resorted to as a substitute; some housewives even attempted to make loaves from potatoes: while nettles were gathered and cooked in lieu of ordinary vegetables.

When prices had attained their maximum, some of the poor, driven almost mad by the misery of their children, made one or two riotous attacks on the stall-keepers in the city markets, and soldiers had to be called in to prevent further outbreaks. No account of the disturbances was published by the newspapers supporting the Government, on the pretext that such intelligence was likely to have a bad effect, but the following item appears in the Corporation accounts: "Paid expenses during the market riots in the month of April, 1801, £117 7*s*. 4*d*." To what extent political discontent prevailed in the city it is now impossible to say. The prosecution of Hardy for high treason had brought out the fact that a "Bristol Society for Constitutional Information," similar to the Radical organizations in other towns, had existed in 1794 ["State Trials," xxiv. 480–484]; but the suspension of the Habeas Corpus Act and other arbitrary measures of the Government had suppressed every indication of popular feeling, public meetings and even lectures being forbidden except by consent of the magistrates. The extreme distress of the lower classes, however, induced many half-famished men to seek relief by resorting to crime, and *Felix Farley's Bristol Journal* announced that highway robberies and burglaries in and around the city were of nightly occurrence. In the hope of checking the evil, justice was administered with relentless severity. After the spring assizes of 1801 three criminals were executed at Bristol, six at Gloucester, and nine at Taunton, although in none of the cases were the malefactors charged with murder.

An interesting incident of this disastrous period was the first appearance of the system of co-operative trading. The manufacture and sale of flour and bread were the objects chiefly aimed at by the societies which started up, it being widely believed that millers and bakers were reaping extortionate profits during the general distress. Flour-mills on the co-operative principle were started* in

* A plot of ground for a mill at Baptist Mills was purchased by a few philanthropists; but the project was apparently dropped.

various parts of the country; and the Bristol Flour and Bread Concern is a still existing relic of a movement which for the most part passed away with the dearth. In Bristol, as elsewhere, the wealthier classes contributed largely towards the relief of their famine-stricken neighbours. Mr. John Weeks, the landlord of the "Bush" Hotel, earned great popularity by buying upwards of fifty tons of meat and a corresponding quantity of peas, etc., which were sold to the poor at moderate prices. The extreme severity of the distress rapidly diminished with the advance of summer, which ended in a productive harvest; but the semi-starvation suffered by the labouring classes was followed, according to custom, by a terrible epidemic of fever. "The number of cases," wrote Dr. Beddoes in *The Monthly Magazine*, "was prodigious. . . . Twenty-eight people lay down with fever in one house in Back Street (it is believed they had very little medical assistance), and eight were buried out of a single house in Elbroad Street." During the dearth, the Corporation of the Poor set up a coarse woollen manufactory in St. Peter's Hospital, for the purpose of employing some of the poor who were forced to apply for relief. The plan, however, did not succeed, and the place was closed.

A change of Ministry took place in the spring of 1801, when Mr. Addington (afterwards Lord Sidmouth) became Premier in the room of Mr. Pitt. Lord Eldon is recorded to have complained that although Addington's followers were few in number they all claimed to be officers; and it is clear that Mr. Charles Bragge, one of the members for Bristol, and a brother-in-law of the new minister, was no exception to the rule. Mr. Bragge was already Chairman of Ways and Means; in November he was transferred to the Treasurership of the Navy, thus vacating his seat. No opposition was offered to his re-election. On the evening after his return, "Brother Bragge," as he was contemptuously styled in one of Canning's well-known satires, is reported by an admiring journalist to have treated "the freemen in general with a supper, and liquor to drink his health." Besides being returned at the general election in the following year, Mr. Bragge was again re-elected in 1803, when he became Secretary at War. He took the name of Bathurst in 1804, on the death of a relative who bequeathed to him the Lydney estate.

At a meeting of the Common Council in March, 1801, it was reported that the vestry of Christ Church had applied for the payment of £500, the last instalment of the gift of £2,000 promised by the Corporation in 1784 towards rebuilding the church. A committee pointed out that the vestry had not complied with the conditions on which the subscription was granted, but suggested that if the churchwardens would so far fulfil their engagements as to lay into Broad Street enough ground then covered by houses to widen the thoroughfare to twenty-two feet (!), the money might be paid. It may be presumed that this condition was complied with, as the Corporation, in 1803, ordered the remainder of their gift to be paid in instalments.

The census of 1801, the first attempted in England, was taken in March, greatly to the dissatisfaction of many pious persons, who condemned the numbering of the people as a national sin. The statistics showed that the population of the ancient city was 40,814. The inhabitants of Clifton numbered 4,457; St. George's had 4,038; the district of St. James and St. Paul, 1,897; St. Philip's, outside the city, 8,406; Mangotsfield, 2,942; and Stapleton, 1,541. Adding these suburban districts, the total given by the census-takers was 63,645. Bedminster, which had a population of 3,278, was omitted from the suburbs for reasons unexplained. Much disappointment was felt at the result, local writers having confidently asserted that the city was inferior only to London in point of inhabitants, and that more than 100,000 persons dwelt within its boundaries.

About ten years before this date a project was started for the erection of an imposing crescent at Clifton, and several thousand pounds were expended on the undertaking. The outbreak of war with France, however, had ruinous effects on this and many other speculations,* and the scheme was abandoned for some years. On the 17th of May, 1800, "the pile of buildings called the Royal York Crescent," with the land adjoining, being the sites for the unbuilt houses, was offered for sale in *Felix Farley's Journal,* but without success. In July, 1801, the newspapers announced that the Government intended to buy the site of the unfinished portion of the

* Tyndall's park was sold, in 1790, for conversion into an extensive crescent, and the construction of some houses had begun, when the war broke out and the project collapsed (Bonner's *Bristol Journal*, May 24th, 1794). About the same time, "Mother Pugsley's field," on which St. Matthew's Church and a number of streets now stand, was sold to speculators, who sank the foundation of several houses—part of an immense crescent—but the purchasers were unable to complete the contract, and the turf was restored (Evans' *Chron. Hist.*, p. 202, where the owner is inaccurately styled "Freeman" instead of Fremantle). Several builders became insolvent in 1793, and a great number of unfinished houses in St. James's Parade, Richmond Place, York Buildings, Portland Square, the Mall, Cave Street, etc., were offered for sale.

crescent (about three-fourths of the whole), and to construct barracks there for the accommodation of a large body of troops. The ground, in fact, was actually secured for this purpose, but earnest petitions were forwarded by the inhabitants, urging that the intended building would be ruinous to the fame of Clifton as a watering-place, and the army authorities abandoned the design in July, 1803.* The crescent long remained in a desolate state. In May, 1809, a sale by auction was announced "by order of the Barrack Department," of fifteen unfinished houses, adjoining the first ten already standing at the west end. In the following year another sale was announced of "the remaining twenty-one unfinished houses, with a long range of void ground behind the same." The advertisement of 1809 was accompanied by a notice, by private persons, of a sale of eleven partly erected houses "in the crescent," by which, it may be presumed, was meant the lower or Cornwallis Crescent. This row was also begun in the prosperous years before the war, the first leases being granted by the Merchants' Society in November, 1791, but was left in an equally forlorn condition. In October, 1805, a local newspaper stated that the number of permanent residents in Clifton was becoming greater every season, "so that we should not be surprised if, in a very few years, the present ruinous piles of unfinished houses were to offer a lucrative speculation to the builder." The last gaps in York Crescent, however, were not filled until about 1818. Cornwallis Crescent was still longer in hand, nine of its unfinished houses being advertised for sale in July, 1824. In Saville Place, described in an advertisement as "in the centre of the village," there were eleven houses partially finished in June, 1796. Some were not completed until a much later date. Richmond Terrace contained several unoccupied houses at the close of 1799, when a gang of thieves attempted to steal the lead from the roofs, "which was only prevented," according to a local journalist, "by one of the gang being caught in a man-trap, which, from the quantity of blood left on the trap and premises, must have severely wounded him." Another row of dwellings which remained long incomplete was Bellevue. "Eight of the unfinished houses" there were offered for sale in July, 1810.

* The result was disappointing to the liquor interests. The minutes of the Court of Aldermen for February, 1808, record the presentation of a petition from "several distillers, rectifiers, maltsters, etc., praying that the mayor and aldermen would recommend to Government the building barracks in or near this city. And it is agreed not to recommend the said petition."

On the petition of several tanners and curriers in the city, the Common Council, in June, 1801, resolved on the establishment of a market in the Back Hall for the sale, every Wednesday and Saturday, of hides and skins, and every Thursday of leather.

The Council at the same meeting granted a pension for life of £60 per annum to Mrs. Harris, widow of Alderman John Harris (mayor in 1790-91), who had died a few days before. Two gentlemen, Gregory Harris and Wintour Harris, were about the same time nominated to comfortable offices under the Corporation. Such arrangements were not unusual under the irresponsible system of government. In 1808 a pension of £40 was granted to the widow of Samuel Sedgley, common councillor. In 1817 the widow of Alderman Anderson was granted a life annuity of £100; and a little later Charles Anderson, presumably her son, resigned his seat in the Council, and was elected to the well-endowed office of collector of town dues. J. H. Wilcox (who twice filled the office of mayor) relinquished his aldermanic gown under financial reverses about the same time, and became deputy-chamberlain. In 1820, upon the death of Mr. Joseph Edye (mayor 1801-2), his widow was voted a pension of £60 yearly. Other cases occur in the minutes, and will be mentioned hereafter. Another singular item occurs regularly every six months in the civic accounts. The following is an example: —"1800, September 29, paid sundry coachmen for attending with their masters' carriages on public days; half-year to this day, £32 12*s*." Then there are numerous payments for the robes and cocked hats of the petty officers of the Corporation, who were freshly caparisoned every other year. On the other hand, the Corporation declined to pay more than £26 12*s*. towards lighting the city. For this sum a lamp was lighted at Wine Street pump, four at the Drawbridge, as many in the centre of Queen Square, and three each at the Mansion House and Council House.

The tidings of the signature, at Amiens, of preliminaries of peace with France were received, in October, 1801, with enthusiastic tokens of joy. At Bath, the populace took the horses (which on this happy occasion were ten in number) out of the mail coach which brought the news, and insisted on dragging the vehicle as far as Twerton. Through the delay thus caused, the intelligence reached Bristol by a stage-coach, whereupon arrangements were made for meeting the mail and escorting it into the city. The procession, which to a later generation may have a somewhat ludicrous air, consisted of a troop of cavalry stationed in the city, some civic officials, Mr. Weeks of the Bush, in a gig, magniloquently styled a curricle, accompanied by a "musical gentleman," the "delightful sounds" of whose trumpet greatly affected the newspaper chronicler, and some thousands of the commonalty, whose continuous cheers were re-echoed by the spectators stationed along the route. This spectacle occurred about noontide on a Sunday, but the chronicler hastens to observe that the demonstration "did not trench upon the duties or decencies" of the day. On Monday, however, the air was rent with bell-ringing and cannon firing, and the irrepressible Weeks appeared on the balcony of his hotel "habited as a sailor, and delivered a string of appropriate toasts and sentiments, which were each of them preceded by an air from the band of the Oxfordshire militia, and by the plaudits of the populace." At night the city was ablaze with tar barrels, oil lamps, and tallow candles, Mr. Weeks coming out again triumphantly with an illuminated allegorical group representing Britannia, Cupid, the arts and sciences, Hercules, Fortitude, Minerva, a French *sansculotte*, and various other astonishing personages.* The popular joy broke forth afresh upon the proclamation of peace in the following May. Unprecedented crowds flocked into the city from the surrounding districts to witness the ceremony, which was carried out according to ancient precedent, the proclamation being read on the site of the High Cross, at St. Peter's pump, at St. Thomas's Church, at Queen Square, and lastly opposite the Exchange. A large platform, covered with crimson cloth, for the use of the civic authorities, was carried about in the procession from place to place. In the evening the city broke into a general illumination, *Felix Farley's Journal* remarking that so numerous were the emblematical transparencies that a full detail would occupy "nearly every column" of the pigmy newspaper.

---

* Although Mr. Weeks's demonstrations were sometimes rather grotesque, his fellow-citizens had reason to be grateful to him. In an advertisement published in 1814, he stated that when he entered upon the Bush, in 1772, there was no coach from the city to London, Exeter, Oxford, or Birmingham which performed its journey in less than two days. After ineffectually urging the proprietors to quicken their speed, Weeks started a one-day coach to Birmingham himself, and carried it on against a bitter opposition, charging the passengers only 10*s*. 6*d*. and 8*s*. 6*d*. for inside and outside respectively, and giving each of them a dinner and a pint of wine at Gloucester into the bargain. After a two years' struggle his opponents gave in, and one-day journeys to the above towns became the established rule. Another of Weeks's boasts was, that he had "the honour to conduct Lord Rodney into the city in 1782," which cost him the sum of £447.—*Bristol Journal*, June 11, 1814.

Considerable difficulty was found in filling the civic chair in 1801. Three gentlemen, Messrs. Gordon, Page, and Anderson, were successively elected mayor, but each in turn refused to accept the office, and paid the fine of £400. After a long delay, Mr. Joseph Edye was appointed.

. The urgent need of improvement in the shipping accommodation of the port had been widely felt for many years before this date, and many schemes for that purpose were devised during the last half of the previous century. So early as 1765, Smeaton, the greatest engineer of the time, proposed to convert the lower part of the Froom into a dock, the estimated outlay being only about £20,000. Two years later, William Champion, an ingenious Bristolian, produced a scheme for damming up the Avon, the cost of which he estimated at £35,000. This was followed by a dock project, designed by John Champion. The completion of the merchants' dock, near Rownham, in 1768, which was the work of W. Champion, and was regarded as a great improvement, temporarily shelved the question; but the complaints of shipowners gradually became pressing, and numerous fresh schemes of improvement were promulgated towards the end of the century.

It was not, however, until 1802 that the citizens began to consider the matter seriously. Early in that year a plan was laid before the Corporation and the Merchants' Company, who agreed upon referring it to Mr. William Jessop, an engineer who had some nine years before suggested a floating harbour by means of a dam at Rownham. That gentleman having approved of the project, it was brought before the inhabitants generally; and on the 1st May a subscription was started to carry out an undertaking the boldness of which exceeded any engineering work hitherto attempted in the kingdom. Jessop proposed to cut a new course for the Avon from Prince's Street to Rownham, and to form the old channel into a dock; which he estimated could be done for about £150,000. If this plan had been adopted, vessels would have had the option of entering the new harbour, or of taking up berths in the old river at the Grove and Welsh Back, as before. But the promoters of a floating harbour declined to sanction an arrangement which would have allowed merchants to escape the charges intended to recoup the cost of the undertaking. They preferred, at a great additional expense to themselves, to monopolize the whole of the ancient harbour; and their engineer was requested to alter his plan so as to extend the float to Temple

Back, a "cut" for the Avon being thus required from Rownham to Netham.

Vast as was the addition thus made to the intended excavations, Mr. Jessop, with the light-heartedness of his profession, estimated that the outlay for the cutting and locks would still not exceed £212,000, or, including the cost of the land, £300,000. It being arranged that the shareholders in the proposed company should receive 4 per cent. per annum for six years and 8 per cent. in perpetuity, a subscription covering £250,000 of the proposed capital was eventually obtained. An application to Parliament for the necessary powers was made in the session of 1803, when a lively opposition was manifested. The assent of the Corporation to the bill—which, besides imposing a tax upon every ship entering the port, levied an annual rate amounting to £2,400 (equal to sixpence in the pound) on the fixed property within the city—had been given by a majority of only one vote; and, as was natural, the difference of opinion in the Council largely prevailed out of doors. Many local shipowners, amongst whom were found the influential names of Bright, Gibbs, King, Baillie, Protheroe and Pinney, urged before the House of Commons' committee that at all the other ports where docks had been established the use of such accommodation was optional, the proprietors being content to look for profit from those who voluntarily came to them, whereas, if the proposed float were carried out, ships could not discharge their cargoes at Bristol without been mulcted for works which many of them did not require. Other opponents of the scheme submitted that an impost on house property for the benefit of private individuals was as unjustifiable as it was unprecedented. The legislature thought proper, however, to treat the scheme in an exceptional manner, and the bill received the royal assent. Under its provisions a company was incorporated under the title of the Bristol Docks Company, consisting of the Corporation, the Merchants' Company and the subscribers to the sum of £250,000. The total capital was fixed at £300,000.

According to the original draft of the bill, approved by the Common Council, the Corporation estates were made liable for the payment of one moiety of the interest on the intended loan of £50,000. The Court of Aldermen, however, denounced the proposed mortgage as unjust and dangerous, and, after the bill had passed the Commons, a successful appeal was made to the Upper House to strike out the provision. Parliament also rejected an audacious clause levying dues on shipping trading to Newport. Twenty-seven directors were appointed, comprising the mayor and eight members of the Common Council, the master and eight members of the Merchants' Company, and nine gentlemen chosen by the shareholders. It was stipulated in the Act that the two corporate bodies were to have no interest in the dividends.

The excavation of a new bed for the Avon from St Philip's Marsh to Rownham was necessarily the first portion of the intended works, and was of itself an undertaking of a gigantic character. The first sod of "the cut" was turned in a field near Mr. Teast's shipbuilding yard, at Wapping, on the 1st of May, 1804. The hour of five in the morning, then the usual time at which labourers began work, was fixed for the ceremony, which was performed by Mr. G. Webb Hall, in the presence of the directors and many influential shareholders. The tax on the city came into operation on and from this date. At a meeting of the Company in the following year it was reported that the directors had been unable to borrow the £50,000 authorized by the Act, and that the share capital was deficient by £14,500, owing to some of the subscribers having withdrawn their names before the bill became law. It was thereupon determined to augment the amount of the existing shares from £100 to £135 each, thereby supplying the required sum. (£12 9*s.* was afterwards added to each share by dividing the forfeited capital, making the total £147 9*s.*) As a sop to the proprietors for this compulsory demand upon them, the board promised that the interest named in the Act should be raised from 4 to 6 per cent.; and a bill to legalize this arrangement passed soon afterwards.

This, however, was but the beginning of the company's financial difficulties. The estimates originally framed, both as to the expense of the works and the time required for their completion, proved altogether deceptive. The task of constructing the lock and basin at Rownham had been especially underrated, and it was at last found necessary to contract the area of the basin by one-third. Even after making this reduction, the time fixed for the completion of the works was exceeded by a year, while the original capital of £300,000 defrayed only one-half of the total expenditure. To meet this formidable deficit, the directors, in 1807, promoted another bill, empowering them to raise fresh capital on the security of greatly enhanced charges on shipping and goods: the coasting trade, which had originally been exempted from dues on goods, being now deprived of its immunity. Through the slovenly manner in which private legislation was conducted at that period, the bill was presented and made some progress in the House of Commons before the citizens, or even the Common Council, became acquainted with its character; but the underhand proceedings of the Dock Board having been at length discovered, an opposition was organized in the city, and was supported by the Corporation and by the petitions of several seaport towns. The scheme was ultimately rejected in the Commons by 88 votes against 55. But in 1808 another bill, deemed less objectionable in some of its details, and giving powers for the erection of a toll-bridge and caisson near Prince's Street, was allowed to pass unopposed. The capital was raised by this Act to £500,000. Under a fourth statute, obtained in 1809, the amount was increased to £600,000. During the parliamentary struggle the works had been slowly progressing, and it was not until January, 1809, that the Avon was diverted into its new channel. On the 2nd of April the first vessels passed up and entered Bathurst Basin —so called in honour of one of the city members. Finally, on the 1st May following, the docks were certified as completed.*

To commemorate this striking event in the history of the city, a thousand of the labourers who had been employed on the works were entertained to dinner in a field opposite Mardyke. The principal items of the bill of fare consisted of two oxen, roasted whole, a proportionate weight of potatoes, and six hundredweight of plum pudding, a gallon of strong beer being also provided for each guest. The excessive supply of liquor led, as might have been expected, to a general fight between the English and Irish parties amongst the labourers, who had always been on bad terms. The Irishmen, according to a reporter, attempted to take possession of a cart bringing up a fresh supply of "stingo," and, being defeated in their attempt, ran off in a rage to their head-quarters in Marsh Street, whence they reappeared armed with shillelaghs. The Englishmen, equally

* At Gloucester summer assizes in 1809, the proprietors of a local brass manufactory (names carefully suppressed by the newspapers) claimed £40,000 damages from the Dock Company for depriving their factory of water during the construction of the floating harbour. The jury awarded the plaintiffs £10,000. Another dispute, which long remained unsettled, arose out of the practical destruction of the water-mill on St. James's Back, by the damming up of the Froom. The mill, which belonged to the Corporation, let for £48 a year. It was not until 1822 that the Dock Company consented to pay £992 to the Corporation and £50 to the tenant.

eager for the fray, having followed them up, the hostile camps met in Prince's Street, and a battle royal ensued immediately. As the civic guardians of the peace were ridiculously inadequate to meet the emergency, the "press gang," a social institution already referred to, was called in to arrest the leaders of the two factions, and the tumult was suppressed. The new "Float," eighty acres in extent, entirely removed the greatest defect of the port—the stranding at every ebb tide of the vessels awaiting discharge or loading, a test of strength which few ships save those built at Bristol were able to endure with impunity. The benefit conferred on local commerce by the dock was, however, in the opinion of some, outweighed by the extortionate dues imposed by the directors in their short-sighted and self-destructive efforts to realize large dividends for the shareholders. Complaints respecting this policy soon made themselves heard, and they increased from year to year; but, as will subsequently be seen, they long failed to produce the least effect upon the Board. No dividend on the share capital was paid until 1823.*

It has been already observed that the barbarity of the law in the reign of George III. afforded some excuse for the brutality which characterized the habits of the people. But for the indisputable testimony on which the following statements rest, they might well be deemed incredible by modern readers. In April, 1802, two women were executed at St. Michael's Hill gallows for infanticide. The bodies, according to the judge's sentence, were taken for dissection to the Infirmary, in an open cart, followed by an immense mob. Some of the surgeons were in attendance, and after the bodies had been at least partially stripped, a "crucial incision" was made in the breast of each, in the presence of as many of the rabble as were able to crush into the room. On the following day, at the request of the mayor and aldermen —who were present—the brain of one of the women was dissected and lectured upon by Mr. Richard Smith. The authority for this story is a manuscript note by Mr. Smith himself, who appears to have revelled in operations upon malefactors. Although somewhat out of date, another inci-

* The Dock Company obtained authority in one of their Acts to employ the waste water of the Float in driving mills, which were intended to be constructed at the "overfall" near Cumberland Basin. An advertisement appeared in the *Bristol Journal* of November 22, 1810, of a sale by auction of this water power, and of the foundations of three "thoroughs," for powerful mills. No later reference to the subject has been discovered.

dent relating to this gentleman may as well be added. In April, 1821, a man named John Horwood was hanged at the usual place, for the murder of a girl, and his body also fell into Mr. Smith's hands. The following tradesman's account is the first manuscript contained in a book in the Infirmary library:—"Bristol, June, 1828. Richard Smith, Esq., Dr. to H. H. Essex. To binding, in the skin of John Horwood, a variety of papers, etc., relating to him, the same being lettered on each side of the book, 'Cutis vera Johannis Horwood,' £1 10*s*." Perhaps all that can be said in excuse for such an act is, that it had been surpassed in a neighbouring county a few years previously. According to the *Bristol Journal* of May 11, 1816, after a man named Marsh had been hanged in Somerset for murder, his body was flayed, and his skin sent to Taunton to be tanned.

At the general election in the summer of 1802, John Baker Holroyd, Lord Sheffield, who had represented the city during two Parliaments in the Whig interest, announced his intention to retire. He had been promised an English peerage, to which he was promoted a few weeks later. Lord Sheffield gained much credit for his exertions in suppressing the riots in London in 1780, but he will be chiefly remembered by posterity as the correspondent and literary executor of Gibbon. Sir Frederick M. Eden, a supporter of the Addington Ministry, attempted to secure the vacant seat, but being unknown to the freemen, he met with a cold reception and speedily withdrew. The Whig party found a champion in Mr. Evan Baillie, ex-Colonel of the Bristol volunteers, and a wealthy local banker. Mr. Bragge was again the nominee of the Tories. There being no opposition, the two candidates were elected on the 5th of July.

A somewhat astonishing illustration of the character and conduct of ecclesiastical dignitaries in the Georgian era is afforded by an incident which occurred in the summer of this year. During some trivial reparations in the cathedral, the dean and chapter resolved that the lectern, which had been presented by a sub-dean in 1683, should be removed and sold as an inconvenience and obstruction. A firm of brassfounders was consequently called in, and the eagle, which weighed about the third of a ton, was disposed of as old brass at the rate of 9½*d*. per lb. The only person who appears to have been shocked by this procedure was a gentleman named William Ady, residing in St. James's, who rescued the eagle from the melting-pot by offering an advanced price. His attempt to awaken better feelings in the chapter by proffering to return it for the sum paid down, proved, however, fruitless, and in August the lectern was advertised for sale by auction at the Exchange Coffee Room. Clergymen, churchwardens, and persons contemplating benefactions to their parish churches were especially invited to attend; but the advertiser, apparently dubious of finding a buyer in this direction, pointed out that "traders with foreign parts may find it worth their while to purchase, as a like opportunity may never occur again." It was not until the scandal had reached this stage that Dean Layard and his colleagues thought fit to offer an explanation to the public. According to a brief statement published in *Felix Farley's Bristol Journal*, the eagle, which "had not been used for many years," had been removed simply to accommodate the congregation; and the authorities promised the introduction of "something in its stead of equal or greater value and ornament." There is no evidence to show that this promise was ever performed. On the contrary, there is reason to believe that other articles, more especially two large candelabra that once stood on the communion table, disappeared about the same time. Churchmen, however, were almost as indifferent as the chapter. At the auction Mr. Ady could not get a bidder for the eagle, and he finally presented it to the authorities of St. Mary-le-port, on condition that it should be "placed in the chancel, there to remain for ever." The conduct of the cathedral officials can scarcely have been approved by the citizens, but the only audible expression of censure is reported to have been uttered by one of the half-witted paupers then allowed to wander about the streets. Being rebuked by Dean Layard for disturbing the peace of the college precincts, the vagrant made an inquiry as to bird-stealers which effectually silenced the irritated dignitary.

Felix Farley's Bristol Journal of February 5, 1803, contains the following singular paragraph:—"On Saturday last, in order to decide a bet for 200 guineas which had been made dependent on his grace's presence there, the Duke of Norfolk dined with a party of gentlemen at what is commonly known in this city by the name of the *stone kitchen*, at the Rose and Crown, in Temple Street, where the evening was spent in the utmost conviviality and good humour." From another paragraph in the same paper, it appears that the duke had been presented a short time previously with the freedom of the city by the Corporation. "Jockey of Norfolk," as he was styled by his convivial contemporaries, had for some reason a strong liking for the West of England, and especially for the city of Gloucester, of which he was elected mayor in 1798, afterwards becoming its recorder, lord high steward, and on two later occasions chief magistrate. His visit to the "stone kitchen" is said to have been brought about by one of his sporting friends in Herefordshire, who had been invited, during a brief sojourn in Bristol, to one of the tripe and beefsteak feasts given every Saturday, for which the inn was famous. In despite of its name and locality, the place, which is said to have been occupied by a family named Sloper for nearly two centuries, until they died out in 1841, was the resort of several "well-seasoned" members of the Common Council and other leading citizens, amongst whom was the royal academician, Bird, who painted a large rose upon the ceiling of the "kitchen." * In accordance with the terms of the wager, no alteration was made in the usual fare on the day of the duke's attendance, but his grace thoroughly enjoyed the entertainment, which indeed was congenial to his tastes, and is said to have "eaten like Ajax, and drunk with twenty-aldermanic power." There is a further tradition recorded by an old contributor to the *Bristol Times*, namely, that the convivial nobleman, on his departure, was being conducted through a narrow alley which enabled visitors to avoid the front tavern, when his grace, whose size was proportioned to his gastronomic capacity, knocked over an oyster stall, and was objurgated by the choleric virago who owned it as a pot-bellied old brute. The duke, it is added, was profuse in his apologies, and assisted the angry dame in gathering up her stock-in-trade.

A sad incident, peculiar to the time, occurred one Sunday afternoon in March, 1803. On the previous night a large press-gang had scoured the city and seized upon upwards of two hundred able-bodied men, who were carried off to the "rendezvous," or headquarters of the impressment service. On Sunday the gang, aided by a party of marine infantry, were conveying the unfortunate captives to Rownham, in order to their being shipped on board a frigate lying in Kingroad, when a mob attacked the guard in Hotwell Road, pelting the officers and soldiers with mud, stones, and broken bottles. Some of the marines, injured by the missiles, retaliated by firing into the crowd, with the effect of killing a boy. A woman was also shot in the breast, and a man had

* It appears from Dr. Bruce's Handbook to Newcastle-upon-Tyne, that a "stone kitchen" also existed in that town about the same date, and that it was equally popular amongst the leading merchants.

an ankle fractured by a bullet. At the inquest on the boy, the jury, after hearing evidence as to the provocation offered by the mob, returned a verdict of justifiable homicide.

A musical festival, extending over three days, took place in Easter week. The morning performances were given in St. Paul's Church, and consisted of a selection from Handel's works, and the oratorios of "The Creation" and "The Messiah." Two miscellaneous evening concerts were given in the theatre. Mrs. Billington, "The British Syren," was the leading vocalist, and excited general admiration.

War with France having again broken out in the summer, the Bristol volunteers, who had been disbanded with scant courtesy after the Peace of Amiens, forgot the affront, and were forthwith reorganized, a subscription of several thousand pounds being raised by the citizens in support of the movement. Owing to the arrogant language of Napoleon, and his stupendous preparations for invading England, the ardour shown in defence of the country rose to enthusiasm. It was at first proposed to enrol only 1,000 infantry volunteers, but 1,100 citizens pressed forward to join, and similar zeal was shown in volunteering for the local cavalry and artillery, the total number of effectives having soon reached 1,474. The following gentlemen were appointed as officers: Infantry—Colonel, Evan Baillie, M.P.; lieut.-colonels, William Gore and Thomas Tyndall; majors, Thos. Kington and Thomas Haynes; adjutant, Geo. Bradshaw; quarter-master, Stephen Cave; captains, G. Goldney, S. L. Harford, R. Vaughan, junr., Thos. Cole, Robert Bush, C. Payne, A. P. Collings, P. Baillie, J. Gordon, and J. Haythorne. Light horse—Major commandant, Henry Dupont; captains, Levi Ames, junr., Robert Kingsmill.* Artillery—Captain, W. Innis Pocock. Corps numbering about 200 each were also formed in Clifton, Westbury, and Bedminster, the two former being united in a battalion. In a short time more than 16,000 men were enrolled in Gloucestershire and Somerset—a notable fact when it is remembered that the entire population of the two counties was little more than half a million. In order to make use of the waterside community, a corps of about 150 Sea Fencibles was established, having its head-quarters at Pill. The commandant was Captain Sotheby, R.N. The Common Council voted 400 guineas towards the establishment of the various corps, and also offered £300 in bounties of £3 each to the

* The cavalry corps, having become greatly diminished in numbers, was dissolved in July, 1813.

first hundred sailors who volunteered to enter the Royal Navy. Finally, Sir John White Jervis, then living in Clifton, undertook to raise at his own expense a volunteer rifle corps, two companies of which were soon organized. It may be observed in parenthesis that the land volunteers were exempted from service in the militia, then compulsory on persons capable of bearing arms, and that the pilots and watermen enrolled in the Fencibles secured protection against the ruthless press-gangs. The colours of the Bristol infantry were consecrated by the Rev. Sir A. Elton after a service in the cathedral; a "war anthem" being composed by the organist for the occasion. Telegraphs and beacons were erected on the principal hills of Somerset, Gloucestershire, and the neighbouring counties;* and the Duke of Cumberland, who had been appointed military commandant of the Severn district, visited the city to inspect the volunteers and to "fix on spots best calculated for the erection of batteries on the Avon." The freedom of the city was presented to him on the occasion. A more lasting honour to a prince who was destined to be the most unpopular of his family, was the adoption of his name for the new tidal basin constructed a few years later at Rownham, in connection with the floating harbour. In October the "Royal Bristol Light Infantry" were engaged in guarding 500 French prisoners from Wells to Stapleton prison [now the Bristol workhouse]. These captives, who had marched from Plymouth, were followed from time to time by several thousand others consigned to the same place. In December a meeting was held in the Guildhall, at which General Tarleton, who had succeeded to the Duke of Cumberland's command, laid before the mayor (Mr. D. Evans), and other leading citizens, the defenceless state of the port in view of the threatened invasion. After a discussion, it was resolved to provide for the security of the harbour by gunboats, for the construction of which it was resolved to apply for an Act to raise £20,000, to be cleared off by a tax upon the citizens. This project, however, met with such decided disapproval at the parochial meetings which followed, that it was promptly abandoned. The volunteer regiments of each locality were called upon to perform permanent duty for a few weeks yearly, being generally quartered in some neighbouring town. During

* The Corporation voted £200 for the erection of four of these signal posts, "fifty feet long, with halyyards" at "the snuff mill on Clifton Rocks, Dundry tower, Kingsweston Down, and Hobbs' Hill, above Portishead battery," for the security of the city.

this period the men received military pay. In September, 1804, when it was believed that a French landing might occur at any moment, it was arranged that the Bristol corps, on receiving a signal, should march on Burford, while the Somerset and Gloucestershire corps should be directed on Marlborough, measures being taken for the subsequent transport of the whole force eastwards by carts, to take part in the defence of London. Early in 1805, the city Guard-house in Wine Street, which had been for some years in a ruinous state, underwent a thorough repair in order to accommodate the garrison. About the same time the War Office entered into a contract for a magazine for 20,000 stand of arms, "to be erected in the Gloucester Road, without Lawford's Gate." This building, locally known as the Armoury, has long disappeared, but its memory is preserved by the name of Armoury Square, given to the dwellings now standing on its site.

The Common Council was specially convoked in August, 1803, owing to a mournful event of an unusual character,—the death of the mayor, Mr. Robert Castle, during his year of office. According to ancient precedent, the chair was taken by the senior alderman, Sir John Durbin, who announced the cause of the meeting. The quaint official minutes continue as follows:—"And the robes, swords, and other insignia belonging to the office of mayor, which the late mayor died possessed of, being laid upon the table in order to be disposed of to such person as should be elected," three gentlemen were nominated, and David Evans was chosen. "Then the mayor-elect, there putting on his scarlet gown and the scarlet robe (always worn by the mayors of this city at their swearing), with the old sheriffs and the rest of the Common Council, also in their scarlet gowns, removed out of St. George's Chapel to the High Desk in the Guildhall," where the oaths were administered by the mayor of the preceding year. "After which all the insignia were in the usual manner delivered to Mr. Mayor, who in the scarlet robes aforesaid was, with the sword and pearl scabbard borne before him, attended by the others of the Common Council (in their scarlet gowns) to the Council-house, where they separated." Only four years later, the Corporation had again to regret the loss of its head, Mr. Henry Bright having died in November, 1807, in the second month of his mayoralty. Mr. Samuel Birch was appointed his successor in December, when the above ceremonies were repeated.

Puritanic views and practices respecting the sanctity of

the first day of the week lingered long amongst local guardians of order. *Felix Farley's Journal* of Feb. 2, 1804, contained the following paragraph :—"Several boys were on Sunday taken to Bridewell for playing in the streets in St. James's parish during the time of morning service." In the following year the corporate accounts record a payment of £1 1*s.* 10*d.* "paid George Merrick, costs in prosecuting a man for prophaning the sabbath."

Down to the year 1804, the only thoroughfare from Broad Street to Nelson Street, for foot-passengers as well as for vehicles, was the central archway under St. John's Church tower, now appropriated to carriages. Serious accidents were consequently of frequent occurrence. In March of this year, the Corporation purchased a lease, granted by the feoffees of the parish, of the premises adjoining the west wall of the tower, and opened in 1805 what a contemporary journalist called a "noble" (though it was really a very mean) archway as a footpath for the public. In 1827, the parochial vestry resolved upon restoring the tower and removing the cistern attached to the south side of the church (the appearance of which is shown in plates in Mr. Seyer's and the Rev. J. Evans's histories), with the view of opening another footway on the east side of the tower. The entrance to the church, previously inside the great archway—as may still be seen from existing remains—was removed to the spot previously occupied by the cistern and fountain, and the latter was set up on its present site. While these alterations were in progress, the vestry memorialized the Common Council, pointing out that the gateway under the tower had been "for many years complained of as a great public nuisance, fraught with danger and difficulty from its extreme narrowness and the multitude of carriages and passengers passing through the same; and that by proper and adequate footways on each side of the tower the grievance would be greatly diminished." To effect this, it would be necessary to take down the house abutting upon the west side of the tower, and the property being leased by the Corporation, the petitioners prayed that the Common Council would surrender its interests, in order that the site might be sold and the proceeds devoted to the improvement. The Corporation having assented, the building, which contained some window mouldings and other slight relics of the church of St. Lawrence (the roof, according to J. Evans, was remarkably perfect in 1824), was swept away. The alterations, which were generally approved, were finished in 1829.

In February, 1805, four habitual thieves, captured under peculiar circumstances, were committed to Newgate prison charged with a burglary in St. Augustine's parish. A local journalist wrote:—"They had converted a cavern in Cook's Folly wood, called St. John's Hole, into a kind of store-room, which was well supplied with bacon, cheese, etc., and were in the act of cooking when detected." Crime was exceedingly prevalent about this time, and the Corporation had made the following payment only a few weeks before:—"Paid Wm. Gibbons, Esq., and Co., for 86 dozen hard Hand Cuffs for city use, £130 19*s.*"

Amongst the ill-advised fiscal laws passed during the struggle with the French, the tax on salt was probably the most oppressive and injurious. In seeking to lighten its severity on the poor, many of whom lived mainly on vegetables, and consequently consumed more of the condiment than the wealthy, Parliament resorted to singular devices. At the city quarter sessions in March, the justices, in compliance with the statute law, fixed the price of "rock salt, otherwise Bristol salt," at fivepence per pound, and 1*s.* 4*d.* per quarter-peck. The penalty upon a tradesman charging a higher price was £20 for each offence. One conviction is recorded about the same date.

During the summer it was currently reported that George III., whose most extensive journeys had previously been to Cheltenham and Weymouth, intended to make a tour in the West of England. The Corporation was immediately on the alert, and Sir John Durbin, Alderman Noble, the two sheriffs, and the town clerk were sent off to London with an invitation to his Majesty to visit the city. If the king had ever contemplated a "progress," however, he had changed his mind. The expenses of the deputation amounted to no less a sum than £282; but the details are unfortunately wanting.

The religious delusions of a semi-lunatic Devonshire woman, named Joanna Southcott, attracted much attention about this time. Joanna had many enthusiastic followers, and probably some relatives, in Bristol. In 1805 and 1806 her "inspired writings" were advertised as on sale at "Mr. Southcott's, 69, Broad Quay." Shortly afterwards her votaries announced that "there was a place in Bristol" where her inspirations "were publicly read and explained; which opens every Sunday evening at 6 o'clock and every Friday evening at 7." Further information was to be had of "the expositor, the Rev. Samuel Eyre." The place rented by the fanatics, at £25 a year, was a large room in what has been called Colston's house in Small Street, then chiefly occupied by the printing office of the *Mirror*. Joanna died in 1814, and the discovery of imposture upon a surgical examination of her body so shook the faith of her Bristol admirers that the furniture of the room was seized for rent, and sold in the street. The more infatuated section of the Southcottites nevertheless retained the belief that their prophet would reappear; and the rent of the chamber was paid until 1854, when the death of Mr. Eyre, "of Stokes Croft," put an end to the occupancy.

On Sunday, the 15th of Sept., 1805, the date fixed by the charter of Queen Anne, Mr. John Foy Edgar, a member of the Common Council, was elected mayor, but refused to accept the office, and was fined £400 for his contumacy. The fine was paid, although the refusal may have been due to the declining fortunes of Mr. Edgar, who had twice filled the then costly office of sheriff. In 1818, he relinquished his seat in the chamber, and was appointed sword-bearer. Mr. Edgar, who was descended maternally from Sir Robert Cann, a masterful mayor and member of Parliament occupying a conspicuous place in the city annals, was of a different stamp from the ordinary ruck of civic officials. Educated at Christchurch College, Oxford, he was found an acceptable acquaintance by young men of high social and intellectual position; and when the Earl of Liverpool and Mr. Canning paid a visit to Bristol, in 1825, they recognised and cordially saluted their old companion at the university—the Premier and his colleague, it is said, making offers of assistance which the fallen merchant was too proud to accept. Mr. Crabb Robinson, who visited Bristol in 1836, after recording in his diary a call upon Joseph Cottle, wrote:—"Here, too, was living a man I became acquainted with through Flaxman—Edgar, a man of accomplishments and taste. A merchant once enjoying wealth, he was the patron of Flaxman when little known. Adversity befell him, and then, though he was a Conservative, and the Radicals were in power,* they behaved, as he himself said, with generosity towards a political adversary, allowing him to retain the office of sword-bearer on terms more liberal than could have been required. He was an F.S.A., and possessed an unusual degree of antiquarian knowledge."

It would appear that the Common Council found it im-

* There is obviously some error in Mr. Robinson's reminiscence of the facts. Mr. Edgar was president of the Anchor Society in 1798.

possible to fill the civic chair except by promising to increase the salary attached to it. At all events, Mr. Daniel Wait had no sooner been elected in the place of Mr. Edgar, than the sum annually granted to the mayor, which had been increased from £1,200 to £1,500 in 1800, was further augmented to £2,000. Yet a twelvemonth after, Mr. Wm. Fripp refused the office, and was fined £500. Four years later, in 1810, Sir Henry Protheroe also paid the same fine rather than accept the chief magistracy, and indicated the cause of his refusal by giving notice of a motion for raising the salary to £2,500, to which amount it was actually advanced in September, 1813. Two gentlemen, Levi Ames, junr., and W. Inman, had declined the costly honour in 1811, and paid a fine of £500 each.

Intense public emotion was caused in November by the naval victory of Trafalgar and the death of Nelson at the moment of his greatest triumph. On the occasion of the national thanksgiving, in December, the collections made on behalf of the Patriotic Fund at the places of worship in the city amounted to over £1,000. The largest gifts were made at St. James's and St. Paul's Churches and Lewin's-mead Chapel,* each of these collections slightly exceeding £100.

On the 20th of February, 1806, the ironwork of the bridge intended to carry the Bath road over the new course of the Avon suddenly collapsed when it was on the point of completion. Two of the workmen were mortally injured. The art of iron bridge building being then in its infancy, the faultiness of the design escaped attention, and the bridge was rebuilt on the original plan. As had frequently been predicted, it fell a second time, many years later (see March, 1855).

The account books of the Corporation for the month of March contain the following item, which is eloquent enough to speak for itself:—"Paid John Noble, Esq., for wine sent as a present to the High Steward, members in Parliament, and Recorder, by order of Common Council, £295 9*s*." The gifts, which were made every year, consisted of a butt of sherry to the two members, another to the Lord High Steward, and a hogshead to the Recorder. The fortunate purveyor, "John Noble, Esq.," was one of the aldermen of the city, and a Whig, as were the majority of the municipal body at that date. Mr. Noble was appointed one of the

* The congregation of Lewin's Mead Chapel at one time consisted of so many leading citizens that, with one exception, its members included the whole aldermanic bench. Of the feoffees of the Unitarian almshouse in Stokes Croft in 1785, eight had been mayors and three sheriffs.—*Bristol Times*, April 9, 1853.

Auditors of public accounts during the ministry of Lord Grenville (1806), and afterwards lived in London, but retained his aldermanic gown until his death in 1828.

The foundation-stone of the left wing of the Infirmary was laid in June by Mr. E. Protheroe. Prior to commencing the work the committee had collected a fund sufficient to provide for the cost of the building, and had also obtained by a public subscription the sum of £10,500, which was invested as an endowment for maintaining the new wards. For some inscrutable reason, the whole of the Infirmary buildings were painted black, and presented a most lugubrious appearance. Prince Puckler Muskau, who visited the city in 1828, noted the fact with astonishment, and compared the place to "an enormous mausoleum." It was not until more than thirty years later that the doleful aspect of the institution was removed at the expense of Mr. H. A. Palmer.

A bill for amending previous local Acts relating to the sewerage, cleansing, paving, and lighting of the city, received the royal assent during the parliamentary session of 1806. For several years previous to this date, the Corporation was looked upon by the ratepayers with extreme distrust, and every effort made to extend its powers over the citizens had been obstinately resisted. On the present occasion the Common Council, in order to carry a bill unquestionably desirable, proclaimed its willingness to delegate the powers of the statute to a body of commissioners. This announcement was received with as much approval as surprise; but upon looking into the matter, the citizens found that the concession was rendered delusive by a provision under which the Corporation retained its predominance under disguise. The bill provided that the ratepayers of each parish should nominate ten persons, from whom the Council were to select two at their discretion—an arrangement by which the authorities doubtless expected to eliminate all who were likely to be critical or hostile. An influential body of ratepayers, acting as parochial delegates, combined to oppose this clause; but the corporate officials, after promising to delay the measure until the objectors had laid their case before Parliament, pushed the bill through its final stages, and then coolly laughed at their dupes. The latter held an indignation meeting to denounce the conduct of the authorities and protest against the blow struck at the rights and interests of the citizens; but the triumph of the Corporation was not the less complete, the commissioners being always the subservient instruments of the Common Council. A sum of £2,230 in consols, being the surplus of the trust for repairing and lighting Bristol Bridge, was handed over to the new body, which continued to exercise its functions as a highway board, and to levy rates throughout the ancient city until so late a date as 1851, when it was superseded by the adoption of the Health of Towns Act by the Council.

The short-lived Whig Ministry of 1806 succeeded in passing through Parliament a bill for the suppression of the inhuman slave-trade between Africa and the West India colonies. The measure was opposed by Mr. Bathurst, one of the members for Bristol, where the trade had flourished exceedingly during the previous century. Public opinion, however, had nearly brought about its extinction, a paper in the *Monthly Magazine* for May, 1799, observing that it was "just expiring" in Bristol; and Mr. Protheroe, M.P., stated that when the Act passed not a single slaver hailed from the port. A reference to Clarkson's work on the subject will prove that the conversion of local merchants had been remarkably rapid. Slavery was even recognised in England. In *Sarah Farley's Bristol Journal* for Jan. 9, 1768, was the following advertisement:—"To be sold, a healthy Negro Slave, named Prince, 17 years of age, 5 feet 10 inches high, and extremely well grown. Enquire of Joshua Springer, in St. Stephen's Lane." So late as Dec. 8, 1792, a local journal reported that a wealthy citizen had just sold a "black servant girl, who had been many years in his service," into perpetual bondage, and that the price of the unhappy woman, who was shipped to Jamaica, was £80, colonial currency. When she "put her feet into the fatal boat at Lamplighters' Hall, her tears ran down her face like a shower of rain."

The three election contests in 1780, 1781, and 1784 were long remembered for their extreme costliness. In 1780, the Prime Minister, with the consent of George III., contributed £1,000 from the king's private purse with the object of defeating Burke and his Whig colleague, Cruger. This gift was but a drop in the bucket, however, and in 1781, upon the death of one of the successful Tory members, the local leaders, exhausted by the previous struggle, made an earnest appeal for further assistance, and secretly received £5,000 from the royal bounty. About the same time the king's income was drawn upon to the extent of £2,000 on behalf of the Tory party in Gloucestershire (see "Correspondence of George III. and Lord North," vol. ii., p. 425). The still more expensive struggle in 1784 ended in a drawn battle, each side returning a candidate, and the rival camps appear to have thereupon mutually agreed to avoid further conflicts upon the basis of a divided representation. Thus for many years there was not even the semblance of a struggle. A general election took place in October, 1806, when Mr. Bathurst, the Tory nominee, and Colonel Baillie, the representative of the Whigs, were re-elected. Parliament was again dissolved in the spring of 1807, and as the old compromise remained in force, Mr. Bathurst (who had just been appointed Master of the Mint) and Colonel Baillie were nominated for the third time. The intended unanimity of the proceedings at the Guildhall, on the 5th of May, was, however, interrupted by a man named Henry Hunt, who had recently started a "Clifton genuine beer brewery" at Jacob's wells, and who afterwards obtained national notoriety for his demagogic oratory in support of annual parliaments and universal suffrage. Hunt presented himself on the platform to propose Sir John Jervis, a popular lawyer, and afterwards Lord Chief Justice of the Common Pleas; but the sheriffs refused to accept the nomination, on the ground that its proposer was neither a freeholder nor a free burgess of the city. During the chairing of the members, Hunt's followers, who had on the previous night demolished the windows of the Council House and White Lion Hotel, pelted Mr. Bathurst so vigorously with mud and sticks that he was forced to leave his gilded car and beat a retreat. Another attack was being organized against his hostelry, the White Lion, when Hunt successfully diverted the attention of the mob by offering to distribute two butts of beer at his brewery. In the evening, the windows of the Council House and the neighbouring hotel were again assailed by a drunken crowd.

A new hotel was opened during the summer in a large mansion in College Place, for many years the residence of Alderman Noble. The opening dinner of "Reeves's Hotel" took place on the 25th of June, the mayor, Mr. (afterwards Sir) Richard Vaughan, presiding. The company, twenty-two in number, consisted chiefly of aldermen and common councillors, and the bacchanalian powers of the party may be judged from the "wine bill" drawn up by the chairman, and religiously preserved by Mr. Reeves.* The items were as follows:—Dinners, at 25*s.*, £27 10*s.*; 12 bottles of sherry, at 5*s.* 6*d.*, £3 6*s.*; 12 bottles of port, at 5*s.*, £3; 12 bottles of hock, at 10*s.* 6*d.*, £6 6*s.*; 20 bottles of claret, at 11*s.*, £11;

* "MS. Annals," City Library, ii., 388.

with 6 bottles of champagne (paid for by the mayor). The total was sixty-two bottles for twenty-two persons. Mr. Reeves, who was famous as a caterer, made a fortune of £20,000 before retiring from business.

The Prince of Wales, accompanied by the Duke of Sussex, having arrived at Berkeley Castle during a short tour in the West, his royal highness responded to an invitation of the Corporation by paying a visit to Bristol on the 6th of October. Attended by his brother, his noble host, and a numerous party of friends, he entered the city by Park Street, and was conducted by the sheriffs, Sir H. Protheroe and Mr. Haythorne, to the Mansion House, amidst the usual tokens of rejoicing. An address was there presented, in which the Corporation assured the prince that while they contemplated the blessings they enjoyed under the paternal reign of his father, "the true principles of greatness which adorn the character of your royal highness encourage us to hope in the prospect of their continuance." A suitable reply having been made, the prince was presented with the freedom of the city in a gold box. The royal visitor explained that his entrance into the city in a close carriage—which, says the reporter, had greatly disappointed the spectators, and especially the fair sex—was due to his suffering from a swelled face, and he then condescended to inspect the guard of honour in front of the house, and to show himself to the populace. Having partaken of a sumptuous banquet at the Merchants' Hall, the royal party left for Berkeley, the visit having lasted about four hours. The entertainment cost the city £1,225. The Duke of Sussex also received the freedom of the city shortly afterwards, and a similar compliment was conferred upon the Duke of Gloucester in the following year.

The small dome surmounting the tower of All Saints' Church,—a grotesque whim of churchwardendom in the previous century,—having become dilapidated, was replaced in January, 1808, by the existing structure, which is not less incongruous with a Norman fabric than was its predecessor.

On the 25th March, 1808, a double duel took place amongst four of the French war prisoners at Stapleton, two of whom were mortally wounded. A verdict of manslaughter against the two survivors was returned by the coroner's jury; but at the Gloucester assizes in the following month they were acquitted. In July, 1809, another fatal duel took place in the prison. Two of the captives, a naval and a military officer, quarrelled over a game of marbles, by which they were seeking to beguile the dreary monotony of the place, whereupon a duel was arranged to come off in the chapel. Ordinary weapons being of course out of their reach, the antagonists fought with sticks, to the ends of which they had contrived to fix sharp pieces of iron, and one of the men was mortally injured. The coroner's inquest resulted in a verdict of wilful murder against the other; but at the ensuing summer assizes at Gloucester the jury acquitted the prisoner, who, it was deposed, acted in self-defence. A contemporary local newspaper stated that not less than 150 duels had been fought amongst the prisoners, averaging about 5,500 in number, during the previous three years. Owing to the enforced idleness of the unhappy men, gaming became a passion amongst them; and it was not uncommon to find a prisoner reduced to nakedness through wagering away the clothes upon his back.

An additional butcher market in Nicholas Street was opened on the 25th of June, 1808. The building had cost the Corporation upwards of £5,000.

The local journals for the early weeks of September contained an advertisement of the intended sale by auction, by order of the mayor (Mr. S. Birch) and the other surveyors of the city lands, of "the materials of Temple Gate, now standing at the top of Temple Street." This step was determined upon in consequence of a petition addressed to the Common Council by residents in the neighbourhood, setting forth that the gate was very narrow and ruinous, a great impediment to traffic, as well as dangerous and inconvenient, and that its removal would considerably improve the street. Strangely enough, none of the newspapers appear to have noticed the sale itself, nor the destruction of a building which, though neither ancient nor beautiful, was still identified with the history of the city. From the diary of a citizen published in the *Times and Mirror* (March 15, 1884), it appears that the materials were bought by a Mr. Wilmot, carpenter, for £107. The city arms were on the outside of the gate, and the royal arms on the inside. The structure was removed shortly afterwards, much to the convenience of public traffic. In September, 1869, workmen came upon some remains of the gate, or possibly of its predecessor, when excavating the foundations of the bridge connected with the harbour railway.

A proposal to establish a Commercial Coffee Room, on the pattern of Lloyd's Coffee Room in London, was circulated during the autumn of this year. The project having been favourably received, a meeting was held in November, the mayor (Mr. J. Haythorne) in the chair, when it was stated that £10,000 would be required to carry out the undertaking in a manner worthy of the city. The value of the shares was fixed at £25 each, and a subscription having been started, the entire sum was guaranteed within twenty-four hours. A design by a Mr. Busby having been selected, the foundation stone of the building was laid in March, 1810, by Mr. George Dyer, treasurer, in the presence of most of the leading citizens. The rooms, which cost about £17,000, were opened in September, 1811, when the original title was altered, the word "coffee" being suppressed. The number of members at the outset was about 500, but they increased in a few months to over 600.

A heavy snowstorm occurred early in the year 1809. Being followed by an unusually rapid thaw, the greatest flood ever remembered took place in the valleys of the Avon and the Froom, and caused great damage in the city. The water spread over large portions of Newfoundland, Callowhill, Milk, King, and Merchant Streets, St. James's Back, and Broadmead, some houses being inundated to the depth of six feet. Provisions had to be conveyed to imprisoned families by means of boats. A temporary bridge over the Float, for use whilst the drawbridge was under repair, was carried away, some passengers having a narrow escape.

Up to this time both of the assembly rooms established in Clifton for balls and entertainments were in the neighbourhood of Dowry Square, which, through the increasing number of residences on the brow of the hill, was ceasing to be patronized by fashionable visitors. The need of a suitable public building in a commodious situation had been recognised in 1792, when a scheme was started to build an assembly room and hotel by means of a tontine, but the project collapsed. Having been revived, the foundation stone of the Mall Assembly Rooms, to which a new hostelry, to be called the Clifton Hotel, was to be attached, was laid in the spring of 1806. In January, 1809, the structure, which was of an imposing character, and occupied the whole east end of the Mall, was roofed in, when, says a contemporary diarist (*Times and Mirror*, March 15, 1884), "the proprietors had an ox roasted whole, and gave it to the populace." The Assembly Room was opened in November, 1811, with the most brilliant ball ever known in Clifton. A room attached to the York Hotel (on the site of Clifton Down Hotel) which had occasionally served for balls, was rarely used after this date.

A fatal duel took place in a field near the Montagu Hotel on the 1st of March, 1809, and caused a lively sensation in the district. The parties, who, it was reported, had quarrelled at the theatre, were Mr. Henry Smith, attorney, a member of an old Bristol family, and Mr. Richard Priest, a tailor in Clare Street. The latter was mortally wounded in the thigh, and died within a few hours. [The account of the affair given in the local newspapers does not occupy half a dozen lines.] Smith fled to Portugal, but surrendered at the assizes in April, 1810. No indictment, however, was presented against him, and after being arraigned upon the verdict of the coroner's jury, a convenient informality was found in the document, upon which he was at once discharged.

In consequence of the occupation of Spain by the armies of the French emperor, and the enormous destruction of sheep by the foreign invaders, Spanish wool, which had previously formed one of the largest imports into Bristol, rose in this market to wholly unprecedented prices. The highest rate known before the war for fine Spanish wool was 6*s*. 9*d*. per lb.; but at a sale in the Exchange Coffee Room in the spring of 1809, Mr. Lane, a broker, disposed of a lot at 20*s*. 6*d*. per lb. A few days later, a cloth manufacturer of Wotton-under-Edge offered 21*s*. per lb. for a parcel, which was refused. One large transaction took place at 30*s*. per lb.; but the purchaser, discovering that he had been deceived by false representations, forced the vendors to return him a considerable sum. Some flocks of merino sheep were afterwards brought from the Peninsula, and sold at exceedingly high prices on being landed at Shirehampton. The Spaniards, through carelessness and blundering, subsequently allowed Germany to wrest from them the supremacy they had long enjoyed in the fine wool trade; and Bristol suffered much by the loss of this branch of her commerce.

One of the earliest railways, if not actually the first, projected in the West of England, was a proposed line to connect the Bristol with the English Channel. The promoters, whose scheme is mentioned in the *Bristol Gazette* of October 18, doubtless contemplated the laying down of a horse tramway, similar to the colliery lines then common in Northumberland; but the severe financial exigencies of the war rendered the project abortive.

Notwithstanding the gloomy condition of British affairs, international as well as domestic, the commencement of the fiftieth year of the reign of George III. was celebrated on the 23rd of October with much rejoicing. A triumphal arch was erected in Corn Street near St. Werburgh's Church, under which the mayor and members of the Corporation passed in procession on their way to the mayor's chapel. Large congregations also attended divine service in the various places of worship. Subsequently, as the result of a liberal subscription, to which the Corporation contributed £220, distributions of meat, etc., were made to several thousand poor people, the children in the endowed schools were treated with cake and wine, and about twenty miserable debtors were liberated from Newgate. In the evening a gigantic bonfire was lighted on Brandon Hill, and lighted tar-barrels were kicked about in Corn Street. A more permanent memorial of the king's "happy reign" was devised in St. Paul's parish, the foundation-stone of an obelisk being laid during the day in Portland Square, in the presence of the volunteer corps of the city and neighbourhood. In the following April the obelisk was superseded by what the newspapers termed "a very fine statue of his Majesty," the pedestal of which bore an inscription expressive of the gratitude of the subscribers for "the blessings enjoyed under the best of kings." The size of the figure is not recorded, but the editor of the *Gazette* asserted that in point of execution it was equal to the work of "Flaxman and Nollekens." On March 23, 1813, the night after one of "Orator Hunt's" demagogical performances on one of the brazen pillars at the Exchange, a party of eight or ten men entered the inclosure in Portland Square and flung down the statue, which was so much injured that it was never replaced. One of the perpetrators of this act was sentenced, at the ensuing quarter sessions, to twelve months' imprisonment.

The death of the Duke of Portland, then Prime Minister, in 1809, caused a vacancy in the office of Lord High Steward of Bristol. The Common Council, in March, 1810, appointed as his successor another eminent statesman, Lord Grenville. The new High Steward visited the city in May, 1811, and was magnificently entertained by the Corporation on being presented with the freedom of the city, the outlay, as shown by the civic accounts, being no less than £1,396. Many prominent citizens were excluded from this banquet because of their Tory principles, much to the discredit of the ruling party in the Corporation. Lord Grenville was also present at a banquet given by the Whig Club. Another guest at the latter feast was the Duke of Norfolk, the eccentric gastronome already referred to [p. 19], who was toasted as "our friend and fellow-citizen." Lord Grenville held the office of Lord High Steward until his death, in 1834.

Shortly after the appointment of Lord Grenville, the Whig party in the Common Council lost its predominance. Some old Whigs, following the example of Burke, had previously changed sides, but the final defeat of the party in the civic chamber seems to have been due to the reckless conduct of its leaders, who lost the sympathy of the younger Whigs out of doors. A strong feeling had grown up amongst the citizens that the revenues of the Corporation, instead of being squandered in useless pomp, should be made subservient to purposes of public utility. The Corporation, on the other hand, showed a disposition to devote a continually increasing amount on enjoyments monopolized by themselves and their friends. The advance in the mayor's salary to £2,000 at a time of much national distress has been already recorded. The proceeding was followed by similar liberality towards the sheriffs, who had been previously allowed £420 each. This amount was found to be far from adequate to meet the expenditure on dinners, etc., expected from the functionaries in question; and when a gentleman was patriotic enough to serve the office twice, it became the custom to allow him a larger honorarium. In 1808, Sir Henry Protheroe was granted £974 12*s*. 3*d*., and Mr. J. Haythorne £840 on this account; they subsequently got a further vote of £84 between them, being the cost of a piece of plate presented by them to the mayor (H. Bright), who died during the municipal year. In 1811, the sheriffs' salaries were raised to £630 each; yet one of the functionaries of that year, W. Inman, was thought deserving of £213 18*s*. 4*d*. additional, for having served a second time. Adding to the salaries of the mayor and sheriffs the expenditure on the Mansion House, about £1,000 per annum, it appears that fully a fourth of the civic income was expended on display and feasting at a period when the mass of the inhabitants, in common with the country at large, were suffering under the burdens and misfortunes of the long struggle with the French emperor. The effect on public opinion in the city was manifested when it became necessary to fill vacant seats in the Common Council. Although a fine of £300 was imposed on gentlemen refusing to accept office after being elected, the repudiations became numerous after 1805. Five years later the difficulty assumed a form which strikingly illustrated the disgust of intelligent lookers-on. In August, 1810, upon the death of two common councillors, Messrs. J. B. Bence and

J. Thomson were elected, but they both refused to serve, and were fined. Messrs. W. Dowell and R. Bush were next chosen, only to pursue the same course. Messrs. J. Fowler and J. Vaughan were thereupon elected, and the former took his seat. Mr. Vaughan refused, and the gentleman elected to succeed him, Mr. C. Hill, refused also. At this point another councillor died, and fresh efforts were made to fill the two vacancies. Remembering that the Corporation was one of the wealthiest and most distinguished in the kingdom, it is not a little significant that fourteen gentlemen were successively appointed and successively paid the fine rather than accept what was once regarded as an honour. Their names were J. Cave, J. Sutton, Tim. Powell, C. Saunders, G. Thorne, J. R. Lucas, J. Hurle, Jos. Powell, T. Stock, Jer. Hill, W. Dowson, J. Nicholas, G. Gibbs, and T. Hellicar. Finally, after a delay of two years, two gentlemen were found willing to accept the equivocal distinction—Messrs. George and Abraham Hilhouse. They were supposed to be Whigs by Alderman Bengough, who was then all-powerful in the Corporation; but a few months after their election they joined the Tory camp, which by their help obtained a majority, and Alderman Daniel, its leader, a strong-willed disciplinarian, gradually obtained so complete a predominance in civic affairs as to be styled by his admirers the "King of Bristol." Bad as had been the system of local government, the change of autocrats cannot be said to have wrought any improvement. In 1812, at the close of the shrievalty of Messrs. E. Brice and B. Bickley, who had served twice, they were awarded £1,687 16*s.* 8*d.*, as well as a further sum of £150, the fee paid to a barrister for acting as their assessor during the first election of that year. In 1813, the salary of the mayor was increased to £2,500, and in 1816, Sir W. J. Struth was voted £3,346 for his second term of office.* A few years later, as will be seen hereafter, the extravagance of the new *régime*, maintained as it was by crushing imposts on the trade of the port, excited a fierce storm of indignation amongst the leading Tory merchants, and the mayor's allowance was reduced (doubtless with much unwillingness) to £2,000. Returning for the present to the difficulty experienced in recruiting the Council, a remarkable resolution was adopted

* Sir William claimed and received a further sum of £120 14*s.* for earthenware left by him at the Mansion House. The breakage there must have been enormous, for only a few months later a tradesman was paid nearly £40 for another supply of crockery.

in June, 1813, at the instance of the mayor (Mr. R. Castle), who moved that application be made to the Crown for a supplementary charter to the Corporation, empowering them to augment the fine for refusing to serve the office of mayor, alderman, sheriff, or common councillor, to any sum not exceeding £2,000, exemption being granted only to persons willing to swear that they were not worth £8,000. It was thereupon ordered that proper measures should be forthwith adopted for obtaining such powers; but the only further reference to the subject in the records is a payment to the city solicitors of £51 17*s.* "for the intended new charter," after which the project was abandoned owing to the determined opposition of influential citizens of both political parties. For some years Alderman Daniel appears to have easily obtained new adherents, a result probably due, in some measure, to the system of admitting freemen which was adopted under his rule. In the early years of the century the fee imposed on "foreigners"—that is, men not free burgesses—on taking up the freedom averaged about 15 guineas. But in 1815 the fee of Mr. Joseph Reynolds (son of the philanthropist) was fixed at £84. Shortly after, Mr. R. Blakemore, Mr. George Grenfell, and Mr. C. Hare were severally required to pay £105 before their admission. On the other hand, the fees demanded from Mr. Gabriel Goldney, Mr. C. L. Walker, Mr. C. Pinney, and Mr. F. Savage, who all became town councillors, and were elected mayors (the last named refused the chief magistracy), were reduced to 12 guineas. Towards the close of the reign of George IV., when the Corporation had become, if possible, more unpopular than ever, it again became difficult to induce leading citizens to enter the Common Council.* Several gentlemen paid the fine rather than serve; and seven seats were vacant in December, 1829, of which only three could then be filled. The Whig element in the chamber had by that time dwindled away to insignificance; but Alderman Daniel was sagacious enough to prevent its entire extinction, and could easily afford to grant it an occasional recruit.

Great popular discontent, arising partly from the distressed state of industry and partly from the repressive measures adopted by the Government, existed in the spring of 1810. The feeling was much exasperated by the arrest of Sir Francis Burdett—a refined "Orator Hunt"—for expressions

* So early as 1822, three out of the eleven aldermanic seats long remained vacant—one of them for upwards of eighteen months.

that in later days would pass without remark, and by the shooting down of several persons in the streets of London whilst the frothy baronet was being conducted to the Tower. Unfortunately the protests of the people against arbitrary rule too often assumed a violent character. On the 16th of April, 1810, the day fixed for opening the assizes, Sir Vicary Gibbs, the Recorder (who, as Attorney-General, had made himself highly unpopular by his informations against the press), was received by the populace on his entry into the city with groans and hisses; and in the evening, whilst he was being entertained at the Mansion House, the windows were destroyed by stones amidst shouts of "Burdett for ever; no Tower!" The mob afterwards visited the Council House and Guildhall, where the windows were also demolished. In fact, but for the action of the authorities, disasters similar to those of 1831 would probably have occurred. On this occasion, however, the danger was faced with a courage and firmness which should have been an example twenty-one years later. The *Bristol Gazette* eulogizes "the temperate and dignified behaviour of the mayor and aldermen, who went among the people and reasoned with them on the impropriety of their conduct;" and praise is rendered to "the spirited exertions of a number of gentlemen who volunteered as constables," these combined efforts being successful in suppressing the disturbance.

At this assize, Sir Henry Lippincott, bart., a somewhat debauched representative of the old Bristol family of Cann, was arraigned upon a charge of felonious assault upon a woman, whom he was alleged to have decoyed from the cathedral. Sir Vicary Gibbs summed up strongly in his favour, and the jury returned a verdict of acquittal. In another case two men, one of them a sheriff's officer, were convicted of a disgusting offence, and were sentenced to two years' imprisonment, and to stand in the pillory in Wine Street. The latter part of the sentence was carried out a few days later, when one of the men, according to the contemporary diarist already referred to, "was very near being killed."

It would require a vivid imagination on the part of any one now traversing the Pithay and the sordid neighbouring thoroughfares lying between Broadmead and Tower Lane, to represent to himself the locality as a place of public recreation and fashionable resort. No more singular testimony of the local changes effected by time could well be adduced than is to be found in an advertisement published in the Bristol papers in May, 1810, announcing the sale of twenty-nine void old houses in the Pithay and Bowling-green, in the parish of Christ Church. Amongst the lots were "the timber and materials of the Old City Assembly Room, situated in the Bowling-green aforesaid," and "the timber and materials of the Old City Assembly Room Tavern," in the same place. Both those buildings had been last in the occupation of a basket-maker. The property belonged to All Saints parish, which afterwards disposed of the ground—now occupied by Wellington Street and All Saints Street.

The advantages of Weston-super-Mare as a watering-place appear to have dawned upon a speculative innkeeper about this time. In July, 1810, an advertisement in the Bristol newspapers announced that an hotel had been opened in that village for the accommodation of bathers. The house was stated to have about forty bedrooms, so that it could have sheltered, on an emergency, the entire population of the parish, which contained less than forty families. The enterprise came speedily to ruin; in about nine months the hotel-keeper failed, and the furniture was dispersed by auction. The fact was, that the mercantile and trading classes had not yet acquired a taste for the seaside. Their utmost desire in that direction appears to have been a stroll or sail towards the mouth of the river. From an advertisement published in June, 1810, it seems that Lamplighters' Hotel—a house built about half a century before by one Swetman, an oil-man of Small Street, out of his profits as a contractor for lighting several Bristol parishes by means of oil-lamps, who reared his hostelry in full view of the picturesque beauties of Pill—was in especial favour; the landlord stating that his house was "so much frequented on Sunday" that he was "under the necessity of engaging additional waiters from Bath." "Ordinary every Sunday at 2*s*." The Weston hotel does not appear to have been reopened until the summer of 1814, when a couple of coaches commenced plying to and from Bristol "every Saturday during the season."*

One or two aërial ascents by means of the Montgolfier system of heated air had been made in Bristol a quarter of a century previous to this date. The announcement by a Mr. Sadler, in September, of a balloon which was to be raised by hydrogen gas, was deemed still more astonishing, and nearly 20,000 of the inhabitants thronged to the Assembly

* Clevedon did not obtain much patronage until a later date. The village is mentioned as a "newly established" watering-place in Phelps' "History of Somerset," published in 1836.

Room to see the "machine." On the appointed day, almost the whole population, and many thousands from the suburban villages, flocked to Stokes Croft and the adjoining high ground to witness the marvel. Coal gas being still in the future, the cost of providing the needful supply of hydrogen was considerable, upwards of three tons of iron filings and a proportionate quantity of sulphuric acid being placed in twenty-five large casks. The arrangements, however, were satisfactorily carried out, and the balloon arose about the time appointed, amidst the firing of cannon and the applause of the spectators, not a little astounded at the spectacle. The voyage of the two aëronauts, Mr. Sadler and a citizen named Clayfield, proved of a highly perilous character. The balloon sailed down to near Woodspring Priory, when it crossed the Channel to Cardiff; then it was again driven over the sea, nearing both shores alternately, till it approached the coast of Devon, where a large escape of gas caused it to descend rapidly, until the car floated on the water, four miles from land. After remaining three-quarters of an hour in this perilous plight, the voyagers were happily rescued by a boat from Lynmouth.

In December of this year the Kennet and Avon Canal, completing the water communication between Bristol and London, was opened for traffic. The canal had been originally proposed so long ago as 1661; but bills for its construction were frequently rejected by Parliament, owing to the vehement opposition of the landed interest and of the townspeople of Chippenham, Devizes, and other places, who declared that if corn, butter, and cheese reached the inland districts from the ports, the country markets would be destroyed, husbandry discouraged, the breed of horses deteriorated, and carriers and innkeepers ruined. The undertaking was eventually accomplished at a cost of a million sterling. The competition which it opened with the older Thames and Severn Canal was so disastrous to the latter concern that the original £100 shares were sold in 1814 for £1 each. The route of the link between the Kennet and Avon was not, however, well chosen, the summit level being 404 feet above the basin at Bath, necessitating the construction of seventy locks, exclusive of forty-four more on the rivers Thames, Kennet, and Avon. This obstacle greatly impeded traffic, and it was stated before a committee of the House of Commons, in 1834, that the average time required to pass goods from London to Bristol, even in fine weather, was seven days, while during frosts and floods there was generally a delay of a month, although the distance to be traversed was only 150 miles. The Kennet and Avon Canal was transferred to the Great Western Railway Company in September, 1851.

In January, 1811, the Floating Harbour was frozen over for the first time, affording the citizens an unprecedented opportunity for recreation on the ice, of which numbers availed themselves. The frost continued for several days.

The second census of the kingdom was taken early in 1811, when the population of the "ancient city" was found to be 46,592. In the suburbs Clifton contained 6,984 (showing an increase of over 50 per cent. in the previous ten years); St. George's, 4,909; the District, 2,427; St. Philip's out parish, 10,702; and these, with Mangotsfield, 2,901, and Stapleton, 1,921, brought out a total of 76,433. Bedminster, excluded by the eccentric enumerator, had 4,577 souls. The increase over 1801 was greater in Bristol than in any provincial town except Liverpool and Manchester. In many towns, and notably in Newcastle and Hull, the population had diminished, owing to the effects of the war.

Nearly all the ports in Europe being at this time closed against English vessels, through the despotic influence of the French emperor, imports of grain became almost impracticable, notwithstanding the urgent demand for supplies owing to successive bad harvests at home. Bread therefore advanced to excessive rates, the average price throughout the year being 1*s.* per quartern loaf. Butter during the spring rose to 2*s.* 6*d.* per lb., which provoked a riot in the city markets, a mob of colliers and labourers seizing the farmers' baskets and selling the contents for 1*s.* a pound (though many of the purchasers re-sold the butter at 2*s.*). Finding that the attempt to regulate the price of bread made matters only worse, the magistrates abandoned the system during the summer. The harvest of the year was again disastrous, and bread advanced to 1*s.* 8*d.* per quartern loaf, causing terrible distress amongst the poor.

During the parliamentary session of this year an Act was passed for constructing a canal from Bristol—or rather from Pill—to Taunton. Although warmly supported for a time, the required funds were not forthcoming, and by an Act of 1823, the canal from Pill to the parish of Kenn was abandoned. The company were then constructing the canal between Taunton and Bridgwater.

The first attempt in Bristol to resort to coal gas for purposes of illumination was made this year by a Mr. Briellat, a dyer in Broadmead, who is supposed to have seen the gas apparatus erected by Robert Murdoch, some years earlier, at the Soho works, Birmingham. The following advertisement appeared in the *Bristol Gazette* of the 6th of September:—"Lecture and Exhibition of the Gas Lights. J. Briellat respectfully informs the nobility, gentry, and public that he intends for a short time to exhibit every evening at his own house a specimen of the above interesting discovery, accompanied with a descriptive lecture, this present evening, Thursday, at 7 o'clock. For particulars see handbills. No. 56, Broadmead." After having lighted up his shop, Mr. Briellat set up a few lamps in the street, thereby giving Bristol precedency over London in the use of gas for thoroughfares, the first experiment of the same kind in the metropolis being made at Westminster Bridge in 1812. It seems strange that the Bristolians who witnessed Briellat's success should have been reluctant to abandon their flickering and malodorous tallow candles; but for some time the Broadmead dyer passed amongst the vulgar as a man having unholy dealings with an infernal power, while the upper classes treated the innovation with contemptuous indifference. The aristocracy, indeed, were decidedly hostile to gaslighting. In 1816, Lord Lauderdale, in the House of Peers, protested strongly against an invention which threatened to ruin the whale fisheries. Even some scientific men were not less opposed to the new system. When it was proposed to place gas lamps in the streets of London, Sir Humphrey Davy sneeringly asked whether the promoters were going to convert the dome of St. Paul's into a gasholder. It was not until 1816 that the Bristol Gas Company began operations, Mr. Briellat being engaged as manager. The views of the promoters must have been singularly modest, for the capital of the undertaking was fixed at £5,000; but great exertions were needed to raise even that paltry sum. A serious difficulty next arose with the Corporation. The company, after having erected a small gasometer near Temple Back, applied to the authorities for leave to lay pipes in the streets; but the Court of Aldermen (October, 1816) expressed grave apprehensions of danger from the proximity of the gasometer to the city depot of gunpowder (at Tower Harritz), and "considered it their imperative duty to withhold any measures being taken in the streets, the gasometer being in its present situation." The obstacle having been, however, overcome by some means, a few shops were lighted up in May, 1817, and lamps were placed in the principal streets in the following December. In the same month, Lewin's Mead chapel, the first public building in which the novelty found favour, was opened for evening service. In March, 1818, it was proposed to extend the gas pipes into the Commercial Rooms, where the annual cost of oil and candles was £140. As the new company asked £120 for the supply, however, the members of the rooms stuck to lamps and dips until 1825. Although the charge for gas was 15*s*. per 1,000 feet, the undertaking gradually won its way against prejudice, and the company was incorporated by an Act passed in 1819, the authorized capital being fixed in the statute at £50,000. Complaints were raised from time to time, and not without reason, against the offensive odour and the poor illuminating power of the new agent, the purification of which was then very defective; and in September, 1822, a rival establishment was started, styled the Bristol and Clifton Oil Gas Company, which undertook to produce a superior article. In spite of the vigorous opposition of the original company, the rival concern obtained an Act of Parliament in 1824, and, its capital of £30,000 having been subscribed, works were started near Limekiln Lane. The price of oil gas was 40*s*. per 1,000 feet; but its producers asserted, amidst the angry denials of the coal gas directors, that its illuminating power was four times greater than that of coal gas. Unfortunately for the rival establishment, the price of oil advanced considerably, and no dividend was paid for ten years. In 1835 it was admitted that the system of manufacture from oil was a failure; and an Act was obtained to permit distillation from coal, though not until severe restrictions had been imposed in the interests of the original company. Both concerns then reduced the price to 12*s*. per 1,000 feet, further concessions being made subsequently. The competition went on until 1853, when the undertakings were amalgamated under a new Act. By this time the apparatus for purification had greatly improved, and the rapid introduction of gas into houses brought in handsome profits, notwithstanding repeated reductions in price. In 1878 the company (whose capital had increased to £550,000) purchased forty acres of land near Stapleton Road, for the extension of their works. The first contract—for one-sixth of the buildings proposed to be constructed, was let for £80,000. It included a retort house capable of making a million cubic feet of gas daily, and a gasometer capable of storing 1½ million cubic feet. The old works at St. Philip's and Limekiln Lane then yielded 5½ million cubic feet daily. The foundation stone of the new building was laid in March, 1879. On its completion, the mains of the company were extended to Westbury, Shirehampton, and Avonmouth.

During the year 1811 water pipes were laid from Sion Spring to most of the houses in the neighbourhood, which had previously been supplied from it by means of water-carts. The spring was capable of yielding 33,560 gallons per day, and, as the quality was irreproachable, the owner was patronised by nearly every household within the range of his pipes. In 1845, during the Health of Towns inquiry, it was stated that 304 dwellings were thus supplied. The spring was soon afterwards purchased by the Bristol Water Company.

The practice of "stealing the common from the goose" was in great vogue during the early years of the century, when the landlords were rolling in wealth through the high prices occasioned by the continental blockade. Large tracts of commonable land in the parishes of Henbury and Westbury were inclosed this year under the provisions of an Act promoted by Mr. E. Sampson, solicitor, of Henbury, on behalf of himself and other landowners, who appropriated nearly the whole extent, with the utmost indifference to the claims of the resident labourers and of the public at large. Similar inclosures—for the most part unauthorized by Parliament—had been made in other suburban parishes, those in Clifton being especially obnoxious to Bristolians; but except a few timid grumbles in the newspapers, nothing was said or done in defence of public rights. In 1813 another Act swept into the hands of landed gentry a large extent of commonable land in the parishes of Long Ashton, Wraxall, Nailsea, and Bourton, and further extensive inclosures were made at Portishead, Dundry, and Almondsbury by subsequent statutes. Even before those "conveyances" were effected, a writer in the *Bristol Gazette* of August 13, 1812, says:—"They who remember Ashton, Leigh, Westbury, Kingsweston, Clifton, and Stapleton twenty years ago, will need no description to recall to their minds the delightful and healthy walks now untrodden by vulgar feet—then open to the public for exercise or pleasure."

An Act was passed this year for authorizing the cutting of a canal between Bristol and Bath, and the construction of works for supplying Bristol with water. The canal was to have been without locks, and the western terminus was intended to be in Temple Meads, adjoining the Floating Harbour. The proposed waterworks excited signs of life in a concern which had long lain dormant and forgotten—the old company formed in the seventeenth century for supplying water from the Avon at Hanham. The local newspapers for June and July contained announcements of an intended sale by auction of "all the right, title, and privilege of the Bristol Waterworks Company to supply the inhabitants of Bristol with fresh water, granted to them by an Act passed in the reign of William III., and also all their leasehold land situate near Bristol, and a small piece of leasehold land near Hanham Mills." A reservoir belonging to the company then existed at Lawrence Hill; but the supply of water had ceased for about half a century—it is supposed from want of funds to renew the pipes, which were formed of hollow trunks of trees. The projects authorized by the Act of 1811 were never carried out, and the land purchased for a depôt and warehouses at Temple Meads was bought by the Great Western Railway Company, and forms part of the site of the existing terminus.

The death was announced in October of the Rev. Charles Lee, who had been head-master of the Grammar School for forty-seven years. Having, when a young man, married the daughter of Alderman Henry Dampier, an influential member of the Corporation, his father-in-law induced the Common Council to remove the Grammar School from Bartholomew's Hospital, Christmas Street, to the large mansion in Unity Street belonging to the City School, the boys in the latter being sent to dwell in the unhealthy premises near the then open Froom. Mr. Lee is stated to have been a good classical scholar, and during the early years of his management the Grammar School was largely attended by the sons of respectable citizens. For a long period before his death, however, the institution "sank into disrepute," to use the expression of a contemporary newspaper; and there is a tradition that for some years the head-master had only one pupil, commonly known as "Lee's chick." In 1805 his friends in the Common Council endeavoured to induce that body to grant him a pension of £200, more than double his salary, but the proposal was rejected, as was another to the same effect in 1809. His death afforded the Corporation an opportunity of introducing regulations calculated to restore the school to its former popularity; but the recommendations made by a committee appointed to consider the matter were little adapted for such a result. The trust-deed of the founder, Nicholas Thorne, in 1561, declared that no charge was to be made for education other than fourpence on the admission of every scholar. This fee was raised in the reign of Charles II. to five shillings. It was now determined to increase it to £4. By the regulations of 1666, each boy was required to pay ten shillings yearly for firing, and the same sum for sweeping the school. For these charges the committee recommended the substitution of a yearly fee of £6 6*s*., but the Common Council made no change under this head. The new master was permitted to take as many boarders and day scholars as he thought fit, and was left at liberty to fix his own terms for such pupils. The only other regulation worthy of notice was, that the scholars were, as under the old rules, to answer to their names at seven o'clock in the morning in the summer half year, and at eight o'clock in the winter months. The person chosen in March, 1812, for the post of head-master, was the Rev. John Joseph Goodenough, who, like his predecessor, had married a daughter of a member of the Common Council, and who lost no time in converting the institution into a private high-class school. Fortified by a judgment of Lord Chancellor Eldon in the Highgate case, Mr. [afterwards Dr.] Goodenough refused to teach the "free" scholars, who were exclusively the sons of freemen, anything save Greek and Latin; and the natural, as it was the intended, effect was, to reduce the endowment to a sinecure. The complacent Common Council spent upwards of £220 in 1815, on the construction of a gallery in the mayor's chapel "for the Grammar-school boys," in other words, for the head-master's private boarders, who were generally thirty-five in number. In 1820, in flagrant violation of the regulations, Dr. Goodenough was permitted to take a Church living in Buckinghamshire, his memorial for the leave of the Corporation asserting, with perhaps unintentional irony, that his acceptance of the incumbency "would not in any way interfere with the duties of his situation in this city." In 1828, when the school—as a grammar school—was practically deserted, the Charity Commissioners addressed a letter to the Corporation on the state of the institution, with the effect of obtaining a reduction of the entrance fee to its original amount. The opportunity was taken, however, to shut out the sons of free burgesses living beyond the limits of the "ancient city," and as the lowered charge was unaccompanied by any alteration in the system of teaching, it wrought no change in the condition of the school. How the abuse was remedied will be narrated at a later date.

Clifton churchyard having become much too small as compared with the population of the parish, a piece of ground near Bellevue—part of the site of an old quarry—was obtained about the close of 1811, and was laid out as an additional cemetery.

Towards the end of 1811 the Assembly Rooms in Prince's Street * underwent considerable internal alteration, and were in the following year reopened under the name of the Regency Theatre. For some time the entertainments consisted chiefly of concerts, but during the summer it was announced that a Mr. Lawler, from London, having taken the management, a company had been engaged for pantomimes and burlettas, and a "prodigious expense" had been incurred to make the theatre worthy of public patronage. The first performance took place on the 24th of August; but Mr. Lawler's efforts were unsuccessful, and at the end of eight weeks the house was closed. A Mr. Clark became manager in November; and although he complained that he sustained heavy losses, the competition affected the receipts of the old theatre, which had now opened for the regular season. Alarmed at the attack upon their chartered rights, the proprietors and manager of the latter applied to the magistrates in January, 1813, and a warrant was issued against Clark under the old law placing stage-players under the category of rogues and vagabonds. The public, strongly resenting this proceeding, lent its patronage to the new enterprise. The law, however, could not be evaded, and the Regency shut its doors. When it was next noticed in the newspapers, in the following autumn, it had sunk to giving entertainments on the "musical glasses."

The social condition of the Kingswood district,† early in the year 1812, is graphically illustrated in an address pub-

* Local annalists having overlooked the story of this building, it may be stated that in March, 1754, the Corporation granted a lease of four tenements to Cranfield Becher, John Heylyn, Morgan Smith, and others, at a rent of £5, and a fine of £100 on renewal every fourteen years, on condition that they pulled down the old buildings and erected a large room suitable for an assembly room, with convenient appurtenances. The Corporation reserved a right to the free use of the premises for six days every year, should they be needful for the entertainment of members of the royal family visiting the city.

† A large part of this district lay in the parish of Bitton, a fact that explains the following anecdote, the date of which is ascribed to the closing years of the previous century. Mr. Justice Heath, while sitting in the Crown Court at Gloucester, asked a lying witness from what part of the county he came, and being answered "From Bitton, my lord," he exclaimed. "You do seem to be of the Bitton breed, but I thought I had hanged the whole of that parish long ago." (*Campbell's Lives of the Chancellors*, vi. 154.) A Bristol newspaper of April 8, 1786, stated that, including two men then under sentence of death, ten persons from the parish of Bitton had been hanged at Gloucester within three years. They had all belonged to the "Cock-road gang," which regularly received black-mail from the neighbouring farmers at the annual fair on Lansdown.

lished in the local journals by a committee of the respectable inhabitants. The document stated that robberies, burglaries, and other crimes were daily committed by an extensive combination of villains, who extended their ravages for miles around. "This scheme of enormity has been maturing for a long series of years, and whole families are dependent on this combination for their maintenance, and many hundreds of the younger branches are well known to be in training for the like purposes. Labourers are decoyed from employment and admitted into the society; great numbers of hucksters are in alliance with them, and the vendors of the [stolen] goods are seen passing with cart-loads by night, none presuming to interrupt them." The address goes on to say that many of the malefactors were known, but that the terrorism they exercised deterred honest persons from giving information, "and when it is recollected that thousands are connected, by receiving and vending the goods, it will not appear surprising that very few remain sufficiently virtuous or courageous to unite with us." Appeals were therefore made to the citizens of Bristol and Bath for subscriptions to crush the gigantic conspiracy. Funds having been obtained, patrols were established in the district, which had a temporary effect in intimidating depredators. Nevertheless, throughout the severe distress which occurred during the winter of 1812–13, the number of robberies and burglaries in Kingswood exceeded anything before known. In 1813 the Wesleyan body, desiring to strike at the roots of the evil, started a school at Cock-road, in which locality seven-tenths of the children were found to be ignorant of the alphabet. Owing to lack of funds, however, the school for several years could not be kept open on week days. Improvement under such circumstances was necessarily slow. In August, 1814, a Bristol journalist compared the state of the honest population in and near Cock-road to that of loyal persons in some parts of Ireland. "They are frequently obliged to sit up all night with loaded muskets by their side to guard against assaults, depredations, and even murder." An account follows of the firing of two guns into the bedroom of a constable who had been summoned to Gloucester assizes to give evidence against some captured ruffians. A few days later, when a gang of robbers was arrested, with a quantity of plunder in their possession, the constables were nearly killed by the friends of the thieves, who attempted to rescue them.

As the time drew near for the renewal of the East India

Company's charter, a movement sprang up in the leading provincial ports for the abolition of the monopoly so long enjoyed by the Company in the trade between India and this country. The mercantile interest in Bristol bestirred itself vigorously in the matter; and the Corporation, at a meeting in June, contributed £200 towards the subscription started for pressing the subject upon the attention of Parliament. The agitation was successful, an Act for throwing open the trade being passed in 1813. The first two Bristol vessels bound for Hindostan sailed in April, 1814, amidst various demonstrations of rejoicing. On the 27th of October, 1818, a ship arrived in Cumberland basin bringing the first East Indian cargo imported into Bristol. About 5,000 spectators greeted her appearance, and the bells rang merry peals when she passed into the Float. The hopes entertained of a large development of commerce in this direction were, however, disappointed. In August, 1862, when a vessel arrived with a cargo from Calcutta, it was stated in one of the local newspapers that no importation direct from India had been made into Bristol for twenty-five years.

Mr. Bragge Bathurst, M.P., obtained another ministerial promotion in June, 1812, being appointed Chancellor of the Duchy of Lancaster, and a vacancy was thus created in the representation of the city. From some unexplained cause, the understanding which had long existed amongst local politicians was broken up, and as a costly struggle threatened to take place at the ensuing general election, Mr. Bathurst declined to offer himself for re-election. Three candidates presented themselves for the vacancy—Mr. Richard Hart Davis, M.P. for Colchester, who resigned that seat at the request of the Bristol Tories; Mr. Henry Hunt, the former brewer at Jacob's Wells, but now a blacking maker in London; and the well-known William Cobbett. The name of Cobbett was withdrawn, and the candidature of Hunt was merely the idle outcome of his vanity, the respectable Whigs holding aloof from him. With a recklessness that later days would deem criminal, Mr. Davis's friends set no limit to the corruption employed on behalf of their nominee, spending over £1,000 a day during the fortnight for which the poll was kept open. The numbers at the close of the voting were:—Mr. Davis, 1907; Mr. Hunt, 235. Owing to the floods of beer dispersed by the Tory committee, fights between the partisans of the rival candidates were almost continuous throughout the contest, and the city was kept in a state of constant agitation. Hunt's mob, on the night of the first day's poll, smashed the doors and windows of the Council House, and then proceeded to Mr. Davis's residence, Mortimer House, Clifton, where similar destruction was committed. The military were called out, and in the confusion one man was killed and many wounded. It was deemed advisable to retain a guard of soldiers at the powder magazine at Tower Harratz until after the close of the polling. Amongst the items of corporate expenditure caused by the conflict was one of £437, "paid to J. H. Wilcox, mayor," expended in entertaining the military and peace officers, and for "beer for guards mounted in the city during the election"; a further sum of £158 4*s.* 6*d.* being reimbursed to the sheriffs, "what they expended for constables, etc." The repair of the Guildhall and Council House windows cost £108 more. In October, the general election threatened to bring a renewal of disorder, and a large body of special constables was enrolled at an outlay of £516. Mr. Davis was again the nominee of the Tories. Mr. Baillie, the late Whig member having retired, Mr. Edward Protheroe came forward in the "old Whig" interest, whilst the progressive Whigs, or Reformers as they were beginning to be called, styled Mr. Protheroe a Tory in disguise, and nominated Sir Samuel Romilly, the distinguished lawyer. Finally, Mr. Hunt, whose hand was against all respectable parties and persons, offered himself as the champion of democracy. Owing to a coalition between Mr. Davis and Mr. Protheroe, or at least between the two political sections of the West India interest, which heartily concurred in detesting the anti-slavery principles of Romilly, the latter withdrew at the close of the ninth day's poll, when the numbers were: Mr. Davis, 2,895; Mr. Protheroe, 2,435; Sir S. Romilly, 1,683; Mr. Hunt, 523. This was another costly contest. To insure success, the Davis and Protheroe parties were at the expense of placing about 1,100 freemen on the burgess roll, at an outlay of about £2,500. About 600 more freemen were entered by the Romilly party. [Amongst the total were seventy-five men who had obtained qualifications by means of marrying the widows of deceased freemen. It was said that many of these unions were merely colourable, the parties separating at the church doors.] In ordinary years the average number of burgesses taking up their freedom did not exceed fifty. Mr. Hunt petitioned against the two members, one of his leading points being that the payments for freemen were acts of bribery, the value of the freedom being considerable. In support of this contention before a committee of the House of Commons, he showed that the mayors of the two preceding years had been paid £42 each out of the civic purse, "for not having nominated a freeman" during their official term, as they were entitled to do by ancient custom. [This item occurs in the civic accounts every year until the Corporation was reformed.] It was unquestionable that corruption had also extensively prevailed. Oxen ornamented with blue ribbons had been paraded through the streets, and every "blue" voter who claimed his "rights" had an allowance of fourteen pounds of beef, three quartern loaves (then selling at about 1*s*. 6*d*. each), and 7*s*. 6*d*. in money. Bludgeon men, styled constables, took possession of the entrance to the Guildhall on the nomination day, denying admission to all but their employers' partisans, and about 1,500 bludgeons, painted blue, were seen to be carried to the house of one of Mr. Davis's agents. It was alleged, moreover, that charity money had been corruptly dispensed by the parochial churchwardens, who were all active canvassers in the "blue" interest. The conduct of the Protheroe Whigs was not less demoralizing than that of their allies, and the printed evidence offers the reader a glimpse of Sir Henry Protheroe scattering his money at the Mulberry Tree Tavern,* and damning "French principles"—an allusion to Romilly's Huguenot descent. The Commons' committee, however, declared the members duly elected, to the unbounded delight of their chief supporters in Bristol, who forthwith repaired to a tavern, and emptied a gigantic bowl, containing twenty-eight gallons of punch, "suitably decorated with blue," in honour of the victory. The *Bristol Times* of August 2, 1862, published a detailed account of the outlay of the Tory party at the above two elections. The total amounted to the sum of £29,429 14*s*. 7*d*., paid through the Steadfast Club. The first election, although never in doubt, cost £14,362, of which nearly £3,000 were distributed in money amongst the "constables" (voters), and over £2,000 at public-houses in entertaining the so-called guardians of order. The cost of blue ribbons supplied at the first contest was £3,366, yet £2,318 more for the same frippery were squandered three months later. "This money," says the above authority, "seems to have been distributed amongst all the constitutional mercers in the city." The expenses of the chairing were formidable, one Charles Smith, "the great physical force purveyor,"

* An etching inaccurately professing to give a view of this hostelry having been recently published, it may be useful to state that some remnants of the tavern may still be seen at the back of Guildhall Chambers, Broad Street.

being alone paid £2,577. The blue umbrella held over Mr. Davis's head figured for £6 13*s*., and £7 12*s*. were paid for the gaudy dress of the man who bore it. There were also charges for "the gold banner," gold fringe, etc. The entertainment of the committee at the White Lion Hotel cost £2,182, besides which there was a heavy disbursement for the expenses of the various parochial committees. Towards defraying the total charge, Mr. Davis contributed £10,000. The balance was liquidated by means of subscriptions, several wealthy Tories giving £500 each.*

A piece of ground at Clifton, somewhat less than ten acres in extent, was sold in September for building sites, and brought what was then regarded as the extraordinary sum of £15,000. The houses erected upon it were called Richmond Hill, and an advertisement in September, 1814, shows that certain sanitary arrangements were limited to a short sewer and a cesspool. Clifton was still, so far as the elevated district was concerned, a mere village, and all its arrangements were primitive. An aged correspondent of the *Times and Mirror* (May 26, 1883), recalling the appearance of the place in 1813, stated that the post office was near Saville Place—a mere cottage with two small shop windows. The postmaster was a tailor, who used to sit at his work on the shopboard in one window, while his wife, at the other side, sold gingerbread and sweets. There were two letter carriers, one of whom was a woman, and the work of carrying the letter bags to and from Bristol, and of delivering the contents, was divided between them.

The Prudent Man's Friend Society, for the then novel object of encouraging thrift amongst the poor, founded by the philanthropic Richard Reynolds, Mr. T. Sanders, and a few friends, came into existence in December. To this society the city is indebted for the establishment of the Bristol Savings Bank, which was opened a few weeks later at No. 20, Small Street, although the title it now bears was not assumed until 1815. The society made great exertions to promote economy among the labouring community, but only seventy-three persons opened accounts at the bank during the first nine months of its existence, and as their deposits averaged over £7 each, very few could have belonged to the class it was designed to benefit. It was not indeed until 1817,

* Not content with his demagogic displays in this city, Hunt made excursions to Bath, with the effect of exciting serious rioting in that city. The power of choosing members for Bath was vested solely in the Corporation, consisting of thirty persons, self-elected, and irresponsible.

when the first Savings Bank Act was passed, that artisans and servants were attracted to the institution. Progress was afterwards rapid, and by 1827 the accumulated deposits amounted to over £300,000. It was not, however, until twenty-six years later that the aggregate exceeded £400,000, and the increase in the fund has been still slower since the introduction of the postal institutions. Soon after its establishment the Savings Bank was removed to Bridge Street, whence it again removed, in December, 1831, to St. Stephen's Avenue, where a building had been specially erected for it at a cost, including site, of £3,500. The premises have since been reconstructed on an enlarged scale.

In the course of the year 1812, the Rev. Samuel Seyer, who was then engaged upon his valuable history of the city, published "The Charters and Letters Patent granted by the Kings and Queens of England to the City and County of Bristol, newly Translated, and accompanied by the Original Latin." In the preface to the work it was stated that the manuscripts forming the text were found in the Bodleian collection, but that Mr. Seyer, fearing verbal errors or omissions in those copies, addressed a memorial to the Common Council, praying to be permitted to have access to the originals for the purpose of collation. The response was a point-blank refusal, although the charters were, as Mr. Seyer went on to remark, "open letters," granted to the burgesses generally, and for their benefit, and ought to have been accessible to all of them as members of the Corporation. It appears from the official minutes of the Common Council that the rejection of the reverend gentleman's request was due to the Recorder, Sir Vicary Gibbs, whose advice was solicited by the Corporation.

A "grand gala fête," in honour of the British victories over the French armies in Spain, took place in September, 1813, "in the gardens of the Three Blackbirds tavern, near Stapleton." In the following year the name of the place was changed to the "Wellington Gardens," under which it became a fashionable resort for many years. The galas were of a somewhat exclusive character. The price of admission was half a crown; gentlemen were expected to appear in full evening dress; and livery servants were excluded. The gardens remained popular notwithstanding the opening of the Zoological Gardens at Clifton, though that event greatly altered the status of those who resorted to them. The latest notice of the place that has been found in the newspapers occurs in 1847, when there was a large attendance at a balloon ascent.

A somewhat singular accident occurred in September, 1813, at Cumberland Basin. A heavily laden West Indiaman, named the *William Miles*, was entering the basin by the upper lock, when a press-gang was seen approaching for the purpose of seizing the crew. After having been many months absent from home, the men were by no means disposed to be captured, and instantly fled. Unfortunately the ship had not cleared the entrance, and as the tide rapidly ebbed, she remained suspended in the lock, the weight of the cargo crushing the hull out of shape and firmly fixing it between the walls. The lock thus became impracticable for other vessels until the obstruction was removed, which was not effected for upwards of three weeks.

Mr. Bathurst, late member for the city, who had retreated to the cheaper and less arduous representation of Bodmin, was presented by his Bristol admirers, in September, with an elegant piece of plate, valued at 700 guineas, in gratitude for his lengthened services.

The *Bristol Journal* of September the 4th contains the following advertisement:—"For sale, a Tyburn Ticket, exempting the holder from serving the parish and ward offices of the parish of St. Paul and ward of St. James. Apply to Mr. Evans, Bridewell." The same newpaper a few weeks later announced that "two Tyburn tickets for the parish of Clifton" were for disposal. These ominously named documents had their origin in the statute 10th William III. c. 12, which enacted that, after the 20th of May, 1699, every person convicted of burglary, horse stealing, or theft from a shop to the value of five shillings, should be debarred from benefit of clergy—that is, should be hanged; and that every person who should apprehend such an offender and prosecute him to conviction should be entitled to a certificate to that effect from the judge who tried the case, such certificate to discharge the holder from fulfilling all manner of parish and ward offices in the district where the felony was committed. The ticket was capable of being assigned to another person, but only once. The privilege was abolished by an Act passed in June, 1818. Only three months previously, according to the *Stamford Mercury* for March 17, 1818, a Tyburn ticket was sold in Manchester for £280. A copy of one of the tickets is given in *Notes and Queries*, 2nd series, xi. 395.

Up to this time the income of the bishopric of Bristol does not appear to have exceeded £600 or £800 a year—not a twentieth of the revenue of one of the episcopal prizes of the English Church. The irregularities which then prevailed in the value of the various sees were considered to "work well." A spiritual lord in the reign of George III. might find it difficult to make ends meet at Bristol, Exeter, or Llandaff; but he knew that preferment would come sooner or later if he offered himself as a submissive instrument to the royal or ministerial will. The distinguished Bishop Newton, declining to be a "king's friend," was left in the cold at Bristol for twenty-one years. But in the next twenty-seven years he had eight successors, though only one vacancy was caused by death. If the fact proved that the system "worked well" for those who lived long enough, it was silent as to those who dropped by the wayside. At a meeting of a local clergy society so recently as 1860, it was stated that a former bishop had left a daughter absolutely penniless, and that, after having kept a small parish school until old age rendered her incapable, she had applied for relief to the society, having not a farthing to live upon save £5 a year granted by a charity in London. Going back to 1813, it would appear that the leaders of the Church were not wholly satisfied with "the system." In the course of the year an arrangement was effected, at the instance of the Archbishop of Canterbury, by which the rectory of Almondsbury was united to the bishopric of Bristol. The effect of this union, according to the contemporary press, was to increase the income of the see from £600 to £2,000 per annum; but this estimate appears to have been greatly exaggerated. A significant incident of the affair was, that neither the primate, the bishop, the Government, nor the newspapers appear to have bestowed the slightest thought on the fact that the living of Almondsbury existed for the benefit of the parishioners, and that the non-residence of a rector—even though a bishop—was a scandalous abuse. The living was again detached from the see by Order of Council in July, 1851, when Bishop Monk was granted, in compensation, an additional income of £650 yearly.

Bristol Exchange, never very popular amongst mercantile men, was entirely abandoned by them upon the opening of the Commercial Rooms. The Corporation, in September, directed the south row of the deserted quadrangle to be converted into a corn market, an institution of which grain merchants and the neighbouring farmers had long felt the want. The market was opened on the 18th of October.

A Bristol newspaper editor of this year gravely speaks of pugilism as an "elegant and fashionable science." That it was fashionable was beyond dispute, as the memoirs of

George IV., of Mr. Windham, and of other notabilities of the time bear witness. In Bristol "the ring" was especially popular, several of the leading "bruisers" being natives of the city or of its environs. Of these, early in the century, the Belchers, one of whom was "champion," and Nichols, the "Game Chicken," another "champion," were the most conspicuous. A Bristol paper of 1805 stated that Miss Belcher, a sister of the heroic brothers, had a fight with another woman in one of the streets of the city, seconded by her mother, the combat lasting "more than fifty minutes." Tom Belcher, who won eight great battles and lost only three, retired from the ring in 1814, but survived as a reputable London publican until December, 1854. Another favourite pugilist was William Neat, famed for many arduous victories, though, being at length unsuccessful in an encounter with Spring, in 1823, he was denounced by his former admirers for having "sold the fight." Neat was prevailed upon to quit the "ring" by Mrs. Fry, the celebrated philanthropist. A local annalist, in recording Neat's death, in 1858,* states that 30,000 persons were present at his last battle, which took place near Andover. A large contingent had come from Bristol, every available horse in the city, including the black horses employed at funerals, being hired for the occasion. A still more famous combatant was John Gully, in youth a Bristol butcher. After having won national fame in "the ring," he betook himself to the congenial, though not yet so miry, "turf," where he was patronized by the Duke of York, and made a large fortune as a "betting man." In 1832 Gully, then metamorphosed into a country gentleman, was elected member of parliament for Pontefract, in the neighbourhood of which town he resided. He died in 1863, aged 80 years.

On the 21st of December, 1813, the Prince Regent was pleased to confer the honour of a baronetcy on Mr. Nathaniel William Wraxall, whose claims to such a distinction were much criticized by his contemporaries. Wraxall was the son of a Bristol merchant, and was born in Queen Square, on the 8th of April, 1751.† At the age of eighteen he entered the service of the East India Company, and sailed for Bombay; but he relinquished that employment on attaining his majority, and after returning to Europe he occupied himself for seven years in travelling, extending his tour from Italy

* "Local Annals," City Library, iii. 37.

† Another Nathaniel Wraxall, probably a cousin, was swordbearer to the Bristol Council in 1768. A third, holding the same office, died in 1781.

to Lapland. During a portion of his ramblings he was employed by an unfortunate princess, Caroline, wife of Christian VII. of Denmark, to seek the support of her brother, George III., to a conspiracy for placing the queen on the throne. Wraxall afterwards alleged that the English king was so pleased with his services as to order him to be presented with 1,000 guineas; but it is clear from his majesty's letter to Lord North ("Correspondence," ii. 359), that the negotiator was treated with great indifference, and that his mission was unsuccessful. In 1775 Wraxall published an account of his travels, under the title of "Cursory Remarks," the easy style of which carried the book through several editions. Other works, chiefly on the history of France, followed at intervals, but excited little attention. In 1815, however, he produced a work in three volumes, entitled "Memoirs of My Own Times," which caused some sensation in political circles, and which the literary critics of the day concurred in condemning as throwing equal discredit on the author's head and heart. For a libel on the Russian Ambassador, printed in this book, Wraxall was fined £500 and sentenced to six months' imprisonment. The general charge of mendacity levelled against the author is, however, denied by Carlyle in his "Life of Frederick the Great." After revising the "Memoirs" for a second edition, Wraxall published nothing more, though he enjoyed vigorous health until his eightieth year. He died on the 7th of November, 1831, whilst preparing for an extensive continental tour. In 1836 was published "Posthumous Memoirs of My Own Times," in three volumes, which in character resembled the previous work, and which, as the author virtually confessed, had been held back until he should be beyond the reach of those whom he assailed. A new edition of both the above works has been published within the last few years. One of Sir Nathaniel's grandsons and successors, Sir C. F. Lascelles Wraxall, devoted himself to literature with considerable success. Having served in the Crimea with the Turkish contingent, the result was a book called "Camp Life," which was perhaps the best of his productions. "The Armies of the Great Powers," a "Life of Caroline of Denmark," "The Second Empire," and several novels also issued from his pen. On his death, in his thirty-seventh year, in 1865, the title reverted to his brother, Horatio Henry, who followed the vocation of a "betting man," but died in a lunatic asylum in 1882, having been for some time chargeable as a pauper to the Union of Southwark. The baronetcy is still in existence.

A frost of extreme severity and unusual length was experienced in the opening months of 1814. The Floating Harbour from end to end was so thickly covered with ice as to permit of general locomotion upon it, and some thousands of persons are said to have enjoyed the novel experience of passing under Bristol bridge on foot. Owing to heavy snowstorms, the roads in all parts of the kingdom were drifted up, communication by coaches was cut off, and the mails were everywhere delayed for some days. So extensive a dislocation of traffic had not before occurred since the establishment of mail coaches.

On March 16, 1814, whilst workmen were sinking a vault near the vestry in St. Mary-le-port Church, under a mural monument in the Early Tudor style, they came upon a lead coffin, the ancient appearance of which was thought worthy of the inspection of local antiquaries. A group of amateurs was soon assembled, and it was forthwith decided that the remains were those of Robert Yeamans, one of the "royal martyrs" executed in 1643, though there is incontestable contemporary testimony to prove that the unfortunate man was buried in Christ Church. Assuming, however, that the supposition had been correct, its authors displayed their admiration of the victim of Puritan vengeance in a remarkable manner. Mr. Richard Smith, surgeon, who was always foremost in such affairs, cut up the body, which was in excellent preservation, and removed the heart as a precious addition to his "anatomical museum." The incumbent, the Rev. W. Waite, carried off a slice of the shirt. Mr. Henry Smith possessed himself of a portion of the same garment, and further made prize of part of the handkerchief that bound up the head. The spoil of the other members of the party is not recorded, but it is highly probable that they followed the example of their leaders. Mr. Richard Smith subsequently published a characteristic account of the proceedings.

A musical festival for the benefit of the Infirmary took place in June, three oratorios, "The Messiah," "The Creation," and "The Mount of Olives," being given in St. Paul's Church, and two evening concerts at the theatre. The chief vocalists were Madame Catalani, then at the summit of her fame, and the equally celebrated Mr. Braham. The surplus receipts, including collections, amounted to £845.

Bristolians, in common with Englishmen generally, were profoundly stirred at this time by the mighty events occurring on the Continent. The battles of Leipsic and Dresden, the general rising of Germany, the successive victories of the English army on the Franco-Spanish frontier, and the final downfall of Bonaparte caused repeated illuminations and other tokens of rejoicing.* When the newspapers became almost hysterical, and shouted, as did the editor of *Felix Farley's Bristol Journal*, "Huzza! huzza! huzza! the Dutch have taken Holland!" one may imagine the fervour which animated the masses. The intelligence of the conclusion of a definitive treaty of peace, closing a war with France which had lasted, with a brief interval, for twenty-one years, was received with transports of joy. The mail coach conveying the news was stopped at Totterdown by the populace, who removed the horses, and dragged the vehicle through the streets amidst a whirlwind of cheers. The customary proclamations were made by the civic authorities on the 27th of June, the details of the ceremony being identical with those of 1801. In the evening the city was illuminated. A lofty triumphal arch, erected in Corn Street in front of the Commercial Rooms, was, when its pictorial embellishments were lighted up, an especial attraction; but the inhabitants of the chief streets appear to have vied with each other in the production of fanciful allegories, the description of which fills many columns of the newspapers. Probably the most picturesque and effective displays were the illumination of the battlements of the tower of St. Mary Redcliff, and the huge bonfire on Brandon Hill. Immediately after the peace, the volunteer infantry were disembodied by order of the Government. After the final parade, when Lieut.-Colonels Gore and Goldney took farewell of the regiment, the colours were deposited at the house of Colonel Baillie, in Park Row, and the weapons stored at the Armoury in Stapleton Road. Lieut.-Colonel Gore died within a fortnight of these events, deeply regretted by his regiment, which at once resolved to give £3,000, part of the fund subscribed and invested for the use of the corps, to the widow and five children of the deceased, "in respectful testimony of his meritorious conduct." A further sum of £200 was ordered to be spent in striking silver medals to commemorate the services of the regiment, one of which was given to each officer and private. Colonel Baillie was presented by the Common Council with

* The statue of William III. in Queen Square was brilliantly illuminated upon the evacuation of Holland by the French. The Corporation contributed £20 towards the expense. Another item in the civic accounts is £7 6*s*. 6*d*. for "500 fagots, *haling*, etc. to Brandon hill, to make a bonfire on the arrival of the glorious intelligence that the allies had obtained a decisive victory over the enemy of mankind."

a piece of plate, value £200, for nearly twenty years' services in connection with the regiment. In November, 1816, a cenotaph to the memory of Colonel Gore, bearing his portrait in *basso-rilievo*, was placed in the cathedral at the expense of the volunteers.

During the brief sojourn of the allied sovereigns in London in 1814, the Common Council sent off a deputation to invite the Prince Regent and his imperial guests to visit Bristol. The arrangements of the illustrious strangers rendered the step abortive; but the deputation by some means succeeded in spending £378 of the corporate money in performing the duty imposed upon them.

The close of the mayoralty of Mr. James Fowler was marked by an unusual scandal in the history of the Corporation. At the usual meeting in December, 1814, a motion that the ex-mayor should receive such a sum as would raise his receipts from fees and perquisites to £2,500 was rejected in favour of an amendment to limit the payment from the civic chest to such an amount "as should appear to the mayor and aldermen to have been expended." The inferential censure having been ratified by a majority, the case was investigated by the Court of Aldermen in the following month, when, after an examination of the accounts and vouchers, it was resolved "that the sum of £2,000 should be paid to Mr. Fowler as a full and ample reimbursement for the expenses incurred by him." Mr. B. Bickley was at the same time voted £844 for his third shrievalty. Some stories respecting an exceedingly parsimonious mayor early in the century probably date from this year. It is said that a large placard was posted upon the walls of the city, notifying that a cat had just brought forth kittens in the kitchen grate of the Mansion House, and was doing well. "The only fear is that the kittens may suffer from cold, as a fire has not been for some time lighted in the said kitchen grate." A few mornings later, three dead rats were found suspended to the knocker of the civic residence, with the label: "Starved out of the Mansion House."

On the 16th of January, 1815, the death occurred in London of a Mr. Samuel Gist, a wealthy planter in Virginia, but who was educated, three-quarters of a century earlier, in Queen Elizabeth's Hospital. The remains of the deceased were buried, at his own request, at Wormington, Gloucester. By his will he left the sum of £10,000 in consols, upon trust, to maintain six poor men, six poor women, and six poor boys in Queen Elizabeth's Hospital, and to maintain and educate six poor girls. It being impossible to carry out this bequest in the manner directed, an application was made by the Common Council to the Court of Chancery, which in 1820 decreed that the income should be distributed in payments to three male and three female annuitants, who were to receive £115 16*s*. amongst them; £100 to Queen Elizabeth's Hospital, for the maintenance of three boys; and £72 to the Red Maids' School for three girls. Mr. Gist's will also directed that his 300 slaves should have their freedom, and he devised a large sum for the education and religious instruction of their descendants, as well as for food and clothing to such as might become destitute.

A war with the United States, which, though of brief duration, had been exceedingly disastrous to English shipowners through the ravages of the enemy's privateers, was brought to a close by the Treaty of Ghent, in the spring of 1815. A congratulatory address to the Prince Regent was sent up by the Corporation, two of whose representatives, Mr. W. J. Struth, then mayor, and Alderman Richard Vaughan, received the honour of knighthood. The expenses of the deputation were, as usual, excessive, the amount paid out of the civic purse being £195 10*s*.

The close of the long continental struggle caused an almost immediate collapse in the artificial system which had grown up whilst nearly all the great foreign ports had been closed against us, and whilst prices had been almost continually rising under a factitious paper currency. When wheat rarely sold at under 80*s*. per quarter, and meat advanced to 10*d*. per lb., or three times its price before the war, the rent of land naturally rose in proportion, estates more than doubled in value, and the price of labour in many trades was notably enhanced. The opening of the ports brought down prices of food with a crash, wheat falling to 56*s*. per quarter, and meat to 4*d*. per lb. As a natural consequence, the highly-rented farmers could no longer earn a profit, and every branch of industry felt the reaction. The panacea of a parliament of landlords was the prohibition of imports of corn whenever the domestic rates were under 80*s*. per quarter. Bristol, like all the commercial towns, strongly condemned the proposed law, and a petition signed by 40,000 of the inhabitants prayed the Commons for its rejection; but in the then state of the popular chamber all such efforts were futile. The attempt to bolster up prices, however, failed, and the first to feel the effects were the labouring classes. The workmen endeavoured to combine against reductions of wages, but trades unions were illegal, and were sternly put down. On the other hand, it was equally illegal for employers to unite against their servants, and two master plasterers in Bristol were brought to trial charged with combining to lower wages. It transpired during the hearing that the journeymen did not earn more than 16*s*. per week throughout the year. The counsel for the two parties agreed to leave the matter to the bench, which decided that the old rate should be continued; but the masters refused to employ their former hands. The workmen of other trades, especially the tailors, took advantage of another old law, which forbade employers to hire any person who had not served an apprenticeship of seven years. The effect of this movement, however, was the abolition by Parliament of an obnoxious restraint on natural rights. The manufacturers and tradesmen of the city were so rejoiced at the relief, that they presented a piece of plate to Serjeant Onslow, who had framed the measure and conducted it through the House of Commons.

"The newspapers of Great Britain may be reckoned among its noblest spectacles," modestly observed the *Bristol Journal* of September 9, 1815. The assertion was made in connection with the Budget of the year, which increased the stamp tax on newspapers from threepence-halfpenny to fourpence per copy. A discount of 20 per cent. was allowed on this oppressive impost; but the concession was counterbalanced by the duty of 3*d*. per lb. on printing paper, which was charged in addition to the stamp. Newspaper proprietors were consequently obliged to advance to sevenpence the price of each copy, the largest of which in Bristol contained much less than half the typography of the penny journals of later days. The Eldon and Sidmouth party, which at that time was supreme in the Cabinet, had always shown hostility towards the press, and it was suspected that the tax was increased not so much for the sake of the revenue,—which was only slightly benefited,—as to check the circulation of political intelligence amongst the people. The duty on advertisements was raised simultaneously to 3*s*. 6*d*. upon each announcement, a sum practically prohibitory to poor persons in search of employment.

At a meeting of the Bristol turnpike trustees, in December, 1815, Mr. John Loudon McAdam was appointed general surveyor of the roads belonging to the trust. Mr. McAdam was a Scotch country gentleman, who migrated to Bristol early in the century and engaged in mercantile pursuits. In

July, 1805, the Common Council assented to his becoming a freeman on paying a fine of thirty-eight guineas. After making practical experiments in road construction, at an expense to himself of several thousand pounds, he invented the system which is now known by his name throughout the civilized world. It was long, however, before he could overcome the dead weight of prejudice and the hatred of innovation which have so often obstructed great public improvements in this country; and the Bristol trust had the credit of being the first to appreciate the value of his labours. Some idea of the state of the turnpike roads prior to McAdam's improvements is furnished by a letter in the *Monthly Magazine* for August, 1804. "The usual method of making or mending roads," says the writer, "consists in breaking stones taken out of neighbouring quarries into masses not much less than a common brick, and spreading them over the line of road. It may be conceived with what pain and difficulty a poor horse drags a carriage over such a track." The change effected by McAdam in the roads of this district was too notable to be denied even by the admirers of "ancient ways," and in the course of a few years "macadamization" spread into the most secluded parts of the island, everywhere working a beneficent revolution. It is painful to add that the section of local trustees representing the Corporation of Bristol, and animated by its reactionary spirit, attempted, in September, 1824, to summarily dismiss Mr. McAdam, without giving him a hint of their intention, and that a motion to that effect was negatived only by the casting vote of the chairman. Mr. McAdam's salary from the trust barely covered his travelling expenses. In an address to the trustees, he pointed out that he had accepted the post with no view to profit. When he entered on his work, the roads in the district were all but impassable in bad weather, and the trust was on the verge of bankruptcy. Through his exertions its funds had become flourishing, and the roads had been made "an example that has been followed and imitated from one end of the kingdom to the other." Mr. McAdam resigned his office in the following year, protesting against what he termed the "mean persecution" of his enemies in the Common Council. He was then nearly eighty years of age. About the same time, the House of Commons, regarding him as a great benefactor, both to the public and to beasts of burden, voted him a grant of £10,000. In 1827, the Metropolitan road trustees (who had not adopted McAdam's system until 1823) gladly appointed him their superintendent. Mr. McAdam died in 1836, in comparative poverty, aged ninety years. His son, many years surveyor of the Bristol roads, died in 1857.

From the time when the philanthropic Howard undertook his beneficent crusade in favour of prison reform down to the period now under review, numberless records exist as to the abominable condition of Newgate, the Bristol gaol. Howard himself describes it as white without and foul within. Criminals, he says, were allowed to mix with unfortunate debtors, and men with women; and although the place reeked with filth, yet the authorities made no allowance for mops, brooms, or towels. The accommodation was lamentably insufficient for the number of prisoners; and partly from this cause, and partly for security, a place called the "dungeon," or "pit," some twelve feet below the level of the soil, to which scarcely a ray of light could penetrate, was used for the detention of the worst class of felons. Seventeen persons slept nightly in this den, which was only fourteen feet square, neither straw nor rugs being provided for them, and the stench arising each morning on its being reopened turned the stomachs even of the warders. There was no employment to break the monotony of detention; but the chapel, on week-days, was used as a tippling room, and during the service on Sundays drinking and smoking went on in the galleries. It would appear that the city authorities provided nothing in the shape of food except two-pennyworth of bread daily per head. The local papers consequently contained almost every week an acknowledgment of gifts from the public to "the poor felons in Newgate," who sometimes declared themselves to be "in great distress for the necessaries of life." Besides numerous donations of money, the journals record the receipt, between 1785 and 1787, of many sacks of potatoes, various cartloads of coal, and doles of beef, salt fish, herrings, vegetables, "136 sixpenny loaves," and "a dozen towels." In 1792 the prisoners were even allowed to affix a box near the gaol door for the reception of donations; but many undoubtedly perished from want and fever. Another class of unhappy wretches consisted of those dragged to prison under the law of mesne process, and to these were added a great number of persons immured for non-payment of their debts. Under the mesne process system, any man could be arrested for a debt exceeding £10, and detained in prison until the cause was heard, which might not be for several months. It was notorious that this power was often used for iniquitous purposes, and the legal abuse was rendered still more grievous by the fact that, even if the victim proved at the trial that the claim was unfounded, he could not obtain release except by an expensive course of procedure beyond the means of the poor. So late as 1820, nearly 3,700 persons were languishing in prison under the law of mesne process; and the filthy Bristol gaol contained its full share of them. As for the ordinary class of prisoners for debt, the penalty to which they were liable was, until 1813, detention for life. But the condition of Newgate was so horrible that local philanthropists frequently raised subscriptions for paying the debts of poor labourers, and thus obtained their removal from horrible surroundings. The state of Bridewell was no better. Howard found the place shockingly offensive from open sewers, and a Mr. Neild, who visited it in 1807, stated that so numerous were the rats that a cat was kept in each room at night to prevent the vermin from gnawing the prisoners' feet. Howard's revelations having excited general disgust, the Corporation, in 1792, obtained an Act to build a new gaol on the site of Bristol Castle; but as the authorities proposed to levy a county rate upon the citizens for the future maintenance of the prison, the statute was threatened with universal opposition, and ultimately became a dead letter. In the meantime, the condition of the gaol became an ever-increasing reproach to the city through the increase of the population. Felons convicted of atrocious crimes and untried striplings charged with venial offences were locked up promiscuously, as if the object of the authorities was to provide for an unfailing succession of housebreakers, ruffians, and thieves. In April, 1813, the grand jury at quarter sessions, having received a report from four eminent physicians of the city, to the effect that "it was almost impossible for any building to be worse calculated" for its purpose, drew up an unanimous presentment, declaring that "any measure short of rebuilding the prison would be of no effect as to remedying those great evils so long and so justly complained of." The Corporation soon after announced that it would apply to Parliament for powers to erect a new gaol near Castle Street, provided the citizens would consent to pay for the structure and relieve the Council of the burden of maintaining it; but the proposal was indignantly scouted at meetings held by the ratepayers. Nothing having been done, Mr. J. S. Harford published a pamphlet in 1815, in which the practice of herding together degraded people of both sexes was denounced as monstrous. The author added:—

"I saw the irons put upon a little boy ten years old, who had just been brought in for stealing a pound and a half of sugar; he was then introduced into the felon's court, crowded with wretches among the most abandoned of their class." Yet in spite of this and other protests, it appears from an incidental remark in a local newspaper that untried prisoners were kept in fetters in 1817. In the following year, Mr. (afterwards Sir) T. F. Buxton visited the gaol and published his experiences. In the too notorious "pit," lying in a very dirty bed, was "a wretched human being who complained of severe illness. This was his infirmary—a place one short visit to which affected me with nausea for two days. The preceding night eighteen persons had here slept, and some of them were *untried*. A person only accused of crime may wear heavy irons and sleep in the 'pit,' and this a whole year before his trial." By this time, however, the scandal was in process of being removed. In the session of 1816 a committee of citizens had promoted a bill for building a new gaol on a proper site; but as the scheme repudiated the claim of the Corporation to control the expenditure, it was stoutly opposed by the civic oligarchy, who wrote secretly to other close corporations asking their help to resist the invasion on chartered "rights." The discovery of this proceeding caused a commotion in the House of Commons, and the Common Council, dreading that further obstinacy would end in a defeat, reluctantly came to terms with the promoters of the bill, consenting to abandon the Castle Street scheme, permitting the ratepayers to nominate some of the commissioners charged with supervising the new erection, and confessing the liability of the Corporation to maintain the prison establishment, as in the past. Newgate, with its site, was moreover given up to the commissioners. The measure received the royal assent in June, 1816. The estimated cost of the new gaol, £60,000, was raised by a rate on the ancient city, and the site chosen was in Bedminster parish, between the new course of the river and the floating harbour. A singular dispute with the revenue officials arose in November, 1817, soon after the works were begun. Some of the stone intended for the walls, brought from Blackrock quarry, on the Avon, was seized by a customs officer, who contended that it was liable to the duty imposed by the Customs Consolidation Act of 1809, which imposed a tax of £20 per cent. *ad valorem* on limestone. The customs authorities also asserted that the stone brought from Hanham and Bath was liable to the same duty. The claim, however, was soon afterwards abandoned. On the completion of the new building, in August, 1820, the prisoners in Newgate "were removed in a wagon to their new quarters." The site of the old gaol was thereupon re-purchased by the Corporation for £682, and the materials were sold for £500. As will be seen hereafter, the new gaol was itself condemned as unfit for the purpose for which it was constructed.

Great local rejoicing took place upon the 2nd May, 1816, upon the occasion of the marriage of the Princess Charlotte of Wales, heiress expectant to the throne, with Prince Leopold of Saxe Coburg (maternal uncle of Queen Victoria). The Common Council sent a deputation up to London, to present an address to the Regent on the happy event. As the expense of the trip was £166 11*s*., the emissaries appear to have enjoyed themselves. Unhappily the hopes which were excited by the union were speedily blighted; and the princess's death in the following year evoked a manifestation of national sorrow such as had never been witnessed since the accession of the House of Brunswick.

Bull-baiting was still a popular amusement amongst the lower classes. A paragraph in a local journal for June 8, 1816, gives the reader a brief but vivid glimpse of the manners of the time:—"A poor animal was led through our streets on Monday, with blue ribbons to its horns, for the savage purpose of being baited on Clifton Down. One of the ill effects of such an assemblage was a quarrel, in which the parties agreed to fight, when a man of the name of Donald was killed upon the first blow by a postboy of the name of Lambert." There is no record that Lambert was brought to trial for the homicide. A few weeks later a parochial constable complained in the newspapers that after he had arrested a ruffian for an assault, the only two resident aldermen, as well as the mayor, proved to be out of town, and he was thus forced to release his prisoner. The latest case of bull-baiting in Bristol noticed in the local press occurred in 1822; but as the "sport" was continued at Wells until 1839 or 1840, it is not unlikely that the newspaper record is defective.

On the 27th July, the Duke of Wellington, the idolized hero of the time, paid a visit to Bristol in response to an invitation from the Common Council, which had sent deputies to Cheltenham for that purpose. His grace's entry was by Redland, where the sheriffs were in attendance to welcome him to the city. In the procession which was then formed, the duke's carriage was followed by the barouch of "that old veteran, John Weeks," whose mode of displaying his enthusiasm was not less characteristic than it had been years before (see p. 12). In the midst of laurels, roses, leeks, and shamrocks, six ladies were seated in his vehicle, displaying banners inscribed with mottoes in honour of the great captain and his brother officers, while Weeks himself performed the feat of bearing an Irish harp, a royal standard, and three other national flags. On arriving at a handsome triumphal arch erected across Park Street, surmounted with "a figure of the genius of Bristol"—whatever that may have been,—the horses of the noble visitor were removed by a party of sixty men, whose habiliments would probably appear grotesque to later eyes, but which, it is believed, formed the customary garb of those who bore the members for Bristol during the triumphal ceremony of chairing. The men were "dressed in black hats, white shirts over their waistcoats, ornamented with white ribbons, black breeches and white stockings." After being dragged to the Mansion House, the duke was received by the mayor, aldermen, and councillors in the banqueting room, surrounded by the grandest state paraphernalia. The mayor (Sir W. J. Struth) in a brief address—the turgidness of which excited some ridicule out of doors—presented his grace with the freedom of the city in a gold box; and a similar gift was made, in much more graceful terms, by the Merchants' Company through their master. After a brief adjournment to the drawing-room to gratify the curiosity of a large gathering of ladies, the distinguished guest was conducted to the Merchants' Hall for dinner. A sumptuous repast having been followed by a few toasts, the duke left early in the evening to undergo a similar reception at Gloucester. The cost of the entertainment, including £100 for the loan of plate to decorate the tables, £63 for the gold box, and £50 spent by the deputation to Cheltenham, was £925 17*s*. Much dissatisfaction was expressed by the members of the Merchants' Society at the conduct of the corporate officials, who, after borrowing the Company's hall for the banquet, excluded its owners from the feast.

The next public ceremonial in the city was of a more touching character. On the 10th of September Richard Reynolds, who has been styled "the greatest of Bristol's great philanthropists," expired at Cheltenham, where he was sojourning by the advice of his physicians, and ten days later his remains, which had been removed to Bristol, were conveyed from his house in St. James's Square to the burial-ground attached to the Friends' meeting-house in the Friars. The attendance of mourners included many of the resident clergy, dissenting ministers of every persuasion, prominent citizens of every sect and party, the staffs of the various charitable institutions of the city, to which the deceased had been a munificent patron, the children of the parish schools of St. James's and St. Paul's, and great numbers of the poorer classes, who displayed much eagerness to pay a token of respect to the remains of their departed friend. A more affecting ceremony was probably never witnessed in the city. Mr. Reynolds was a native of Bristol, having been born in Corn Street in 1735; but he left the city in early life, and his wealth was accumulated during his long residence at and near Coalbrookdale. In 1804 he returned to his native town, where he soon distinguished himself by diffusive and universal benevolence, though from his solicitude to escape notice only a few of his munificent acts could be clearly traced. Of these may be mentioned a fund of £10,500 invested in the hands of trustees for the benefit of seven local charities, gifts of £2,000 and £4,000 for augmenting the weekly payments to the inmates of Trinity almshouses, and a donation of £2,600 for an extension of the Infirmary. These instances, however, do little to show the extent of his liberality. During one of the famine crises which occurred during the great war, he remitted £20,000 to an agent in London, and throughout his residence in Bristol he employed four almoners charged to inquire into the state of the poor and to distribute relief to the deserving. From statements made by Mr. Rathbone, who published a sketch of his career, Mr. Reynolds seems to have bestowed during his life upwards of £200,000 in acts of charity, exclusive of anonymous gifts of which no record appeared in his private accounts. A few days after the funeral, a meeting was held at the Guildhall, the mayor (Mr. J. Haythorne) presiding, when it was resolved to establish a Reynolds' Commemoration Society, for continuing relief to objects of his bounty, for assisting the charities of the city, and especially for succouring an institution founded by the deceased—the Samaritan Society. Unfortunately the support extended to the Commemoration Society has never been worthy of its objects.

During this year, the Freemasons of the city purchased a house in Bridge Street for £1,600, and fitted it up for the use of the craft at a further expense of £2,000. The removal of the Freemasons' hall to Park Street will be recorded at a later date.

An interesting paper on the declining popularity of the Hotwell Spring, with suggestions for its revival, was addressed, in 1816, to the Society of Merchant Venturers by Dr. Andrew Carrick, then one of the leading physicians of Clifton. The paper did not reach the public until nearly half a century later, being first published in the *Bristol Times* of October 18, 1862. The following are extracts: "Seven and twenty years ago (viz. 1789) when I first became acquainted with the place, the Hotwells during summer was one of the best-frequented and most crowded watering-places in the kingdom. Scores of the first nobility were to be found there every season, and such a crowd of invalids of all ranks resorted to the waters that it was often difficult for them to provide themselves with any sort of lodgings. About that period a considerable number of lodging letters had in the course of a few years realized very handsome fortunes, without any complaint of extortionate exactions. [Matthews' Guide to Bristol and Clifton, written in 1793, states that the general price of lodgings was 10*s*. per week in the summer and 5*s*. per week in the winter half year; boarding 16*s*. per week; servants' rooms and boarding half price.] Three extensive taverns were constantly full, and two spacious ballrooms were profitably kept open. There was a well-attended ball, a public breakfast, and a promenade every week, and often twice a week. The pump-room was all day long the resort of invalids, who left with the keeper of the well many hundreds a year in voluntary donations, and from twelve to two o'clock was generally so crowded that there was often some difficulty in getting up to drink the water. The walk adjoining was in the meantime filled with fashionable company, to whom the sublime scenery of the cliffs was enlivened by the sounds of a band of music. The downs and all the avenues to the Hotwells were filled with strings of carriages, and with parties on horseback and on foot." Having drawn this graphic sketch from personal experience, Dr. Carrick proceeded to contrast it with the condition of the place in 1816: "The silence of the grave, to which it seems the inlet. Not a carriage to be seen once an hour, and scarcely more frequently does a solitary invalid approach the neglected spring. One of the ballrooms and taverns has been long ago shut up, and the other with great difficulty kept open. The lodging-houses, or such of them as still remain open, almost entirely empty in summer, and not very profitably filled even in winter." He went on to say that "not one tenth of the visitors of rank and fortune, and of invalids perhaps a still smaller proportion" then resorted to the place; that the letters of lodgings became "almost universally bankrupt in a few years," though visitors complained of "bad usage and exorbitant charges;" and that the value of houses at the Hotwells had "vastly depreciated—many houses, and even whole rows, are unoccupied and as it were deserted." "With great difficulty can a ball be supported once a fortnight at Clifton; no public breakfasts; no promenades, or none deserving the name. At the Hotwells nothing of the kind." Dr. Carrick attributed the declining fortunes of the spring, chiefly, to the fact that about 1790 its proprietors (the Merchants Company) let the place at a price vastly beyond its value, and allowed the tenant to impose an exorbitant price—26*s.* a month from each individual—for permission to drink the water. People in health refused to pay the impost, and betook themselves to other resorts. The charges thus restricted the use of the water to those who were suffering from consumption, and who were in fact incurable, and the high rate of mortality amongst the drinkers cast discredit upon the spring itself. "From the day that the Hotwell became practically a fountain sealed to the lips of every one but the actually moribund, the fame of the place began rapidly to decline. None who drank of the Lethean waters were thenceforth found to recover; because none did drink of them but such as were past recovery. It was now one uniform black list of disappointment and death; and in the course of a very few years it became all over the kingdom a source of horror and despair, instead of hope and confidence, to be ordered to the Hotwells, from whose awful bourne no traveller now returned." A subsidiary cause of the decline was said to be the "difficult and dangerous" descent from Clifton to the well. "To many the hire of a carriage twice or thrice a day, at the increased charges of such conveyances, presented an insuperable obstacle. To others the fatigue and the terror of riding up and down the precipitous track (for it even now scarcely deserves the name of a road) of Granby Hill was an objection not to be overcome." Dr. Carrick concluded by suggesting that a commodious footpath might be made from Prince's Buildings to the bottom of Granby Hill, and that a carriage road should be constructed from the Hotwell house to the downs. The latter, he urged, would not be difficult, as "the space at the foot of St. Vincent's rocks is already practicable for carriages, or nearly so."* If this thoroughfare were made, and the tollgate [which then stood opposite the site now occupied by Camp House] removed to the edge of the downs, Dr. Carrick believed the improvements would offer "a material accommodation to that part of the parish, and a powerful incitement to the use of the waters." The worthy doctor, however, did not make allowance for the popularity of Continental watering-places that arose after the conclusion of the long French war, a popularity which struck a permanent blow at all the English resorts of the wealthy classes.

On January 17, 1817, whilst workmen were engaged in improving Leigh Down, the inclosure of which had been recently effected, they discovered a large quantity of Roman coins, which had apparently been buried about six inches below the turf. It was believed that about 1,000 pieces of silver were found; but the labourers lost no time in disposing of their booty, and about 500 coins at once disappeared. The specimens seen by Mr. Seyer, who gave a lengthy account of them in his history (vol. i. 164–173) ranged from the reign of Nero to that of Constantius II., so that the treasure was probably buried about the year 350.

From the beginning of the century the deteriorated condition and scarcity of the silver coinage had been painfully felt by the trading classes and the poor. In some districts employers of labour, unable to obtain coins for the payment of wages, issued cards which were equivalent to notes for a given number of shillings; and these billets passed with comparative ease when confidence was placed in the issuers. Forgeries, however, were often perpetrated, to the great injury of the labouring community, as tradesmen made heavy deductions on the value of the primitive notes to secure themselves against loss. At a city meeting in Bristol, in 1803, it was stated, as the result of an extensive experiment, that forty of the sixpences then current were not by weight

* Dr. Carrick here refers to operations which were proceeding at the time he wrote. Down to 1816, St. Vincent's rocks protruded almost to the brink of the Avon at high water, there being only a narrow path on the verge of the river to admit of the towage of vessels. In 1816–17, when extreme distress prevailed amongst the poor, owing to deficient harvests and the high price of food, a subscription was raised for employing labourers, to which the Corporation subscribed £241; and the Merchants' Society having granted permission to quarry the projecting rocks, a large quantity of stone was removed and broken for the roads around the city. [Redcliff Hill was lowered about three feet by another party of labourers, the wages in both cases being provided out of the fund.] The widening of the path continued for several years; and it will be seen hereafter that Dr. Carrick's suggested road was constructed in 1822.

worth more than 10*s.* 9*d.*, and twenty of the current shillings not more than 14*s.* 5*d.* A memorial to the Government praying for a new coinage was adopted, but nothing was done; and the old coins becoming steadily worse from year to year, most of them at length became mere smooth pieces of silver of less than half their assumed value. The difficulty was exasperated in 1810–11 by the depreciation of bank notes through excessive issues. A 20*s.* note being really worth only about 14*s.* or 15*s.* in gold, many who got possession of silver coin naturally refused to part with it in exchange for paper, and thus shillings and sixpences became scarcer than ever. Many persons now ventured to issue "tokens," generally of about half their nominal value, undertaking to redeem them for the sum they represented. Knavish people followed this example, issuing debased tokens, which were not intended to be, and which never were, redeemed; and the Government, whose short-sighted mismanagement had caused extreme embarrassment and distress to the retail trade of the country, was forced to shut its eyes whilst large profits were thus reaped at the expense of the community. Another source of public injury was the issue of 10*s.* notes by various persons, in spite of their illegality; but several convictions took place in Bristol in 1815, which put an end to the system in this locality. At the close of the war, when bank notes rose in value, the hoarded silver money reappeared, and the currency of tokens became illegal after December, 1814. Nearly all the silver coin in circulation, however, was so much worn as to be perfectly smooth on both sides; and in July, 1816, owing to mischievous rumours as to the intentions of the Government, a panic arose in Bristol market, and rapidly spread to Bath and other neighbouring towns, the refusal of many farmers to accept the "smooth shillings" in payment for their produce causing an almost complete suspension of business. The Ministry at length saw the necessity of action, and a large coinage was ordered. On January 27, 1817, says the diary of a contemporary citizen (*Times and Mirror*, April 11, 1885), "sixty boxes of the new silver coinage, of the value of £36,000, were sent from the Mint to the mayor, to be circulated in this city, which were deposited in the Council House till the 13th February, when inspectors were appointed to examine the old silver and give the new in exchange, which was done at the Council House, Guildhall, and Merchants' Hall, for the space of fourteen days." Although every genuine coin, however worn and defaced, was exchanged at its full value,* many people, especially country-folks, neglected the opportunity, and retained their hoards until after the old coinage was declared an illegal tender. The Bristol journals contain numerous advertisements of a later date, in which tradesmen offered to allow their customers *4d.* for old sixpences, *9d.* for shillings, and *2s. 1d.* for half-crowns—the latter being soon scarce and curious.

The first steam vessel seen in Bristol made its appearance in the Float in June, 1813, and is reported to have been constructed under the direction of Mr. Theodore Lawrance, one of the city coroners. It was called the *Charlotte*, and was intended to carry passengers and goods between Bristol and Bath. The boat had accommodation for twenty cabin passengers, who paid half a crown each, the steerage fare being *1s. 6d.* A few months later it was announced that the journeys of the boat had been suspended during the rebuilding of Keynsham bridge, but that it would resume work shortly, a larger and quicker vessel being also promised at an early date. The enterprise, however, proved a failure. In the *Bristol Journal* of May 3, 1817, is a paragraph stating that the *Britannia* steam-packet had arrived in this port from Swansea, "making the passage against the ebb tide in twelve hours." This vessel was built for the Dublin and Holyhead service, and it is fair to surmise that the builders sent her to Bristol in the hope of stirring up a feeling of emulation amongst the citizens which might not be unprofitable to themselves. If so, they were disappointed, for the mercantile classes here made no effort to compete with their northern rivals, who for several years had a monopoly of steam traffic with Ireland. An advertisement in the Bristol papers of July 28, 1821, at last announced that "the steam-packets *Talbot* and *Ivanhoe*, so well known on the Holyhead station"—where, it may be suspected, they had been replaced by larger vessels—had "commenced plying between Bristol and Cork;" and a paragraph of the same date adds that the voyage was to be made in thirty hours. The first steamboat from Bristol to Dublin started in May, 1822, for the summer season only, calls being made at Tenby and Wexford on the outward, and at Liverpool on the return voyage. A daily steamer to Newport started at the same time. From inferential remarks in the contemporary press,

* The Corporation had old silver in the city chest to the large amount of £356 *7s. 6d.* It sustained a loss in the exchange of £3 *12s.*; in other words, coins representing that sum proved to be counterfeit.

it is evident that many travellers refused to trust their lives to these dangerous novelties, in spite of difficulties and discomforts attending the old mode of transit which seem almost incredible in the present age. Mr. S. C. Hall, the well-known art critic, in a little work published in 1861, wrote:—"In the year 1815 it was my lot to visit Ireland. I was then a schoolboy in Bristol; my family resided in Cork; and the voyage from one port to the other occupied just six weeks. . . . The packet boat under the best circumstances was miserable enough. There was no separate accommodation for ladies. To undress was out of the question. Each passenger took his own sea store. Salt junk and hard biscuit were the only food to be obtained if the voyage lasted above three or four days. Imagine the wretchedness . . . of those who had to bear it for weeks! The case I have stated was by no means rare. The voyage from Holyhead to Dublin often consumed a fortnight." It is not surprising that in the face of such miseries old-fashioned apprehensions of steam rapidly died out. In 1823 the owners of the Irish steamers, in a petition to the Common Council, stated that they proposed to run three vessels weekly, but that the mayor's dues on the vessels would amount to £359 yearly, and they prayed relief from a burden which was not imposed either at Dublin or Liverpool. Similar appeals were made by other companies; and the Corporation, though declining to abate the charge, voted a sum of money to a committee, which practically refunded the dues at the end of the season. By 1824 steamers had come into general use for passenger traffic, and the Bristol Steam Navigation Company, which was established in 1837, soon possessed a numerous fleet. The slowness with which Bristol is charged by her critics was, however, remarkably exemplified in her attitude towards steam-tugs. Although vessels of this class had been started on the Clyde in 1803, and were soon after introduced on the Tyne, Mersey, and Thames, and although the cost of towing by men and horses, whether on entering or leaving the Avon, was £9 for a vessel of only 100 tons, many years passed away before Bristol shipowners thought of resorting to steam power, by which the cost would have been largely reduced. The Chamber of Commerce vainly pointed out, in 1824, that tugs were successfully employed at all the other leading ports. Two well-known Bristolians, Mr. C. Claxton and Mr. M. Whitwill, showed by actual experiment that steam power was equally applicable here, but their arguments for its adoption met with no response; and the Common Council passed a resolution affirming that its members "at present were not capable of forming any accurate judgment of the expediency of the proposed plan." The *Great Western* steamer was designed about ten years later for opening rapid communication with America, yet local bigwigs refused to admit that either time or money would be saved by substituting steam-tugs for men and horses on the Avon. In short, it was not until 1836 that a little vessel called the *Fury* was brought into operation between Kingroad and Bristol. Her appearance excited disturbances at Pill amongst the labourers who gained a scanty living by acting as towers. In February, 1836, the *Fury* was seized by a party of these men, who attempted to scuttle her, but finally set her adrift on the Severn. The vessel, however, soon returned to work, and her success being beyond dispute, the old arrangements at last became a matter of history. [The *Fury* was destroyed in Kingroad, by the explosion of her boiler, on the 21st September, 1859.]

On the night of the 23rd October, 1817, the sailing packet *William and Mary*, which had left Bristol a few hours previously for Waterford, with a number of passengers, struck on a rock near the Flat Holmes, and almost immediately sank. Out of about sixty persons who were on board only twenty-three were saved. The night was clear, with only a gentle breeze blowing, and the disaster was unquestionably due to the flagrant misconduct of the mate, who had been left in charge by the captain. The inhuman criminal saved his own life by forcing some ladies to quit the only boat—holding four persons—belonging to the packet. Most of the survivors were rescued by Pill pilots.

Queen Charlotte, wife of George III., being on a visit to Bath for the purpose of drinking the waters, was invited to this city by the mayor and Corporation, and responded to their request by driving over on the 17th December, accompanied by the Duke of Clarence, afterwards William IV., and the Princess Elizabeth. After breakfasting at the Mansion House, the royal party crossed Prince's Street bridge, and proceeded along the "newly formed road" by the side of the New Cut to the Hotwells. They then returned to College Green, ascended Park Street, and drove through Berkeley Square to Clifton, "passing under the York Crescent, up Sion Hill, and through the turnpike to the Look-out (Wallis's Wall),* on Durdham Down;" returning

* Now called Sea Walls.

through another part of Clifton to Colonel Baillie's residence* in Park Row, where "every delicacy and luxury of the season" was "served up in the drawing-room on a most costly service of embossed plate." On returning, the queen was to have gone over the Drawbridge and through Clare Street and Corn Street; but as the procession approached, the rigging of a small vessel passing the bridge, which was then really a drawbridge, got entangled in the lifted structure—an accident of common occurrence. The royal carriage was consequently stopped; and as the Float was then the receptacle of the city sewage, the overpowering odour of the water is said by a local poet to have forced her majesty to "snuff her royal nose." ["Rhymes, Latin and English," by the Rev. John Eagles.] Her majesty had at last to be taken to Bristol Bridge by way of Nelson Street, Union Street, and Dolphin Street, the beauties of which thoroughfares she had an opportunity of admiring, as the *cortége* proceeded at "a slow rate." The queen, who died in the following year, was far from popular, and a courtly newswriter in the city noted, with assumed "surprise," that the tradesmen in the principal streets manifested no tokens of mourning on her demise.

An illustration of the bibulous habits of the Regency is afforded by a tavern bill paid by a Bristolian in August, 1817, to the landlord of the Montagu Hotel (communicated to the *Times and Mirror*, May 24, 1873). The dinner, which was for twelve guests, and included venison and turtle, was charged 14 guineas; dessert, 2 guineas. The giver of the feast supplied twelve bottles of wine from his private cellar. Beside this, the guests drank claret costing £7; Madeira, £1 18*s.*; two bottles of hock, £1 8*s.*; two bottles of champagne, £1 14*s.*; and two bottles of port, 12*s.* Altogether the party must have swallowed about three bottles of liquor per head. The hotel bill amounted to £31 7*s.*, exclusive of the wine privately supplied.

At a meeting of the Common Council in August, Alderman Daniel announced that a citizen of Bristol, Thomas Bonville, had authorized him to express his willingness to transfer into the hands of the Corporation, for charitable purposes, several sums of money invested in Government securities, subject to the life interest of himself and others. The Council accepted the proposed trust. In February, 1822, Alderman Daniel announced that Mr. Bonville proposed to hand over—subject

* Site of the Prince's Theatre.

to a similar proviso—a further considerable sum, which was also accepted. Altogether the donations amounted to about £32,800 in three per cent. stock, ten shares in the Bristol Dock Company, and £1,200 in dock bonds; producing a revenue of upwards of £1,000 per annum. Upon the decease in April, 1842, of Mrs. Bonville, widow of the donor, the Charity Trustees, who had taken the place of the Corporation, came into possession of nearly all the income, and the last annuitant died in 1866. The receipts, in accordance with Mr. Bonville's trust deeds, are distributed yearly in sums varying from £5 5*s.* to £21 amongst 124 poor housekeepers and residents in the "ancient city," of a station of life superior to that of recipients of parochial relief. In some remarks on charitable bequests in the *Bristol Times* of April 4, 1874, the editor said: "Benevolent deeds done to the world at large while there are those of our own family who are in need can scarcely be an acceptable offering either to heaven or society. There is on our local list of charities one—that of Bonville's—the founder of which got the money which he bequeathed through marriage with a lady, some of whose relations were poor when he passed them over to endow strangers."

The Common Council were informed by Mr. H. Bright in December, 1817, that a member of the Corporation "taking into consideration the length of time (now 400 years) since any member hath endowed a hospital as a perpetual place of refuge for the aged and infirm," proposed at his own charge to execute a deed granting to the Corporation in perpetuity the reversion and inheritance of a freehold estate purchased by him for the purpose, and situate in the parishes of Nempnett and Blagdon, the rack rental of which, subject to several leases for lives, was estimated at £600. The donor proposed that the Corporation, pending the existence of the leases, should allow the income to accumulate, and that when the entire property had fallen in hand an almshouse should be erected for the residence of poor aged people, in the proportion of three women to one man, half of the inmates to be members of the Church of England, and the remainder Dissenters. The Council, in accepting the trust, expressed its opinion that the gift reflected the highest honour on the Corporation. As was announced by Mr. Bright at the next meeting, the benevolent donor was Alderman Bengough—long the ruling member of the civic body—who was then suffering from an illness which proved fatal. On his demise, in the following April, it was found that the alderman, though a Unitarian, had expressed a wish in his will to be buried in the Mayor's Chapel, and had left a large sum for the erection of a monument there to his memory. The Court of Aldermen gave the required permission for the interment, and it appears from the civic records that the inscription upon the monument was achieved by Mr. Bengough's former colleagues. His intentions with reference to the hospital, which legally were void under the statute of mortmain, were, under the provisions of his will, fulfilled by his nephew and heir, George Bengough, who executed a conveyance of the estate in September, 1818. The last of the leases expired in 1878, when the accumulated profits exceeded £11,000. The trustees shortly afterwards proceeded to the erection of a handsome almshouse in the Queen Anne style, a piece of ground in Horfield Road being purchased for the purpose from the Merchants' Society. The building cost about £5,500, and the site £3,500. A peculiarity of this charity—suggested by its founder—is that some of the inmates are aged married couples.

At the December meeting of the Common Council it was reported that the accounts of the late chamberlain, Wintour Harris, who had died a few months previously, showed a serious deficiency. The sureties were called upon to make good the sum of £3,600, which was subsequently reduced to £3,000 on the surrender by Mrs. Harris of certain securities. The new chamberlain, John Langley, was deprived of his post in 1822, on the ground that he had allowed his sisters to claim and collect the rents of a small property in Portwall Lane, which really belonged to Whitson's charities. The matter is obscurely recorded in the civic minute books, and it is significant that a common councillor forthwith resigned in order to take the office of deputy chamberlain, in the place of Mr. Garrard, promoted. The defalcations of the new chamberlain will be noticed hereafter.

In January, 1818, Sir Vicary Gibbs, Lord Chief Justice of the Common Pleas, resigned the office of Recorder of Bristol, owing to ill health. His lordship was notable in his time as a stickler for the maintenance of his personal dignity, and always had an officer to gallop before his carriage on his to and fro journeys between Bath and Bristol. He was also famed for an acrid temper, which earned him the name of Sir Vinegar, and for extreme harshness towards offenders tried before him. On one occasion a criminal named Lewis received the following sentence:—"You are to be whipped at a cart's tail from Newgate to the Gallows Field" [the site of Highbury Chapel]. The prisoner having rashly retorted:

"Thank you, my lord, that is all you can do," Sir Vicary coolly added, as if he had been interrupted, "and back again." He was a favourite, however, of the Corporation, which in 1816 paid Mr. Owen, R.A., £131 for painting his lordship's portrait. The new recorder was Sir Robert Gifford, then Solicitor-General, and subsequently Lord Chief Justice and a peer. At this period, and down to 1827, the recorders were accustomed to hold only one assize yearly, to the great injury of persons committed for trial, some of whom, after lying in the filthy and unwholesome gaol for nearly twelve months before their cases were decided, were found guiltless of the crimes imputed to them.

The Bristol Crown Fire Office, established in 1718, became extinct through effluxion of time early in 1818. A new company, however, was established under the name of the Crown Fire Office, and an advertisement soliciting continued support appeared on the 17th January. A portion of the old proprietors seceded, and started a new concern called the Bristol Union Fire Office. The latter company, the last local institution of the kind, resolved on discontinuing business on the 3rd of May, 1844. The goodwill of the concern was purchased by the Imperial Company, which had in January, 1840, bought up the business of the Crown office.

During the month of January, 1818, an altar tomb, bearing an effigy, which had been plastered over early in the present century, when the building was repewed, was discovered in a recess in the south aisle of St. James's Church. The local Monkbarns of the time forthwith rushed to the conclusion that the tomb was that of Robert, Earl of Gloucester, the builder of Bristol Castle and founder of St. James's Priory; and an inscription to that effect, bearing the alleged arms of the earl, was placed over the monument. Scientific antiquaries are agreed in repudiating the authenticity of the effigy, which is of later date than the period assigned to it, and clearly represents a civilian.

In the year 1818, the Attorney-General, at the instance of several corporate towns interested in Sir Thomas White's charities, filed an information against the Corporation of Bristol in reference to its management of the estates. In the year 1562, Sir Thomas White, an alderman of London, gave £2,000 to be laid out in the purchase of land for charitable uses, to produce "six score pounds or more," the Mayor and Corporation of Bristol being appointed trustees. Sir Thomas ordered that, for the first ten years £100 yearly were to be advanced for the benefit of poor apprentices in

Bristol, to be selected by the Council; then, for twenty-four years, the same number of English Corporations were in succession to receive £104 each, to be applied to a similar purpose; and finally, at the end of thirty-four years, the rotation was to recommence. No provision was made for the application of the surplus, and it was supposed that the donor intended it to provide for contingencies. But in the course of years the estates originally producing about "six score pounds" were estimated to be of the value of £3,500 a year, and the question raised by the information was whether the surplus should be appropriated by the Corporation of Bristol, as had hitherto been the case, or should be divided amongst the Corporations benefited by the original gift. The Bristol Council, contending that it was entitled to the balance, raised a demurrer, which was overruled by the vice-chancellor; but the cause was then carried on appeal to Lord-Chancellor Eldon, whose strong sympathies with Corporations overpowered his customary love of delay, and led to the immediate reversal of the previous judgment.

At the general election in 1818, Mr. R. H. Davis again came forward in the Tory interest. Mr. Protheroe's votes in support of Lord Sidmouth's repressive system of government (the Habeas Corpus Act had been again suspended in the previous year) had offended many of the Whigs, and, finding that they proposed to start Colonel Hugh Baillie, who was a parliamentary reformer, and an opponent of the laws against Roman Catholics, he declined to offer himself. Some of his supporters, however, insisted upon nominating him, and after a poll of four days, ending on the 20th June, during which many Tories split their votes in his favour, he was elected. The numbers were: Mr. Davis, 3,377; Mr. Protheroe, 2,250; Colonel Baillie, 1,684. The friends of the rejected candidate petitioned against the return, on the ground that the sheriffs, by prematurely closing the poll, had prevented nearly a thousand non-resident freemen from voting. The petition was unsuccessful. A few months later a serious misunderstanding arose between Mr. Protheroe and his committee (of which Mr. W. Fripp, jun., was chairman), respecting the expenses of the election, and the former announced that he should not again solicit the representation of the city. Mr. Fripp's name subsequently appeared in the list of leading Tories.

An Act of Parliament having been passed this year appropriating the sum of one million sterling of the national funds towards the erection of additional churches in populous places, an early application was made to the Ministry by the authorities of St. Augustine's parish, for a grant in aid of the erection of a proposed church near Brandon hill. A donation, equal to one-third of the cost of the building and site (£7,000), having been made in October, the work was begun shortly afterwards, the workmen in the first place removing seven houses partially erected on the spot many years before, but never finished. [Other uncompleted houses in the neighbourhood remained in ruins many years after this date.] The church was consecrated in September, 1823. In December, 1832, a portion of St. Augustine's parish was separated from the mother church, and formed into an independent parish, called St. George's, the incumbent of which became a vicar. The new church, as originally built, was destitute of a chancel, but an annexe, after the model of some ancient basilicas, was erected in 1871.

The punishment of whipping appears to have been still highly approved by the local justices, and continued so for several years. The *Bristol Journal* of December 4, 1819, contained the following:—"A man who has been loitering about our city for some days, and who was taken to the Council-house charged with being a nuisance, was publicly whipped on Tuesday at the pump in Wine Street, and immediately after passed to his parish. We cannot too highly applaud the conduct of the magistrates." The same paper of May 12, 1821, stated that "three men were flogged yesterday at Wine Street pump, being apprehended as rogues and vagabonds." A month later, it is recorded that "a man was placed in the stocks in St. James's churchyard last week for drunkenness." In August, 1823, to quote the same authority, a man and two boys were flogged through Bedminster for stealing fruit from a garden. To give one more example, the *Journal* of April 22, 1826, reported that a man convicted of stealing a piece of meat had received forty-eight lashes at Wine Street pump. "During the exhibition several persons in the crowd had their pockets picked."

The Bristolians who ventured at this early period to "trans-parish" themselves to Clifton must have found that suburban enjoyments were not without a drop of bitterness. The *Bristol Journal* of November 27, 1819, after recording several highway robberies in the suburbs, added:—"The roads leading to Clifton are so infested at night with desperadoes that few gentlemen think it safe to walk about alone or unarmed; and yet we hear that at a vestry meeting of the parish on Thursday, to propose measures for lighting and watching it, a majority determined that it was unnecessary." Repeated attempts were made without success to overcome the inveterate conservatism, or perhaps the parsimony, of the parishioners. At length, however, a Watching and Lighting Act was obtained during the session of 1824, and a sprinkling of gaslights and a few night-constables were established during the ensuing winter. Another great improvement dates from the year now under review. The roads in Clifton had hitherto been in as unsatisfactory a state as was the police of the parish. But amongst a number of roads which became turnpikes under an Act obtained in 1819 were "the road from the top of Bridge Valley, along the southern side of Durdham Down, to the top of Gallows Acre Lane" (Pembroke Road), and "the road from the bottom of Granby Hill to the Hot-well pumping room." The construction of several new roads was authorised by the same Act, amongst them being "a new road to lead from . . . the Hot-well pumping room, to lead or pass by the river side, and up the hill, into the road leading from Clifton to Pill Passage, at the top of Bridge Valley." Dr. Carrick's suggestion (see p. 72) was thus adopted, and the new thoroughfare, laid out in 1822, afforded Cliftonians a point of view which has ever since been a theme of admiration.

A few references to the coaching arrangements of this period may not be unworthy of record. On the 6th April. 1819, a new coach began running from the Bush Hotel to Exeter, the time occupied in the journey, 74¾ miles, being fourteen hours—less than 5½ miles an hour! In June, 1820, another new coach started for Manchester, performing the journey in two days—the intervening night being spent at Birmingham. To accomplish the first half of the task, the vehicle left Bristol at half past eight in the morning, and reached Birmingham, 85½ miles, in thirteen hours. Finally, an advertisement published in December, 1821, headed "speed increased," informed the public that the Regulator coach left London daily at 5 a.m., and arrived at the White Hart, Bristol, at five minutes before nine at night—the speed being barely seven miles an hour.

Great consternation was caused in the city and neighbourhood on the 5th July, 1819, by the failure of the Tolzey Bank, the proprietors of which were Messrs. Worrall and Pope. Though of recent origin, the bank had issued a great number of notes for 20*s*. and 30*s*. each, and the disaster affected all classes in the locality, causing a "run" upon some of the other banks, then eleven in number. The town clerk, Mr. Samuel Worrall,* being one of the partners in the Tolzey concern, was obliged to resign his office a few days later, on being declared a bankrupt. He was succeeded, on the 22nd July, by Mr. Ebenezer Ludlow, afterwards a serjeant-at-law. At a meeting of the Common Council, in December, it was ordered that, in consideration of Mr. Worrall's faithful services for thirty-two years, the sum of £400 should be annually paid to the mayor and aldermen, in trust for the use of the late town clerk and of his wife and family, for the remainder of his life. Mr. Worrall, who died in November, 1821, was in his prosperous days a man of great entertaining powers in convivial society, which led to his introduction to the Prince Regent, and he was a frequent guest at Carlton House. On the other hand, he was rude and coarse to his inferiors, and gained in some way the name of "Devil Worrall," of which he seemed proud. The present town clerk, Mr. D. Travers Burges, has been good enough to furnish the following anecdote, preserved in one of his late father's note-books, which affords an illustration of the social habits of the upper middle class in the early years of the century:—"Worrall lived for many years in a house opposite the Council House, and on one occasion, upon coming home from a party a little 'elevated,' as he was getting out of the hackney coach his foot slipped, and he fell to the ground. A crowd immediately assembled, and amongst them a very harmless and quiet silk mercer who resided in High Street, of the name of Camplin. Worrall, still on his back, fixed his eyes on the unfortunate mercer, and pointing at him said, 'That's the man that knocked me down,' upon which the crowd took part with the town clerk, and poor Camplin, protesting his innocence, was obliged to run." To fully realise this scene it must be remembered that the bibulous official presided on the magisterial bench at every quarter sessions.

In July, 1819, the Common Council increased the allowance to the master of Queen Elizabeth's Hospital—who then fed and educated the boys by contract—to £20 per head. This was the last of several advances made in consequence of the great rise in prices in the early years of the century. Down to the outbreak of the French war, the master received £12 per head for the food and instruction of the boys. In

* In addition to his high position in the Corporation and his business as a banker, Mr. Worrall held the Government appointment of distributor of stamps, and the patent office of publisher of the Bristol presentment in connection with the custom house.

the years of scarcity which followed, the Council allowed him an extra lump sum of £70. This being found inadequate, an advance of £3 per head instead of the gratuity was made in 1805, £2 additional was voted in 1806, £1 more in 1813, and £2 more, as stated above, in 1819. A year or two later, "in consequence of the reduction in the price of provisions," the grant was again fixed at £17 a head, but the master received a further allowance of £50 for instruction. The contract system was also adopted in the Red Maids' and Colston's Schools, and from some reminiscences of "old boys," published in the *Bristol Times* in November, 1856, it appears that the fare in the latter institution down to the end of the Regency was of a somewhat Spartan character. On Saturdays the dinner of the boys consisted of milk gruel, with bread only. On Mondays they were regaled with water gruel, and bread and butter. For the rest of the week they had meat, with bread or vegetables. Breakfast always consisted of bread and butter; for supper there was a double allowance of bread, with butter or cheese. Table beer was given with each meal. The boys were required to mop and scrub the schoolroom, dormitories, and hall, and performed various other menial duties. Details are wanting in reference to the Red Maids' School, but if the accomplishments of the mistresses are to be inferred from the caligraphy of one of them appointed about this time, and whose signature is found in the aldermanic minute book, there can have been little ground for the old-fashioned complaint that the girls were "spoilt by education."

Edward Bird, the only artist resident in Bristol ever honoured with the title of Royal Academician, expired after a protracted illness on the 2nd November, at his house in King's Parade. His interment took place a week later at the cathedral, when about two hundred leading residents attended to mark their respect for a man whose distinguished talents had conferred honour on the city. A subscription was subsequently raised for the relief of the deceased's family, to which Prince Leopold, husband of the late Princess Charlotte, to whom Bird was appointed historical painter, sent £100. The Earl of Bridgwater gave £650 for a picture of "the embarkation of Louis XVIII.," the last great work of the artist. In the memoir of Bird published in Cunningham's "Lives of British Painters," strong charges were made against the citizens of Bristol for their alleged neglect of the painter, but these statements were controverted in *Blackwood's Magazine* for December, 1833, in a paper by

Bird's friend, the Rev. J. Eagles. Subsequently the charges were revived by Mrs. S. C. Hall in the *Art Journal* for April, 1843, when Mr. Eagles again stigmatised them as untruthful in the *Bristol Journal* of the 22nd April of the same year.

The death of George III. occurred on the 29th January, 1820. The proclamation of his successor took place five days afterwards, and as no such event had occurred within the memory of nineteen-twentieths of the population, it excited some interest. The members of the Corporation assembled at the Council House in their black robes, but after proclaiming the new king at the site of the High Cross, they returned to their place of meeting and donned their scarlet habiliments. A procession was then formed, the mayor (Mr. W. Fripp, junr.) and sheriffs taking their places in "a splendid car, carried by twenty-four men," and proclamation was made at the customary sites. At three of these—St. Peter's pump, St. Thomas's conduit, and the Quay pipe—a hogshead of wine was distributed to the populace, and four hogsheads of porter were given away at other places. Altogether, the Corporation spent £279 over the ceremony. Drinking appears to have been thought the most appropriate manner of inaugurating the new reign. According to the accounts of the Commercial Rooms for that year, the committee spent £67 18*s*. 11*d*. of the proprietors' money on wine "drunk on the night of his majesty's accession"! Perhaps these and other excesses brought about a certain amount of reaction. Down to this period it had been the custom, on the evening of the king's birthday, for the mayor and aldermen to invite many of their friends and acquaintances to drink his majesty's health at the Council House. A company of soldiers, standing opposite to the building, fired salutes at intervals, and a military band, stationed on the stairs, rendered musical honours to the carousal. Unseemly results had frequently arisen from this custom, which was also regarded by many as a gross misappropriation of the civic revenue; and the entertainment, which generally cost from £80 to £90, was now abolished.

The general election caused by the demise of the crown found both political parties in Bristol in a state of disorganisation. In the previous year, Mr. R. H. Davis, the Tory member, had been plunged in financial embarrassments by the ill success of a funding scheme, which, it is said, the Chancellor of the Exchequer (Mr. Vansittart) had adopted under his advice, though some contemporaries gave the credit or discredit of the suggestion to Dr. Beeke, the Dean of Bristol, another private friend of the minister. In either case, Mr. Davis, having lost heavily by speculations connected with the scheme, had withdrawn from the local banking, mercantile, and manufacturing firms of which he was a partner, and the Steadfast Society (which claimed the right of nominating the "blue" candidate), under the belief that the honourable gentleman would be unable to continue his former profuse expenditure at elections, did not invite him to come forward. Mr. Davis, deeply hurt, consequently announced his retirement, observing in his address to the electors that "under the painful recollections of the past year, an invitation would have poured balm into a wounded mind." Mr. P. J. Miles was chosen by the Steadfast Society as their champion, but his acceptance of their proposal was briskly followed by a withdrawal. Much difference of opinion became apparent in the party, the friends of Mr. Davis being indignant at the action of the society; and the latter at length declined to nominate a candidate unless the late member refused to offer himself. In the meantime, Mr. Davis had found sympathisers whose "liberality," to use his own words, had "removed the obstacles which originally opposed" his candidature, and he again took the field. These incidents excited much irritation, and greatly shook the influence of the Steadfast Club, which had been allowed for many years to nominate persons for Government appointments. (The value of the offices under its "patronage" was estimated at upwards of £20,000 a year.) On the other hand, the division caused amongst the Whigs by the contest of 1818 continued to rankle. Mr. Henry Bright having offered himself, a discontented section of the party nominated Mr. J. E. Baillie without obtaining his consent, and insisted on demanding a poll. In the result Mr. Bright had 2,997 votes; Mr. Davis, 2,250; and Mr. Baillie, 115. Mr. Davis refused to be chaired, by which he saved his friends an expenditure of about £2,500. Mr. Bright, however, continued the old practice, and John Evans states that "he appeared in a procession of splendour without example on similar occasions." [*Chron. Hist.* p. 316.]

The Common Council were informed in June that Mr. Alderman Ames, who died a few weeks previously, had devised the sum of £1,200 in consols to the Corporation, in trust to purchase for the night constable and nine night watchmen of the ward of St. Mary-le-port "a good and substantial great coat, a good strong pair of boots, and a good strong hat, every two years." Mr. Ames had been many years alderman of the ward. On the establishment of the present police force, the Corporation, on the pretext that the kind-hearted gentleman's bequest could no longer be applied in accordance with his intentions, thoughtlessly threw the £1,200 into the borough fund, and without doing any appreciable good to anybody the donation was irrecoverably lost.

Much inconvenience being caused by the want of a trustworthy public clock in the city, the Corporation ordered the erection of a timepiece at the Exchange. The clock, which was set up during the spring, cost £166 9*s*.

The forced withdrawal of the Bill of Pains and Penalties against Queen Caroline was hailed by a majority of the citizens with demonstrations of delight. In spite of a circular issued by the magistrates "earnestly recommending" the inhabitants to abstain from "a measure which might disturb the peace of the city," a spontaneous illumination took place on the 13th November; and it was remarked by the unsympathetic editor of the *Bristol Journal* that the display extended to, and was most general in, the districts inhabited by the labouring classes. "The splendour of the dwellings of the out-door paupers," wrote the angry scribe, "announced that the whole week's allowance from the workhouse had been expended in honour of Queen Caroline." On the other hand, the upper class Tories displayed their affection for George IV. by keeping their houses in darkness. A congratulatory address to the Queen on the defeat of her persecutor was afterwards adopted at a meeting in the Guildhall, and this again was followed by a gathering of the king's friends, at which an address expressing fidelity to the monarch, and horror at the "treason and blasphemy" abetted by a "licentious press," was agreed upon with enthusiasm.

The following paragraph, from the *Bristol Journal* of December 16, 1820, indicates the miserable inefficiency of the police of the city at this date: "We hear that the inhabitants of College-green and its vicinity have enrolled themselves, for the purpose of patrolling the neighbourhood nightly, during the winter, by an alternate watch of four hours each, armed with a bludgeon, dirk, and pistol. Were this plan generally adopted, it would doubtlessly be the means of preventing many depredations." Although the Common Council regarded this scandalous state of affairs with perfect indifference, it allowed one of its members,

Mr. J. George, the exorbitant sum of £903 10*s.* 4*d.* for serving the office of sheriff a second time during this year.

A controversy between the Corporation and Mr. Edward Griffith, steward (judge) of the Tolzey Court, broke out about this time. It appeared from the complaints of the Bristol solicitors that Mr. Griffith, having succeeded in obtaining an appointment as a stipendiary magistrate in London, had taken up his residence in the capital, and persistently neglected his duties in the Tolzey Court, although continuing to receive the fees of his office. Remonstrances being without effect, the Common Council resolved, on the 6th January, 1821, that as Mr. Griffith had left the city, caused great inconvenience to the public by absenting himself from his court, and ignored the summons to attend that meeting, he should be "amoved and removed" from his functions. Mr. Griffith had the audacity to appeal to the superior courts in support of his claim to the judgeship, but was unsuccessful, and thenceforth dropped out of sight.

Much to the displeasure of many residents in the neighbourhood, four rows of lime trees, standing upon that part of the quay still known as the Grove, were removed about the close of 1820. It may be worth while to add that five or six large trees remained in front of the Apple-tree Inn, Broadmead, a door or two to the eastward of Union Street, so late as 1828 or 1829.

On the 28th February, 1821, the Royal Commissioners appointed under an Act of 1819 to inquire into the condition of the charities of the kingdom opened their investigations in the Council House, the charities under the control of the Corporation being the first subject of inquiry. The Commissioners paid another visit to the city in March, 1822, when they dealt with the parochial charities. The result was given in two thick Blue-books, known as the sixth and tenth reports of the Commissioners, of which the portions relating to Bristol were locally reprinted, in two quarto volumes, by Mr. T. J. Manchee, in 1831.

The *Bristol Journal* of March 11 stated that a few nights previously "a brother of Mr. Southey, the Poet Laureate, performed the character of Sir Robert Bramble in the comedy of 'The Poor Gentleman,' at our theatre. He is from Exeter theatre, and will be an acquisition to the company." No further allusion to him, however, was made in the *Journal*. About two years later the same paper had an announcement of the publication of "The History of the West Indies," in three volumes, by Captain T. Southey, R.M., another brother of the poet.

The census of 1821 credited the ancient city with a population of 52,889. To these figures Clifton added 8,811; St. George's, 5,334; the district of St. James and St. Paul, 3,605; St. Philip's out-parish, 11,824; Mangotsfield, 3,179; and Stapleton, 2,137, making a total for the city and suburbs of 87,779, an increase of 15 per cent. on the return for 1811. The population of Bedminster was now 7,979, and the tything of Stoke Bishop, in Westbury parish, was credited with 1,883.

A local journal of the 23rd June records that on the Monday previous, "as some workmen were removing a monument at the east end of the south aisle of our cathedral, they discovered an elegant altar-piece, similar to that which was lately found in the Mayor's Chapel. At the east end of the north aisle was also discovered a very superb piece of workmanship, the gilding and colours of which were remarkably bright, and the fluted columns very perfect. There are niches on each side with small pedestals." There is no appearance of an "altar-piece" in the south aisle at the present time, a recess for a tomb occupying the place designated; but the existing work is not ancient, and as there was no outrage on the integrity of a building which chapters of the Georgian era were not capable of committing, the above account is probably correct. As regards the altar-piece, or reredos, in the north aisle, which is supposed to have been walled up during the civil war, its relics still attest the richness and beauty of the original workmanship and the barbarism of the authorities by whom it was brought to light. In 1821 the seventeenth century monument of the Codrington family was in the chancel, near the tomb of Abbot Morgan. But the chapter resolved upon fixing it to the reredos in question, and a large hole was hacked in the tabernacle work for the purpose! Four tablet monuments are also fixed in the reredos, little of which can now be seen.

The coronation of George IV. took place on the 19th July, but was not celebrated in Bristol with the liberality that had marked a similar event sixty years previously, there being no record of fat oxen roasted whole, or of fountains running wine or beer. The members of the Corporation, accompanied by the parochial clergy and officials, the Society of Merchants, the Freemasons, and representatives of various trades* walked in procession through the principal streets to the

---

* The incorporated companies were by this time practically extinct. The *Bristol Journal* states that the company of wire workers and pin makers was the only chartered one which took part in the procession.

cathedral to attend service. The building was filled, but it was believed that the only person who had attended a similar service at the coronation of the last king, and who now applied for a seat, was the Dowager Lady Smyth, who had been the reigning "toast" of her generation. The procession returned to the Council House by a circuitous route. The most remarkable feature of the parade was a triumphal car bearing a crown, and a man cased in armour of the time of Henry V. In the afternoon there was a dinner at the Assembly Rooms, the Mayor presiding, after which the company were called upon to drink thirty-five toasts, that of "Our glorious and inestimable Constitution in Church and State" being followed by the glee "With a jolly full bottle." At night the Corporation gave a ball, which cost upwards of £700. The public buildings and many private houses were illuminated, but one gentleman dyed his candles black on account of "the unmerited exclusion of my queen." On the Sunday following the coronation, Prebendary Randolph, then in residence at the cathedral, took as the text of his sermon two verses from the Book of Daniel, beginning: "Belshazzar the king made a great feast to a thousand of his lords," and ending with a reference to the said monarch's "wives and concubines."* The prebendary, it has been alleged, was a disappointed courtier; but a more probable explanation of his impropriety is, that he was a warm sympathiser with Queen Caroline, and had been irritated, like many other Whigs, by the political tergiversations of George IV.

Mention having been made of one of the cathedral dignitaries of the period, the opportunity may be taken to notice some of his ecclesiastical contemporaries. In touching upon some of the abuses of the age, however, it is only fair to observe that the functionaries in question ought not to be judged by the standard of the present day, but by that of their own generation. In an interview which once took place between Sydney Smith and Mr. Gladstone, the witty canon frankly observed to the then youthful statesman that "whenever you see a clergyman of my age, you may feel certain that he is a bad clergyman;" and allowance must be made for the habits of a time when nearly the whole profession was apathetic, slothful, and self-seeking. These conditions being premised, the prebendary entitled to precedence on the ground of seniority is the Rev. F. W. Blomberg, on whom the favours

* "Local Annals," City Library, vol. i. p. 282.

of royalty were abundantly showered. Very soon after his ordination he was appointed to the valuable living of Shepton Mallet, in the gift of the Prince of Wales, to whom he was chaplain and private secretary, generally living at Carlton House. In 1790, in his 28th year, he was appointed Prebendary of Bristol. A few years later he became Prebendary of Westminster, Vicar of Bradford, Wilts, and Vicar of Banwell. His next elevation was to a canonry of St. Paul's, by right of which he obtained the vicarage of St. Giles's, Cripplegate, one of the richest livings in London. In addition to all this preferment,—for much of which he rendered no service whatever,—*Felix Farley's Bristol Journal* of November 2, 1816, announced that he had "lately been presented to a very handsome estate, which had become the property of the Crown in default of an heir-at-law." Such abundant favour exciting curiosity, an explanation was offered, with the alleged approval of Dr. Blomberg himself. His father, it was said, was an officer in the army, who had made a secret marriage with a lady that died in a few years, whereupon the two children of the union were nursed in an obscure part of the country. During the wars the father died abroad, but immediately afterwards his ghost presented itself to a fellow officer, and gave him instructions where to find the children, and how to put them in possession of a valuable estate. This having been done, the marvel reached the ears of Queen Charlotte, who sent for the youthful Blomberg, and had him brought up and educated with the royal children. If the narrators of this story obtained it from the person chiefly interested, it is singular that their versions, three in number, should be utterly irreconcilable respecting the date and the place of the ghost's appearance, the locality of the deceased's estate, and every other detail into which they enter. Cynical people offered a perfectly unromantic explanation of Dr. Blomberg's good fortune. That he was brought up at Windsor appears certain, and it was generally agreed that in features he strikingly resembled the royal family. Dr. Blomberg's successor as Prebendary of Bristol was Lord W. G. H. Somerset. His lordship had been an officer in a cavalry regiment during the long war, but upon the army being reduced after the fall of Napoleon, he applied for ordination and entered the Church, when he was rapidly promoted by the head of his family to four rectories—Tormarton, Llangattock, Crickhowell, and Conduc. After obtaining a stall at Bristol, his income from the Church was estimated at £3,000 per annum. It was stated by those acquainted with him that he never wrote a sermon; but there is a tradition that he preached twice in the cathedral in the course of twenty-three years. On the other hand, he had all the skill of his family for driving a coach and four, which it was his constant practice to do after morning service during his periods of residence here; and the stables he built at Tormarton were much more imposing than was the rectory. The Rev. John Surtees, appointed to a seat in the chapter in 1821, and holding two valuable Crown rectories in Norfolk, had no other claim to wealth and dignity than the fact that he was a relative of Lady Eldon, wife of the Lord Chancellor. He was as guiltless of sermon-writing as was his noble colleague, but he preached at intervals when in Bristol. If report is to be credited, he bought his discourses from one of the minor canons, but eventually availed himself of a cheaper market, though the reduced price and inferior quality of the article did not induce him to increase the quantity. During the latter half of his connection with the cathedral, which extended over thirty-six years, his irregularity of attendance and slovenly performance of his duties became almost proverbial. "Belshazzar Randolph," as he was sometimes called in consequence of the escapade reported above, was the son of a Bristol physician, residing in Trinity Street. He was forty years a prebendary, holding for much of the time the lucrative rectory of St. Paul's, Covent Garden, London, the gift of his friend the Duke of Bedford, and also the vicarage of Banwell, Somerset. He was famous for his courtly manners, but through having misdelivered, in early life, a letter written by the Princess of Wales to a friend, sarcastically commenting on the English royal family, he destroyed his prospects of higher advancement in the Church. One of his contemporaries, the Rev. F. Simpson, held a prebend for nearly twenty years, but nothing is recorded of him save that he had three rectories and a vicarage in various parts of the kingdom. Another was the Rev. H. J. Ridley, a brother-in-law to Lord Chancellor Eldon, and described by Sydney Smith as "worldly-minded, vain, noisy, and perfectly good-natured." Ridley was succeeded by the Rev. Edward Bankes, who, having married a daughter of the Lord Chancellor, had more than the usual share of favours extended to the great lawyer's connections. In addition to his prebend at Bristol, he had another at Gloucester, and a good living in Dorset. Although he became enormously rich upon the death of his father-in-law, Mr. Bankes continued to hold his preferments for some years after he was incapable of performing the duties attached to them. This was, however, natural enough, seeing that he had rendered very perfunctory service when in his vigour. In a letter addressed to the Archbishop of Canterbury, of which a copy appeared in the London *Sun* of the 13th January, 1834, a citizen complained of "the general neglect and almost total abandonment of our cathedral service." "We have had," added the writer, "neither dean nor prebendary in residence for many months." The defaulting officials at this date were, it was understood, Messrs. Surtees and Bankes. The dean, Dr. Beeke, who was then in his 84th year, was a finished scholar, and, before age disabled him, an energetic promoter of literature and science in the city. His only shortcoming, apparently, was his stature, Sydney Smith alleging that if Bishop Gray stood on the dean's shoulders their combined height would not equal that of the Archbishop of Canterbury. As to Sydney himself, it must be added that, although a political reformer, he was a zealous champion of abuses in the Church. Soon after becoming a prebendary of Bristol, he claimed by rotation the chapter living of Halberton, Devon, a place he is supposed to have never visited except to go through the legal formalities needed to secure the income. Non-residence in those days was so common as to excite little remark. Hannah More, writing from Cowslip Green in 1790, remarked that "thirteen adjoining parishes had not so much as one resident curate, much less rector." And according to a parliamentary return printed in 1829, out of the 443 clergymen holding livings in the diocese of Bath and Wells, only 177 were resident. Bishops were content to follow the customs of their inferiors. Dr. Kaye, who held the see of Bristol from 1820 to 1827, was also Master of Christ Church College, Cambridge, Regius Professor of Divinity, and the incumbent of a valuable rectory. So indifferent was he to episcopal duties that on one occasion he is said to have compelled the local candidates for ordination to take a journey to Cambridge. His successor, Dr. Gray, was a prebendary of Durham, which was more valuable than his bishopric, whilst Bishop Monk held the deanery of Peterborough and two or three other preferments.

A musical festival was opened on the 30th October, 1821, in St. Paul's Church, when, after a sermon by the Dean of Bristol, Handel's oratorio of "Esther" was performed. On the following day a selection of sacred music was given, and the third morning performance was devoted to "The Messiah." Evening concerts also took place at the Assembly Rooms and theatre. Madame Catalani, equally famous for her voice and her rapacity, was the "star" of the festival, which was financially successful. The receipts from the first performance, indeed, reached only £59, which says little for the persuasiveness of the Dean's discourse; but "The Messiah" was especially productive, and the aggregate amounted to £1,856. Including the collections made at the doors, the Infirmary secured £587 by the gathering.

The minutes of the Common Council for the 9th of February, 1822, contain a reference to a local undertaking the story of which has been strangely neglected by Bristol annalists. Little more is recorded of the first Bristol Water Company than that it was formed about 1695 under a special Act of Parliament, that it undertook to pay the Corporation a septennial sum of £166 13*s*. 4*d*. for the privilege of supplying the city, that a supply of water obtained from the Avon at Hanham Mills was driven to the higher level by means of a remarkable atmospheric engine near Conham, that there was a reservoir at Lawrence Hill, and that the pipes into the city were formed of the hollowed trunks of trees. It has been stated that the company "soon failed;" but the Act of 1760 for rebuilding Bristol Bridge contained a clause requiring the bridge trustees to lay down new and sufficient pipes if they removed those belonging to the waterworks, and empowered the company to repair their pipes on or near to the bridge. Yet it is difficult to imagine how service pipes could be attached to trunks of trees, and there is no record of reservoirs for dispensing the water in another manner. The sixteenth septennial payment to the Corporation was made in 1807. The Common Council, on the day mentioned above, ordered "that the city seal should be affixed to a deed of release, from the Corporation to the proprietors of the waterworks, of the payments and covenants contained in a certain deed bearing date the 10th day of August, 1695, in consideration of the sum of £500 to be paid by the said proprietors to this Corporation." It may be presumed that this release was obtained in order to enable the proprietors to dispose of their land at Lawrence Hill and other places. In 1848 several trunks of elm, hollowed with a very large bore, were discovered during excavations in Old Market Street, and a similar pipe was disinterred in West Street in March, 1886.

The West India interest was about this time in a seriously depressed state. In a petition of the West India merchants of Bristol, presented to the House of Commons in April, 1822, it was stated that owing to the prohibition imposed by Parliament on intercourse between the islands and the United States, the planters were compelled to ship nearly the whole of their rum and molasses to this country, and that, as the supply exceeded the demand, the price of rum barely cleared the expense of distillation, while the low price of sugar, owing to the increased imports from our eastern colonies, left no return for capital after defraying the cost of production. The petitioners therefore prayed for a renewal of the free intercourse formerly existing between the settlements and the continent of North America. In response to this and other similar appeals, the Ministry brought in and passed a Bill for abolishing the restrictions complained of, the colonies being permitted to trade both with each other and with the American States. This was the first great inroad on the old Navigation Laws, and, although disapproved by the ultra-Tory party, was highly applauded by most of the mercantile community.

The Easter holidays of 1822 were thus recorded in the *Bristol Journal* of April 13: "The annual scenes of rude festivity, and, we may add, of low debauchery, known by the name of 'the Bedminster revels,' took place on Monday, as usual at this period of the year; and a fight of no interest was exhibited on Durdham down, between two combatants of 'little note and less skill.'" The following equally singular indication of the changes effected by time is found in the same paper three weeks later: "May-day was celebrated this year with more than its wonted gaiety. Soon after sunrise there was an unusually strong muster upon Clifton down . . . 'to sport the light fantastic toe.' . . . During the morning kings and queens out of number paraded the streets. The chimney sweeps, too, made a splendid appearance. The next and most attractive 'bit of life' was on Clifton down to see the racing. Here was life in all its variety. . . . The Fancy [pugilists] too, mustered pretty numerously. [An account of the racing follows]. A better day's sport was never witnessed. After the races, a ring was formed, and Jacky Cabbage *shewed* to challenge Hazell for a bellyful. Some interruption, however, occurred by the appearance of a Deputy *Beak* in the ring, so it was off. There was some milling afterwards. . . . A [dinner and] ball concluded the evening." It is rare to find the old-fashioned editor descending from his stilts in this way to notice the manners and customs of the time. In addition to the above seasons of revelry, a correspondent of the *Times and Mirror*, whose memory carried him to about this period, recently stated that on Boxing Day a pleasure fair was held "outside the gate," and was known as the "Horn Fair." "It took its name from a grotesque-looking gingerbread cake known as 'the horn,' which was made to represent a man's head and shoulders, with two trumpets branching out from his back; they varied in size from a few inches to a yard long. . . . The fair was held in Wade Street. Stalls were pitched on the sides of the road . . . gilt horns were everywhere by hundreds. It was a wild, noisy affair, notable for petty gambling. . . . From morning till night groups of pleasure-seekers wandered up and down amongst the stalls, staking their pence until their pockets were emptied. On New Year's Day a similar fair was held in West Street, from Bullpaunch Lane [famous for bull baiters] to Gloucester Lane."

Coronation Road, Bedminster, a new turnpike road from Harford's Bridge to the Ashton road, was opened on the 23rd April, 1822, with some ceremony. The Dowager Lady Smyth, of Clift House, in a coach and four, preceded by Captain Smyth's troop of Yeomanry, took part in the inaugural ceremony. The road, which had been under construction for about a year, had received its name when the workmen employed upon it were regaled on the coronation day of the new king.

In July the Prince and Princess of Denmark made a brief visit to the city during their incognito tour in the West of England. Being waited upon by the Mayor (Mr. A. Hilhouse) at their hotel in Clifton, they went down to the Mansion House and were sumptuously entertained. Subsequently they visited Mr. Ricketts's glass house and Mr. Hare's floorcloth factory. The prince also accompanied the Mayor to the Guildhall, where the quarter sessions were proceeding, and subsequently visited the new gaol.

The parish church of St. Andrew, Clifton, a small and mean edifice, rebuilt during the Commonwealth, had long been inadequate to accommodate even a tithe of the inhabitants. Much difficulty, however, was encountered in obtaining funds for its reconstruction on a scale worthy of the parish, and it was at length found necessary to guarantee to each subscriber of a certain amount a freehold right to a pew in the best portions of the new church. More than two-thirds of the pews on the floor of the edifice were disposed of in this way. The foundation was laid in the summer of 1819, another site being selected in order that the old building should remain until its successor was finished. The edifice—a characteristic specimen of Georgian mock Gothic—was consecrated on the 12th August, 1822, by the Bishop of Bristol. An admission fee of four shillings each was demanded from all save a limited section of the poorer inhabitants. A "capital dinner" afterwards took place, at which, says the reporter, "the utmost harmony and gentlemanly deportment prevailed," the compliment being doubtless an indirect slap at the dubious amenities of Clifton parochial life sixty years ago. The freehold pews—locked up against the invasion of the vulgar—soon became a scandal. Many of the subscribers, on leaving the parish, sold their "property" by auction, and a "good family pew" was eagerly bought up for from £100 to £150; others were let at heavy rents. In 1844, when Mr. Leech wrote his "Church-goer," he spoke of Clifton church as being "not to any extent the church of the parishioners; the rich and the non-resident occupy the reserved seats, and those few that are nominally free are filled with powdered footmen." Further reference to the subject will be found under the year 1863.

Amongst the social incidents of the reign of George IV., the practice of stealing human bodies for anatomical purposes, which was then constantly resorted to by agents of the surgical profession, was perhaps the most revolting. The *Bristol Journal* of the 26th October, 1822, narrated that, a few nights previously, a body was stolen from a grave in St. Augustine's churchyard, and conveyed to the "dissecting-room," a chamber hired by two or three Bristol surgeons, and situated in the precincts of the cathedral. A quarrel having arisen betwixt the "resurrection men" and their employers, a crowd gathered near the house, the door of which was eventually forced, and the crime discovered. The churchwardens were bound over to prosecute the ostensible occupier of the room, but no result is recorded, the surgeons having doubtless succeeded in hushing up the matter. Less than a fortnight after this affair, three parish constables, in consequence of private information, visited Bedminster churchyard at midnight, and found six persons busily engaged in raising the recently interred body of a young woman. A severe struggle followed. "There were pistols snapped and rapiers drawn, bloody noses and broken heads. The battle was long and severely contested before the patrol was able to secure five; the sixth escaped." The prisoners were committed for trial, but the result has not been found. Offences of this character could not have been committed with impunity in populous localities if the streets had been adequately guarded. As a matter of fact the police regulations were farcical. In the newspaper recording the Bedminster outrage is the mock trial of a gentleman, a stranger in the city, charged with whistling in the public thoroughfares between eleven at night and two in the morning, thereby preventing the watchmen from enjoying their accustomed slumbers. One of the injured fraternity, "about sixty years old, and decrepit in the extreme," is made to depose that "he had originally been in the employment of a member of the —— [Corporation], but his infirmities having unfitted him for labour, he was appointed watchman." As regards "body snatching" in rural parishes, there is evidence that it was frequently practised, to the great horror of country people. A ghastly affair of this kind occurred about 1824 or 1825. Three medical students connected with "the college dissecting room" started one dark evening in a gig for Long Ashton churchyard, for the purpose of disinterring the body of a person whose malady had excited professional interest. One of the youths being left in charge of the vehicle, his companions entered the cemetery and began operations, when one of them was almost frozen with terror on seeing, or imagining he saw, the ghost of the intended "subject." His companion became infected with his panic, and both fled to their conveyance, in which they hurried homewards. On the following day, the Long Ashton authorities offered a reward for the discovery of the body, which had been stolen during the night; and the students are believed to have had ocular evidence that they had been frightened away by the trick of a gang of professional "resurrectionists," who did not relish the interference of amateurs. The youth who supposed he saw a spirit, however, died shortly afterwards, having never recovered from the mental shock. He was the son of a dissenting minister in Bristol. His companion in the churchyard, long a member of the Infirmary staff, recounted the story, under feigned names, in *Once a Week* for October, 1860.

During the year 1822 the old Hotwell house, overhanging the river, built about 1696, and the resort of so much fashionable company for several generations, was removed, to admit of the construction of the new Bridge Valley road to Clifton Down. A handsome pump room, in the Tuscan style, was shortly afterwards erected, a suite of baths—the want of which had always been complained of—being added to the building. The improvement came too late, however, to arrest the declining popularity of the spring; and with few exceptions visitors resorted to the well rather from curiosity than from belief in its medical efficacy.* In June, 1867, the new pump room was in turn closed and demolished, in order to carry out Mr. Howard's plan for the removal of Hotwell Point—an inconvenient prominence on the right bank of the Avon. As the spring reached the surface in the projecting rock, it became entirely inaccessible to the public after March, 1868, and remained so for about ten years. At length, owing to the reasonable complaints of the inhabitants, pipes were laid down in the summer of 1877, and a pump was erected in a cavern hollowed out of the neighbouring cliff; but Dr. F. W. Griffin, in a letter addressed to a local paper in July, 1880, expressed his belief, as the result of analyses, that the true spring had been lost, or that it was subject to variable admixture from other sources. In any case, the distance between the source and the pump caused the water to lose its characteristic temperature before it reached the consumer, and the title of "hot" well—a misnomer from the outset—became wholly inapplicable.

Soon after the accession of George IV. the beautiful little church of St. Mark's, College Green, commonly known as the Mayor's Chapel, having been again allowed to fall into ignorant and presumptuous hands, became the victim of destructive "restorations" carried on for upwards of seven years. Strange to say, no reference to the subject appears in the records of the Common Council; but the cash-book of the city treasurer contains so many brief yet eloquent items that it is possible to form a chronicle of the devastations. The first payment occurred in August, 1822, when Mr. Thomas Clarke, sometimes called a sculptor and sometimes a mason, received £100 for "repairing vestry room, etc." From an item in the following month, it appears that the renovators had resolved on pulling down the great west window of the church—an interesting specimen of the last era of Decorated architecture. For producing and setting up a copy of the original work, Mr. Clarke received £180. The old masonry was given to Mr. J. Cave, then or soon after a member of the Common Council, who had it placed in a mock ruin in his park at Brentry, where, after being buffetted by the storms

* The management appears to have been of an illiberal character. Threepence per glass was charged for the water, equivalent to a shilling a day for average drinkers, and only paupers were allowed to draw from a tap in the back yard. In 1831 this tap was removed, but in 1837 a free pump was erected in consequence of the public discontent.

of more than sixty years, its sound condition still demonstrates the recklessness of those who expelled it from its original site. The next payment to Mr. Clarke is £25 4*s*. for "repairing tombs." The erection, in 1815, of a gallery for the accommodation of Dr. Goodenough's private pupils has been already mentioned [see p. 47]. In 1823 it was determined to construct a new gallery, and Mr. Clarke received £185 3*s*. for carrying out the order. At this point Mr. William Edkins, a house-painter, begins to figure often in the accounts. This gentleman was entrusted with the task of designing the gallery and superintending the "sculptor's" operations, for which he received £10; and he had £21 more for "superintending the erection of the altar screen"—the original work having been "restored" by Clarke after the removal of a huge and unsightly fabric, in the Dutch style, with which the church was "beautified" about 1721. These works, completed in 1824, were merely preliminary to the grand "embellishment" which the authorities had been induced to sanction through the persuasion of the city chamberlain, Mr. Thomas Garrard, a well-meaning collector of antique curiosities, but as ignorant of Gothic architecture as was the churchwardendom of his time. Having obtained practically unlimited powers, the amateur architect's first efforts were directed to the collection of stained glass of various styles and dates. One lot, costing £166, was obtained at a sale of the effects of Sir Paul Bagot, a Gloucestershire baronet; another, for which £192 were paid, was bought at the great sale at Fonthill: a third lot was purchased in London for £45; and "the figure of a bishop," the original locality of which is not mentioned, cost £8. In 1828, the so-called renovation of the church began in earnest. The west window of the south aisle was reconstructed, the "cieling" underwent great alterations, a new gallery was built for the City School boys, the church was fresh paved, and the windows were "scraped." Worse than all this, however, the house-painter already mentioned designed, in conjunction with Mr. Garrard, an "ante-chapel," with wooden columns and mock vaulting, and was allowed to introduce into the building itself a mass of lath-and-plaster ornamentation, in imitation of carving, bedizened with gold and colour, but in execrable taste, and glaringly incongruous with the true character of the fabric. Upon this paltry gingerbread work alone nearly £1,400 were squandered. The entire "renovation," including a new organ, a picture over the communion table, by Mr. King, a local artist, and a quantity of "velvet with cloth of gold fringe for the pews," entailed a cost of over £5,500. The chapel was reopened in October, 1830, when the Mayor and Corporation attended in great pomp. The organ at that time was placed over the "ante-chapel," where it blocked up the western window. It was removed to a more suitable position in 1870, and it may be hoped that the time is not far distant when the chapel will undergo a real restoration in intelligent and sympathising hands.

It has been already observed that the high charges imposed on shipping by the Bristol Docks Company became the subject of complaint soon after the completion of the Floating Harbour; and there can be no question that those burdens, aggravated as they were by the exorbitant town and mayor's dues levied by the Corporation, crippled the commercial progress of the port, and diverted trade to places more liberally managed. A striking illustration of the shortsighted rapacity of the local bodies had been furnished in October, 1818, when a consignment of 400 flasks of quicksilver was sent from Cadiz to Bristol for a Liverpool consignee. The dock dues charged were £15; the town dues, £14 11*s.* 4*d*; and the wharfage dues, £3 14*s.* 9*d*; making a total of £33 6*s.* 1*d.* The owner protested against the charges, observing that at Liverpool the total dues demanded would have been only £10 8*s.* 4*d.*; but the authorities curtly replied that "it was not in their power to make any alteration." It was stated, again, that Bristol might have carried on a large business in indigo, which was extensively used by the west of England clothiers; but that the charges on a chest of about 3 cwt. being 16*s.* 5½*d.*, against 2*s.* 4½*d.* levied at Liverpool, the trade was almost entirely diverted. The mayor's dues on a vessel, imposed without reference to burden, were £2 5*s.*, so that an Irish trading sloop of 60 or 80 tons, making twelve voyages yearly, paid £27, while a West India sugar ship of ten times the tonnage paid only £2 5*s.* on her annual entry. With a view to pressing for relief from these and other grievances, several influential firms co-operated in the spring of 1823 in establishing a local Chamber of Commerce, of which Mr. Joseph Reynolds was the first president, Messrs. Thomas Stock and Joseph Cookson being appointed vice-presidents. The new institution lost no time in appealing to public opinion on the subject. A paper showing the duties payable on leading imports at the chief ports, bringing into relief the enormous excess of taxation at Bristol, was published by the Chamber, and made a profound impression. When the new body memorialised the Common Council, however (in September), urging for a remission of the taxes, the document was contemptuously "laid on the table." The Chamber soon after returned to the charge, whereupon the Council, in January, 1824, passed a resolution condemning the acts of its critics as "hasty, premature, and animated by hostile feelings." The result was a petition to the House of Commons, praying for an inquiry into the causes of the languishing condition of the city. The Corporation met the threatened attack by introducing a Bill into Parliament, ostensibly for the purpose of enabling it to reduce its dues, but really—its opponents asserted—with the object of obtaining legislative sanction for taxation which many merchants held to be illegally imposed. The Bill was withdrawn through the opposition offered by the Chamber of Commerce, supported by the citizens generally, who subscribed £3,000 to carry on the struggle. It was, however, revived in 1825, when a prolonged conflict took place between the civic authorities and the mercantile and trading interests. The latter, after laying bare the real motive of the promoters of the scheme, and asserting that the proferred abatement in the dues still left them excessive as compared with those of other leading ports, made a powerful attack on the Corporation itself. It was shown that the Common Council was self-elected and irresponsible, that it rendered no services in return for the taxes it imposed on shipping, that it published no accounts, and administered the revenues of which it was trustee with a wanton disregard for the opinion of the citizens. The oath of secrecy imposed on its members was, it was added, a practical avowal that its proceedings would not bear the face of day. What lent the greatest weight to these charges was the fact that they were supported by the testimony of influential citizens of both political parties, some prominent Tories being even more zealous in the attack than were their Whig colleagues. The Corporation, however, defiantly retorted through their parliamentary counsel, that the port dues, as well as all their other estates, though applicable to public purposes at their discretion, were their personal property—"as much so as any estate belonging to any peer"—and that no one had a right to demand an account as to how the revenues were administered. Mr. Serjeant Ludlow, the town clerk, scornfully declared to the Commons' committee that it was a new thing to contend that the law courts, or even Parliament itself, could control a Corporation in the expenditure of its own money. He flatly denied that the people of Bristol had any interest in the corporate funds, and against such a principle, he said, the Corporation would struggle to the utmost extremity. What answer a reformed House of Commons would have made to these insolent pretensions may be left to the judgment of the reader. Even the Legislature of 1825, dominated as it was by aristocratic influences, repelled the attempt of the Common Council to exchange a doubtful prescriptive title for one resting on an Act of Parliament. As the Chamber of Commerce had suggested, power was given to reduce the dues without trenching on the question of legal rights, and in this form the Bill passed. A Government Commission to inquire into the collection and management of the revenue having visited the city in November, one of its members, the Hon. Mr. Wallace, deploring the differences between the authorities and the inhabitants, offered to remain in Bristol with a view to effecting a reconciliation. The Merchants' Society and the Chamber of Commerce cordially accepted the overture; but the Council forwarded Mr. Wallace a resolution in December, declaring that negotiation was useless, seeing that the differences "wholly consist of hostile aggression on the one hand on the revenue and constitutional government of the Corporation, and on the other on the necessary defence and maintenance of rights established for centuries." By the alterations effected under the new Act, the obnoxious corporate imposts * were reduced nearly two-fifths, or from £5,500 to about £3,500. But the results justified the apprehensions of those who had contended that the concessions would prove inadequate to revive the commerce of the city, inasmuch as they left the port charges in excess of those of more enterprising rival towns. The question again became a burning one in 1833.

For some time previous to this date the Corporation had been perplexed how to administer the increasing revenues of Dr. Thomas White's charities with a due regard for the wishes of the donor. According to Dr. White's will, the Corporation were yearly to devote £100, part of the surplus income of his estate after providing for his collegiate endowment, to repairing the highways leading to the city of Bristol. But whilst the general introduction of turnpikes rendered this expenditure unnecessary, the rents of the property continued to increase, and though large sums were spent on

* Previous to the passing of the Bill, the dues on a packet of woollen cloths exported from Bristol were £3 16*s.* 8*d.*, whilst at Liverpool they were sixpence. —*MS. Annals*, City Library, 1824.

roads which were not turnpikes, the unexpended surplus accumulated from year to year. The recorder, Sir Robert Gifford, having advised the Corporation that they were not justified in spending more than £100 per annum on roads, it was determined in 1820 to apply for a scheme to the Court of Chancery, by which they might spend £200 in that way, and devote the remaining surplus to introducing additional almspeople into Dr. White's hospital in Temple Street—the inmates of which they had already increased from twelve to twenty-four. The court having objected to some of the details, a new scheme was suggested, which was ultimately sanctioned, and which the Common Council in March, 1823, formally approved, and ordered the mayor and aldermen to carry into effect. By this plan the surplus applicable to roads (£479) was distributed as follows:—£100 to roads; £100 to loans and gifts similar to those created by Dr. White; £162 to eight additional almspeople; £83 to augmenting the pay of those in the hospital; and £34 for contingencies. The fund in hand, £3,400, was to be spent in renovating and extending the almshouses. To avoid recurring to the subject again, it may be added that through the alterations made in the laws respecting highways, the last appropriation of money for the repair of roads was in 1860, when about £5 were paid to the Local Board towards the cost of repairing a footway to Bedminster. The fund having accumulated afresh to nearly £3,900, the Charity Trustees, in 1859, obtained an Act, under which £700 were applied to augment the endowment of Queen Elizabeth's Hospital, £1,200 to the Grammar School endowment, about £100 towards repairs at Trinity Hospital, and the balance towards the exhibition fund of the Grammar School. It was further enacted that future surpluses should be invested for the benefit of the last-named institution.

Much consternation was excited amongst the West India interest in the spring of 1823 by an attempt of certain East India merchants to obtain the abolition of the heavy extra duties on sugar imported from our Eastern settlements. The Common Council adopted a petition to Parliament, asserting that as the West India trade was the most important branch of local commerce, and had largely absorbed the capital of the citizens, the project to deprive the sugar industry of the islands of its ancient protection had excited serious alarm. The Council expressed its belief that "from the ruinous prices of sugar of late years, the slightest further depression would lead to the total and speedy ruin of the planters, and the extinction of West India commerce"—with consequences disastrous to Bristol. [The wholesale price of raw sugar was then about 4*d*. per pound.] Notwithstanding this and similar protests, the Government, in 1826, admitted Mauritius sugar at the West India rates, and in 1830 reduced the extra burden on Bombay sugar to 8*s*. per cwt., to the great grief of the interest previously "protected."

Some curious illustrations of the old law of deodands occur in the civic accounts about this time. According to the immemorial custom of the realm, any personal chattel which was the immediate occasion of the death of a man or woman (but not of a child) was forfeited to the king or to the lord of the manor, the value being applied, prior to the Reformation, to the purchase of prayers for the soul of the person snatched away. Thus, if a man fell from a ship in fresh water, and was drowned, ancient legal sages had laid down that the vessel and cargo were, in strictness of law, forfeited as a deodand. The absurdity of the system had, however, been mitigated by the juries empannelled to inquire into the cause of death, who took upon themselves to fix the value of the article forfeited to the lord of the franchise; and the Corporation of Bristol are thus found receiving one shilling as the value of a wagon and team of horses. In another case a ship is valued at two shillings; and in a third the jury assessed a ship and its contents as worth only one shilling. Reformers long protested against a law which practically forced coroners' juries to trifle with their oaths. Deodands were not abolished until 1847.

The Bristol Philosophical and Literary Institution was founded in 1817 by a few public-spirited citizens who felt the want of a local organisation for the promotion of science. Funds having been subscribed for the construction of a building suitable for the purpose in view, a site was purchased in Park Street, and the foundation stone was laid by the mayor (Mr. W. Fripp, junr.) in February, 1820. The edifice, which was much more imposing in its appearance than commodious in its arrangements, cost £11,000. It was finished and opened early in 1823. A dinner was given on the occasion, and some merry local gossips have recorded that, during the dubious "feast of reason" which followed the banquet, Mr. Samuel Lunell, an energetic promoter of the institution, in order to teach his scientific hearers humility, let an apple drop from his hand, and asked why it fell rather than rose, concluding with the poser: "What keeps the moon up in the sky?" The inconvenient querist received no response, save a request from an alderman to "pass the decanters."

In an Act for "preventing encroachments, annoyances, and other nuisances," obtained by the Corporation in 1788, power was taken for placing barriers at each end of Broad Street during the time business was being transacted at assizes and quarter sessions. This provision does not appear to have been exercised between 1793 and 1818, but after the election to the town clerkship of Mr. Ludlow, that fretful official caused the street to be blocked at every sitting of the court. After submitting to the annoyance from 1819 to the summer of 1823, the tradesmen of the city complained loudly of the interruption to business; and the Court of Aldermen, after a brief attempt to maintain the obstruction, advised that the portion of the street in front of the Guildhall should be macadamised. The only subsequent occasion on which the barriers were raised was in 1832, during the sitting of the special commission for the trial of the rioters.

A new assessment of the city was laid before the Court of Aldermen in May, 1823. The total annual value of the property within the ancient boundaries was £186,756.

During the mayoralty of Mr. James George, 1822–3, he was presented by his wife with an addition to his family. It was resolved by his brother corporators to commemorate an event so rare at the Mansion House by the presentation of a "silver cradle," value 100 guineas; and the gift was soon afterwards made through the sheriffs, Messrs. Cave and Goldney.

The Council House, a modest but not ungraceful structure erected in 1704, had been long condemned, as inconvenient in its arrangements and unworthy of the wealthy body to whom it belonged. So early as 1788 an Act had been obtained for rebuilding the house on an enlarged scale by the absorption of the site of the disused church of St. Ewen's (the south aisle of which had been appropriated for the original Council House) and by the purchase of what was formerly known as Forster's Coffee House, together with an adjoining dwelling in Corn Street. The church was dismantled in 1791, but for some reason the Corporation took no further steps until the date now under review, when it obtained from the then celebrated architect, Sir R. Smirke, a design for a spacious and stately edifice in the classical style, comprising not only a Council House but a new Guildhall. The desirability of throwing back the municipal building in order to widen Broad Street and Corn Street led, however, to the rejection of the plan; and it was suggested that a Council House, assize court, etc., should be erected in the centre of Queen Square. Eventually Smirke produced a design for a Council House only on the old spot, suggesting that the streets could be widened to the extent desired by the authorities if the two adjoining houses in Corn Street were removed. This scheme was approved in 1823, and the houses in Corn Street were afterwards bought for £2,740, but only one was then demolished. The foundation stone of the new civic premises was laid by the mayor (Mr. J. Barrow)* in May, 1824. A grand procession, including the members of the Corporation, the Merchants' Society, the Incorporation of the Poor, the clergy, citizens, schoolchildren, etc., marched from the Guildhall by Broad Street, Quay Street, St. Stephen Street, and Corn Street, to the vacant ground; and his worship, after duly laying the stone, delivered an appropriate little address. As the building progressed, it became a subject of general remark that the lines of Smirke's design did not harmonise with those of Corn Street and Broad Street. Amongst the epigrams to which the fact gave rise, the following appeared in the high-Tory *Bristol Journal*:—

> " Why yonder mansion stands awry,
> Does Bristol wondering seek?
> Like to its councils is its site,
> Oblique, oblique, oblique!"

During the reconstruction of the council chamber, the Corporation held its sittings in a large room between Small Street and Broad Street, appertaining to the (former) Mulberry Tree tavern.† The Council House, which cost about £16,000, was completed and occupied in February, 1827, when a figure of Justice by the Bristol-born sculptor, Bailey, R.A., was placed over the front in Corn Street. The aldermanic body was not held in much esteem, and a joke, to the effect that the statue was only too faithfully symbolic of the bench, inasmuch as it was armed with a sword but was destitute of a balance, had widespread success. The court for magisterial business designed by Smirke was so badly lighted that it was condemned, and another was subsequently erected at the west side of the Council House, and finished in November, 1829, at a further cost of about £1,400. To improve the approach to this court, "Forster's Coffee House," the second of the quaint old houses in Corn Street purchased in 1823, was demolished in 1834.

* Mr. (afterwards Alderman) Barrow was educated in Colston's School (*MS. Annals*, City Library), and was, it is believed, the only Colston boy who attained the chief magistracy.

† The Corporation bought the premises for about £1,500.

Mr. Matthew Brickdale, eighteen years Member of Parliament for the city, and long the senior member of the Common Council, resigned his seat in the latter body in January, 1824. He had been in early life a wealthy woollen draper in High Street, but impoverished himself by profuse expenditure at four contested elections. During the closing years of his life he was chiefly supported by his daughter, who obtained the modest situation of housekeeper at the Custom House. On his resignation being read to the Council, it was suggested that he should be granted a pension of £200. The gift was, however, limited to a single vote of £200. Mr. Brickdale died in 1831, aged 97. Mr. Cruger, Brickdale's Whig rival, and once his colleague in the representation, surrendered his aldermanic gown in 1792, when he returned to his native city, New York; but he retained the office of Common Councillor until his death in 1827. An interesting letter from Cruger to Brickdale will be found in Mr. Leech's "Brief Romances of Bristol History," p. 237.

In February, 1824, in the course of some reparations on the first floor of the house in College Green adjoining the western side of the Mayor's Chapel, a small oratory was discovered in the thickness of the party wall, proving that the place had originally formed part of the monastic buildings. A piscina was found intact, and remains of paintings were observed on the walls, some of which were supposed to represent the Nativity and the Resurrection. In one corner was a double-sighted squint or hagioscope, by which an inmate would have been able to see the performance of Mass at the high altar of the church.

The foundation stone of the Arcade leading from St. James's Barton to the Horsefair was laid in May; and the building, which was esteemed at the time as remarkably ornamental and graceful, was finished and opened in 1825. The Lower Arcade was completed soon after.

For the purpose of making a street improvement in the neighbourhood, the Corporation during the spring purchased the interest of a Mr. William Player in the Castle Mill, for £453 10*s*. 10*d*., and the building, which represented the most ancient industrial institution in the city, was soon afterwards removed.

Locomotive steam engines had been employed upon two colliery railways near Newcastle-upon-Tyne for nearly ten years previously to this date, but the surpassing importance of the invention of Hedley and Stephenson remained unrecognised by even the keenest and most enterprising men of business. At length, during a speculative mania which was to end in widespread disaster, the matter excited attention, and in December, 1824, a prospectus appeared of the Bath and Bristol Railway Company, which proposed to avail itself of "that grand improvement, the locomotive steam engine," for the conveyance of passengers and merchandise. The cost of the proposed undertaking was estimated at £8,000 a mile, and a prospect was held out of travelling from Bristol to Bath in the incredibly short space of one hour. The scheme was received with much approval, and applications were made for shares to the amount of double the proposed capital of £100,000. Shortly afterwards a meeting was held, the mayor (Mr. T. Hassell) presiding, at which it was resolved to form a company, to be called the Bristol, Northern and Western Railway Company, for opening communications with the midland and western counties. The capital was to be £800,000 in £50 shares. The capital reserved for Bristol was subscribed within an hour, and equal enthusiasm was shown in Birmingham and other towns. This prospectus was followed by that of the London and Bristol Railroad Company, with a proposed capital of £1,500,000 in £100 shares. The celebrated road improver, Mr. McAdam, had made a preliminary survey of the country for this undertaking, which he recommended should follow the course of the White Horse Valley, characteristically suggesting that a new turnpike road should accompany the railroad from end to end, by which the distance to London would be reduced from 120 to 110 miles. The shares of this company were taken up before even the prospectus was printed. Next, some enterprising people at Taunton proposed the construction of the "Grand Western" railway from Bristol to Exeter, the cost of which was estimated at only £200,000. The whole of these magnificent schemes, in common with hundreds of others less substantial, collapsed in the panic which is about to be noticed.

Early in the year 1825, the Earl of Liverpool, Prime Minister, and Mr. Canning, Secretary of State for Foreign Affairs, who were sojourning at Bath in the hope of recovering health—though the life and labours of both were fast hastening to a close—accepted an invitation from the mayor and Corporation to pay a visit to Bristol, and arrived accordingly on the 12th January. The distinguished guests were first presented with the freedom of the city. In reply to the town clerk, who in a well-turned speech communicated the intention of the corporate body, Lord Liverpool expressed his thanks. He had, he observed, some patrimonial claims upon the city which would have rendered such an honour desirable to him, but he preferred receiving it as a testimony of public approval. Mr. Canning having also briefly acknowledged the compliment, the two statesmen were then presented with the freedom of the Merchants' Company, and afterwards received an address from the Chamber of Commerce, thanking them for the reforms recently effected in the commercial code of the country. In his reply to the latter, Mr. Canning expressed his belief that "a free and liberal policy in regard to trade was increasing throughout the world." In the evening the guests were entertained to dinner at the Mansion House, after which twenty-eight toasts were drunk. (The entertainment cost the Corporation £665.) The Prime Minister returned to Bath after dinner, but Mr. Canning slept in Clifton, and viewed the scenery of the neighbourhood next morning, before his departure.

The early months of 1825 are memorable in English history for a speculative mania as unreasoning and as widespread as that which seized the nation during the South Sea frenzy in the previous century. People of all classes rushed into joint-stock enterprises which were expected to bring in oceans of wealth; and gambling operations in shares, fomented by the madness of the hour, actually enabled some to make fortunes, which they forthwith invested in new bubbles. The rage could not have extended so far had not the Bank of England, in spite of continuous exportations of gold, enormously increased its issues of paper money, in which course it was followed with still greater recklessness by the provincial bankers, who in a few months more than doubled the previous circulation of their notes by making free advances to speculators. At length, in September, the London issues were materially reduced, and the inevitable collapse which followed brought about the most overwhelming revulsion of commerce ever known in the country. In December two large London banks stopped payment, and about seventy country banks became insolvent within a few weeks. The only failure in Bristol (December 20) was that of Messrs. Browne, Cavanagh & Co., whose establishment—the Bullion Bank—stood nearly opposite to the Exchange. Intense alarm being caused by the suspension, there was a rush upon the other banks to demand payment of their notes. A declaration of confidence in these establishments was, however, rapidly signed by the leading firms of the city, and the panic subsided. The crash nevertheless brought about a notable reduction in the local banking houses. In June, 1826,

Messrs. Pitt, Powell & Fripp, Bridge Parade, retired from business. Messrs. Cave, Ames & Cave, Corn Street, about the same time joined the Old Bank of Messrs. Elton, Baillie, Tyndall & Co. A few weeks later, Messrs. Ricketts, Thorne & Courtney, whose premises—the curious house at the corner of Wine and High Streets—were known as the Castle Bank, also withdrew, and their example was immediately afterwards followed by Messrs. Worrall and Gold, who had an office in the Exchange. Half the private banks in Bristol thus disappeared in less than a twelvemonth. In December, 1828, the firm of Savery, Towgood, Yerbury & Towgood, Wine Street, also relinquished business.

In 1824, a few promoters of education amongst the poor, the most prominent of whom were Dr. Birkbeck and Mr. (afterwards Lord) Brougham, suggested the establishment of Mechanics' Institutes in populous towns. The movement found local supporters in the following year, and in June, 1825, an institution on a modest scale was opened in some rooms in Prince's Street. Projects of this character were then regarded with suspicion by old-fashioned politicians. The *Bristol Journal* denounced the "mania for raising the lower orders above their proper sphere," and gave prominence to an article extracted from a London paper, a brief extract from which may be amusing. After remarking that "there only wants a few years' working of Mr. Brougham's infidel college [University College, London], to enlist the shopkeepers on the side of the rabble, and thus sever the only remaining bond by which poverty, ignorance, and numbers are held in subordination to rank, wealth, and knowledge," the able editor, referring to mechanics' institutions solemnly added: "A scheme more completely adapted to the destruction of this empire could not have been invented." Unfortunately for the working classes, their educational training was so deficient at that period that comparatively few could avail themselves of the advantages of the institution, which was mainly supported by tradesmen and their families. In November, 1832, it was removed to a new building erected for the purpose in Broadmead, but when the attraction of novelty had passed away, the subscribers who had been gained by the change of site gradually fell off. After languishing for some years, the institution was dissolved, and its library was transferred to the Athenæum, founded in February, 1845.

An interesting religious body—descendants of the Huguenots who fled from France and settled in Bristol after the revocation of the Edict of Nantes—disappeared in the summer of 1825. The original fugitives were for some years permitted to use the Mayor's Chapel for their weekly worship; but in the reign of George I. the Corporation resolved on resuming occupation of the building, and offered the French Protestants a plot of ground in Orchard Street at a nominal rent, upon which they built a chapel of their own. It was highly characteristic of the old Corporation, that the land thus disposed of was not its own property, but was held in trust for charitable purposes, being part of the estate of Queen Elizabeth's hospital. A lease, renewable every 14 years at a small fine, was granted in September, 1729, to Jacob Peloquin, merchant, and Peter Panon, stuff-maker, at a yearly rent of £1 17*s*. 6*d*. The congregation were negligent in securing renewals of the lease, but on several occasions no advantage was taken of their carelessness. In 1797 the lease seems to have lapsed, but the Rev. Francis de Soyres, chaplain, was allowed to rent the chapel at a charge of two guineas yearly. His successor, the Rev. J. S. Pons, had a similar grant in 1823. The rent was paid up to June, 1825, when the congregation, which, though once numerous, had been constantly diminishing, was finally broken up. The chapel, in 1832, was granted at the old rent to Dr. Kentish, Dr. Davies, and Mr. Wm. Mortimer, who fitted it up as a medical library. Having been again vacated about 1850, it was taken in 1856 by a congregation of Plymouth Brethren at a rent of £25 per annum.

The merchants, shipowners, and others who had agitated for the reduction of the town and mayor's dues, observing the impracticable tactics of the Corporation, resolved about this time upon trying whether the rights and privileges claimed by the civic oligarchy were not assailable in the law courts. It is noteworthy that the movers in this experiment were for the most part leading Tories, and that they were zealously supported by the *Journal*, one of the chief organs of the party, which denounced what it called "the system of favouritism perpetuated by a select body who have by degrees elected themselves into close and tyrannical family compacts." The Whig *Gazette*, on the other hand, was the organ and apologist of the Corporation. Towards the close of 1825 an application was made in the King's Bench for a writ of *quo warranto*, calling upon the mayor and sheriffs to show by what authority they exercised their offices. The promoters of this proceeding contended that in the reign of Edward III. the mayor and sheriffs were elected by the burgesses of the town, and that this right of the inhabitants generally had been filched from them by the help of an illegal charter obtained from Charles II. For the Corporation it was contended that the governing charter of the city was that of Queen Anne, by which the right of self-election was distinctly given to the Common Council; and this defence was upheld in May, 1826, by the Court of King's Bench. Whilst this case was pending, the assailants of the Corporation commenced another action, directed against the town dues. It appeared that whilst the civic archives were being explored in reference to the *quo warranto*, a charter of Edward IV. was found, which, in conferring upon the Corporation the power to levy dues on shipping, directed that the receipts should be applied to the reparation of the quays, pavements, etc., of the city. In consequence of this discovery, application was made for a *mandamus* against the Corporation, requiring them to pay over to the commissioners of paving, in aid of their funds, the income derived from the town dues. In May, 1826, the Corporation put in the technical plea that they had never been asked to do so. In reply the promoters pointed out that, as all the paving commissioners were nominees of the Common Council, there was no independent official capable of taking action on behalf of the ratepayers; but the judges, whose sympathy for privileged bodies and vested rights was in those days carried to excess, held the plea of the Corporation to be sufficient, and the rule for a *mandamus* was discharged. The Corporation's law costs in the above cases exceeded £3,500. In November, 1826, the Chamber of Commerce, changing the object of its attack, requested the Society of Merchants, who held a lease of the wharfage dues of the Corporation for the sum of £10 yearly, to permit an examination of their accounts, it being urged that the dues were grievous to commerce, and produced a revenue enormously in excess of the expenditure incurred in maintaining the quays and wharves of the port. The society's emphatic refusal of this demand was warmly applauded by the Common Council.

"Cabriolets," or "flys," drawn by a single horse had been introduced into London shortly before this time, and had in a large measure superseded the old lumbering "hackney coach." The Common Council in March, 1826, sanctioned a similar innovation in Bristol, but limited the number of the new vehicles to forty.* The number was doubled four years

* The Common Council had of course no jurisdiction in Clifton, where

later. As another novelty in locomotion, it may be stated that passenger "wherries" began to ply from Cumberland Basin to Prince's Street bridge in 1824, and proved so popular that bye-laws fixing the fares were passed by the Common Council in 1827.

Many thousand persons assembled on the banks of the Avon, near the Hotwell, on the 22nd May, 1826, in consequence of an announcement of an American, named Courtney, that he would take a "flying leap" from St. Vincent's rocks to the opposite side of the river. A rope stretched from the highest point of the rocks, above Giant's Cave, was made fast to a tree on the opposite side of the stream; and at the time fixed Courtney appeared, suspended below the rope in a horizontal position, and accomplished the descent, 1,100 feet, in a few seconds, amidst great applause. The feat was repeated on the 5th June with equal success. It may be added that it had been achieved nearly a century earlier, by a man named Thomas Kidman—immortalised in Hogarth's engraving of "The Fair,"—who visited Clifton in April, 1736.

A general election took place in July, and promised at the outset to pass off quietly in this city. The sitting members, Messrs. Bright and Hart Davis, had informed their respective parties that they should prefer to resign rather than bear the onerous expenses of a contest; whereupon the local leaders resolved to avoid a struggle by re-electing the old representatives, and started private subscriptions for defraying the cost. This amicable arrangement, however, was promptly denounced by the more advanced section of the Whig party, who were discontented with Mr. Bright's votes on religious disabilities and other questions, and who determined to nominate Mr. Edward Protheroe. Though the latter declined to stand, he was brought to the poll, to the great joy of the freemen, who regarded economy in election matters as "robbing them of their rights." A serious riot took place on the nomination day, during which the Bush Hotel, Mr. Bright's head-quarters, was partially sacked by the mob. The poll (the last taken in the Guildhall) was kept open for a week, and resulted as follows: Mr. Davis, 3,887; Mr. Bright, 2,315; Mr. Protheroe, 1,873. The names of 999

---

ladies chiefly depended upon sedan chairs. The *Bristol Times and Mirror* of October 5, 1875, published a reminiscence to the effect that the chairmen of Clifton were so alarmed at their interests being imperilled by a fly which a daring individual started, that they assembled at night, broke open the door of the outhouse where the revolutionary vehicle was kept, and hurled it (the vehicle) over St. Vincent's rocks.

persons were added to the burgess roll during the contest, doubtless at the expense of the candidates' committees.

The noxious condition during the summer months of the Floating Harbour, which, as has been already observed, was then the receptacle of nearly all the sewage of the city, had for several years provoked loud complaints on the part of citizens whose dwellings or places of business lay near its banks. The dock directors, however, treated appeals for improvement with contemptuous indifference. In 1825, when the weather was exceptionally hot, and when the Float was described in one of the local journals as a "stagnant mass of putridity," the intolerable character of the nuisance at last stirred up the citizens to co-operate for their own relief. In February, 1826, the Attorney-General applied to the Court of King's Bench for a *mandamus* against the Dock Company, requiring them to make proper provision for carrying the sewage into the tidal river, as it was held they were under an obligation to do by their original Act. It was stated in court that nearly six miles of sewers drained into the Float. The directors denied their liability, but a *mandamus* was granted in modified terms, ordering them to make such alterations as were necessary. Attempting to evade this requirement by delay, further proceedings were taken against them in the following year, when a peremptory order was issued. They then set about the construction of a culvert, known as Mylne's culvert, from the name of its designer, by which, at a cost of about £7,000, the filthy waters of the Frome were diverted from the harbour, and conveyed by a tunnel under the old bed of the Avon to the New Cut.

The latest record of punishment by the stocks in this city occurs in August, 1826, and the incident throws some light on the habits of the lower classes of that generation. One Sunday afternoon fourteen labourers entered St. Mary Redcliff churchyard, took possession of a form which had been placed at the south porch preparatory to a funeral, and carried it away to the lower part of the burial ground, where they held a noisy carousal. On being brought before the magistrates, two of them, refusing to pay a small fine, were ordered to be "exposed for three hours in the stocks on Redcliff Hill," and the sentence was forthwith carried out.*

The recordership of the city became vacant in September

* The stocks belonging to St. James's parish were in existence in 1837, when the Corporation took a lease of the ground now used as a hay market, the stocks and parish watch-house being reserved.

through the death of Lord Gifford, in whose room the Common Council elected Sir John Copley, Master of the Rolls. A few months later, on the break up of the Liverpool Ministry, Sir John was appointed Lord Chancellor, and raised to the peerage under the title of Lord Lyndhurst. It is said that Mr. Canning's despatch, offering him a seat in the Cabinet, was delivered to the recorder during morning service in Henbury church. The assize of 1827 was certainly held a day or two before the reconstruction of the Ministry. On the election of a new recorder some members of the Corporation appear to have had presentiments as to the danger of appointing a violent political partisan. At a meeting of the Common Council on the 11th July, 1827, a resolution inviting Sir Charles Wetherell to accept the office was lost, the votes for and against it (eleven) being equal. Another meeting on the 21st had a like result, thirteen votes being given on each side. A week later, however, the opposition was withdrawn, and Sir Charles was unanimously elected.

On the 28th of May, 1827, appeared the first number of a daily journal of four pages (about the size of *Punch*), styled *The Bristolian: Daily Local Publication,* and published at 16½, Broad Street, price three-halfpence. Its proprietor and conductor was a person named James Acland, who had recently taken up his residence in the city. The contents were almost exclusively of a local character, reports of police cases being a prominent feature. The newspaper—for it was unquestionably a newspaper—did not bear the stamp (costing nearly fourpence) required by law, the editor coolly alleging that the work was a pamphlet; and for a few days the Stamp Office authorities were content to receive the pamphlet duty of 3*s.* on each publication. On the 5th June, however, they decided that the *Bristolian* was a newspaper, whereupon Acland next morning produced what he called a new work, *The Bristolian: Daily Literary Publication,* all the local intelligence being suppressed. Though in this form it escaped the duty on newspapers, it ceased to be attractive to local readers, and the proprietor on the 14th June boldly revived his police intelligence. The case reported that day is still worthy of note. A sailor named Redding, who had served about twenty years in the navy, was convicted of having brought with him from Ireland a two-gallon keg of whisky, which he had bought of a spirit dealer at Cork. Irish whisky could not then be imported in less quantities than 100 gallons, and Redding, convicted of the "offence," was sentenced to "five years' compulsory service on board a king's ship"—the punishment imposed by an Act passed in 1825. The indignation excited by the decision was not lessened by the fact that Alderman Fripp, jun., one of the presiding justices, anxious to prevent the case from coming to the public ear, had insisted on expelling Acland, the only reporter present, from the court. As the latter naturally made the most of the affair, public feeling was so strongly stirred that Redding was eventually liberated; and the prisoner and his champion enjoyed a triumphal procession through the streets. In the meantime, however, Acland's newspaper had come to grief. The anger of the Government officials at the infraction of the stamp laws was aggravated by Redding's case, which redounded so little to the credit of their employers; and on the 18th June—in the nineteenth daily number of the *Bristolian*—Acland announced its cessation, but promised to produce a pamphlet every Wednesday and Saturday. In that form, owing largely to the personality in which its compiler indulged, the periodical attained a large circulation. Up to that time no Bristol newspaper had reported the business in the police court, although evidence is not wanting that the aldermen sometimes conducted themselves in a manner open to public criticism. To the extreme irritation of those gentlemen and their officers, the cases heard at each sitting were not only narrated at length by Acland, but were embellished with remarks far from complimentary to the dispensers of justice, Alderman Sir Richard Vaughan being for some time an especial target for banter. Orders were at length given to exclude the censor, and as, by some means, Acland still contrived to get information, a sergeant was placed at the door of the court, with orders to prevent the admittance of every one not concerned in the day's business. This aggression on public rights gave the *Bristolian* new matter for attack, and its conductor boldly assailed the entire Corporation as unjust, tyrannical, and corrupt. These charges provoked the Court of Aldermen to institute a criminal prosecution against their author, who was tried before Mr. Justice Park at the assizes in August, 1828. On being called on for his defence, Mr. Acland, in a speech occupying nearly three hours in delivery, contended that the conduct of the justices had been indefensible, and that he had not trespassed beyond legitimate criticism. He also commented strongly, and it must be confessed justly, on the circumstance that several of the jurymen were related to members of the Corporation, or were closely connected with them in business. He did not know—though it is now apparent in the civic cash-book—that no less than

£532 had been spent in bringing him to trial. A verdict of guilty being returned, the defendant was subsequently sentenced to two months' imprisonment in Gloucester gaol. In the following year Acland had the effrontery to petition the Common Council to be admitted a free burgess. His appeal was, of course, rejected, and the scribe revenged himself by renewed libels on prominent corporators in his *Bristolian*, which continued to appear twice a week until the spring of 1831. During a portion of this period of his career Acland got up a Bread Association, and one of the advertisements in his periodical stated that "pure flour and bread (4 lb. loaves at 10*d.*)" were sold at the *Bristolian* office, at 4, All Saints' Street. Being threatened with another prosecution by the aldermen, Acland removed to Hull, where he set up a journal of a similar character, and where his acrimony against the aldermen was quite as bitter as before. Three prosecutions for libel having resulted in convictions, he was sent to prison for fifteen months. Shortly afterwards his wife, who had continued the Hull newspaper, was sentenced to a term of imprisonment for publishing additional libels. And no sooner was Acland at liberty than he began to print another unstamped journal, for which he underwent incarceration for half a year more. A copy of probably his last local production, dated September 29, 1832, is in the City Library. It is a newspaper, styled *A Free Reporter*. To evade the stamp duty, its publisher added to the title, "Left to read six months, for three-halfpence."

A branch of the Bank of England, for which premises had been purchased at the east end of Bridge Street, was opened for business on the 12th July, 1827. The institution was regarded with great disfavour by the private bankers of the city, and appears to have been long disliked by many members of the mercantile community. In April, 1844, the bank purchased two picturesque old houses in Broad Street, which were pulled down, and the existing heavy-looking edifice was erected on the site.

The city chamberlain's cash-book contains the following curious item: "August 1st, 1827. Paid James Poole for a scarlet and black gown and a pair of gloves, the property of Mr. George King, late a member of the Common Council, £12." There is no reference to the matter in the minute books, but it seems probable that the payment was made to avoid scandal. The robes were purchased three years later, at the same price, by a new councillor, Mr. H. W. Newman.

The foundation-stone of the new asylum for orphan girls,

at Hook's Mills, replacing the building in which the charity had been established in 1795, was laid by the mayor (Mr. T. Camplin), on the 22nd August, in the presence of a numerous gathering of citizens. The chapel attached to the institution was consecrated a few months later by the bishop of the diocese.

The Drawbridge, a cumbrous structure, raised and lowered by a winch, which had been condemned by the Council so far back as 1808, was replaced in August by a new bridge, on the swivel principle. The opening of the latter—which cost £2,000—took place on a Sunday, the first to pass over being the mayor and sheriffs as they proceeded to morning service at the Mayor's Chapel.

Much public interest was aroused about this time by a Mr. Gurney's invention of a steam carriage, intended to supersede passenger coaches on turnpike roads. One of the vehicles, which was intended to run between London and Manchester, was of twelve-horse power, and carried six passengers inside and fifteen outside, exclusive of the guard, the promised rate of speed being from ten to twelve miles an hour. The *Gentleman's Magazine* for November, 1827, announced: "A steam-coach company are now making arrangements for stopping places on the line of road between London, Bath, and Bristol, which will occur every six or seven miles, where fresh fuel and water are to be supplied. There are fifteen coaches built." Owing to the conservative prejudices of many turnpike trustees, who imposed inordinate tolls on steam carriages, the inventor was unable to make any practical progress. The threatened competition moreover stirred up the coach proprietors, whose vehicles were still going at a jog-trot of six or seven miles an hour, and a notable increase of speed took place throughout the country. Mr. Gurney had also to contend with the ignorant passions of the poor. On one occasion, as a steam carriage was on its way from London to the west, it was stopped on its arrival at Melksham by a crowd of agricultural labourers, at that time greatly irritated by the introduction of thrashing machines and other rural apparatus. Believing that the steam coach was likely to injure manual labour, they attacked it with stones, amidst shouts of "Down with machinery!" its occupants narrowly escaping serious injury.

A still more remarkable locomotive novelty than that of Mr. Gurney excited local attention about this time. An ingenious schoolmaster, Mr. George Pocock, residing near St. Michael's church, discovered that by fastening a kite to the string attached to another kite already in the air, the combined power of the two toys, when elevated in a good breeze, was sufficient to drag a considerable weight along the surface of the ground. After many experiments, Mr. Pocock invented a vehicle somewhat similar in form to the modern tricyle, and found that one of these, capable of carrying four persons, could be drawn by two kites of twelve and ten feet in height respectively—the speed attained with a brisk wind being about twenty-five miles an hour. With kites of twenty feet and twelve feet, a carriage loaded with six persons was drawn with equal rapidity. When, by further developments, the kites were made capable of "tacking," the carriages could be used in any wind which was not directly opposed to the intended line of advance. In June, 1828, the novel vehicle was exhibited at Ascot races before George IV. In the following month Mr. Pocock was at Liverpool, and made an experiment to show the use of kites for drawing a ferry boat across the Mersey. The *Liverpool Mercury*, recording the results, observed that with a good wind "a boat furnished with one of the largest pairs of kites would be able to make the passage from and to Birkenhead, whatever might be the state or the strength of the tide," thus avoiding the great detentions which frequently occurred before steam power was adopted. The same paper stated that the kites could draw the boat in a direction "less than five points from the wind." On another occasion a yacht was hired, and after the sails had been replaced by kites, a numerous party cruised for three weeks in the Bristol Channel off the coasts of Wales and Devon. In 1836, during the visit of the British Association to Bristol, a kite carriage was shown on Clifton Down, and amongst those who tried its remarkable powers was Prince George of Cumberland, afterwards King of Hanover. The local journals stated that a gigantic kite, thirty feet high, capable of drawing four cars with four persons in each, had been prepared, but that owing to some accident to the tackle it could not be used. Mr. Pocock obtained a patent for his kites and carriages, by which he and his family travelled about for many years. A not unimportant advantage of the vehicles, was their immunity from turnpike tolls, a heavy tax upon locomotion in those days. According to a "Treatise on the Aeropleustic Art, with a Description of the Charvolant, or Kite Carriage," published by Longman & Co., the travelling kites were shown in operation daily at Ealing, Middlesex, during the Great Exhibition of 1851.

A partial revival of the project for constructing a railway from Bristol to Birmingham [see p. 111] occurred in 1828, when an Act was obtained for making a colliery tramway from Coalpit Heath to St. Philip's, Bristol, on the line of country laid out for the previous undertaking. The promoters of this modest work adopted the name of the Bristol and Gloucestershire Railway Company; but their energy was scarcely equal to the pretentiousness of the title, for the nine miles of tramway, which cost about £77,000, were not opened until August, 1835. The line was worked by horses until 1839, when an Act was passed for adapting it to locomotive engines. In the meantime another tramway, styled the Avon and Gloucestershire railway, had been laid from Coalpit Heath to the Avon, near Bitton, at a cost of £46,000, the promoters being under the belief that they could supply coal by canal boats to Bath and other inland towns at rates which would defy competition. This line had been originally contemplated so early as 1803, but the £23,000 then required for its formation could not be obtained. In 1843, after long negotiations, the first-mentioned tramway was absorbed in the undertaking of the Bristol and Gloucester Railway Company, which had been formed to construct a narrow-gauge line between the two cities. The new company, however, fell under the control of the Great Western board, in consequence of which that portion of the tramway between Lawrence Hill and Fishponds was converted into a broad-gauge railway, and became part of the new line to Gloucester. The Avon and Gloucestershire line opened out a considerable coal traffic; but its temporary success was succeeded by complete failure, and the works have long lain in ruins.

During the session of 1828 an Act was obtained, under the auspices of the Corporation, for constructing a cattle market at Temple Meads, power being also obtained to suppress the market previously held in Thomas Street, and to build a new wool hall. Compensation was to be paid (out of the receipts from tolls) to the feoffees of St. Thomas's parish for the relinquishment of their rights. The new market provided accommodation for 2,000 cattle, 7,000 sheep, 300 horses, and 500 pigs. Thomas Street market was held for the last time on the 28th January, 1830, and its successor was opened a week later. One of the first sales, according to a local newspaper, was that of the wife of a fellow named Gardner, of Felton, who "knocked her down" for £5 10*s*. The market cost £17,400, and the new wool hall £4,400. Towards these sums the Corporation advanced to the trustees on loan £10,800, besides selling them four acres of land at £600 per acre. The remainder of the outlay was defrayed by the feoffees of St. Thomas, the Act providing that the interest on the loans effected by them should be a first charge on the tolls. It was further enacted that the feoffees should be entitled to a yearly sum of £300 out of the receipts before interest was paid on the Corporation debt. In the result, the profits of the market failed for many years to meet the preferential claims, and the Corporation received nothing. The place has since undergone great alterations. Part of the site was absorbed for the Bristol and Exeter railway station, and a still larger portion was appropriated under the Act for constructing the Joint Station, the railway authorities giving up other ground in the immediate neighbourhood. The new wool hall appears to have been a financial failure, and it was closed in 1834.

Mr. Francis Freeling, who had filled the appointment of Secretary to the General Post Office for more than thirty years, was created a baronet on the 11th March, 1828, in recognition of his services to the State. Sir Francis, the son of a journeyman sugar-baker, is said to have been born on Redcliff Hill in 1764, and was educated in Colston's School. He held a subordinate position in the Bristol Post Office in 1784, when the introduction of mail coaches, at the instance of Mr. John Palmer, of Bath, caused a mutiny amongst the clerks in the London establishment, who declared that the daily despatch of mails at a fixed hour was utterly impracticable. Freeling, whose energy had been remarked, was sent to the capital, where he succeeded, in spite of the antagonistic attitude of all the old-fashioned superior officers, in bringing the new system into successful operation. In reward for his exertions he was soon afterwards placed at the head of the department, and thoroughly justified the appointment by indefatigable devotion to his duties for thirty-eight years. The Corporation of Bristol presented him with the freedom of the city in 1822. Sir Francis died on the 10th July, 1836.

In April, 1828, the Society of Merchants granted to Mr. Wm. West, a local artist, at a nominal rent, the ruins of an old windmill, known as the snuff-mill, on Clifton Down, which had been destroyed by fire, October 30, 1777. Mr. West built a dwelling house on the spot, and reconstructed the tower, which he fitted up in 1829 with telescopes and a camera-obscura, and styled an observatory. Some years later, at considerable expense, he excavated a passage from the building to the well-known "Giant's Cave." This was opened in July,

1837. Photography appears to have been introduced to the people of Bristol at Mr. West's abode. In an advertisement in a Bristol newspaper of April 27, 1839, it was announced that "various kinds of photogenic drawing" might be seen, and that "superior photogenic paper" was sold at the observatory.

The Corporation about this period appears to have experienced alternate fits of economy and extravagance. Having undertaken the re-erection of the Council House without possessing funds in hand adequate to meet a fourth of the expense, there was for a time a tendency towards retrenchment. In June, 1824, the Common Council reduced the salary of the future mayors from £2,500 to £2,000, while that of the sheriffs was curtailed from £1,260 to £800; but in the latter case the saving was comparatively small, the Corporation undertaking charges amounting to about £200 which had previously been borne by the two functionaries. Here, moreover, frugality ended, and two years later, when the works in hand had drained the treasury, the civic income was suddenly diminished by the serious sum of £2,000 a year through the reduction of the town dues. The advance made by the bankers at length became so large that they refused to increase it, and the Corporation, in extreme embarrassment, was obliged to borrow £5,000 from Mrs. Harford, the mother of the deputy chamberlain, and nearly as much more from other persons. Previous to that time the Common Council had rarely allowed its expenditure to exceed its income, the bonded debt in 1825 (excluding charity moneys which it had no power to pay off) being only about £5,000. But having once deviated from the proper path, it lost little time in plunging deeper, and a further sum of £10,000 was borrowed in 1827–8. Gratified by the ease with which troubles were thus overcome, the Common Council adopted a proposal the nature of which will be best explained by an entry in the city cash-book: "May 24 [1828]. Paid the first cost, freight, duty, bottling, etc., of four pipes of Madeira and four pipes of port, placed under the Council House for the purpose of supplying the mayor for the time being with wine on his entering into office, the cost of which is to be repaid on the same being delivered, £802 0*s.* 10*d.*" In the following year six pipes of port and two of Madeira were added to the stock, at a cost (excluding bottling) of £554 7*s.* 5*d.*; in 1830 the purchases consisted of two pipes of port and two of Madeira, costing (with £113 for bottling) £393 4*s.* 11*d.*; and in 1832 and 1834 two butts and a hogshead of sherry were obtained for £302. On the other hand, Mr.

Cave paid £188 19*s.* 5*d.* for a pipe of port and another of Madeira consumed during his mayoralty (1828–9), and Mr. Savage, who held office for two years, paid £199 2*s.* 9*d.* But the next mayor, Mr. Stanton, accounted for only £27 11*s.* 6*d.*, and no repayments by later mayors have been found. Though the amount due for wine may have been deducted from the annual honorarium of each chief magistrate, it does not seem that the new system effected any saving to the city treasury. Economy, however, was less than ever in fashion since the Common Council had become accustomed to the easy process of borrowing. The vast expenditure squandered upon the Mayor's Chapel has been already mentioned. In September, 1828, the sum of £286 16*s.* 0*d.* was paid for a new gold chain for the use of the mayor, the ancient ornament being sold as old metal for £50. The law expenses incurred from 1826 to 1828 inclusive, amounted to over £8,500. In 1829, as will shortly be shown, upwards of £5,200 were paid for an intended new Mansion House, and about the same sum was soon afterwards disbursed for building a hotel at Portishead, while the grants made towards erecting new churches about this time amounted to nearly £3,000. As the ordinary revenue scarcely met the customary expenditure, further loans to the extent of £13,650 were made in 1829–30, yet the balance due to the Chamberlain's bankers frequently exceeded £10,000. One ingenious mode of raising money remains to be noticed. Under a pretence—wholly fictitious as will afterwards be shown—that Queen Elizabeth's hospital was largely indebted to the city, the Corporation, acting as trustees, made frequent raids upon the income of the charity, the appropriations amounting to £5,500 between 1828 and 1832, and £6,700 more between the latter date and 1836. In the same manner, an estate called the Bartholomew Lands was declared by the Common Council to belong to the Corporation and not, as had been previously held, to a charity, and a sum of nearly £4,000, accumulated income, was carried into the civic treasury. In spite of these "conveyances," a financial equilibrium could not be effected, and more than £16,000 were borrowed between 1831 and 1833. Adding to the bonded debt the amount derived by sales of city property, it appears from a statement made before the reformed Council on the 22nd July, 1837, that the civic estate was impaired to the extent of £74,733 between the years 1824 and 1835, irrespective of over £16,000 improperly withdrawn from the charities—an aggregate exceeding £90,000.

A racecourse was improvised on Durdham Down in May, 1828, and a number of horses started for the prizes offered. Though the quality of the animals was indifferent, the affair attracted a great attendance. The meeting was continued for some years, the last taking place on the 9th and 10th May, 1838, when Mr. Blagden Hale and Mr. J. Coulston officiated as stewards. An interesting reminiscence of these gatherings is preserved in a picture by Miss Sharples, containing portraits of several Bristolians of the time, to be seen in the permanent collection at the Fine Arts Academy.

At a meeting in September, the Common Council resolved to apply to the Court of Chancery for a scheme for altering the regulations of the Loan Money Fund—investments derived from the charitable bequests of fourteen donors at various dates, but which had become almost inoperative owing to the smallness of the sums which the founders had directed to be advanced to individuals. An order approving of a scheme, by which loans varying from £50 to £300 were authorised to be lent to persons carrying on business in the "ancient city," was confirmed by the Master of the Rolls in March, 1831.

In October, 1828, the interesting crypt of St. John's church, which, according to a contemporary newspaper, had been used at intervals as an engine-house, a sugar warehouse, and finally as an auctioneer's wareroom, was cleansed and put in decent order at a cost of £60.

On the 5th November, the Rev. Sydney Smith—termed by Lord Macaulay the greatest master of ridicule that has appeared in England since Swift—who had been appointed a prebendary of Bristol by Lord Chancellor Lyndhurst in the previous January, delivered a sermon in the cathedral which created a sensation not merely in the city but throughout the country. It had long been the custom for the Mayor and Corporation to attend the cathedral in state on the Gunpowder Plot anniversary; and the occasion had usually been seized by the dignitary in residence to pronounce a hearty denunciation of popery and a denial of the political rights of its adherents; after which the ecclesiastical and civic functionaries dined together at the Mansion House, and toasted Protestant Ascendency with mutual fervour. Mr. S. J. Reid, in his memoir of Mr. Smith observes: "Writing to inform one of his friends of his approaching duty on Guy Faux day, the Canon states: 'All sorts of bad theology are preached at the cathedral on that day, and all sorts of bad toasts drunk at the Mansion House. I will do neither the one nor the other, nor bow the knee in the house of Rimmon.' He kept his word, and preached what he styled an 'honest sermon' on those 'rules of Christian charity by which our opinions of other sects should be formed.' He delivered a noble and closely reasoned plea for toleration in reference to the religious scruples of others. The sermon, as might have been expected, gave great offence, for the Corporation of Bristol included at that time many rigid and uncompromising Tories, and though some of them must have realised that the cause of bigotry was already lost, that fact increased rather than lessened their animosity towards a preacher who had compelled them for once to listen to a clear and dispassionate statement of the facts of the case.* . . . Bristol Cathedral was crowded during the delivery of Sydney Smith's sermon; and so great was the interest which it excited that he seldom stood in that pulpit again without looking down on a sea of upturned faces. The preacher became the talk of the town. . . . The newspapers took up the controversy, and in leading articles and letters the old warfare was waged. Sydney Smith was attacked at public dinners and declaimed against from the pulpit; but when the storm was past it was apparent that the cause of justice had been strengthened." The sermon exists as a local pamphlet, four editions of which were issued in about ten days. It also appeared in the collected works of the author. The original manuscript of the preface, with a letter to the local printer, Mr. Manchee, is preserved in the City Library.

The announcement at the beginning of 1829 that the Prime Minister, the Duke of Wellington, and the leader of the House of Commons, Sir Robert Peel, had changed their views on the long pending "Catholic question," and that the Cabinet had prepared a Bill for enabling Romanists to sit in both Houses of Parliament, caused much excitement amongst Bristolians, a great majority of whom were opposed to the scheme. On the 12th February one of the largest meetings ever remembered was held in Queen's Square, to denounce the proposed concession. The petition against the scheme, adopted by acclamation, was forthwith signed by 25,000 inhabitants. All the parochial vestries and the local clergy, with only one or two exceptions, forwarded similar petitions. Even many Dissenters, whilst exulting that their own rights of conscience had just been secured by the repeal of the Test

* In a letter written shortly afterwards to a friend, Sydney Smith remarked that "they looked as if they could not keep turtle on their stomachs."

and Corporation Acts, showed an eagerness to maintain the fetters on Roman Catholics. Mr. Bright, the Whig and Nonconformist member for Bristol, voted against the Bill, and the Rev. W. Thorp, minister of Castle-green chapel, was amongst the most active of its local opponents. The friends of religious liberty also addressed a petition to Parliament, but could muster no more than 1,700 adherents. When it was seen that the measure was likely to pass both Houses, the Corporation forwarded, through Lord Eldon, an address to the King, denouncing his ministers for their intention to subvert Protestant ascendency, and this was soon followed by a second appeal to his Majesty, emanating from a public meeting, begging him to dissolve Parliament, Lord Eldon being again the intermediary. The Corporation, in the meantime, stamped the ex-Chancellor's efforts at Westminster with its approval by forwarding him the freedom of the city in an oak box (which cost £11 6*s*.). Almost the only member of the Ministry who refused to abandon his old opinions at the behest of his leaders, was Sir Charles Wetherell, then Attorney-General and Recorder of Bristol. He was consequently dismissed from his lucrative post in the Government; but his firmness brought him great popularity amongst those who agreed with him in politics. In April, on his arrival in Bristol to hold the gaol delivery, Sir Charles was welcomed by a large crowd at Totterdown, and continual shouts of "No Popery! Wetherell for ever!" greeted his progress to the Guildhall. Similar scenes took place every morning and evening during the assizes. The mob, not satisfied with these demonstrations, broke the windows of the mayor (Mr. J. Cave) and of other prominent supporters of the Bill, and committed much destruction at the Roman Catholic chapel in Trenchard Street, and amongst the dwellings of the Irish "Papists." How fleeting was the popularity of the Recorder will shortly be seen.

Although the population of the suburban districts had greatly increased during the half century previous to this date, the accommodation for public worship offered by the Established Church had been increased only by the chapel-of-ease of St. George, near Park Street. The wants of Clifton were first brought before the public, it being pointed out that while the place contained nearly 12,000 inhabitants, the only provision for public devotion consisted of the parish church and a small chapel in Dowry Square. A subscription having been started, Mr. T. Whippie (who had given £2,000 towards the re-building of the church, and subsequently built a Wesleyan Chapel in Hotwell Road at his sole expense,) contributed £6,000; and £4,000 more were given by other benefactors. A site was obtained in Hotwell Road, upon which a large church, dedicated to the Trinity, was rapidly constructed, and the edifice, (the last in the city designed in a debased Italian style) was consecrated by the Bishop of Llandaff on the 10th November, 1830. [A district was attached to this church by an Order in Council in January, 1864.] In the meantime the spiritual destitution of the populous out-parish of St. Philip, in which, it was stated, 15,000 souls were living without a single place of religious worship, had also excited attention, and assistance was sought from the State grant for building new churches, already referred to [p. 82]. The Commissioners charged with its administration made a donation of £6,000 for the erection of a church, afterwards styled Holy Trinity, St. Philip's; and the Corporation, who claimed the patronage of the living, granted a site and subscribed £1,000. The cost of the edifice was £8,200, of which only a trifling sum was given by laymen. A similar application was made on behalf of Bedminster, where the parish church, of extremely narrow dimensions, was absurdly inadequate to meet the requirements of twelve thousand parishioners. In this case it was resolved to form a chapelry of St. Paul. The State provided all but £2,000 of the cost of building (£9,796), the offering of the lay element being again insignificant. The promoters had even to purchase a site, at the rate of £200 per acre, from the wealthiest landlord of the locality. The foundation stones of both churches were laid in September, 1829. St. Paul's was consecrated in October, 1831 (five days before the Bristol riots), by Dr. Law, Bishop of Bath and Wells, who, in consequence of his votes against the Reform Bill, was treated with much indignity by the rabble of the parish. Trinity Church was consecrated by Bishop Gray, of Bristol, in the following February. Ecclesiastical districts were soon afterwards allotted to each of the new edifices.

At a meeting of the Common Council on the 4th July, 1829, it was announced that Mr. William Weare, the senior councillor, and a member of a family long connected with the Corporation, proposed to pay into the city treasury the sum of £10,000 as a free gift, on condition that the Corporation should pay him £500 yearly for life, and the same sum to Henry Weare for life in the event of his surviving the donor. The gift having been accepted, its object was declared in a deed entered into between the parties, in which Mr.

Weare expressed his wish that the money should be applied, either immediately or after his death, to the widening and improving of Redcliff and Baldwin Streets, the opening of a new street from St. Augustine's Place to Trenchard Street, and the altering and improving of the thoroughfares at the lower end of Park Street. The Corporation resolved upon investing the money, which, as will afterwards be seen, was transferred to an Improvement Fund. All the schemes suggested by Mr. Weare were eventually carried out by the new Corporation.

The imposing design of another liberal-hearted citizen came prominently into notice during the summer. In 1753, seventy six years before the time under review, Mr. William Vick, a spirit merchant of Bristol, who is often, but erroneously, styled an alderman, devised the sum of £1,000 to the Merchant Venturers' Society, directing that it should be invested and suffered to accumulate until it reached £10,000, when it was to be devoted to the building of a bridge over the gorge of the Avon at Clifton, if such a design should be adjudged practicable. In 1829, when the fund had swollen to about £8,000, and when Telford's recent achievement at Menai Strait was one of the topics of the day, a proposal was started for carrying out Mr. Vick's project by the construction of a suspension bridge. The suggestion having been considered and approved by many influential citizens, a committee was formed, comprising the mayor, the president of the Chamber of Commerce, several members of the Common Council and of the Merchants' Company, and others; and as it was found that a stone bridge could not be constructed for less than £60,000, it was resolved to apply to Parliament in the session of 1831, for a Bill authorising the erection of an iron structure, the funds required to eke out Vick's bequest to be raised by loans and donations. In the meantime the committee invited engineers to send in plans for the work, and one of the first to respond was Mr. Telford, who produced a beautiful, but not quite satisfactory, design. Believing that the space from cliff to cliff was too wide to be prudently spanned at a bound, he proposed the erection of two enormous gothic towers on the river banks, so as to narrow the central opening to 360 feet. His estimate of the cost being £52,000, the promoters solicited designs from other leading engineers; and those of Messrs. Brunel, jun., Rendel, Brown, and Hawkes, together with that of Telford, were submitted to Mr. D. Gilbert, M.P., a distinguished authority on the subject of suspension bridges. Mr. Gilbert gave his decision in favour of Brunel's plan, the cost of which was estimated at £57,000. The Bill, which was factiously but fruitlessly opposed by Mr. James Acland, received the royal assent in May, when the trustees were chosen, and some preliminary operations were begun during the summer. Owing to the hostile attitude of Sir John Smyth, the under-sheriff of Somerset summoned a court at Failand, to determine the value of four and a quarter acres of land, required for an approach to the bridge from the turnpike road to Leigh. The land in question formed part of an extensive common which had been enclosed by Sir John's predecessor in the baronetcy, who, when the Act was obtained, alleged that its value was ten shillings an acre. It was now alleged on behalf of Sir John that the new road would deprive him of the private use of 170 acres, which he could have thrown into his park; and one of his witnesses estimated the compensation due to him at £3,775. The trustees had offered £1,200, which had been scornfully rejected. The jury fixed the value at £1,107. The first turf for the approach on the Clifton side, the land for which was given by the Merchants' Society, was cut by Lady Elton. The gifts and loans promised on behalf of the undertaking representing only £32,000, or £20,000 short of the amount required, the trustees appointed under the Act thought it advisable to proceed with circumspection; and the disastrous riots of the following October caused the complete suspension of the project for four years. In 1835, when the passing of the Great Western Bill gave a stimulus to local spirit, Mr. Brunel suggested that the outlay might be reduced to £35,000 by contracting the width of the bridge and dispensing with some ornamental features. The trustees temporarily adopted this proposal; but in consequence of the strong disapproval of the public they reversed their decision in favour of the original plan. At a meeting held in January, 1836, it was reported that a sum of £17,000, in addition to the £33,000 already guaranteed, would finish the work, and as £9,000 were soon after forthcoming, operations were recommenced. On the 27th August, during the visit of the British Association to the city, its president, the Marquis of Northampton, laid the foundation stone of the south pier in the presence of many thousands of spectators; and at a breakfast which followed (at the Gloucester Hotel, on a service of china bearing views of the bridge, which was eagerly bought up and divided amongst the guests) it was believed that all difficulties were surmounted. For the convenience of the workmen, measures were taken to connect the two sides of the river by a car, suspended from an iron bar 800 feet in length. The first attempt to carry out this plan was unsuccessful. Owing to the breaking of a hawser, one end of the ponderous bar fell into the river as it was being drawn into its place, blocking up the navigation; and though on the following day it was raised and secured in its intended position, the iron was so much bent in the middle as to be practically useless. In September a new bar was passed over, and the communication was opened by Mr. Brunel, accompanied by a boy named Claxton. The novelty of the contrivance attracted crowds of visitors desirous of making the airy journey, and the trustees found it necessary to impose a toll of five shillings, subsequently reduced to half a crown, and afterwards to a shilling. The income received from this traffic was £142. On one occasion, it is reported, a bride and bridegroom on their wedding day resolved on taking a trip over the fragile bridge; unfortunately the hauling ropes got out of order just as they reached the middle of the bar, and they were left for some hours to discuss the beauty of the scenery, with a prospect—not less moving, but happily avoided—of remaining suspended for the night. It may be observed in parenthesis, that the bar remained in its place until 1853, and that some political jokers availed themselves of it during the general election of 1852 to suspend over the Avon an effigy of one of the candidates. The figure being unapproachable, the services of a skilful rifleman were called in to sever the rope. The construction of the piers proceeded slowly, but the core of each—intended for an ornamental incrustation which was never applied—was finished in 1840, when a contract was entered into for a portion of the ironwork. In February, 1843, the public were informed that £40,000, including Mr. Vick's bequest, had been spent, and that no less than £30,000 more would be required to carry out the undertaking. The statement, which caused equal surprise and dissatisfaction, was regarded as the death-warrant of the project; and though the trustees made repeated appeals to public liberality, it was found impossible to obtain further subscriptions. The contractors for the chains, etc., at length pressing for the balance of their claim, it was resolved in 1851, when £47,400 had been expended, to sell the ironwork and plant, and in February, 1853, the former was purchased by the West Cornwall Railway Company, nothing then remaining visible of the abortive scheme save the two unsightly piers which deformed the landscape. The story of the bridge for a lengthened period was of the dreariest character, various plans for completing the structure being produced, apathetically discussed, and incontinently dropped. After a lapse of seventeen years from the collapse of 1843, brighter days set in; but for the remainder of the tale the reader must be referred to 1860.

About the time when the suspension bridge project was first mooted, the Merchants' Society set about the improvement of the path leading from the bank of the river near the Hotwell to Clifton Down. The path, which was little more than a track, was approached at the back of the Colonnade by a long and steep flight of steps, and was almost impracticable in wet weather. The new footway, termed the Zigzag, was deemed a great acquisition. It was much improved in the autumn of 1849.

In the closing months of 1829, a new road was formed "from the top of St. Michael's Hill, through the Gallows' field, to Cotham." The road in question was afterwards known as Cotham New Road. According to a contemporary writer (MS. Annals, City Library, vol. i., p. 159), the workmen found the base of Bewell's Cross in the Gallows' field (a small portion of which was sold by the Corporation), and the stone was imbedded in the south wall of the road (now enclosing Highbury Chapel). But Roque's large map of the city, dated 1741, shows the cross to have stood nearly one hundred yards farther to the north-west.

A design of the leading members of the Corporation, carefully concealed from the citizens at large, was cautiously introduced into the Common Council in December, 1829, when it was resolved that the mansion and grounds of Mr. Richard Bright, at the southern end of Great George Street, should be purchased at a cost not exceeding £5,250. At a meeting in February, 1830, it was announced that the property had been acquired for the above-named sum, but no hint of the purpose it was intended to serve appeared upon the minutes. Three months later, on the motion of Alderman A. Hilhouse, it was resolved that the building should be converted into a Mansion House, and that the City Lands' Committee should make the needful additions and alterations to the dwelling and provide new furniture. In June the committee reported that the required additions would alone cost £5,000, exclusive of furniture and stabling. Alderman Hilhouse thereupon moved that his original proposal should be carried out in its entirety; but an amendment, proposed by Mr. E. Protheroe, to the effect that the committee should look out for a house which could be made serviceable at a moderate expense, was approved by a majority. No further mention of the subject appears in the minutes until September, 1831, when the committee recommended that as "the site of the present Mansion House" was "most desirable for the public convenience," the building should be retained, provided some increased accommodation could be secured. The adjoining house, added the committee, was offered for £2,050, and they advised that it should be bought without delay. The outbreak of the riots, a few weeks later, blew the project into the air.

The month of January, 1830, was remarkable for a protracted snowstorm, which blocked up the roads in all parts of the country, communication between many towns being almost wholly suspended for several days. A local newspaper, in recording the incidents of the season, stated that on the 25th January a party of nineteen labourers dragged into the city a wagon containing upwards of two tons of flour, which they had succeeded in hauling from Melksham, a distance of twenty-five miles. They had been promised by a baker, and received, 28*s.* 4*d.* (being 1*s.* 8*d.* per sack) for performing this arduous task.

Sir Thomas Lawrence, President of the Royal Academy, expired on the 7th January, 1830, and his remains were honoured with a stately public funeral a fortnight later in St. Paul's Cathedral. Various inaccurate statements as to the place of his nativity have appeared in print, but the parochial records show that he was born at No. 6, Redcross Street, Bristol, and was baptised at St. Philip's Church on the 6th May, 1769. His father, a few months later, became landlord of the White Lion Hotel, Broad Street, whence he removed in 1773 to the Bear Hotel, Devizes, and after his failure there, in 1780, to Bath. Whilst almost an infant, the son manifested extraordinary indications of genius, and some drawings executed in his eighth year, which still exist, afford ample evidence to justify the admiration which he excited in cultivated circles. Before he had reached the age of twelve, his studio at Bath was the resort of many noble and fashionable persons who then frequented the city, so that he may be said to have become famous before establishing himself in London, which he did at the age of eighteen. On the death of Sir Joshua Reynolds, in 1792, Lawrence was appointed to succeed him as portrait-painter in ordinary to the king, and thenceforth he was never able to keep abreast of the work which poured in upon him. There was scarcely a single upper-class family in the kingdom which did not solicit his services, and engravings of his most successful portraits had an unexampled sale. When the presidency of the Royal Academy became vacant by the death of Sir B. West, the fashionable favourite was immediately appointed to the distinguished office, and received the customary honour of knighthood. In 1826, when Lord Gifford resigned the recordership of Bristol, the Corporation resolved upon having his portrait, and aware of the peculiarity of Lawrence, who with a princely income was always in an inexplicable state of impecuniosity,* they remitted 200 guineas with the order. Lord Gifford, however, died soon afterwards, and the painter eventually returned the money.

On the 15th June, Zion Chapel, Bedminster,—to which an interesting story attaches—was opened with a sermon by the celebrated Scotch divine, Dr. Chalmers. The chapel, which cost £4,000, was erected at the sole expense of Mr. John Hare, the founder of an extensive floor-cloth manufactory in the city, in pursuance of a long-cherished design. In an address delivered by one of his descendants at the centenary of the factory in August, 1882, it was stated that Mr. Hare was born at Taunton in 1753. When in his twentieth year, at a time when the Government were forcing men into the army in the hope of reconquering America, he left home for Bristol with a few shillings in his pocket. On reaching the southern suburbs of the city he got over a dwarf wall, resolving to rest a few hours, and on awakening was so struck with the beauty of the spot that he felt he should like to build a house there. By dint of patient perseverance, prudence and skill, he ultimately became wealthy, but the impression formed on that early morning of his youth was never effaced, and about fifty-seven years after his arrival he erected the above-mentioned edifice on the scene of his slumbers. The chapel had not been occupied many years before serious dissensions arose amongst the congregation. During a debate in the Council, October 17, 1836, it was stated by the mayor (Alderman Fripp), that the trustees of the chapel had refused Mr. Hare a pew in the edifice which they owed to his liberality.

The death of George IV. in June, 1830, was followed a few days later by the usual civic ceremony of proclaiming his successor. The proceedings were marked with a few

* "Cannot think what keeps him so poor," said George IV. to Croker in 1825; "I have paid him £24,000, and have not got my pictures. The Duke of Wellington is £2,800 in advance to him. All the world is ready to employ him at £1,000 a picture, yet he never has, I am told, a farthing."—*Croker's Correspondence*, ii. p. 88.

deviations from precedent. At noon a "large and handsome car," covered with a pall, was drawn by four grey horses to the site of the High Cross, when the mayor and members of the Corporation, in black robes, preceded by the civic sword covered with crape, marched to the spot uncovered, and solemnly walked round the car in testimony of their respect for the deceased monarch. Their worships then returned to the Council House, donned their scarlet habiliments, and set off in state to make proclamation of the new king at the customary sites, the car being now stripped of its mournful panoply and adorned with a gorgeous crown on a velvet cushion. Two hogsheads of porter and three quarter-casks of sherry were distributed to the populace, the proceedings of the day costing the city treasury £240. A corporate deputation, sent to London to congratulate the new monarch, spent £90 additional.

In accordance with the law at that time, there was a general election in the following month. The retiring Tory member, Mr. Richard Hart Davis, was again nominated by his party. His Whig colleague, Mr. Bright, retired, being unwilling to bear the expense of a contest, and the Liberals —as they were now beginning to be called—were, as usual, unable to agree upon the choice of a successor, an unbridgeable gulf being still open between the slavery and anti-slavery sections of the party. The West India interest nominated Mr. James Evan Baillie, the candidate of 1820, Mr. C. Pinney, who seconded that gentleman, asserting on the hustings that five-eighths of the trade of the city depended upon the islands. The progressive camp brought forward Mr. Edward Protheroe, junr., son of a former member for the city. To give a fillip to the excitement, or perhaps to his newspaper, Mr. James Acland, of the *Bristolian*, who had just been released from gaol after suffering imprisonment for libel, also made his appearance in the field. The polling (which took place for the first time in booths erected in Queen Square), continued for five days, and was marked by violent disturbances. On one occasion the windows of Mr. John Hare, of Temple Gate, an earnest Liberal, were smashed by a pro-slavery Whig mob, who entered and did much damage to the factory. The Bush Hotel, Mr. Protheroe's head quarters, underwent its usual fate at elections, while on another occasion the friends of the same gentleman were attacked by a party of gentlemen on horseback, armed with bludgeons. After one of many street affrays, twenty-seven persons were so much injured as to require treatment at the

a year, put in repair, and fitted up for the reception of a considerable number of paupers. The experiment proving satisfactory, the building, in 1837, was purchased for £2,000. Further extensive alterations being found necessary, the guardians raised £6,512 by the sale of their estate at Shirehampton (bought in 1701 for £1,600 for the purpose of employing paupers as farm labourers). The Armoury, which had been rented at £200 a year by the Corporation of Bristol, was also disposed of, though there was a loss on this transaction of £1,100. Thanks to these windfalls, the Stapleton workhouse was placed in satisfactory working order without any sensible cost to the ratepayers. As time went on, the propriety of removing the entire pauper establishment from St. Peter's became gradually recognised, and between 1861 and 1865 nearly £26,000 were spent in enlarging and improving the buildings at Stapleton. Some four years later, a fever hospital was constructed there at a further outlay of £4,200. To meet a portion of the expenditure, the guardians, in 1865, disposed of part of the premises at St. Peter's for £5,195, reserving only the interesting and picturesque mansion of the Nortons for their board-room and financial offices.

The absence in Bristol of an institution capable of providing a complete system of higher education had long been deplored by the more intelligent citizens. A movement for supplying the want was started in 1829, by the distinguished physician, Dr. J. C. Prichard, Mr. J. Naish Sanders, the Rev. J. Eden, Mr. J. C. Swayne, Mr. S. S. Wayte, Dr. Carrick, and others, who suggested the erection of a college, with an efficient staff of masters and lecturers, theological instruction according to the doctrines of the Church of England being also provided for such pupils as might desire to avail themselves of it. The proposed capital was £15,000, to be raised by £50 shares, the proprietors of which were to nominate a student for each share. The required sum could not, however, be obtained from the public,—owing in a large measure to the hostile attitude of the Bishop of Bristol, Dr. Gray,—and the promoters had to content themselves with hiring a large house in Park Row, "formerly occupied by Matthew Wright, Esq.," and since swept away for modern improvements. A competent staff having been engaged, "Bristol College" was opened on the 17th January, 1831, with about thirty pupils, the principal being Dr. J. H. Jerrard, and the vice-principal Mr. Charles Smith, both graduates of Cambridge. The Rev. W. D. Conybeare, F.R.S., afterwards

Dean of Llandaff, was visitor, and undertook to preside at the examinations. The terms of admission were £18 for the nominees of shareholders, and £21 for other students. Though comparatively few in number, a large proportion of the youths educated at the College attested in after life the value of the institution. Amongst them were Edward Fry, afterwards Lord Justice, the Rev. S. W. Wayte, who became President of Trinity College, Oxford, G. G. Stokes, senior wrangler of his year, and afterwards Lucasian Professor at Cambridge, Walter Bagehot, eminent as a writer on financial and constitutional questions, and the Rev. G. Swayne, a well-known Greek scholar. The college, in fact, might have afforded the city all the advantages which were to be offered by Clifton College, thirty years later. But its promoters were a generation before their contemporaries, and the institution was of too liberal a character for the age. Although great care had been taken to avoid ruffling theological prejudices, the college had not been long in operation before a section of the clergy, vehemently opposed to the admission of Dissenters to the Universities, began to protest against the sons of Nonconformists being allowed to attend the school without participating in the religious instruction provided for Churchmen. The cry of "godless education" was a formidable one in that day; and the persons who raised it at length found a sufficient number of local sympathisers to encourage them to set up a rival institution, from which the unorthodox could be debarred. The new Bishop of Gloucester and Bristol (Dr. Monk) having lent his patronage and support to this movement, a "Bishop's College" was opened in August, 1840, in a house in Bellevue, Clifton, from which it was removed in October, 1841, to extensive premises at the top of Park Street (designed for the Red Maids' School), purchased by Bishop Monk from the Charity Trustees for £9,750. The competition at once proved fatal to Bristol College, which closed its doors at Christmas, 1841. The successor of the first principal had been the Rev. J. E. Bromby, D.D., who left to establish a school in Clifton, but afterwards emigrated to Australia, where he became Warden of the Senate of Melbourne University. The last head master, holding the office only a few months, was Dr. J. Booth. Bishop's College began its course under the head mastership of the Rev. H. Dale, the second master being the Rev. J. R. Woodford, one of the most eloquent preachers of his time, who, before his death in 1885, became Bishop of Ely. The institution was not, however, successful. At a meeting of the proprietors in 1851, it was reported that the school was carried on at a loss, and that the interest due to the Bishop on the purchase money was unpaid. His lordship having requested the return of his loan, it was resolved that he should be left to exercise his power of sale. The college languished on until 1861, when the premises were purchased by the promoters of a Volunteer Club. The two last head masters were Dr. Robertson and the Rev. T. Bowman.

The death, on the 21st February, 1831, of the Rev. Robert Hall, one of the most celebrated pulpit orators of his time, occasioned widespread regret amongst the members of every Christian denomination. Mr. Hall, who is said to have declined high preferment in the English Church from Mr. Pitt while Prime Minister, accepted the pastorate of Broadmead Baptist Chapel in 1826, and officiated until within a few days of his death. His remains were removed, on the 2nd March, from his residence in Ashley Place to the burial ground adjoining the chapel, in the presence of a great concourse of mourners. Mr. Hall's body, with others buried at this place, was removed to Arno's Vale Cemetery some years after this date.

On the night of the 16th March, the steamboat *Frolic*, plying between this city and Haverfordwest, was wrecked on the Nash Sands, on the coast of Glamorganshire, whilst on a return voyage to Bristol. Fifty persons, including General Macleod, Colonel Gordon, Major Boyd, and several respectable tradesmen of Haverfordwest lost their lives by the calamity.

In consequence of the defeat of Lord Grey's Ministry upon an important detail of the Reform Bill, the Parliament of 1830 was dissolved in the following April, after an existence of less than nine months. In Bristol, as in almost every constituency uncontrolled by what were called borough-mongers, the current of opinion in favour of "the Bill" swept away even the appearance of opposition. Mr. Davis, who in the previous year had been supported by five-sixths of the voters, and who solicited re-election, soon found that his resistance to Reform had wrecked his chances of success, and he speedily quitted the field. The Whigs and Liberals, divided at the previous contest, had been welded together by the popular passion of the hour, and their candidates, Mr. J. E. Baillie and Mr. E. Protheroe, were unanimously elected. The most telling illustration of the general enthusiasm was furnished by Dr. Lant Carpenter in the *Monthly Repository* of the following December. "The expenses of the preceding election," he wrote, "were estimated at not short of £30,000; this time, on the part of Mr. Protheroe, up to the day of election, they had not amounted to £200." The ceremony of chairing, omitted in 1830, was revived, and was the occasion of an unprecedented demonstration, almost the whole operative class in the city, accompanied by great numbers of tradesmen, taking part—at their own expense—in the triumphal procession of the two members. In the evening the city was illuminated. This was the first occasion on which two Whigs had been returned together for Bristol since 1774.

The census of 1831, taken in the spring of that year, for the first time gave a population exceeding 100,000 to Bristol and its suburbs. The "ancient city" was found to contain 59,074 souls. Clifton, which had nearly trebled its numbers within thirty years, returned a total of 12,032; St. George's, 6,285; the District, 4,495; St. Philip's out, 15,777; Mangotsfield, 3,508; Stapleton, 2,715; making altogether 44,812, and, with the city proper, 103,886. Bedminster, which through some caprice was still excluded from the reckoning, had a population of 13,130, being more than fourfold the numbers of 1801. The tything of Stoke Bishop, in Westbury parish, which the enumerator also ignored as a suburb, contained 2,328 persons.

Langton Street Chapel, built by Lady Huntingdon's connection, was opened in August. The building, which cost about £4,500, is remarkable only as being the first in Bristol in which a mediæval style was adopted for a dissenting place of worship.

The death of the Rev. Samuel Seyer took place on the 25th August. Mr. Seyer was a native of Bristol, being the son of a rector of St. Michael's parish who had been also head master of the Grammar School. After being educated at Oxford, he opened a school in the Royal Fort, at which the sons of many respectable citizens enjoyed the benefit of his classical attainments. His translation of the "Charters and letters patent granted to Bristol" has been already noticed [p. 54]. In 1881, after many years' laborious study, Mr. Seyer commenced the publication of his "Memoirs of Bristol," two quarto volumes, comprising the history of the city, illustrated with many beautiful engravings, being eventually issued from the press. Towards the expense of this work the Corporation subscribed £200. The second and more interesting section of the work, containing the topography of Bristol, was left in manuscript, owing, it was supposed, to apprehensions as to the pecuniary risks attendant on its production. Mr. Seyer was also the author of a Latin grammar, a few other school books, and one or two religious tracts. An original member of the Bristol Library Society, Mr. Seyer was its active vice-president for upwards of thirty years. His useful life, however, passed away ignored by the Corporation, one of whose numerous livings might have been gracefully conferred on native merit of no ordinary character. The reverend gentleman, according to a friend who contributed a brief biography of him to a local journal, was one of the few surviving members "of a well known club of literary gentlemen who for many years, during the winter months, assembled by the sound of the mail horn in the Bush Tavern," of which reunions he is said to have been a distinguished ornament. His remains were interred at Shirehampton.

The coronation of William IV. was celebrated in Bristol on the 8th September with more than usual enthusiasm, his Majesty being at that time very popular amongst the working classes on account of his attitude towards the Reform Bill. Shortly after midday, an imposing procession was formed at the Council House, consisting of the members and officials of the Corporation, of the Society of Merchant Venturers, and of the Incorporation of the Poor, the Dean and clergy of the city, the boys in the endowed schools, the Freemasons of the district, and the workmen of the various trades, bearing emblems of their respective crafts. With these were mingled certain so-called "heralds," "knights" accoutred in ancient armour, a "crown and cushion," and innumerable flags and banners, the general appearance of the pageant being picturesque and attractive. The procession made its way, by High Street, Queen Square, and the Quay, to the cathedral, where the civic dignitaries attended service, leaving their followers in College Green. Afterwards the procession was again formed, and returned by a circuitous route to the Council House, which was reached about half-past five o'clock. Besides the enormous crowds of citizens who lined the streets, it was calculated that 30,000 persons had been attracted from the neighbouring districts to witness the civic parade. In the evening all the public buildings and a great number of private houses and places of business were gaily illuminated. The civic expenses on the occasion amounted to £257 16*s.* 10*d.*

Some months previous to this date a proposal had been started by a few philanthropic persons, chiefly members of the Society of Friends, for the establishment of a medical and surgical institution for the southern districts of the city, and at a meeting held at the Guildhall on the 21st September the creation of the General Hospital was definitely resolved upon. The project was deprecated by many friends of the Infirmary, who argued that the receipts of the existing charity were barely able to cover the expenditure, and that a fraction of the money proposed to be spent on a new building and an additional staff would enable the older institution to meet all the needs of the inhabitants. The promoters of the Hospital, who objected to the interference of the medical officers in the administration of the Infirmary, proceeded with their work, and having purchased some property in Guinea Street for £3,725, they had the premises suitably fitted up, and opened them for the reception of patients in 1832. In 1850, in consequence of the dilapidated state of the property, and of the insufficient accommodation available for patients, it was resolved to build a large and appropriate hospital near the same spot. Mr. Joseph Eaton, one of the original promoters, subscribed £5,000, and upwards of £15,000 were offered by other friends. On the completion of the new hospital, in 1858, it was found that the outlay, £28,000, had exceeded the funds in hand by several thousand pounds. At a meeting held in May, 1858, Mr. Eaton increased his gift to £6,500; Mr. George Thomas, another earnest Quaker supporter, augmented his donation to £6,000; Messrs. Finzell gave £300, and Mr. Greville Smyth £100. These and other contributions cleared off the debt. A few days after the meeting, Mr. Eaton suddenly died. He left by will £3,500 to the hospital, making with former gifts £10,000. [His almost equally munificent friend, Mr. Thomas, died on the 7th December, 1869.] The patients were removed from the old to the new hospital in August, 1858. In 1873 a new out-patients' department was added to the building at a cost of £9,000; and in 1882–3, at an outlay of £9,000 additional, the hospital underwent extensive alterations to improve its sanitary condition. Notwithstanding the intentions of the founders, however, the medical staff of the institution have succeeded in acquiring much of the power which was originally withheld from them.

An "affair of honour" was arranged to take place on the 24th September at Wimbledon, between Mr. E. Protheroe, junr., M.P. for the city, and Lieut. Claxton, R.N., who afterwards held the office of corn meter under the Corporation. The cause of the intended duel was a letter on the slavery question, addressed by Mr. Protheroe to the freemen and

[illegible]

[illegible] Charles Wetherell, had held the office of recorder for about four years, and down to 1830 had been popular with the [illegible] owing to his [illegible] opposition to the Roman Catholic [illegible] policy. On the question of Reform coming to the front, Sir Charles was found to be as vehement and abusive in his condemnation of that Bill as he had been of the other. If he had confined himself to attacks on the general principles of the ministerial scheme, the extravagance of his speeches and demeanour might not have excited more attention in Bristol than elsewhere. In spite of the coarseness of his invective, his speeches were often amusing, whilst his extraordinary display of "gymnastics" in delivery, forgetful of the downward shrinking of his unbraced nether garments, wrought effects on his costume which caricaturists were delighted to reproduce. "He had no interval of lucidity," said a witty senator after one of his exhibitions, "save the interval between his waistcoat and his breeches." The declamation of men of this kind is seldom taken seriously. But Sir Charles was indiscreet enough to perorate as a self-constituted representative of Bristol. During a debate in the spring of 1831, he stated that the citizens were indifferent to Reform, an assertion which evoked indignant denials, and which led, upon his entering the city for the April assize, to emphatic demonstrations of popular disapproval. Far from taking warning from this incident, however, the recorder, on the 27th August, assured the House of Commons that "the Reform fever had a good deal abated in Bristol." Mr. Protheroe, one of the members for the city, forthwith rose to declare that this assertion was the very reverse of the fact, inasmuch as local feeling in favour of the measure had increased rather than diminished; but Sir Charles, reminding the House that he was the senior alderman of the city, said "he felt quite sure that the Bill did not stand so high as it did in the Bristol thermometer." His belief may have been founded on the assertions of the local organ of ultra Toryism, or on the communications of some of his brother aldermen, who, living out of the city, and keeping aloof from all but their own select circle, represented facts, not as they were, but as they wished them to be. In either case, the truth was, that since the recorder's previous misrepresentation, as the election had borne witness, public feeling in support of the Bill had become far more intensely enthusiastic than before, and the news of this second and wholly unjustifiable offence excited great irritation. It was pointed out, that whilst Sir C. Wetherell was using every device to obstruct the progress of a measure demanded by the country (the *Mirror of Parliament* credits him with 180 addresses against the Bill during the two sessions of 1831), he was in no legitimate sense of the term a popular representative at all. He was, in fact, one of four members, nominally elected by a small rural parish in Yorkshire, but actually the nominees of the Duke of Newcastle, who, if he had chosen to follow the example of another noble borough-owner referred to by Earl Russell in the introduction to his collected speeches, could have dictated the election of his negro valet. The connection of Sir Charles with Bristol, again, was not one to challenge public criticism. His selection for an office which gave him powers of life and death over the prisoners brought before him was the work of a self-elected coterie, entirely out of harmony with the opinions of the citizens. The claim of such an official to interpret the political views of Bristolians was therefore regarded as an impertinent challenge, which the advocates of Reform were called upon to take up; and it speedily became known that the recorder, on his next visit, would be furnished with unmistakable proofs of the inaccuracy of his assertions. Matters became still more critical at the beginning of October, when the House of Lords, taking the course which Sir Charles had conjured them to follow, and perhaps putting faith in his and other allegations about popular reaction, rejected the Reform Bill by a large majority. A few days later, following the course adopted in all the great towns, the local supporters of the measure convened a meeting at the Guildhall (but which was adjourned to Queen Square owing to the unexampled attendance), when intemperate speeches were made by Mr. Protheroe, M.P., and others, amidst enthusiastic cheering. The historians of the time are agreed that a large majority of the middle and working classes were prepared for a national convulsion rather than submit to a continuance of the so-called borough-mongering system, and there is no evidence to show that Bristolians were less in earnest than the rest of their countrymen. They had, moreover, special reasons for discontent, which their political opponents in the city, jubilant at the action of the Peers, were ill-advised enough to throw into relief by taunts and defiance. The members of the Corporation, becoming alarmed at the ferment, took steps which made matters only worse. After the Queen Square meeting, and about a fortnight before the day fixed for the assizes, Lieut. Claxton, R.N., the gentleman mentioned in a former page, privately solicited signatures to a requisition calling on the mayor to convene a meeting, at which the seamen of the port might "express their loyalty to the king." The mayor assented to the request, and a meeting was accordingly held on board a West Indiaman belonging to the mayor, Lieut. Claxton, and others. In the course of the proceedings, however, Mr. Claxton, who had taken the chair, admitted that the real object of the gathering was to organise the sailors as a body-guard for Sir Charles Wetherell on his approaching visit. The avowal met with a reception little expected by the agent of the Corporation. The sailors present refused to be employed in a manner which would identify them with the anti-reformers, and, being forthwith ordered out of the ship by the discomfited chairman, they held another meeting on shore, where they passed a resolution expressing loyalty to the king, but declaring that they "would not allow themselves to be made catspaws by the Corporation or its paid agents." Baffled in this direction, the aldermen thought of postponing the assizes, but found that Sir Charles Wetherell would not consent to such a course. Application was then made to the Home Secretary (Lord Melbourne) for a military force to support the civil authorities. The Secretary of State, before assenting to this request, asked the opinion of Mr. Protheroe, M.P., then in London, when that gentleman replied that it was not to be supposed that the reformers of the city would fail to manifest their disapproval of the recorder's political conduct, since, if they remained silent, the opponents of Reform would assert that the alleged reaction was triumphantly proved; he would not be answerable for tranquillity if military force were employed, but, if the Corporation would assent, he would conduct Sir C. Wetherell to the Guildhall in his own carriage. Treating this proposal with scorn, the corporate officials persisted in their request for troops, and Lord Melbourne assented. The next step of the civic body was to direct the chief constables of the wards to swear in 300 inhabitants as special constables. The result afforded a striking illustration of the feeling entertained towards the Corporation. With rare exceptions, the gentlemen and tradesmen summoned refused to attend, and almost the only persons forthcoming were very young men, zealous anti-reformers, who, according to a contemporary historian, "viewed the lower classes with contempt, as a troublesome rabble, and rather relished an occasion for defying and humbling them." Even with this risky assistance, only 200 constables could be marshalled, and it was necessary to have recourse to a still more questionable class—the rough labourers who were hired as "bludgeon men" at elections. Whilst the preparations were still proceeding, Mr. Alderman Daniel, who was not only the guiding spirit of the Common Council, but the head of the local Tory party, entered into negotiations with Mr. Wm. Herapath, the president of a numerous working-class organisation known as the Political Union, with the object of obtaining the help of the latter body in the preservation of order. Mr. Herapath, who was kept in ignorance of the approach of troops, consented to lend his assistance; but the arrangement with Lord Melbourne becoming known a few hours later, the committee of the Union, expressing strong censure on the conduct of the authorities, refused further cooperation, requesting the Unionists, however, to assist individually in maintaining the public peace. The day fixed for the opening of the assize—Saturday the 29th October—at length arrived, and the state of the streets from an early hour manifested the excitement of the populace. The aldermen, in the hope of lightening the difficulty, had arranged with the recorder that his state entrance should take place at 10 o'clock in the morning, instead of at the usual hour in the afternoon; but the change of time had become known to many persons on the previous evening, and the gathering of the special constables in the Exchange early in the day put all classes on the alert. The promised cavalry—a troop of the 3rd Dragoons and another of the 14th Hussars—were known to be quartered in the suburbs; and though they were moved to the cattle market and the gaol with the least possible display, their presence tended to increase the excitement. At the time appointed, between one and two thousand persons, chiefly labourers, had assembled at Totterdown, where it was customary for the recorder to leave the private carriage in which he had driven from Bath, and to take his seat in the state coach of the sheriffs; and when Sir Charles made his appearance he was received with a loud burst of hisses and groans. The change of vehicles having been made, however, the constables closed around the civic coach in a somewhat disorderly manner, and the procession started for the city, accompanied by the mob, which vented its wrath in continuous yells. On reaching Temple Street the crowd, increasing at every step, became so dense as almost to choke up the narrow thoroughfare, while a number of women of the lowest class, flinging mud at the carriage, shrieked invectives at the recorder, and upbraided the men around them for the cowardice of their inaction. At Bristol Bridge another vast crowd had assembled, and the groaning and hissing became more furious than ever, occasional stones being flung towards the carriage, but without doing any injury. Amongst ever-increasing numbers and amidst whirlwinds of yells, the procession at length reached the Guildhall, where the constables with great difficulty cleared a passage and enabled the recorder to alight. Sir Charles was naturally somewhat agitated by so emphatic an expression of public feeling, but after taking his seat in court he recovered his equanimity, rebuked the tumultuous rabble that filled the gallery, and threatened to commit any disturber of order. The usual preliminaries of an assize having been achieved, and the court adjourned to the following Monday amidst cheering for the king, another critical task had to be faced—the procession to the Mansion House in Queen Square. A dense crowd occupied the entire route, and the cries and groans were not less boisterous than before; but beyond the flinging of a few stones by the crowd gathered in the square there was no symptom of violence, and the civic residence was reached in safety.

The situation at this moment was very similar to what it had been twenty-one years before on the entry of another unpopular judge [see p. 39]. Unhappily the magistrates did not now display similar vigour to that which restored tranquillity on the previous occasion. A large portion of the crowd, thinking that the protest against the recorder's offence had been sufficiently explicit, soon dispersed, and many more would have left the square if an appeal had been made to their reason. Even as it was, the commotion so much settled down that the magistrates actually discussed the propriety of proceeding to church in the accustomed pomp next morning. The advisability of confronting and remonstrating with the noisy assemblage before the house was not thought of; and the special constables were left to exercise their discretion—or rather indiscretion—with truly calamitous consequences. Some of the young guardians of order, without leadership, eager to display their zeal for the established order of things, and destitute alike of prudence and forbearance, had been hit by some of the missiles which greeted the recorder's arrival at the Mansion House. No sooner were the civic authorities in safety than the constables, in retaliation for these insults, rushed into the crowd, which for the most part fled at their approach, and, after belabouring those that could be reached with their heavy staves, carried off a few prisoners in triumph. Desultory incursions, of the same character, and with similar results, were made at intervals by parties of constables for two or three hours, and, as was to be expected, the people who were maltreated by the officers were rarely the most mischievous or ill-intentioned of the rabble. It was equally natural that the hap-hazard administration of bludgeon law by men crying, "We'll give you 'reaction!'" should excite a desire for revenge; and whilst the constables were exulting over the success of their raids, it was evident to cooler-headed observers that a strong feeling of exasperation was rising in the crowd. Intelligence of the situation was moreover quickly spread about the city by those who fled bleeding from the scene of action, while the removal of wounded men to the Infirmary, and the dragging of prisoners to Bridewell, were perilous advertisements of the strife. The captives in many cases were rescued, whereupon they returned to the square, in company with enraged sympathisers who added fresh elements of danger. Nevertheless the situation did not cause great anxiety within the Mansion House. The town clerk, Mr. Serjeant Ludlow, it is true, expressed an opinion that some of the troops should be brought to the spot; but Sir Charles Wetherell disapproved of the suggestion, and his view of the matter prevailed. A little later, when the fiercer spirits amongst the crowd were searching the neighbourhood for sticks and missiles, a large body of the special constables, having been many hours without food, were permitted to return to their homes for refreshment, but with instructions to collect again in the evening at the Guildhall. Observing their departure, and unacquainted with its cause, the more disorderly section of the populace attributed the retreat to fear, and acted as ruffians are prone to act at such a moment. A rush was made against the constables remaining on duty, who were quickly scattered; the railings in front of the Mansion House were then torn down; and the whole of the windows on the ground floor were demolished with stones and brickbats.

At last thoroughly alarmed, some of the magistrates made their appearance, and the mayor (Mr. C. Pinney), who, being a Reformer, was not personally unpopular, with great difficulty obtained a hearing. The earnest remonstrances he addressed to the people on the folly and wickedness of their conduct, and the warnings he added as to the consequences of further tumult were, however, of no avail, and his entreaties to disperse were interrupted by a shower of missiles. The reading of the Riot Act, which followed, was received with howls of derision, whilst such of the constables as had re-assembled were attacked, disarmed, and mercilessly beaten—one of the luckless band being compelled by threats to fling his staff through the windows of the Mansion House, whilst another was driven into the Floating Harbour, and narrowly escaped with his life. Every vestige of defence being swept away, a general assault was made on the Mansion House, the broken railings of which became destructive weapons in the hands of the wreckers. A neighbouring wall was soon pulled down to furnish materials for the assault, and beams of timber were brought up and used as battering rams. The door and window frames being reduced to splinters, the rabble made their way into the ground floor of the building, the furniture, mirrors, chandeliers, and other contents of which were demolished in a few minutes. The kitchens, where a great civic feast was in preparation, were next entered, the cooks driven away, and joints, fowls, game, and pastry were carried off and devoured by the rioters, amidst the cheers of hundreds of spectators. All that the imprisoned mayor and his colleagues could do was to protect themselves from missiles in the upper rooms by barricading the broken casements with feather beds, the whole resources of the establishment being applied to this purpose. Complete ruin having been wrought in the basement apartments, straw and faggots were collected by the mob and carried into the dining room for the purpose of setting fire to the house. That end, it is said, was temporarily averted by a singular obstacle—the inability of the rabble to procure a light, (lucifers being still in the future). Their villanous intentions, however, were manifested by the attempts which were begun to barricade the entrances to the square with planks and paving stones, with the view of preventing the interference of the military.

It was about this point that Sir Charles Wetherell resolved

on making his escape. The rioters, apprehensive that he would take flight, had surrounded the Mansion House as far as the adjoining dwellings permitted, and no doubt destined him to the fate they were preparing for the building itself. The recorder, however, guided by his friends, got upon the flat roof of the dining room, clambered from it by a ladder to a window of the next house, and ultimately made his way to a stable at the back. Here he changed clothes with a postillion, and succeeded so easily in passing through the crowd, and reaching a house at Kingsdown, that he is said to have taken a voluntary stroll through the streets at a later hour in the evening, to ascertain the state of the city. Finding the disturbance showed no signs of abatement, he ordered a chaise and left for Newport, which he reached early on the following morning.

Ignorant of the evasion, the rioters continued their preparations for a fire, when, about six o'clock, in response to the request of the magistrates, the two troops of horse soldiers were brought into the square by Lieut.-Colonel Brereton, the resident Inspecting Field Officer of the Bristol recruiting district, who, by virtue of his rank, had assumed the command. Their arrival put an end to the attack on the house, but the rioters, far from showing fear of the troops, received them with cheers, and sang "God save the king!" Colonel Brereton had already had an interview with the besieged mayor and aldermen. After perambulating the square, he returned to the house, and a lively discussion ensued as to the steps that should be taken. The aldermen and the town clerk advocated the instant employment of force to clear the square; and the mayor told the officer he must order his men to fire if the tumult could not otherwise be suppressed. But Major (afterwards Sir) Digby Mackworth (aide-de-camp to Lord Hill, commander in chief), who had shortly before returned from the Forest of Dean after putting down some agrarian disturbances, urged that no firing should take place, for the sake of the innocent who would certainly suffer, and expressed his conviction that by combining the civil and military forces the populace might be dispersed. Colonel Brereton also strongly disapproved of bloodshed. After again going into the square, he reported on his return that the mob were in good humour, and that he should be able to disperse them by simply walking his troops about. This he sought to do for some hours. But although, whenever he appeared, the rabble received him with cheers, many of them seizing and shaking his hand, the crowd continued in the square with but little diminution. During one of the colonel's numerous calls at the Mansion House, the town clerk, who seems to have made himself the mouthpiece of the authorities, expressed much dissatisfaction at the delay, and told the colonel that the magistrates required the square to be cleared. To this the officer more than once replied that if his men were to fire he must have an explicit order to that effect. In giving evidence afterwards, Serjeant Ludlow admitted that "he was not aware that any explicit orders were given." However, about an hour before midnight, the situation remaining unchanged, Colonel Brereton gave directions to Captain Gage, of the 14th Hussars, to clear the streets by force, and the troops thereupon made a charge on the populace, striking only with the flat of their sabres. Though the rioters instantly scattered, the traditional obstinacy of a Bristol mob was nevertheless visible. Many ruffians, taking refuge in narrow alleys, pelted the soldiers with stones and pieces of iron, and Captain Gage, returning to the Mansion House, asked for orders to fire. The mayor hesitated; Colonel Brereton refused to give the order on his own responsibility; and Captain Gage, resuming the command of his troop, had to be satisfied with clearing the interior of Queen Square; while the special constables, organised by Major Mackworth, were posted around the house, which now seemed secure against attack. Major Mackworth subsequently stated that when he left the building, about two hours later, "the crowds had nearly all dispersed, and I thought the worst of the riot was over." In the meantime, however, some of the populace had repaired to the Council House, the doors and windows of which were assailed, and Captain Gage was sent off to take such measures for its protection as he deemed expedient. A scene of great confusion ensued, the troops making dashes at the crowd, while the more determined rioters, ensconcing themselves in narrow lanes which the cavalry could not enter, hurled volleys of missiles on the troops. Exasperated by their injuries, some of the soldiers at length fired, and one man, a peaceful ostler returning from his stable, was killed at the head of the Pithay. Sabres were also vigorously wielded, and several men were wounded, one of them mortally. The effect of the charges was, however, decisive. The rioters wholly disappeared, and for some hours all was quiet.

During the night carpenters were employed to board up the breaches in the Mansion House, where a few soldiers remained on guard, and the work was completed without interruption. The mayor remained at his post, though rest was of course impossible; but the aldermen, the town clerk, in fact the whole civic body with the exception of Mr. Sheriff Lax, quietly disappeared. The special constables followed the example, and when Major Mackworth returned early on Sunday morning, the force of 250 which he had drilled the night before had "dwindled to about a dozen, and were even then diminishing in number." Their defection sealed the fate of the civic mansion. Soon after dawn about a score of the rioters gathered in the square, and by eight o'clock the knot of men had increased to a crowd, almost wholly composed of the most vicious class in the city. Through another of the many blunders incidental to this deplorable affair, the handful of troops patrolling the square was about this time withdrawn, and the moment the stage was clear the rioting recommenced. The newly-constructed defences of the Mansion House having been quickly demolished, a number of ruffians dashed into the premises, clambered to the upper rooms, and threw the furniture, bedding, etc., into the square, where much was carried off and the rest wantonly destroyed. Amongst the articles found were Sir Charles Wetherell's judicial robe and wig, which were forthwith torn to fragments and distributed amongst the plunderers as souvenirs of their triumph.

Just before the capture of the house, the mayor, accompanied by Major Mackworth, effected his escape, by getting out of an attic window, crouching along between the double roofs of eight or nine houses for concealment from the mob, kicking out a pane of glass in the Custom House to raise a sash, and then quietly leaving that building for the Guildhall. Regardless of the fate of the inmates of the Mansion House, and even of Sir Charles Wetherell himself—whose escape was still unknown—the rioters lost no time in making their way to the wine cellars, which were reported to be well stored. Several hundred bottles of port, sherry, and Madeira were forthwith stolen and carried into the square, where an astonishing orgie was soon in full swing. A crowd of men, women, and boys were to be seen staggering about, madly intoxicated, yelling, swearing, singing, and vociferating threats against the recorder; whilst scores, too drunk to stand, were rolling on the ground, where those not already insensible from their excesses were re-echoing the maledictions and menaces of their companions. Intelligence of the debauch spread with remarkable quickness into all the low-class quarters of the city, and the concourse in the square was rapidly reinforced by those eager to share in the saturnalia. Some of the cavalry having been brought back at the request of the mayor, the Riot Act was three times read by one of the aldermen. No order to fire was, however, given, and Colonel Brereton, in spite of the scene before his eyes, declared that fire-arms should not be used, and that the troops were so exhausted as to absolutely require rest. Having remarked, moreover, that the rabble, whilst cheering the dragoons, were intensely exasperated against the hussars, in consequence of the charge in Wine Street on the previous night, Colonel Brereton told Captain Gage that his troop was the sole cause of the renewed disturbance, and directed him to take his men out of the city, Keynsham being selected as their future station. The colonel's order excited great indignation, not merely in the city but throughout the country. It is only fair to state that Major Mackworth, in his "personal narrative," remarked that the hussars were in absolute need of rest, and that, though "they might have executed a few charges, unless supported by some other description of force they could have done no permanent good, and would soon have been so exhausted as to leave the city wholly defenceless." Their retreat was not effected without bloodshed. The unpopular cavalry, being first directed to their quarters in College Place, were violently attacked with stones on St. Augustine's Back, when some of them, painfully injured, fired in self-defence, killing one rioter and wounding seven or eight others. They soon after left for Keynsham, whereupon Colonel Brereton returned to Queen Square, and, in response to the cheers with which he was greeted, addressed the mob, begging them to disperse, but adding that there would be no more firing, and that the hussars had been sent away.

Such language was not calculated to discourage the rioters, and though the dragoons prevented further plundering in the wine cellars, the mob went on carousing as before. In a short time the bells began to chime for Sunday morning service, and, incredible as it now seems, the attendance at the churches and chapels was so nearly of an average character that a stranger could not have suspected the actual condition of the city. This was doubtless largely due to the singularly isolated position of Queen Square, surrounded on three sides by water, and to the ignorance of the great bulk of the respectable inhabitants of the events that had transpired. But it was partly attributable, as will be shown, to the unpopularity of the Corporation. The mayor and some of the aldermen had assembled early at the Guildhall, where they received offers of service from some of the army pensioners. There were about 250 of those disciplined veterans in the city; and if, as Major Mackworth had counselled the mayor, they had been called out before the recorder's arrival, the tumult in Queen Square would have been suppressed at the outset. Even after the experience of the previous night, however, the magistrates were unable to appreciate the value of these auxiliaries, who met with so cold a reception that they withdrew. About eleven o'clock the mayor issued a placard stating that Sir Charles Wetherell had left the city, and another announcing that the Riot Act had been read. Handbills were also sent to the churches and chapels, describing the perilous state of affairs, and earnestly calling upon the citizens to support the mayor in maintaining order. His worship's appeal was made known to most of the congregations at the close of the service; but although Dr. Carpenter estimated that some 20,000 persons were in attendance, only about 200 gentlemen assembled at the Guildhall. Many of the absentees, according to a subsequent deposition, excused themselves by asking: "Why should we protect the Corporation's property? Let them protect their own property." The muncipality, it was argued, instead of being a public institution for the public security, claimed to be a private monopoly, and had shown itself contemptuous of public opinion [see p. 104]; it had no right to complain when almost the entire community showed its discontent and distrust by holding aloof. The gathering of citizens was so small that after multitudinous plans of action had been discussed—"every one differing from his neighbour," according to Major Mackworth—it was finally determined that each gentleman should go home, endeavour to obtain the cooperation of his neighbours, and return in the afternoon.

The three o'clock meeting was not more numerously attended than its forerunner, owing in some degree, perhaps, to thoughtless arrangements, entrance into the hall being obtainable only by a side-door unknown to the general public. The mayor, who presided, stated that the mob had been in possession of the city for some time, and were then in the act of burning down Bridewell. Being asked if he had any plan to propose, his worship answered in the negative, and upon further questions being put, Mr. Serjeant Ludlow, with his habitual garrulity and self-sufficiency, undertook to speak for the magistrates. Having delivered himself of his views on political affairs, the town clerk, however, vouchsafed no information or advice except that "every man must act on his own discretion and responsibility." Some of the gentlemen present offered to act as constables if a few soldiers were sent in company with them; but Colonel Brereton, who arrived at this point, declared that his men were then too fatigued to go out. After further desultory conversation, in which union and energy were as conspicuously absent as in the morning, Serjeant Ludlow declared that nothing more could be done, that it would shortly be dark, and that it was high time to take care of themselves—a rule which the learned gentleman faithfully followed throughout. The mayor next observed that being without an efficient civil force, and the military being untrustworthy, the best advice he could give was that each person should go home and take care of his own property. The meeting was nevertheless adjourned to the Council House, and continued some hours longer in a disorderly and unfruitful fashion. But it is useless to dwell further on the melancholy exhibition of feebleness and indecision, and the scene must be shifted to the centre of the disturbance, in Queen Square.

After Colonel Brereton's imprudent remarks already recorded, no change in the aspect of affairs occurred for two or three hours. The official placard announcing that Sir Charles Wetherell had left the city was followed by another to the same effect, posted by the Political Union; but the mob put no faith in either document, and the Mansion House continued to be rigorously watched. At length, about one o'clock, Mr. S. Waring, a respected Quaker merchant, addressed the crowd, assuring them that the recorder had departed. After some hesitation, the men who assumed the position of ringleaders said they would "believe the Quaker," adding: "We will do no more here; we will go to Bridewell, and release the prisoners taken last night; and then we will go to the gaol, and release those Sir Charles was to have tried." Mr. Waring at once went to Alderman A. Hilhouse to acquaint him with the purpose of the rioters, and urged the necessity of immediately guarding the prisons; but the alderman treated the warning very lightly, asserting that the walls and gates "were strong enough." Little time was lost by the rioters in carrying out their design, and a gang of desperadoes was soon in front of Bridewell. The buildings forming the prison at that time stood on both sides of what was called Bridewell Lane, the gaoler, Mr. Evans, residing on one side, while the prison proper, on the other, was connected with the dwelling-house by two strong archways, each of which could be closed by a heavy gate. The position was so strong that a dozen resolute men could have kept an unlimited number of ragamuffins at bay; but the gaoler had only himself and two under-officers to depend upon. On the approach of the mob, Evans armed himself and his subordinates with swords, drove the front rank of the assailants from the space between the two buildings, and closed the gates. The garrison, however, was too weak to withstand the pressure of a multitude, and in a few minutes the mob succeeded in lifting the gates from their hinges and in throwing them into the Froom—then uncovered at Bridewell Bridge. Evans, in spite of the threats and missiles showered upon him, next appeared armed with a blunderbuss at one of the windows of his house, and for a further time kept the assailants at a distance. Sledge hammers had however been obtained from a neighbouring smithy, an entry into the gaoler's house was effected through a window, and as Evans had his wife and family, as well as the wife and children of the turnkey, in the building, he found himself compelled to order the warder to surrender the keys. He managed, however, to send a messenger to the magistrates, describing the peril of the prison; and the man assured the aldermen that he could still protect the place with twenty constables and ten soldiers. The answer which the messenger swore to having received was:—"You say they have released the prisoners: pooh pooh! there will be nothing more done." The issue was very different. As soon as the criminals in custody were set free, the rioters set fire to the chapel and cells, which were speedily consumed. The gaoler's house for the time escaped destruction.

Having carried out this part of their plan, the rioters proceeded to the gaol, then only a few years old, and standing on the southern bank of the new river. Mr. Waring, who had made another reconnoitre, had already warned Alderman A. Hilhouse that an attack was imminent, but met with no better success than before. About half an hour before the mob reached the prison, Mr. Humphries, the governor, made his way to the Guildhall, and asked whether he was to defend the place or release the prisoners. No answer was given, and it was not until the question had been pressed two or three times that Alderman A. Hilhouse informed the governor that "he was to use his own discretion; the magistrates gave him no directions." After further consultation, however, the above alderman, accompanied by Alderman Savage and a few other gentlemen, went down to the gaol to see if anything could be done; but the mob, which was making for the spot, refused to listen to them, and drove the party away with stones.

The reader will find it difficult to produce before his mind's eye a glimmering picture of the state of the city during that wet and murky October afternoon. Let him add, however, to the following rapid sketch of the rioters by Dr. Carpenter a few pallid and anxious spectators on the dingy pavements, and he may faintly conceive the scene :—"They could not have been more than from five to six hundred, and the number might have been less. I saw them about a quarter after two, as they were coming down Clare Street on their way. They were a compact body, without stragglers or attendants. They moved with great expedition; and their object was well known. Most of them had bludgeons; some had hatchets; and others were armed with iron palisades, from the front of the Mansion House. All I noticed were the dregs of the city; and a large part were under twenty years of age. . . . The sledge hammers with which they broke [the gaol] open, they procured at a neighbouring manufactory; and the proprietor told me they brought all back but two."

The outer gates of the gaol were of great strength, and the place was even more capable of defence than Bridewell. Though no defence was attempted, the assailants had to ply their hammers and iron bars for three quarters of an hour before a hole was made sufficiently large to admit of the entrance of one of the mob. But this once achieved, the ringleaders were soon within the archway, whence they attacked the inner iron gates, which were comparatively weak. Resistance being hopeless, one of the warders unlocked the gates, and in a few minutes about 300 of the criminal crew penetrated into every nook of the building, destroyed the doors of the cells, and liberated the prisoners, about 170 in number, several of whom stripped themselves of their gaol dress, and ran off to their former haunts in a state of nudity. As the main object of the rioters was being achieved, a body of about twenty dragoons trotted to the prison, led by a young cornet named Kelson, whose account of what occurred was afterwards given on oath. He was, he said, ordered by Lieut.-Colonel Brereton to go with a party of men to the gaol. He had asked the colonel what he was to do when he got there, and was told that, as a magistrate was not to be found, he must on no account use violence, but simply go and return. The soldiers therefore advanced to the gates, where the officer could see the mob "knocking things to pieces," and then the troops, who had been welcomed with cheers by the rioters, and had waved their caps in return, were marched back to College Green, where Colonel Brereton, on receiving the cornet's report, told him he had acted "perfectly right." About the same time, Mr. Herapath and other members of the Political Union remonstrated with the mob, but were roughly told by its leaders that they knew their own business and would attend to it. After the prisoners had been set free, the governor's house was sacked, a large portion of the contents, including the prison records, being thrown into the Avon amidst the cheers of thousands of the labouring class who lined the river banks. The devastation was completed by setting fire to the buildings—every part that would burn, including the governor's dwelling, the chapel, and the treadmill being speedily destroyed.

Whilst the flames were still raging, the ruffians held a council in the gaol yard to consider their next point of attack. Several public buildings were marked out for destruction, but it was eventually determined to burn the toll-houses near the Floating Harbour, and then to break open the Gloucestershire House of Correction at Lawford's Gate, where several prisoners were known to be detained. The firing of the toll-houses was the work of only a few minutes, though the rioters allowed the toll-collectors a brief interval to remove their furniture. About seven o'clock in the evening, the rabble reached Lawford's Gate prison, the gates of which were quickly demolished by hammers and other weapons; and as soon as the prisoners had been released the building was set on fire, and speedily burnt down. Simultaneously with this outrage, a small band of ragamuffins, not exceeding thirty in number, and chiefly Irish boys, returned to Bridewell, and completed the havoc in that quarter by burning the gaoler's house.

The gang which committed the latter wanton piece of mischief next moved towards the Bishop's Palace, situated on the south side of the cathedral. Bishop Gray, who had made himself unpopular amongst the working classes by his speech and vote against the Reform Bill in the House of Lords, had preached in the cathedral at the morning service, but had left his residence during the afternoon from apprehensions as to its fate, and the more valuable contents had been removed. Notice of the intended attack was in this case also sent to the magistrates; and several gentlemen, who had gone to the Council House to offer their services, addressed Alderman Savage, requesting him to authorise them to defend the palace. The alderman, however, replied:— "We can give no such permission: we are advised to call out the *posse comitatus* to-morrow morning; and can do nothing until then." The first gang which entered Lower College Green, according to the evidence of Jones, the bishop's butler, who displayed much courage, consisted of about a hundred men and boys; but other witnesses estimated the number at not more than thirty. The account in the *Bristol Mirror* describes them as "a mere handful." On reaching the Green, about eight o'clock, this body, with the hammers brought from Bridewell, attacked the gate leading into the cloisters, which was soon broken down. The door into the palace, which Jones refused to open, was next demolished, and the rioters rushed into the apartments in search of plunder. The arrival of a party of troops in the Green, however, caused a panic; and the mob, who had flung the red-hot cinders in the grates about the fine old dining parlour and some of the bedrooms, took to flight, carrying off such portable articles as had attracted their cupidity. Cornet Kelson, in command of the cavalry, was invited by Jones to dismount and enter; but he replied that Colonel Brereton's orders did not permit him to do so. A few minutes afterwards he received instructions to leave for Queen Square; and no sooner had the troops departed than the rioters, reinforced by many of the gang from Lawford's Gate, burst afresh into the palace, drove Jones from his post, thoroughly sacked the premises from the attics to the cellars, and finally kindled fires in several places at once. The bishop's wine, cleared out from the cellars, is said to have been sold in the Green at a penny or twopence a bottle. The chapter house was next broken into, and a library of 6,000 volumes, together with some valuable manuscripts, was recklessly tossed about, the major portion of the books being flung through one of the windows into the burning palace, while a bonfire was made with several hundred others in the cloisters. The rest were chiefly stolen, or flung into the harbour. The rioters now resolved to burn the chapter house and cathedral, but were resisted for a time by Phillips, the sub-sacrist. The exertions of that worthy official would, however, have been fruitless but for the courage of four or five gentlemen (Dissenters) who ventured into the crowd. Mr. B. Ralph, the most energetic of the party, faced the ringleader of the incendiaries, and told him that no Reformer would destroy the people's property; whereupon the ruffian, shouting for Reform, said they would not burn the college, and the flames in the chapter room were extinguished. Before they quitted the neighbourhood, the rioters had the insolence to make an attack on Reeves' hotel in College Place, the head-quarters of the dragoons; but upon a few of the cavalry turning out, the assailants decamped, after demolishing some windows.

Whilst those scenes were being enacted in St. Augustine's, more extensive devastation had begun in Queen Square. The liberation of a horde of hardened criminals from the prisons had doubtless a serious influence on subsequent events. Political feeling had brought about the demonstration of Saturday, but the mass of those who took part in it had withdrawn, and the undisguised purpose of the vicious crew who had succeeded them, consisting, according to the *Mirror*, "entirely of low Irish," was outrage with a view to plunder. During the attack on Lawford's Gate, a crowd had remained in front of the Mansion House, for the protection of which, strangely enough, the magistrates had made no provision throughout the entire day, but had contented themselves with removing the plate and several valuable pictures. For some hours the rabble were prevented from doing serious mischief by a picket of seven soldiers which perambulated the thoroughfare; but the intention of the ringleaders was in no doubt, for they were seen by Father Edgeworth in one of the adjoining by-streets preparing balls of pitch and flax, which, according to his deposition, "they significantly held up to the people and the soldiers." When the handful of the latter were despatched for the so-called protection of the bishop's palace, a few desperadoes again burst into the Mansion House wine-cellars, and ransacked the cupboards etc., on the ground floor. The testimony of Father Edgeworth, who had been drawn to the spot by a desire to keep his Irish flock in order, affords a graphic idea of the scene. The plunderers, he said, hesitated before mounting to the upper floors of the house; but a boy, of about thirteen years, with a candle in his hand, ran up a few of the stairs and cried out, "Why do you not come on; are you afraid?" whereupon about twenty or thirty, chiefly lads of about sixteen years, followed the boy with a cheer. Everything which could be carried away was then stolen; the larger pieces of furniture were knocked to pieces; and the raiders finished the work by setting fire to most of the chambers, a quantity of wine and spirits being thrown upon the straw in the cellar before it was lighted. A few remained upstairs in search of plunder until retreat was no longer practicable; and the remains found in the ruins showed how dearly they had paid for their villany. So rapid was the progress of the flames, that the dragoons directed to Lower College Green saw, on arriving there, the Mansion House in a blaze. Believing that the palace was no longer in danger, the troops returned to Queen Square—only to behold, immediately afterwards, that the episcopal residence had shared the same fate. A little before ten o'clock, Cornet Kelson, who was left without orders, and believed that nothing more could be done, ordered his slender force to their quarters; and the rioters were left to work havoc at their discretion. "Not a fire engine was present," wrote Mr. Somerton, proprietor of the *Bristol Mercury*, a spectator, "nor do we hear that any made the attempt. The firemen of the different companies alone, armed with their fire hatchets, would have been more than sufficient to have routed the mob at this or any subsequent time during the evening." The special constables had disappeared early in the day; and the only regular officers of police, the mayor's and sheriffs' sergeants, were so panic-stricken that they hid themselves in their houses, taking the name-plates off their doors in order to escape attention.

A new illustration of the mental condition of the authorities was given about this time. The magistrates had despatched expresses in various directions for military assistance. Amongst others, the Dodington troop of Gloucestershire Yeomanry was summoned; but no arrangements were made for the quartering of that or any other body. The troop in question having arrived about ten o'clock in the evening, the commander, Captain Codrington, marched to the Council House; but no magistrate was in attendance to give him instructions. The captain next proceeded to the recruiting office in College Green, in search of Colonel Brereton; but that officer declined to give him orders to act until he had the co-operation of a magistrate. Later on, Captain Codrington and his men made their way to Queen Square while the Mansion House was in flames; but they could still obtain no intelligence of a guardian of the law. In a letter, addressed next day to the Home Secretary, the captain wrote:—"Having paraded through the principal streets of the city for more than two hours, without being able to find a magistrate; hearing that they had in fact left the town after withdrawing both his majesty's troops and the police; finding ourselves thus unsupported, and without a hope of being in any way serviceable, the city being actually in the uncontrolled power of the populace, I had no alternative but that of withdrawing also my men, and we returned home about five o'clock this morning." Soon after his interview with Captain Codrington, Colonel Brereton retired to bed, apparently washing his hands of all responsibility. If he supposed that the rioters would be satisfied with the havoc they had wrought on public property, he was soon undeceived.

The Mansion House was still burning fiercely when it became apparent to the thousands of persons hitherto looking on with indifference, that the ringleaders were preparing to fire the adjoining houses. The attack commenced by beating in the ground-floor windows and forcing the doors; admission having been gained, the rooms were ransacked and the lighter furniture and effects thrown into the thoroughfare; finally, the heavy furniture was broken to pieces, piled in a heap, and set on fire. Most of the apartments being lined with wainscot, and combustible articles being kindled on every storey, the flames spread with astonishing rapidity. Indeed, before midnight the range of dwellings between the Mansion House and the Custom House, including several houses at the back, formed one immense conflagration. The occupiers, having received from the rioters a brief notice to leave, had carried off a portion of their more valuable effects; but much of the salvage was deposited in other houses, then supposed to be out of harm's way, and eventually also destroyed.

The sack and destruction of the Custom House were the next flagrant incidents of the night. After an entry had been effected, a band of wretches, including a few women, allowing the officials to pack up and remove the documents and books, rushed upstairs to the dwelling rooms, where, finding a quantity of provisions and liquor, they deliberately sat down to regale themselves, whilst a more active gang pursued the work of destruction in the adjoining apartments. A dreadful fate befell many of the carousers. In the midst of their brutal revelry, the fires lighted by their companions reached the staircase, which soon became impassable. Some of the revellers slid from the balcony outside and escaped; others jumped from the windows and fell crushed on the pavement; one or two leaped upon the portico, the leaden roof of which was already in a molten state, and, being held fast by the viscous metal, were literally roasted to death. [At the Bristol meeting of the British Association in 1836, Dr. Buckland perpetrated a grim joke on the geological section by producing for inspection a bone, which he said had just been handed to him, and which he described as part of the rib of a mammal, found upon the red sandstone. The relic having greatly puzzled the learned gathering, the doctor at length explained, that it was a bone of one of the rioters who perished at the Custom House. The animal matter had been decomposed by intense heat, and the cavities were filled with melted lead.] About four or five fell back into the flames, and their bodies, half reduced to cinders, were afterwards found in the ruins. Their ghastly end, however, made no impression on the bulk of the rioters. As an avenue separated the Custom House from the remaining dwellings on that side of the square, the spectators, estimated at from 15,000 to 20,000, hoped that the incendiaries would now be satisfied with their devastations. But this was far from their thoughts. The houses on the western side of the avenue met with precisely the same fate as those in the eastern wing. The proceedings of the miscreants were of the simplest character. A brief notice was given to the occupants to leave. If a house were abandoned and shut up, it was entered by boys through the windows in the manner already described; portable articles of value were carried off, others were thrown into the square to be picked up by confederates; and then fires were lighted in most of the rooms. The whole row was in flames about an hour after midnight; and from the thoroughly effectual way in which the villains pursued their operations, the destruction was as rapid as it was complete. Besides the property in Queen Square, some warehouses were burning in King Street; and from a bonded store, containing about fifty puncheons of rum, the ignited spirit poured into the street, forming a "hedge of fire" in front of several dwelling houses, the inmates of which were saved by the courage of a party of sailors.

Most of the older criminals were by this time in a brutal state of drunkenness, from the quantity of liquor which had been consumed during their raids. But the fury of the younger gang was insatiable, and the western side of the vast quadrangle, beginning with the Excise Office, was next vowed to ruin, a number of neighbouring warehouses fronting Prince's Street being destined to the same fate. Nearly all the mischief in this locality was committed by young boys, whose number, according to one witness, did not exceed fifty, while many respectable persons reduced the total to about thirty. Mr. Somerton wrote:—"We saw three urchins, apparently not more than ten or eleven years of age, who, when their retreat from the attic floor of one of the houses had been cut off, and while the flames were bursting out beneath them, coolly clambered along a coping, projecting not more than three inches, and, entering an adjoining house, immediately set fire to a bedstead and furniture." Language cannot do justice to the extraordinary scene which the city presented at this time. Almost the entire population was afoot, and in spite of a continuous drizzling rain, every eminence dominating the burning square was crowded with a terror-stricken multitude of all ages. Charles Kingsley, at that time a boy of thirteen, residing in a boarding school on St. Michael's Hill, was one of the units of this great mass, and twenty-seven years afterwards narrated to a Bristol audience his reminiscences of the spectacle. "One seemed," he said, "to look down upon Dante's Inferno, and to hear the multitudinous moan and wail of the lost spirits surging to and fro amid that sea of fire." After a graphic sketch of Brandon Hill, tinged with diversified tints of colour, he added:—"Higher and higher the fog was scorched and shrivelled by the fierce heat below, glowing through and through with red reflected glare till it arched itself into one vast dome of red-hot iron—fit roof for all the madness down below; and beneath it, miles away, I could see the lovely tower of Dundry, shining red." How dazzling was the refulgence may be imagined from the statement of an inhabitant of Beachley, near Chepstow, who averred that the illumination of the sky enabled him to read a book in his garden. The most bewildering scenes, however, were in Queen Square itself. Scores of rioters in the last stages of drunkenness were rolling about in front of the burning property, or carousing in groups, or grovelling on the sward; now and then a barrel of wine or beer was brought out of one of the houses to keep up the brutal debauch; a few lads were rushing with torches or burning brands from one doomed house to another; and about one hundred and fifty older and more wily villains were engaged in gathering up the plunder extracted from the dwellings—many of them selling it openly in the square and adjoining streets, amidst the ruddy glare from the blazing buildings. Mr. Somerton saw "what appeared to be a beautiful silver teapot offered for a shilling, and feather beds, mahogany tables, and a variety of costly and valuable articles of furniture were offered at the same rate." According to the *Mirror*, a handsome pianoforte taken out of the Mansion House was bought by a gentleman for four shillings. The enormous quantity of stolen goods could not, however, be got rid of in this way, and a number of fellows might be seen busily piling their spoil upon wagons, cars, carts, and trucks, a stream of which came and went as deliberately as if they had been engaged at a gigantic auction, whilst thousands of citizens of all classes, apparently paralysed at the spectacle, looked helplessly on. How little courage would have been needed to trample down the riot, may be judged from a few facts elicited during the subsequent trials. Whilst the incendiaries were at the height of their triumph, a porter named Mills, employed by Messrs. Bartlett & Mogg, wine merchants, saw some of the gang attempting to remove the padlock from one of his masters' warehouses, when he wrested a hammer from one of the men, set his back against the door, and threatened to knock out the brains of any one who should come nigh him. The ruffians at once went off; and the warehouse was saved for the time. In another case, Martha Davis, servant to a Mr. Cross, living in Queen Square, withstood the rioters who entered the house; and though she was knocked down insensible by a blow, she on recovering seized one of the crew by the collar, and eventually drove out the whole party, shutting the door in their faces. Similar bravery was shown near Lawford's Gate prison by Mrs. Mack, wife of a publican, and by her brother, William Field. The mob which set fire to the prison had afterwards burst into Mack's house, and attempted to burn it; but Field and his sister resisted them so stoutly that Mr. Justice Taunton, who tried three of the criminals at Gloucester, declared that if twenty men had acted like Field, the riots would have been suppressed.

It is now time to return to the doings of the authorities. As already stated, the troops had been ordered to their quarters, and Colonel Brereton had gone to bed. No evidence is forthcoming as to what had become of the aldermen. The mayor, though exhausted from want of rest, declined to leave the city, but had some difficulty in obtaining shelter, being refused admission at the house of Mr. Sheriff Lax, in Park Street, by the servants left in charge (the family, like many others, had fled from the city), whilst he was virtually turned out of that of Mr. Granger, a surgeon. He at last found refuge at Mr. Daniel Fripp's, in Berkeley Square, whence a letter was sent to Colonel Brereton, notifying where he was to be found. About two o'clock on Monday morning, Mr. Samuel Goldney, surgeon, a relative of one of the aldermen, was in Queen Square, and satisfied himself, as he afterwards deposed, that the actual number of rioters was only between fifty and a hundred, and that a single vigorous effort would put an end to the havoc. He accordingly went to the cavalry stables, where he found Cornet Kelson eager to act if he could obtain a proper order to that effect. Mr. Goldney then proceeded to Mr. Fripp's, where, after great hesitation, that gentleman admitted him, and heard his report, which he conveyed to the mayor. The latter thereupon wrote a note, bearing the vague address, "Bristol, 3 o'clock, Monday morning," requiring the officer in command of the troops to use the most vigorous measures to suppress the riot. Mr. Fripp, in delivering this missive to Mr. Goldney, remarked, "You are particularly requested not to say where the mayor is." The letter was taken to Leigh's stables, and delivered to Captain Warrington, who was technically in command of the dragoons during Colonel Brereton's absence. The captain at first declined to open the letter, on the ground that it was not directed to him, but ultimately consented to do so. He then said that his superior officer would return in two or three hours, and that, although willing to turn out the troops on the receipt of proper orders, he would not move except in company with a magistrate. Mr. Goldney made no reply, as he did not know where an alderman was to be found, and was unwilling to mention the whereabouts of the mayor. Through this unfortunate error of judgment on the part of Captain Warrington, which was the ruin of his professional career, the rioters remained unchecked for nearly two hours longer, during which the devastation was greatly extended. About four o'clock, Mr. Alderman Camplin found his way to Captain Warrington, and requested the troops to be brought out; but the captain, though expressing a desire to act, would not give orders until he had seen Colonel Brereton. He and the alderman, however, roused up the colonel at his lodgings in Unity Street; and although the commanding officer still protested that a few jaded troops could do no good against such a mob, he was at last prevailed upon to order out the dragoons, who arrived at the scene of ruin between five and six o'clock.

At this time, a large warehouse in Prince's Street was in flames, the whole of the western side of Queen Square—excepting two dwellings which the rioters were pillaging*—

* The *Mirror* states that these houses escaped destruction through the exertions of Mr. B. Ralph and a young man named Thomas. They still stand in the middle of the western side, immediately below the central avenue.

was burnt or burning; and an attack had just commenced against the corner house on the southern side, which had been sentenced to the same fate as the northern and western façades. The dragoons had begun to patrol the square, as before, when Major Mackworth arrived. "It immediately struck me," he afterwards wrote, "that if this house were fired, the shipping would soon be in a blaze, and nearly the whole city must inevitably be burned. It was no longer time to consider numbers or await magistrates' orders. I called out 'Colonel Brereton, we must instantly charge,' and without waiting for his answer (he could not but approve), I called out, 'Charge, men, and charge home.' The troops obeyed with the utmost alacrity, Colonel Brereton charging with great spirit at their head. . . . Numbers were cut down and ridden over; some were driven into the burning houses, out of which they were never seen to return; and our dragoons, after sabring all they could come at in the square, collected and formed, and then charged down Prince's Street, and again returned to the square, riding at the miserable mob in all directions; about 120 or 130 of the incendiaries were killed and wounded here." In the meantime a party of public-spirited citizens, who had gradually collected (amongst whom Mr. B. Ralph was again prominent), offered themselves to Colonel Brereton, who readily accepted their services. They first entered the two unburned houses on the western side, from which they dislodged the plunderers by main force, one of the gang having his neck dislocated, while others were cut down by the soldiers outside. Strengthened by a few volunteers, the salvage party advanced to the house of ex-Sheriff Claxton, at the west end of the south side, which was being stripped by the rioters in the usual manner, prior to being set on fire. As a further evidence of the astonishing weakness of the horde that had perpetrated so much ruin, it may be stated that the band found wrecking this house numbered only sixteen persons, of whom five were women and young boys. After a smart conflict, during which Mr. Henry Smith, solicitor, received two stabs, while Mr. Claxton's negro servant threw one of the thieves clean out of an upstairs window, the villanous crew were driven off, and the fires they had kindled in three rooms extinguished. With the pertinacity they had displayed throughout, however, the rioters, though repeatedly charged by the dragoons, retreated into the little courts railed off in front of the houses; and about half past six o'clock about fifty ruffians actually attempted to renew their work; but the armed force, slender as it was (21 men), prevented further acts of violence. Major Mackworth, moreover, had already galloped off to Keynsham, bearing Colonel Brereton's order for the return of the 14th Hussars, and these troops were joined in trotting back by about fourteen of the Bedminster Yeomanry—whose "discretion" throughout the crisis excited some uncomplimentary criticism. [It was stated in a newspaper, that they had been for some time shut up in the riding-house in Portwall Lane, to keep them out of harm's way.]

Before the hussars reached Bristol, effectual help had arrived from another quarter. Major Beckwith, commanding a portion of the same regiment stationed at Gloucester, had hurried from that city on receiving a demand for assistance, and reached the Council House about seven o'clock, an hour and a half in advance of his troops. He was received by the mayor, three or four aldermen, and the town clerk; and his description of the civic authorities, afterwards given on oath, is deserving of record. They appeared, he said, bewildered and stupified with terror, the mayor being the most collected of the party. Having requested that one or two magistrates would accompany him on horseback, they individually and positively refused to do so. "One of them stated it would make him unpopular; another, that it would cause his shipping to be destroyed; another, his property. They also informed me that none of them knew how to ride on horseback, except one gentleman, and they pointed to the tall alderman [A.] Hilhouse. Mr. Hilhouse said he had not been on horseback for eighteen years, and he would hold anybody responsible who said a second time that he could ride." [Major Beckwith subsequently stated that he had mistaken the identity of the alderman who used these expressions. A contemporary writer, in defending the Corporation, alleged that at ordinary times most of the aldermen could be seen riding into the city every morning.] The major having demanded written authority sanctioning any steps he might take, the required document was signed by the mayor. He then went to Queen Square to have an interview with Colonel Brereton, and, expressing his astonishment at the scene before him, he asked what had become of the 14th Hussars. Colonel Brereton said that they had been sent away, but were about to return; that the magistrates would not authorise him to use force; that he had too few men to put down the tumult; and that he should go to his lodgings to dress, which he incontinently did. Major Beckwith had a further conversation with him pending the arrival of the squadron from Gloucester; and it may be presumed from the major's subsequent acts that he resolved, in spite of his inferior rank, to take his own measures for suppressing the riot, regardless of the opinion of his superior officer. Colonel Brereton calmly submitted to this military offence, contenting himself with declaring that Major Beckwith must take the whole responsibility. Just as the troops from Gloucester reached the city, a report was received that the cellars of the bishop's palace were being again pillaged; but the charges of the fresh troops, which were made wherever the rabble collected, and in which Colonel Brereton again took part, brought the atrocious disorders to an end in less than two hours.

Unhappily order was not restored without much bloodshed. Major Mackworth stated that he saw "at least 250 rioters killed or wounded" in the concluding charges. And, as is usual in collisions of this kind, several innocent pedestrians, unexpectedly encountering the troops, were grievously injured. The officers of the public hospitals recorded a total of twelve deaths arising from the riots—four from shots or sword cuts, six from burns, and two from excessive drinking. The wounded under treatment numbered 96, of whom 59 were injured by the troops, and 37 from various other causes. It was known, however, that these figures far from represented the aggregate casualties, either fatal or otherwise. Some of the mortally injured were not taken to the hospitals, and some bodies, it was suspected, were secretly thrown into the Avon. Probably at least a dozen rioters were burnt to ashes in the destroyed houses. The relics of five or six others were dug out of the ruins. They were not corpses, said Mr. Kingsley, but "corpse fragments," and he added, "there was one charred fragment, with a scrap of old red petticoat adhering to it, which I never forgot." (One man was disinterred alive, but had an arm entirely burned off.) A great number injured in the charges of the troops, again, were concealed by their friends, through fear of recognition if they were removed to the infirmary. There is every reason to believe, however, that Mr. Eagles' assertion, that five hundred of the rioters paid for their crimes with their lives is a ridiculous exaggeration. In addition to the hussars from Keynsham, some troops of the North Somerset Yeomanry from Frome, Wincanton, and other places soon after arrived, and the magistrates, reassembled at the Council House, resolved on calling out the *posse comitatus*, and appointed a number of deputy sheriffs, amongst them Mr.

Herapath, whose proffered assistance of the members of the Political Union was at last welcomed. By these measures upwards of 4,000 citizens were soon embodied, wearing a strip of white calico round the right arm as a distinguishing badge. In a few hours the streets were deserted except by the guardians of the peace, while the ringleaders of disorder, already dreading discovery, hid themselves in obscure dens—one of the worst of the ruffians, however, having the audacity to assume the badge of a constable, which he was wearing when arrested.

The restoration of order had not come a moment too soon. The news of the devastation had spread far and wide, and all the evil characters of the western counties were flocking to the city to share in its plunder. The lower labouring class in the suburbs had already become demoralised. On the night of Sunday, when the city was illuminated by the gigantic fires in Queen Square (which were seen for forty miles around), gangs of low ruffians attacked and entered the public houses in almost every part of the town, demanding unlimited supplies of liquor with horrible menaces, recklessly breaking open barrels and wasting more than they consumed. To say nothing of many such outrages in the heart of the city, Mr. Somerton stated that there was scarcely a tavern from Queen Square to Easton that was not more or less ravaged. "In Wine Street," he added, "the houses of respectable tradesmen were visited, and money was demanded under threats of murdering the owners in case of refusal; and in some instances—such was the terror in which the wretches were held—handfuls of silver coin were thrown to them from the upper windows." After many of the rioters had fled into the country in consequence of the charges of the hussars, news was received that they were plundering houses near St. George's, and cavalry had to be sent there before they would disperse. A despatch had been previously sent to Bath for military aid; but the populace of that city forthwith broke into disturbance, and did so much damage at one of the hotels * that it was deemed prudent to retain the troops. Again, when two or three companies of infantry sent from Cardiff were about to embark in a steamer at

* The hotel in question, the White Hart, was threatened with the fate of the Bristol Mansion House. The mob were rushing in after destroying the windows. "They however met with a warm reception, a charge being made by the inmates with red hot pokers, previously prepared, which had an admirable effect in causing the assailing party to beat a precipitate retreat."—*Mainwaring's "Annals of Bath,"* p. 375.

Newport, a mob in sympathy with the Bristol rioters attempted to cut the boat adrift, and even threatened a regular attack on the troops. These soldiers (for whom no accommodation had been provided in Bristol,* and who took shelter in the Guildhall and the White Lion dining-room) had to be sent back to Wales two or three days later, owing to an apprehension of riots at Merthyr Tydvil, where some of the Bristol fugitives were reported to have fled. Such facts suffice to show the widespread peril of the crisis, and the urgent need of the vigour which was so tardily displayed. Until the arrival of a large body of troops, including artillery, which were promptly despatched by the military authorities, watch and ward were kept by the special constables, the parish churches being lighted up nightly for use as head-quarters for each district. Even so late as the 5th November it was deemed advisable to close the markets at six o'clock; though, from the co-operation of all supporters of order, danger had then disappeared.

With the return of security came arrangements for detecting the ringleaders, and for recovering as much of the stolen property as could be traced; and extraordinary were the results of the investigation that followed. Mr. John Mills, editor of the *Bristol Gazette*, a man thoroughly acquainted with all classes of the population, stated in his journal that the great bulk of the rioters had sprung from the Irish colonies located in the slums of the city; and his assertion was confirmed by those engaged as searchers. In Marsh Street, the denizens of which were nearly all Irish, an almost incredible quantity of stolen property was discovered, many of the houses being crammed with goods. Many cartloads were collected in Lewin's Mead; two loads were taken out of a dwelling in Host Street; and still larger stores of booty came to light in the low alleys in St. James's, the Pithay, the Dings, Baptist Mills, Bedminster, and Kingswood. The aggregate is said to have loaded forty wagons, and occupied so much space that the parish churches were opened for its reception, the quadrangle of the Exchange being also full of recovered property of every kind, piled up in heaps several feet high. Many stratagems for secreting their prey, or for getting rid of it when discovery became threatening, were resorted to by the freebooters. Some property was found

* A few days later the Armoury in Stapleton Road, hired from the Corporation of the Poor, was fitted up for the accommodation of the troops sent down by the Government, and additional barracks were temporarily formed in the Wool Hall and in a warehouse in Thomas Street.

buried in back yards, laid upon roofs, and lodged in water cisterns and pigsties. In other houses, the constables found fragments of valuable furniture burning in the grates, while occasionally the thieves divested themselves of their ill-gotten booty by throwing it into the Float or the Avon.

One recovery will long be memorable, the article saved—a massive sixteenth century silver salver—forming an interesting item in the collection of civic plate. The salver, accidentally forgotten when the rest of the plate was removed from the Mansion House, was purloined by a rioter named Ives, who cut it into no less than 169 pieces. Supposing its identification would thus be impossible, Ives offered a portion of it for sale to Mr. Williams, a silversmith, who, suspecting a robbery, asked to see the remainder before making a purchase. Next day, when Ives brought the rest of his spoil, he was captured, and was soon after sentenced to fourteen years' transportation. The whole of the salver was recovered save two minute fragments, and by Mr. Williams's ingenuity it was so successfully riveted together that its original beauty remains intact, while it has acquired an additional historic value.* Of the valuable cathedral library about eleven hundred volumes were rescued from marine stores, old clothes shops, etc., but only two or three works were recovered entire. The discoveries of stolen goods led to the capture of several more of the leading rioters, some of whom were caught whilst carousing on the liquors they had carried off. One Irishman, when apprehended, was wearing three shirts, three jackets, and three pairs of trousers, while an Irishwoman was indebted for the "interesting condition" in which she posed, to two silk waistcoats and a pair of blankets wrapped around her waist. About forty of the criminals who had been liberated from prison were also arrested; and in a few days the gaol, having undergone hasty repair, contained nearly 240 inmates compromised in the tumults.

In the then existing state of the city political party spirit might well have been hushed. On the 1st December, however, a meeting took place of local anti-Reformers, Alderman Daniel presiding, when an address to the king was adopted, in which, according to the London *Times*, it was argued that anarchists, atheists, robbers, and incendiaries were the only allies of Lord Grey's Ministry. Shortly afterwards, a so-

* Ives returned to Bristol after undergoing his sentence, and had the effrontery to call at the Council House and ask permission to see the restored salver.

called history of the riots was published, professedly from the pen of "a citizen," but really compiled by the Rev. John Eagles, then living in a secluded village in Somerset, who reproduced the most extravagant rumours and gossip of the time. Ignoring the obligations of his sacred calling, the author boldly avowed that his object was to excite a belief that "the perpetrators of the [Reform] Bill"—in other words the Ministry—"were in connection with the perpetrators of the plot," which "had been long in preparation, and had been carried out by hirelings from Birmingham." The reverend censor was of course unable to produce a vestige of trustworthy evidence in support of his assertions. So far from the mob being led by hired desperadoes prepared for slaughter and destruction, it does not appear that a single rioter was possessed of a lethal weapon until he stole one during his search for plunder; and the idle tales reproduced in the book about incendiary powders, cakes, pastes, liquids, and so forth, found no support in the testimony of the witnesses at the trials, excepting that one fire-raiser was believed to have had a pocket bottle of spirits of turpentine. [It is only fair to add, that in his later years, Mr. Eagles, seemingly ashamed of the work, endeavoured to escape from the stigma which attached to its authorship.]

To the great indignation of the citizens, the Corporation proposed that the rioters should be tried before Sir Charles Wetherell; but the Government resolved on issuing a special commission directed to Lord Chief Justice Tindal, Mr. Justice Taunton, Mr. Justice Bosanquet, and the Duke of Beaufort (lord high steward of the city), ordering them to proceed with their task on the 2nd January, 1832. The recorder was indignant at being excluded from the commission, and had the courage to demand, "as a matter of right," that his name and that of his brother aldermen should be added to the list. His request was rejected by the Government, as "simply a claim by the Corporation to sit as judges on their own cause," and Sir Charles vented his rage at the rebuff by a characteristic outburst in the House of Commons. Due preparations were made for receiving the judges with a solemnity worthy of the occasion. The whole of the ratepayers were again sworn in as constables, a body of policemen was formed for the special protection of the judges, and detachments of troops were posted at various points in case of emergency; though, as may be supposed, there was no indication of disrespect or ill-feeling. The trials occupied twelve days, during which 102 prisoners were brought up. Of these 81 were convicted and 21 acquitted. In addition to these cases, 12 indictments were rejected by the grand jury, and on 13 others no evidence was offered. Of the criminals convicted, 5 were left for execution; sentence of death was recorded against 26, but it was commuted to transportation for life; one was sentenced to transportation for fourteen years, and 6 for seven years; while the remaining 43 suffered various terms of imprisonment with hard labour. [Four of the aldermen had the courage to take their seats on the judicial bench whilst the Lord Chief Justice passed sentence on the criminals. Their intrusion appears to have been looked upon as a notable manifestation of bad taste.] Richard Vines, one of the five capitally convicted, received a reprieve, owing to his semi-idiocy. On behalf of the others—Christopher Davis, for destroying the gaol; William Clarke, for destroying the gaol and Bridewell; and Thomas Gregory and Joseph Kayes, for destroying private houses—a petition for a commutation of the punishment was addressed to the Crown by about 10,000 citizens, including many of the highest respectability. Especial exertions were made on behalf of Davis, a man who had amassed a small competence in his former business as a carrier, but was addicted to violent language when excited by liquor. It was pleaded that he had been guilty of no act of violence, his crime consisting in cheering on the rabble by waving his hat on an umbrella, in cursing the bishops and the Corporation, and in expressing hopes of their downfall. He had, however, boasted that he had drunk some of the wine stolen from the Mansion House. Owing to the detestable jurisprudence of the age, Davis's counsel was not allowed to address the jury, and the culprit had not the ability to plead for himself. The Government resolved that the law must take its course, and the convicts were executed at midday on the 27th January, in front of the gaol, in the presence of a vast concourse of spectators. Besides the prisoners tried in Bristol, six men were convicted at Gloucester, of attacking and attempting to burn a public house and other premises near Lawford's Gate prison. Sentence of death was recorded against them, but it was commuted to transportation.

In the meantime inquiries had taken place by order of the Commander-in-chief into the conduct of the officers who had held the command of the troops during the tumults. The court-martial in the case of Lieut.-Colonel Brereton was opened on the 9th January, 1832, when a series of eleven charges was formulated against him by General Sir Charles

Dalbiac, who acted as prosecutor, and who described them as "bearing on their face every character of culpability unprecedented in the case of a British officer." The proceedings were abruptly brought to a close, after four sittings, by the suicide of the unhappy defendant, whose mind gave way under the weight of his misfortunes. Colonel Brereton, who had been major of a West India regiment, took up his residence in Clifton some years before the riots, on being appointed Inspecting Field Officer of this recruiting district. He resided at the time of his death at Redfield house, St. George's, and is stated to have been highly esteemed by his friends and acquaintances. The trial of Captain Warrington, who commanded the troop of dragoons, followed a few days later. The chief charge against him was his refusal to instantly comply with the order of the mayor, under circumstances already narrated—a refusal which unquestionably enabled the incendiaries to greatly extend their devastations. It was proved, however, that the defendant was so ill at the time as to be almost unfit for duty. The court adjudged him guilty, and ordered him to be cashiered, but accompanied the sentence with a recommendation to mercy, on the ground that his offences were mere errors of judgment. The Crown approved the sentence, but allowed Captain Warrington to dispose of his commission.

The last prosecution was that directed against the mayor and aldermen for their conduct during the riots. Immediately after the restoration of order, the apathetic action of the magistrates was condemned by the respectable classes in the city, regardless of party—a meeting of merchants, etc., at the Commercial Rooms, and a still larger gathering at the Assembly Rooms, being practically unanimous in their expression of disapproval. (Mr. J. Mills, at the former meeting, endeavoured to apologise for the aldermen, but was stopped by general cries of "off, off.") The parliamentary battle on the Reform Bill was, however, then raging violently, and party spirit throughout the country—furious to a degree unknown since the time of the Stewarts—speedily laid hold of the events in Bristol. As Liberals were vehement in their accusation of the local authorities, Tories began to feel themselves bound to defend the cause of the magistrates, and to throw the guilt of the havoc on the Ministry and their scheme of Reform. It was even alleged by enemies of "the Bill" that the object of the Government in prosecuting the justices was to strike at the independence of the municipalities. As the trials were fixed to take place before a jury of Berkshire landowners, a large majority of whom were known to be anti-Reformers, the result was never in much doubt. The Corporation, however, was more than usually prodigal in making preparations to defend its incriminated members, and upwards of £3,800 were paid out of the civic treasury. The trial of Mr. Pinney began in the Court of Queen's Bench on the 25th October, 1832, and occupied seven days, the chief counsel employed being the Attorney General (Sir Thomas Denman) with the Solicitor General (Sir W. Horne) for the prosecution, and Sir James Scarlett (afterwards Lord Abinger) for the defence. The summing up of the judge (Mr. Justice Littledale, in the absence of Lord Tenterden, who was seized with fatal illness during the trial) was criticised by the Liberal press as being rather a speech for the defendant than an impartial comment on the facts; but it was highly lauded by the organs of the Opposition, and was doubtless satisfactory to the jury. They not merely acquitted the defendant, but declared their opinion that circumstanced as he was, "unsupported by any adequate civil or military force, and deserted by those from whom he might reasonably have expected assistance," the mayor "discharged his duty with zeal and personal courage." The Government thereupon withdrew the indictments against the aldermen. Whatever might be the opinion of the Berkshire gentry, however, the ratepayers of Bristol seem to have held strong views as to the conduct of the authorities. Shortly after the riots, at parochial meetings held for the purpose, it was declared that the Corporation had forfeited the confidence of the citizens. A later generation, exempt from the party spirit of those agitated times, can have little difficulty in forming a sound opinion on the subject.

Immediately after the opening of Parliament, in December, 1831, Mr. Protheroe gave notice of his intention to introduce a Bill for altering and amending the charter of the city. The Reform question, however, then exclusively absorbed the attention both of the House of Commons and the country, and it is not improbable that the member for Bristol received a hint that the work of reforming the English corporations was under the consideration of the Government. His scheme was at all events dropped. In the meantime the Corporation, calmly ignoring its unpopularity, promoted a Bill by which it was proposed to establish a police force on the system introduced a year or two previously in London. The chief part of the cost was to be borne by the ratepayers, while the Common Council was practically to have the control of the force. This project being scouted by the public, the authorities proposed that commissioners should be elected by the citizens for the management of the constabulary, and that a stipendiary magistrate should be appointed for the city; towards which purposes they undertook to contribute £1,500 a year providing the remainder were raised by a county rate. The matter was earnestly discussed at meetings of each parish, and delegates were appointed by those gatherings to watch the proceedings of the Common Council in the interest of the ratepayers, the renewed attempt to establish a county rate—which by law would have been assessed by the aldermen —being unanimously condemned as depriving the ratepayers of all control over their money, and as "opening an illimitable field for future taxation." The relations of the rulers and the ruled were not improved by an announcement that the Corporation had commenced an action against the city to recover £25,000, the alleged value of the corporate property destroyed during the riots, and that the imposition of a county rate was contemplated for the purpose of rebuilding Bridewell. The ratepayers' delegates protested strongly against this policy, urging that it ought first to be shown that the civic revenue was insufficient to bear the proposed charge; but the Corporation haughtily denied the alleged liability, and refused to permit the delegates to look into the civic accounts. In answer to the demand for an abandonment of the projected county rate, the authorities availed themselves of a threadbare subtlety. The citizens knew that the magisterial bench was filled exclusively by the aldermen, and that these aldermen were supreme in the Council Chamber. But the Corporation argued that the magistrates had no control over civic affairs, and that if they thought fit to establish a county rate, the Council had no power to restrain them. The controversy was still pending when an apparently self-elected committee of influential inhabitants, nearly all of whom were closely related to members of the Council, announced that they had been allowed to examine the civic account books, and to publish a summary of receipts and expenditure. From this document it appeared that the average ordinary outlay for the seven previous years had been £18,329, against an average income of only £15,474, leaving a deficit of nearly £3,000 per annum. The publication of this statement merely increased public distrust, the ratepayers professing their inability to understand how the Corporation could guarantee a yearly contribution of £1,500 towards the cost of the proposed police, seeing that the civic income was already unable to provide for ordinary expenditure. After further abortive negotiations, the authorities were threatened with "universal passive resistance" against the collection of the contemplated rate, and the opposition of the inhabitants became so formidable that the Bill was abandoned. Another Police Bill had been framed to carry out the views of the ratepayers. But the King's Speech at the opening of the session, after referring with regret to "the scenes of violence and outrage" that had occurred in this city, intimated the wish of the Ministry to improve the municipal police of the kingdom generally, with a view to prevent the recurrence of such commotions, and the local project was therefore withdrawn.

One important legislative scheme affecting the city became law, however, during that stormy session, namely, the Bill to provide for the losses occasioned by the riots—afterwards generally known as the Compensation Act. As originally drawn under the direction of the Common Council, it contained several clauses that were deemed objectionable by the ratepayers—a renewed attempt to insinuate powers for a county rate being especially unpopular. But through the exertions of the parochial delegates referred to in the preceding paragraph, the offensive proposals were removed, and the scheme, as it eventually passed, met with general approval, and worked to the satisfaction of all parties. Under its provisions a board of twelve commissioners, elected by the ratepayers, was empowered to make private arrangements with persons entitled to damages, thus avoiding a great amount of costly litigation. When the commissioners began their labours, no fewer than 121 actions at law had been instituted against the city, the aggregate amount of compensation demanded by the plaintiffs being nearly £150,000. Negotiations were forthwith opened with the claimants, and large reductions were soon effected. The Corporation, which had first estimated its loss at £25,000, and afterwards at about half the amount, consented to accept £5,000. For the destroyed Custom-House and Excise Office the Government had put in a claim for £10,500, but ultimately relinquished its right to compensation. The private suitors, with a single exception, came to terms with the commissioners, the total sum paid in liquidation of their claims being £42,783. The exception was Dr. Gray, the bishop of the diocese. His lordship accepted an offer of £2,040 for the loss of his furniture, but was unyielding in the prosecution of his claim for the destroyed palace, the value of which was estimated by his agents at £10,000. The case came before a jury, empannelled at Bridgwater, when a verdict was given for £6,000, but the city had to bear the heavy costs attending the trial. The net result of the commissioners' labours was to reduce the original total of the compensation claims from £150,000 to £55,824. A sum of £7,424 was, however, expended in legal charges, and £4,960 more in obtaining the Act and carrying it into operation, so that the aggregate charge was £68,208. The immediate liquidation of even the reduced burden would, nevertheless, have been almost impracticable, seeing that it would have necessitated the exaction of a tax equal to nearly ten shillings in the pound on the rateable value of the "ancient city." On an appeal made by the commissioners, the Government proffered a loan of about £58,000, bearing interest at the rate of 2½ per cent., repayments being made in yearly instalments of £10,000. To clear off this annual amount the Corporation of the Poor levied an additional rate of about 1*s.* 6*d.* in the pound. As will be explained hereafter, the passing of the Corporations' Reform Act in 1835, by which Clifton, St. Philip's out-parish, and other populous suburbs were placed under the new municipality, caused a modification of the above arrangement. The commissioners, whose energy and skill effected so sensible a relief to the city, had before that time concluded their labours, their final report bearing date the 11th January, 1835. Their names were: James Wood (for All Saints' Ward); Richard Jones (St. Stephen's); Robert Suple (Trinity); William Herapath (St. James's); William Watson (St. Ewen's); Thomas Carlisle (St. Maryleport); William Evans (Castle Precincts); George Jones (St. Michael's); Benjamin Ogden (St. Nicholas'); John Kerle Haberfield (Redcliff); Edward Kidd (Temple); and Thomas Sanders (St. Thomas's). The committee of parochial delegates, who had so largely contributed to the economy and efficiency of the system adopted, dissolved in September, 1835. Their expenses, during upwards of three years, had been only about £200.

The following were the heaviest claims made against the city—those mentioned above excepted. The amounts actually paid are appended in parentheses:—

P. H. Ashworth, warehouse, etc., King Street, £1,000 (£275); Fulke T. Barnard, furniture, etc., 3, Queen Square, £2,000 (£722); Jesse Barrett, house and furniture, 57, Queen Square, £1,490 (£855); Benjamin Bickley, furniture and stock, 54, Queen Square and Prince's Street, £3,500 (£2,042); Cambridge & Williams, warehouse, etc., Avenue, £1,000 (£400); J. B. & E. W. Clift, warehouse, etc., King Street, £1,290 (£585); Cooke & Turner, stock, behind 51, Queen Square, £1,000 (£327); Thomas Crocker, furniture, 52, Queen

Square, £1,100 (£52); Richard T. Coombe, houses, 6 and 7, Queen Square, and warehouses behind, £2,900 (£2,050); Daniel & Haythorne, house, 51, Queen Square, lofts, etc., £1,500 (£950); Fryer, Gosse & Pack, oil in warehouses, Prince's Street, £1,000 (£793); Joseph S. Fry & Co., cocoa in warehouse, Prince's Street, £6,900 (£2,400); William Gibbons, houses, 54, Queen Square, 4, Prince's Street, and warehouses, £4,000 (£1,752); Martha Harford, house, Excise Avenue, and furniture £1,600 (£908); William Humphries, furniture in gaol, £1,300 (£900); James Johnson, warehouses, King Street, etc., £1,500 (£963); Maria Jones, house, 50, Queen Square, £1,600 (£930); Richard Lambert, two houses, 45, Queen Square, £1,150 (£1,005); Langley & Arding, share in 43, 44, 52, Queen Square, and 9, Prince's Street, £1,700 (£660); Joseph Lax, spirits, etc., in warehouses, King Street, etc., £3,000 (£387); Philip John Miles, house and warehouse, 61, Queen Square, wine, etc., £3,500 (£1,312); Mogg & Bartlett, wine, etc., in warehouse, Avenue, £1,000 (£493); John Morgan, house and warehouse, 3, Queen Square, £1,690 (£1,000); Charles Pinney, china, wine, etc., Mansion House, £2,000 (£714); James Room, furniture and books, 61, Queen Square, £3,000 (£1,172); Henry Rumley, share of house and furniture, 46, Queen Square, £1,779 (£605); Joseph Richardson, furniture, 45, Queen Square, £2,000 (£381); Henry B. Smith, houses and furniture, 59 and 60, Queen Square, £4,649 (£2,938); William C. Stephens, furniture, 53, Queen Square, £1,600 (£309); Thomas Sheppard, furniture, 5, Queen Square, £1,100 (£712); William Strong, furniture, 63, Queen Square, £2,000 (£336); Robert Thomas, shares in 43, 44, 52, Queen Square, and 9, Prince's Street, £1,700 (£285); M. M. J. & E. Vigor, furniture, 6, Queen Square, £1,000 (£450); Thomas Webb & Co., wines, spirits, etc., 4, Queen Square, £2,000 (£652); George Worrall, house, 5, Queen Square, £2,000 (£1,016); John Tilladam, house, 4, Queen Square, £1,000 (abated by plaintiff's death); Samuel Webb, houses, 47 and 48, Queen Square £1,800 (abated by plaintiff's death). The report to which these statistics are appended states that the law prevented claimants from receiving any compensation for articles stolen, when they were carried off and destroyed elsewhere, though these reductions pressed with great hardship on many sufferers. In other cases, abatements were caused by the remission of excise duty on spirits, etc., and it is added: "In justice to the plaintiffs generally, the commissioners expressly state that blame is not imputable to them for the discrepancy between the sums claimed and those accepted."

To the great indignation of many citizens, the Common Council resolved, soon after the riots, upon the establishment of a new Mansion House, for keeping up the convivialities and entertainments previously in vogue. Notwithstanding the financial distress of the city, and the recently avowed embarrassment of the civic treasury, the house in Great George Street already referred to [see page 134], was fitted up and furnished at a heavy cost. [After the reconstruction of the corporate body under the Municipal Reform Act of 1835, the new Mansion House was closed, and the furniture and stock of wine were sold by auction, producing £2,232.] Some attempts at retrenchment were, however, made. At a meeting of the Common Council, in December, 1831, the customary motion to present a butt or pipe of wine to the lord high steward, and another to the members for the city, was negatived, but Sir Charles Wetherell was voted his annual hogshead. In June, 1833, the salary of the mayor was reduced from £2,000 to £1,604, his worship being recommended to curtail the number of his banquets. In 1835, however, a vote of £350, in addition to the usual sum of £400, was passed to Mr. J. N. Franklyn, who had served the office of sheriff a second time. The extra allowance granted to Mr. T. Hassall in 1827, on the same ground, was only £125. Amongst the very numerous items of civic expenditure caused by the riots may be noticed the following: Sundry expenses to April 11, 1832, £1,188, 8*s.* 11*d.*; Tolzey, keeper, for entertaining magistrates during the disturbances, £300; providing accommodation for troops at Armoury, wool hall, warehouse in Thomas Street, and premises [for an hospital] in Great Gardens, rent, gas, etc., £2,293. [The troops remained in these temporary barracks until about September, 1833. The Government refunded £326 8*s.* 11*d.* of the above amount.] Special constables, £437 15*s.*; city solicitor's expenses, £734; subscriptions on behalf of sufferers, whose losses were £30 or under, £500; expenses in connection with the trial of the mayor, £3,871 15*s.* 10*d.*; repairing pictures, £59 12*s.*; Mr. Williams, for repairing the silver salver, £55; law proceedings against inhabitants for compensation, £581.

On December 31, 1831, the old mill on the left bank of the Avon, nearly opposite to the Hotwell House, was destroyed by fire. The building was used in 1761 as a lead smelting-house, but was converted at a later date into a cotton mill, and afterwards to other purposes.

Upon the passing of the Reform Bill, in June, 1832, its local supporters resolved upon a "grand demonstration" to celebrate their triumph. Accordingly, on the 18th June, many thousands of tradesmen and working-men belonging to the city, reinforced by large contingents from St. George's, Bitton, and other districts, assembled at Lawford's Gate, and marched in procession through the principal streets, the artisans of each trade displaying models, emblems, etc., illustrative of their respective crafts, while music and banners lent further animation to the display. The date had probably been fixed upon on account of its being the anniversary of the battle of Waterloo—the yearly return of which was then always hailed with bell ringing. The clergy of the city, however, had been unanimously hostile to the Reform Bill; and they won a small victory over their political opponents by locking up the belfries. On the 14th August the leading Reformers provided a dinner for 5,500 working-men on Brandon Hill. Unfortunately for the success of this affair, a rough mob assembled round the tables and seized upon the viands, causing great tumult and confusion. Some of the fireworks prepared for the evening were also stolen or destroyed.

The Reform Act effected important changes in the city and its constituent body. The boundaries of the borough were largely extended, the parish of Clifton, the district of the out-parishes of St. James and St. Paul, the out-parish of St. Philip, and parts of the parishes of Bedminster and Westbury,—embracing an aggregate population of about 50,000,—being added to the "ancient city." Up to this time the franchise had been enjoyed exclusively by freeholders and freemen, whose right to vote was not impaired by non-residence. Those classes retained their privilege, so far as concerned persons living in, or within seven miles of, the city; and to them were joined all men rated for and occupying premises of the yearly value of £10. The immediate effect of the extensions was less than modern readers might suppose, the population of the suburban parishes being then insignificant as compared with the central mass. Already, however, there was a tendency on the part of both rich and poor to remove to the outlying districts; and before the Reform Act had attained its jubilee, the population of the added parishes was about three times greater than that of the old borough. The register of electors for 1832 contained the names of 5,301 freemen, 862 freeholders, and 4,215 householders.

The passing of the Reform Act necessarily caused a fresh appeal to the constituencies, and a general election took place in December. The victory of the united Liberal party at the previous contest had been followed by a re-opening of the old division in reference to the slavery question. Mr. Baillie at first proposed to retire into private life; but the West India Whigs insisted on his candidature. The anti-slavery Liberals thereupon nominated, in conjunction with Mr. Edward Protheroe, junr. (the former member), Mr. John Williams, an eminent barrister who soon afterwards was raised to the bench, both those gentlemen being ardent advocates of slave emancipation. The Tories found a champion in Sir Richard R. Vyvyan, a Cornish baronet, who had manifested his uncompromising hostility to change by moving the rejection of the Reform Bill. Ultimately a coalition was formed between the supporters of Vyvyan and Baillie. The poll at the close stood as follows: Sir R. R. Vyvyan, 3,695; Mr. Baillie, 3,160; Mr. Protheroe, 3,028; Mr. Williams, 2,739. The result was alleged to have been due to unjustifiable means. The *Bristol Mercury* of the following week published a view of a house (No. 8, King Street) at which bribes were said to have been distributed wholesale to the poorer classes of voters after the poll; whereupon it was jubilantly retorted in the *Bristol Journal* that, according to a decision of the Court of King's Bench, the giving of money to electors after they had voted did not constitute bribery. A number of gentlemen who petitioned against the return undertook to prove that upwards of a thousand electors were paid by the committees of the successful candidates for attendance at the nomination proceedings, and that more than twelve hundred voters received tickets at the "bribery box" in King Street, entitling them to 23*s.* each after polling for Vyvyan and Baillie. A list was also given of twenty-six public houses at which liquor was distributed gratis for some weeks previous to the contest. It was further asserted that a so-called charity, called the Conservative Operatives' Association, had enrolled 1,200 freemen by promising them, in return for their votes, relief when sick or out of work, and 7lb. per head of "blue beef" at Christmas, the funds being provided by certain "honorary" members, whose names remained a secret. No proof, however, was forthcoming that the successful candidates had been privy to corruption, and the return was upheld by a committee of the House of Commons. Mr. Richard Hart Davis, who had refused to be nominated at this election, was soon afterwards presented by his admirers with a service of plate valued at £750.

Indian cholera, which made its way to this country for the first time in 1831, by way of the northern coal ports, gradually spread over the island, to the intense terror of the people, and reached Bristol in the following summer. The first case was reported to have occurred on the 11th July, in Greyhound Court, near the Stone Bridge, a region then reeking with sewage and filth, and rarely free from epidemics. As already stated, the malady worked deadly havoc in the overcrowded wards of St. Peter's poor-house [see p. 139]. The numerous burials in the neighbouring churchyard of St. Philip's appear to have driven many of the poor of the locality out of their senses. A delusion became prevalent that the authorities were burying paupers alive; and on one occasion a mob broke into the burial ground, and tore up some of the recently interred bodies. A similar frantic occurrence took place in Temple churchyard, where thirty-one victims of the disease were buried in a single day. Owing to the crowded state of the parochial cemeteries, a piece of ground was inclosed near the Cattle Market, and those who afterwards died at St. Peter's Hospital were removed there by water, so that the interments might escape public notice. The disease disappeared in October, when there had been 1,521 cases, and 584 deaths. Clifton was almost wholly deserted by the wealthier class of residents during the epidemic. To prevent the influx of strangers, St. James's fair was forbidden to be held this year by an Order in Council. The precaution did not prevent the disease from penetrating into the rural districts, in some of which it was comparatively more fatal than in Bristol. At the village of Paulton, for instance, there were no less than 229 cases in sixteen days, and forty deaths in eight days.

The Corporation resolved during the autumn upon establishing a body of twelve day constables or policemen, after the London model. The wages of the men were fixed at 15*s.* weekly per head, so that the total annual charge, irrespective of clothing, amounted to the modest sum of £468. The night watching continued in the hands of the inefficient old "charleys."

Owing to the great abuses existing in the administration of the poor rates, the Government appointed a Commission to inquire into the subject, and sub-commissioners were directed to make local investigations in various districts. One of those gentlemen, the Rev. H. Bishop, visited Gloucestershire and Bristol, and a few extracts may be given from his report, written on the 22nd September 1832. With respect to Kingswood, it was stated that the miners seldom earned 12*s.* a week. Boys of ten or eleven years earned 4*d.* to 6*d.* a day. "During the summer months women may earn above ground 10*d.* a day; girls from 6*d.* to 8*d.*" Agricultural wages fluctuated between 8*s.* and 12*s.* a week. In Clifton the administration of poor relief was described as profuse and corrupt. "A man who gains 10*s.* or even 20*s.* a week will come, after a few days' indisposition, for relief, and obtains it. . . . The overseers and select vestrymen are very frequently tradesmen enjoying the custom of those who have been lavishly assisted. . . . Those paupers who are in the employment of the parish are paid at a public house, and are expected to promote the 'good of the house' by expending in liquor a portion of their parish earnings. . . . Above the age of fifty the paupers claim permanent relief, which is regarded as a sort of pension, so certain that it may be sold or mortgaged. It is no uncommon thing for apprentices to be receiving relief for three or four children." The writer goes on to detail particular instances of indiscriminate and scandalous waste in the administration of parochial and charitable funds. Abuses also extensively prevailed in Bedminster. The parish contained 14,000 persons, but the rates were made to fall on only 831 householders, and many of these escaped; "the whole weight of local taxation is thrown upon about 330 individuals." Mr. Bishop mentions incidentally that Bristol was then taxed £1,200 a year for paying the passage money of Irish vagrants sent back to their own country, and this charge, he added, did not nearly represent the whole expense which those paupers entailed upon the citizens.

One of the earliest ameliorative measures proposed by Lord Grey's Ministry to the reformed House of Commons was a Bill for the abolition of slavery in the English colonies. Mr. Stanley (afterwards Earl of Derby) explained the scheme on the 14th May, 1833, its chief features being that the slaves should undergo a period of apprenticeship, and that the planters should be granted a loan of £15,000,000 to provide against the loss they might sustain at the outset. To the latter proposal the slave-holding interest in Bristol, as elsewhere, refused to listen; and as the result of the pressure brought to bear on the Ministry, the loan was converted into a gift, and was ultimately raised to £20,000,000. The Act came into force in the colonies on the 1st August, 1834. According to a parliamentary return issued in 1838, the principal firms and persons in this district owning slaves received compensation as follows: Messrs. Thos. & John Daniel, £55,178; Messrs. H. J. D. E. Baillie & G. H. Ames, £23,024; Sir C. Codrington, Bart., £29,867; Mr. James E. Baillie, £12,968; Mr. Philip John Miles, £9,076; Mr. James Cunningham, £12,357; Mr. Richard Bright, £8,092; Mr. Robert Bright, £3,820; Messrs. Charles Pinney & E. Case, £3,572. The list does not include payments under £3,000. The *Bristol Times* of April 8, 1854, stated that Messrs. Daniel & Sons, who had a house in London as well as in Bristol, "obtained not much less than a quarter of a million" in compensation for their slaves.

By this time the country had recovered from the effects of the great panic of 1825–6, while the absurd alarm created amongst the moneyed classes by the concession of the franchise to the trading community had largely passed away. With the return of confidence came a revival of the railway projects which had come to grief seven years before. About the close of 1832, when the shares of the Liverpool and

Manchester railway were selling at double, and those of the Stockton and Darlington line at treble, their original cost, a few public-spirited Bristolians resolved upon making a renewed effort for the construction of a railway to London. There is a tradition that the Great Western Company was projected in a small office in Temple Backs. However that may be, it is certain that Messrs. George Jones, John Harford, T. R. Guppy, and William Tothill were the most energetic in promoting the undertaking. Animated by their appeals, in January, 1833, the Corporation, the Merchant Venturers' Society, the Dock Company, and the Bristol and Gloucestershire railway company severally appointed three gentlemen, empowering them to inquire into the best mode of procedure, and furnishing them with funds for the purpose. This committee* directed Mr. J. K. Brunel and Mr. Townsend to make a survey of the country, and in a few months elaborate plans were produced by the two engineers, who estimated the cost of the undertaking at the modest sum of £2,805,000. On the 30th July a meeting was held in the Guildhall to evoke the sympathy of the citizens. The promoters urged that if the advantages of cheapness and speed which railways offered should only double the existing carriage traffic the line would yield a clear yearly profit of about 14 per cent. Though the response of the public does not appear to have been very enthusiastic, the company was soon after formed, the title of "Great Western" being assumed in the following September. One half of the directors were nominated by London capitalists; the other moiety were Bristolians, whose names and subscriptions were as follows: Robert Bright, £25,900; John Cave, £17,900; Henry Bush, £8,000; C. B. Fripp, £15,500; George Jones, £20,000; Peter Maze, £23,000; Fred. Ricketts, £10,000; William Tothill, £14,000; John Vining, £11,500; Charles L. Walker, £6,000; George Gibbs, £14,000; Thomas R. Guppy, £14,900; John Harford, £11,900; William S. Jacques, £12,000; James Lean, £1,000; Nicholas Bush, £11,900. A Bill authorising the construction of two sections of the line—from London (where the station was originally fixed at Vauxhall and afterwards at Brompton)

* Some of the members of this committee possessed so remarkable a foresight into the future of railways that it deserves to be noted as unique in that generation. They recommended that a quadruple line of rails be laid down, "two lines for light carriages to convey passengers at a rapid pace, and two for heavier vehicles carrying goods at a slower rate," the advantage of which arrangement, "as a means of preventing both delays and accidents, is too obvious to be insisted upon."—*Common Council Minutes, Feb.* 1833.

to Reading, and from Bristol to Bath—was laid before Parliament in 1834. Railway projects, however, were exceedingly unpopular amongst the aristocracy and landed gentry. Lord Eldon's last speech and vote in the Upper House were against what he called "the dangerous invention of railways," and the old Tory chief found many of kindred views amongst his hearers. The country squire, again, dreaded danger to his game, farmers were afraid that the smoke of the locomotives would injure the wool of their sheep, and breeders of horses predicted that they would be ruined if coaches and posting carriages were superseded. In addition to the rural clamour against railways generally, the Great Western Bill was resisted by the canal companies and turnpike trusts of the district, and encountered formidable opposition from the authorities of Eton College, who alleged that the line would excite revolutionary ideas in the minds of the schoolboys. After an obstinate struggle of fifty-seven days in committee, the Bill passed the House of Commons by a small majority, but it was rejected in the Lords by 47 votes against 30. Public opinion, however, became rapidly converted to the arguments in favour of the new mode of travelling, and the company's second Bill, authorising the construction of the trunk line and branches to Bradford and Trowbridge, with some modifications to soothe Eton and squirearchal susceptibilities, received the royal assent in August, 1835. A competing scheme, which proposed a railway from Bath to Basing, was rejected; and an attempt made in the House of Commons by Mr. (afterwards Sir William) Miles to prevent Great Western trains from running on Sundays was defeated by a large majority. The parliamentary campaign during the two years cost the company £90,000. The line, as sanctioned by the legislature, was to join the London and Birmingham railway near Acton, whence the trains were to run to the station of the latter undertaking in Euston Square, London; but the Great Western board subsequently resolved on having an independent terminus at Paddington, for which powers were obtained in the session of 1837. The land for the station at Bristol was purchased of the Corporation for £12,000. Operations having been vigorously prosecuted at both ends of the system, the section from London to Maidenhead was opened in May, 1838, and that from Bristol to Bath on the 3rd July following. Intermediate sections were completed from time to time, and finally, on the 30th January, 1841, the line was opened throughout, and the coaches, which had formed so striking a feature both of town and country life, disappeared. (In October, 1837, there were twenty-two coaches running daily between Bristol and London, and twenty-seven others passed between this city and Bath every twenty-four hours.) One coach, however, obstinately held its ground in spite of the railway, continuing to carry passengers from and to London and Bristol, at the rate of a penny per mile, until October, 1843. Perhaps the wretched accommodation afforded on the new line to second and third class passengers may have partially accounted for this sustained opposition. For several years the only trains carrying third class passengers from Bristol started at four o'clock in the morning and nine o'clock at night, offering the travellers —who were wholly unprotected from the weather—an alternative of miseries. What is more surprising, the second class carriages, down to May, 1845, were also open to the elements, both as regards roof and sides, and according to a statement in a contemporary newspaper, were "dangerous not only to health but to life." In the year 1844, to the intense wrath of the railway interest, Parliament insisted on covered carriages being provided for third class travellers at the rate of a penny per mile; but the boards revenged themselves by inventing a "horse-box" for the obnoxious caste, and by reducing the speed of the cheap trains to twelve miles an hour. The first of these trains on the Great Western line started on the 1st November, 1844, the journey from Bristol to London being timed at nine hours and a half.* A history of the Great Western Railway is not within the province of this work, but a few facts concerning an enterprise so closely connected with the city may not be out of place. The time has long passed away since there was any difference of opinion as to the deplorable error of the original board in neglecting the sober-minded, practical, and economical engineers of the North, already deservedly famous, and in preferring to them an inexperienced theorist, enamoured of novelty, prone to seek for difficulties rather than to evade them, and utterly indifferent as to the outlay which his recklessness entailed upon his employers. The evil consequences of his pet crotchet, the "broad gauge" system, on the commerce of Bristol will have to be noticed hereafter. For the present it will suffice to show the fallaciousness of Mr.

* The commercial classes were so dissatisfied with the charges imposed on the transit of goods that in 1855 a steamer, called the *Pioneer*, was built for the purpose of trading between London and Bristol. The vessel plied regularly until February, 1865, when it was wrecked off Penzance. The average passage was made in sixty-eight hours, equal to ten miles an hour.

Brunel's estimates. The original share capital was fixed by his advice at £2,500,000. Before the line to London was completed, the directors had to ask for votes bringing up the expenditure to £6,300,000, which did not include any part of the outlay for the permanent station at Paddington. In 1844 this vast sum was increased to £8,160,000, inclusive of loans. As may be suspected from the figures, the directors were even more imprudent than was their subordinate. For several successive years there seemed to be no limit to their aggressive designs. In 1845 they obtained Acts for making no less than 574 miles of new railways; and in November, 1847, their notices of intended applications for Acts in the following session are said to have numbered forty-seven. That the war against rival companies—possibly quite as pugnacious—was carried on for many years with unflagging pertinacity is sufficiently proved by the fact that between 1851 and 1855 alone the board spent an aggregate sum of £188,421 in legal and parliamentary expenses. Nor was this the worst. The lines constructed in the neighbourhood of Oxford, Birmingham, Dudley, etc., in rivalry with the North-Western Company, and consequently unprofitable, cost £6,600,000, while the unfruitful Shropshire lines, competing with the same undertaking, required an additional capital of £3,300,000. In the meantime, Bristol proprietors complained that an undertaking intended to develop the trade and industry of their own city and district was recklessly squandering its resources in the construction of vast works at Plymouth, Milford Haven, and Birkenhead. The consequences of this policy were such as might have been expected. In its early days the Great Western board was able to declare a dividend at the rate of 10 per cent. per annum, and the shares, when only £80 were paid up, were quoted in the market at 236. On the other hand, the directors' report for the first six months of 1858 recommended that no dividend should be declared. The subsequent meeting at Bristol (the last held in the city, whose moiety of directors had already vanished) was of a stormy character, the exasperation of the shareholders being increased by the fact that during the previous half year, when the dividend was only 5*s.* per share, the board had carried a grant of £5,000 to the secretary, Mr. Saunders, who had previously received a similar present, though his salary was £2,500 a year. In July, 1862, the accounts showed that the net profits of the previous six months had been only £992, but a reserve brought forward produced a dividend of 5*s.* per cent. Affairs improved in the following years; but for the last half of 1866 the dividend was only 10*s*. per cent. The embarrassment, it transpired, arose from a floating debt of about £1,250,000, which the board had allowed to grow up, and upon which the interest for the first half of the year had averaged £8 7*s*. per cent. per annum. The directors appealed to the Government and to the Bank of England for the loan of a million to clear off pressing obligations, but the relief was refused. An appeal was then vainly made to the shareholders to take up a six per cent. stock, to prevent the company from being thrown into liquidation; and as a last resource, the board issued six per cent. bonds for the amount of preferential interest then due. These were offered in the Stock Exchange at the rate of 16*s*. in the pound, the shares of the company being quoted for a considerable period at 40, and sometimes lower—a memorable example of the results of reckless management on a substantial and once prosperous concern. Happily the lesson was not wasted on the board, and the company have since enjoyed a career of continuous prosperity. As has been already stated, the original capital was under three millions; it is now [1887] upwards of seventy-six millions. The line first sanctioned by Parliament was 114 miles in length; the board have now upwards of 2,350 miles under their control, while the employés, a mere handful at the outset, now number little short of 30,000.

The conflict which began in 1823 between the mercantile interest of the city and the Corporation, in reference to the heavy charges imposed by the latter on the commerce of the port, has been recorded in a previous page. It will be remembered that after a struggle of two years, the Common Council had to be content with obtaining an Act authorising it to reduce the civic dues, the clause conferring a parliamentary title on those imposts being struck out in the House of Commons at the instance of the Chamber of Commerce. The concessions made under this statute proved insufficient to bring back the trade which had been blindly driven away; and in the hope of securing a larger measure of relief, Mr. Henry Bush, one of the leaders of local Toryism, supported by many influential firms, refused to pay the town dues, thus challenging the Corporation to prove their legality in a court of law. The case was heard before Lord Chief Justice Tenterden, in the Court of King's Bench, in July, 1828. The judge, who had a superstitious reverence for privilege and prerogative, was alleged by the mercantile party to have acted throughout the hearing rather as a counsel for the Corporation than as an impartial expounder of the law. He summed up, according to the newspaper reporter, "decidedly in favour" of the plaintiffs; and the jury, submitting to his influence, gave the verdict he desired. But although the Common Council exulted over this affirmation of a dubious title, its members can scarcely have seen without misgivings the gradual and continuous decline of the shipping trade of the port. The value of English goods exported from Bristol, which had been £315,000 in 1822, sank in 1833 to £205,000; the once magnificent fleet of foreign-going ships belonging to the city was reduced in number to about thirty; whilst the warehouses, once filled with produce, offered accommodation so much in excess of the demand that their formerly prosperous owners could not realise one per cent. on the capital invested in the buildings. The depression in fact became so severe that it provoked another agitation against the port charges, the Chamber of Commerce again taking the lead by forwarding memorials to the Corporation and the Dock Company, pressing for a mitigation of the burdens. The dock directors were the first to acknowledge the reasonableness of the complaints; and in July, 1834, reductions were announced in the dock dues on certain classes of goods. The concessions, however, were regarded by the suffering interests as illusory, the commodities relieved producing but a small revenue, while, so far as concerned the chief branches of local commerce, the dock rates still exceeded those of Liverpool to the extent of about 50 per cent. on sugar, 70 per cent. on tobacco, 157 per cent. on wine, 200 per cent. on foreign spirits, and 1,100 per cent. on wool. The dues were still more oppressive as regarded foreign goods imported coastwise; for, whilst the Liverpool authorities contented themselves with half the rates imposed on direct foreign imports, the Bristol board imposed the full rates. According to another table published by the Chamber of Commerce, showing the comparative charges on all the leading articles of import, the duties at Bristol were 20*s.* as compared with 11*s.* 5*d.* at Liverpool, 7*s.* 3*d.* at Hull, and 6*s.* 2*d.* at Gloucester. The Dock Company, nevertheless, refused to grant any further relief, urging in excuse that the shareholders were receiving less than 2¼ per cent. per annum in dividends, and held a deaf ear to the retort that the inadequate profits were the natural fruit of unreasonable exactions. The pressure placed on the Corporation had more satisfactory results. One of the last important acts of the unreformed Common Council was to order a large reduction in the town dues, which were wholly abolished as regarded exports. Unhappily the latter concession was not made until the export trade of the city had almost disappeared, the civic receipts from this source in the previous year having been only £466. Concurrently with these remissions, the Common Council abolished the tolls on fish, which were obnoxious to fishermen yet practically unproductive. The mayor claimed one hundred oysters from each oyster boat, and six mackerel, a pair of soles, and twelve herrings from each fishing boat. The sheriffs had fifty oysters from each cargo. Nearly the whole of the fish collected were distributed amongst the petty officials of the corporate body.

It had been understood throughout the agitation of 1831–2 that one of the first efforts of a reorganised House of Commons would be directed to the reconstitution of the municipal corporations of the country,—most of which, for more than a century, had been the object of widespread complaint—and the establishment of a system of local government based on the opinions and interests of the urban community. With a view to these ends, a royal commission was issued in the summer of 1833, to inquire into the constitution and working of the existing bodies. Twenty gentlemen, for the most part experienced barristers, were chosen for this purpose, and in order to hasten the proceedings, the corporations in England and Wales were divided into nine territorial districts, in which investigations took place simultaneously. The formation of this tribunal excited violent indignation amongst the class who had monopolised authority in many towns. Protests were raised against what was styled "the Radical Inquisition," and the Corporations of Dover, Lichfield, and a few other notoriously misgoverned places, set the commissioners at defiance, denying the legality of their powers, and refusing them access to the civic archives. This course was also followed by the Merchant Venturers' Society of this city, and by the Bristol Dock Company. In a great majority of cases, however, the municipal bodies, though exceedingly irritated at being called upon to render an account of their proceedings, prudently submitted to the royal request. The commissioners allotted to this district, Mr. E. J. Gambier and Mr. J. E. Drinkwater, opened their court at Bristol on the 7th October, and continued their sittings until the 2nd November. The complaints of the inhabitants against the Corporation were laid before the commissioners by Messrs. Visger, Manchee, Thomas, and other prominent members of the Liberal party, while the Common Council was defended by the town clerk (Mr. Serjeant Ludlow), Messrs. Brice & Burges, and other officials, who afforded every facility to the visitors during the progress of the inquiry. The proceedings were miserably reported in the local newspapers, but it appears that the chief grievances adduced against the corporate body were, that it was constituted on the closest principles of self-election, that the members, bound together by an oath of secrecy, claimed to be irresponsible in administering the large public revenues entrusted to them by the city charters, that they refused to produce accounts, that, as was natural under such circumstances, their transactions had been frequently marked with mismanagement and extravagance, and that the declining prosperity of the port was largely due to their neglectful and mischievous conduct as conservators, and to their imposition of taxes on shipping and goods for which they made no beneficial return. Offices in the gift of the Common Council were, it was alleged, often filled by decayed members of the body, or by relations and connections. The legal jurisdiction of the aldermen extended to life and death, but it was shown that, although the residence of those functionaries in the city was compulsory under the charters, only the mayor and one alderman lived in Bristol, while the town clerk, with a salary of £1,000 a year, was a practising barrister in London.* The result of those abuses, it was asserted, had been to excite and perpetuate a general distrust and contempt of the magistracy, and to taint with suspicion the administration of justice. With regard to the great charity funds vested in the Corporation, it was complained that large sums of money were distributed under the recommendation of the parish churchwardens, themselves chosen by self-elected vestries, and acting at parliamentary elections as canvassers and local managers of the party to which most of the members of the Common Council were attached. Much dissatisfaction was expressed at the management of the Grammar School and of Queen Elizabeth's Hospital. Finally, it was declared that the establishment maintained by the Corporation, consisting of upwards of forty salaried officers, was not merely overgrown and expensive, but inefficient; that the civic pomp assumed amidst declining prosperity was idle and unseemly, and that the confession wrung from the officials of a heavy debt offered convincing evidence of the evil system that had prevailed.

* The commissioners do not seem to have been aware that Serjeant Ludlow also held the office of auditor to the Duke of Beaufort.

The net result of that system was alleged to be, that the Corporation was generally distrusted and unpopular, the desertion of the authorities by the ratepayers at the time of the riots being adduced as an unmistakable proof of the feeling inspiring all classes. From the report drawn up by the two commissioners, it may be inferred that they regarded this indictment as substantiated. It had been shown, they said, by accounts which the Corporation produced for the first time in the previous year, that the civic expenditure had been for a long period in excess of the receipts, the bonded redeemable debt having increased from £5,140 in 1825, to £54,949 in 1833. That much of the outlay was unnecessary was regarded as proved by the fact that when the Corporation attempted to carry their Police Bill through Parliament in 1832, they promised to effect such retrenchments as would permit them not merely to establish a financial equilibrium, but to grant £1,500 a year towards the maintenance of the police. The commissioners commented severely upon the transaction by which the Corporation, about half a century previously, had handed over the wharfage dues—popularly supposed to produce some £2,000 a year—to the Merchant Venturers' Company, on a lease for 99 years, for the trivial consideration of £10 per annum. The police arrangements of the city were stated to be utterly insufficient even in the central districts, while no protection whatever existed in the southern and eastern suburbs. As to paving and lighting, the Corporation denied that such matters came within their province. In their concluding "general remarks," the two commissioners observed that the Corporation of Bristol offered a very unfavourable specimen of the results of self-election and irresponsibility. Although there had been no improper appropriation of public funds, the Corporation could not be acquitted of mismanagement and profusion. In the face of a sinking and overburdened trade, its large resources had been unprofitably squandered in the maintenance of an overgrown establishment and in the display of state magnificence. Its ruling principle had been the desire of power, and each of its applications to Parliament to extend or prop up its privileges had become a topic of general discontent. So intense a spirit of opposition and distrust had been aroused, that it seemed doubtful whether an act of real liberality on the part of the governing body would not arouse suspicion and reproach. As owners and guardians of the port, the conduct of the Corporation was condemned as indefensible. They had suffered burdensome charges of every description to be accumulated upon trade, of which they were the last to see the impolicy, and had placed out of their own control—for a nominal consideration—a heavy and oppressive tax, which in its beginning was at least applied to the purposes of the harbour. They had procured a parliamentary title for their lessees, from whom they could demand no account, and had suffered the tax, imposed for public services, to be absorbed in paying the debts, incurred in other speculations, of those who now claimed to be a private and irresponsible company. "We are informed," added the commissioners, "that the same political party has not always held the ascendency in the Council House. We should not seek for a stronger proof that the fault is inherent in the system itself." [For further details the reader is referred to the Appendix to the First Report of the Municipal Corporations' Commissioners.]

The Kingsweston estate, late the property of Lord de Clifford, deceased, was purchased in July, 1833, by Mr. Philip John Miles, of Leigh Court, for £210,000. Sir R. Southwell, Lord de Clifford's ancestor, bought the estate shortly before the Revolution from its former owners, the Hookes, a family long connected with Bristol. The story to be found in some local histories, to the effect that a walled-up room (shut up during the civil wars) was discovered in the mansion during the last century, containing records of a barony granted to the Southwell family by Henry III., is therefore untrustworthy.

During the summer of 1833 the trustees of the Bristol turnpikes, with a view to improving the chief southern entrance to the city, caused a deep cutting to be made at Totterdown, near the junction of the Wells road with that from Bath. A very steep hill there, much disliked by stage coachmen, was thus practically removed. A similar improvement was effected at the same time near Clifton church, a new road being cut in front of Goldney House.

The death was announced, on the 7th September, of Hannah More, who expired at her house in Windsor Terrace, aged 88, having outlived not only all the celebrated literary friends of her youth, but, to a certain extent, her once considerable reputation as an author. Her funeral was of a private character, only four mourning coaches and as many private carriages following the hearse to Wrington, where the sisters of the deceased had been already interred. There being no near relatives surviving, Mr. J. S. Harford and Mr. J. Gwatkin acted as chief mourners. Miss More, after making many charitable bequests, left the residue of her estate (about £3,000) to the church of Trinity, St. Philip's. Extensive parochial schools in the neighbourhood of the church were erected by subscription in 1838–9, and dedicated to her memory.

The Bristol Medical School began its first session on the 14th October. The institution, first located in King Square, but removed to Old Park in 1834, was founded upon two private schools which had been in existence for some years —one of which has been already noticed in connection with a ghastly story [see p. 100].

In February, 1834, the Common Council appointed the sixth Duke of Beaufort Lord High Steward of Bristol, in the place of Lord Grenville, deceased. His grace held the office for only a brief period, having died in November, 1835. His son, the seventh duke, was shortly afterwards elected to the vacant dignity.

Amongst several sales of property effected by the Corporation about this time, the well-known island in the Bristol Channel—the Steep Holmes—was disposed of to Colonel Tynte, of Cefn Mably, Glamorganshire.

In the early months of 1834 the Rev. Francis Edgeworth, then officiating at St. Joseph's Chapel, Trenchard Street, the only Roman Catholic place of worship in the city, resolved upon the erection of a gigantic church in the classical style, to be dedicated to the Holy Apostles. Having purchased a field lying to the east of a large quarry called Honeypen Hill (on which Meridian Place then looked), the foundation stone of the intended edifice was laid in October, and the mason-work slowly progressed for some years. In the meanwhile a small chapel was built within the area, and Mass was performed there in 1842. Unfortunately for the reverend promoter, two or three landslips took place, and his pecuniary difficulties became at last so serious that operations were suspended. Father Edgeworth, declared a bankrupt, fled to Belgium (where he died in 1850), and the unfinished building was in June, 1844, advertised for sale by auction. Although saved from this fate by the exertions of the faithful, the fabric long remained in a state of semi-ruin. In 1847, Bishop Ullathorne purchased the land and building from the mortgagees for £2,500; but it was not until 1848, when all hope of completing the church according to the original plan was abandoned, that a portion was fitted up for worship. The opening ceremony, marked with the customary pomp of the Romish Church, took place on the 21st September, the officiating prelates being Bishops Hendren and Ullathorne, the existing and previous vicars-general of the western district. A convent and chapel dedicated to St. Catherine of Sienna, for the use of nuns of the order of St. Dominic, were added in 1849. The church was termed a pro-cathedral after the revival of the English episcopate by Pius IX. in 1850, and shortly afterwards a mansion of mediæval design was erected near it for the "Bishop of Clifton." Several years later an eastern extension of the church was made in an incongruous Lombardic style. One of the most stately ceremonials that have taken place in the "pro-cathedral" occurred in February, 1855, on the death of the bishop at Plymouth, when a chapter was held, under the presidency of Cardinal Wiseman, for the selection of three ecclesiastics worthy of the Pope's consideration in filling the vacancy.

During the session of 1834, a measure for the amendment of the poor laws passed both Houses of Parliament, and received the royal assent. At the instance of the Bristol Incorporation of the Poor, that body, and a few others of the same character, were permitted to retain the privileges granted them under their special Acts; but this exemption, as will be recorded under the year 1857, was subsequently withdrawn. One effect of the Poor Law Reform Act was to constitute the "Clifton Union," including, besides several rural parishes, Clifton itself, the parishes of Westbury and Horfield, the district of St. James and St. Paul, and the out-parish of St. Philip*—all forming part of the municipal borough of Bristol. The parish of Bedminster, similarly situated, and several other parishes in Somerset, formed another new union, called after Bedminster. The title of "union" given to the confederations was somewhat of a

* Each parish, up to this time, had provided relief for the poor in its own way—which was generally a bad one. In 1823 the authorities of Winterbourne offered the poor of that parish "to be let by tender" for a year to any person willing to "farm" them (*Bristol Journal*, August 30). In June, 1835, Mr. C. Mott, Assistant Poor Law Commissioner, visited St. Philip's workhouse, in Pennywell Road, and reported on it in these terms:—"I was ill-prepared to find in a parish with nearly 17,000 inhabitants, expending annually £6,000 for the support of the poor, and immediately adjoining one of the most cleanly and well-ventilated establishments in England (St. Peter's Hospital), such a disgraceful instance of neglect and mismanagement. The state of the workhouse was filthy in the extreme; the appearance of the inmates dirty and wretched. There was no classification, men, women, and children being indiscriminately huddled together." A dismal filthy room, as dirty as a coal cellar, contained, he added, a poor distressed lunatic as dirty as the floor, clothed in rags, and with feet protruding through his shoes. The poor creature had never quitted the den for years. Another room contained a young lunatic, almost in a state of nudity, who had been detained there for four years.

misnomer, for each parish continued to defray the cost of its out-door poor. As a necessary consequence the local rates varied considerably, and the anomalies appeared the more unjust inasmuch as the taxation was lowest where the inhabitants were wealthy, and highest where the ratepayers were least able to endure the burden. For example, in Bedminster, in 1849, the yearly charge was nearly 5*s*. in the pound on the rental, while in Westbury it was 7½*d*., and in Clifton only 7*d*. In 1858 an agitation was started for amalgamating all the suburban parishes with the Bristol union, but the movement was unsuccessful, and though it has been revived in later years it has hitherto met with no better success. The passing of the Union Chargeability Act, however, did much to remove the previous inequalities in local taxation.

The prospectus of the West of England and South Wales District Banking Company was published in August. The shares—50,000 of £20 each—having been subscribed for, the bank opened its central office on the 29th December in the Exchange, Bristol, branches being also established at Bath, Bridgwater, Taunton, Exeter, Barnstaple, Newport, Cardiff, and Swansea. In 1854 the directors purchased and demolished the once great coaching hostelry, the Bush, opposite to the Exchange, together with some adjoining houses, and built on the site a remarkably ornate edifice, in the Venetian style, the cost of the site and building exceeding £40,000. The new bank was opened for business in February, 1857. A local paper stated that the Corporation of the Poor assessed the building at £2,000 per annum, which was £50 more than the assessment of all the other bank premises in the city put together

For some years previous to this date, the Court of Aldermen, which had the management of the Red Maids' School, seems to have been much exercised as to the desirability of removing the institution from the old premises in Denmark Street. Complaints had been made as to the inconvenience of the building, but the governors, in November, 1830, resolved that it was inexpedient to alter the site, and plans were soon after approved for reconstructing the house. Three months later the position of the school was condemned; and in September, 1831, it was resolved to buy part of the property in Great George Street which had been acquired for a Mansion House [see p. 134]. The matter then dropped out of sight until March, 1833, when the last motion was rescinded, and it was again determined to rebuild on the old site, if the adjoining premises could be obtained for an extension. This condition having turned out to be impracticable, the Common Council in the following September sold 1 acre and 22 poles of Tyndall's Park (part of "King's Orchard"), belonging to the Corporation, to Whitson's trustees for the new school.* The authorities then selected a design of an imposing and expensive character, and building operations had proceeded for some time when the progress of the Municipal Reform Bill suggested the desirability of suspending operations. Nothing further was done until the appointment of the Charity Trustees, who made an inquiry in January, 1837, and discovered that the cost of the school buildings and site would be nearly £17,000, a sum which could not be raised except by disposing of part of the hospital estates, and permanently reducing the income of the charity. A few months later the trustees had under consideration a project for removing the City School to the spot in question, but this scheme was also rejected. The property was at length sold to Bishop Monk, for the purposes of the Bishop's College [see p. 141]. The Charity Trustees rebuilt the school in Denmark Street in 1842.

The new Blind Asylum, adjoining the intended Red Maids' School, was also progressing in 1834, the remainder of the King's Orchard having been purchased of the Corporation for £1,850. The asylum was founded in 1792 by a few Quaker philanthropists, the manager and secretary being Messrs. Fox and Bath. Until 1803 it was located in a disused Quaker meeting-house in Callowhill Street; but the building, together with adjoining premises called the Dove House [the columbarium of the ancient friary?], was then offered for sale (*Felix Farley's Bristol Journal*, March 3), and the asylum was removed to Lower Maudlin Street, where it remained until its present habitation was finished. The chapel erected for the use of the inmates, and also designed to serve as a chapel-of-ease to St. Michael's, was opened on the 20th November, 1838. At a meeting held after the inaugural service, it was stated that the new asylum had cost £15,000, and the chapel £5,000. A new wing was added to the asylum in January, 1883.

With some appreciation of the signs of the times, the

* The price fixed was £1,270. Some want of forethought was shown in the transaction. The thoroughfare in front of the plot was too narrow for the traffic; and some years later, when the Council wished to buy a narrow slip of the land to widen Queen's Road, the Rifles' Headquarters Company, who had become the owners, asked £600 for a few square yards.

Common Council gave an order during the year to Mr. Pickersgill, R.A., to paint the portrait of Alderman Daniel, to commemorate the long connection of that gentleman with civic affairs. Excepting four individuals, the entire body of aldermen and common councillors owed their position in the municipality to the influence or passive assent of the autocrat of the Corporation; and seeing that the balance due to their bankers exceeded £10,000, it would have been creditable to the authorities if their manifestation of gratitude had come out of their own pockets. In December, however, the artist received 150 guineas for his picture, and the alderman was paid his expenses in journeying to London to sit for it—£24 8*s*. 3*d*.

A general election occurred unexpectedly in January, 1835, owing to the summary dismissal of Lord Melbourne's Ministry by William IV. The result in Bristol, as in many other places, indicated a marked reaction in favour of the Tory party—now first called Conservatives. At the formal nomination of candidates, that party, desirous of avoiding a contest, put forward only Sir Richard R. Vyvyan. But in consequence of the Liberals unexpectedly proposing two gentlemen—Mr. J. E. Baillie and Sir John Cam Hobhouse (son of a candidate of 1796, a Bristolian by birth, and a member of the two previous Ministries), Mr. P. J. Miles was brought forward as a second "blue" candidate, without being formally nominated before the sheriff. Both the Conservative nominees were triumphantly returned, the numbers being: Mr. Miles, 3,709; Sir R. R. Vyvyan, 3,312; Mr. Baillie, 2,520; Sir J. C. Hobhouse, 1,808. Two Tory candidates had not been elected simultaneously since 1780.

In April, 1835, the monopoly of the China trade, previously held by the East India Company, having been abolished by Parliament, a cargo of tea was brought into Bristol direct from Canton. An attempt was afterwards made to establish a Bristol Tea Company, with a capital of half a million, for the purpose of carrying on an extensive trade with the Celestial Empire; but the project met with slender encouragement from local tea merchants, and was dropped. A few more cargoes were afterwards imported by the same firm—Messrs. Acraman, Bush, Castle & Co.—who built extensive warehouses in Prince's Street especially for this trade. Subsequently a London merchant named Robertson continued for some time to import tea by way of Bristol. Grocers, however, preferred to follow the old ruts of the trade, and Mr. Robertson's enterprise proving unprofitable, it was discontinued in 1843.

A charge of murder, which had caused intense excitement in the city, was opened at the assizes on the 10th April, 1835, and occupied the court two days. The case was tried before Sir Charles Wetherell, recorder, who had not held an assize since the riots in 1831. It appeared that on the 23rd October, 1833, an elderly woman named Clara Ann Smith, who had lodged for some time with one Mary Ann Burdock, the occupier of a lodging-house in College Street, suddenly died. The relatives of the deceased, having had no tidings from her for upwards of a year, at last made inquiries, and finding that Mrs. Burdock would not give a satisfactory account of her death, or of the considerable property which she was known to have possessed, application was made to the police, and the body was disinterred fourteen months after the burial. Identification was difficult after such a lapse of time, but two fellow lodgers of the deceased swore to certain marks on the stockings, and the undertaker proved that he had supplied the coffin. The stomach was thereupon handed to Mr. Herapath, who discovered that it contained arsenic, and three medical witnesses testified that the quantity of poison detected was sufficient to cause death. The purchase of arsenic by a person in Burdock's house also came to light, as well as the fact that Mrs. Burdock had alone administered food to the deceased, and had cautioned a servant not to eat of what remained after each meal. It further transpired that the murdered woman had received £800 shortly before her demise, and that Burdock became suddenly rich after that event. Other circumstantial evidence pressing against the woman was adduced, and, the jury having found her guilty, she was sentenced to be hanged. Her subsequent indifference to her fate was another strange feature in the case. She ordered her brother not to spend more than £2 upon her coffin, which she desired to have by her bedside on the night before her execution, and she gave especial directions to be provided with a "warm, comfortable shroud." The wretched woman was hanged at the gaol on the 15th April, in the presence, it was computed, of 50,000 spectators.

St. Matthew's Church, Kingsdown, which had just been finished at a cost of about £7,900, including a sum set apart for the endowment, was consecrated by Dr. Ryder, Bishop of Lichfield, on the 23rd April. A peal of eight bells, the gift of Mr. John Bangley, a liberal contributor to the church, was subsequently placed in the tower. In July, 1882, Mr. George Gay, builder, presented the parish with a handsome villa and garden in Cotham Park, for the use of the vicar and his successors.

Brunswick Square Chapel, built at a cost of £5,000 by some seceders from the congregation of Castle Green Chapel, was opened in May, when a sermon was preached by the Rev. Dr. Raffles, of Liverpool. The first marriage celebrated in a dissenting place of worship in Bristol took place in this building shortly after the passing of the Marriage Act of 1837.

The Corporation cash-book contains the following item dated the 14th May: "Paid John Willis for various embazonments (*sic*) to embellish the Mayors' Kalendar, £23 15*s*." The payment can refer only to the coats of arms which have been placed against the names of many of the mayors and sheriffs of later times—often, it may be suspected, at the fantasy of the illuminator.

The new Bridewell, entirely rebuilt after the deplorable events of 1831, was finished in July, 1835, at a cost of £7,800. The new prison was constructed entirely on the northern side of Bridewell Lane. The ground on the opposite side,—on which the old Bridewell chiefly stood,—was a few years later made available for a central police station. In 1842 it was reported that the prison was deficient in accommodation, there being 100 prisoners confined in it, whilst the cells were constructed to contain only 56. The Council subsequently resolved to enlarge the building, and appropriated some adjacent void ground for the purpose. The alterations cost the city upwards of £4,000. The abolition of the prison will be recorded under a later date.

After having been for some time contemplated by a few public-spirited citizens, the Bristol and Clifton Zoological Gardens Society was definitely established in July, 1835, the capital being in the first instance fixed at £7,500 in £25 shares. It was originally proposed to lay out a garden at Pyle Hill, Bedminster, where a plot of ten acres was actually purchased, and planting commenced. A change of plans, however, took place, and the present site—about twelve acres—having been purchased of Mr. F. Adams for £3,456, about £5,300 more were spent in laying out the ground and erecting the necessary buildings. The gardens were opened to the public on the 11th July, 1836. According to the original proposal, annual subscribers were admitted into the grounds on Sundays, in common with the proprietors. A section of the latter, a few years later, endeavoured to close the gardens entirely on that day, but met with a decisive defeat. On directing their attack against those who had no votes, however, they were quite successful, a resolution depriving the subscribers of their former privilege being adopted in April, 1841. Forty-five years later, in April, 1886, the society returned to its original policy, a vote to admit subscribers on Sundays being carried with only one dissentient voice.

During this year a monument to the memory of Dr. Gray, Bishop of Bristol, who died on the 28th September, 1834, was erected in the cathedral at a cost of £260.

The last of the few public improvements effected by the old Corporation, whose extinction is about to be recorded, were made in the autumn of 1835. Maudlin Lane was widened, by pulling down some old houses and removing the small inclosures which stood in front of others. A more important work was effected in Bridewell Lane, by opening through it a street from Nelson Street to the Horse Fair, covering over part of the Froom, and pulling down some old dwellings which contracted the thoroughfare. The total cost was about £3,000. The dean and chapter about the same time improved the appearance of the cathedral by removing some ugly houses adjoining the west end of the building, and demolishing others built upon the cloisters.

In November, 1835, Lord John Russell, then Home Secretary and leader of the House of Commons, having won extensive popularity from the manner in which he had conducted the Reform Bill and other important measures through the Lower House, was entertained to dinner at the Gloucester Hotel, Clifton, by his admirers in this district. The occasion was seized to present his lordship with a handsome piece of plate, purchased by a sixpenny subscription, commemorative of his services to the cause of civil and religious liberty. An amusing illustration of the political acrimony of the time was furnished by a local newspaper, which recorded that the parochial authorities, "to their honour," refused to allow the church bells to be rung on the Home Secretary's visit to the city.

The report of the Municipal Corporations' Commission, occupying five bulky folio volumes, was laid before Parliament in the spring of 1835. Even before the production of the entire work, the irresistible proofs of corruption, extravagance, and inefficiency that had become public in the course of the inquiry had extorted an avowal from Sir Robert Peel, then Prime Minister and leader of the Tory party, that it would be impossible to resist a thorough reform of abuses, and the concession of popular election and control in municipal affairs. A change of Ministry having taken place soon afterwards, the question returned to its original hands, and early in June Lord John Russell, in producing a Bill, described to the House of Commons the plan of municipal government which the Cabinet intended to provide. So great was the effect produced by the commissioners' report, that the measure was read a second time without opposition; nor was any resistance offered to the principle of the Bill when it underwent examination in committee. A few of the old corporations, however, amongst which those of Bristol and Liverpool were especially conspicuous, continued to maintain that a scheme which would deprive them of the enjoyment of property and privileges derived from royal charters was both oppressive and unconstitutional; and when the Bill reached the House of Lords they petitioned to be heard against it by counsel. The Ministry, opposed by an overwhelming majority of peers, were forced to give way, and in July and August Sir Charles Wetherell, recorder of Bristol, supported by other counsel,* protested against what he termed the tyrannical annihilation of ancient rights, and poured a flood of insulting invective on the commissioners, the Government, and the House of Commons. The Opposition peers next moved that Sir Charles should be permitted to call evidence on behalf of his clients, it being hoped that at so late a period of the session (August 3rd) the Ministry would abandon the Bill, rather than continue the sittings. The point having been carried, Mr. Daniel Burges, one of the solicitors for the Corporation of Bristol, Alderman Fripp, an ex-mayor of the city, and officials representing about thirty other close bodies, were examined, but with little other result than to show that they approved of the existing system, and that the proposed reforms were in their opinion unadvisable. The noble opponents of the Government appear to have been disappointed at the emptiness of this testimony, for only the Duke of Newcastle and one or two other uncompromising enemies of change advised the Tory majority to reject what they termed an "atrocious and revolutionary Bill." But though this counsel was ignored, many of the clauses were, to use Lord Brougham's expression, "butchered" by the Conservative peers, with the avowed purpose of checking the control intended to be conferred on the ratepayers. The most unpopular of those "amendments" was that reviving the body of aldermen, who were to be chosen, as far as practicable, from the existing aldermen, and to be elected for life. Other

* The expenses were divided amongst the petitioning Corporations. The share paid by Bristol was £210 18*s*. 9*d*.

alterations, strongly opposed by the Government, were the introduction of property qualifications for councillors, and the rejection of the clauses conferring power on councils to nominate magistrates and to grant public-house licences. The Ministry were for a time undetermined whether to proceed with or to drop the Bill in what they regarded as a mutilated form; but the House of Commons was ultimately invited to sanction most of the changes. The aldermanic tenure was however reduced to six years, and the provision in favour of the old dignitaries was rejected. The House of Lords having assented to the modification, the Bill received the royal assent in September.

The passing of the Act, which excited great interest amongst all classes in the city, revolutionized the existing system, and involved a number of initiatory steps prior to the establishment of the new order of things. In the old Corporation, vacancies in the Common Council (of thirty members) were filled by the aldermen and councillors, while on the death of one of the twelve aldermen his successor was appointed by the mayor and aldermen only, the opinions of the citizens counting for nothing in such affairs. Under the new Act the municipal boundaries of the city were made conterminous with its parliamentary limits by the inclusion within the "city and county" of Clifton, the district of St. James and St. Paul, St. Philip's, and the urban portions of Westbury and Bedminster parishes, thus increasing the area from 755 to 4,879 acres. The rated male inhabitants, or rather such as had been rated for three years, were required to elect a body of forty-eight councillors. Those councillors were then to appoint sixteen aldermen—chosen either from amongst themselves or from qualified ratepayers—and the aggregate body of sixty-four, entitled the Council, was charged with the responsible administration of municipal business and of the corporate revenues. Under the old system the aldermen and common councillors were elected for life. The new aldermen were to sit for six years, and the councillors for three years, but were eligible for re-election; and in order that the council might keep touch with public opinion, it was arranged that one third of the councillors should retire every year on the 1st November, and one half of the aldermen every three years on the 9th November—the day fixed for the annual election of the mayor. Under the ancient charters, the Corporation could spend its revenues at the caprice of the majority, and contract debts at its discretion. The new Act contained stringent provisions against financial abuses, and the Council was unable to borrow money except with the consent of the Treasury, and for purposes manifestly beneficial to the community. Finally, the jurisdiction of the old sheriffs was preserved, but the Bristol custom of appointing two such officers, in puerile imitation of London, was abolished. As the reformed system did not come into operation until the end of the year, the old Corporation had in the first place to appoint a mayor and two sheriffs for the three months which intervened between the retirement of the existing officials at Michaelmas and the creation of the Council. This was easily arranged, however, by the re-appointment of the gentlemen then in office.* Another indispensable work was the preparation of the "Burgess Roll"—a register of the qualified rated inhabitants—a task for which there was but scanty time, owing to the late date at which the Act passed. Equally urgent was the division of the borough into wards, which was to be effected by barristers nominated by the Government for the purpose. These functionaries did not reach Bristol until the 28th October. The importance of the work confided to them does not appear to have been generally appreciated, and their proceedings were almost ignored by the inefficient newspaper reporters of the age. It was not, indeed, until the wards had been created that the supporters of the new system opened their eyes to the fact that the interests of the ratepayers had been deeply compromised by the arrangements effected. The following were the divisions as settled by the legal visitors.

	Burgesses.	Rated value.	Councillors.
Bristol (or Central) .	870	£41,446	9
Clifton	494	25,348	9
Redcliff	517	27,508	6
St. Augustine's. . .	335	20,157	6
Bedminster	177	8,500	3
District	314	18,285	3
St. James's	413	14,976	3
St. Michael's . . .	305	7,926	3
St. Paul's	336	15,614	3
St. Philip's. . . .	432	15,310	3

* The last meeting of the old Common Council took place on the 9th December. It would have been interesting to possess some description of the expiring throes of the old *régime*, but the mystery which shrouded its career was maintained to the last. Curiously enough, even the official minutes are defective. A resolution was passed to grant the sheriffs an extra allowance for their additional period of service, but the amount to be paid them was never filled in; and the mayor, forgetful of invariable custom, neglected to sign the record.

The net result was that the first four of the above wards, with just over 2,200 burgesses, had thirty representatives, whilst the rest of the city, with nearly 2,000 ratepayers, was allotted only eighteen. The distribution was the more extraordinary inasmuch as it was a flagrant deviation from the arrangement proposed by the Royal Commissioners on Corporations, who in their report on Bristol (page 39) had advised the formation of sixteen wards, with three councillors each, by which St. Philip's, Bedminster, and the District would each have had six representatives. The Liberal newspapers—when it was too late—commented warmly on the disproportionate number of councillors awarded to the parishes where the Tory party was known to be most influential. The critics admitted that the division did not seem so unjust when the rateable value of the respective wards was taken into account; but on the other hand, it was pointed out that while three out of the four favoured wards were practically built over, the suburban districts were certain to rapidly increase, both in population and rateable value. Application was eventually made to the Government, which admitted the unfairness of the distribution, and promised redress by legislation, but never carried out its pledge. It will afterwards be seen how excessive the disproportion became before a remedy was applied. The preparations for the elections having been completed, the field became open for candidates, of whom a great number made their appearance, including many members of the old Corporation. Eventually ninety went to the poll, nearly every seat being contended for by representatives of both political parties. The elections took place on the 26th December, and two days afterwards the results were declared by the mayor (Mr. Charles Payne), whose functions thereupon terminated. The following summary gives the results in each ward, the names of members of the old Common Council being distinguished by an asterisk. Further evidence of the unequal distribution of representatives is afforded by the number of voters which is appended to the name of each ward.

Bedminster (177 voters).—Robert Phippin (C.), 93; John Drake (L.), 92; Samuel Brown (L.), 79. Defeated: Henry Glascodine (C.), 58; James Bartlett (C.), 56; James Powell (L.), 46.

Central (870 voters).—James Wood (L.), 388; William Edward Acraman (C.), 379; Thomas Stock (L.), 377; Fred. Ricketts (L). 366; Peter Maze (C), 366; Charles B. Fripp (L.), 344; Henry Bush (C.), 335; James Lean* (C.), 322; John Savage* (C), 315. Defeated: Rich. Bligh (L.), 314; Thomas Carlisle (L.), 307; William Terrell (L.), 302; George W. Franklyn (C.), 291; Samuel Waring (L.), 289; Samuel Morgan (L.), 272; William Watson* (C.), 268 William Plummer (C.), 246; A. J. Drewe (C.), 238.

CLIFTON (494 voters).—Charles Payne* (C.), 274; Gabriel Goldney* (C.), 268; James N. Franklyn* (C.), 258; Joseph Cookson (C.), 238; Abraham Hilhouse* (C.), 223; William S. Jaques (L.), 204; Robert E. Case (C.), 204; James Ford (C.), 204; Michael H. Castle* (L.), 198. Defeated: John Warne (L), 196; Joseph Lax* (C.), 184; John Vining (C.), 184; James Johnson (L.), 177; L. McBayne (L.), 165.

DISTRICT (314 voters).—James E. Lunell* (L.), 221; Thomas R. Sanders (L.), 131; Richard Ash (L.), 127. Defeated: Robert H. Webb (C.), 124; George Shapland (C.), 119.

REDCLIFF (517 voters).—Christopher George* (L.), 236; Henry Ricketts* (L.), 236; Richard P. King (C.), 228; George Thomas (L.), 228; William O. Gwyer (C.), 222; George E. Sanders (L.), 222. Defeated: John Hare, jun. (L.), 213; William Fripp* (C.), 209; William Tothill (L.), 206; Robert Fiske (L.), 182; Nicholas Roch* (C.), 175; Henry R. Llewellyn (L.), 166.

ST. AUGUSTINE'S (235 voters).—Thomas Daniel* (C), 152; Charles Hare (C.), 149; Richard Smith (C.), 147; James E. Nash (C.), 145; P. Maze, jun.,* (C.), 134; Thomas Powell (C.), 124. Defeated: Charles Pinney* (C.), 90; John Manningford (L.), 72; James Reynolds (L.), 69; Richard Ricketts (L.), 68; Joseph F. Alexander (L), 68; James Jenkins (L.), 54.

ST. JAMES'S (413 voters).—James Cunningham (L.) 224; Samuel S. Wayte (L.), 214; John W. Hall (L.), 208. Defeated: Thomas Menlove (C.), 118; James Moore (C.), 111; M. H. Castle* (L.), 54.

ST. MICHAEL'S (305 voters).—John Howell (C.), 208; James George* (C.) 156; Charles L. Walker* (C.), 136. Defeated: John Mills (L.), 115; John Irving (L), 87.

ST. PAUL'S (336 voters).—Nehemiah Moore (L.), 170; Thomas R. Guppy (L.) 164; William Harwood (L.), 137. Defeated: Robert T. Lilly (C.), 129; Thomas H. Riddle (C.), 106; Edward Harley (C.), 105.

ST. PHILIP'S (432 voters).—Thomas Harris (L.), 302; William Herapath, (L.), 242; Edward B. Fripp (L.), 236. Defeated: Samuel G. Flook (C), 107; John Winwood (C), 92.

The net result of the struggle being the return of twenty-four Tories and the same number of Liberals, extreme interest turned upon the election of aldermen, which was fixed for the 1st January, 1836. On this occasion, Mr. Thomas Daniel, senior ex-alderman, was voted into the chair, as a compliment due to his long connection with civic affairs; after which Mr. Stock, one of the leading Liberals, appealed to gentlemen of both political parties to discard party feelings, and to concur in the nomination of a moiety of the aldermanic body from each side. His proposal, however, met with no response from the Conservative ranks. Much discussion followed as to the best mode of procedure, the Tories being desirous of proposing sixteen candidates in a batch, while their opponents urged that a member should be nominated alternately by each party. A division took place on this point, but as the numbers were equal, and the chairman had no casting vote, the Council were unable to make any progress. It being at length determined to resort to alternate nominations, Mr. Wm. Fripp was proposed by the Tories,

Mr. Charles Pinney by the Liberals, Mr. T. H. Riddle by the Tories, and Mr. Richard Ricketts by the Liberals; and in each case the election was unanimous. The third Conservative candidate was Mr. Wm. Bushell, who was also chosen without opposition. But the nomination of the third Liberal, Mr. Wm. Tothill, one of the most respected members of the party, brought about a defection which had been partially anticipated from the outset. Mr. Christopher George, a member of the old Corporation, had won some popularity three or four years before by his ardent advocacy of Reform principles. But, as frequently occurred amongst old-fashioned Whigs about that period, Mr. George's admiration of political improvements came to an end when they threatened to affect his own interests and position. The abolition of rotten boroughs was all well enough, but the purification of effete corporations, of one of which he was a member, was not to his taste. His election into the Council gave him an opportunity of revenging himself upon the party to which he had hitherto professed attachment, and the time had arrived for the blow that had been secretly concerted with his new allies.* A division was called for by the Tories, and as Mr. George voted with them, Mr. Tothill was rejected by 25 votes against 23. Mr. Wm. Watson was next nominated by the Conservatives, and elected; but when the Liberals proposed Mr. J. Reynolds, son of the distinguished philanthropist, he was also rejected by the vote of Mr. George. Mr. John K. Haberfield (Tory) owed his election to the same gentleman. Mr. J. Maningford (Liberal) and Mr. J. Gibbs (Tory) were also successful. Another desertion then took place from the Liberals, Mr. Henry Ricketts, the last gentleman admitted into the old Corporation, following Mr. George's example and voting against Mr. R. Castle. After this change of sides, only one gentleman on the Liberal list was elected—Mr. Thomas Stock. The remaining Conservative nominees appointed were Messrs. N. Roch, Edward Harley, George W. Franklyn, J. Winwood, Wm. K. Wait, and John Vining. As Mr. Pinney, though proposed by the Liberals, immediately joined the Tory camp, the issue of the election was the return of 13 Conservatives and 3 Liberals, giving the former an overwhelming preponderance in the Council.† On the fol-

* Mr. George was a brother-in-law of Alderman Fripp, who had become a convert to Toryism a few years earlier, and had now been selected by his party for the mayoralty.

† One of the Liberal aldermen died; the other two were refused re-election in 1838. According to an interesting series of papers by the Rev. A. B. Beaven,

lowing day, January 2, the jubilant victors carried the election of ex-Alderman Daniel as mayor, 38 votes being recorded for him against 22 given for Mr. Stock. Immediately afterwards, Mr. D. Cave (Tory) was elected sheriff by 35 votes against 25, the latter representing the supporters of Mr. G. Bengough (Liberal). [Mr. Daniel refusing—as was anticipated—to accept the chief magistracy on account of his advanced age, Mr. William Fripp, another alderman of the old *régime*, was shortly afterwards appointed in his place. Mr. Fripp's qualification being contested, an application was made to the Court of King's Bench in the following month for a writ of *quo warranto;* but for some reason the judges did not grant the document until November, when the new mayor's term had expired.] Finally, Mr. Serjeant Ludlow was re-appointed town-clerk; but upon being called in and informed of his election, he stated that for the present he should neither decline nor accept an office which, as defined under the Act, was entirely different from that which he held under the old Corporation, and he must be allowed time for reflection. The learned gentleman continued to maintain this attitude for some weeks. The explanation of his conduct was obvious. For a great number of years Serjeant Ludlow had converted his office into a practical sinecure, his only service consisting in his direction of the aldermanic justices at the quarter sessions. As the recorder would thenceforth be required to fulfil the duties of judge, Mr. Ludlow's object was to induce the Council to dismiss him, when he would be entitled to compensation under the Act. According to a letter he addressed to the Council, his average income from the town-clerkship had been £913 per annum, and he claimed a lump sum of £5,336. In the course of the controversy, Mr. Ludlow, whose hastiness and impatience were as marked as his legal abilities, took offence at some strictures passed upon him by the ex-mayor, Mr. C. Payne, and made the customary preparations for an "affair of honour;" but the explanations that were tendered were accepted as satisfactory. Eventually the town-clerkship was declared vacant, owing to Mr. Ludlow's refusal to fulfil the duties, and the Council consented to pay him a life annuity of £533 yearly, which he

---

published in the *Times and Mirror* in 1880, the three places were filled by Conservatives, and of the 52 gentlemen elected to fill vacancies between 1838 and 1880 there were only 4 Liberals—appointed at distant intervals—against 48 Tories. Of the 68 aldermen appointed up to the same date, Mr. Beaven's statistics show that 27 had been rejected by the ratepayers when they offered themselves for the office of councillor.

enjoyed until his death in March, 1851. [During his later career he was one of the commissioners in bankruptcy for the city, and chairman of quarter sessions for Gloucestershire.]

The Council lost no time in facing the formidable labours which lay before it. Committees were appointed to inquire into the financial position of the Corporation, into the duties and emoluments of the official staff, and into the measures to be taken for the establishment of a police force; and those subjects each underwent lengthy discussion in the chamber. With respect to salaries, it was resolved to reduce the amount paid to the mayor from £1,604 to £700,* the Council also providing him with a carriage. The two sheriffs had previously received £400 a year each; there was now to be only one sheriff, without a salary. The recorder had received £105 for each assize, and a hogshead of wine; but as he was thenceforth to preside at quarter sessions, the salary was increased to £500, and £200 more were added on his becoming judge of the Tolzey Court. The chamberlain and deputy chamberlain had enjoyed incomes of £1,200 and £500 respectively; these were reduced to £700 and £350, and the title of treasurer was adopted for that of chamberlain. Mr. Daniel Burges was appointed town-clerk in the place of Mr. Ludlow,† and Messrs. Brice & Burges were selected as city solicitors, the salaries for these offices being fixed at £2,150, which was to include the cost of providing clerks, etc., while Messrs. Brice & Burges surrendered the fees and other emoluments attached to their functions. This arrangement, it was stated, would be productive of a considerable saving. Economies were effected in other departments. The Mansion House was given up, and many of the useless officials maintained for purposes of "state," including four mayor's serjeants, four sheriffs' serjeants, four sheriffs'

* The salary was reduced to £460 in the autumn of 1837, when the Council was in financial straits, but it was again raised to £700 in November, 1843.

† Mr. Burges (the son of a gentleman of the same name who had held the office of city solicitor for some years when he died in 1791) held the appointment of mayor's clerk, and in conjunction with Mr. Brice that of city solicitor, from 1819 until the end of the old Corporation. His long experience in civic affairs was of great value to the new body; and it was largely through his tact and ability that the antagonistic parties in the Council were brought into harmonious action. Upon his retirement, in 1842—when he was succeeded by his son, Daniel Burges, jun.—he received many marks of respect both from members of the Corporation and his fellow citizens; and a costly and beautiful piece of plate was presented to him in recognition "of his personal worth and public service during a long and honourable life." Mr. Burges died in April, 1864, in his 89th year.

yeomen, two mayor's marshals, the mayor's beadle, two sheriffs' beadles, four wait-players, etc., were suppressed. The aggregate savings were estimated by the mayor at about £6,600. With respect to finance there was an initial question of considerable gravity. Under the scheme for providing compensation to sufferers from the riots of 1831, the ratepayers within the "ancient city" were required to pay a sum of about £10,000 a year. On the other hand, the householders in the districts added to the borough were now entitled to share in the advantages derived from the city estates, whilst they were exempt from taxation under the Compensation Act. This arrangement being obviously inequitable, the Finance Committee recommended that an Act should be obtained, empowering the Council to sell corporation property and apply the money to discharge the amount of compensation still outstanding—about £35,000, after the current year's rate had been collected. Their report was adopted, in despite of the opposition of some of the Clifton councillors, and the proposed Bill received the royal assent. The debts of the old Corporation were stated by the mayor to amount to £110,000, including about £30,000 accepted on condition of paying interest for charitable purposes; and nearly the whole of the total was required at once, partly to meet the claims of the bankers and of bondholders, and partly for the purpose of transferring the charity estates to a new body of trustees, of whom mention will shortly be made. The Corporation, however, possessed large resources. According to an estimate presented to the Council, the landed estates in various parts of the country (3,816 acres) were worth £144,400; ground in the city and suburbs, £14,000; capital value of chief rents, £39,060; premises in Bristol (gross rental £3,620), £57,940; the city markets (producing £2,155 yearly)* £38,772; town dues (producing £1,582 per annum) £31,640; reversions of property, £65,200; and the Mansion House, £4,760; making a total of £395,772, exclusive of public buildings in the city, valued at £80,000, and of the advowsons belonging to the Corporation, estimated at £27,000 more. The work of liquidation necessarily occupied some time. The advowsons, which were first offered for sale, produced £27,753, the separate amounts being as follows: Portis-

* Four markets, the oyster, Welch, and cheese markets and the corn market on the Back, were stated to produce little or no income, and had no value affixed to them. The last-named market, however, lingered on until 1839. The oyster market was demolished in 1844. The cheese market, after long costing more than it produced, was closed about 1850, and entirely disappeared in 1885.

head, £8,050; Christ Church, £4,555; St. James's, £2,555; St. Paul's, £3,210; St. Michael's, £1,710; Temple, £1,510; St. George's, £2,003; St. Peter's, £930; St. John's, £605; St. Philip's, £510; Trinity, St. Philip's, £1,010; Stockland, £1,105. Two estates at Aldmondsbury brought in £16,420, another at Ashton, £2,200, and certain fee-farm rents and properties in Bristol nearly £12,000; by which the compensation charge was cleared off and some pressing bondholders satisfied. Later on, with a view to wiping off the old debt and meeting the first claims of the Charity Trustees, the estate of Stockland (708 acres) was sold for £36,368; the rectorial estate of Nether Stowey (65 acres) for £2,677; the farms at Gaunt's Earthcott (654 acres) for £20,866; and the estate at North Weston (521 acres) for £16,443. These alienations, however, gravely reduced the income of the Corporation at a moment when new and heavy expenditure had to be provided for. The creation of an efficient police force was obligatory on the Council, and in conformity with the recommendations of the Watch Committee, the constabulary, numbering 232, were duly enrolled, and commenced their duties on the 25th June, 1836. [The first superintendent was Mr. Joseph Bishop, who had been an officer in the Metropolitan police. The central station was established at the Guardhouse, in Wine Street, much to the discontent of the leading tradesmen there, and in 1842 the building was condemned by the Council as inconvenient and unhealthy. A more commodious station, erected opposite to the new Bridewell, and upon the site of the old one, was completed in 1844. The force, after being slightly increased in strength in 1845, and again in 1857, was augmented in 1872 to 357 officers and men, of whom 13 were specially charged with the protection of the Floating Harbour. The pay of the civic army has also been raised at intervals, and the annual expenditure under this head, estimated at £9,000 in 1836, has amounted of late years to £32,000.] It was originally intended to defray the cost of the police establishment by means of a watch rate; but difficulties arose out of the peculiar circumstances of the districts added to the city, and the Council was driven to resort to a borough rate, and to submit to restrictions in administering the corporate revenues which such a rate imposed upon it under the Corporations Act. A new assessment of the city was therefore ordered, the result of which was reported to the Council in January, 1837, as follows. [The town-clerk having been kind enough to furnish corresponding statistics for 1886 they are appended for the purpose of showing the progress effected during half a century of representative local government.]

	1836.	1886.
Ancient City . . .	£198,865	£377,503
Bedminster . . .	31,919	101,591
Clifton	83,645	196,800
St. Philip's, out . .	34,125	133,472
Westbury, part of .	10,347	92,201
District	24,414	71,813
	£383,315	£973,380

Only one other matter arising out of the change in local government remains to be noticed—the appointment of borough magistrates in the place of the superseded aldermen of the old Corporation. The Municipal Reform Bill originally contained a clause vesting the nomination of justices in the local councils, but the provision was rejected by the House of Lords. Lord John Russell, Home Secretary, in advising the Commons to assent to the alteration, promised that the Ministry would receive the suggestions of the municipalities with the utmost consideration, and a meeting of the Bristol Council took place in February, 1836, to select a list of persons deemed worthy of the local bench. At the beginning of the discussion it was proposed that the two political parties should each suggest twelve names; but some of the Conservative members showed so decided a determination to claim a majority that Mr. Cunningham, a leading Liberal, advised his friends to leave the room and permit their opponents to act at their discretion. Conciliatory counsels thereupon prevailed, and twelve gentlemen were selected from each side of the chamber, in despite of the opposition offered to three Liberal nominations by an extreme section of their opponents. Shortly after the list had been forwarded to the Home Office, the mayor received a notification from Lord J. Russell that only eighteen names had been accepted, six of the Tory candidates, Messrs T. Daniel, C. L. Walker, J. George, A. Hilhouse, N. Roch, and J. N. Franklyn—comprising four of the old aldermen and two common councillors—being rejected. The announcement was received with intense indignation by the local Conservatives, and gave rise to a debate in the House of Commons on the 29th March, in the course of which Sir R. R. Vyvyan charged Lord J. Russell with corrupt practices, while his lordship stigmatised his assailant as a calumniator. By order of the Speaker, the two gentlemen pledged themselves to refrain from "an affair of honour," and the matter dropped.

The prospect of direct railway communication being opened with London at an early date inspired an enterprising Bristolian, Mr. T. R. Guppy, with the happy thought of connecting the port with the United States by means of a regular service of steam vessels, which had not hitherto been attempted by the most adventurous spirits on either side of the Atlantic. The proposal having found many supporters, a prospectus appeared, early in January, 1836, of the Great Western Steamship Company, with a capital of £250,000, and the project was received with a cordiality which augured success. The design of the first transatlantic steamer, the *Great Western*, was furnished by Mr. Brunel, and the building of the vessel, which was to be of 1,340 tons measurement, having been confided to Mr. William Patterson, of Wapping, the stern frame of the ship was raised on the 28th July amidst much rejoicing. The builder proceeded with so much vigour that on the 19th July, 1837, the *Great Western* was launched; in the following month she left for London, to be fitted with engines of 440 horse power; and in April, 1838, she returned to Bristol, having made the return journey (about 670 miles) in fifty-six hours. The vessel cost her owners £63,000. On the 8th April the ship, big with many hopes, left Kingroad for America, seven passengers risking their lives in an enterprise which many scientific men and ancient mariners declared to be impracticable. Before her departure, however, an adroit scheme was devised in other quarters to deprive the city of the credit which was undoubtedly due to its undertaking. A large steamer called the *Sirius*, usually plying between London and Cork, was despatched under Liverpool orders from the Thames to the Irish port, whence, after receiving a fresh store of fuel, she left for New York on the 4th April, having a start over the *Great Western* of four days and over 250 miles. Notwithstanding those advantages, the race was very close. The *Sirius* arrived at Sandyhook at midnight on the 22nd April, but being unable to proceed further until she had obtained coal, she did not reach New York until midday on the 23rd. The *Great Western* arrived two hours later, with eighty tons of coal on board. The result of the experiment had been awaited with intense interest in America; and both vessels were greeted with characteristic enthusiasm by the New Yorkers. The superiority of the Bristol ship was manifest, and it was again attested by the return voyage. The *Sirius* left on the 1st May and reached England on the 18th. The *Great Western*, with sixty-six passengers and 20,000 letters, started on the 7th May in the presence of 100,000 spectators, and arrived at Bristol on the 22nd, having solved the great problem in spite of winds, waves, and philosophers. Instead of consuming 1,480 tons of coal, the minimum fixed by scientific calculators, the engines had required only 392 tons on the return journey. The second voyage was still more satisfactory, the outward passage being made in fourteen days sixteen hours, and the homeward run in twelve days fourteen hours.* The practicability of steam navigation across the Atlantic being triumphantly established, the policy which should have been adopted by the Bristol company seems now obvious. Three or four additional vessels of the *Great Western* type, rapidly placed on the line, would have enabled the concern to establish a weekly service between this port and New York, and the passenger traffic between the two continents would unquestionably have flowed towards the route which was not only first established but which was shorter than that of Liverpool by little less than a day. The merchants of the Mersey were not long in perceiving the danger; and the construction of a fleet of steamers fitted for a regular service was ordered by Mr. Cunard and his friends during the autumn. It was not until late in the following year that anything was resolved upon at Bristol to supplement the *Great Western*. And the step at length taken was as imprudent as it was tardy. In lieu of pushing forward two or three more *Great Westerns*, it was determined, to use a homely proverb, to put all the company's eggs into one basket—to build, in fact, a single ship nearly three times the capacity of the *Great Western*, and to leave Mr. Brunel full scope and leisure to indulge his passion for experiments and novelties. The consequence was a series of disasters. The *Great Britain* was to be constructed of iron, and as no engineers could be found willing to undertake the task by contract, the company were induced by their scientific guide to establish works of their own—at a cost of £52,000, and with financial results that the sagacious antici-

* A keen rivalry for early intelligence existed at this time between two London journals, *The Times* and *Morning Herald*. Both concerns engaged boats at Portishead to board the *Great Western*, and their messengers were carried at racing speed in posting carriages from Bristol to Maidenhead, where special trains were in waiting for the rest of the journey.

pated. The colossal ship was laid down in July, 1839; at a subsequent date, Mr. Brunel determined that she should be propelled by a screw instead of by paddles; other alterations followed, and it was not until four years later, July, 19th, 1843—when the Cunard company had long had four steamers on the transatlantic service, besides having two more nearly ready—that the ship was launched. [The ceremony will be noticed hereafter.] By putting the engines into the vessel at the works, it was found, at the end of March, 1844, that the hull was so deeply immersed as to be unable to pass out of the Float, and seven months more elapsed before the requisite alterations could be made for its release. It was not, indeed, until December 11—nearly seventeen months after launching, and five and a half years after her inception—that the *Great Britain* left Cumberland basin for an experimental cruise. That she then proved an excellent sea-boat was nothing to the purpose. Liverpool had recovered the supremacy which the *Great Western* had temporarily shaken, and the competition of Bristol was at an end. The *Great Britain's* career as an Atlantic steamer was, moreover, prematurely cut short. In September, 1846, a few hours after leaving Liverpool on her second voyage, the great ship stranded on the coast of Ireland, and remained there for over eleven months, which certainly proved the wonderful strength of her frame—if that was any consolation to her luckless proprietors, whose loss by the wreck exceeded £20,000. Their works, as well as the *Great Western*, had been already offered for sale. The *Great Western* was ultimately disposed of for £24,750 to the West India Royal Mail Company, and Messrs Gibbs, Bright & Co. bought the *Great Britain* in 1850 for £18,000, her original cost to the company having been £97,154. Both vessels were sent to ply in the trade of rival ports. In fact, they had been driven from Bristol long before. The dues charged by the Bristol Dock Company on the *Great Western* amounted to £106 on each voyage (as much more being levied on the cargo), although the ship was forced to remain in Kingroad owing to the defective accommodation in the Floating Harbour, and had even to proceed to Milford for some repairs.* The Dock

* The local author of "Rambling Rhymes" [J. R. Dix] commented on the subject as follows:—

> "The *Western* an unnatural parent has,
> For all her beauty;
> Her mother never *harboured* her, and yet
> She asks for *duty*.

Board was appealed to for somo reduction in its demands, owing to the admitted inadequacy of its works; but the cold response was, that the directors had no power to make abatements. It was then proposed to provide the required accommodation at a lower point in the Avon. A joint committee was formed, representing the Corporation, the Merchant Venturers, and the Steamship Company, and Mr. Brunel, who was called on to advise as to what should be done, suggested a dock at Sea Mills and a pier at Portishead.* This, however, would have involved an increase in the capital of the Dock Company, who were not disposed to spend money, and who appear to have thought that the tolls on the *Great Western* would continue in any case to flow into their coffers. An attempt to secure a reduction of the town dues imposed on the cargo having been also unsuccessful,* the proprietors of the steamship resolved in February, 1842, that the vessel should sail alternately from Bristol and Liverpool, and as the expenses at the latter port were found to be less by £200 per voyage, the *Great Western* was shortly afterwards removed entirely from Bristol, as was the *Great Britain* from the outset of her career. The fate of the spirited company which started this local enterprise may be imagined from the facts already recorded. The *Bristol Journal* of February 14, 1852, remarked: "The accounts of the company show some very disastrous results. The whole of the original £100 shares are written off as a total loss. The loss on the *Great Britain* alone was £107,896, and on the works £47,277." The *Great Western* and the *Severn* (another Bristol built steamer) were sold by the Royal Mail Steamship Company in October, 1856, to a shipbreaker for £11,500.

An official statement was published early in 1836 of the excise duties which had been collected in Bristol during the previous year. The figures, which illustrate not only the fiscal system of the age, but also the industries of the city, were as follows:—spirits, £175,980; soap, £52,304; glass, £47,085; malt, £65,662; bricks, £2,003; paper, £5,660; licences, £13,868; auctions, £3,452.

The popularity of the Great Western Railway scheme, then in course of construction, naturally gave rise to a project

---

Hull, Liverpool, and other ports aloud
Cry 'Go a-head!'
A certain place that I know seems to say
'Reverse!' instead."

* "The Corporation of Bristol and its Trade and Commerce." By L. Bruton, pp. 10, 43.

for extending the new system westwards. The Bristol and Exeter Railway Company, with a capital of £2,000,000, was started under influential patronage; the shares were quickly taken up; and a Bill for the construction of the undertaking passed both Houses of Parliament without difficulty, receiving the royal assent in May, 1836. The line, like its forerunner, was laid out by Mr. Brunel, who again adopted his pet theory of the broad gauge. The work of construction proceeded very slowly, the board having encountered much difficulty in obtaining the necessary loans. It was indeed at one time seriously discussed "whether it would not be the wisest course to wind up and abandon the undertaking, or, if it should be continued, whether the construction of a single narrow gauge line to Bridgwater was not the extent to which the works could be conducted" (Directors' Report, 1850). The confidence of capitalists was, however, restored by an arrangement made with the Great Western Company, under which the latter advanced £20,000, and undertook to lease and work the line for a term expiring in April, 1849. The first section, between Bristol and Bridgwater, was opened on the 1st June, 1841, amidst much rejoicing in the district. The section to Taunton was completed in July, 1842, and the entire undertaking was finished and opened on the 1st May, 1844. As if to give a new illustration of the unpractical mind of the engineer, the station erected in Bristol was placed at a right angle with the Great Western terminus, occasioning extreme annoyance to through passengers, and great delay. The blunder was partially remedied under an Act passed in 1845, a junction railway being then formed to connect the two lines. This, however, necessitated a third set of booking offices for the through trains—a monument of Mr. Brunel's ingenuity which excited general derision. In 1845, the boards of the two companies came to an arrangement for the absorption of the Bristol and Exeter line into the Great Western system. But the proprietors of the former, who were to receive a dividend of six per cent. in perpetuity, were greatly irritated by the announcement, and when the scheme was laid before them, in November, it was rejected with indignation. The shareholders had reason, however, to regret their decision. When the lease terminated, and the line had to be worked independently, the first year's dividend was only three per cent.; for several years afterwards the distribution did not exceed five per cent.; and, as will be seen hereafter, the concerns were at last amalgamated in 1876 on terms which by no means recouped the shareholders for the loss they had brought on themselves. It must be added, that throughout its career as an independent concern, the company was complained of for the extreme illiberality of its system of management. So late as September, 1869, only one third-class train was run from Exeter to Bristol, while the second-class fare was higher than some companies charged for first-class accommodation; yet at the same time the board carried Bristol excursionists to and from Weston at the rate of about one farthing per mile, declaring that such trains paid "as well as any they had."

The 21st April, 1836, will long be memorable as the date of the foundation of the most remarkable charity of which the city, and indeed the kingdom, can boast—the great orphan houses at Ashley Down. The story of its author, the Rev. George Müller, has been narrated by himself, and it is unnecessary to enter into it in detail. Born at Kroppenstaedt, Prussia, in 1805, and educated at the university of Halle, Mr. Müller came to this country when in his twenty-fourth year, with a desire to labour as a missionary of the Society for the Conversion of the Jews. After studying for some time with a view to fitting himself for the position, he had a serious illness, and was ordered to Devonshire for change of air. There he encountered Henry Craik, an able and earnest minister, with whom he formed a life-long friendship. Beginning to entertain doubts as to the course of life he had fixed upon, Mr. Müller resigned his studentship, and accepted the ministry of an Independent congregation at Teignmouth, with the modest salary of £55 a year. In a short time, however, he felt conscientious scruples about accepting a stipend derived from pew rents, and he thereupon resolved as his rule of life to place his entire reliance upon Providence, and "never to ask for money from any human being." In 1832 he left Devonshire for Bristol, where Mr. Craik had already been favourably received as a preacher, and the two friends laboured together as ministers of Gideon Independent chapel, in Newfoundland Street. Subsequently, Bethesda chapel, near Brandon Hill, was temporarily hired as an experiment, and the results were so satisfactory that it was permanently retained. [In June, 1857, Mr. C. W. Finzel purchased the chapel, and presented it to Messrs. Müller and Craik's congregation.] In 1834 Mr. Müller established a Scriptural Knowledge Institution, the objects of which were to circulate the Scriptures, to promote education amongst the poor, to aid in missionary enterprise, and—most remarkable and successful of its ends—to feed, clothe, and educate destitute orphan children. Mr. Müller's diary for October, 1835, contained the first notice of the extraordinary undertaking he had resolved upon, for it was his purpose from the outset to ask no help from the public for the immense family he was soon to draw around him. He next recorded that the first donation he received after intimating his purpose was a shilling, which came to hand in December. Soon afterwards a friend undertook to pay £50 for the rent of a house, and nearly £500 were soon forthcoming for fitting it up. The necessary preparations being completed, the orphanage, furnished for thirty female children, was opened on the 21st April, 1836, in the house No. 6, Wilson Street, St. Paul's, near which Mr. Müller resided. Three weeks later the founder resolved upon establishing another orphanage for infants, and this was opened on the 15th December following, at No. 1, Wilson Street. In October, 1837, a third house in the same street was hired and fitted up as an orphanage for boys, and before the close of that year Mr. Müller had seventy-five young children dependent on him. "Several more are daily expected. During the last twelvemonth, the expenses have been about £240, and the income about £840." Seven months later, the fund in hand was reduced to £20, but so far from feeling apprehension, "we have given notice for five children to come in, and purpose to give notice for five more." The entry characterises the story of the institution for several of its early years, evolving an uninterrupted series of trials and deliverances. Oftentimes there were not funds or stock to provide for twenty-four hours in advance, yet help always came in time; a debt was never contracted; and Mr. Müller neither doubted nor desponded. As time went on, and the phenomenal character of the institution became more widely known, subscriptions from distant places—in fact from all parts of the world—began to flow in. The funds accumulating, a fourth house for girls was opened in the same street in July, 1843. Ordinary dwelling houses were necessarily ill-adapted for Mr. Müller's requirements; and the inhabitants of Wilson Street remonstrated against the inconveniences to which the institutions exposed them. In 1845, accordingly, the philanthropist resolved on building an orphanage large enough to accommodate 300 children. The announcement appears to have alarmed his usual supporters, for scarcely any donations were offered for some time. At length, however, two gifts of £1,000 each came in, and Mr. Müller entered into a contract for the purchase of seven acres of ground at Ashley Hill, the owner of which accepted £120 an acre out of sympathy with the object. No further pecuniary difficulty was encountered; and in June 1849, when the building was finished at a cost of £14,500, the whole of which, with £500 to boot, had been provided, the children were removed and the houses in Wilson Street abandoned. The housekeeping expenses of the new institution, when it became fully occupied, were £70 per week; and many people condemned the founder for what they termed his rashness and presumption in trusting upon casual gifts for the maintenance of so great an undertaking. In point of fact, the enlarged hospital was scarcely ever threatened with the embarrassments that hung so long over the Wilson Street establishments; and within eighteen months from its opening Mr. Müller determined on the erection of a second and much more spacious building, capable of accommodating seven hundred additional orphans. The estimated cost was about £35,000. Subsequently the plan was extended, and it was determined to erect two new orphanages, one for 400 infants and girls, and the other for 450 girls. The former was begun in 1855, and opened in 1857; the other was finished in 1862. Enormous as had become the responsibilities and expenditure of the institution, Mr. Müller felt an inward conviction that his work was not accomplished; and he next declared his intention to construct two additional houses, to accommodate 900 children, about equally divided between the sexes, and raising the total number of orphans to 2,050. One of these was finished in 1868, and the other in 1870. [Those who are unacquainted with the institution may form an idea of its extent from the following figures, published in 1868, giving the quantity of materials consumed in the construction of the last two orphanages only:—building stone, 36,000 tons; freestone, 15,000 tons; lime and ashes, 14,000 tons; timber, 10,000 tons; deal boarding, 2 acres; paving, 1½ acre; plastering, 10 acres; slating, 2 acres; painting, 4½ acres; glazing, ¼ acre; rainwater pipes, 1¾ mile; drain pipes 3 miles.] The total expenditure for buildings had then been raised to about £115,000. The annual cost of the establishment has since been nearly £25,000. The sole conditions of admittance, which have never varied from the outset, are that a child be a legitimate orphan, destitute, and deprived of both parents by death. According to the yearly report published in August, 1886, the amount forwarded to Mr. Müller for the various objects of his Scriptural Knowledge Institution then exceeded £1,086,000, of which about £700,000 were for the orphanages. No debt was ever incurred on behalf of the charity, which is still, as when its benevolent head began the work, entirely dependent on the liberality of the Christian world. The number of children confided to Mr. Müller had reached 7,294 in May, 1886. The contributors are of all classes. Sometimes a poor person sends a few pence; rich sympathisers occasionally forward from £1,000 to £5,000, and as much as £11,000 have been presented at once. Ostentation, moreover, cannot influence the givers, for their names never appear in print. Mr. Müller relinquished his personal superintendence of the orphanages in 1872, when he delegated his labours to his son-in-law, Mr. Wright.

The population of the city at this date was probably ten or twelve times greater than it had been during the middle ages. Nevertheless the extent of the parochial churchyards had remained practically unaltered, the only addition of any importance being the cemetery attached to Trinity Church, St. Philip's; and as only a few Dissenting bodies had made provision for interments, the urgent need of increased space had long been painfully known to all classes. In May, 1836, the Bristol General Cemetery Company, with a capital of £15,000 in £20 shares, was formed for supplying this want. According to statistics published by the promoters, the area of the existing churchyards, including the sites of the churches, was only fourteen acres. An Act of Parliament having been obtained in 1837, about twenty-eight acres of ground were purchased at Arno's Vale, a moiety of which was laid out as a cemetery, and a portion was consecrated in October, 1840. The entire cost was £16,387. Owing to a clause inserted in the Company's Act through the interference of Bishop Monk, a fee of ten shillings was reserved to the clergy of the city on each body interred in the consecrated portion of the ground. As this cost doubled the charge on every simple interment, its effect was almost prohibitive. The number of burials in 1842 was only twenty-five, and the average for the first seven years was under 100. The closing of the city churchyards under the Health of Towns Act, however, wrought a complete change in the position of the company. In 1860 the remaining half of the land was included in the cemetery, and as this was rapidly appropriated, an Act for obtaining additional ground was obtained in 1880.

The reorganisation of the Established Church, with a view to the better application of its revenues to the altered conditions of society, was another of the great questions which were pressed upon the reformed House of Commons by the constituencies. Amongst the defects most urgently demanding amendment were the anomalous incomes and position of the English sees. The Bishop of Durham, with the supervision of two thinly populated counties, had an income of about £21,000 a year, besides extensive and valuable patronage. The bishopric of London was worth £15,000, and the bishopric of Ely £11,000 a year, to say nothing of the opportunities they afforded to their occupants of enriching relatives and friends. On the other hand, the sees of Bristol, Carlisle, and Gloucester were endowed with only about £2,200 apiece, while the Bishop of Rochester had only £1,500, and the Bishop of Llandaff barely £900. The diocese of York, again, contained a population of nearly a million and a half, and that of Chester nearly two millions; while Ely, with its excessive wealth, embraced only 126,000 souls, and several others had less than 200,000. In March, 1836, the Ecclesiastical Commissioners, to whom those gigantic anomalies had been referred with a view to legislation, recommended, amongst other matters, a rearrangement of dioceses and the creation of two new bishoprics—Manchester and Ripon—for the supervision of the swarming population of Lancashire and Yorkshire. It was, however, one of the cherished theories of the Churchmen of that age that every bishop must be a member of the House of Peers; and as the feeling of the popular chamber was known to be decidedly hostile to the increase of the ecclesiastical lords, the Commissioners proposed to avoid the difficulty by suppressing two of the old sees. The diocese of Bristol, it was suggested, might be conveniently amalgamated with that of Llandaff (or, as it was subsequently proposed, with Wells), while Bangor could be united with St. Asaph. A few months later, a further report recommended the blending of the sees of Bristol and Gloucester, and in despite of several local protests the plan was forthwith sanctioned. A death which unluckily occurred in the episcopal body allowed the Commissioners' scheme to be carried out without delay. Dr. Allen, appointed Bishop of Bristol in 1834, on the death of Dr. Gray, was transferred to the vacant see of Ely, whereupon Dr. Monk, Bishop of Gloucester, added the archdeaconry of Bristol to his former diocese under the direction of an Order in Council of the 17th October, 1836,—the county of Dorset, the remaining part of the diocese of Bristol, being added to Salisbury. [About the same time the prebendaries of Bristol—thenceforth styled canons—were ordered to be reduced from six to four, but the existing functionaries retained their places for life or until they received promotion.] The episcopal arrangement was loudly condemned by Churchmen in Bristol, and, being regarded as a slur on the dignity of the city, it was far from approved by many Dissenters. To soften the blow, an implied promise was made that Bishop Monk and his successors should reside in or near Bristol during a part of each year; and the Ecclesiastical Commissioners took measures for providing the bishop with a second palace for that purpose. Stapleton House, the property of Isaac Elton, Esq., with about sixty acres of adjoining land, was eventually selected as the most convenient and desirable site, and the estate was purchased in April, 1840, for £11,500. Towards the payment of the purchase money the Commissioners had £6,000 paid by the citizens in compensation for the palace burned during the riots, and £1,450 more obtained in 1837 by selling the site and garden of the ruined edifice.* The charge incurred for the new residence might therefore have been inconsiderable. But the Commissioners, whose reckless profusion in reference to episcopal palaces was frequently criticised in the House of Commons, were not content to make the modest alterations suggested by Bishop Monk, the cost of which need not have exceeded £3,000; and in spite of his lordship's remonstrances they set about a wholesale reconstruction, designed by their London architect, who rapidly raised the total expenditure on the mansion to £23,908.† To put a climax to their extravagance, it was resolved, on the death of Dr. Monk, to rebuild the palace at Gloucester, on which £14,411 were soon afterwards squandered. The latter transaction was sought to be veiled by a so-called economy, —the abandonment and sale of the palace at Stapleton, in defiance of the promises that had been held out to the citizens of Bristol. After standing for many years unoccupied, Stapleton House, with the land, was sold in October, 1858, to the trustees of Colston's School for £12,000—almost exactly half its cost. The steps recently taken for the restoration of the bishopric will be recorded hereafter.

The sixth annual congress of the British Association was held in Bristol in August, when upwards of 1,100 members took part in the proceedings. The sections into which the

---

* The Commissioners displayed characteristic shortsightedness in disposing of this ground. In August, 1884, apprehensive that a noisy or offensive factory might be built on the portion abutting on the cathedral, the Commissioners purchased of the Corporation (which had recently acquired the site) a strip of 1,580 square yards (less than a fourth of the whole) for the sum of £1,100.

† Parliamentary return, 1847; Report of Commons' Committee, 1848.

Association was divided were accommodated as follows: Mathematics (President, Professor Whewell), in the Merchants' Hall. Chemistry (Professor Cumming), Grammar School. Geography and Geology (Dr. Buckland), Institution. Zoology (Professor Henslow), and Botany (Dr. Roget), Colston's School. Statistics (Sir Charles Lemon) Cathedral Chapter House. Mechanics (Mr. Davies Gilbert) Merchants' Hall. Amongst the crowd of distinguished men present were the Marquis of Northampton (who presided in the absence of the Marquis of Lansdowne), Lord King, Sir David Brewster, Sir John Rennie, Sir W. Hamilton, and Messrs Faraday, Sedgwick, Murchison, Wheatstone, De la Beche, Hallam, Cubitt, Lubbock, Fox Talbot, Brunel, and the poets Moore and Bowles. The general committee met in the Chapter House, and reunions took place nightly at the theatre. The meeting was especially interesting to geologists, owing to the extensive cuttings made in the district for the construction of the Great Western railway. Another prominent feature of the proceedings was the laying, by the President, of the foundation stone of the south pier of the Suspension Bridge. In order that this ceremony might not interfere with the work of the sections, it took place at the unusual hour of seven in the morning. The "wise week" of 1836 is now chiefly memorable for an unlucky prediction, uttered by Dr. Lardner in the course of a lecture at the Institution on the subject of steam communication with America. The lecturer and his audience were aware that a few enterprising Bristolians were building a steam vessel in the hope of establishing a more rapid system of transit between the two continents. The learned doctor, however, contended that such an enterprise was "Quixotic," and produced voluminous calculations to show that "2,080 miles was the longest run a steamer could encounter; at the end of that distance she would require a relay of coal." At the conclusion of the discourse, Mr. Brunel, the designer of the new ship, briefly observed that the lecturer had founded his conclusions upon the performances of old vessels; but the Doctor was not to be shaken from opinions which he had repeatedly affirmed in his "Encyclopædia" and elsewhere. In December of the previous year he had lectured on the subject at Liverpool, where he affirmed that the project of direct steam intercourse between that port and New York was "perfectly chimerical; they might as well talk of making a voyage from New York or Liverpool to the moon." Some half dozen years afterwards, Dr. Lardner proceeded to the United States by the system of navigation he had deemed practically impossible. He had previously admitted his mistake by urging the establishment of steam communication with India.

Amongst the local papers read during the above congress was one on education, by Mr. C. B. Fripp, which records some noteworthy statistics. Mr. Fripp showed, that while the population of the city was over 112,000, of whom 20,000 ought to be attending school, the actual number receiving instruction in Bristol was only about 5,200. In 1882, when the population had not quite doubled, the number of children on the school registers was 30,000, and the average attendance 22,170.

One of the provisions of the Municipal Corporations Act having transferred the judgeship of the court of quarter sessions and of the local courts of record to the Recorder, Sir Charles Wetherell in his new capacity opened the ancient Court of Piepoudre according to ancient forms, in the Old Market, at the time of the September fair. According to immemorial precedent, toast, cheese, and metheglin were provided for the entertainment of the official staff and their friends, beer and cider being also distributed to the commonalty. The scene was, as usual, a disorderly one, a portion of the victuals and liquor being thrown about in a roisterous way amongst the populace. Sir Charles Wetherell, however, maintained his gravest demeanour on the occasion, having previously ordered that all the old customs of the court should be strictly maintained. The summoning of a long roll of people "to come forth and do suit and service"—although they had been dead for centuries—was another farce of this ancient tribunal; but Sir Charles never relaxed a muscle when, in reply to the clerk, he declined to fine the defaulters for non-attendance, seeing that, as he was informed, they could not be found. The yearly disturbance arising from the feast ultimately led to its suppression, and the holding of the court was discontinued after 1870.

During the parliamentary contest over the Municipal Corporations Bill, it was found impossible to make arrangements for the future administration of the charity estates which the old corporations, in their capacity of trustees, were alleged to have abused for political purposes. Towards the end of the conflict between the two Houses, it was accordingly determined to insert a clause in the Act leaving the charities in the hands of their former governors until August, 1836, after which date, if Parliament had not otherwise directed, new trustees were to be appointed by the Lord Chancellor on petitions from each locality. In the session of 1836 a Bill was brought in for the administration of the charities by boards chosen by popular election, but this proposal was not unjustly condemned by the Conservatives as highly objectionable, and it was rejected by the House of Lords. As the Ministry refused to assent to the request of the Tory peers for a further delay of a year, the Lord Chancellor became entitled to exercise his jurisdiction. Some Liberal members of the Bristol Council thereupon petitioned his lordship for the creation of a board of trustees, composed of eighteen members, half of whom, it was suggested, should be Conservatives. The proposal was approved at a meeting of the Council in September, and the names of nine Tories and nine Liberals were forwarded to the Chancellor. At another meeting, a week later, it was reported that the Master in Chancery to whom the case had been referred wished the board to consist of an uneven number of trustees, whereupon the promoters of the trust requested the Conservatives to increase the names on their list from nine to ten, stating that they should themselves select eleven. Most of the Tories who had been nominated were greatly offended at their party being refused predominance in the trust, and requested that their names should be withdrawn. Other members of the majority, still more irritated, flung aside the dictates of prudence, and a resolution was angrily passed, at the instance of Mr. Pinney, by which the Council refused to take any further steps in the formation of a charity board. In consequence of this unfortunate resolution the matter was thrown entirely into the hands of the Liberals, and the desire of the latter party to avenge their treatment at the aldermanic election prompted them to a policy as indefensible as was that of their opponents. Another petition to the Chanceller was forwarded by Mr. R. Ash and Mr. G. E. Sanders, and in October, 1836, his lordship confirmed the appointment of the gentlemen they had nominated, namely: Richard Ash, George Bengough, Samuel Brown, Thomas Carlisle, Michael H. Castle, James Cunningham, Thomas Davies, Robert Fiske, Charles Bowles Fripp, John Kerle Haberfield, William Harwood, William Herapath, Thomas Powell, George E. Sanders, John Savage, Richard Smith, W. P. Taunton, George Thomas, William Tothill, Harman Visger, and James Wood. Only three of those gentlemen—Messrs. Haberfield, Smith, and Savage—were Conservatives, against eighteen Liberals, a disproportion obviously inequitable in every point of view. The board lost no time in entering upon its work; Mr. James Cunningham being appointed chairman, and Mr. T. J. Manchee (the compiler of a useful work on Bristol charities) secretary. Inquiries were forthwith set on foot with reference to the estates and accounts of the various charities; and the results soon threw a singular light on the asserted honest and faithful administration of the old corporate body. The manipulation of the funds of Queen Elizabeth's Hospital by the Common Council had provoked some strong reflections from the Royal Commissioners. But those officials, it was now discovered, had been allowed a very imperfect acquaintance with the true facts of the case. In the year 1767 the boys of the hospital, then located in a stately house in Orchard Street, erected at the expense of Colston and other benevolent citizens, were transferred to inconvenient and unhealthy premises in Christmas Street, previously appropriated to the Grammar School. The pretext for this transfer was, that the Orchard Street school would accommodate "twice the number of young gentlemen" who attended in Christmas Street; but the real motive of the change—as has been already shown at page 46—was to give a better and more fashionable domicile to the head-master of the Grammar School, who had married the daughter of an influential alderman. Not content with depriving the charity of its "stately house," the Corporation proceeded to acts still more unjustifiable. For some years previous to the above transfer, the Common Council had been spending more than its income, and money had been borrowed from the hospital funds to supply the deficiency; "seals" (bonds) to the total amount of £4,715 being outstanding in 1771. The Corporation paid no interest on this debt, as it ought to have done. On the contrary, it being convenient to make the most of so productive a milch cow, the boys in the hospital were reduced from forty-eight to forty, in order to liberate a larger portion of the yearly income. Matters proceeded in this way until 1781, when the Corporation was in serious pecuniary embarrassment, and owed the hospital £2,400 for interest alone. The difficulty was surmounted by the ingenuity of Alderman Harris, at whose instigation the Common Council resolved on a financial masterstroke. When the hospital was established, the Corporation, to further the designs of its benevolent founder, made certain gifts, amounting to £3,000, towards the work—claiming the praise of Queen Elizabeth for the munificent spirit which had actuated them. Alderman Harris's device, —cordially approved by his colleagues—was to treat those gifts as loans, and to charge the hospital compound interest on the so-called debt, at rates varying from ten to five per cent. per annum. The result of this operation was to bring the charity under enormous liabilities; and the corporate body thereupon quashed the "seals" due to the hospital, together with the arrears of interest, and ordered the scholars to be reduced to thirty-six. As all the proceedings of the Corporation were transacted in private and under an oath of secrecy, nothing was publicly known of this financial legerdemain until the Charity Commissioners examined the accounts in 1821. The Corporation then unblushingly asserted that the hospital was indebted to their treasury in the sum of £46,499. Such were the facts which the Charity Trustees had to deal with. It was impossible to restore the ancient schoolhouse to the charity, since an Act of Parliament had been astutely obtained to legalise the transfer; but the manipulation of the funds admitted of different treatment. A skilful accountant, Mr. Joshua Jones, made a thorough examination of the civic accounts on behalf of the trustees, and he eventually reported, in October, 1837, that, so far from the hospital being hugely indebted to the city, as was still contended at the Council House, the Corporation owed the charity a capital sum of £57,916, which, if simple interest were added at the rates charged by the Common Council on their fictitious claim, would be increased to £240,569. The Council had also engaged an accountant, Mr. Fletcher, and that gentleman produced his version of the facts in February, 1839, asserting that £21,000 were due to his clients. This calculation, however, appears to have been universally discredited. Various abortive efforts were made to effect a compromise, during which the local newspaper which had at first ridiculed as a "mare's nest" the claim of the trustees, began to violently assail them for endeavouring to "ruin the ratepayers." The trustees having at length commenced proceedings in the Court of Chancery, some influential members of the Council, warned by legal advisers of the hopelessness of the defence, entered into private negotiations with the plaintiffs, who made large concessions, and the matter was finally arranged in January, 1842. The basis of the agreement was that—in this as in other cases—the property belonging to the charity should be surrendered by the Corporation, which should also refund the revenue received subsequent to the Municipal Reform Act coming into operation. As regarded this hospital, the Common Council paid off the old bonds for £4,715 already referred to, with interest from January, 1836, and returned £1,200 received from rents; two crown-rents amounting to £61 3*s*. 5*d*. per annum were surrendered; and "Alderman Barker's gift" of £103, with several years' arrears, was refunded. In all, £7,174, and crown-rents of a capital value of £1,500 were returned to the charity. During the later days of the management of the old Corporation the number of boys in the school was forty-two. The trustees at once increased the number to 120, and afterwards augmented it to 220.—Another dispute arose between the Council and the trustees with reference to the Bartholomew Lands, which the latter body held to be the property of the Grammar School. It appears from the minutes of the Common Council that on the 15th September, 1814, it was resolved that the rental of an estate at Brislington, part of the Bartholomew Lands, and previously carried into the city chest, should be thenceforth transferred to Foster's Almshouse, to which the property was held to belong. In July, 1827, however, an alderman, emulous of the fame of Mr. Harris, moved for a committee to investigate the title of the entire estate. This body, of whom the alderman in question was the guiding spirit, having produced a report "after careful investigation," asserting in effect that the Bartholomew Lands vested absolutely in the Corporation, subject to a small payment to the Grammar School, the Council, in December, 1827, again inspired by the alderman aforesaid, declared the resolution of 1814 to be rescinded, and decreed the funds in hand (about £4,000) to be the sole property of the Corporation. It must now be added that the prime mover in this transaction was Mr. Alderman Fripp (jun.), who testified before the House of Lords in 1835 that the Corporation had piously, honourably, and discreetly administered the charities which had been confided to its control. The Charity Trustees, in 1837, commenced a legal suit for the recovery of the estate; and after lengthy proceedings in Chancery, that court, in January, 1842, with the consent of the defendants, gave judgment in favour of the trustees. The Council accordingly surrendered the property, and returned about £1,260, being the mesne profits from January, 1836, with interest.—Another and more remarkable litigation arose out of what was known as "Codrington's gift" to Trinity Hospital. Previous to the year 1572, Francis Codrington (sheriff in 1544) bequeathed £50 to his friend and fellow merchant, William Carr, requesting him to invest the money in land, and to apply the profits to maintaining the bedding in Barstaple's (Trinity) Hospital, which then provided entertainment for poor travellers. In pursuance of this bequest, Carr purchased nearly 210 acres of land at Portishead for £48, and soon after leased the estate for 1,000 years to the Corporation of Bristol, upon trust that the lessees would devote the entire receipts arising therefrom to the maintenance of the hospital. This trust was fulfilled for some forty years. But about 1616 the Corporation bought a large estate at Portishead on its own account, and thenceforward appropriated the rents of the whole property, Codrington's gift included. The malfeasance escaped the notice of the Charity Commissioners in 1820; and it was not until the misappropriation had continued for nearly two centuries and a quarter that the Charity Trustees discovered the facts. The Codrington estate then yielded over £200 a year. Application for relief was made to the Court of Chancery, which —by consent of the litigants—ordered the property to be transferred to the Charity Trustees, its legal owners; £708 being refunded in the shape of arrears. In all the above cases, the vast misappropriations of the old Corporation, which certainly exceeded a quarter of a million sterling, including interest, were condoned in the interest of the ratepayers, who had possessed no control over the Common Council, and who reasonably protested against being victimised for its misdeeds. Still another case remains to be noticed. In 1553 Dr. George Owen granted certain lands in Redcliff and other parts of the city to the Corporation, in order to increase the number of inmates in Foster's Almshouse by ten poor men, the cost being estimated by the donor at £15 3*s*. per annum. In course of time the property in question greatly increased in value; but in order to diminish the yearly proceeds it became the custom of the Common Council to grant leases upon lives at very low annual rents, while the fines on renewals, which were proportionably large, were coolly carried to the corporate treasury. This estate was also claimed through the Court of Chancery by the Charity Trustees, and after a struggle the Council consented to yield up the entire property (estimated to be worth £1,200 a year after the leases had expired), and also paid over arrears from 1836, amounting to £1,027. [By a scheme confirmed by Lord Chancellor Lyndhurst in 1843, five-sixths of Owen's estate were applied to the use of the Grammar School, and the remainder to the support of Foster's Almshouse.] This brief summary of the proceedings of the Charity Trustees during the early years of their existence will suffice to show the true character of that system of charity administration which was described by Alderman

Fripp in his evidence before the House of Lords as wholly irreproachable. It is needless to state that the members of the reformed body did no more than their duty in defending the interests committed to their charge. The proposal for a compromise of the disputes on the terms actually adopted was informally made by the Charity Trustees about the close of 1841, when the Council applied to Sir Charles Wetherell for his advice upon the subject. The recorder having, on the 5th January following, recommended the acceptance of the proposal, the corporate committee who had charge of the matter recommended the Council to sanction the arrangement, which "would terminate a painful and irritating litigation, and would in its results relieve the inhabitants not only from the expenditure attending its continuance, but also the risk of a much larger pecuniary sacrifice." A resolution adopting this report was formally passed by the Council on the 12th January, 1842, and was confirmed by the Lord Chancellor in a judgment delivered on the 27th of the same month. By the decree of the latter, the Corporation retained the management of the "gifts" left by the following persons—chiefly for sermons or church poor: Thomasine Harrington, Alderman Long, — Powell or Powl, — Silk, — Wheatley, W. Spencer, W. Carr, Lady Rogers, J. Bagod, M. Brown, P. Matthews, Sir J. Young, — Fownes, J. Griffin, W. Gibbs, and E. Cross; also "the Mayor's gift." After all the disputes had been settled, the Charity Trustees passed a vote of thanks to their solicitor, Mr. Meshach Brittan, to whose unwearied zeal and judicious counsel the recovery of the funds was largely due. In 1851, when the number of trustees had been much diminished by death, the political majority in the Council, who had long repented of their hasty action in 1836, petitioned the Lord Chancellor to appoint nine new members, all the persons suggested to him being Conservatives. The Liberal majority of the trustees—to prove, perhaps, that wrongheadedness was not peculiar to any political party—applied to be recruited by gentlemen from their own camp. In the following year, Lord St. Leonards, implying a rebuke to both sides, selected four names from the Council's list, and five from that of the trustees. This reconstruction of the board put an end to the charges of party animus which had been frequently, though groundlessly, made against the trust by exasperated party writers.

The last local duel of which any record has been found in the newspapers was fought on the 24th January, 1837, upon Durdham Down. The antagonists are described as "a gentleman of the Hotwells, and a foreigner residing in this neighbourhood." After an exchange of shots, the seconds succeeded in effecting an arrangement.

The manufacture of cotton cloth was established in Bristol in 1793, when about 250 hands were employed in a factory in Temple Street. The price of the poorly-printed goods intended for ladies' dress was at that time about four shillings a yard. In the *Bristol Journal* of July 6, 1805, "a capital cotton manufactory in Temple Street carried on for several years past" was advertised to be let. There were seventy looms on the premises, and the advertiser added: "There is a cotton mill and bleaching-field in the neighbourhood, where good twist and weft may be had." No further mention has been found of this establishment, and it was probably discontinued. In 1835 another attempt was made to add cotton-spinning to the industries of the city, a cotton twist and cloth company being proposed, with a capital of £200,000. The scheme was abandoned, owing to insufficient support; but in the spring of 1837, a party of ten influential gentlemen, in conjunction with a Mr. G. B. Clarke, of Manchester, started a private company under the style of Clarke, Acramans, Maze & Co. A little later, this concern merged into a joint-stock adventure, and assumed the name of the Great Western Cotton Company. A piece of land having been purchased at Barton Hill, the foundation stone of the intended factory was laid on the 18th April, 1837. A twelvemonth later a *fête* took place on the completion of the building. The first piece of cotton manufactured by the company was presented to the mayor (Mr. Haberfield) in January, 1839. The company, which had been already once or twice reorganised owing to the death of its proprietors—always a limited number—was again reconstructed in the spring of 1885, when the capital was fixed at £100,000 in £20 shares. Mr. [Sir] J. D. Weston became chairman of the new company, in which several wealthy citizens held an interest.

The new Custom House, Queen Square, erected upon the site of the building destroyed during the riots, was opened for business purposes on the 14th March, 1837. During its construction the work of the department had been conducted in a large house in St. Augustine's Place, near Colston's School, once the mansion of the Swymmer family, whose ultimate heiress married Thomas Fane, who about the middle of the eighteenth century was clerk to the Merchant Venturers' Company, but afterwards succeeded to the earldom of Westmoreland. [This fine old house, since demolished for the formation of Colston Street, contained a quantity of carved oak wainscoting, etc., which was purchased by Mr. W. Carne for beautifying some of the chief rooms in St. Donat's Castle, near Cowbridge.]

The destruction of spring garden produce in 1837 by repeated frosts gave rise to a new trade between Cornwall and this port. Mr. Dupen, master of a steamer plying to and from Hayle, brought on one occasion about fifty Cornish brocoli, which Bristolians eagerly purchased. About fifteen dozen were brought in on his next trip, and sixty dozen in the following week, a portion of the last being sent to Bath, where they were quickly sold. Mr. Dupen carried on the trade for some years, and gave a great impetus to market-gardening in Cornwall. A local journal of March, 1859, in stating that the quantity of brocoli received from that county each spring had swollen to from 30,000 to 40,000 dozen, added: "This week the *Cornubia* brought 880 baskets, containing from fifteen to eighteen dozen each."

In April, 1837, the churchwardens of St. Stephen's, exercising the power vested in them by the law, seized part of the furniture of a Mr. Brown, of Queen Square, a respectable Dissenter, on account of his refusal to pay the sum of 9*s*. demanded for church-rates. The seizure occasioned some excitement, and so large a crowd assembled at the Albion Tavern, Prince's Street, where the property was to be sold, that the auctioneer was afraid to proceed. The goods were disposed of privately, however, and the rate, with the costs, was recovered. Church-rates were then levied in nearly all the parishes of the city, and the defeats of dissenting minorities at the annual vestry meetings were invariably reported in the *Bristol Journal* as "victories of the Establishment." A more sagacious view of the matter, however, gradually prevailed. The above case is the latest recorded of an enforced payment by means of bailiffs, and, some years before the law was altered to meet the wishes of Nonconformists, the compulsory system was abandoned in Bristol, except in the parish of St. Augustine's.

The death of William IV. took place on the 20th June. His successor, Queen Victoria, whose majority in the preceding month had caused general rejoicing, was proclaimed in Bristol on the 24th; and the ceremony offered a great contrast to the cold pageants which had marked the accession of the two previous monarchs. Much of the "state" of the old Corporation—including the "knights in armour" —had, indeed, disappeared; but, in addition to the civic officials, a number of the local clergy and ministers, the magistrates, the Charity Trustees, and many respectable inhabitants joined in the procession, much sympathy being felt for one called to the cares of sovereignty at so early an age. It must be added in the interests of truth, that the attachment of the people to the monarchy had been rudely shaken by the experience of the previous quarter of a century; and the opinion expressed about this time by Sir Robert Peel, that the throne was visibly hastening to its fall, denoted the critical condition of the public mind. Chartism, which really meant republicanism, had many supporters amongst the working classes in Bristol, but there was little open manifestation of hostility during the proceedings of the day. Proclamation was made at the seven accustomed places from a car drawn by grey horses, the red cloth-covered rostrum of Georgian days being superseded.

At the general election in July, caused by the demise of the king, the two Conservative members of the previous Parliament retired into private life—Mr. Miles on the ground of his advanced age; Sir Richard Vyvyan from his disgust at the attitude of the leaders of his party, who in his opinion were pusillanimously truckling to new-fangled principles and ideas. The local heads of Conservatism nominated in their room Mr. Philip W. S. Miles, a youthful son of the late senior member, and Mr. William Fripp, an ex-alderman of the old Corporation, and first mayor under the Municipal Reform Act. The Liberal party selected the Hon. Francis Henry F. Berkeley. After an exciting contest, the poll was declared on the 25th July, as follows: Mr. Miles, 3,838; Mr. Berkeley, 3,312; Mr. Fripp, 3,156. In lieu of the old ceremony of chairing, the Liberals celebrated their victory by a procession of the trades of the city, in which some thousands of artisans took part. A petition against the return of Mr. Berkeley was presented on behalf of the defeated candidate. It alleged extensive bribery and treating, and further affirmed that certain agents of Mr. Berkeley, being also Charity Trustees, had been openly guilty of corruption and undue influence, by giving or promising charity gifts in order to secure votes against Mr. Fripp. On the publication of this document a declaration was made by nineteen out of the twenty-one trustees, including two who had voted for Mr. Fripp, asserting that the charge made against them was "entirely unfounded, calumnious, and false." The committee of the House of Commons appointed to hear the case assembled in February, 1838. After a three days' hearing the petition was abandoned, whereupon the chairman of the committee announced that they were unanimously of opinion that nothing had been proved against the Charity Trustees. Concurrently with the proceedings in Parliament, Mr. Fripp's supporters* brought actions at law against a number of Mr. Berkeley's friends, to recover penalties for bribery, and the trials took place at the ensuing Gloucester assizes. The juries in three cases having returned verdicts for the defendants, the remaining actions were withdrawn. Shortly afterwards, a woman named Verrier, who had deposed before the Commons' committee to an act of bribery committed by Mr. Berkeley, was tried for perjury, and convicted of the offence. In commenting upon this case, the editor of the *Bristol Journal*, who had been for some time noted for his acrimonious personal attacks, published gross charges against three of the Charity Trustees. Those gentlemen retorted by instituting actions for libel, and challenged their accuser to prove his assertions. The trials, which took place in July, 1839, resulted in the defendant being cast in damages in each case—for £400, £175, and £150 respectively—with heavy costs. The oldest of the Bristol newspapers, and once the most powerful, never recovered from the blow. It lingered on for several years, but its place was taken by more ably conducted Conservative organs, and on March 26, 1853, after a career of one hundred and one years, *Felix Farley's Bristol Journal* appeared for the last time.

The Bristol Teetotal Society celebrated its first anniversary in June, 1837. It then boasted of about a thousand members. A Temperance Society, which required a pledge from its adherents to abstain from spirituous liquors, was started about seven years earlier; but "mere temperance" was bitterly denounced and caricatured by the total abstinence party, and the moderate camp appears to have succumbed under their attacks.

At a meeting held on the 25th November, 1837, it was resolved to form a company, with a capital of £25,000, for the construction of a bridge across the Avon from Temple Back to Queen Street, St. Philip's. The company paid the Corporation £2,157 in compensation for the ferry which had previously occupied the site, the number of passengers over which had been ascertained to be 115,500 per annum. An Act of Parliament to carry out the undertaking having been

* Who are said to have spent £12,000 on the petition and subsequent trials. —*Ms. Annals, City Library*, ii. 118.

obtained in the session of 1838, a temporary bridge was built and opened during the autumn, and 342,000 persons passed over it during the first twelvemonths of its existence. The permanent bridge was opened by the mayor (Mr. G. W. Franklyn) on the 1st December, 1841. It had cost £11,000. The remainder of the company's capital, and a further sum raised by loan, were expended in the purchase of property for, and in the construction of, the approaches. [One of the buildings destroyed was a fine sixteenth century house, which in its later days had been known as the Giant's Castle Inn.] As the new bridge was a great improvement upon the old ferry, the public spirit of the shareholders, who received slender dividends for several years, was much commended by the residents of the neighbourhood. In course of time, however, the halfpenny toll came to be regarded as a grievance, and a movement was started to secure its abolition. The agitation gradually acquired strength, and in consequence of memorials addressed to the Council on the subject, that body, in November, 1873, resolved to enter into negotiations with the proprietors with a view to the purchase of the bridge. Legal difficulties then arose, causing a lengthened delay; but in the closing months of 1874 it was agreed that the Council should lease the property in perpetuity, paying the shareholders a yearly sum equivalent to 6 per cent. on their investments. The Corporation was also to take over the debt (£5,000) on the bridge, and to pay £2,000 to cover compensations, etc. An Act of Parliament having been obtained to sanction this arrangement, the toll on foot-passengers was abolished on the 31st July, 1875. The bridge was shortly afterwards widened at a cost of £5,000.

The first serious disaster in connection with the steamship service between Bristol and Ireland occurred on the 20th January, 1838, when a vessel named the *Killarney*, whilst on her passage from Cork to this city, struck during a heavy gale upon the Rennie rocks, near Youghal, and became a total wreck. Twenty-nine of the passengers and crew were drowned. The survivors, thirteen in number, succeeded in clinging to the slippery rocks, where they remained for two nights and a day, enduring extreme suffering from cold and hunger, before means for their rescue could be devised. One of the passengers, styling himself Baron Spolasco, published a local pamphlet, narrating the details of the disaster.

The foundation-stone of the Victoria Rooms was laid on the Queen's birthday, May 24th, 1838, by the mayor (Mr. Haberfield). The building,—which is the noblest classical erection in the city, and for the first time provided the inhabitants with spacious and convenient apartments for public entertainments,—was built at the expense of a body of Conservative citizens, and cost about £23,000. It was opened on the 24th May, 1842, with a dinner, at which the mayor (Mr. G. W. Franklyn) presided. A fine organ was placed in the large saloon about 1873.

The coronation of the youthful Queen, on the 28th June, was celebrated in Bristol with many demonstrations of joy. On previous occasions the expense of the festivities had been borne by the Corporation. Such an expenditure of public funds was no longer legal, but the voluntary subscriptions of the citizens were largely offered to meet the outlay, and the rejoicing was all the more genuine inasmuch as it was entirely spontaneous. At noon an imposing procession started from the Council House for the cathedral, headed by a troop of the North Somerset Yeomanry, a "champion" on horseback accoutred in full armour, and the boys of Queen Elizabeth's Hospital. Then followed the officers of the Corporation, the mayor and members of the Council, the foreign consuls, the local clergy and Dissenting ministers, the boys of Colston's School, the master and members of the Merchants' Society, the governor and members of the Incorporation of the Poor, the parochial officials, the Freemasons, and finally the workmen of the various trades, with banners, devices and emblems, etc., of their crafts. Two more "knights in armour" were strange fish in these modern waters, but they at least lent variety to the interesting pageant, the concluding divisions of which consisted of the members of the principal benefit societies, the firemen, and a troop of Gloucestershire Yeomanry. The procession passed through all the chief thoroughfares of the ancient city. So great was its length that its two extremities encountered each other in Dolphin Street, the main body then occupying Peter Street, Castle Street, Lower Castle Street, the Broadweir, Merchant Street, Broadmead, and Union Street. Whilst the members of the Corporation attended service at the cathedral, the procession passed up Park Street, Berkeley Square, etc., and then returned to the Council House, where it separated. Various public dinners were held in the afternoon, and the festivities concluded with a general illumination.

At a meeting of the Council on the 16th July, 1838, the fair annually held in St. James's Churchyard in the month of September, as well as the March fair held in Temple Street, was abolished; and fairs for the sale of live stock exclusively were ordered to be held in the cattle market on the two first days of March and September. The decree put an end to saturnalia of which but a faint conception can be formed in our times. That St. James's fair in the seventeenth century had been very extensively resorted to is proved by a letter of the Mayor of Penzance, forwarded to the Government in 1636, stating that twelve Turkish men of war, bearing English colours, were lurking in St. George's Channel to capture travellers to the fair. In the same year the Corporation of Bristol wrote to the Privy Council, pointing out that the manufacture of goods for the fair was being carried on in parts of London then infected with the plague. Obtaining no protection from this danger, the Corporation resolved to prohibit the entry of the perilous commodities, whereupon the wholesale traders of London also appealed to the Government, declaring that they—"drapers, skinners, leather sellers, and upholsterers"—yearly turned over "many thousand pounds" at the fair, and had "the chief part of their estates owing them by chapmen who meet nowhere else but at Bristol." The local inhibition was thereupon quashed. According to an official report to the Admiralty, a royal ship had "convoyed all the vessels from Bristol fair to Tenby and Milford," in 1657; and ten years later a Government official at Bridgwater reported that the Channel had been in great danger from French pickaroons, but two of the king's frigates had scared them. "It was feared they would have done mischief at Bristol fair." Down even to the close of the first quarter of the present century, the influx of wares and merchandise from all parts of the kingdom was astonishing, having regard to the defective means of communication. Blankets and woollens from Yorkshire, silks from Macclesfield, linens from Belfast and Lancashire, carpets from Kidderminster, cutlery from Sheffield, hardware from Walsall and Wolverhampton, china and earthenware from Staffordshire and other counties, cotton stockings from Tewkesbury, lace from Buckinghamshire and Devon, trinkets from Birmingham and London, ribbons from Coventry, buck and hog skins for breeches, hats and caps, millinery, haberdashery, female ornaments, sweetmeats, and multitudinous toys from various quarters arrived in heavily-laden wagons, and were joined by equally large contributions from the chief industries of the district. To these again were added nearly all the travelling exhibitions and entertainments then in the country—menageries, circuses, theatres, puppet shows, waxworks, flying coaches, rope-dancers, acrobats, conjurors, pig-faced ladies, living skeletons, and mummers of all sorts, who attracted patronage by raising a fearful din. It need scarcely be added that the scene attracted a too-plentiful supply of pickpockets, thieves, thimble-riggers, and swindlers of every genus. To make purchases or to gratify curiosity, the population of the surrounding district, from the family of the Duke of Beaufort down to the children of the Kingswood colliers, thronged into the city, and from early morning until late in the evening the alleys between the stalls and standing-places (which, being built and covered with wood, took a month in construction) presented a busy and often an amusing scene. As time went on, the places of business rapidly diminished, while the shows, entertainments, and general disorder increased; and as liquor was sold at a number of "bush" [unlicensed] houses, the fair, which by charter lasted nine days, but was generally permitted to continue a fortnight, became a centre of corruption and demoralisation. Strong vested interests were long, however, arrayed in support of the nuisance. About 1813 Mr. E. B. Fripp, then a vestryman of the parish, made an effort for its suppression, he and his friends offering £3,000 to the vestry as a compensation for the loss of tolls; but the receipts were so large that the proposal was contemptuously rejected. In 1837, when the "foreign" tradesmen had dwindled to less than a dozen, and the tolls scarcely defrayed the cost of erecting standings, the vestry gladly listened to terms; and Mr. George Thomas, one of the Quaker founders of the General Hospital, was largely instrumental in effecting an arrangement, having, with the aid of a few friends, raised a sum of about £1,000 for laying out the ground for a hay and coal market, and for compensating the vestry. The Corporation thereupon took a lease for ninety-nine years, at a rent of £150 per annum, of the open plot to the south of the churchyard. To this place, in May, 1841, the hay market was removed from Broadmead. The attempt to establish a coal market on the spot seems to have failed from the outset.

Up to this time, owing to the post office authorities measuring the distance between Bristol and London by way of Bath, the postage of what was called a "single" letter—that is, a single sheet of letter paper without envelope or enclosure —from or to the capital, was tenpence. In September, 1838, however, the officials discovered that the distance of Bristol from London by way of Marshfield was not over, but under, 120 miles, and the single letter postage was consequently reduced to ninepence. A letter enclosing a slip of paper, such as a cheque, was charged 1*s.* 6*d.*, one enclosing two cheques, 2*s.* 3*d.*; more numerous enclosures, not exceeding an ounce in weight, 3*s.* A system of penny postage for letters and small packets had been established for some years between the city and a few of the neighbouring villages, but the arrangement was of a very arbitrary character. For example, although Oakhill and Axbridge were each eighteen miles from Bristol, the charge for a four ounce packet to the former place was a penny, while to the more important town the postage was 6*s.* 8*d.* During the session of 1839, Lord Melbourne's Ministry succeeded in passing an Act for carrying out the penny postal scheme of Mr. Rowland Hill; and in December a uniform charge of fourpence per half-ounce came into force as regarded all letters on which the postage had previously exceeded threepence. In the following January the rate was reduced to a penny per half ounce. The new system was strongly condemned by the political opponents of the Cabinet. The *Bristol Journal* of December 7, 1839, feared that "this new plan of Whig Reform will be a more serious evil to the country than even any one of their more flagrant jobs." On the first adhesive stamp (printed in black ink) and the first envelope coming into use in the following year, the same paper of May 16 said: "Fortunately those who send letters have still the option of prepayment, and are not obliged to use the contemptible cover or black patch which the Government have been asses enough to sanction. Both patch and envelope are beneath criticism. How long is the revenue of this once powerful country to be entrusted to the hands of the nincompoops who are now wasting it?" The actual results of Mr. Hill's scheme, so far as regards Bristol, will be shown later on. The editor's shortsightedness was, however, pardonable, seeing that the heads of the postal service in London predicted the certain failure of the cheap system. [In 1844 a "national testimonial" to Rowland Hill was started, and resulted in a subscription of about £13,000. The sum contributed in Bristol was £292.]

On the 16th December, in conformity with a decision of the ecclesiastical tribunal of the diocese, two persons, living in Pomphrey's Court, Christmas Street, performed penance in the vestry room of St. John's Church, between the hours of morning and evening service. The punishment inflicted was the result of a cross suit between the parties in the above court.

A new survey of the city took place towards the close of

the year, when the rateable value of the various districts was assessed as follows: "Ancient city, £213,318; Clifton, £69,822; St. Philip's, out, £36,364; District, £20,310; part of Westbury, £10,457; part of Bedminster, £28,005.

Much discontent, arising largely from the depressed state of trade, prevailed amongst the working classes at this time, and Chartism had many followers in Bristol, as in other large towns. On the 26th December a meeting of the party took place on Brandon Hill, when Mr. Feargus O'Connor, a noisy platform orator, made a violent speech. For some months afterwards gatherings took place on the hill almost nightly, and owing to the tumultuous character of the proceedings, and the threats occasionally uttered to resort to physical force, the agitation excited some anxiety amongst the citizens. At length, early in May, 1839, the magistrates issued a circular prohibiting further nocturnal assemblies, and a number of the ratepayers were sworn in as special constables. This action had the desired effect, and, in spite of the unhappy outbreak at Newport in the following November, the peace of the city was undisturbed.

A discovery of some interest in connection with the Roman occupation of this part of the island was made in January, 1839, at Ashton Waters, near Long Ashton, during the excavation of the ground for the Bristol and Exeter railway. The workmen came across the remains of a building, the foundations of which extended for a considerable distance; and a number of coins, including one of Julius Cæsar, another of Diocletian, and several of Constantine, were disinterred. Two bronze spoons, a portion of the capitals of two columns, and various broken articles were also found. About the same time the remains of a villa, with a large tesselated pavement, were disinterred near Newton St. Loe.

Although two short sections of the Great Western railway had been opened in 1838, the question of gauge, which from the outset had excited much controversy, had not been definitively settled. On the 9th January, 1839, a great meeting of the proprietors was held in London to consider the reports of two eminent engineers, Mr. (afterwards Sir John) Hawkshaw, and Mr. Nicholas Wood, and to determine the problem on which those gentlemen had been consulted. Mr. Wood, whilst disapproving of Mr. Brunel's seven feet gauge, recommended that, in view of the outlay already incurred, it should be retained. Mr. Hawkshaw, though regretting the narrowness of the north country gauge, decidedly condemned the introduction of another, on the ground that it would be a serious impediment to the working and development of the railway system of the country. The directors, in a report commenting upon the objections of the two engineers, declared them to have "little weight," and the shareholders were confidently assured that Mr. Hawkshaw's assertions would prove groundless. A member of the board having moved that Mr. Brunel's system be adhered to, an amendment was proposed condemning it as wasteful and injudicious; but the result of the voting was in favour of the original motion by a majority of 7,792 against 6,145. The only excuse that can be offered for those who adopted a shortsighted resolution is, that unlimited confidence was placed by many wealthy shareholders in Mr. Brunel's genius. When Mr. George Stephenson was asked about the same time what gauge should be adopted on two lines, one near Leicester and another near Canterbury, he at once pronounced in favour of the system adopted on the Stockton and Darlington and the Manchester and Liverpool railways. "Though they are," he observed, "a long way apart from each other now, they will be joined together some day." Brunel, on the other hand, assured the Great Western board that their undertaking "could never have any connection with any other of the main lines," three or four of which, he felt assured, would suffice for the traffic of the country. This opinion rapidly proved to be a delusion, and the natural effect of the break of gauge was to excite the then existing directorates to fight for the territory which lay between them. A fierce war thus broke out, which lasted for several years, with deplorable consequences to the shareholders. So long as the two gauges were apart, the public of course felt no inconvenience. But in 1844, when the Bristol and Gloucester line (then broad gauge) was opened, it came in contact at the latter city with the Birmingham and Gloucester narrow gauge railway, and whilst through passengers complained of the trouble and loss of time involved in a change of carriages —often in bad weather and in the darkness of the night—the stoppage in the transit of cattle, minerals, and goods through the necessity of unloading and reloading the trucks excited widespread discontent. The merchants of Bristol speedily felt the grievance. Birmingham manufacturers, finding that their wares forwarded for shipment at this port were delayed or mislaid at Gloucester, and that the distance between their factories and Bristol was as difficult of transit as in the days before railways, forwarded their goods to Liverpool or London, where no such difficulty arose. In a lesser degree a similar impediment to Bristol traffic was experienced at Worcester, Warwick, Rugby, Salisbury, and Dorchester, at each of which places broad gauge wagons came in contact with narrow gauge lines, and could travel no farther. In short, the West of England was as completely isolated from other parts of the country as if a river too wide to be bridged lay between it and the rest of the kingdom. And this, according to Mr. Brunel and the Great Western board, was to go on for ever along a boundary line 200 miles in length, running on both sides of the railway. The grievance became the more crying when Mr. Brunel himself laid out plans for several narrow gauge lines, and the matter at length came to be viewed in commercial circles as a public calamity. At the instance of Mr. Cobden, a royal commission was appointed to consider the subject, and a lengthened inquiry commenced in August, 1845. The result was an overwhelming mass of scientific testimony in condemnation of Mr. Brunel's theory, which had no supporters but himself and two Great Western officials. The Commissioners consequently recommended that the narrow gauge should be used on all future railways, and that some equitable means should be devised for producing an entire uniformity of gauge throughout the kingdom. Parliament practically adopted the first of those suggestions, but it was estimated that the alteration of the Great Western lines would involve an expense of a million sterling, and the legislature, declining to lay any burden upon the public for the reparation of the company's blunder, left the directors to their own devices. The board had in the long run to admit that their favourite theory was deeply injurious to the interests of the shareholders. In August, 1868, it was determined to convert all the broad gauge lines north of Oxford into narrow gauge. In 1871 it was resolved to abandon the broad gauge on the South Wales section of the railway, and to lay the narrow gauge from Didcot to Milford Haven. This was obviously but the beginning of a general change in the western districts. In June, 1874, a similar alteration took place between Bristol and Bath, and towards the end of the same year the narrow system was extended throughout the trunk line, the old gauge being retained for express trains only. The Bristol and Exeter board being then forced to take action, the "mixed gauge" was completed from Bristol to Exeter in May, 1877.

The Royal Western Hotel, College Place, a building of some architectural pretensions, but erected on an ill-chosen site (previously occupied by Reeves's hotel, see p. 30), was opened on the 18th April. A public dinner in celebration of the event took place soon after, the mayor (Mr. Haberfield) presiding. The house, built by Messrs. Rogers, ceased to be an hotel in April, 1855. Some five years later, Turkish baths were fitted up in the building by Mr. Bartholomew.

A gigantic tusk of a mammoth was discovered in June by some workmen engaged in excavating in St. Philip's Marsh. The tusk, which was nearly six feet in length, was forwarded to the museum of the Bristol Institution.

The foundation-stone of a monument dedicated to Chatterton was laid on the 13th November, 1839, in St. Mary Redcliff churchyard.* The site chosen was the angle between the tower and the north porch. The statue, which was universally condemned as mean in execution and absurdly diminutive as compared with its pedestal, was erected on the 30th April, 1840. In February, 1846, the vicar of the parish, the Rev. M. R. Whish, whose eccentricities brought him frequently before the public, suddenly gave orders for the removal of the monument, asserting that it had been erected without his sanction. As the reverend gentleman—whose action was applauded by a few contemporary bigots—was omnipotent in his churchyard, the structure was taken down, and disappeared from public view for some years. In July, 1857, however, it was re-erected on the (unconsecrated) spot where it now stands, a few members of the parochial vestry having defrayed the cost of the restoration.

In the course of this year some negotiations took place between the Corporation and the dock directors, with a view to the purchase of the Floating Harbour by the city, and thus to get rid of the shortsighted exactions by which the commerce of the port was weighed down. It was intimated to the dock board that the Council were prepared to pay interest at the rate of 2¼ per cent. on the share capital if the transfer were effected; but the offer was rejected as inadequate, and the matter was suffered to drop.

About this time the land known to all Bristolians as Mother Pugsley's Field, together with some adjoining plots, was disposed of in sites for building. Pedestrians had enjoyed access from time immemorial to the spring in Pugsley's Field; but, to use the language of a local journalist, Sir Thomas Fremantle, the owner of the land, flourished his title deeds in the face of the public, and nobody had the spirit to defend

* So early as September, 1805, a movement was started in the city for the erection of a "magnificent cenotaph" to the unfortunate boy poet. The scheme, however, found few supporters, and was soon dropped.

the rights of the community. A builder, named Hucker, who purchased part of the property, enclosed the spring—which had a reputation for healing virtues amongst the vulgar—for private use at his residence, Spring Villa, Nugent Hill.

Bristol Cathedral was reopened in February, 1840, after undergoing partial "restoration." The most important alterations were the removal of a large screen in the Greek style erected behind the communion table, and the construction of a richly decorated central recess corresponding with those on each side. No vestige remained of the original decorative work at the back of the altar, so that the arrangement is merely the conception of a modern architect. It would appear from the view of the reredos in the frontispiece to Britton's account of the cathedral, that the renovator took great liberties with the beautiful work of Abbot Knowle. The Corinthian screen was purchased by the Irvingites for their church on the Quay. Although the chapter showed an improved taste in this proceeding, its ideas of seemliness were still somewhat chaotic. A letter in the *Bristol Journal* of the 5th April, 1845, stated that "a cast-iron stove, with an immense black vertical flue, passing through the beautiful groined roof," had just been placed in the choir of the cathedral!

The lighthouse at the mouth of the Avon, erected by the Corporation of the Trinity House, was completed in April, 1840, and was lighted up in the following June.

In June, 1840, the royal assent was given to a Bill "for regulating the buildings and party walls within the city, and for widening and improving certain streets." The Corporation by this statute obtained power to open a new street [Phippen Street], and to widen and improve the thoroughfares in that neighbourhood. Power was taken to borrow £15,000 for those purposes, and a sum of £10,000, given some years previously by Mr. William Weare (see page 130) to further various improvements, was ordered to form part of a fund, to be called "the Improvement Fund."

In July, 1840, the Society of Merchants undertook to remove one of the greatest obstructions to the navigation of the Avon—the Round Point, a little below St. Vincent's rocks—and obtained the consent of the Corporation, as conservators of the river, to carry out the necessary work. It was announced that the undertaking would involve the removal of 25,000 cubic yards of rock. The operations of the Society, however, must have been of a limited nature, for in March, 1852, after the *Demerara* disaster, the removal of the Round Point was reported to the Council to be urgently necessary, and in the following September a resolution was passed authorising the docks committee to carry out the needful improvement at an expense not exceeding £5,000. The Merchants' Society having been asked to contribute to the cost, in consideration of the large revenue they derived from the wharfage dues, subscribed £1,000. Upwards of 30,000 tons of rock were cut away on this occasion, and about the same quantity was removed from the projection on the Somerset bank, a portion of the hill on each side being also taken down to open the line of sight upon the river. Even after this was done the place continued to be very dangerous; and under Mr. Howard's improvement scheme of 1864 another and much more costly effort was made to straighten the river, Bridge Valley Road, which overhung the Avon at the "point," being carried farther back, and many thousand tons of rock being blasted away under high-water mark. Nevertheless, in 1884, the obstruction was still complained of, and once more the Council ordered excavations, which were continued for several months at low tides, the electric light being employed to facilitate operations during the night. In 1885 similar operations were begun on the opposite shore, and are still unfinished. Even now the state of the Round Point leaves much to be desired.

Another disastrous wreck of an Irish passenger steam vessel occurred on the 18th November, 1840. The ship in question, *The City of Bristol,* had left Waterford on the previous night, and was driven during a violent storm on the Welsh coast, near Worm's Head. Of the twenty-seven persons who were on board only two survived to tell the lamentable story.

Up to this time the citizens were very scantily provided with public rooms fitted for meetings or social gatherings. With the exception, indeed, of an inconveniently situated Assembly-room, in Prince's Street, and two halls of the ancient trading companies, there was no place in the city where the inhabitants could meet together in large bodies. In December, 1840, a spacious public room, called the Hall of Science—built by the admirers of the then celebrated socialist, Robert Owen, and intended for the dissemination of his doctrines—was opened in Broadmead, when a lecture was delivered by Mr. Owen. Its founders being unable to meet the expenditure, the building was purchased in January, 1843, by a few members of the Liberal party, and was subsequently known as the Broadmead Rooms. Until the erection of Colston Hall, this place, in spite of its inconvenient access, was the favourite spot for popular gatherings in the city. It subsequently reverted into the hands of the Corporation, which in 1875 granted a lease of it at a rental of £100 per annum, the lessee undertaking to build a factory on the site.

In December, 1840, the newly-appointed mayor, Mr. Robert Phippen, revived the custom of attending the Mayor's Chapel in state, which had been discontinued for some years. In anticipation of the pageant his worship was presented by his friends with a state robe and gauntlets, similar to those worn in the old Common Council, and their use was afterwards continued. The cost of maintaining divine service in the Mayor's Chapel had, from 1836 to this time, been provided by private subscriptions, the Liberal section of the Council having protested against the application of the corporate funds to denominational purposes. In 1841, however, the Conservatives formed an overwhelming majority of the civic body *, and on the 22nd March it was resolved, by forty votes against six, that the chapel should be "supported and maintained in the same manner, to the same extent, and for the same purpose in all respects, as before the passing of the Municipal Act." The expenditure originated by this decision was set down at £260 in the accounts for the year. As a complement to the resolution, the aldermen and a large majority of the councillors revived, in December, 1850, the ancient custom of wearing scarlet robes when attending the chapel on state occasions.

At a meeting of the Council on the 3rd February, 1841, a matter was brought to light which provoked much criticism in Dissenting circles. It appeared that a few months previously an application had been made on behalf of a Wesleyan congregation in the parish of Dyrham, for a lease, at the full value, of a plot of ground on which it was intended to erect a schoolroom, to be used occasionally for religious services. The Finance Committee had at first expressed its willingness to assent, and had directed the surveyor to fix the rental, whereupon the rector of Dyrham forwarded an earnest request that the lease should be refused, observing that great evils would arise from the introduction of schism, and that there was ample accommodation for the parishioners in his church. The reverend gentleman omitted to state that the village of Hinton, where it was proposed

---

* In October, 1843, the Council consisted, according to the *Bristol Journal*, of fifty-three Conservatives and eleven Liberals.

to build the schoolroom, was nearly a mile and a half from the church, and that an existing small building used by the Wesleyans was inconveniently crowded every Sunday. The Finance Committee at once complied with the rector's wishes, and several of its members defended its action in the Council, Mr. Powell, of St. Augustine's, asserting that only two or three itinerant Wesleyan preachers, who "sent the hat round every Sunday, and made a good thing of it," were at the bottom of the scheme. The Council having referred the matter to the committee for further consideration, a report was presented a month later, recommending that the lease be granted; but the Council rejected the advice by 28 votes to 12. The subject was revived in 1845; but the application for a lease, at a rental to be fixed by the Corporation, was again rejected by 26 votes against 14. Yet in October, 1847, when a piece of ground valued by the corporate surveyor at £500 was selected as the site for St. Matthias' Church on the Weir, the Council, by 24 votes against 9, resolved to reduce the purchase money to £150. The Lords of the Treasury, however, put a veto on this transaction, and the price was ultimately fixed at £300.

The opening of the Great Western Railway between Bristol and London took place, as has been already recorded, on the 30th January, 1841. Amongst the incidental difficulties connected with the introduction of rapid travelling, the question of "time" was amongst the most perplexing. Down to this period each provincial town kept its own time, which was generally determined with accuracy by some scientific resident, and coaches found no trouble in accommodating themselves to local arrangements. But the railway lines starting from the capital naturally fixed on Greenwich time, and adopted it throughout their respective systems. There was thus a difference between Bristol time and railway time of about ten minutes; and a few years later, when the line was extended to Plymouth, the time of that town varied seventeen minutes from that of the railway station. The authorities in Bristol, doubtless with an intention to accommodate the public, had two minute hands placed on the clock at the Exchange, and a similar plan was adopted at Bath; but as local time continued to be recorded by the church clocks, the public seem to have been more puzzled than instructed. The people of Exeter, on the other hand, obstinately refused for some years to recognise "cockney time." As will hereafter be noted, the introduction of the electric telegraph quickly routed provincial prejudices on the subject.

The church of St. John the Evangelist, near Redland, was consecrated on the 27th April, 1841, by the bishop of the diocese. The remarkable change which has since occurred in that district is illustrated by the fact that, in the appeals made to the public on behalf of the building fund, it was stated that the church was intended to meet the spiritual destitution of a locality almost exclusively inhabited by the poorest class of labourers, and that a large proportion of the sittings would in consequence be free. In course of time, the free seats in the choir were calmly appropriated by the middle-class families which had come into the district; and in 1864 a fresh set of free seats was provided in less fashionable parts of the church. Dr. Benson, Archbishop of Canterbury, is said to have preached his first sermon as a deacon in this building.

At a meeting of the Council on the 5th May, a committee, to whom the subject had been referred, reported that it would not be advisable to make alterations in the Guildhall, but that the most advantageous course would be to take down the edifice, together with some adjoining houses, and to erect a more commodious hall upon the site. A hope was held out that the sale of the surplus ground would sensibly diminish the cost of the new structure. The Council gave power to the committee to carry out the recommendations of the report. After the subject had been postponed for nearly two years, the Guildhall committee, on the 12th April, 1843, presented a fresh report, accompanied by plans prepared by Mr. R. S. Pope. It was proposed that the new building should comprise, in addition to an assize court capable of containing 1,000 persons, two bankruptcy courts, a Court of Requests, a mayor's parlour, and other apartments. The cost was estimated at £10,000, but it was supposed that an income of £428 would be derived from rents. It was objected in the Council that the principal hall shown in the plans would be one-third less than the Guildhall then in existence, which was often found too small for election nominations and public meetings. Nevertheless, Mr. Pope's design was, with slight modifications, adopted, and in June workmen commenced demolishing the old building. [The large traceried window in that part of the structure known as St. George's Chapel was shortly afterwards re-erected in the grounds of "The Grove," Stapleton. On removing the roof of the chapel, in the space between the modern ceiling and the rafters, a row of pointed window arches was found in the walls on each side, showing that the building had originally been lofty and finely formed.] On the 30th October, 1843, the foundation stone of the new Guildhall was laid by the mayor (Mr. James Gibbs). It had been intended to mark the event with much ceremony, and the Freemasons of the district were invited to take part in the proceedings; but torrents of rain fell at the appointed hour, and the procession, which was to have passed through the principal streets, dwindled to an undignified "scuttle" down Broad Street. During the construction of the building the assizes and quarter sessions were held in Coopers' Hall, King Street. The new court was used for the first time on the 28th July, 1846, when the sessions were opened by Sir Charles Wetherell (who died less than three weeks afterwards). The interior of the structure excited a universal wail of disappointment. The feeling of the public was embodied in homely but explicit doggerel:

> "They pull'd down the old hall, because it was too small,
> And now they've built a new Guildhall, with no hall at all."

Only one opinion was expressed as to the arrangements by those called upon to make use of the building; and Mr. Justice Coleridge's remark, that the place was "the perfection of inconvenience," was re-echoed by jurors, counsel, litigants, witnesses, and reporters. Defective as it was, the Guildhall was in some respects an improvement on its predecessor. The shortcomings of the latter were described from recollection by Mr. Leech in the *Bristol Times* of July 17, 1858. The writer remarked: "Justice was at times administered with anything but gravity and decorum. The chief portion of the great hall was occupied by the sessions, and once a year by the assizes, whilst at the lower end was a smaller court, where the late Mr. A. Palmer administered justice in matters whose gravity did not exceed the weight of forty shillings. The division between the two courts was an imaginary line, which led to an occasional collision between the two jurisdictions. . . . Sometimes a message would be sent down to urge the necessity of the actors in the inferior tribunal conducting their proceedings *sotto voce*, . . . and it might be that the herald would receive an answer couched not merely in strong language, but actually in phrase not to be repeated to ears polite. Bankruptcy was administered in lofts upstairs, and the barristers robed in an old garret magnificently furnished by the city with a tenpenny looking-glass. Rows in the Guildhall we all remember, when blue and yellow roared and fought around the door for the possession of the premises on the election nomination days; and then, when the point had been carried by a column headed by the Game Chicken, or some other local champion, with what a rush and a bellowing up the flight of stone steps burst the strugglers." The additional assize court and other buildings fronting Small Street will be referred to under 1865.

The fifth decennial census of the population was taken on the 7th June, when the city of Bristol, as extended by the Municipal Corporations Act, was found to contain 123,188 souls. For the purpose of comparison with previous returns, it may be added that the ancient city had a population of 64,266; Clifton, 14,177; the District, 6,139; St. Philip's, out, 21,590; St. George's, 8,318; Mangotsfield, 3,862; Stapleton, 3,944; Bedminster, 17,862; and Stoke Bishop tything, 2,651.

On the dissolution of Parliament in June, 1841, the previous members, Mr. P. W. S. Miles, and Mr. F. H. F. Berkeley, offered themselves for re-election. The Conservatives proposed to oust the latter by again nominating Mr. W. Fripp; but at the close of the poll, which took place on the 29th June, the numbers were found to be: Mr. Miles, 4,197; Mr. Berkeley, 3,743; Mr. Fripp, 3,689. Much irritation was caused amongst Mr. Fripp's friends by Mr. Miles's disclaimer on the hustings of a coalition, and an angry controversy took place on the subject, which, as will afterwards be seen, ended in a temporary disruption of the Conservative party in the city. The polling had hitherto taken place in Queen Square only; but on this occasion the sheriff resolved on erecting forty-three booths in various parts of the borough, much to the convenience of the electors.

As an illustration of the manner in which elections were still conducted, the following extract from an article published in the *Bristol Journal* on the eve of the contest is not unworthy of preservation: "Remember that a Conservative Government will be the inevitable result of the coming elections, and that all the situations in the Customs and Excise will be in their gift, on the nomination of Miles and Fripp.* Freemen of Bristol! The following is a list of the gifts in

* "A meeting of Mr. Miles's committee was held on Monday, Sir. J. K. Haberfield in the chair, when the following appointments were made to fill up vacancies in our Custom House: Mr. Baber, son to our well-known and respected fellow citizen, Mr. Harry Baber, was appointed to a clerkship in the Long Room; Mr. William Ross Davis to a weigher's situation, and Mr. George Collins as tidewaiter."—*Bristol Journal*, May 22, 1852. In the same newspaper for the following week it is stated that the appointment of a postmaster for Clifton by Mr. Hale (M.P. for Gloucestershire) had caused great dissatisfaction amongst the dispensers of Government patronage in Bristol.

the hands of the Conservative churchwardens and vestries of this city: All Saints, 19; St. Augustine's, 56; Christ Church, 25; St. Ewen, 5; St. James's, 66; St. John's, 26; St. Leonard's, 6; St. Maryleport, 10; St. Mary Redcliff, 46; St. Michael's, 48; St. Nicholas' 60; St. Paul's, 6; St. Peter's, 45; St. Philip's, 45; St. Stephen's 31; Temple, 62; St. Thomas's, 61; St. Werburgh's, 14—631. This is a goodly array of gifts which are in the power of the Conservatives to bestow, and will no doubt brighten the eyes of many a poor freeman." It was true, continued the writer, that the Charity Trustees, who were abusing the powers confided to them in the interests of Liberalism, had 129 gifts at their disposal. But a Conservative Government would "displace every one of these men in the very next session" of Parliament, and Liberal electors "having already had such a large picking, must in common justice give way to the claims of those who now vote for Miles and Fripp." In the meantime the "poor freemen" were assured that "our generous Conservative mayoress, our Conservative Town Council, our Conservative churchwardens, our Conservative vestries, our Conservative Merchant Venturers would not turn a deaf ear to their supplications."

Christ Church, Clifton, the finest example of the Early English style of architecture in the city, was consecrated by Bishop Monk on the 8th October. It had cost about £10,500, including the purchase of the site. In 1858, the then incumbent urged that the building should be enlarged by the addition of aisles, but the parishioners preferred to add the tower and spire, according to the original design. These graceful ornaments were completed on the 22nd November, 1859, at a cost of £2,400 (a workman celebrating the fixing of the capstone—which weighed a quarter of a ton—by standing upon it on his head, at a distance of 212 feet from the ground). In 1884 the aisles were again projected, and the proposal caused fresh dissension and some litigation, several influential residents being of opinion that the additions, if carried out, would irreparably destroy the beauty of the edifice. Their opponents, however, prevailed, and the new aisles, which cost upwards of £4,000, were opened by Bishop Ellicott in September, 1885.

The Bristol Deaf and Dumb Institution was established in the course of this year. In the case of this charity, the city did not occupy its customary position amongst the great towns of the country. Edinburgh founded a Deaf and Dumb Institution in 1760, and the example had been largely followed before Bristol entered the field. The charity, which was for many years located in Park Row, was removed in August, 1874, to the entrance to Tyndall's Park, where a building in the Tudor style had been erected for it at an outlay of £7,000.

Under the Cathedral Acts passed in 1841 and 1842, the bishop of this diocese was authorised to appoint, at the rate of two per annum, twenty-four honorary canons of Bristol. An equal number was awarded to Gloucester.

In March, 1842, workmen commenced the removal of the old houses which earlier generations had allowed to cluster against the north side of St. Mary Redcliff Church, some encroaching on the west front of the edifice being also demolished, with the object of laying out a new street, which was called Phippen Street, in honour of the mayor for the previous year. By the destruction of several miserable dwellings, the north front of the parish church, the details of which had been concealed for two or three centuries, were thrown open to public view. [The statue of Chatterton (see p. 249) was re-erected on the site of one of those hovels.] The cost of the property destroyed (about eighty-six tenements), with other expenses, was upwards of £20,700; but by the sale of ground rents the expenditure was reduced to about £8,700. In May, 1843, a further improvement was effected near the church by the lowering of Redcliff Hill, a commencement being also made with the widening of Redcliff Street, by the setting back of one or two houses. These works raised the total amount spent in the locality to £13,500.

On the 18th March, a man styling himself Signor Irving walked across a rope stretched over the Floating Harbour, from a warehouse on Redcliff Back to the Welsh Back. The feat attracted a great concourse of spectators. Three days later, the precursor of Blondin was repeating the performance, when the rope broke, and he was seriously bruised by falling upon a barge.

On the 7th July, 1842, an exhibition of machinery, works of art, etc., promoted by the members of the Mechanics' Institute, was opened in a building at the top of Park Street, and continued on view, with a short interval, until the end of October. Amongst the visitors was H.R.H. the Duke of Cambridge, who expressed himself much pleased. The exhibition was very popular, upwards of 74,000 persons paying for admission; and the net profits, nearly £800, sufficed to wipe off the debt of the Institute.

The Royal Agricultural Society opened the fourth of its annual country meetings at Bristol on the 12th July. The site selected for the exhibition of implements is now occupied by the Triangle, while the show ground for animals was in the fields which then lay immediately behind the Victoria Rooms, about six acres being enclosed for the purpose. Amongst the miscellaneous articles on view was a gigantic cheese, weighing nine hundredweight, made at West Pennard, Somerset, and intended by the dairy farmers of the district as a present to the Queen. [The cheese subsequently got into the Court of Chancery.] The showyard was visited by 33,000 persons. The trials of implements took place in a field at Sneyd Park. Amongst the crowds of distinguished personages who visited the city on the occasion, were the Duke of Cambridge, the Prince of Saxe Meiningen, the Dukes of Richmond and Beaufort, the Marquis of Downshire, the Earls of Ilchester, Somers, Ducie, Spencer, Essex, Chichester, Fortescue, and Zetland, the Hon. E. Everett, United States minister, H. Handley, Esq., president of the Society, etc. The annual dinner of the Society was held on the 14th July in a pavilion capable of accommodating about 2,500 persons. On the same day a single train from London brought down 2,115 passengers. The receipts of the Great Western Railway for the week were £20,627, which by a generation accustomed to coach travelling was deemed a truly marvellous amount.

About this date a curious official seal or die of the reign of Henry VIII. was found in a sewer near Castle Street. It was of copper, gilt, about three inches in diameter, and bore an effigy of the king in his robes, seated under a canopy, and holding a sceptre and orb. The inscription was as follows: "Anno Regis Henrici Octavi 34, racium (?) anno gracia, 1542."

The local journals of the 30th July published a long and earnest appeal to the citizens on behalf of the venerable parish church of St. Mary Redcliff, then crumbling to decay through the neglect and parsimony of previous generations. The appeal, which was signed by the Rev. M. R. Whish, vicar, and Thomas Proctor and John Farler, churchwardens, stated that the objects to be kept in view were the solid and substantial repair of the fabric, the restoration of its ornamental parts, and such alterations, chiefly internal, as might be necessary to restore the church to its ancient and pristine beauty. The services of Mr. Britton, the eminent antiquary, had been obtained for the restoration, and Mr. William Hosking, professor of architecture at King's College, had co-operated in the preparation of plans and drawings illustrative of the work to be accomplished. The cost of the restoration was estimated at "very nearly £40,000." The response of the citizens to this document was of a frigid character; and although the promoters of the work nevertheless persevered in pressing it upon the public, they long failed to shake the apathy of the wealthier classes. At a meeting in March, 1845, it was reported, that although the ruinous state of the church was daily becoming more alarming, the total amount subscribed (less a vote of £2,000 made by the vestry and £1,000 contributed by the committee) was only £2,400. Urgent appeals were repeatedly made through the press; and in the following September, in the hope that if the work were once begun it would not be suffered to drop, Mr. George Godwin was appointed architect. A contract was also entered into for the restoration of the east window and of one section of the church. The foundation-stone of the new works was laid on the 21st April, 1846, by the mayor (Mr. Haberfield), a long masonic procession accompanying his worship to the spot. In the course of carrying out this contract, which was completed in September, 1847, some brickwork blocking up an arch between the chancel and the Lady Chapel was removed, when a beautiful but much-mutilated stone screen was exposed to view. [Another interesting discovery was made some years later in the south aisle of the nave, namely, the original tombs of William Canynges and his wife. The face of these beautifully canopied recesses had been ruthlessly cut away and wainscoted over in the reign of Queen Anne, when the church was repewed. It was supposed that the effigies then lying in the south transept had been removed from the recesses by the perpetrators of the mutilation, and in 1852 the figures were replaced in their original position.] In January, 1848, the Canynges Society was formed for the purpose of helping forward the restoration, directing its efforts in the first instance to the chancel. In the summer of the same year an anonymous contributor, signing himself "Nil Desperandum," began to forward money for the restoration of the north porch, the cost of which was nearly £2,600. [On the death of Alderman Proctor, in May, 1876, his executors discovered—as had long been suspected—that he had effected this work at his sole expense, besides contributing largely to the subscriptions for the church]. The assistance of the public continued to be rendered grudgingly for several years; and but for the exertions of the Canynges Society, and its auxiliary, the Commercial Association (which rebuilt the south porch), little progress could have been effected. At the close of 1857, after nearly sixteen years' efforts, less than

£13,000 had been obtained from every source. More interest, however, began to be shown by the wealthier classes after that date; and in 1860 a stimulus was given to the work by the offer of Mr. S. W. Lucas, of Birmingham, to give £1,000 provided £4,000 additional were collected. The result was a subscription exceeding £5,500, which enabled the committee to make considerable progress during the following five years. In the meantime, the freemasons of the city resolved upon restoring the Lady Chapel at their sole expense. The first stone of this work was laid on the 28th August, 1861, when the masonic body in full regalia assembled in the Exchange, and walked in procession through the streets, the unusual pageant exciting much public interest. The stone was laid by Mr. Henry Shute, P.G.M. At the close of 1865, when the treasury was again exhausted, another subscription was set on foot, Alderman Proctor, Mr. R. P. King, Mr. J. Lucas, and the Rev. H. G. Randall offering £500 each, to which the public added about £4,000. In 1870 it was announced that this fund, which had reached £7,500, was absorbed. The restoration of the Lady Chapel was completed in the same year. Only £5,000 additional were now asked for to complete the restoration, including the spire, and as about £2,000 were soon forthcoming, the committee began operations for "crowning the edifice" in the summer of 1871. No time was lost in prosecuting the task, for on the 9th May, 1872, the capstone of the spire—a piece of Portland stone thirteen feet in girth, and weighing about a ton—was laid by the mayor (Alderman W. P. Baker), who was accompanied to the summit, 276½ feet above the ground, by the mayoress, the vicar, and some officials of the parish. The vane, which stands 15½ feet above the capstone, was fixed a few days later. In the closing months of the year an illuminated dial was placed in the tower, and the peal of bells was increased from ten to twelve. In October, 1874, a "final appeal" was made by the Canynges Society, who stated that up to that date £45,000 had been expended in the restoration, of which sum £2,000 remained as a debt. Various details were also left uncompleted, and for these £4,000 more were required. The incumbrance was shortly after cleared off, and the additional works were undertaken and finished at intervals.

On the 1st August, 1842, Lord Langdale, Master of the Rolls, gave judgment upon an information filed by the Attorney-General against the Society of Merchant Venturers in the matter of Colston's School. The question at issue was the disposition of the surplus of the funds left by Colston after the expenses of the school had been provided for, it being argued by the Society, that as they were liable for deficiencies, they were entitled to appropriate the surpluses which might remain in hand. A particular transaction appeared to have led to the information. The Merchants' Society had demised to one Edward Bowyer and his wife a portion of the Colston property on lease, at a yearly rent of £315; but subsequently, in consideration of the lessees undertaking to pay down £2,500, the rent was reduced to £5 per annum. The lessees had actually paid only £500 of the promised amount; for the balance of £2,000 the Society obtained as security the manor of Stogursey, which subsequently, saving certain rights of Eton College, passed wholly into their possession, when the profits were retained by themselves. Lord Langdale, in giving judgment, said the Society were not entitled to deal with the funds of the school for their own benefit. There must be an inquiry, and the Society must be charged on account of the £2,500, but the inquiry was not to go further back than the date of the information. There was, his lordship added, much to be urged for the defendants, considering the difficulties imposed upon them by Colston's executors. The Society appealed against the decision, but the Lord Chancellor, in January, 1848, confirmed the judgment of Lord Langdale. During the hearing of the case it was stated by counsel that certain estates, ground-rents, etc., given by Colston to the school, and producing £1,280 at the time of the foundation, had become worth more than £3,000 a year, and that the surplus had been retained for many years by the Merchants' Society.

The conversion, in 1786, of the Weavers' Hall, Temple Street, then a Methodist chapel, into a Jewish synagogue, is recorded in Barrett's history of the city. On the 18th August, 1842, the Jews opened a new synagogue near the same spot, having purchased and decorated a chapel built for the Society of Friends, but which had been for some years hired by the Wesleyans, who were thus twice succeeded by the Jews. The Weavers' Hall, again vacated by the removal of the synagogue, was bought soon after by the authorities of Temple parish for the purpose of being converted into a school.

About the end of September a local case, marked by astonishing credulity on the one hand and of rarely matched baseness and treachery on the other, excited widespread attention. The main features of the story were as follows: At No. 5, Cumberland Terrace, Cumberland Road, resided

Mr. John Woolley, a timber merchant, considerably advanced in years. After the death of his wife, in 1838, his house had been managed by his sister-in-law, Mary Bryers, whom he was said to have adopted whilst a child, and to have treated with much kindness. Woolley, however, was vain, weak-minded, and greedy; and the housekeeper, who was inordinately fond of finery and display, resolved upon gratifying her tastes by playing upon his weaknesses. Her first essay, made about a year before this date, was to induce him to believe that his personal charms and amiable disposition had won the heart of a young lady with a fortune of £5,000, and large "expectations" from a wealthy aunt, who knew of and sympathised with her niece's affection. Woolley thereupon began to write amorous letters to his Dulcinea, the missives being placed in the hands of Bryers, who quickly concocted responses calculated to keep up his delusion. The sympathetic aunt was also made to play a part in the farce. Under the pretence that her large income came in irregularly, loans of money were requested in letters to Woolley, who advanced some £70 on being made the custodian of a pretended will, by which the dupe was promised a legacy of £5,000. Feeling that further imposture in this direction might lead to exposure, Bryers now devised a fresh and more daring scheme. Her brother-in-law was informed that another young lady—a Miss Poole King—with a fortune of £47,000, had conceived so ardent a passion for his person, through having seen him frequently passing her house in Redcliff Parade, that she was ready to throw herself and fortune into his arms. Although, as in the former case, Woolley was wholly unacquainted with his reputed adorer, he seemed to have accepted her advances as a matter of course, and the first charmer was so completely neglected that Bryers was enabled to forge a letter purporting to come from that lady, upbraiding him with inconstancy, and declining further correspondence. Released from this difficulty, Woolley fell eagerly into the new web of fraud framed by his impudent relative, who obtained a gold watch from a tradesman on the credit of his name, induced him to believe that it was a present from Miss King, and secured his own watch for an imaginary exchange of love tokens. A correspondence was next started, Bryers producing letters from the lady expressing the warmest attachment—accompanied on one occasion with a request for a loan of £20 to meet an emergency, which met, of course, with a prompt response. Eventually, on being told that Miss King's family were violently opposed to her marriage, Woolley expressed his willingness to assist in her elopement; and one Sunday evening Bryers informed him that the lady had taken refuge in his house, but declined to see him. A pretended fugitive did, in fact, remain in the house until the following Wednesday, Bryers in the meanwhile obtaining money from her complacent employer under various pretexts. All preparations having been made, Woolley was at length permitted to see his intended bride; and though the slightest perspicacity would have sufficed to convince him that the alleged lady was of the vulgarist materials, the gull appears to have been perfectly satisfied. A post-chaise having been obtained, the party set off for London, where the "fair one," to Woolley's great satisfaction, undertook to make over £27,000 of her fortune. A licence being next obtained, the couple were married at Southwark on the 12th September—the bride being so "overcome" when her signature was required in the vestry that Bryers had to guide her hand. A week having been gaily spent at an hotel, the party returned to Bristol, where, on the pretence that the lady was going to Redcliff Parade to prepare her home for her husband's reception, the two women took to flight, with certain luggage belonging to Woolley. The wretched man soon after discovered that he had not only been robbed of his valuables, but had been united to a girl of low origin, named Mary Ann Morgan, who had earned her living as a domestic servant. About a fortnight later, Bryers and her tool were captured in London, and were taken before a magistrate; but Woolley, overwhelmed by the roar of popular ridicule excited by his tale, ultimately declined to prosecute, and was left to ponder for the rest of his life over his egregious credulity.

In the autumn of this year public attention was called in the local press to the destruction of the natural beauties of Leigh Woods and of the Somerset bank of the Avon by the proprietors of the property. From the statements made in newspaper articles and correspondence, it appeared that a portion of the ancient British camp had been converted into a potato garden; the wood was let as a rabbit warren; many of the large trees were cut or thrown down; and sylvan spots of eminent beauty, open to the public from time immemorial, were hedged off from pedestrians, who were insultingly driven away by the man who had taken possession of the place. All this was done, it was added, in order that "the poor annual pittance of some £20 sterling" might fall "into coffers already overflowing"; and letters addressed to the owner of the estate were contemptuously ignored. On the river bank, the destruction worked on another property by pickaxe and blasting powder was playing still greater havoc with scenery of surpassing grandeur and beauty. A Conservative editor remarked: "Of the unintelligent, unscrupulous, and merely mercenary and vulgar character of the general invasion of which this fine scenery has long been the victim, there can be in every generous and feeling mind but one opinion." The protests of the public were, however, of no effect. A toll was demanded of every one entering Leigh Woods, while on the other estate every large tree was cut down in the wood overhanging the river from Stokeleigh camp to opposite Cook's Folly. In July, 1849, the restrictions imposed upon pedestrians frequenting Leigh Woods were abandoned, and the boorish potato grower disappeared. In the summer of 1879, on the other hand, an ancient foot and bridle path from Leigh road to the wood overhanging the Abbot's Pond, was closed by the owner of the land, and as no one felt called upon to resist his action, the right of the public was surrendered. In the meantime the devastation of the riverside scenery had gone on, as it still goes on, without interruption. The *English Illustrated Magazine* for November, 1886, contains the indignant protest of a well-known literary citizen against the destruction of the "waving forest that had been the nursery of art to W. J. Müller, Danby, Pyne, and Turner, and the scenery that has given character to Clifton," which had become "only a record of an utilitarian age, whose sordid spirit could convert so choice a piece of landscape into crumbling stones for the sake of their value in money."

An interesting geological discovery was made in November, 1842, in one of the quarries which were then worked in the middle of Durdham Down, the workmen having found an opening into a cavern containing a quantity of the remains of animals for ages extinct in this country. The cavity, though narrow, was of some extent, being traceable to a depth of ninety feet. The bones had belonged to about twelve hyenas, a bear, two rhinoceros, several hippopotami, numerous examples of wild bulls, about five deer, and five or six elephants, besides the relics of animals of later date. The bones were nearly all fractured into small pieces, and the proportion of teeth and horns to other parts of the body greatly preponderated. Taking this fact into consideration, together with the marks of gnawing on the bones, and the certainty that the cave could not have accommodated more than a small fraction of the animals represented by the vestiges, scientific observers concluded that the den had been the retreat of hyenas, which had carried to it portions of their prey. By comparison of the teeth of the hyena and bear with those of the present races, the larger size of the early animals became strikingly apparent; those of the hyena testified that the beast had been bigger than the largest known species of tiger. The appearance of the remains suggested the hypothesis that a considerable movement had taken place in the sides of the fissure since the animals had lived there; and this, it was presumed, had produced the closure of the orifice, and the consequent high preservation of the bones.

In February, 1843, the Government purchased a plot of land, part of Horfield Court Farm, the property of Mr. A. M. Storey, for the purpose of erecting cavalry and infantry barracks on the site, and so avoiding the quartering of troops on the publicans of the city—a system which had long been condemned both by the victuallers and the public. The foundation-stone of the new buildings was laid with masonic ceremony on the 3rd June, 1845, and the completed premises were handed over to the Board of Ordnance on the 26th April, 1847. The barracks, which cost £57,000, were constructed to accommodate four companies of infantry and two troops of cavalry. In 1873 considerable additions were made to the buildings, which became a "local military centre" under the Army Re-organization Act. A field opposite to the barracks was also purchased, to serve as a camping ground for the Gloucestershire militia during the annual period of training.

Robert Southey, one of Bristol's most distinguished sons, died on the 21st March, 1843, at Keswick, Cumberland. A detailed notice of the literary labours of one of the most indefatigable and voluminous of English writers would be inconsistent with the character of this work, but it may be interesting to record a few local facts connected with his career. Born on the 12th August, 1774, at No. 9, Wine Street, where his father carried on business as a draper, at the sign of "The Hare," Southey received the elements of instruction from various teachers in and near the city, and showed at an early age such strong indications of ability and genius that an uncle, the Rev. H. Hill, undertook to bear the expense of his education at a public school. At Westminster the boy soon found congenial associates, amongst whom was Mr. Charles W. Wynn, afterwards for nearly half a century a highly esteemed member of the House of Commons. Southey's career at the school was cut short by an unlucky essay on corporal punishment, published in the school magazine which he had contributed to establish, the lucubration being supposed by the servile head-master to reflect upon the inhuman floggings which were then of constant occurrence in the army and navy. The punishment was expulsion; and, as the elder Southey failed in business about the same date, the lad's prospects would have been seriously compromised but for the continued protection of his uncle, Hill, who provided means for sending him to Oxford. It was during his college life, 1792-4, that he encountered Coleridge, then, like himself, a Unitarian and a republican, and the new friends a little later found themselves at Bristol, disgusted with scholasticism and with the superannuated customs of old world civilization, and eager to form a Utopian "Pantosocracy" in America—a bubble which happily soon burst. The dreamers, moreover, fell in love with two young Bristol ladies named Fricker, daughters of a maker of sugar-loaf moulds at Westbury, who had died in embarrassed circumstances. Being themselves in sorry pecuniary plight, the amorous youths resolved on giving a course of lectures in the city—Southey selecting historical, and Coleridge political and moral subjects. For the former's course of twelve lectures, tickets, 10*s*. 6*d*. each, were "to be had of Mr. Cottle, bookseller, High Street," from whose published reminiscences it appears that the experiment met with liberal patronage.* A few months later, Cottle, who was himself a poet, was so pleased with "Joan of Arc," Southey's first important work, that he offered £50 for the copyright, promising also as many gratis copies of the book as the author should obtain subscriptions for. While the poem was passing through the press, Southey accepted an invitation of his generous uncle, who lived at Lisbon, to spend six months in the Peninsula, Mr. Hill being doubtless wishful to break off his nephew's love affair. On the day of his departure, however (in November, 1795), the enthusiastic young man effectually baffled this intention by marrying Miss Edith Fricker at St. Mary Redcliff, the parties separating at the church door. Such was the bridegroom's poverty at the moment that Cottle furnished the money to buy the wedding

* Southey's fourth lecture was to be "On the Rise, Progress, and Decline of the Roman Empire," a theme which so excited Coleridge's imagination that he asked permission to deal with it himself. The room was thronged on the occasion; but Coleridge, with customary absence of mind, never made his appearance, and the assembled citizens were forced to go lectureless to bed.

ring, and paid the fees of the ceremony; yet no union was ever more happy, and Southey wrote forty years later, that his partner had always been "the life of his life." On his return from the Continent, in 1796, the young couple established themselves in lodgings in Bristol, where Southey wrote his "Letters from Spain and Portugal," Cottle, who bought the copyright, advancing money on account, and thus keeping the wolf from the door. Shortly afterwards, Mr. Wynn, though not a rich man, granted Southey an annuity of £160 a year (which was continued until the generous giver was able to obtain for him a Government pension of an equal amount); and Southey, who had had brief flirtations with the clerical, the medical, and finally the legal professions, definitely resolved to devote himself to literature. In 1797, out of sympathy for the sister and niece of the unfortunate Chatterton, who had been shamefully defrauded and left destitute by a literary charlatan—Sir Herbert Croft—Southey undertook an edition of the works of the youthful genius. The liberal-hearted Cottle was again the publisher (as he had already been of two volumes of Southey's minor poems), and the effort resulted in a clear profit of £300 for Chatterton's relatives. A year later, Southey, whose health was impaired, took a house at Westbury-on-Trym, which he styled Martin Hall from the number of those summer visitors that hovered around it, and there he spent, as he afterwards said, "one of the happiest years of his life." "I never before or since produced so much poetry in the same space of time." There, too, he formed the acquaintance of Humphry Davy, who, when scarce twenty years old, had come to Bristol to superintend Dr. Beddoes' Pneumatic Institution, and whose brilliant career was predicted by his new friend. Another visit to the Peninsula and a brief official charge in Dublin followed the sojourn at Westbury. In 1802 Southey was again living in Bristol; but the loss of a child while in the city caused him profound grief, and in the following year, having gone with his wife to see Mr. and Mrs. Coleridge at Keswick, he was so charmed with the locality that what was intended to be a temporary visit turned out to be a permanent settlement for life. His labours from that date belong to the literary history of the century. In 1813 he was appointed poet laureate, which added £90 a year to his income but nothing to his fame. In later years he was offered a seat in Parliament and a baronetcy, but wisely eschewed both distinctions. He accepted, however, a further pension of £300, which was gracefully offered by Sir Robert Peel in

1835. Southey's poems, deemed imperishable by himself, have been long forgotten; but as a prose writer he sometimes displayed talent of the highest order; and Thackeray's eulogy on the true nobility of his life, his indefatigable industry, and his self-sacrificing devotion to his relatives and dependants, will remain a monument to his memory so long as the English language endures.

The singular cavern known as Pen-park Hole, which excited much interest in the previous century, was explored in April, 1843, by Mr. Richard Rowe, of St. Agnes, Cornwall, and a party of working miners from that county. After descending about 140 feet, the party reached a large body of water, and it was found necessary to take down a boat before any progress could be made. The piece of water was stated to be eight fathoms deep, twelve fathoms long, and fifteen fathoms broad; though on the last previous occasion on which the cavern was visited—in the autumn of 1776—Mr. George Catcott estimated the pool to be "not more than four yards over, and its greatest depth not above six feet." The explorers obtained some fine specimens of lead ore, which were afterwards stated to have yielded more than 75 per cent. of metal. The results were deemed so satisfactory that it was proposed to form a company in Cornwall for the purpose of regularly working the mine; but from some reason the project was abandoned.

On the 19th May a commission of preliminary investigation was opened in the chapter house of the cathedral to inquire whether there were sufficient grounds for proceeding in the Episcopal court against the Rev. M. R. Whish, vicar of St. Mary Redcliff, and the Rev. D. V. Irvine, his curate, and also chaplain of Bridewell, for a breach of church discipline. The alleged offence consisted in Dr. Irvine having solemnized the marriage of two persons living in the parish of Nailsea, the woman being a sister of the deceased wife of the man. The proceedings were instituted by Archdeacon Thorp, who conducted the case. After a hearing which extended over two days, Dr. Phillimore, the presiding commissioner, declared that there were sufficient grounds for instituting further proceedings against Dr. Irvine, who loudly protested that he was the victim of a High Church persecution. The charge against Mr. Whish fell to the ground. The parties having agreed that Bishop Monk should pronounce sentence in Dr. Irvine's case, without further proceedings, his lordship suspended the curate for a year, his licences being also revoked. Petitions in the reverend gentleman's favour were presented to the bishop by the visiting justices of Bridewell and the parishioners of Redcliff, but Dr. Monk refused to make any remission.

Some quaint old houses in Baldwin Street (a view of which is preserved in Prout's Sketches) were demolished about the end of May for the purpose of widening that thoroughfare, which was in some places exceedingly narrow. The net cost of the improvement was about £2,700. The premises built upon the sites were tasteless in the extreme. About the same time a picturesque old house was pulled down in Broad Street, in order to open a communication into Small Street through Albion Chambers.

The first mention of tricycles found in the newspapers of this part of the kingdom occurs in the *Bath Gazette* of the last week in May. The paragraph stated that two descriptions of three-wheeled self-propelling machines were then traversing the streets of Bath. One of them was propelled by the rider "rising up and down, after the manner of horse exercise"; the other, invented by a local artisan, was worked by treadles which moved a crank close to the small guiding wheel. "The inventor lately came on it from Bristol to Bath in an hour and a half." Bicycles came into favour about 1860, and caused much astonishment in the rural districts. One Somerset peasant, dumbfoundered by their speed and inexplicable mode of propulsion, is recorded to have described a party of excursionists as being "the cheeribums as Daniel seed."

The stately chapel on St. Augustine's Back, erected in 1840 by the Irvingite denomination at a cost of about £14,000, was purchased for £5,000 in the summer of 1843 by the Roman Catholics of the city, and was consecrated, under the name of St. Mary, on the 5th July, by Bishop Baines, vicar apostolic of the western district. Dr. Baines expired during the night following the ceremonial at his residence, Prior Park, Bath. In 1871 the chapel was purchased by the fraternity of Jesuits.

Highbury Chapel, Cotham, erected on the ground where three unhappy Protestants were burned to death for their religious opinions during the reign of the intolerant Mary, was opened on the 6th July by the Rev. William Jay, of Bath. It had cost £3,000, exclusive of the site, which was given by Mr. Richard Ash. The original design appears to have included a western tower, which was never carried higher than the roof of the chapel. During an enlargement which was made in the autumn of 1863, another tower, in a style uncommon in this district, was erected on the south transept of the building. The outlay on the additional buildings exceeded the cost of the original edifice.

On the 19th July, the day fixed for launching the *Great Britain* [see p. 219], his royal highness Prince Albert paid a brief visit to the city, on the invitation of the proprietors of the Great Western Shipbuilding Company, and was received with many demonstrations of joy. The train which brought the Prince down from London performed the distance in what was then deemed the astonishingly short space of three hours and ten and a half minutes. On arriving at Bristol Terminus, the royal visitor was presented with an address by the mayor (Mr. James Gibbs) on behalf of the Corporation, to which he made a courteous reply. The Merchants' Society also presented an address, accompanying it with the freedom of the Society in a gold box. The Prince (who was accompanied by the Marquis of Exeter, Lord Wharncliffe, and the Earl of Lincoln) was then conducted by Temple Street, High Street, and Corn Street, College Green, Park Street, and Clifton Church to the Downs, thence by Bridge Valley Road to Hotwell House, and finally along Cumberland Road to the shipbuilding yard at Wapping. Triumphal arches had been erected at judiciously selected spots; and the visitor was greatly pleased with the appearance of the city and with the adjacent scenery. On nearing the rude towers of the unfinished suspension bridge, some men, by means of a basket-car, traversed the bar which united the two banks of the Avon, much to the wonder of the Prince and his attendants. On reaching the gigantic vessel, his royal highness inspected the platform on which the ship was to descend, and expressed his admiration of the "magnificent sight." A banquet followed, in a saloon fitted up for the purpose, Mr. Thomas Kington presiding. At its conclusion the Prince named the ship the "*Great Britain*" in the customary manner, and the colossal vessel glided into the water amidst a whirlwind of cheers. The Prince's return journey was accomplished with as much celerity as his morning trip. It was estimated that, in addition to the crowds which lined the sides of the Floating Harbour, about 30,000 persons assembled on Brandon Hill to witness the launch. A medal was struck to commemorate Prince Albert's visit to the city. Whilst the *Great Britain* remained in the Float, a number of royal and distinguished personages visited Bristol, to inspect what was then termed the "monster" vessel. Amongst them were the Duke of Bordeaux ("Henry V." of France), the King of Saxony, and

Prince William of Prussia (afterwards Emperor of Germany). The Queen visited the ship when it was fitting out in the Thames.

The steamer *Queen*, whilst on her passage from Bristol to Dublin, was totally lost on the Welsh coast near Milford Haven, during a dense fog, on the night of the 1st September. All the passengers, with the exception of one who was drowned in his berth, were taken off by a passing sloop; but, owing to the fog, they had to remain for twenty-four hours without food or shelter before they could reach the shore. The crew had previously made off in the steamer's boats. The *Queen* belonged to the Bristol Steam Navigation Company, and was said to be worth about £15,000.

During the autumn of 1843, whilst alterations were being made in the pews and other internal arrangements of All Saints' Church, the authorities thought the opportunity a favourable one for endeavouring to ascertain where the remains of Edward Colston were deposited, the site of his grave having been for many years in doubt. After some unsuccessful attempts, the matter was supposed to have been cleared up on the 2nd September, in the presence of the vicar (the Rev. H. Rogers), the churchwardens, and a few of the leading parishioners. From a memorandum written by Mr. H. Penton, a churchwarden, and published in the local journals, it appeared that at the suggestion of Mr. Garrard, the city treasurer, who had discovered that Alderman Colston (ob. 1597) was buried in a vault opposite "the little vestry door" [discovered during the alterations], a search was made at the place indicated. The vault in question was found packed with coffins, the uppermost being within a few inches of the surface. One of the last bodies interred had been that of Sir Stephen Nash, LL.D., sheriff in 1785–6. "The rotten remains of several wooden coffins" having been removed, two others were found at the bottom of the vault. One was supposed to be that of Sarah Colston, the philanthropist's niece, who was buried in 1721, but no name could be traced upon it. "The larger coffin of the two," wrote Mr. Penton, "was evidently that of a man of good stature, and was on the left of the vault. It appeared to be found necessary, when the body was interred, to excavate a portion of the rock, to admit of length sufficient for the foot of the coffin. The falling away of the wood from the sides disclosed a leaden case of substantial thickness, which it was determined to bring to the surface, the vault being deep. The treasurer, vicar, churchwarden, and myself concluded to open the upper part of the coffin, when to our great surprise and gratification, we found it was the immortal Colston himself, lying in all the apparent tranquillity of sleep. The features were so perfect as to be readily recognised; so much so (*sic*) that it is not improbable that a cast of his head was taken for the celebrated monument of him in the church, sculptured by Roubillac! The face was covered with a sheet quite strong and perfect, and a diaper cap or napkin on his head: his cravat and shirt exactly of the make and form of those shown on the same admirable monument in front of the vault. The whole was sacredly and immediately closed and replaced; a leaden plate being soldered on, inscribed—'Edward Colston, 1721.'" If the vicar and churchwardens had, at the beginning of their operations, a fitting sense of the "sacred" character of the remains, they appear to have speedily lost it. A fortnight later, on the 14th September, the contents of the vault were again disturbed, and Colston's coffin was opened a second time to gratify the curiosity of Mr. F. E. Colston, of Roundway Park, Wilts, grotesquely styled by the *Bristol Journal* a "lineal descendant" of Colston, but really the representative of a collateral branch of the family. The church, in fact, was turned into a sort of show, and "about a hundred gentlemen" were permitted to witness the exhibition. The repulsive extent to which curiosity was pushed may be divined from the account of the journalist mentioned above. "The body," he says, "was clothed in a shirt, drawers, and stockings [some portions of which were purloined and appropriated by persons who were present], all of which were yet strong and perfect; the enamel of the teeth was scarcely discoloured. On a portion of the upper part of the shirt being removed, the breast appeared almost of the colour of living flesh, and was firm to the touch. The face and arms were very dark; the only portions of the grave clothes that bore any marks of decay were the gloves that covered the hands." The alleged discovery gave rise to much controversy, it being maintained by several persons that the remains could not have been those of Colston. One argument adduced by the sceptics was, that, according to an inscription formerly in the church, the text of which is preserved in Barrett's History, the body was laid in a vault "in the first cross alley, under the reading desk"—which, down to 1757, stood against the north column of the chancel arch, whereas the vault near "the little vestry door" was in the south aisle. It was also shown that the body of Ann Colston, Edward's sister, was brought from Mortlake, and interred with his own, according to his express directions, but no such coffin was in the opened vault. Finally, the head of the exhumed body contained a set of teeth in excellent preservation, which was not to be expected in the case of a man who had reached his eighty-fifth year. The question at issue was never authoritatively settled.

The "Old Castle" tavern, one of the oldest buildings in Castle Street, and chiefly constructed of wood, was destroyed by fire on the night of the 6th September. The occupier, Mr. Thomas Worthington, who was an invalid, perished in the flames, and one of his relatives afterwards died from the effects of her injuries.

St. Barnabas' Church, Ashley Road, was consecrated by Bishop Monk on the 12th September. The building cost the modest sum of £2,200, of which only £175 appear to have been contributed by the citizens. St. Luke's Church, Barton Hill, was consecrated on the 20th of the same month, having just been finished at an outlay of £2,700. The proprietors of the adjacent cotton factory, for whose workpeople it was chiefly intended, contributed largely to the building fund.

The last coach between Bristol and London ceased to run in October, 1843. The *Bristol Journal* of March 30th, 1844, announced: "The Bush coach office, where an extensive business has been carried on for, we believe, more than a century, has this week closed." But in April, 1849, in consequence of the Great Western railway board having reduced the number of trains, and discontinued return tickets, two coaches ran daily to and fro between Bristol and Bath, and were well patronised during the summer months.

The Charity Trustees having resolved to remove the boys of Queen Elizabeth's Hospital from the unhealthy premises in Christmas Street, and to erect convenient school buildings in a more salubrious locality, submitted a scheme to the Lord Chancellor, praying for his assent. His lordship, in January, 1844, deputed a London architect to inquire into and report upon the eligibility of the plans, and, the result being satisfactory, the scheme was approved. The site selected was on the north-west side of Brandon Hill, on land once used as a cemetery by the Jews. The scholars took possession of the new premises, which cost £14,000, on the 27th September, 1847. The abandoned hospital in Christmas Street was occupied for some time by a cooper; but in the early months of 1856 it was taken by the local branch of an association for improving the dwellings of the industrial classes; and after being partially reconstructed, was opened in the following October as an "establishment of model dwellings." The association about the same time constructed another range of buildings in Limekiln Road. The scheme, however, was unprofitable, and the old "Bartholomew's" was subsequently converted into a shoe factory.

In consequence of the increasing traffic through Baldwin Street, the Council, at a meeting in February, 1844, ordered the removal of the Fish Market, an ugly building standing on St. Nicholas' Back, opposite to the church. The fish dealers appear to have removed to the Welsh Back. [See June, 1872.]

Miss Ann Dimsdale, of Frenchay, who died about this time, bequeathed by will the sum of £26,000 to local charities and religious societies. Miss Dimsdale was a member of an old Quaker family.

During the spring of 1844, nine quaint old houses in Broad Street, between the Council House and the entrance to Albion Chambers, had their projecting gabled fronts removed, for the purpose of widening the thoroughfare. The Corporation effected this improvement for £630. Three projecting houses on the opposite side, adjoining Christ Church, had been thrown back in 1835. The last old houses in the western row were purchased, as already stated, by the Bank of England, whose banking house, erected on the site, was opened in November, 1847.

In May, whilst workmen were engaged in repewing St. Stephen's Church, a richly canopied altar tomb, bearing two effigies, was discovered plastered up under one of the windows of the north aisle. The male effigy was habited in civil costume, but bore a studded swordbelt of the peculiar fashion of the later half of the fourteenth century. It was suggested that the effigy was that of John Shipward, elected mayor in 1455, who built the magnificent tower of the church; but the dress of the figure, as well as the style of the tomb, clearly indicated an earlier date. A few days later, another male effigy was discovered in the south wall. Both figures are engraved in the *Archæological Journal,* vol. iii. pp. 82, 83. [The church was repewed, in a more tasteful manner, in the autumn of 1886.]

On the 14th June, the ministry of Sir Robert Peel met with a severe defeat in the House of Commons, upon an amendment brought forward by Mr. P. W. Miles, one of the members for Bristol, on the question of the sugar duties. Up to this time, the duty on foreign grown sugar was 63*s.* per cwt., while the tax on our colonial product was 24*s.* The Ministry proposed to reduce the former duty to 34*s.*, giving the West India interest a protection of 10*s*. per cwt. Mr. Miles objected to this reduction as inexpedient and as wanting in finality. After entering into lengthy details to show the depressed condition of the colonies, and contrasting their former prosperity with their late decay, he said: "He wished the Chancellor of the Exchequer could pay a visit to his (Mr. M.'s) estates in Jamaica, and view a state of things which was the sad spectre of what it once had been." Already many estates had been thrown up; and he called on the agriculturists of England, whose cause with that of the West Indies was a common one, to save the colonists from the very great distress which the ministerial proposal would create. He concluded by moving that the duty on British sugars should be reduced to 20*s*. per cwt. The Opposition, on the ground that the amendment, if carried into effect, would be more advantageous to the consumer than the Government proposal, supported Mr. Miles, and on a division the Ministry were defeated by 241 votes against 221. The result caused great excitement in political circles. Three days later, Sir Robert Peel moved a resolution annulling the effect of the previous vote, and restoring the duty to 24*s*.—a proposal much condemned by several speakers, and especially by Mr. Disraeli, who charged the Premier with "laying down a tariff of political disgrace." Mr. Miles also sharply complained of the conduct of the Ministry, and declared that he should continue to defend the interests of the West Indies. Sir Robert Peel's resolution was however carried by 255 votes against 233. About forty of the members of Mr. Miles's previous majority either absented themselves or changed sides.

The Bristol and Gloucester railway, which had been under construction about two years [see p. 123] was opened to the shareholders on the 6th and to the public on the 8th July. The first six days' traffic on the line (which was closed on Sundays) amounted to £735. Of the seven coaches which had been running between the two cities, six were immediately withdrawn; and on the 22nd July the time-honoured "north mail" left Bristol for the last time—the horses' heads surmounted with funereal plumes, and the coachman and guard in equally lugubrious array. The portion of the railway between Stonehouse and Gloucester had been made by the Great Western Company; the rest of the line (which had cost about £500,000), though originally intended to be of the narrow gauge, had been laid down on the broad gauge, under the advice of Mr. Brunel, the company's engineer. The result of this arrangement was, that although the opening of the railway completed the chain of communication between Bristol and Newcastle on Tyne and all the leading towns on the route, every train was stopped at Gloucester as if a wall had been built across the way. In the course of the year, negotiations were set on foot for an amalgamation of the new line with that of the Gloucester and Birmingham Company (who had completed their task in December, 1840), and an arrangement between the two boards was soon after effected. The united companies then received offers of alliance from the Great Western and Midland directorates—each eager to secure the valuable territory. The rivalry of the two great concerns was close and keen; but the Midland Company, then under the rule of Hudson, "the railway king," were eventually the successful bidders, their offer of a guaranteed dividend of six per cent. per annum in perpetuity being accepted in February, 1845. In the following year, to escape from obligations to the Great Western board, the Midland Company resolved to make a new line from Gloucester to Stonehouse, alongside that of their competitors, but so obstinate was the opposition of the latter that an Act for the purpose was not obtained until 1848. Preparations were then made to extend the narrow gauge system to Bristol; but further obstacles were successfully raised by the Great Western magnates, and for several years the passenger and goods traffic between the West of England and the manufacturing districts was brought to a dead stop at Gloucester. The narrow gauge carriages did not, in fact, reach Bristol until the 22nd May, 1854.*

A meeting of the friends and admirers of Robert Southey was held at the Institution, Park Street, on the 13th July, for the purpose of raising a subscription for the erection in his native city of a monument to the memory of the distinguished writer. The mayor (Mr. W. L. Clarke) presided over a scanty gathering, which appointed a committee to carry out the project, with an understanding that the artist of the memorial should be another distinguished Bristolian—Mr. E. H. Baily, R. A. It was found that £500 would suffice to erect a monument which would be worthy of the object and creditable to the city; but the subscriptions, excluding £20 by Mr. Baily and £30 by literary men unconnected with Bristol, amounted only to about £50. The subsequent dona-

* The Midland board subsequently gained much popularity by its cheap excursion trains. On August 6, 1855, about 7,000 Bristolians were conveyed to and from Birmingham, a distance of 182 miles, for 1*s*. 6*d*. each.

tions were so trifling that the committee abandoned the idea of a monument in College Green, which Southey had hoped for during his declining years, and contented themselves with obtaining a bust of the poet, which was placed in the north aisle of the cathedral in December, 1845.

About this time, the condition of the south lock at Cumberland Basin having occasioned some anxiety, the directors of the Dock Company applied to Mr. Brunel for his opinion as to the course to be taken. That gentleman reported that repairs of a costly character were indispensable, and that, considering the insufficient breadth of the lock (45 feet), it was advisable to entirely reconstruct the entrance, enlarging it to 52 feet, which he thought would adequately meet the future requirements of the port. The cost was estimated at £22,000. This report was approved by the directors, who communicated their intentions to the Council. The latter body, at a meeting on the 15th July, passed a resolution expressive of its gratification at the liberality of the Dock Company, and cordially concurring in their plan. The lock, afterwards known as Brunel's lock, was constructed of a width of 54 feet.

At the sale of the Chew Magna and Dundry estates of Mr. John Harford, which took place in Bristol in July, the Charity Trustees purchased farms and land at North Chew and Littleton, of the area of 207 acres, for which £11,500 were paid.

A company was formed in July, with a proposed capital of £8,000 in £20 shares, for the construction of a swivel bridge from Redcliff Back to the Grove. The shares were taken up, but in April, 1845, a resolution disapproving of the scheme was carried in the Council by 21 votes against 18. The project was consequently suffered to drop.

By the Bank Charter Act, passed in the session of 1844 at the instance of Sir Robert Peel, the issue of notes by provincial banks was limited to the average amount of their circulation during the previous two years. From an official return published in the *London Gazette* in September, it appeared that the average circulation of the local banks had been as follows: Bristol Old Bank (Messrs. Baillie, Ames & Co.), £89,540; Bristol Bank (Messrs. Miles & Co.), £48,277; West of England and South Wales District Bank, £83,535; Stuckey's Banking Company, £356,970.

Up to this time the guardians of the Clifton poor-law union had maintained three workhouses for the indoor paupers of the district—at Clifton for the aged and infirm, at Pennywell

Road for the able-bodied, and at St. George's for children. A proposal was now brought forward for the erection of one large establishment, with a view to economy in management. At a meeting of ratepayers, at Clifton, in October, it was stated that since the union was founded a new workhouse had been built in the parish at a cost of £4,000. It was contended that this building fulfilled the requirements of the locality; but the Pennywell Road workhouse was admitted to be a disgrace to the union [see p. 200]. A resolution was passed to agitate for a separation of Clifton from the other parishes if the guardians persisted in the new project. At a meeting of the board, a few days later, however, it was resolved by a large majority to negotiate for the purchase of land near Stapleton, upon which to erect a workhouse capable of accommodating 1,180 inmates. An area of about seventeen acres was obtained for £3,500, and the builder's contract for the workhouse amounted to £10,916. The premises were first occupied in September, 1847, but they were at once found inadequate, and in December, 1848, the Poor Law Board authorised an expenditure of £25,000, including the cost of site. Additional buildings have been added from time to time, and the total outlay has been probably not less than £40,000. In spite of these extensions, the workhouse now accommodates only 1,161 inmates, recent regulations insisting on an increased cubic space for each pauper. The workhouse at Clifton, after its abandonment, was hired from the overseers, and became the Clifton Wood Industrial School. A vestry hall and parochial offices were built on part of the site in Pennywell Road, the rest of which was sold, as was the workhouse at St. George's.

In November, 1844, a prospectus appeared of the Wilts, Somerset, and Weymouth Railway Company, with a capital of £1,500,000 in £50 shares, for the construction of a railway from Corsham to Trowbridge and Westbury, with diverging lines from the last-named town to Salisbury and to Weymouth. The Great Western board, which promoted the scheme, undertook to work the line on a lease, and guaranteed a minimum yearly dividend of 4 per cent. The proposal excited strong disapproval amongst Bristol traders, on the ground that it threatened to obstruct if not destroy their extensive business in the commercial districts of Wilts and East Somerset, and measures were taken to oppose it in Parliament. The Great Western directors, however, undertook to establish direct communication between Bristol and the towns in question, and the Bill passed. Subsequently, an

Act was obtained to carry out the promise of the board, but the construction of the additional line was postponed from year to year, and the directors at last attempted to repudiate their pledges. The Court of Queen's Bench was eventually applied to for redress, when the construction of a railway from Bathampton to the above line at Bradford was declared to be obligatory on the Great Western Company. Another Act was obtained in the session of 1854, and the junction line was opened in February, 1857. The line to Salisbury had been finished in June, 1856, and the Weymouth section was completed in December of the same year. The cost of the Wilts, Somerset, and Weymouth system to the concern which absorbed it was over £3,000,000—a sum exceeding the original capital of the Great Western Company.

The urgent need of providing the city with an additional supply of water had for some years before this time become a pressing public question. The state of the poor in many districts was lamentable in the extreme; and the high rate of mortality which generally prevailed was held to be largely attributable to the consumption of impure water, and to the dirt and squalor that prevailed amongst the labouring classes. At length, in March, 1840, a meeting was held, the mayor (Mr. J. N. Franklyn) presiding, when it was proposed to form a Bristol and Clifton Waterworks Company, with a capital of £60,000 in £50 shares. The scheme, however, failed from want of support. In November, 1841, notice of an intended application for parliamentary powers was given on behalf of the Merchant Venturers' Company, who proposed to obtain a supply from springs in various suburban parishes, though it was understood that the chief source depended upon was the lower hot-well spring, near Black Rock. The subject was brought before the Council by a far-sighted member, who urged that the work of supplying the city ought to be undertaken by the Corporation; but the majority, sympathising with the Merchants' Company, refused to take any action. The Bill was shortly afterwards dropped, and nothing was done for some years. In the meantime Bristol was described in an official report as "worse supplied with water than any great city in England." About a hundred houses near Richmond Terrace were supplied from wells known as Richmond and Buckingham springs; some 400 dwellings were connected with Sion spring, while a few families in and near College Green were provided from Jacob's Wells, the pipes from which were the property of the dean and chapter. The poor, excepting those living near the public conduits, were generally without any provision. Water-carrying was therefore a common and lucrative trade, and as many thousand poor families had to pay on an average a penny daily for a scanty supply, it was not surprising that they should be stigmatised as extremely dirty in their habits. Unfortunately, too, much of the water drawn from private wells was affected by neighbouring cesspools, and was pernicious to health. Early in 1845, the Merchants' Society set about the construction of works for tapping the springs near Black Rock, an engine-house * of somewhat fantastic design being erected near what was known during the previous century as the "New Hot Well," while excavations for a reservoir were made in the ancient British camp on Clifton Down. It being obvious that this supply would be inadequate to meet the wants of the city, a company was started in April, 1845, to bring in a copious provision from more distant sources. The result was an obstinate and expensive struggle between the rival parties before a parliamentary committee in 1846, the Merchants' Society seeking to obtain exclusive powers for the supply of Clifton and the adjoining parishes. The committee of the House of Commons eventually approved of the more comprehensive scheme, and the company's Bill received the royal assent on the 16th July, 1846, the capital sanctioned being £200,000 in shares, and £66,000 in loans. [In order to buy off opposition when the Bill was before Parliament, negotiations were opened with the proprietors of the chief springs in Clifton, and the following sums were ultimately paid: The Merchants' Society for the river-side springs, machinery, and plant, £18,000; Mr. Coates, for Sion House spring, £13,500; Mr. W. Hamley, for Buckingham spring, £2,196; Mr. J. Coombe, for Richmond spring, £4,950; and for Whiteladies' spring, £400; total, £39,046.] Various sources of supply having been examined, it was resolved to have recourse to certain springs at Barrow Gurney and Harptree Combe, with others forming the head of the river Chew, at Litton and Chewton Mendip, the first two being about five, and the latter nearly sixteen miles distant from Bristol. Operations having been begun and continued with great vigour, the water from the Barrow springs was brought into the city for distribution on the 1st October, 1847. The remoter sources necessitated more

* This building, which was a puzzle to strangers owing to its bizarre architecture, was removed in February, 1864, during the construction of the railway to Avonmouth. It was at one time suggested that it should be converted into a church for the use of sailors and bargemen.

costly operations. The springs at Litton and Chewton were conveyed by several branches to a principal aqueduct, proceeding for upwards of two miles towards East Harptree, where it entered a tunnel about a mile and a quarter in length. Emerging from the rock of the hill, the aqueduct was carried over Harptree Combe (where it met with a feeder) by means of an iron tube supported at intervals by masonry. The valley having been bridged, the water passed into a line of pipes of thirty inches diameter and upwards of four miles in length. At their termination was a tunnel of three-quarters of a mile through North Hill, followed by stone aqueducts over valleys at Leigh Down and Winford, and those were succeeded by the Winford tunnel, a mile long. The total length from Chewton Mendip to the Barrow reservoir was eleven miles, and it will be seen that most of the route necessitated costly operations. The springs brought to the store reservoir were calculated to yield four million gallons daily, and the reservoir being 25 acres in extent, it was estimated that the works as a whole would meet more than double the probable demands of the inhabitants. Three service reservoirs were also constructed for maintaining a constant supply throughout the city; the first at Bedminster Down, for that portion of the borough south of the Float; the second near Whiteladies Road, for the rest of the lower parishes and the suburbs; and the third on Durdham Down, at an elevation of 300 feet above high water mark in the Avon, for the service of the more elevated districts. The first of these was finished in 1847, and the others came into use in the following summer. The water flowed from Barrow to Whiteladies Road by simple gravitation, and was then driven up to Durdham Down by powerful pumps. The water rates fixed by the Act were moderate; for example, the charge upon a house of £20 rental was £1; on £50 rental, £2, and on £100 rental £3. For shops and offices the rate was 5*s*. per year for rentals under £20, and 8*s*. if under £50. To owners of small tenements a reduction was offered on the ordinary rates. The terms of the company were nevertheless far from being enthusiastically received, the water rents during the second year of its existence amounting to under £3,000. Up to February, 1850, only 3,152 houses were supplied throughout the city, of which 75 per cent. were rented at upwards of £20. The number, however, increased steadily after that date. In 1854 the company encountered its first serious difficulty. Early in the year a leakage occurred in the Barrow reservoir, which had to be emptied before the repairs could be executed. A drought, unexampled for nearly sixty years, then set in, and from May to October the supply of water to the city was very limited, much to the wrath of the consumers. Throughout this era of the company's existence, the proprietors received no dividend on their capital, and it was not until March, 1856, that the directors were able to recommend a distribution at the modest rate of 14*s.* per cent. The average return of each of the three following years was only 2 per cent., and the £25 shares naturally sold much below par, the quotation being for some time between £8 and £9. Despairing of an adequate return under the original arrangement, the company, in the session of 1862, under a pretext of seeking for powers to construct a new reservoir at Barrow, promoted a Bill intended to materially change their relations with the inhabitants. The directors in applying for their first Act had undertaken to furnish a constant supply of water to consumers. It was now sought to cut off the supply for nine hours daily. Under the plea that it was necessary to prevent waste—it being alleged that through the carelessness which prevailed the whole freshwater current of the Avon would not suffice for the city—the scheme proposed that every family should be compelled to use and pay for a meter, to be supplied by the company. Finally it was proposed to levy an increased rate of 1½ per cent. on the rental of houses standing 200 feet above the level of Bristol Bridge. To the dissatisfaction of many citizens, the parliamentary committee of the Council manifested a marked sympathy towards the proposals of the company, and the Council itself was charged with indifference to the interests of the inhabitants. The clause abolishing constant service was approved with trifling modifications, and an extra rent of 1 per cent. on the high level dwellings was also conceded. The directors could well afford, under those circumstances, to abandon the clause enforcing the use of meters; and in this form the Bill became law. The new system had not been long in force, however, before the company had to encounter a fresh embarrassment. The spring and summer months of 1864 were accompanied by an unprecedented drought in the south and west of England. During the five months ending August, the rainfall at Clifton was only about 6½ inches, or less than half the average of the ten previous years. The company's springs produced only a small fraction of their usual supply; and as the store in the reservoirs rapidly diminished, the directors were compelled to make repeated deductions in the period of service. This was for some weeks limited to one or two hours a day, but in various parts of the city the supply ceased altogether. Fortunately the drought broke up at the beginning of September, and the *Bristol Times* of the 10th announced that, on and after the 12th, the citizens would have "at least two hours' supply daily." Additional sources were tapped to alleviate the pressure, a well in the coal measures at Bedminster being especially useful in supplying 160,000 gallons daily. Another source made available was the old "boiling well" at Ashton, which yielded no less than 200,000 gallons daily. In spite of these aids, however, the above newspaper of the 8th October, referring to the "water famine" in Clifton, said: "Several housekeepers have been driven to such straits that in some cases we have actually seen Paterfamilias start in a fly with an empty barrel by the side of the driver, and go in seach of a supply to the nearest spring, which is in some instances a mile off." A week later the same writer reported that the "boiling well" was the only source of supply for Clifton and the upper districts, the Mendip springs having dried up. Urged by the Corporation, which bore the expense, the company opened Richmond spring, from which a valuable contingent could have been obtained; but the residents in the neighbouring houses, protesting against the noise that would be caused by a steam-engine, threatened to apply to Chancery for an injunction, and the preparations were dropped. It was not until December that the board were able to extend the supply to six hours a day. They intimated about the same time that they should insist upon payment of the full rates for the current six months—an announcement which did not contribute to their popularity. In the following session application was made to Parliament for powers to appropriate additional springs at Chelvey and other places, and to construct fresh reservoirs at Barrow and Knowle. It was also sought to largely increase the scale of charges then in force. The proposed advance in the rates varied from 30 to 66 per cent., but on this occasion the Council resolved on opposing the demands of the company, and the increase in the rates was eventually limited to about 20 per cent. An attempt to reduce the hours of service to ten per day was also resisted and defeated. That the directors were ungenerous in framing their Bill was proved by the subsequent progress of the undertaking, the dividends of which soon rose to ten per cent., while the shares attained a premium of nearly 180 per cent. In January, 1877, the Council, tardily repentant of its apathetic policy in 1841, adopted by a large majority a resolution brought forward by Alderman Jones, affirming the desirability of the Corporation acquiring the water works; and a committee was appointed to negotiate with the company. After protracted labours, the committee reported in November. The directors, it appeared, had proposed that the entire capital of the undertaking, including a large sum not paid up in respect of new shares, and an additional £100,000 demanded in compensation for arrears of dividend, should be converted into £1,400,000 four per cent. bonds. On the other hand the committee had suggested that the Corporation should pay 10 per cent. yearly on the ordinary stock of £200,000 until 1883, and thereafter 12 per cent. on that stock and 10 per cent. on later issues. The directors subsequently offered concessions, and the differences were so narrowed as to give hopes of a compromise, when the committee, considering the year too far advanced to permit of legislation in the ensuing session, suspended their labours and reported progress to the Council, adding as an expression of their opinion that the transfer would be beneficial to the city. From the outset of the negotiations a section of the citizens had warmly opposed the purchase, and resolutions condemning the scheme had been passed at some thinly attended ward meetings. Certain persons interested in a project for partially supplying the city with water from old mine workings at Frampton Cotterell were especially active in their hostility. (A Bill for carrying out that speculation was rejected by the House of Commons in 1878.) The Council, moreover, had become indifferent about the matter. The report of the committee was simply "received," and, as the committee was not re-appointed in the following year, the question dropped. In March, 1882, at the request of a public meeting, the Council again manifested a desire to acquire the works; but the directors peremptorily declined to reopen the negotiations. During the same year the company, which by that time had extended their mains to many suburban districts, finding it again advisable to increase their supplies, obtained parliamentary powers to acquire certain springs near Chewton Mendip and the Sherborne springs flowing into the Chew, and also to take an increased quantity from the Kenn, near Chelvey. These works were expected to give an additional supply of two and a half millions of gallons daily. The capital of the company, by Acts of 1850, 1853, 1862, 1865, and 1872, had been increased to £800,000. The new Bill asked for power to raise £400,000 more at the rate of 7 per cent.

per annum, by which the proprietors, whose £25 shares were already quoted at £70, would have been insured a luxuriant bonus on the new stock. Similar powers had been obtained on previous occasions, and most of the capital raised by loans had been converted into shares bearing a high rate of interest. But the Corporation, which had hitherto been strangely apathetic, now awoke to the interests of the citizens, and appealed to the House of Lords against the proposed rate of profit as unreasonable and extortionate. The Upper House reduced the rate of interest to 5 per cent. Amongst the works undertaken under this Act was the laying of a large conduit from the Sherborne springs for a distance of over thirteen miles, including a tunnel about a mile in length, near Whitchurch. The water from this source reached the city in 1885.

The perennial discontent of the commercial classes at the charges on vessels entering the port was the subject of a discussion in the Council in January, 1845, when it was stated on behalf of Messrs Hilhouse and Hill that the dues on Australian wool were seven times greater at Bristol docks than they were at London and Liverpool. Mr. N. Acraman had also represented to the Finance Committee that the charges on guano were 2*s.* 4*d.* per ton in Bristol, while they were only 2¼*d.* at Liverpool. Mr. F. Green said that the local dues on shipping were 3*s.* a ton, against 1*s.* 6*d.* in the Mersey docks. The Council forthwith reduced the town dues on guano from 8*d.* to 1*d.* per ton, but had no power to deal with the wharfage due of 8*d.* levied by the Merchants' Company, or with the dock due of 1*s.* imposed by the dock board. At the same meeting it was announced that the Corporation had no power to expend the borough funds in enforcing the restoration to the public of Mother Pugsley's well [see p. 249] or in resisting similar encroachments. It appeared that a clause to enable the Council to make payments out of the borough fund in defence of public rights to footpaths, etc., would have been inserted in the last Improvement Act, but that the Dock Company threatened such strenuous opposition at every stage of the Bill as to render it prudent to withdraw the clause in order to prevent the loss of the entire measure.

A proposed branch of the Bristol and Exeter railway, from Yatton to Clevedon, received the approval of the shareholders at a meeting on the 16th January. The line, which cost about £40,000, was opened on the 4th August, 1847.

The establishment of the Bristol Academy for the promotion of the Fine Arts was announced in the local newspapers of the 18th January, 1845. A lady named Sharples headed the list of donors with a gift of £2,000, the president, Mr. J. S. Harford, and the vice-president, Mr. P. W. Miles, M.P., subscribing £100 each. The first exhibition of pictures was opened at the Institution, Park Street, in the following April. The Academy met with very feeble support from the citizens, and there seemed no probability that it would be furnished with funds for erecting a building suitable for its intended purposes. In 1848 it was suggested that the Institution should give up a portion of its premises to the Fine Arts Society, in consideration of a payment of £3,000; but the proposal was strongly opposed by Mr. J. N. Nash, on account of the weakness of the new organisation. It had begun, he pointed out, with sixty-three subscribers of a guinea each, and already they had dwindled to nineteen. The plan having been abandoned, the annual exhibitions of the society were held for some years in St. Augustine's Parade, in the large house fronting the drawbridge. Under the will of Mrs. Sharples, who died in 1849, the society eventually came into possession of the bulk of her estate, amounting to about £3,500; and the construction of an Academy of Art was determined upon in 1855. A building with a façade in the Italian style, but far from convenient in its internal arrangements, was erected near the Victoria Rooms, and opened on the 12th April, 1858. The society, nevertheless, did not make much progress in public favour. At the annual meeting in 1863, Mr. P. W. Miles observed: "It really seemed as if the people of this neighbourhood did not care in the least about the fine arts. Though there was a good collection of pictures on the walls, he always found the rooms perfectly empty. No amount of effort to bring pictures of the first class there seemed to be of any avail." The net proceeds of the exhibition of that year were under £25. The situation does not appear to have been much more satisfactory in 1882, when Mr. R. Lang stated at the annual meeting that the total amount of donations for the previous thirty years had not averaged £4 annually. "That was Bristol love of art. They had tried year after year to get up a fund to buy some pictures, but the results had been pitiful. More recently, he had endeavoured to purchase some of the late Charles Branwhite's pictures, which it would have been an easy thing to do; but the sum promised was so ridiculous that he was forced to give up the project." It ought to be added that Mr. Lang had himself offered a noble example to the wealthier class of citizens by presenting the institution with a number of valuable paintings, chiefly by Bristol artists. His gift, however, remains unique.

St. Andrew's Church, Montpelier, was consecrated by Bishop Monk on the 31st January, 1845. It had cost only £2,428 in erection. The building was much enlarged in 1878, owing to the greatly increased population of the district. The ecclesiastical parish created for this church was subtracted from those of St. Paul and Horfield.

About this time the efforts of an Early Closing Association were successful in releasing a number of young men from business at an earlier hour than had previously been the rule,* and the necessity of an institution in which such persons could find instruction and innocent amusement soon became apparent. A committee having been formed, a course of lectures was delivered during the winter, and this experiment having proved successful, a meeting was held on the 24th February, the mayor (Mr. R. P. King) presiding, when it was resolved to found a literary institution under the title of the Bristol Athenæum. Negotiations were soon afterwards opened with the committees of the Mechanics' Institute and of the Clergy Book Society, both of which organisations were in a declining state, and the overtures resulted in their consolidation with the new body, their libraries, apparatus, etc., being also taken over. The Athenæum thus came into active operation in September, 1845, the rooms of the Clergy Book Society, in Broad Street, being fitted up for the accommodation of the members. In the following year the library was removed to a large room in a house in Corn Street (on the site now occupied by the bank of Messrs. Stuckey & Co.). The institution gradually became very popular; and in 1850, when the members numbered nearly 1,000, and when the scantiness of the accommodation provided was painfully felt, the directors recommended the acquirement on lease of the Queen Bess Tavern (formerly the residence of Whitson) and certain adjoining property lying between Corn Street and Nicholas Street, the access from the former being through Cypher Lane, and from the latter through Queen Bess Passage. [In removing these old constructions, some beautiful architectural remains were exposed of an edifice apparently erected at the beginning of the thirteenth century. On one side were three bays of semi-circular arches, springing from triple shafts, while the south wall was perforated by a Decorated two-light trefoil

* According to a statement in the *Bristol Journal*, drapers' shops in 1825, and doubtless for many years later, were usually kept open for fourteen hours a day, and the assistants were allowed only one hour for meals.

headed window. Two Romanesque pilasters with sculptured capitals were also found *in situ*. The place had been traditionally styled Alderman Whitson's Chapel, from having adjoined his mansion.] The new buildings, which, with the furniture, etc., cost £6,600, were "inaugurated" by Lord John Russell, President of the Council, on the 25th October, 1854. His lordship spent two days in the city, in the course of which he was entertained to breakfast by the mayor (Mr. J. G. Shaw), to a public soirée in the Victoria Rooms, at which 1,500 persons were present, and to a grand dinner by the members of the Council, to which the Duke of Beaufort and the Earl of Ducie were also invited. Party spirit, however, was still so strong that the bells of the city churches were all silent, and many Conservative members of the Council refused to contribute to the cost of the dinner, which was about £400. The Athenæum became so popular in its new quarters that in 1855 the members numbered 1,577; but after a brief period of prosperity, the roll rapidly diminished, the desertions being partially due to a violent attack made on the committee by the Rev. J. B. Clifford, of St. Matthew's, because they refused at his dictation to remove the *Westminster Review* from the library tables. Unfortunately, too, a debt of £2,000 had been left unprovided for; and in 1861 the bankers threatened to take possession of the property and to recoup themselves by a sale. By dint of strenuous exertions, the liabilities were at length wiped off.

The Bristol Stock Exchange was founded on the 17th March, 1845, at a meeting of brokers, Mr. R. H. Webb presiding. Mr. J. K. Haberfield, an honorary member, was the first president and treasurer of the Exchange, which was opened on the 16th April. The "railway mania," destined to end in a disastrous collapse, attained its highest development during this year; and amongst the extravagances to which it gave rise were two schemes for linking Bristol with Dover, two for railways from London to the Land's End, a line from Bristol to Norwich, etc. Writing some years after the fever, a contributor to the *Bristol Times*, who could be easily identified, observed :—"Fairy legends had no wonders for us like that time. You saw a man to-day in the streets of Bristol whom you would not trust with the loan of a five-pound note; to-morrow he splashed you with the wheels of a new Long-acre carriage. He was as suddenly transformed from a twenty pound house to a mansion in the country, and though small beer refreshed him during the greater part of his life, he now became critical in the taste of Bordeaux. A railway, in fact, was not a means of transport but a thing to bet and gamble about. . . . Once in the height of the sorrowful farce, I had occasion to call on a couple of 'bold brokers' in a certain street not a mile from the centre of Bristol. The flavour of old Havannahs and new scrip filled the place; the clerks were having chops and tomato sauce, and a silver-necked bottle proved they enjoyed at least a reversion of the Saint Peray from the principals' apartment, into which I was summoned. Softly I trod on a Turkey carpet; a tray well furnished stood on a sideboard; and piles of prospectuses flanked the fine ponderous bronze inkstand of the man of projects, who sat in a richly cushioned chair. Voices issued from the neighbouring room, where the second principal saw others on business, and the click of plates and occasional flying of corks proved how actively the business of allotments was progressing. But they came like shadows, and so departed."

The commercial interests of Bristol in South Wales being seriously threatened by the construction of railways connecting the Principality with London and the midland districts, a prospectus was issued in April of the Bristol and South Wales Junction Railway Company. The proposed capital was £200,000, and so popular was the scheme, and so eager the desire to invest during the mania then prevailing, that the shares soon commanded a preposterous premium. According to the plan of the promoters, for which an Act was obtained, the line was to proceed from the Great Western terminus to the Old and New Passages by way of Baptist mills, Horfield Down, and Almondsbury. In connection with this railway, a second scheme was propounded for a railway from the northern shore of the Severn to Chepstow and Monmouth. Another prospectus, issued about the same time, was that of the Bristol and Liverpool Railway Company, with a capital of two millions, which proposed to construct a bridge over the Severn. This project had the support of the mayor and sheriff of Bristol, and the subscriptions for shares far exceeded the number proposed to be issued. None of these designs were, however, carried out, the two latter being abandoned before application was made to Parliament. In 1851, after about a third of the share capital had been spent, it was acknowledged by all concerned that the South Wales Junction scheme was in a hopeless condition; but difficulty was encountered in dissolving the company, owing to the invariable absence of a quorum when a statutory meeting was convened. In October, 1853, the undertaking was formally relinquished. Nevertheless, in 1854 a new scheme was started, having the same end in view, but proposing to construct a line to the New Passage by way of Queen Square, the Hotwells, Sea-mills, and Shirehampton, with a floating bridge over the Severn by which entire trains were to be carried across, and unloading avoided. The capital was fixed at £600,000. The proposal was approved at an influentially attended meeting, and the Council intimated its assent, but the paucity of subscriptions and threatened opposition led to the project being dropped. In July, 1856, another prospectus was issued by the party of Bristolians who had all along urged the necessity of action. The original line of country was, with modifications, adopted; the capital was fixed at £300,000; and "floating steam bridges" were to be devised by Mr. Brunel for crossing the Channel. An Act authorising the project was obtained in 1857, but it was not until October, 1858, that the contractor began operations, the tunnel of 1,242 yards at Patchway being first undertaken. The New Passage ferry was bought soon after for £2,700, and the construction of the immense wooden piers followed. The tunnel was completed in July, 1860, and the line was formally opened on the 25th August, 1863. In 1867 an arrangement was made by the directors with the Great Western board, under which the railway and works at the end of three years became the property of the latter company. Originally constructed on the broad gauge, the line was altered to narrow gauge in August, 1873.

At a meeting of the Council on the 13th August, 1845, the Improvement Committee presented a report strongly condemning the narrow, inconvenient, and dangerous streets between Bristol Bridge and the railway station, and recommending the construction of a new thoroughfare, to be called Victoria Street. The expenditure required for this purpose was estimated at £84,510, but it was anticipated that £44,200 would be recovered by the resale of building sites, etc. The commmittee also recommended an extensive alteration of the road from Cumberland Basin to St. Augustine's Back, including improvements in the Jacob's Wells road, the gross expense of which was estimated at £63,900 and the net outlay at £26,250. The widening of Bristol Bridge at a cost of £8,000, the improvement of the road from Park Street to the Victoria Rooms at an expense of £4,200, and the arching over of a part of the malodorous Froom, set down at £3,400, also formed features of this report, the comprehensiveness and boldness of which were without precedent in local annals.

In the following year the Improvement Committee suggested various alterations in the scheme, and added to it a project for a new street commencing in Nelson Street opposite Bridewell Street, and having terminations in Wine Street and Broad Street. This plan, which was intended to sweep away a quantity of wretched habitations, was expected to cost £38,000. A Bill to authorise this and other improvements was introduced into Parliament in 1847. [At the sitting of the inspectors sent down by the Government to inquire into the merits of the scheme, the town clerk stated that Bristol then contained 250 streets, 50 lanes, and 390 courts and alleys; the number of houses was about 20,000. In regard to the number and area of places for public recreation, he said that Queen Square had an area of over 6¾ acres, College Green about 4½ acres, Brunswick Square 1¼ acre, Portland Square 2¼ acres, and King Square nearly 1¼ acre. Brandon Hill was 19½ acres in extent, and £800 had been recently collected by private subscription for the purpose of forming walks there.] The Bill—which empowered the Council to levy a yearly Improvement Rate not exceeding twopence in the pound—received the royal assent; but owing to the financial charges attending the transfer of the docks to the city the proposed works were not popular, and in 1849 the more costly schemes were indefinitely deferred. The Council resolved, however, on widening portions of Hotwell Road, Limekiln Lane, and Bread Street, broadening the roadway at the Stone Bridge, and effecting some minor improvements in the out-parish of St. Philip's. In March, 1852, when the powers of the Act in reference to Victoria Street, Bristol Bridge, etc., were about to expire from effluxion of time, the Council determined upon undertaking a portion of the new street at a net cost of £11,300; but the intention was strongly condemned at ward meetings of the ratepayers, and the resolution was rescinded a few weeks later.

Queen Adelaide, widow of William IV., paid a brief visit to Bristol on the 20th August, stopping one night at the Royal Hotel, Mall, Clifton, and spending a few hours on the following day at Blaize Castle and Kingsweston.

William James Müller, the greatest painter to which Bristol has given birth, expired at the residence of his brother, Mr. E. G. Müller, on the 8th September, aged 33. Mr. Müller was born at No. 13, Hillsbridge Parade, on the 28th June, 1812. His father, a Prussian of good scientific abilities, had fled from Germany upon the occupation of the country by the French, and found his way to Bristol, where he married a Miss James, a member of an old family in the city, and was for some years curator of the Bristol Institution. The son showed artistic talent whilst very young, and a promising original picture, executed in his fourteenth year, was accepted and shown at the Bristol annual exhibition of works of art. Shortly afterwards he was apprenticed to Mr. J. B. Pyne, a meritorious artist then residing on St. Michael's Hill; but the connection was broken at the end of about three years, and young Müller thenceforth became his own master. His first picture exhibited at the Royal Academy, in 1833, "The destruction of old London Bridge," was painted when he was little more than twenty years old. Before that date he had produced some hundreds of sketches, chiefly of quaint old buildings in Bristol and picturesque spots in the neighbourhood, most of which were disposed of to local collectors at a few shillings each. Eager for a wider field, he accompanied another local artist, Mr. G. Fripp, in a tour through Germany and Italy. But he seems to have had an early longing for the East, and as soon as his circumstances permitted, he departed for Greece, following up this tour with another in Egypt, and subsequently a third in Asia Minor, and producing works on each occasion which gained him high repute in the artistic world. One of these pictures, "Chess Players in Cairo," was sold at the dispersion of the Gillott gallery for upwards of 5,000 guineas. Unhappily Müller's constitution was never robust, and it is not improbable that the effects of an Eastern climate and the fatigues of travelling brought about the malady which cut short his career. He had removed from Bristol to London in 1839. He returned here in the summer of 1845, in the hope of recovering strength in his native air; but he came back only to die. His remains were interred in the Unitarian cemetery in Brunswick Square. Shortly afterwards his sketches, etc., were sold in London, and produced £4,242. An interesting biography of Müller, written by his friend, W. Neal Solly, was published in 1872.

Upon the death, in September, of Dr. Law, Bishop of Bath and Wells, the parish of Bedminster was detached from that diocese, and came under the episcopal jurisdiction of the Bishop of Gloucester and Bristol. The change did not take place without manifold protests in the press and elsewhere on the part of the rector, the Rev. M. R. Whish; but when that eccentric gentleman, who was noted for his pertinacity, followed them up by reading a document from the pulpit of his church, denying the jurisdiction of his new diocesan, a suit was raised against him in the Prerogative Court of

Canterbury. On his making a formal apology, however, the freak was condoned.

Towards the close of Mr. King's mayoralty, and chiefly at his instigation, another attempt was made by the Council to purchase the rights of the Dock Company over the port and harbour. At a meeting of the civic body on the 19th November, it was reported by the special committee appointed to negotiate with the directors, that their efforts had been fruitless. Although the annual dividends of the company for the previous twenty-three years had averaged only £2 2*s*. 3*d*. per cent., the committee had proposed that the city should guarantee the shareholders £2 10*s*. per cent.; but the directors demanded 3 per cent. The Council approved of the steps taken by the committee; and in the following February renewed its efforts for a solution by proposing to the directors that the amount of dividend to be guaranteed should be fixed by arbitration. The company maintaining its attitude of stolid resistance, the matter again fell to the ground.

The details of a dispute which threatened to culminate in an "affair of honour," were laid before the public in the *Bristol Gazette* of the 10th December. It appeared that a few days previously a paragraph appeared in the *Bristol Times*, stating that a situation in the Custom House had been conferred upon an Irishman, and that this was the second or third instance in which—probably through the remissness of those who were expected to look after such matters—the patronage of the Government offices had been snatched by other localities. At a meeting of the True Blue Club (formed in 1844 with a view to promoting unity in the Tory party), the honorary secretary, Mr. Charles Blisset, of Clifton, characterised this statement as "a wilful and deliberate falsehood." Mr. Leech, the proprietor of the *Times*, forthwith requested an explanation, but Mr. Blisset only replied that the committee of the club were of the same opinion as himself. Mr. Henry Shute, the "friend" of Mr. Leech, thereupon requested Mr. Blisset to appoint a "friend" also, with a view to a hostile encounter; whereupon Mr. Blisset wrote that he "peremptorily declined the challenge; first, because I can substantiate the charge, and, secondly, because every member of the committee who adopted my opinion would be liable to a similar attack, so that Mr. Leech, in addition to his title as a public slanderer, may have to add that of a murderer also." The writer went on to assail Mr. Leech's character in acrimonious terms, and concluded by declaring that so long as the editor of the *Bristol Times* criticised the True Blue Club, he

(Mr. B.) would continue to expose his treachery. The correspondence having been published for the edification of the public, Mr. Leech, in commenting upon the charges of treachery and falsehood, said "they are comprised in the offence of my wishing to have an independent opinion of my own, and determining not to be made the means of gratifying the personal animosities of two or three individuals." His explanation was briefly as follows. In November, 1844, the chief promoters of the True Blue Club published a poll book of the municipal election for Clifton Ward, with the avowed object of depriving Liberal tradesmen of Conservative patronage. This, it appeared, Mr. Leech had condemned, whereupon, "the fiat went forth, that the paper that would not defend exclusive dealing was unworthy of confidence, and must be crushed." This retort led to an animated correspondence on the part of Mr. Henry Bush and others, and had doubtless the effect of exasperating the discord already prevailing in the party since the election of 1841, and ending, as will shortly be seen, in the complete rupture of 1847.

The old almshouses in Barrs' Lane, belonging to St. James's parish, having been taken down for reconstruction, the Council, in February, 1846, succeeded in purchasing the site, and were thus enabled to widen the thoroughfare—afterwards called Barrs' Street. About the same time the Council determined on buying some houses in Barton Alley, leading from St. James's Barton to the churchyard, in which, as a committee reported, two persons carrying umbrellas could not pass. Property was also acquired in Bridewell Street, and the widening of both thoroughfares was commenced. The Bridewell Street improvement was soon finished, but owing to the obstinacy of one or two persons, Barton Alley was not opened for vehicles until some fifteen years later.

During the memorable debates in the House of Commons on Sir Robert Peel's proposal for the abolition of the corn-laws at the end of three years, one of the members for Bristol, Mr. P. W. Miles, was selected by the Protectionists to resist the motion of the Ministry for going into committee on the subject. After an unusually protracted struggle, Mr. Miles's amendment was defeated on the 27th February by 337 votes against 240. In the course of the discussion, the junior member for the city, Mr. Berkeley, excited amusement by reading to the House a letter to a Bristol merchant in which Mr. Miles had declared that "it would be better for all parties that the repeal [of the corn laws] should be immediate," and that he should not oppose such a motion if it were made. Mr. Berkeley presented a petition in favour of the ministerial scheme, signed by 18,000 Bristolians, "Conservatives equally with Liberals." There was no petition from the city in a contrary sense.

About the month of April, the large mansion in Dighton Street, commonly known as Harford House from having been formerly the residence of the Harford family, was purchased by certain Roman Catholics, who established in it a convent dedicated to "Our Lady of Mercy." The nuns subsequently established an orphanage for sixty children, and added a large school-house.

In May, the mansion known as Cotham Lodge, which had been evacuated a short time before by Mr. William Fripp, was razed to the ground, the estate having been purchased for conversion into building sites. The place was afterwards called Cotham Park. The only relic of the original buildings is a lofty "observatory" or tower, erected in 1779 on the base of a windmill, and commanding a very extensive prospect.

Persons who have grown up since the creation of educational machinery embracing all classes of society can with difficulty realize the ignorance prevailing amongst the poor at the period now under review. A year or two earlier, a committee had been formed in the city to promote unsectarian education; but, as the Roman Catholic priests and the Unitarian ministers were forthwith excluded from the work, the chief effect of the movement was to demonstrate the prejudices of its leaders. In the summer of 1846, Miss Mary Carpenter and a few kindred spirits, taking compassion on the "gutter children" or "street Arabs" which prowled about in great numbers, resolved upon opening a room in Lewin's Mead, then notorious for the degraded character of its inhabitants, and offering free instruction to the waifs who would attend. On the first morning (Sunday, August 2nd), three boys presented themselves, and in the afternoon the attendance exceeded a dozen. A short extract from the master's diary will afford an idea of the difficulties of the enterprise in which he had engaged: "That afternoon I shall never forget. Only thirteen or fourteen boys present; some swearing, some fighting, some crying. One boy struck another's head through the window. I tried to offer up a short prayer, but found it was impossible. The boys, instead of kneeling, began to tumble over one another, and to sing 'Jim Crow'." From one of the promoters of the school we further learn that "none of the lads had shoes or stockings;

some had no shirt and no home, sleeping in casks on the quay or on steps, and living by petty depredations." By untiring patience and kindliness, however, the teacher obtained such influence over many of his reckless pupils as to secure the regular and orderly attendance of thirty boys, several of whom made good progress, and some, after being reclaimed from moral degradation, were enabled to earn an honest livelihood. A visible improvement was effected in Lewin's Mead, which had previously been the scene of almost constant disorder. Gratified with the results of this experiment, the promoters of the "Ragged School" hired the historic old chapel in St. James's Back, to which the institution was removed in December. A night school was then added, bringing in "a swarm of young men and women, whose habits and character almost caused even the stout heart of Mary Carpenter to quail. Early in 1847 the numbers one Sunday evening amounted to two hundred; the attempt to close the school with prayer was baffled by mockery, and the court beneath resounded with screams and blows." Nevertheless, through the devotion of Miss Carpenter, the institution gradually became a centre of enlightenment and civilisation, and it is difficult to overrate its effects on the miserable district in which it was situated. The experience gained in it by its foundress led her, a few years later, to widen her aims in reference to the youthful semi-criminal population, and the result was the establishment in 1852 of a Reformatory school at Kingswood—in the house once hired by John Wesley. This was followed, two years later, by the creation of a second institution of this class for girls, in the Red Lodge, Park Row, which was purchased for the purpose by Lady Byron, and placed under Miss Carpenter's sole control. For an adequate account of the indefatigable efforts of this remarkable woman on behalf of the juvenile poor, the reader must be referred to the memoir written by one of her nephews. In October, 1877, four months after her death, a meeting, notable for the total absence of sectarian spirit displayed by its promoters, was held in the Guildhall for the purpose of taking measures to found a suitable memorial of her philanthropic exertions. The chief speakers were Canon Girdlestone, the Rev. Dr. Percival, the Rev. Dr. Caldicott, the Rev. A. N. Blatchford (Unitarian), the Rev. U. Thomas (Independent), and Mr. L. Fry (Friend). It was resolved to extend the operation of the Home for boys established by Miss Carpenter, to establish a Home for girls, and to erect a monument to her memory in the Cathedral. The subscriptions for these objects amounted to about £2,700. The monument bears a profile bust of Miss Carpenter by Mr. J. H. Thomas, a Bristol sculptor.

Sir Charles Wetherell, recorder of Bristol, died on the 17th August, 1846, in consequence of injuries sustained by having been thrown from a phaeton. Sir Charles was 76 years of age, and, according to a notice of him in the *Bristol Times* of July 17, 1858, he was in the constant habit, for some years previous to his death, of going to sleep whilst trying prisoners at quarter sessions. The vacant office (no longer in the gift of the Corporation) was conferred by the Government on Mr. Richard Budden Crowder, Q.C., who, on becoming a judge in March, 1854, was succeeded by Sir Alexander Cockburn, then Attorney General, the salary being reduced from £700 to £600 a year. In November, 1856, the office again became vacant, its occupant having been appointed Lord Chief Justice of the Common Pleas. The salary was then further reduced to £500. Mr. Serjeant Kinglake, the new recorder, held the office until his death, in July, 1870. Sir Robert Collier, Attorney General, was his successor; but during his re-election as Member of Parliament for Plymouth, rendered necessary by the appointment, he was so severely censured by his constituents for holding dual offices that he forthwith resigned the post. The recordership was thereupon conferred upon Mr. Montague Bere, Q.C., who relinquished it in July, 1872, and was succeeded by Mr. Thomas Kingdon Kingdon, Q.C., who died in December, 1879. Mr. Charles Grevile Prideaux, then recorder of Exeter, and son of the late Mr. N. G. Prideaux, solicitor, Bristol, was appointed to the vacancy.

The exactions of the Dock Company, and the consequent depression of the commerce of the city, became the more insupportable at this time from the rapid progress which was taking place in the neighbouring ports. The Council having shown an unwillingness to take action, notwithstanding memorials from the ratepayers, a great meeting of merchants, traders, and others was held on the 29th September, 1846, Mr. Robert Bright presiding, when it was resolved to form a Free Port Association, with the view of emancipating the city from the thraldom under which it groaned. The movement was enthusiastically welcomed by a large majority of the inhabitants, meetings of whom were convened in each ward to consider the question. At each of those gatherings a demand for an equitable arrangement was loudly urged, and two gentlemen were delegated to co-operate with the promoters of the association, while at meetings of the various trades cordial support was offered to the agitation by the establishment of an Operatives' Free Port Association. Subsequently a committee of the Council was nominated to act in conjunction with Mr. Bright and his friends, and at a meeting of the municipality, on the 1st January, 1847, this body presented a report which displayed the wrong-headed policy of the dock board in striking colours. From a table showing the dock dues and charges on vessels entering inwards at the leading ports, it appeared that the charges at Bristol amounted to 2*s.* 7*d.* per ton, as compared with 9½*d.* at London, 1*s.* 7*d.* at Liverpool, 3½*d.* at Southampton, 3*d.* at Cardiff, and nothing at Gloucester. As regarded the import charges on the principal articles of commerce, they were found to be 8*s.* 8*d.* at Bristol, against 4*s.* 6*d.* at Liverpool, 2*s.* 10*d.* at Gloucester, 1*s.* 7½*d.* at Hull, and 1*s.* 3½*d.* at Cardiff. After prolonged negotiations with the dock directors a bargain was at last struck, and the Council, on the 25th of October, 1847, by a majority of 42 votes against 4, approved of a scheme by which the dock estate was to be transferred to the Corporation, on the latter undertaking to pay the proprietors a rent charge of £2 12*s.* 6*d.* per cent.* on the original shares of £147 9*s.* each (redeemable at any time at the sum of £96 15*s.* 6*d.*), and interest at the rate of 5 per cent. per annum for the first twelve years on the bonds of the company. In order to secure those conditions by an unquestionable guarantee, the dock board demanded that a rate should be imposed on the entire fixed property of the city, and to this the Council agreed, but fixed the maximum rate at fourpence in the pound. The increase of 2*s.* 6*d.* per cent. on the terms offered to the dock shareholders in 1845 was defended on the ground that the company had in the meantime expended two years' income (£30,000) in improvements, and that the net receipts of the dock had increased about £700 a year. The proposed arrangement caused great excitement in the city. At a public meeting on the 14th February, 1848, at which the trading classes were largely represented, an approval of the transfer was subjected to a condition, imposed on the motion of Mr. W. Herapath, namely, that the new dock board should consist of commissioners chosen by the ratepayers, and that a fund of £50,000 should be previously formed by means of subscriptions to provide for repairs and contingencies. The con-

* The dock proprietors received no dividend down to 1822. Between 1823 and 1844 inclusive the average distribution was £2 4*s.* 5*d.* per cent. In 1845 and 1846 no dividend was paid.

troversy almost wholly monopolised local attention for many months, the working classes at repeated meetings expressing approval of the movement. At length, in the session of 1848, the Free Port Association (in which the Chamber of Commerce had been merged) promoted a Bill for carrying the above arrangement into effect. A petition signed by 19,000 Bristolians was presented in support of the scheme, and others praying for its adoption were forwarded from Bath, Stroud, Trowbridge, and other towns. But a formidable opposition had been organised against the clause authorising a rate upon household property; and it was also urged before the House of Commons Committee that it was inexpedient to vest the docks in the Corporation, whose antecedents were declared to have caused discontent amongst the majority of ratepayers. The House nevertheless followed the example of 1803 in reference to the rating clause; but a provision was inserted rendering it imperative on the Corporation to reduce the dues to an extent equivalent to the sum charged upon the ratepayers. As the opposition did not renew the struggle in the Upper Chamber, the Bill received the royal assent on the 30th June, 1848. On the 23rd August following, the deed transferring the docks from the company to the Corporation was formally executed. The capital of the company at that date was found to be £259,954 in shares, and £256,400 in "notes" bearing interest—a sinking fund having reduced the total original capital by £77,665. [In 1860, the docks' committee of the Council paid off the "notes" and issued bonds at a lower rate of interest, thus effecting a saving of £2,500 a year. In 1882 another great financial operation was completed, the rent charge of £2 12*s*. 6*d*. per cent. being redeemed, and the proprietors paid off in corporation bonds or in cash. On the termination of this arrangement the old Dock Company ceased to exist.] Under the provisions of the Act the Council forthwith elected a Docks Committee for the management of its new property. No time was lost by this body in preparing a new table of dues, showing an average reduction of upwards of 50 per cent. on vessels and of 20 per cent. on goods as compared with that previously in force. The dues on 530 articles of merchandise were wholly abolished. [Notwithstanding the remissions, the surplus income in 1851 was reported to be £3,800, and the dues on some imports were further reduced. But the aggregate reductions proved to be too large, the receipts being insufficient to provide for maintenance and repairs, and in January, 1856, the Council slightly raised the charges, so as to obtain an additional income of £3,500. The scale was reduced to its former level in 1861.] The Merchants' Society, soon after the transfer, abolished the wharfage dues on Irish importations, and on the general exports of the port. The new tariff came into effect on the 15th November, 1848, when the event was celebrated by a general holiday, and by a "free port demonstration"—one of the most imposing displays ever known in the city. The mayor (Mr. Haberfield), the members of the Corporation, of the Merchants' Society, and of the Corporation of the Poor, the Free Port Association, and numbers of merchants and traders, assembled at the Cattle Market, where they were joined by the artisans of every branch of local industry, the members of the chief benefit societies, and innumerable bands of music. The immense procession made its way towards Clifton Down through the principal streets, amidst the acclamations of many thousands gathered to witness the parade. The day concluded with numerous public dinners. Notwithstanding the natural elation which characterised the speeches of the "free port" leaders, however, it could not be disguised that the object which gave the organisation its name had not been achieved. The port was far from "free." As a matter of fact, the harbour charges were still higher than those existing at some other ports; and those who had opposed the scheme called upon the successful party to carry out their programme. In the course of the struggle Mr. R. Bright and other free port men had admitted that, in the face of the tax placed on the citizens, the mercantile and shipowning interests ought to make a considerable sacrifice. A subscription of £50,000 was suggested; but although Mr. Bright offered to become responsible for a considerable sum, the appeal generally fell on deaf ears. The association, asserting that it had fulfilled its mission, dissolved on the 1st October, 1850, and nothing more was heard of the mercantile donation. Unfortunately this was not all. The expenses of the association having exceeded the subscriptions by about £650, an appeal was made to the commercial classes to clear off the liabilities; but the response was disappointing, only about £160 being contributed. After some months' delay, Mr. Bright forwarded a cheque for £500 to a member of the executive, observing: "Every effort which propriety and self-respect will permit has now been made to obtain the assistance of our fellow citizens with but imperfect success, and I cannot allow either myself, or a body of gentlemen from whom I received singular confidence, to remain longer in the painful and unfit situation in which we are placed by claims on the association remaining unsatisfied." Subsequently a subscription was started for presenting a testimonial of public gratitude to Mr. Bright as the person chiefly instrumental in conducting the movement to success, and a sum exceeding £700 was contributed. Mr. Bright expressed his desire that the money should be bestowed upon some local institution, whereupon an amusing rivalry broke forth, a crowd of organisations severally making eager demands for the golden prize. The competition eventually led Mr. Bright to withdraw his request, and the fund was devoted to the purchase of a handsome service of plate, the centre-piece of which bore an allegorical group representing Bristol accompanied by Commerce and Prosperity, and under the protection of Commercial Liberty. The plate was presented to Mr. Bright by Mr. P. W. Miles, M.P., at a meeting held in the Council Chamber on the 21st January, 1855. Mr. Bright's portrait was also painted, and presented to the Merchants' Society. Mr. Leonard Bruton, who had acted as secretary of the association, was presented in 1865 with a handsome piece of plate and £500 "in recognition of his zealous, disinterested, and valuable services," the subscribers to the testimonial embracing most of the leading citizens.* It would be interesting to discover the precise effect of the scheme by which the Corporation recovered control over the port; but in adducing statistics on the subject it is necessary to bear in mind that the abolition of the corn and navigation laws, and the great gold discoveries in California and Australia were contemporaneous with the early years of the new system, and that the commerce of the city would probably have largely increased even if no local change had occurred. Keeping these facts in view, the following summary of a statement made by Mr. Bruton before the British Association in 1875 will be found of interest. In the last twenty years of the old dock board the progressive increase of the import trade of Bristol was at the average rate of 33 per cent.; the first ten years following the transfer showed an increase of 66½ per cent., and in the next ten years there was a further advance of over 62 per cent. Comparing 1848 with 1874, the foreign import trade of the port had

* Mr. Bruton became secretary to the Chamber of Commerce on the revival of that institution in September, 1851. In September, 1880, he was presented with £1,000 and an address. The latter, which was signed by the mayor (Mr. H. Taylor), the master of the Merchants' Society (Alderman Edwards), and the President of the Chamber (Mr. C. Wills), stated that the testimonial was offered by nearly two hundred firms and individuals, as a token of the high admiration in which they held Mr. Bruton's "nearly forty years of untiring and unselfish devotion to the maritime and commercial interests of the port and city."

increased 300 per cent. The net rateable value of property had remained almost stationary under the restrictive system; but it had risen from £406,000 in 1841 to £720,000 in 1871. Notwithstanding the reduction in dock dues, the receipts from that source had increased 50 per cent., while the income from town and other port charges was three times greater in 1874 than in 1847.

The famine which afflicted Ireland and the Scottish Highlands during the year 1847 called forth liberal manifestations of public sympathy in Bristol and the neighbourhood. The amount subscribed in this city for the sufferers amounted to upwards of £9,000.

During the autumn of this year the inhabitants of Cotham and Redland appear to have become awakened to the defects in the sanitary and police arrangements of the district. The residents complained of the utter absence of sewers and lamps; and their remonstrances on the latter point led to a resolution of the Council, declaring it expedient that all parts of the city should be lighted with gas, and ordering negotiations with the gas companies with a view to a reduction in their charges. The matter, however, was suffered to drop, and the suburbs remained as dark as before.

Under the provisions of an Act passed in the previous session, the Bristol County Court came into existence in 1847, Mr. Arthur Palmer, jun., the first judge, opening the new tribunal in the Guildhall on the 15th March. The old Court of Conscience, which had existed from the time of William III., was superseded, but the more ancient Tolzey Court was not interfered with. In 1855 Mr. Palmer resigned his judgeship from ill-health, and was succeeded by Sir Eardley Wilmot, bart., who held the office until 1862, when he was promoted to a metropolitan court. His successor here was Mr. W. H. Willes, who died a few days after his appointment. The next judge was Mr. Edward J. Lloyd, Q.C., who resigned in 1874, and was followed by Mr. R. A. Fisher. The latter died in 1879, and was succeeded by Mr. W. J. Metcalfe, Q.C., recorder of Norwich.

Buckingham Chapel, Clifton, erected by the Baptist denomination at a cost of £6,000, was opened on the 2nd June, 1847. The architecture of the building showed a marked improvement upon most of the so-called Gothic erections of the period; and the richness of the front excited much admiration.

At the dissolution of Parliament, in July, a local contest of an unusually exciting character took place. As has been already recorded, the defeat of Mr. Fripp in 1841 caused great irritation amongst many stanch Conservatives, who contended that that gentleman had been unfairly treated by some of the friends of Mr. Miles. The ill-feeling between the two camps had been only aggravated by time, Mr. Miles remaining a firm protectionist, whilst Mr. Fripp approved of the free-trade policy of Sir Robert Peel. As another election drew near, the rival sections seemed to forget their political enemies, and prepared for a fierce contest for supremacy between themselves. There seems to have been dissension in the Liberal camp also, for a Mr. Apsley Pellatt, introduced by some Nonconformists, met with a very cold reception. Mr. Berkeley, the former Liberal representative, was returned at the head of the poll. The numbers were: Mr. Berkeley, 4,381; Mr. Miles, 2,595; Mr. Fripp, 2,476; Mr. Pellatt, 171. Mr. Miles had 970 plumpers, Mr. Fripp 912, and Mr. Berkeley 2,247. The friends of Mr. Fripp loudly complained of the intimidation exercised by the leading supporters of Mr. Miles, and the wounds given in the fratricidal conflict remained unhealed for several years.

An appearance of the celebrated Swedish vocalist, Jenny Lind, at the Bristol theatre, on September 27th, caused such excitement in the locality that the event seems worthy of a permanent record. Notwithstanding the high prices fixed for admission—25*s*. for the boxes, 20*s*. for the pit, and 10*s*. for the gallery—the demand for seats exceeded the supply, and a portion of the stage was railed off for the accommodation, at 5*s*. each, of about 500 persons condemned to stand throughout the performance. The programme consisted of selections from operas, an air from "The Creation," and some Swedish melodies. Mdlle. Lind sang at a miscellaneous concert, given a few evenings later at the Victoria Rooms, at which the prices of admission ranged from 5*s*. to 21*s*.

Two new churches for the populous eastern districts of the city were in course of construction, and a third was resolved upon, in the course of this year. That of St. Simon's, Baptist Mills, was consecrated on the 22nd December; a similar ceremony took place at St. Mark's, Lower Easton, on the 18th May, 1848, and St. Jude's, Poyntz Pool, was opened in June, 1849. The three buildings cost about £2,500 each. The ecclesiastical districts of St. Simon and of St. Jude were taken out of Trinity parish, St. Philip's; the other was abstracted from St. George's and Stapleton. The Rev. J. R. Woodford, afterwards Bishop of Ely, was the first incumbent of St. Mark's.

By the will of Mr. Robert Suple, of the Mall, Clifton (a retired Bristol linen draper), who died in 1847, the sum of £8,300 was bequeathed to various local charities. Amongst the bequests was one of £1,000 to the Infirmary, for providing two annual prizes to medical students in that institution for the encouragement of medical and surgical science.

The parish church of Abbot's Leigh was partially destroyed by fire on Sunday the 20th February, 1848. The flames burst from the building soon after the conclusion of afternoon service, and were attributed to the foulness of the heating flues. The tower escaped with little injury.

During the spring an arrangement was effected by the Improvement Committee of the Corporation and the Charity Trustees, by which the former surrendered certain property in Portwall Lane, formerly known as the Law Ditch, which the trustees had claimed as part of the estates devised for charitable purposes by Alderman Whitson. The trustees gave up part of the frontage for the purpose of widening the thoroughfare, on receiving £350 as compensation.

In April, 1848, Bishop Monk informed the rural deans in his diocese of his intention to surrender a considerable sum of money which he expected to receive from the Ecclesiastical Commissioners, with a view to benefiting the poorer class of livings. The money in question was to be paid for the surrender of the bishop's interest in the manor of Horfield, and the matter soon afterwards excited attention in Parliament. From Dr. Monk's subsequent statement, it appeared that the manor of Horfield had been leased many years previously for three lives. Two of these had fallen in about 1831, in the episcopate of Bishop Gray, but neither that prelate nor his successor, Bishop Allen, had been able to agree with the lessee on terms for a renewal. The matter was complicated by the fact that some of the land was held under the lessee by copyholders, while the double uncertainty of leasehold and copyhold tenures had prevented the erection of houses upon the estate, though from its contiguity to Bristol it was otherwise attractive to builders. Being unwilling to perpetuate the evil, Dr. Monk declined renewing the lease unless the tenures were altered, and the negotiations made no progress for several years. While matters were in this position, the bishop was informed, in December, 1846, that the Ecclesiastical Commissioners had resolved to take possession of the property upon the first vacancy of the see, on the ground that the average revenues of the bishopric were in excess of the £5,000 a year intended to be assigned to it—a statement which Dr. Monk warmly controverted. The decision of the commissioners, however, induced his lordship to think of renewing the Horfield lease, which, as he explained, would give him the command of a considerable sum of money, and enable him to carry out certain objects which he had at heart. As the lessee did not offer acceptable terms, the bishop applied to the commissioners, with whom he concluded a bargain for the surrender of his interests for £11,587. He had originally intended, he said, to present the whole of this sum to the diocese. But the Bishop's College had not proved successful, and the loan he had made towards its establishment threatened to be lost. He therefore proposed to set apart half of the Horfield money to secure the interests of his family, and to devote the remainder—which, with funds remaining unexpended from his previous donations for improving poor livings, would be raised to £9,238—to the erection of parsonages in benefices worth under £200 a year. Obstacles, however, arose to the completion of the arrangements. In the course of an inquiry before a committee of the House of Commons, the secretary to the Ecclesiastical Commissioners insinuated that the bishop had undertaken never to renew the Horfield lease; and it was alleged that the sale of his interest was not consistent with his engagements. These charges were indignantly denied by Dr. Monk, who stated that they had been instigated by the Rev. Henry Richards, perpetual curate of Horfield, the advowson of which living was leased with the manor. Mr. Richards, he added, was the largest copyholder in the parish, and had been solicitous to obtain for himself a new lease of the manor, by which he would have been able to deal with the estate, in the double capacity of lord and copyholder, in a manner extremely to his own advantage. Disappointed in this desire, wrote Dr. Monk, "his indignation exhibited itself in railing against his bishop." Ultimately the Government refused to ratify the bargain made between the commissioners and the bishop, whereupon, after the dropping of the life of the "lord farmer" in 1849—who had held that position for seventy-two years—Dr. Monk granted a new lease for three lives to his secretary. The income of the manor was then £545 a year. This proceeding, though legal, excited much unfavourable comment in Parliament, it being generally held that his lordship ought to have treated the manor as a trust bequeathed to him by his predecessors for public purposes. Dr. Monk's defence was, that he wished to commute the manorial rights, to set an example of good agriculture, and to improve the living of Horfield, which was inadequately endowed; and that these objects could be accomplished only by a lease controlled by himself. In March, 1852, he executed trust deeds conveying the whole of his interest in the estate to five trustees. A rent charge of £192 yearly was directed to be divided, one half towards increasing the income of the living of Horfield, and the other moiety towards the endowment of a new church when the growing population required one. The rents of the demesne lands, and of 320 acres of additional land just awarded to the bishop by the Copyhold Commissioners in lieu of manorial rights (together about £900 a year), were to be devoted to the building of parsonages in poor parishes in the archdeaconry, and to the increase of curates' stipends in small livings in the diocese. Dr. Monk expressed a hope that when the lease lapsed, the Ecclesiastical Commissioners would continue his disposition of the funds. All apprehension on this point was removed, however, in October, 1858, when the bishop's trustees purchased the reversion of the lease from the commissioners for the sum of £5,000. With the emancipation of the district from the copyhold system dates its rise and rapid growth as a suburb. The *Bristol Journal* of May 22, 1852, contained the following: "The National Freehold Land Society has purchased thirty acres of excellent land near Naylor's cottages at Horfield, which will be divided into about 300 allotments, and apportioned to the Bristol members of the society." It was not, however, until about 1860 that building operations became general in the locality.

Complaint having been made respecting the decayed state of the butchers' shambles in the Exchange market, the Council, on the 9th May, 1848, approved of the design of a new market house for meat and vegetables, prepared by Mr. Pope, the city architect. The expense of the reconstruction was estimated at £3,000. The plan included the widening of a portion of Nicholas Street. A restoration of the front of the Exchange took place at the same time, and the works were completed, and the market opened in April, 1849. Only five years later, in May, 1854, the Finance Committee reported to the Council that the Exchange market was not in a state creditable to the city, and a vote of £2,170 was granted for alterations.

The ceremony of consecrating a Roman Catholic bishop as vicar apostolic of the western district took place in the church of St. Mary, on the Quay, on the 10th September. The prelate was Dr. Joseph William Hendren, Bishop of Uranopolis. The sermon was preached by Dr. Nicholas Wiseman, bishop *in partibus*, afterwards a cardinal, and so-called "Archbishop of Westminster."

At a meeting held on the 22nd September, the Dean of Bristol (Dr. Lamb) presiding, it was resolved to raise a subscription for the purpose of erecting in College Green a copy of the original Bristol High Cross, of which the city was scandalously deprived by a dean and chapter of the last century. The cost was estimated at about £630. The foundation stone of the new structure was laid on the 8th August, 1850, by the mayor (Mr. Haberfield), attended by the local Freemasons. The stone selected by the committee was from the Nailsworth quarries; but the vaunted durability of the material was not verified by experience. The cross, which varied in details from the original construction [see Pooley's work on Gloucestershire Crosses], was finished in November, 1851, when the amount expended had been £450. The cost of the eight statues of kings proposed to be introduced was estimated at £480; but the money could not be raised. The solitary statue of Edward III. was placed in the cross in 1855 by the Freemasons of the province.

In December, 1848, to the great surprise of cathedral-goers, the dean and chapter intimated to the minor canons that the priest's portion of the daily services must no longer be intoned, according to the usage of three centuries, but that it must be read, as in all parish churches of that day. The first service under this regulation took place on Sunday, December 10th, when Canon Surtees officiated, the Rev. E. C. Carter, the minor canon on duty, having refused to obey the order on the ground that he should thereby violate the oath taken on his appointment. He was thereupon excluded from the cathedral by direction of the chapter. Another minor canon, the Rev. Sir Charles Macgregor, who had been chosen a few weeks previously, was, it turned out, unable to intone, and it was currently reported that the ancient custom had been abolished for the benefit of an incompetent person. Mr. Carter, who had the sympathy of the precentor, the Rev. R. L. Caley, shortly afterwards appealed to the bishop as visitor of the cathedral, and a memorial in his support was forwarded to Dr. Monk by the mayor and sheriff. No visitation having been held for a great number of years, there was some doubt as to the power of the diocesan, who hesitated to take action. In February, 1849, a majority of the chapter rescinded the order of December; but Dean Lamb, claiming to possess supreme power in such matters, issued a document requiring the officiating clergyman to continue to read the service. The bishop consequently held a court on the 27th February; and a few days later he formally declared the order of the dean to be null and void, enjoining the chapter to maintain the service according to ancient custom. The dean having set this judgment at defiance, a memorial was presented to the bishop by a number of churchmen, setting forth that Dr. Lamb had set at naught the bishop's order, and allowed the service to be mutilated for six months out of twelve. The position becoming untenable, Sir Charles Macgregor resigned in November, and the appointment of a qualified successor brought the dispute to an end. Dr. Lamb, who in addition to the deanery held the mastership of Corpus Christi College, Cambridge, and the rectory of Olveston, died in April, 1850. Down to the period of cathedral reform, the minor canons had been six in number, including the precentor. They were gradually reduced to three by death or preferment, and in March, 1854, the latter number was permanently established by an Order in Council.

In the closing month of 1848, in excavating for a new sewer in Quay Street, the workmen came upon the foundation of the old city wall, which it is probable was once washed by the tide. At a considerable depth from the surface, the workmen discovered a canoe, fourteen feet long and four feet wide, shaped from a single trunk of timber. Unfortunately this relic of antiquity had to be sawn through, as it was found impossible to remove it entire.

At the usual New Year's day meeting of the Council in 1849, Mr. Visger brought forward a resolution for the abolition of the town dues on 325 out of the 350 articles included in the schedule then in force. After stating that half the foreign goods consumed in Bristol arrived coastwise from London and Liverpool, he showed that the commodities he proposed to relieve produced an insignificant revenue (£227), and predicted that, if the duty were abolished on hides and articles used in tanning, the trade of the city would be greatly promoted. The resolution was carried unanimously, and Mr. Visger's prophecy speedily proved to be well founded, one or two large tanning firms having removed soon after to Bristol from other localities, and established extensive works in the city.

At a meeting of the Council on the 9th January, it was resolved to establish cheap baths and washhouses on the Weir, at a cost not exceeding £7,000, to be paid off in twenty annual instalments. It was believed that the annual profits would soon suffice to liquidate the debt. The baths were opened on the 12th August, 1850, but the hope that the undertaking would be self-supporting was destined to prove fallacious, the receipts having been always insufficient to meet the working expenditure. The great benefit which the establishment conferred on the poor being considered to outweigh the loss to the ratepayers, the Council, in June, 1871, resolved on the construction of a more complete building in the Mayor's Paddock, on the north bank of the Avon, for the accommodation of the working classes of Bedminster and Redcliff. These baths, the first cost of which was about £15,500, were opened on the 1st May, 1873, but they were even less successful, financially speaking, than those on the Weir, it being stated in October, 1882, that while £17,000 had been then laid out upon them, and while the working staff were paid £10 a week in wages, the average receipts averaged only £10 1*s.* 2*d.* per week. In 1877 a swimming bath was added to the Weir buildings, at an outlay of about £2,400. In August, 1881, the Council approved of a plan for baths and washhouses at Jacob's Wells, the expense being estimated at about £22,000. The design met with scanty approval amongst the ratepayers, and the residents of the locality intended to be benefited held an "indignation meeting," and were the loudest in condemning the extravagance of the proposal. With the November elections in view, the Council beat a hasty retreat, and the previous resolution was cancelled. In October, 1885, however, a more modest plan for baths at the same spot, to cost about £9,000, received the sanction of the civic body.

During the summer of 1849 some judicious improvements were effected on and near Clifton Down by a committee of gentlemen resident in the neighbourhood. Upwards of a hundred seats were erected in picturesque spots, a few pathways were laid out, trees and shrubs were planted, and a band of music was engaged for the summer months. Although only modest funds were entrusted to the committee, the results of their labours were much appreciated. The promoters of the movement attempted to make further efforts towards increasing the attractions of the place; but the "Clifton Improvement Association," which they established, met with very limited support. Its designs for improvements were moreover threatened with opposition on the part of the lords of the manor of Henbury—ever jealous of their rights and little regardful of the rights of others. Under these discouraging circumstances, the association was dissolved in January, 1855.

A prospectus was issued in August, 1849, of the Clifton Victoria Baths, for which a piece of ground had been secured "adjoining Oakfield House garden." The baths were opened in July, 1850.

At the instance of Bishop Monk, a meeting was held in the Victoria Rooms on the 7th November, 1849, for the purpose of promoting the establishment of a training institution for schoolmistresses, as an adjunct to the training school for masters which was about to be founded in the diocese of Oxford, it being intended that the advantages of the two schools should be equally shared between the two districts. The bishop announced that donations to the amount of £4,300 and yearly subscriptions of about £230 had been already promised. Resolutions in approval of his lordship's scheme were adopted, and the executive committee soon afterwards purchased a site at Fishponds, and proceeded with the buildings, the foundations of which were laid in the spring of 1852. The cost of the erections was about £12,000. The college was opened on the 10th September, 1853.

In the course of this year, a scheme was sanctioned by the Court of Chancery for the administration of the estates of the Merchant Taylors' Company of Bristol. The Company, which in the previous century embraced every tailor in the city, had become extinct in 1824 by the death of Mr. Isaac Amos, its only surviving member. Mr. Amos, so long as he lived, carried out the ancient customs of the guild with great gravity. He yearly elected himself master, and allowed himself £10 10*s.* for serving "an extra time;" summoned himself to committee meetings, and paid himself £12 12*s.* for his attendances; audited his own accounts, and rewarded himself with £2 2*s.* therefor; and finally put into his pocket various trifling gratuities authorised by established precedents. In 1802 the property of the Company—producing about £100 a year—had been placed by deed in the hands of a body of trustees, and the surplus income was devoted to the maintenance of the almshouse in Merchant Street, erected by the guild in 1701. It was feared on the extinction of the Company that most of the estate had escheated to the Crown; but the surviving trustees petitioned to be permitted to apply the proceeds to charitable purposes, and after many years' delay the rights of the sovereign were surrendered. The scheme above mentioned placed the trust on a permanent basis, and some eighteen pensioners are now maintained out of the estate. Some curious details respecting the Company may be found in Manchee's Bristol Charities, and in Mr.

Alderman Fox's privately printed "Account of the Ancient Fraternity of Merchant Taylors of Bristol."

In the closing months of 1849 some five or six local firms engaged in the corn trade resisted payment of the town dues on grain imported by them, alleging that the impost was illegal. A gentleman at the same time claimed exemption from dues on a cargo of timber, on the ground that he was a "Queen's tenant;" while another demanded free entry for a quantity of sugar in his quality as a freeman of London. The corn merchants submitted on being threatened with actions at law. The alleged "Queen's tenant" turned out to be merely an occupier under the office of Woods and Forests, and found his claim to be untenable. The Corporation maintained that a freeman of London could claim exemption only when he paid scot and lot in the city of London, and, precedents being produced in support of this position, the claimant eventually surrendered.

From the time of the great outbreak of cholera in England in 1831-2, a strong suspicion had existed amongst observant men that the terrible mortality caused by the disease was attributable to the evil sanitary condition of the people. It was not, however, until about 1840 that public opinion became sufficiently instructed to give force to the theory that bad drainage, filthy dwellings, and unwholesome water exercised a deplorable effect, not merely in fostering epidemics, but in sapping the human constitution. In 1840 a committee of the House of Commons was appointed to inquire into the state of the public health; and the investigation then made being deemed inadequate, a Royal Commission was appointed in 1844 to make local inquiries into the matter. Two of the commissioners, Sir H. de la Beche and Dr. Lyon Playfair, consequently paid a visit to Bristol; and their report, published early in 1845, drew a very unflattering picture of the state of the city. The mortality, it appeared, averaged 31 per 1,000, which was exceeded by only two towns in the kingdom; while the deaths in places of average salubrity averaged only 20 per 1,000. The causes of the evil were declared to be obvious. Many parts of Bristol and fashionable portions of Clifton were totally without sewerage; others, which were drained, daily discharged a mass of filth into the stagnant harbour—forty-one sewers having no other outlet. House drainage in poor dwellings was almost unknown. With the exception of about 400 houses, inhabited by the affluent class in Clifton, and a few in the neighbourhood of College Green, there was no water laid by pipes into any dwellings, and those of the poor, besides being crowded, were generally filthy; while the well water on which the inhabitants depended was often unwholesome. In despite of the grave nature of this report, little was done to remedy shortcomings; and in 1849 another epidemic of cholera occurred in Bristol. The disease broke out in the city on the 10th June, and did not disappear until the 16th October, between which dates there were upwards of 15,000 cases of sickness and 778 of actual cholera, the deaths from that disease being 444. The scourge effectually awakened the authorities to the condition of the city. In consequence of a resolution passed by the Council, the Government appointed Mr. G. T. Clark, of the Board of Health, to hold another inquiry into the state of the borough; and that gentleman opened his court in the Guildhall on the 13th February, 1850, and continued to take evidence until the 2nd March. His report is a document which future generations will read with profound astonishment. Many of its statements may possibly seem incredible even to youthful Bristolians of the present day. Not merely as an astounding picture of old-fashioned ignorance, supineness, and folly, but as an eloquent testimonial to later energy and public spirit, a few of its salient features are worthy of record. Mr. Clark reported that the management of the paving, cleansing, and lighting of the "old city" was still in the paving commissioners constituted in 1806. The parishes known as "the District" had obtained a local Act in 1842, which created a similar body. But as regarded the 60,000 people dwelling in Clifton, in the out-parish of St. Philip, and in the urban parts of Westbury and Bedminster, there were no sanitary authorities whatever. It is needless to dwell upon the state of the poorer localities in the centre of the city, which, in spite of the sanitary precautions adopted during the then recent cholera visitation, shocked every visitor. No conception of the actual facts could be given without employing terms repugnant to modern habits and good taste. The course of the Froom through the city was simply a sewer, into which scores of small sewers poured their contents; and as a large portion of the stream was uncovered, the stench which spread from it every summer often sufficed to turn weak stomachs. In many other localities were damp, uncleanly courts, unpaved and undrained, without any decent provision for unavoidable wants, and where the only water available was rank with contamination. In a single house in one of the filthiest of these courts, sixty-four people were living during the cholera epidemic; and it was of course in such dens that the disease was most deadly. The dwellings of the poor in all the outlying parishes of the city were found to be equally deplorable, in addition to which, the roads were unmade in many streets; and in some cases, in wet weather, water lodged in the centre of the thoroughfares to the depth of four feet. Not one of the sixty-eight streets in Bedminster was ever cleansed by a scavenger. Still more surprising is the account of the localities inhabited by the middle classes. The sewage from a house in Montagu (now Kingsdown) Parade ran down an open gutter in Montagu Hill. The road at the back of Kingsdown and St. James's Parades was almost always floating with water, which occasionally ran into the dwellings. There were no drains to carry away the filth from those houses, but there were cesspools, the contents of some of which filtered into neighbouring wells. At the back of Highbury Place were two very large pools of sewage, giving out a pestilential odour. The sewage of Clarence Place drained into two great cesspools directly under the houses, and required to be emptied about once a month, causing an intolerable stench. Nearly all the houses in Richmond Terrace, Clifton, drained into cesspools; and to this was attributed a severe epidemic which had recently prevailed there. At Clifton Park, Cambridge Place, Burlington Place, South Parade, and in other high-class thoroughfares, there was no drainage except into cesspools. In the Black-boy district, near Durdham Down, there was only surface drainage. "The Whiteladies Road has an open gutter, down which the house drainage runs into a side ditch, and is most offensive. [This sewer was the subject of many objurgations in the newspaper correspondence of the time.] Above Whiteladies Gate, in the bottom of the valley, several open sewers meet, and their contents are generally complained of. In a field in front of West Clifton Terrace," now the site of Alma Road, "the sewage [from the Black-boy district and West Park] escapes over a large space. Hampton Terrace suffers materially from an old ditch, in which the sewage is collected. From thence it finds its way to the Froom." A resident at Vittoria Place deposed that, owing to the defective drainage, it was almost impossible to support the stench during the night. The road now known as Oakfield Road had only one lamp, and was a "perfect quagmire." "At the back of Park Place is a peculiarly filthy cross-road and a market garden, the stench of which is much complained of." With regard to lighting, about half the old city, Clifton, and the District were imperfectly lighted; while the very populous parishes of St. Philip (out) and Bedminster, as well as the Redland, Cotham, and Kingsdown districts, were not lighted at all. Although numerous tollgates were within the borough, the condition of the turnpike roads was reported to be discreditable. They were badly drained, badly repaired, and badly cleaned; and in Bedminster there was a continuous bank of scrapings a quarter of a mile long and about five feet high. As to the parish roads in that parish and in St. Philip's, they were "scarcely worthy of the name." In all the suburbs were numerous private roads, some of which had been streets for ten or twenty years, which were "mere troughs of mud, into which all the ashes, soil, and house refuse were daily thrown and never removed." Finally, in reference to cemeteries, Mr. Clark reported that there were sixty-one places of burial in the city, of which thirty-seven belonged to the Established Church, and five to private persons (undertakers).* The great majority, being full to repletion, were unfit for further interments; and burials in the vaults under parish churches were also strongly condemned. The Inspector concluded by asserting that the two great evils of Bristol, to which its drunkenness, filth, and excessive mortality were largely attributable, were want of drainage and want of water. No efficient reform was declared to be possible so long as the various outlying districts were separately and irresponsibly governed. Happily a strong conviction prevailed in the city of the prevailing evils, together with an earnest disposition to support the introduction of reforms. The Council lost no time in taking measures to follow out Mr. Clark's recommendations. A Bill enabling the Corporation to apply the powers of the Health of Towns' Act, and to abolish the paving commissioners in the city, and the watching bodies in Clifton and the District, received the royal assent in August, 1851. A committee of the Council was forthwith appointed for sanitary purposes. Under the new statute the Council, as the Local Board of Health, was vested with sole jurisdiction over the city streets, roads (except turnpikes), sewers, lighting, scavenging, and watering, the removal of nuisances, the regulation of slaughter-houses, and other analogous matters. There was no longer any question of want of power, dubious boundaries, or clashing administration, and the effects of

* A correspondent of the *Bristol Times* stated (April 30, 1853), that from "two to three dozen" bodies were buried every Sunday in each of two private burial grounds, belonging to persons named Francis and Wins.

concentrating authority in a single responsible body rapidly became apparent. One of the first and most striking improvements effected, was the efficient lighting of Clifton and the other suburban districts. A survey of the municipal area having been made, a well-considered plan of sewerage, embracing the whole of the borough, and designed to intercept the drains discharging into the harbour, was laid out and approved. In 1855 four great arterial sewers, each averaging nearly a mile and a half in length, were begun, with a view to diverting the sewage of the western suburbs, to a point in the Avon about a mile below Cumberland Basin. [In the carrying out of this work, the contractors were required to make a footpath from Clifton Down to the river, thus forming a second "Zigzag," one of the most picturesque walks in the neighbourhood.] Upwards of three miles of main sewers were constructed in Bedminster, and a still more extensive system was laid down for St. Philip's and the District. The operations necessarily occupied many years. In 1872 it was officially stated that the Corporation had spent during the previous sixteen years the sum of £137,000 on sewerage works alone. A further outlay of about £18,000 was incurred for Bedminster in 1873. The expense was amply compensated by the reduction effected in sickness and mortality. In 1866, when cholera again visited the city, the fatalities from the disease numbered only 29; and, instead of having one of the highest death rates in the kingdom, Bristol has for many years vied with London for the place of honour on the Registrar-General's returns.

In January, 1850, the death was announced of a man named James Ivyleaf, supposed to have been a native of Bristol,* but who resided in Southampton Row, Bloomsbury, London. It soon after transpired that he had left nearly the whole of his property to the trustees of Bristol Infirmary. On making inquiries, however, the trustees were led to believe that the testator died in embarrassed circumstances, and they renounced probate of the will. One Evan Rees, in whose house Ivyleaf had expired, then took out letters of administration, on the plea that he was a creditor, a person named Lloyd, a money-lender, becoming one of his sureties. After a considerable lapse of time, the trustees of the Infirmary, acting on private information, made a second inquiry, and satisfied themselves that Rees and Lloyd had

* A Mr. Ivyleaf, linendraper, High Street, was residing in King Square in 1770.

appropriated nearly £6,000, the proceeds of the sale of Government stock held by Ivyleaf. Legal proceedings were thereupon commenced, but Rees had emigrated to Australia, and Lloyd, after becoming bankrupt, died. It was nevertheless discovered that Lloyd, with about £3,000 of the money, had made advances to the spendthrift heir of the Earl of Wicklow, receiving as security a *post-obit* deed for £25,000, which he had transferred to his wife. The Court of Chancery was therefore appealed to, and in February, 1855, Mrs. Lloyd was ordered to pay the Infirmary £2,800.

At a meeting of the Council on the 12th February, 1850, a discussion took place upon the extensive encroachments which had been recently made upon the valuable common land in the neighbourhood of Clifton. Mr. Visger observed that measures were in progress which would eventually terminate in the inclosure of Clifton Down. A considerable portion, indeed, had been already built upon. "These encroachments," he said, "had all been gradual. When he was a boy a great part of Clifton was open, and consisted chiefly of sheep walks. A few rails were put up, ostensibly to prevent the sheep from wandering. These soon gave way to iron stanchions; by-and-by a wall was built, and then houses were erected. Opposite these houses small shrubs were planted, and under pretence of protecting them, posts were put up. Within a few years the posts were pulled down and regular plantations formed. He well remembered having ridden up and down places that were now inclosed." Mr. Visger's remarks called forth no contradiction; but when Ald. Pinney advised the purchase of the downs, Mr. Powell (St. Augustine's)* protested against the Council interfering with the property of others. If the Merchants' Society, he said, chose to build upon Clifton Down, they would be dealing with their own property, and the Council had no more right to intervene than to pull down Badminton House. It was resolved to represent to the Board of Health Inspector, then holding his inquiry in the city, the great value of these open spaces, and the danger to which they were exposed from systematic encroachments. In the following August, the lords of the manor of Henbury, "doing what they liked with their own," disposed of a portion of Durdham Down to the authorities of St. John's district church, for the purpose

* This gentleman, who held many eccentric opinions, was accustomed to warn the civic body at intervals that Brandon Hill was an old volcano, and that it would some fine morning give renewed proof of its ancient forces by filling up the Floating Harbour.

of building a schoolhouse. Other encroachments were made from time to time, and in 1856 some enterprising individual, as an experiment, built a cottage in one of the five quarries which were then being worked in various parts of the downs. This step excited so much indignation, however, that the building was forthwith removed. In the course of the following year, the Corporation succeeded in purchasing, for £450, a small property at Westbury, to which commonable rights on Durdham Down were attached, whereby it was hoped a title had been obtained to resist further encroachments in that direction. Soon afterwards Mr. Baker, as owner of the Sneyd Park estate, claimed, and apparently made good his claim to, a strip of ground at Sea Walls, which had hitherto been a favourite promenade for pedestrians. In 1859 the public were startled by another unexpected proceeding—the inclosure by a Mr. Samuel Worrall, descendant of a former clerk of the Merchants' Society, of two large pieces of common land which had been popularly considered to form part of Clifton Down. His action was the subject of indignant reprobation in the Council; but according to legal authorities the inclosures could not be prevented, and the utmost the public could claim was a footpath over the plots. Further encroachments being reported as imminent, a committee was appointed to negotiate with the Merchants' Society and the lords of Henbury Manor. In the result, the Society, while refusing to sell their rights over either the turf or the minerals of Clifton Down, expressed willingness to see the public assured of the free enjoyment of the open space, whilst the lords consented to sell in fee simple their estate in Durdham Down, including the quarries, for £15,000. A resolution empowering the committee to arrange with the parties on those terms was passed by the Council on the 24th May, 1860; and an Act of Parliament legalising the settlement received the royal assent a year later. The lordship of the manor of Henbury was divided between two persons, Sir J. Greville Smyth, who held three-fourths, and who therefore received £11,250; and the trustees of Mrs. Colston, of Roundway, Wilts, who obtained £3,750 in right of the remaining quarter. The expense of obtaining the statute raised the total cost of the transaction to £16,296. The area over which the public acquired a right of perpetual enjoyment was 442 acres—230 acres of which belong to Clifton Down, and 212 to that of Durdham. In March, 1862, an excited controversy arose respecting a contract made by the Downs Committee—which under the Act consists of seven members of the Council and seven of the Merchants' Society—for the construction of a carriage road from Belgrave Place to Sneyd Park. Mr. Baker, the gentleman mentioned above, received £550 for the work, but owing to the disapproval expressed by the citizens, the turf was ordered to be replaced, and Mr. Baker not merely retained the contract price, but got £200 more for restoring the ground to its former state. The necessity of a road to Sneyd Park was nevertheless obvious, and the destruction of the grass by carriages, etc., at length wrought a change in public opinion. In 1875 over £1,000 were raised by private subscription for making a road from near Alderman Proctor's fountain to Sea Walls; and a few months later, the drive was extended to the road leading to Combe Dingle. At the same time, by private arrangement, the carriage road from near St. John's School to Down House [formerly the famous summer resort known as the Ostrich Inn, see p. 4], was closed and turfed. In 1879 these improvements were further extended, the Sea Walls road being continued to the Westbury road. A footpath on the site of "Baker's road" was laid down in 1880, and in January, 1882, another was made in the ravine, affording access to the shore of the Avon.

An ecclesiastical district, afterwards styled St. Matthias's parish, was formed out of the parishes of St. Paul, St. Peter, and St. Philip, by an Order in Council in May, 1846; but for some reason the foundation-stone of the new church was not laid until March, 1850. Much difficulty was encountered in the construction of the edifice, owing to the marshy nature of the site. The church was consecrated in November, 1851.

The large mansion known as Arno's Court, near Brislington, came into the market during the spring of 1850, and was purchased for a Roman Catholic body called "The Sisterhood of the Asylum of the Good Shepherd." The nuns established in it a penitentiary, and added a large chapel to the building. In 1858 the penitentiary was converted into a reformatory for youthful criminals of the Romish faith. The remarkable outbuildings formerly attached to the property, which have obtained the local name of Black Castle, and were styled by Horace Walpole "the Devil's Cathedral," were, with the gardens, detached from the mansion and sold in 1821. They are still decorated with the statues depicted in Mr. Seyer's "Memoirs of Bristol."

In the summer of 1849 a small steam vessel commenced to ply as a passenger boat between the Drawbridge and Cumberland Basin; when the novelty and cheapness of the mode of transit caused the enterprise to be very profitable, and naturally brought competitors into the field. In the summer of 1850, seven additional steamers were provided for carrying on the traffic, which had largely increased. On the evening of the 22nd July, one of the vessels, the *Red Rover*, which was said to have carried a thousand passengers during the day, was starting on her concluding voyage from Cumberland Basin, with about fifty persons on board, when the boiler exploded, scattering death and destruction around. Fifteen individuals were either instantly killed or died from the effects of their injuries; several others were seriously maimed. The verdict given at the first coroner's inquest was, "that the deceased had met with his death in consequence of the bursting of a boiler which at the time was in an unfit state for use."

Upon the death, about October, 1850, of Mr. Charles Vaughan, the office of master of the ceremonies at the balls in Clifton became extinct. The want of some recognised official to organize the amusements of the place was soon productive of difficulties. Even in the days of the old Corporation, when Clifton was but a village, there had been struggles on the part of some of the inhabitants to exclude others from public entertainments. One lady, wife of a wealthy alderman, explained to Prebendary Sydney Smith that she and her friends wished to establish a sort of Almacks, "with of course due consideration for the differing circumstances of the locality." "Yes," replied the canon, "the difference, that is, between refined and raw sugar." Two or three years after Mr. Vaughan's death, rival coteries were formed, one of which held its balls in the large room at the Mall, while the second, which did not deem the other sufficiently "exclusive," set up its camp at the Victoria Rooms. The offensive proceedings of the latter party * were productive of so much ill-feeling that balls were discontinued for some years. Another acrimonious controversy occurred in December, 1860, when Mr. W. P. King, a member of one of the leading mercantile houses in Bristol, published a letter complaining that his family, having applied for tickets for certain proposed "private Clifton subscription balls," had been re-

* According to the reminiscences of a correspondent published in the *Bristol Times*, one of the "patronesses" refused to forward tickets of admission to a lady until she had been allowed a sight of the latter's marriage certificate. The response was, that the document would be produced as soon as the "patroness" had exhibited a specimen of the weekly washing bills which she was accustomed to forward to her customers in her younger days.

fused them by one of the promoters—"the son of a London tradesman, his father having been an undertaker." The friends of this aristocratic youth rushed into print in his defence; and the *Bristol Times*, the organ of both the exasperated parties, felt called upon to rebuke a community "composed entirely of traders or sons of traders," who were ashamed of the means by which they had acquired wealth, and were ridiculously "turning up their noses at each other." A twelvemonth later, at a meeting of leading inhabitants, it was stated that the proceedings of the supercilious undertaker's son and of his youthful supporters had had the effect of breaking up society in Clifton, and had caused some families to leave the place. The balls were then arranged to be held under the supervision of a committee. In the winter of 1862, a Mr. Henry Lucas Bean was appointed master of the ceremonies, but appears to have held the post for only a short period.

In October, 1850, an unwonted outburst of national feeling occurred on the promulgation by Pope Pius IX. of a Bull, by which England was carved into thirteen sees—an archbishopric and twelve bishoprics—the prelates appointed to which were designated by territorial titles. By this bull was created the so-called "diocese of Clifton," which included the three adjoining counties. The new bishop, Dr. J. W. Hendren, was enthroned on the 15th December, in the Church of the Apostles, Clifton, which was thenceforth styled a pro-cathedral. In the following July the bishop was transferred to Nottingham, and was succeeded by Dr. Burgess. The Protestant excitement in Bristol was increased by the fact that the Rev. J. H. Woodward, incumbent of St. James's, and his two curates, Messrs. Parry and Todd, "went over" to the Romish Church about the same time. It may be noted that several of the Oxford men who followed Dr. Newman in the same direction came to reside in Clifton, and published tracts there in defence of their conduct.

In the course of this year, during the reconstruction of the house numbered 41, High Street, the remains were discovered of a fifteenth century roof, resting upon corbels of demi-angels. The place was supposed to have been the site of the chapel of an almshouse, known to have anciently existed in that locality.

In conformity with the provisions of the Mercantile Marine Act of 1850, local boards to provide for the examination of masters and mates were established in the principal ports of the kingdom, and commenced their duties on the 1st January,

1851. The first Bristol board consisted of Mr. Edward Drew (Chairman), the mayor (Mr. Haberfield), and Messrs. P. W. Miles, M.P., Richard Jones, Richard P. King, William P. King, William Brass, Richard Rowe, William Patterson, Frederick W. Green, and William Cook.

In January, 1851, Mr. J. Curnock, an able local artist, who had been employed by the Corporation to clean some of the pictures in the Council House, discovered a work of art the disappearance of which had long puzzled the civic officials. Mr. Curnock was engaged upon a portrait of Charles II., the head of which was so miserably executed, compared with the hands, that he was led to examine it attentively. Indications of another wig beneath the surface convinced him that the canvas had been tampered with, and after obtaining leave of the authorities, he proceeded to remove the outer daubing, with the result of bringing to light a finely painted head of James II. This work—attributed to Kneller—was bought by the Corporation in 1686, and is supposed to have been "translated" soon after the dethronement of the would-be despot.

Amongst the financial proposals in the Budget of 1851 was a scheme, soon after sanctioned by Parliament, for the substitution of a house-tax for the unpopular duty imposed on windows. Owing to causes for which it is somewhat difficult to account, the window tax pressed grievously on Bath and Bristol, which bore a share of the burden greatly in excess of their proportional size and population amongst the chief cities in the kingdom. According to a contemporary Parliamentary return, the following were the ten towns which paid the highest amount of duty for the year ending April, 1849: Liverpool, £28,856; Bristol, £22,176; Bath, £21,278; Manchester, £20,575; Brighton, £17,572; Birmingham, £14,986; Plymouth, £11,929; Newcastle, £7,822; Leeds, £7,596; Cheltenham, £6,767.

Seven years before this date, when the population of Clifton was rapidly increasing, a demand sprang up for the establishment of a public market in the district, the sites proposed being Honeypen Hill Quarry, near Meridian Place, and the ground now occupied by the Triangle. The Finance Committee of the Corporation reported in favour of the project in May, 1844, but the Council refused its sanction. In 1851 the proposal was revived, and a strong effort was made to obtain the erection of a suitable building on a site near the church, the cost being estimated at £5,000. The Council, however, disapproved of the proposal. In 1875 another attempt was made, a company being started to erect a market-house on Richmond Mews, near York Place, and a large portion of the capital (£4,000) was at once subscribed. The Corporation, having requested the opinion of the recorder, was advised that it could not concede to a public company its privilege of holding and regulating markets within the borough. The scheme consequently fell to the ground.

A local journal of the 3rd March contained an announcement that the Society of Merchant Venturers had reduced the fee payable upon admission into the company from £200 to £50. This brief statement comprises the only information respecting the inner working of the corporation in question which has been found in the newspapers of the present century. At an earlier period, it is believed, the political party predominant in it, as in the Common Council, was that of the Whigs; but a rapid change took place after the French Revolution. About 1860 there was said to be only one member of the society—Mr. Robert Bruce—who was not a Conservative; and the unanimity brought about by his death has since remained undisturbed.

The honour of knighthood was conferred in March, 1851, upon Mr. John Kerle Haberfield, who was then filling the office of mayor for the sixth time. His worship had subscribed liberally towards the local fund for promoting the Exhibition of the industries of all nations, which took place in London during the summer. [The total amount raised by subscription throughout the kingdom in support of the undertaking was over £76,000, to which Bristol contributed £788.] A few weeks after receiving his new dignity, Sir John Haberfield was presented, in recognition of his public services, with a beautiful dessert service of plate, valued at upwards of £800, being the result of a subscription to which 500 citizens of all shades of politics contributed. On the centre ornament, nearly three feet in height, were the arms of the city and of the mayor, with the inscription: "To Sir John Kerle Haberfield, knight, six times Mayor of Bristol, 1851." Above this were emblematic figures of Justice, Commerce, and Generosity. The other portions of the service were also tastefully ornamented. Some years after the death of Sir John, which occurred in 1857, his widow presented this handsome service to the Corporation, to be used by each mayor during his term of office. A bust of the knight was also obtained about the same time, at the expense of a considerable number of citizens, and was placed in the Mayor's Chapel. A portrait of Sir John, painted during his first mayoralty, was bequeathed to the Corporation by his widow in 1875.

The census of 1851 was taken on the 31st March. The population of the city and county of Bristol was found to be 137,328; the number of persons in the ancient city being 65,716. The population of Clifton was 17,634; the District, 7,935; St. Philip's, out, 24,961; St. George's, 8,905; Mangotsfield, 3,967; Stapleton, 4,840; Bedminster, 19,424, and Stoke Bishop tything, 5,623.

In April, 1851, Messrs. Stuckey & Co., bankers, who then occupied the singular old house at the corner of High Street and Wine Street, purchased premises in Corn Street, consisting of Mr. Harril's sale-room and the apartments occupied by the members of the Athenæum. An old dwelling standing at the corner of Nicholas Street was bought soon after, and a large banking-house was constructed on the sites, a portion being sold to the Corporation for the purpose of widening the adjoining streets. In removing the ancient buildings, the crypt of the demolished church of St. Leonard—the tower of which stood over the end of Corn Street—was exposed to view, much of it being in good preservation.

Some ludicrous incidents in connexion with a proposed "affair of honour" occurred in the spring of 1851. In a debate on the army estimates in the House of Commons during the previous session, Mr. Berkeley, the senior member for the city, had condemned as wasteful the vote granted for the yeomanry cavalry. As an evidence of the inutility of the force, he stated that during the riots at Bristol, when the North Somerset corps was summoned by the mayor to support the cause of law and order, only about ten of the "heroes" appeared, whereupon they were locked up by the authorities to keep them out of danger. No comment was made upon this statement at the time, but a twelvemonth later, when the vote was again under discussion, Mr. W. Miles, M.P. for Somerset, and the colonel of the yeomanry, made a reply, observing that in 1831 seventeen members of the Bedminster troop followed Captain Shute, and that, although they retired to the riding school during the riots on Sunday, as desired by the magistrates, they came in with the regular troops on the following day, and did good service. Mr. Berkeley, in defending his previous remarks, again contended that the yeomanry, in a military point of view, were impostors, and as constabulary were useless. He went on to show, on the authority of the *Bristol Gazette*, that Captain

Shute's troop had been sent for on the first day of the riots, but that only a handful made their appearance after a delay of twenty-four hours, when they were locked up with the consent of the captain, whose name, added the hon. gentleman, amidst much laughter, was not S-h-o-o-t, but S-h-u-t-e. The discussion then dropped, after mutual explanations. Upwards of a week later, Captain Shute wrote to Mr. Berkeley, asking whether that gentleman intended to imply any doubt of personal courage on the part of the writer. To this Mr. Berkeley replied that he had spelt the name in the House to avoid a mistake on the part of the reporters, and that he believed his correspondent to have been "the gallant leader of a miserably small number of gallant men." Captain Shute, dissatisfied with the reply, proceeded to London in company with Mr. Joseph Leech, and indited a second epistle, repeating the inquiry made in his first. Mr. Berkeley thereupon retorted that, after the explanation already given, he did not think himself called upon to make further admissions respecting a personal courage which he had never impeached, and that, if Captain Shute still continued to consider his reputation injured, he might address himself to the writer's "friend," Colonel Dunne. Captain Shute, however, declared that he was now satisfied, and Mr. Leech, approving of the decision, forwarded the correspondence to the *Times* for publication on the 14th April.

During the summer of 1851, the Great Western and Bristol and Exeter railway boards entered into a contract with the Electric Telegraph Company for the construction of a telegraphic line from London to Exeter. The Midland Company had some months previously established telegraphic communications on their system; but the intelligence received by the public by this means was confined to the results of interesting races. In February, 1852, when the line to London and the West was on the eve of completion, the proprietors of the Commercial Rooms consented to set apart a room in their building as a telegraph office. At the meeting for sanctioning this arrangement, it was stated that a telegraphic line had been laid to Shirehampton, towards supporting which the committee of the Commercial Rooms would give the £30 a year they had previously paid to the "Pill warner." Up to this date, when the arrival of a ship at Kingroad was "warned" up to the rooms, notice was sent to the merchant concerned, who had to pay a guinea to the messenger. The intelligence was henceforth furnished for half a crown. The telegraph office was a few months later removed to the Broad

Quay, and subsequently to the Exchange. The new system was for the first time used as a vehicle for conveying reports of Parliamentary proceedings to the Bristol newspapers on the 30th April, 1852. The rapid development of telegraphic business brought into increased prominence the troublesome question of "local time," still registered by the parish clocks, messages from London being received at the Bristol office about ten minutes before the time at which they purported to be despatched. At a meeting of the Council on the 14th September, 1852, it was resolved—three inveterate admirers of ancient ways protesting against the innovation—to regulate the clocks by Greenwich time. The first electric apparatus fitted up in the provinces for private business transactions was ordered by Messrs. Wills & Co., tobacco manufacturers, in February, 1859, in order to communicate between their premises in Maryleport and Redcliff Streets. In a lecture delivered in Bristol in December, 1859, Mr. R. S. Culley, local superintendent of the Telegraph Company, stated that the first electric telegraph line in this country was erected in July, 1837, between Euston Square and Camden Town, London, but that as George Stephenson and other scientific men did not appreciate its value, it was soon after removed. In 1839 Messrs. Wheatstone & Cook constructed a line from Paddington to Slough on the Great Western railway—the first on which the invention was tried. Mr. Culley added that Mr. Brunel wished to extend the line to Bristol; but that at one of the meetings of the company he was overruled, mainly through one of the shareholders denouncing electric telegraphy as wild, visionary, and worthless.

A local newspaper of the 26th July announced that in consequence of the rivalry of two steamboats plying between Bristol and Cardiff, passengers were being conveyed gratis from and to each town. Subsequently fares were imposed—1*s.* for cabin and 6*d.* for steerage passengers. The costly competition continued until April, 1855.

The annual congress of the Archæological Institute was opened in Bristol on the 29th July. Amongst the distinguished visitors were Lord Talbot de Malahide (the president of the Institute), Dr. Wilberforce (Bishop of Oxford), Chevalier Bunsen, and Mr. Hallam. A large apartment in the Council House was fitted up as a reception room for the guests, to whom cordial hospitality was offered by the mayor (Sir John K. Haberfield). The introductory meeting took place in the Guildhall, and a brilliant conversazione was held at the Institution. A record of the work of the week will be found in the yearly volume of the society's Transactions. *

Down to this period the west end of St. James's Church, with its beautiful Romanesque ornamentation, had been concealed from public view by a number of hovels, which had been permitted to accumulate around the edifice during the seventeenth and eighteenth centuries. A subscription was now started by the parochial authorities for the purchase of those excrescences, and, the required amount having been obtained, the ground on which they stood was cleared during the autumn, to the great satisfaction of persons of taste. [An incongruous Corinthian altar piece was removed from the church in 1847.]

A meeting of merchants, shipowners, and others was held at the Commercial Rooms on the 4th September, Mr. Robert Bright presiding, for considering the desirability of reviving the Chamber of Commerce [see page 300]. Resolutions approving of the institution were adopted, but through the indifference of the mercantile classes no progress was effected for some time. In October, 1852, the movement was again started, and, upwards of a hundred firms having offered to become members, the Chamber was resuscitated in the following year. In 1874 it obtained a charter of incorporation.

At a meeting of gentlemen interested in shipping and commerce, held at the office of the mercantile marine board, Prince's Street, on the 16th September, it was resolved to establish a local Sailors' Home—an institution for raising the character and promoting the comfort of seamen which had been already tested with satisfactory results in other large ports. Mr. P. W. Miles, M.P., was elected president. The proposal having met with a large measure of support, the purchase of convenient premises, extending from Queen Square to the Grove, was effected in March, 1852, for £1,300, and over £1,000 more were expended in fitting them up. The home was opened in January, 1853. On the 1st January, 1880, a new building, called the Sailors' Institute, erected in Prince's Street, at a cost of £4,500, by Mr. W. F. Lavington, was opened to seamen, and proved very popular.

An extraordinary accident, which was disastrous to the

---

* Mr. Pryce relates that, in anticipation of this gathering, one of the churchwardens of St. Peter's ordered the beautiful Renaissance monument of one of the Newton family in that church to be bedaubed with yellow wash, observing that "it was a dirty beastly thing, but was now a little decent."—*Notes on Ecclesiastical*, etc., p. 208.

most skilful and enterprising shipbuilding firm in Bristol, and long cast a cloud on the reputation of the port, occurred in the Avon on the 10th November. Messrs. W. Patterson & Co. had constructed for the West India Mail Steamship Company a vessel called the *Demerara*, which, with the exception of the *Great Britain*, was the largest steamship that had then been built, her registered burden being about 3,000 tons. Having been floated out of the building dock on the 27th September, the vessel was partially fitted for sea, and on the day mentioned above she left Cumberland basin in tow of a powerful Glasgow steam-tug, which was to take her to the Clyde for the purpose of receiving her engines. A succession of blunders, however, occurred. The vessel should have entered the Avon some time before high water, so that the most dangerous reaches might be passed with a full tide; but delay occurred, and the current had turned before she was fairly in the river. The steam-tug, again, started at the rate of seven or eight miles an hour, which was much in excess of the speed consonant with safety. Mr. Patterson, on board the new vessel, urgently called the pilot's attention to the danger of this proceeding, but the rate of speed was not sufficiently reduced, and soon after passing the Round Point the bow of the *Demerara* struck violently on the rocky bank of the Gloucestershire side of the river. The tide, ebbing strongly, caused the stern of the ship to swing across the stream to the opposite bank, and all attempts to repair the disaster proved abortive. As the water flowed away the ship settled down, the bolts started, the deck twisted, and there seemed every probability that the wreck would become immovable and that the navigation of the Avon would be wholly blocked up. Great efforts, however, were made in preparation for the next flood tide, and at night, amidst the blaze of tar barrels and torches, presenting a remarkable spectacle to the thousands of persons who had assembled, the exertions of a large body of workmen were successful, the vessel being floated and conveyed to the shore of the river in front of Eglestaff's quarry. It was intended that she should be temporarily repaired at that spot; but about an hour later the ship broke from her moorings, and again swung across the river, receiving further serious damage. It was not until the rising of the tide on the morning of the 11th that the vessel could again be floated and removed to the entrance of Cumberland basin. It was at first believed that the damage sustained was too great to be repaired, and the vessel, which was insured for £48,000 (her cost, including £12,000 for stores), was abandoned to the underwriters as a "total wreck," her value being then estimated at £15,000. On the 13th July, 1854, the *Demerara* was sold for £5,600; the paddle boxes were removed, and she was converted into a sailing ship, which bore the name of the *British Empire*. In September, 1859, the vessel was again sold for £5,400.

On the 12th November a remarkable amateur company of comedians gave a performance at the Victoria Rooms for the benefit of the Guild of Literature and Art—an institution started under the auspices of Sir E. Bulwer Lytton, afterwards Lord Lytton. The pieces represented were the comedy of "Not so Bad as we Seem," by Sir E. Lytton, and the farce of "Mr. Nightingale's Diary," by Messrs. Charles Dickens and Mark Lemon. The chief performers were Charles Dickens (who was manager of the troop), Douglas Jerrold, John Forster, Mark Lemon, Wilkie Collins, Peter Cunningham, R. H. Horne, Charles Knight, J. Tenniel, F. W. Topham, Frank Stone, Dudley Costello, and A. Egg. Every seat in the building had been secured several days before, and, in deference to earnest appeals, the performance was repeated two days later.

Repeated complaints having been addressed to the authorities by the inhabitants of Clifton and Redland respecting the road then leading from the top of Park Street to Whiteladies Road and Clifton Church, which was much too narrow to accommodate the constantly increasing traffic, the Improvement Committee of the Council, in 1844, entered into negotiations with Mr. Tyndall—who had announced his intention to dispose of his park for building purposes—for throwing back the wall of his grounds from the Bishop's College to the park gates, so as to widen the thoroughfare to sixty feet. But after a price had been agreed upon for the ground, the owner insisted that the Corporation should rebuild his wall, park gates and lodge, by which the cost of the work would have exceeded £3,000. The committee, after some delay, adopted an alternative scheme, and bought in 1851 a triangular field opposite to the park, thus securing a sufficient breadth for the thoroughfare (which in 1854 received the name of Queen's Road). This arrangement also facilitated the opening of a new road on an easy incline from Jacob's Wells to the higher level, for which powers were obtained in the Improvement Act of 1847. The Council, in 1852, agreed with Mr. Tyndall for the purchase of another strip of the park, in order to widen Whiteladies Road from West Park to the Victoria Rooms. The line of large elms then standing within the park wall was thrown into the road when the improvement was carried out; and the locality soon became the favourite promenade of the youthful working classes of both sexes on Sunday evenings. [The last of the noble trees was removed in 1885, having become dangerous from age.] Soon after the road had been altered, the neighbouring part of the park was offered for sale, and a row of villas was commenced. One of the first houses built was the Queen's Hotel, which was opened in October, 1854. A further great improvement was effected in the neighbourhood in the autumn of 1857, when, by means of a subscription amounting to £2,000, a number of hovels and petty shops standing on the now vacant ground between the Victoria Rooms and Richmond Hill were demolished, the land being transferred to the Merchants' Society, who undertook to maintain it as an open space. The upper portion of Whiteladies Road continued to be an extremely narrow thoroughfare until 1858, when a strip of the nursery gardens extending from the end of Cotham Road to opposite St. John's Church was thrown into the street.

The tolls on foot-passengers and cattle payable under the Dock Acts at the gates near Totterdown and Redcliff were abolished by the Council in April, 1852. The charge had always been unpopular, and the toll-houses were burned down by the mob during the riots of 1831. The tolls at the Totterdown and Cumberland Basin gates were ordered to be wholly abolished at a Council meeting held in June, 1863.

The death took place on the 7th April, 1852, of the Rev. Martin Richard Whish, M.A., Prebendary of Bedminster in Salisbury Cathedral, and, in right of that office, vicar of Bedminster, rector of St. Mary Redcliff, perpetual curate of St. Thomas, rector of Abbot's Leigh, and perpetual curate of Bishopsworth. A separation of those benefices took place by an Order in Council of the 6th October following, each district becoming an independent parish.

One of the first steps taken by the new vicar of Bedminster, the Rev. H. G. Eland, was to promote a subscription for rebuilding the parish church, a mean edifice of the seventeenth century, capable of seating only 450 persons. Service was performed in it for the last time on the 25th June, 1854, and the new church was ready for consecration in August, 1855. A few weeks before the intended ceremony, a novel feature in the edifice excited a violent outbreak of antagonistic feelings in the two great parties in the English Church. The structure in question was a richly sculptured reredos, placed behind the communion table, and representing the Crucifixion, the Nativity, and the Ascension in highly idealised forms. This screen—said to have been the first of the kind erected in a parish church since the Reformation—had been executed at the expense of Messrs. W. Fripp and R. Phippen (former mayors), and another gentleman whose name did not transpire. The "Evangelical" clergy in the city vehemently protested against the introduction of an ornament which they termed of a papistical character, while their High Church colleagues insisted on the propriety and edifying tendency of the decoration. Excited meetings were held, and the newspapers abounded with acrimonious correspondence. Bishop Monk seems to have been painfully embarrassed by the stormy memorials addressed to him. On the one hand, he refused to believe, with the Low Church protesters, that the carved figures were likely to become objects of idolatrous worship. On the other, he objected to representations varying from the truth and simplicity of the Gospel narrative, and occupying the space on which, according to law, the commandments ought to have been exhibited. He would not order the removal of the reredos, but he did "earnestly and affectionately request" the vicar and churchwardens to take away the ornament. To this appeal, Mr. Phippen, the senior churchwarden, in an intemperate letter, refused to accede, alleging that the removal of the work would throw a slur upon those who had paid for its erection. The bishop reiterated his "request," with no better success than before; and his lordship, unwilling to debar the parishioners from their church, consecrated the building on the 30th October, the occasion being seized by the jubilant High Church clergy to make a demonstration of their local strength.

At the dissolution of Parliament in the summer of 1852, the disunion which still partially existed in the Tory party in consequence of the incidents of the previous contest induced the Liberals to bring forward a candidate in conjunction with Mr. Berkeley. The new aspirant was Mr. William H. Gore Langton, who was then serving the office of mayor. As it was impossible to nominate either Mr. Miles or Mr. Fripp with any chance of success, the Conservatives found considerable difficulty in selecting a representative, the question of free trade throwing fresh fuel on the still glowing embers of the old personal quarrel. The Tory Premier,

Lord Derby, had formally stated that he would not abandon his hope of restoring a duty on corn until after the elections; and the result was that nearly every Conservative aspirant in the counties declared himself a Protectionist, while those in the boroughs were everywhere Free-traders. Mr. Forster Alleyne McGeachy, the gentleman ultimately selected for Bristol, had been an opponent of the Corn Laws, but, his relatives being connected with the West Indies, he was a Protectionist in reference to sugar; and to this qualification he joined the claim of being a native of Bristol. At the close of the poll the numbers were:—Mr. Berkeley, 4,681; Mr. Langton, 4,531; Mr. McGeachy, 3,632.

A lamentable accident occurred near Ealing on the 25th February, 1853, to the express train from Bristol to London, in which several of the directors of the Great Western railway were travelling to attend the weekly meeting of the board. Amongst those gentlemen was Mr. James Gibbs, of Clifton Park, who was killed instantaneously. Mr. Gibbs, who was head of the firm of Gibbs, Ferris & Co., of Union Street, and a chemical manufacturer in St. Philip's, was for some time a member of the Bristol Council, and served the office of mayor in 1842-3. He was subsequently Chairman of the Bristol and Exeter Railway Company, and of the Bristol and South Wales Union Railway Company, and was highly esteemed by his fellow-citizens. The public were never made acquainted with the cause of the accident.

The *Bristol Journal* of March 5 contained the following paragraph:—"Notwithstanding the many failures of the steam-carriage on common roads, it has again made its appearance between Bath and Bristol; and this time, owing to several most ingenious improvements in the machinery employed, has thoroughly realized the expectations of its projectors. The rate of travelling is about twelve miles an hour, and the cost is most trifling—say 6*d*. for the journey." As no further reference to the carriage has been found, it may be inferred that the "expectations of its projectors" again ended in disappointment.

In the early months of 1853, the ruinous old buildings known as "Spencer's almshouse," in Lewin's Mead, opposite to the Unitarian Chapel, were evacuated by the inmates, who were removed to a new house, erected in Whitson [properly Whitsun] Street, near the west end of St. James's Church.

The Bristol Library came prominently before the public about this time. The committee of the Fine Arts Society, then about to erect their building in Whiteladies Road, suggested a union of the two institutions, and the subscribers to the testimonial to Mr. Bright [see p. 302], offered to give £700 to the funds of the Library, on condition that a few deserving members of the working classes were admitted to the privileges of ordinary subscribers. Finally, a committee of the Council suggested that the Library should be converted into a free city library under the provisions of a then recent Act for facilitating the establishment of such institutions. The executive of the Library refused to confer with the committee of the Council, but assented to the two former propositions. Difficulties subsequently arose, however, and both negotiations fell through.

In the meantime, through the exertions of Mr. Charles Tovey and a few other members of the Council, the position of the Library Society towards the city was thoroughly investigated, with results somewhat surprising to the inhabitants. In a clever little work written by Mr. Tovey it was shown that, in 1613, "a lodge adjoining to the town wall, near the Marsh" was given to the Corporation by Robert Redwood, for the purpose of being converted into a library for the use of the citizens. About 1628, Tobias Matthew, Archbishop of York (son of a local mercer, and born on Bristol Bridge), gave a number of books "to the merchants and shopkeepers of the city"—his intention to do so being apparently known to the donor of the lodge; and the store of books received additions by a legacy of Redwood himself, and by purchases of the Common Council. In 1636, Richard Vickris, one of Redwood's executors, gave a piece of ground for the enlargement of the building, and in 1740 a handsome library was erected by the Corporation at a cost of over £1,300, exclusive of the money paid for a further addition to the site. Lastly, about 1,400 volumes of books were bequeathed, in 1766, by Mr. John Heylyn, a relative of the well-known Peter Heylyn, for the use of the citizens. The foundation of a free public library had thus been laid when, in 1772, a few influential individuals resolved on starting a "subscription library," and shortly afterwards petitioned the Common Council for "the use of the Library House and of the books therein deposited." That such a request should be made was perhaps not so remarkable as the fact that the Corporation, entirely ignoring the rights of the citizens, handed over to the memorialists the building and its contents, spent several hundred pounds in renovating the rooms and removing some contiguous stables, and also undertook to pay a portion of the librarian's salary out of the city purse. Such proceedings were, however, a natural outcome of the old system of local government; and all surprise at the civic munificence ceases when it is discovered that several promoters of the Library Society were also members of the Common Council.* In 1784 the rooms were found insufficient for the convenience of the members, whereupon the Common Council granted an adjacent plot of ground at a rent of 2*s.* 5*d.* per year, and made a donation of £100 to the fund opened for building a western wing, which was finished in the following year. The Corporation further undertook to pay the whole of the national and local taxes on the library, which was also insured from fire and kept in repair at the expense of the city. Again, in 1814, when the society proposed to erect a gallery in the western wing for the accommodation of their books, the Common Council subscribed a moiety of the cost, £200. So entirely did the society consider themselves owners of the property, that in 1826 they requested the Corporation to permit them "to remove the city books from the city shelves, in order to make room for books belonging to the society"; but although the citizens had been practically excluded for many years from their own property, the Common Council was offended at the impudence of the demand, and the application was "laid on the table." In 1836, soon after the Council came into existence, Mr. C. B. Fripp moved for a catalogue of the city books (which was furnished), and followed this up by obtaining the appointment of a committee "to consider of the best means to be pursued for rendering the library useful to the public." The committee, however, never presented a report. Matters remained in this state until 1848, when a memorial was addressed to the Council by forty respectable citizens, calling attention to the usurpation of public rights by a small body of private persons, and asking that the books belonging to the city should be made accessible. Nothing was, however, done, and the subject again slumbered until the date at which this record has arrived. The Library Society having refused, as has been already stated, to co-operate with the Council, Mr. Tovey and his supporters urged the latter body to give the society notice to quit the premises in order that

* The society appears to have been worthy of its patrons. In a letter in the *Bristolian* for June 12, 1827, undoubtedly written by John Evans, the city chronologist, it is stated that the name of Dr. Beddoes, the most distinguished local scientist of his age, was "crossed out of the list of members" of the Library Society because he was "not Blue enough."

they might be converted to their original purpose. The Council unanimously adopted this suggestion in February, 1854, to the great indignation of the society, which threatened for a time to hold possession of the building. At the close of the year wiser counsels prevailed, and the property was surrendered, the Corporation paying the society £630 for its interest in the western wing. The society, leaving behind them the books belonging to the city (about 2,000 volumes), removed in August, 1855, to a wing of the Bishop's College, at the top of Park Street. The old building was shortly afterwards fitted up for its original purpose, and was opened as a free library on the 15th September, 1856, Mr. George Pryce, subsequently author of a "Popular History of Bristol," having been appointed librarian. By the gifts of various citizens, and the energy of Mr. Pyrce, about 4,000 volumes were soon after added to the shelves, and Mr. Robert Lang presented a painting by Syer, in the hope that others would follow his example. The development of free libraries in the city will be recorded under 1873.

A faculty was granted in August, 1853, for extensive alterations in All Saints' Church. Under the powers granted by this document, the west front was rebuilt, a new western entrance formed, the doorway in Corn Street converted into a window, and tracery placed in other windows. Further alterations were made a few years later, when the roof and the capitals of the columns were decorated with colour.

On the 20th August, the vestry of St. Mary Redcliff announced by advertisement in the local journals that they were desirous of receiving tenders for the purchase of the three pictures by Hogarth which then hung in the church. The result appears to have been unsatisfactory, as the paintings remained in their accustomed places until the spring of 1858, when the vestry, at the suggestion of Alderman Proctor, offered them to the trustees of the Fine Arts Academy, on the latter undertaking to preserve them carefully. The pictures were shortly afterwards removed from the church.

A singular case of fraud and deception, bearing resemblance in many points to the more notorious imposture connected with the Tichborne baronetcy, was tried at Gloucester assizes on the 8th, 9th, and 10th August, and excited great interest. The cause was in the nature of an action of ejectment, the plaintiff, styling himself Sir Richard Hugh Smyth, baronet, seeking to establish his claim to the title and estates of the Smyth family of Long Ashton. His story was that, although brought up as the child of one Provis, a carpenter, at Warminster, he was really the son of Sir Hugh Smyth by a lady to whom the baronet was secretly married in Ireland in 1796. He further alleged that soon after discovering this fact he communicated it to Sir John Smyth, who had succeeded his brother Hugh through supposed default of male issue, and that Sir John had immediately acknowledged the justice of his claim, but was so much prostrated by the prospect of being deprived of title and wealth that he died suddenly during the following night. Various documents were produced in support of the case, amongst them being a declaration alleged to have been written by Sir Hugh, witnessed by his brother John, and sealed with the family seal, in which the plaintiff was acknowledged as legitimate heir to the baronetcy and estates. To account for the long delay in prosecuting his case, the claimant alleged that he had been taken to the Continent by one of Sir Hugh's servants; that he had long believed that Sir John was his elder brother; and that subsequently he had no funds to carry on a costly litigation. While under cross-examination, in which a huge web of falsehood was being gradually torn to pieces, a dramatic incident occurred. A telegraphic message was brought into court addressed to the defendants' leading counsel, Sir F. Thesiger, who, after perusing the missive, asked the plaintiff whether he had not, in the preceding January, ordered a London tradesman to engrave a crest upon certain rings, and a name upon a broach—the rings and broach in question being alleged family relics on which much of the case rested. The rogue, whose face became livid, stammered out an affirmative answer, whereupon his counsel, Mr. Bovill, threw up his brief, and apologised to the court for having believed in the imposture. The impudent trickster was forthwith committed on charges of forgery and perjury. He had been, in early life, under his true name of Thomas Provis, sentenced to death at Somerset assizes for horse stealing; subsequently he had picked up a mean livelihood as an itinerant lecturer, and by other less reputable avocations. He was tried and convicted of forgery at Gloucestershire spring assizes in 1854, and was sentenced to twenty years' transportation, but died in a convict prison in the following year. The defence against the action of ejectment is said to have cost the Smyth trustees upwards of £6,000.

A meeting was held on the 7th November, the bishop of the diocese presiding, for the purpose of considering the propriety of converting the Diocesan School in Nelson Street into a Trade School. It was stated that the Diocesan School was established in 1812 for the purpose of educating poor children in the principles of the Established Church, but that owing to the springing up in subsequent years of schools in the various parishes, the object of its promoters had been attained in other ways, and it had ceased to be successful. The Rev. Canon Moseley, soon after his appointment to the cathedral, suggested the desirability of converting the building into a Trade School, similar to those which had been largely successful in Germany and other countries; and his proposal was sanctioned by the committee, subject to the approval of the subscribers. Dr. Lyon Playfair, who attended the meeting, congratulated the people of Bristol on being the first in England to contemplate the establishment of a valuable institution. Resolutions authorising the remodelling of the school were adopted unanimously. The new institution was opened by Earl Granville, Lord President of the Council, on the 28th March, 1856. His lordship, after being entertained to breakfast at the Council House, presided at a meeting held in the Merchants' Hall, where he expressed the deep interest felt by the Government in the new enterprise. The development of this school into the Merchant Venturers' School will be recorded hereafter.

A new church in Clifton, dedicated to St. Paul, was consecrated on the 8th November. The edifice, which was a tasteless specimen of gothic architecture, and cost only £4,000, had an ecclesiastical district assigned to it in October, 1859, by Order in Council. On the night of Sunday, the 15th December, 1867, the building, with the exception of the tower, vestry, and porch, was destroyed by fire—probably from the overheating of the flues. The church, considerably enlarged and improved, was rapidly rebuilt at a cost of about £7,000, and was reconsecrated on the 29th September, 1868.

A letter from the Home Secretary's office was on the 18th January, 1854, addressed to the churchwardens of each of the ancient parishes of Bristol, announcing that Lord Palmerston, under the powers of an Act passed in the previous session, had resolved on recommending the Privy Council to forbid interments in the crypts or burial grounds of their respective churches. In addition to the parochial cemeteries, the following were also closed: Francis's burial ground, West Street; Williams's burial ground, West Street; Thomas's burial ground, Clarence Place, Castle Street; Dolman's burial ground, Pennywell Street; Howland's burial ground, Newfoundland Street; Infirmary burial ground,

Johnny Ball Lane; Broadmead Chapel-yard, St. James's parish. Burials were also prohibited in St. Joseph's (Roman Catholic) chapel, Trenchard Street, and in Counterslip Baptist chapel. In the following places one body only was to be buried in each grave: Quakers' burial ground, Friars; Quakers' burial ground, Redcliff Pit; Quakers' burial ground, near the workhouse; Jews' burial ground, St. Philip's Marsh; Jews' burial ground, Temple parish. No burial was to take place within five yards of the adjoining buildings in the cemeteries of the cathedral, St. George's, Brandon Hill, Zion Independent chapel, Portland Street Wesleyan chapel, and St. Paul's, and in the three burial grounds in or near Red-cross Street.

Some interest was excited about this time by an effort made by the Society of Friends to avert the threatened war between England and Russia by means of an appeal addressed directly to the Czar. The persons selected to undertake this novel mission were Mr. Robert Charleton, of Bristol, Mr. Joseph Sturge, of Birmingham, and Mr. Henry Pease, of Darlington. On being introduced to the Emperor, at St. Petersburg, on the 10th February, the deputies presented him with an address from their society, urging the universal application of Christ's commands on all who called themselves His followers. The address added that the signatories had been induced to take this course "by the many proofs of condescension and Christian kindness manifested by thy late illustrious brother, Alexander, as well as by thy honoured mother, to some of our brethren in religious profession." The deputation was treated with great distinction by the Emperor, and was introduced to the Empress and the Grand Duchess Olga. It is scarcely necessary to add that the mission was a failure.

On the 16th March, Henry Charles, eighth Duke of Beaufort, paid a visit to the city in order to take the oath on accepting the office of Lord High Steward of Bristol, in succession to his father, who had died a few months before. The ceremony took place in the Council chamber. After his grace had been sworn in, and some complimentary speeches had been delivered, the company adjourned to another apartment, where a collation had been prepared. The tables were brilliantly decorated, and "a gigantic ship, in sugar, playing in a sea of whipped cream," represented one of the chief elements of local commerce. In October, the members of the Corporation were invited to dine at Badminton, where a party of seventy was served entirely upon silver. According to the *Bristol Times*, however, the guests were much irritated by their frigid reception, and one of them, in a published letter, complained of the huge dish of "cold shoulder" with which they had been regaled. The duke was presented with the freedom of the Merchants' Company, in a gold box, in the following November.

During the month of March, an old building standing upon the Welsh Back, nearly opposite the entrance to King Street, and known to all Bristolians by the name of the Goose Market, was demolished by order of the Council, being an impediment to traffic. It had been used in former times for the sale of Welsh products arriving by sailing vessels, but the introduction of steamers had diverted trade into other directions.

An advertisement in the Bristol newspapers of the 1st April announced that Pile Hill, consisting of nearly thirty acres of freehold land, had been laid out for building purposes. The offer did not meet with much attention until six or eight years after this date, but several hundred dwellings were eventually erected in the locality.

On the 26th April, the Bishop of Gloucester and Bristol, then residing at Stapleton Palace, addressed a letter to the incumbent and churchwardens of that parish, undertaking to rebuild at his own cost the parish church, then "mean in structure and of inadequate capacity." Dr. Monk explained that his motive in making the offer was to put an end to chronic quarrels respecting pews, and to provide accommodation for the poor. In order to insure the latter condition, his lordship forbore from reserving a seat for his own family. The representatives of the lay impropriator, Mr. J. H. Greville Smyth, a minor, gave notice of their intention to oppose the grant of a faculty for demolishing the old church, unless Mr. Smyth's rights in the chancel, including the power of selling or letting pews, were acknowledged. The difficulty was avoided by allowing the old chancel to remain, but it was afterwards rebuilt by Mr. Smyth's trustees. Amongst the last acts of Bishop Monk (who died in June, 1856, before the consecration of the church) was the gift of an organ and a clock to the edifice, which cost him upwards of £5,000, and is probably the most beautiful modern village church in the county. In 1870 Sir J. Greville Smyth, bart., restored to the parish the great tithes, which had belonged to his family for many generations, and which amounted to £250 a year. Half the sum was reserved for the ecclesiastical district of Fishponds, part of the ancient parish of Stapleton.

The once celebrated coaching-house, the Bush Hotel,

Corn Street, was ordered to be demolished in May, to make way for the new West of England Bank. Whilst the workmen were removing the flooring of one of the large rooms, they discovered a canvassing card of Henry Cruger, printed during the contest of 1781, in which that gentleman appealed for support as "a zealous Promoter of Trade, Peace, and Harmony between Great Britain and America."

About the end of August, the Rev. Robert H. Miles, rector of Bingham, Nottingham, and fourth son of the late Mr. P. J. Miles, of Leigh Court, purchased a piece of ground fronting the new course of the Avon, for the purpose of erecting a church—which the founder intended for the use of seamen frequenting the port—and also an almshouse for sailors' widows. The buildings were completed and the church opened in May, 1859. From the outset the religious services were characterised by an ornateness and ceremonial previously unknown in the city; and in the course of a few months the church became the recognised centre of fashionable "ritualists," the seamen for whom the building was designed being conspicuous from their absence. In 1865 it was announced that a series of pictures, representing the Roman Catholic legend of the "Stations of the Cross," had been placed in the building, and at a later period a waxwork representation of the Holy Family in the stable at Bethlehem was set up during the Christmas festival. In 1877 Bishop Ellicott repeatedly urged the chaplain, the Rev. A. H. Ward, to abandon the illegal practices which he had adopted in the celebration of the Communion; but the reverend gentleman replied that he could not conscientiously make any alteration in the services. In March, 1878, the bishop consequently revoked Mr. Ward's licence, and the church, which had never been consecrated, was thenceforth closed.

Another visitation of cholera occurred during the month of October, 1854, but the ravages of the disease were, as compared with former occasions, limited. Amongst the victims was Robert Evans, LL.D., D.C.L., the first headmaster of the reorganised Grammar School, which, through his learning and ability, had been already raised to great estimation. He was succeeded by Mr. C. T. Hudson, who had held the post of second master.

"In October, 1854, the first mission to that most hopeless of all hopeless countries, Patagonia and the Tierra del Fuego, sailed from the port of Bristol, in the schooner called the *Allen Gardiner*, commanded by the gallant and zealous captain of that name, whose melancholy fate, and that of his crew, off that inhospitable coast, in the following year, filled the minds of many Christians with the greatest grief. Yet, notwithstanding the sad casualty which befell the captain and crew, entitling them to a place on the list of martyrs for the cause of religion, the little vessel, having been rescued and brought home to England, and lengthened and refitted at Bristol, has found another captain and crew ready to undertake the responsibilities of this dangerous but glorious enterprise, and is again (1862) about to sail for her destination." *

Consequent upon the outbreak of war with Russia, a meeting of citizens was held in the Guildhall on the 20th November, in support of the Patriotic Fund, established under a Royal Commission, for the relief of the families of soldiers and sailors who should fall during the conflict. The total amount collected in the city was £9,996. At a later period of the war, when the deficiency of the transport service in the Crimea had caused deplorable results, steps were taken for the creation of a Land Transport corps, of which Bristol became the headquarters. The barracks at Horfield being inadequate for their accommodation, many hundreds of the recruits, drawn from the lowest classes, were billeted upon the innkeepers; and great complaints were made as to their disorderly conduct. The corps was reorganised and removed from Bristol on the return of peace.

In December, the Rev. George Madan, vicar of St. Mary Redcliff, a member of what was called the Puseyite party amongst the clergy, made several alterations in the service of his church. Amongst other innovations, he practically suppressed the parish clerk, and appealed to his parishioners to personally perform the part of the service that was set down for them in the Common Prayer Book. It may be now necessary to explain that, until about the middle of the century, in Bristol as elsewhere, the morning and evening services were simply dualistic performances reserved to the minister and his clerk, the congregations being practically silent, and that in most churches there was a monstrous edifice, known as a "three decker," the lowest stage of which was occupied by the clerk, whilst the second was used by the clergyman during prayers, and the sermon was preached from the summit. Mr. Madan's innovation gave much offence to old-fashioned people. But in July, 1856, when the parish clerkship of St. Nicholas became vacant, the vicar, Canon

* "Gloucestershire Achievements," by the Rev. S. Lysons, p. 13.

Girdlestone, an ardent Low Churchman, followed the example of his colleague in Redcliff; and as it was no longer possible to brand the system as "Tractarian," it eventually came into favour amongst churchgoers generally, and the parish clerks, with the "three deckers," gradually disappeared. Whilst Canon Girdlestone's action was still the subject of criticism, the *Bristol Times* stated (August 30, 1856) that when the Rev. J. H. Woodward [see page 321] was appointed to St. James's, he nominated his brother-in-law to the clerkship of the parish, and that the emoluments of the office, about £100 a year, after paying a small salary to a deputy, were received by Mr. Woodward. This arrangement, it was added, still continued, although Mr. Woodward had resigned the living on joining the Romish Church.

At the usual New Year's Day meeting of the Council in 1855, great complaint was made by some of the Liberal members at the strong political colour given to the various committees by those who privately framed the lists for the Conservative majority. It was pointed out that on the Finance Committee there were fifteen of one party and only four of the other; on the Improvement Committee the proportion was fourteen to four; on the Docks Committee, eight to four; on the Watch Committee thirteen to seven, and on the Parliamentary Committee seven to two. "It was now," said Mr. Cole, "only for a Liberal to displace a Conservative councillor, and the latter was immediately made an alderman, or placed in some other post of honour." It was alleged that one gentleman, whose high character and business habits were unquestioned, was a councillor for six or seven years before he was admitted upon any committee; whilst some aldermen, who did not enter the Council House for a year together, were placed on three or four important committees. In reply it was contended that the object of the majority was not to select political partisans, but men who were considered to be best qualified for the duties. The elections were then proceeded with, when the old arrangement was maintained. Owing to renewed complaints on the subject, however, the ruling party promised that two or three gentlemen from each side of the chamber should thenceforth meet previous to the annual election of committees, with a view to effecting arrangements satisfactory to both parties.

On the morning of the 20th March, the iron bridge spanning the new course of the Avon near the railway terminus was totally destroyed by a Cardiff steam barge. The vessel had conveyed a cargo of coke to the railway works, and was returning down the river, in which there was a strong current, when through unskilful management it struck the ribs of the bridge with great violence. The effect was instantaneous, the structure collapsing, according to the expression of an eyewitness, like a child's house of cards. Not a vestige was left standing, and the carts and passengers crossing at the time were flung into the river. Two persons lost their lives, one being a wagoner whose cart was found next day below Rownham. A ferry was established during the rebuilding of the bridge, which was sufficiently advanced on the 5th June to admit of the transit of foot passengers. The new structure cost about £5,700. [See page 27.]

During the month of April, Mr. William Baker, a Bristol builder, purchased an estate at Sneyd Park for the purpose of erecting a superior class of villas on the picturesque site. The editor of the *Bristol Times*, in commenting on the intended new suburb on the 28th April, indulged in some reminiscences of which lapse of time has increased the interest. "Many living," he remarked, "have made hay in Caledonia Place and the Mall. Most of my readers could have done the same not long since in Clifton Park. The little farmhouse where they sell fresh butter, near Litfield Place, will be soon shut out of sight by a cordon of domestic palaces. It seems but as yesterday that the Victoria Rooms and another building were the only edifices in that direction north of Berkeley Square; and the fanciful will, in a few years, amuse themselves with wondering how things looked when a boy was brought before the magistrates for ingeniously milking a cow in Tyndall's Park into a pair of new boots which he was taking home to his master, as we now smile over the entries in the vestry books of Clifton of sums paid for killing hedgehogs that infested the market gardens of Victoria Square. But we need not travel so far out of town for examples of the march of masons. On the left-hand side as you enter Tyndall's Park from St. Michael's Hill, there is a garden tower [still standing]. That which now barely shows its head above the adjacent houses was the country seat of a Bristol merchant of hospitable memory—Alderman Muggleworth, who, within the recollection of one not long dead, left his city residence in Lewin's Mead when 'the dog star burned,' and travelled to his villa by the pleasant park, there to abide until the late autumn made his mansion by the Froom more tolerable and temperate." The population of the new suburb having soon become considerable, arrangements were made for forming the locality into an ecclesiastical district; and the church of St. Mary's, the site of which was given by Mr. Baker, was consecrated on the 12th March, 1860. The building, which cost about £2,300, was considerably enlarged about the end of 1871, at a further expenditure of £3,000.

St. Clement's Church, Newfoundland Road, was consecrated on the 24th April, and an ecclesiastical district was allotted to it in the following June, by an Order in Council. The church, which originally cost £2,000, underwent extensive alterations in 1871.

Arley Chapel, Cheltenham Road, built by the Congregational body at a cost of upwards of £4,000, was opened in June, when the inaugural sermon was preached by the Rev. J. Angell James. This was the last dissenting chapel of any importance erected in the city in the Italian style, the later constructions being of a mediæval type.

The tower known as Cook's Folly, with the neighbouring woods, and a small public house which had been for many years a popular resort, were purchased about the beginning of July by Captain H. Goodeve, who subsequently erected a private mansion adjoining the "Folly." The tavern, known as the Folly Cottage, was closed about 1859. [On August 18, 1855, a little girl named Melinda Payne, living in one of the cottages which then stood on the right bank of the Avon, near the ravine, was sent by her father to this house for some beer, and was murdered whilst returning homewards. The perpetrator of the deed was never discovered.]

On the 24th July, the body of Field-Marshal Lord Raglan, who had died in the Crimea whilst in command of the British forces before Sebastopol, arrived in Cumberland Basin in the naval steamer *Caradoc*. Two of his lordship's brothers having been interred in the cathedral, it was expected that the remains would be deposited in the same building; but the Duke of Beaufort gave directions that the burial should take place in the family vault at Badminton. Great preparations had been made in the city to render fitting honour to the memory of the distinguished soldier. On the morning of the 25th, the coffin was transferred from the *Caradoc* to a small steamboat, on which a platform covered with black velvet, surmounted by a canopy of the same material, had been raised for its reception. On the coffin were placed the coronet, sword, and hat of the deceased, while his lordship's aides-de-camp and a number of artillerymen were ranged on each side. Upon the vessel entering the harbour, forty-two boats, chiefly contributed by the merchant vessels in the port, each bearing a mourning flag, and with crews appropriately attired, were divided into two lines, and formed a guard on each side of the steamer. In this order the procession made its way to the Quay head, where the goods sheds were draped with black cloth and feathers for the reception of the body. At this point were assembled the mayor (Mr. J. G. Shaw), the sheriff, and many members of the Corporation, together with great numbers of the leading citizens, and the children of the public schools. The coffin having been placed in a hearse, amidst the firing of minute guns by a battery of artillery and the tolling of the city bells, a procession was formed, headed by the Gloucestershire Yeomanry and the band of the 15th Hussars, and attended by a guard of honour of the Royal Horse Guards. The mourning coaches containing members of the deceased's family were followed by the pensioners of the district, a detachment of the Land Transport corps, a troop of artillery, the officers of the Corporation, the carriages of the mayor and of many members of the Council, and those of the members of the Merchants' Society, and finally a lengthy procession of pedestrians, including the clergy, ministers, citizens, and members of friendly societies. Many of the houses along the line of march were hung with crape, black cloth, or wreaths of laurel, some bearing flags or mourning tablets with appropriate inscriptions. Altogether the spectacle was one of an unexampled character in the city, and the good taste and public spirit which marked the proceedings evoked sympathetic admiration in all parts of the country.

St. Peter's Church, Clifton Wood, was consecrated on the 10th August. The edifice had been originally built by the Wesleyans, who opened it for Divine worship in November, 1833. In consequence of the largely increased population of the district, the accommodation of this church became insufficient, and a large, lofty, and ornate Gothic edifice was constructed on an adjoining site at a cost of £6,000, and was consecrated in September, 1882. In the following year the old building was bought by the Corporation for conversion into a free library.

In September, 1855, while repairs were being made in the house No. 10, College Green, then standing between the abbey gateway and the cathedral, and occupied by Canon Bankes, the workmen discovered portions of a Decorated shaft, some arch moulding, and a portion of a turret staircase. These relics were supposed to have formed part of the north-western tower of the nave which Abbot Newland intended to construct in the same style as his choir. The house has since been demolished.

Down to this period the pauper lunatics of the city had been maintained in St. Peter's Hospital, although the suitability of that locality for such a purpose had long been questioned. In the course of this year, after receiving reports from official inspectors, the Government insisted upon the construction of a lunatic asylum in the suburbs. As the cost of the building threatened to make a heavy addition to the rates, opposition to the ministerial order was very generally manifested. But unfortunately the local authorities were unable to agree upon a plan which would avert the necessity of a new building. The guardians proposed that the paupers at Stapleton should be brought back to St. Peter's, and the lunatics sent to the vacated workhouse. The Council—which, under a new Lunacy Act, had in January, 1854, taken upon itself the duty of managing the lunatic asylum, previously imposed on the magistrates—contended that the paupers remaining in the establishment in Peter Street should be removed to Stapleton, so that additional room might be at disposal for the lunatics. But the Poor Law authorities set their faces against both suggestions. In the closing months of the year, the Council, the Board of Guardians, and the Chamber of Commerce severally passed resolutions deprecating a large expenditure for a new asylum, and meetings were held in the wards at which motions to a similar effect were carried almost unanimously. Deputations representing the Corporation and the citizens shortly afterwards, had an interview with the Poor Law Board, and asked that permission should be granted to alienate part of the workhouse premises at Stapleton, so as to build an asylum thereon. To this the Board refused its assent, nor would it sanction the conversion of a portion of the workhouse into an asylum. A committee of the Council was therefore appointed to obtain offers of sites and estimates; and in March, 1857, a report was adopted recommending the purchase of. 24 acres of ground at Stapleton, and the erection of an asylum there at a total estimated expenditure of £30,000. The building, which actually cost upwards of £40,000, but was said to be the model asylum of the country, was finished in February, 1861, when it received 113 lunatics from St. Peter's Hospital. In 1875–7, owing to the increased number of lunatics, the asylum was enlarged at a cost of £22,000. A chapel was built a few years later, at an outlay of £3,000. In 1885 it was reported to the Council that the asylum, though capable of accommodating 430 patients, had become seriously insufficient for its purpose, and that it was advisable to make additions so as to provide for a total number of 679 lunatics. The expense was estimated at £6,140 for land, and no less a sum than £59,535 for buildings. The Council deferred the consideration of the subject, in order to enable the committee to submit an approximate estimate of the cost of a new site that would permit the erection of an asylum capable of meeting all demands for fifty years. On the 1st June, 1886, the committee reported that in their opinion the most economical course would be to carry out their previous proposal, and the Council accordingly authorised the Finance Committee to raise the sum of £65,675 by mortgage, for the execution of the works.

In the session of 1854, the advocates of a strict observance of the Lord's Day, supported by the teetotalers, succeeded in obtaining the consent of Parliament to a measure by which public houses were almost entirely closed on Sundays. The operation of the new law having caused disturbances in London, and much discontent amongst the working classes generally, Mr. Berkeley, M.P., in the session of 1855, obtained a select committee to inquire into the working of the statute. The committee almost unanimously reported that its provisions were too rigorous, having regard to the wants and feelings of the labouring community; and Mr. Berkeley thereupon introduced and secured the enactment of a Bill by which the restrictions were relaxed. His action excited much irritation amongst the advocates of total abstinence; and their organ, the *Alliance*, then noted for its intemperance of language, published a series of articles in which the senior member for Bristol was charged with gross corruption, collusive conduct, and perjury. Mr. Berkeley thereupon raised an action for libel; but when the case came on for trial, in February, 1856, the defendants made an apology for statements they admitted to be false, consented to a verdict against them of five guineas, and undertook to pay the costs, estimated at nearly £1,000. In the meantime a movement had been started for raising a national subscription to recognise Mr. Berkeley's legislative exertions on the subject; and on the 24th September, 1856, he was presented at the Athenæum with a silver salver, a carved and ornamented casket, and a purse, the whole representing an offering of £1,012, contributed by about 14,000 persons throughout the country. The casket was made from an oak beam taken from the old north porch of St. Mary Redcliff, and was enriched with some large and lustrous specimens of Bristol diamonds.

During the autumn of 1855 the upper part of Queen Street (Christmas Steps) was widened by the removal of some old buildings on the eastern side, and the stairs were made much more convenient to passengers.

After an existence of twenty-two years, the Bristol Agricultural Society, having lost many of its early and more liberal supporters, and failing to meet with adequate assistance from a new generation, was dissolved on the 12th December.

In the spring of 1856 the gunboats *Earnest, Escort, Hardy, Havoc,* and *Highlander* were constructed at Bristol for the Royal Navy by the shipbuilding firms of Patterson & Son, and Hill & Sons. These vessels formed part of a large fleet of gunboats hurriedly ordered by the Government during the Russian war, and built in all the leading ports of the kingdom. A few years afterwards the condition of the vessels was the subject of a discussion in the House of Commons; and on inquiry it appeared that, with the exception of the Bristol boats and a few others, the builders had committed gross frauds in construction, and that a number of the vessels were utterly rotten and worthless.

According to a local newspaper of the 8th March, 1856, a joint-stock company, under the new Limited Liability Act, was then in contemplation "for raising passengers and goods from the low levels of some parts of Bristol to the more elevated portions of Clifton by machinery." Suggestions of a fixed engine at the top of Park Street, for drawing up wagons and heavily laden carts, were frequently started before the construction of Colston Street and Perry Road.

The *Bristol Gazette* of the 12th March announced, to the great surprise of the city, that a defalcation of upwards of £4,000 had been discovered in the accounts of the treasurer of the Corporation, Mr. Thomas Garrard, who had been for fifty-four years in the civic service. The deficiency was accidentally brought to light whilst Mr. Garrard was temporarily disabled by illness from attending to his duties. The sum was more than covered by the guarantees of the treasurer's sureties, who were themselves secured by life assurances. The defalcation was stated to have arisen from advances made by Mr. Garrard to retrieve a relative from commercial difficulties. It was understood that his successor, Mr. John Harford, allowed him a handsome yearly sum during the remainder of his life.

On the 30th April the ceremony of proclaiming peace with Russia took place amidst formal demonstrations of joy. The mayor (Mr. J. Vining), the sheriff, and other corporate officials, with the boys of Colston's and the City schools, assembled at the Council House, from the steps of which the proclamation was first made at noon, after a blast from the city trumpets and a peal from the neighbouring church bells. Proclamation was afterwards made in the quadrangle of the Exchange, the centre of Queen Square, Bristol Bridge, St. Peter's Pump, and the Old Market. As the terms wrested from Russia were by many people deemed inadequate, the proceedings did not evoke any marked enthusiasm. The same may be said of the day fixed for a national celebration of the peace—the 28th May. No preparations were made to do honour to the occasion, which had little other character than that of a listless holiday. A writer in the local press remarked: "Some guns were fired from ships, and pistols popped off in obscure corners, and men stood at the doors of the Commercial Rooms, as usual, abusing Bristol for want of spirit, and, as usual, they themselves, though items of this much abused Bristol, doing nothing." In the evening, a few gas-lit crowns, royal cyphers, etc., were exhibited on the public buildings, but the private illuminations were few and insignificant.

Upon the death, on the 6th June, of Dr. Monk, the first bishop of the united sees of Gloucester and Bristol, efforts were made in various parts of the two dioceses to obtain their separation. Lord Palmerston's Ministry, however, declined to propose any legislative measure for that purpose; and Dr. Baring, Rector of Limpsfield, Surrey, was soon after named Dr. Monk's successor. The alienation of the palace at Stapleton at this juncture has been already recorded [p. 228].

The Queen, accompanied by the Prince Consort, the Prince of Wales, and her younger children, passed through Bristol on August 15th on her way from Plymouth to Osborne. The royal party remained twenty minutes in the refreshment room of the railway station, which had been hurriedly decorated, tidings of the visit having been received on the previous evening. In the autumn the Prince of Wales made an incognito tour in the West of England, in the course of which, on the 5th October, he attended service at Bristol cathedral. Presumably from no fee having been forthcoming,* the sub-sacrist conducted the stranger to a bench in one

* The greediness of cathedral underlings has always been notorious. A Bristol sub-sacrist, who died whilst Sydney Smith was one of the prebendaries,

of the aisles, where the heir apparent remained throughout the service. In April, 1858, the Prince again paid a brief visit to the city. Having left his yacht at Kingroad, he was rowed up the river, and landed at Rownham, whence he proceeded in a public cab to the railway station, but stopped at the cathedral on his way, for the purpose of inspecting the Chapter House.

The first annual Conference of the National Reformatory Union was held in Bristol—one of the earliest centres of the reformatory movement—on the 20th August and two following days. Amongst the many distinguished persons present were Lord Robert Cecil (now Marquis of Salisbury), Lord Stanley (now Earl of Derby), Sir Stafford Northcote (Earl of Iddesleigh), Sir John Pakington (Lord Hampton), Mr. Adderley (Lord Norton), etc. Visits were paid to the local reformatories at Arno's Court, Kingswood, St. James's Back, Pennywell Lane, and Hardwicke.

The primary schools existing in the city at this time being greatly below the needs of the population, many thousands of poor children grew up uninstructed, and frequently revenged themselves on society for its shortsighted indifference. At the Michaelmas quarter sessions of 1856, Mr. J. Naish Sanders, one of the magistrates, made some remarks before the recorder which afford a glimpse of the habits of the class in question. "Bristol," he said, "has the unenviable reputation of having within her walls one of the most disorderly set of youths in England. Stones are continually thrown by boys in our public thoroughfares, owing to which many lives have been lost—five at least in Clifton parish only. Ornamental plantations, so placed as to benefit the public, are constantly injured, and even the branches carried away for firewood. Young thieves assemble in gangs at each end of Park Street, professedly to drag wheels, but really for worse purposes, as proved in many cases. If the police or private individuals complain, they are assailed in gross and indecent language, revolting to all, and especially to females." Some regret was expressed by the bench at the uncultivated condition of the youth of the lower classes, but the authorities felt themselves impotent, and the matter was suffered to drop.

---

was said to have hoarded £20,000, causing the witty cleric to observe that he at length understood the full force of the text: "I had rather be a doorkeeper in the house," etc. [The text is inscribed upon the tomb of a verger in Salisbury cathedral.] At a quite recent date, it was publicly stated that one of the English bishops had been treated with indignity in Bristol cathedral for having presumed to look at some of the monuments without being "guided" by the officials.

It has been already stated that the Bristol Incorporation of the Poor was, with a few others, exempted from the supervision of the Poor Law Board constituted by the great Act of 1834. In 1844 an amending statute was passed, empowering the central authorities to combine unions into districts for the audit of accounts, thus striking a mortal blow at the financial independence of the privileged bodies. Armed with this Act, the Board soon after issued an order for forming an audit district embracing Bristol and several Somerset unions. The Bristol guardians for some time offered a passive resistance to this measure, and nothing was done for two years. But in September, 1846, the Poor Law Commissioners gave peremptory directions that the local accounts should be revised by the official auditor of the district; and as the guardians refused to submit their books to his inspection, the Government officials in February, 1849, applied for and obtained a *mandamus* from the Court of Queen's Bench. The defendants, in no wise subdued, appealed to the Court of Error, by which in February, 1850, the action of the court below was affirmed. Although beaten on the point of law, the guardians continued to maintain that they had a right to administer relief in accordance with the bye-laws made under their private Act; and though their allowances were greatly at variance with the scale fixed by the central authorities, the contest on this subject was continued for several years. At length, in the closing months of 1856, the members of the recalcitrant corporation were threatened with legal proceedings for the recovery of £23,157, illegally distributed in relief in defiance of the regulations, and were warned that the "surcharge" would be recovered by levies upon them individually. It was now felt that no other course remained but to accept defeat. On the 8th January, 1857, the local bye-laws were repealed, and the "consolidated order" of the central board was adopted in their place. The effect of this resolution was to terminate, for all practical purposes, the existence of the ancient "Incorporation of the Poor," which now became an ordinary board of guardians. The ancient mode of election was, however, maintained. The last governor under the old system was Dr. George Rogers. The first chairman under the new *régime*—Mr. Elisha Smith Robinson—was elected on the 16th January, 1857. The latter gentleman, in a speech delivered March 2nd, 1860, asserted that the saving to the ratepayers brought about by the reorganisation of the union was not less than £4,000 a year—a fact which the public apparently regarded as outweighing the old-fashioned guardians' anathemas against centralisation, oppression, and red tape. It may be worth while to add that, in spite of the increase of population in the city, and the tendency of the poorest class to flow into the central parishes, the expenditure of the board, in respect both to management and relief, has remained stationary. In the year ending March, 1858, the total charge was within a few pounds of £31,000. In the twelvemonth ending March, 1886, the outlay was £30,480. As the rateable value of the ancient city had in the meantime increased considerably more than 50 per cent., the rates had of course diminished in a corresponding proportion.

After having remained vacant upwards of two years, the Roman Catholic bishopric of Clifton was conferred, in the spring of 1857, on the Hon. and Rev. William Clifford, in whose hands it still remains.

At the general election in March, the members for the city in the previous Parliament, Messrs. Berkeley and Langton, were returned without opposition—an incident which had not occurred in Bristol for fifty years, with the exception of the abnormal election of 1831. The dissolution had been caused by a defeat of Lord Palmerston's Ministry, through a coalition of Conservatives with what was called the Manchester school. The conduct of their leaders gave so much umbrage to many local Tories of influence that a contest was found to be impracticable.

Owing to the confusion arising from the diversified names of "places," "terraces," etc., in the chief suburban thoroughfares, the Council, in April, resolved upon the following nomenclature: Queen's Road (from the top of Park Street to Victoria Square); Clifton Road (from Victoria Square to Clifton turnpike-gate—now the site of Alderman Proctor's fountain); Whiteladies Road (from the Queen's Hotel to the Pound, Durdham Down); Redland Road (from the Pound just mentioned to Cutler's Mills); Stokes Croft Road (from North Street to Cutler's Mills); Cotham Road (from Whiteladies-gate, junction of roads, to Cutler's Mills); Hotwell Road (from the White Hart, Limekiln Lane, to Clifton Gate). Limekiln Lane had its name changed to St. George's Road in June, 1862.

On the 18th June, at a meeting held in the Commercial Rooms, Mr. Jose, master of the Merchants' Society, in the chair, resolutions were passed approving of the scheme laid before those present by M. de Lesseps for the construction of the Suez canal, "being of opinion that it is of the greatest importance to the commerce of the whole world." A few days later, in the House of Commons, Mr. Berkeley asked the Ministry if it would support the undertaking, to which Lord Palmerston answered emphatically in the negative, declaring that the project was hostile to English interests.

On the 24th of June a portion of the premises in the Mall, Clifton, which at a previous period had been known as the Royal Hotel (closed early in 1854), was opened as a club-house, under the name of the Clifton Subscription Rooms. The remainder of the hotel premises was converted into shops and dwelling houses. The cost of the conversion was upwards of £4,000. In March, 1882, the association was reorganised, and the property transferred to a new company, with a capital of £12,000 in £75 shares, each holder of a £60 share in the original concern receiving a fully paid-up share.

The Council resolved, in July, to arch over the Froom from St. John's Bridge to the Stone Bridge, and to devote the space so obtained to the construction of a public street. The new thoroughfare, which was subsequently named Rupert Street, was recommended to the Council as the first instalment of a new line of road from the centre of the city to Stokes Croft. In July, 1859, the Council voted £2,000 for covering the Froom between Union Street and Merchant Street, the roadway constructed upon the site being styled Fairfax Street. In 1867 the sum of £2,650 was granted for covering the last open part of the Froom in the central districts—from St. John's Bridge to Bridewell. Finally, in 1880, almost the only remaining uncovered portion of this river within the city boundaries, near Haberfield Street, was also ordered to be arched over.

Soon after the arrival in this country of the Russian war material captured at Sebastopol and other places, some provincial corporation with decorative tastes applied to the Government for one or two of the cannons, proposing to mount them in a conspicuous position as lasting trophies of English valour. The application having been successful, a great number of municipalities followed the example—some of the local bodies being not a little puzzled how to dispose of the prize when it came into their possession. Amongst the rest, a request was addressed to the war minister by the Corporation of Bristol, and at once met with a favourable response, two cannons, thirty-six pounders, nine feet in length, and each weighing three tons, being despatched from Woolwich, together with carriages—the latter being paid for by the city. On the 19th August the guns were conveyed from the railway station by a party of the Military Train (originally the Land Transport corps) through the principal streets to Brandon Hill. Great crowds lined the route, and the spectacle was of an animated character. In the rear of Berkeley Square a portion of the wall had to be broken down to allow the cavalcade to pass; and as the eight horses attached to each gun were unable to drag it to the summit of the hill, the populace lent enthusiastic assistance, the task being soon accomplished by main force. The proceedings terminated with patriotic and congratulatory speeches.

A murder which created unusual sensation in the city was perpetrated in Leigh Woods, on the 10th September, by a man named John William Beale, who had served as butler to some respectable families in the neighbourhood. His victim was a woman named Charlotte Pugsley, who had occasionally been one of his fellow-servants. On the day before the murder, Beale, who had left the district to serve with a gentleman residing near Daventry, went, apparently by appointment, to a country seat at Freshford, where Pugsley was living as cook. She had previously given notice to leave, and she and her companion departed soon after for Bristol, informing the other servants that they were about to marry and emigrate. (The woman was aware that Beale had a wife living.) On the following morning they were seen at Bristol railway terminus, where Beale had his companion's boxes removed to the Midland luggage room, stating that he was going to Liverpool. What became of the parties during the day was not discovered, but in the evening they were observed walking together in the rabbit warren near the top of Nightingale Valley. Next day Beale returned to his employer's at Daventry, with the woman's luggage, stating that it contained the clothing of his sister, whose funeral he had just attended. The body of Pugsley was found on the same day by one of Mr. Miles's gamekeepers. The woman had been shot in the head, which was nearly severed from the body by a gash in the throat, and her remains had then been thrown over the precipice overhanging Nightingale Valley, but had rested on a ledge about twelve feet from the summit. It was not until nearly a fortnight after the murder that the friends of Charlotte Pugsley suspected that she was the victim, and by that time the features of the body were no longer recognisable. Identity was however established by means of the clothing, and by a peculiar decayed tooth. No adequate motive for the deed was discovered. Beale's wife lived in the neighbourhood of

Daventry, and the money possessed by Pugsley did not exceed a few pounds. The murderer was tried and convicted at Taunton assizes in the following December, and was executed in January, 1858, refusing to admit his guilt even on the scaffold.

At the annual election of corporate dignitaries on the 9th November, Mr. John Henry Greville Smyth, of Long Ashton, who had attained his majority in the previous January, was elected sheriff of Bristol for the ensuing civic year. The appointment had been, as usual, determined upon by the secret committee to whom the selection of officers was delegated by the Conservative majority in the Council, and it was persisted in after Mr. Smyth, who had been made acquainted with the intention to nominate him, had intimated that he should refuse to serve. This he formally did after the election had taken place, whereupon the Council applied to the law courts to compel his obedience. A *mandamus* was issued in January, 1858, and the Court of Error consented to pronounce a formal decision in order that final judgment might be obtained in the House of Lords before the close of the session. The law peers, however, refused to give precedence to the case. The Council did not re-elect Mr. Smyth in the following November, and as that gentleman, by consent, withdrew his appeal, a definitive decision on the matter was never delivered.

About this time the authorities of the united parishes of St. Nicholas and St. Leonard found themselves seriously embarrassed by the increasing revenue of the estates confided to them by ancient benefactors for charitable purposes. A property bearing the strange name of the Forlorn Hope, near Baptist Mills, being likely to fall in through the death of the surviving lessees, the churchwardens had the prospect of the existing charity income being raised from £450 to £650 a year. Even as it was, a large portion of the funds being bequeathed for distribution in doles about the Christmas season, a crowd of worthless people were accustomed to flock into the parishes towards the close of each year, and to hire some miserable lodging to entitle them to share in the gifts, much of the money being at once squandered in dissipation. The competition for garrets and dirty back rooms was so great that inordinate rents were freely paid, and the result was simply to transfer a considerable portion of the doles into the pockets of a greedy and sordid class of landlords. In November, 1857, the churchwardens and vestry, urged thereto by the vicar, Canon Girdlestone, and having the sanction of the Charity Commissioners, resolved to abolish the doles, to set apart £200 yearly for the maintenance of fifteen aged women in the parish almshouse, and to apply the surplus to the support of schools. An Act to authorise this arrangement was passed in 1858. A new schoolhouse was built by subscription in Back Street,* on a site previously occupied by ruinous dwellings, one of which was the ancient parsonage of St. Nicholas. The adjoining Rackhay burial ground, belonging to St. Nicholas' parish, was converted into a playground for the scholars. The new schools were opened in July, 1858.

In November, 1857, the Rev. J. B. Clifford, incumbent of St. Matthew's, somewhat astonished the public by denouncing from the pulpit an "institution in the city" for teaching infidelity and atheism. It ultimately turned out that Mr. Clifford had alluded to the Athenæum; and he subsequently admitted that he intended to condemn, not the institution itself, but a discussion class connected with it, in which an essay had been delivered—on the religions of India—which several clergymen declared to contain nothing worthy of reprobation. The class was warmly defended by Mr. Edlin, barrister, its chairman, while Canon Girdlestone rebuked the intemperance of the assailant, who was charged with intolerance in some of the local newspapers, and was significantly left unsupported by his clerical brethren. In the following January, Charles Dickens evinced his opinion on the subject by coming down from London to read his "Christmas Carol" for the benefit of the institution.

In January, 1858, in consequence of the loud complaints raised by the innkeepers of the city against the army billeting system, the War Office obtained a lease of the extensive premises formerly known as the Royal Gloucester Hotel, and converted the building into barracks. The step aroused opposition amongst some inhabitants of Clifton; but the Secretary for War refused to assent to their appeals, and the building was opened for its new purpose in April. Owing to improvements effected in the recruiting system, and other causes, the Government, in April, 1870, removed the military staff established at this depôt.

In the spring of 1858 the Franciscan monks who had conducted the services at the Roman Catholic chapels in Trenchard Street and on the Quay were succeeded by secular

* This ancient street, which like its namesake, the Rue du Bac in Paris, owed its title to an adjacent ferry, was in 1885 inconsiderately, if not foolishly, dubbed Queen Charlotte Street.

priests. Whilst the old books and manuscripts lying in the monks' apartments in Trenchard Street were being examined prior to removal, a perfect copy was discovered of the Hereford Missal. The book, which was stated to contain the only complete ritual of the Hereford "use" extant, was purchased by the trustees of the British Museum for £300.

On the night of the 30th April, the *Brigand* trading steamer, whilst on her way from Bristol to Glasgow, with eleven passengers and a crew of twenty men, got into collision off the Irish coast with a barque called the *William Campbell.* Both vessels sank within a few minutes of the disaster. Only two of the passengers in the *Brigand,* with the captain and six of the crew, were saved.

An abortive attempt to establish a daily newspaper in Bristol will be found recorded at page 118. The subsequent abolition of the tax on public journals enabled a similar enterprise to be undertaken with success. On the 1st June, 1858, the first number of the *Western Daily Press,* price one penny, was issued by Mr. P. S. Macliver, at No 1, Broad Street. The popular taste becoming rapidly educated to the new and cheaper system of publication, Messrs. C. & G. Somerton, proprietors of the *Bristol Mercury,* started, in January, 1860, the *Bristol Daily Post,* published daily from Monday to Friday, the *Mercury* supplying the sixth day's news. (In January, 1878, the two journals were incorporated, and the title of *Daily Post* was subsequently dropped.) In January, 1865, a combination was formed between the two Conservative journals in the city, the *Mirror,* belonging to Mr. T. D. Taylor, and the *Times,* the property of Mr. J. Leech, the result being the appearance of the *Bristol Times and Mirror,* issued daily from Monday to Friday at a penny, and on Saturdays at twopence. A still further development of daily journalism was made by Mr. Macliver in May, 1877, by the publication of the *Bristol Evening News,* price one halfpenny.

A local newspaper of the 12th June announced that the Docks Committee contemplated the widening of Hotwell Road between Limekiln dock and Mardyke ferry, and the construction of a wharf at that spot. It subsequently transpired that the works, which were to extend forty feet into the Floating Harbour, had been resolved upon without the consent or knowledge of the Council. Operations had scarcely commenced when Messrs. Hill & Co., whose shipbuilding yard stood opposite to the proposed wharf, applied to the law courts for an injunction to restrain the Corporation from erecting works calculated to injure their property. Eventually the Docks Committee were obliged to make terms, Messrs. Hill & Co. accepting £1,000 and withdrawing their opposition. The wharf, which the committee had expected to complete for £1,500, actually involved an outlay of about £5,700.

A small church, dedicated to St. Michael and All Angels, was opened at Bishopston, Horfield, on the 20th June. The quarrel of its founder, the Rev. Henry Richards, with Bishop Monk has been already referred to. The prelate's successor, Bishop Baring, had also to publicly protest against the conduct of the incumbent. In a letter dated February 2, 1858, Dr. Baring stated that Mr. Richards had consented to the formation of a new district in Horfield, of which the bishop was to be the patron, but that after Dr. Monk's death he had repudiated this agreement, declaring that he would never allow a Low churchman to nominate a clergyman in his parish. Subsequently, added his lordship, Mr. Richards built a church, and offered to endow it to the extent of £40 a year, provided the patronage was vested in him and his heirs. But as the Horfield manor trustees intended to endow the incumbency to a much larger extent, the bishop refused his assent, to the great wrath of the vicar, who must have foreseen that through the increasing population the value of the living would soon be largely augmented. In consequence of the disagreement, St. Michael's was not consecrated until February, 1862. It was afterwards considerably enlarged. By an Order in Council of July, 1862, a new parish, cut out of Horfield, Stapleton, and St. Andrew's, Montpelier, was attached to this church.

In despite of the benefits secured by the transfer of the docks to the city, Bristolians could not but be sensible that the port lay under peculiar natural disadvantages, which "handicapped" it heavily in the competition with other harbours. The course of the Avon from Hungroad to Cumberland Basin being exceedingly tortuous, accidents to vessels were of such frequent occurrence as to give the river an evil reputation amongst shipowners; and after the lamentable disaster to the *Demerara*, many firms refused to accept charters which would render their vessels liable to similar mishaps. An equally serious drawback had been created by the designer of Cumberland Basin. At the beginning of the century the commerce of the world was carried on by vessels which, while rarely exceeding 800 tons burden, were on the average of less than half that tonnage; and the depth of the locks had naturally been determined by those conditions. But the application of steam power to ships had revolutionised former ideas on the subject, for not only were over-sea steamers necessarily larger in consequence of the stock of fuel they had to carry, but builders of sailing ships, to meet the competition for freights, studied economy by constructing vessels of double or treble the former size. The results had been early felt in Bristol. The citizens had built the *Great Western* only to find that, while they had solved the problem of transatlantic navigation, they were deprived of its profits by the natural defects of the port. By and by, the effects which the vessel had produced on shipowners and shipbuilders also began to be felt. The local public were ever and anon informed that a large vessel bound for Bristol had arrived at Kingroad, but that owing to insufficient depth of water she must remain at anchor until spring tides, perhaps eight or ten days distant. The evil was constantly growing more serious. The *Great Western* was of 1,340 tons register; but the Cunard company had, in 1848, four ships of about 2,000 tons; and at the time under review Mr. Brunel had under construction the *Great Eastern*, of 22,000 tons burden, which he confidently predicted would be the model ship of the future. The prospect naturally caused anxiety; and on the 24th June, 1858, a joint committee, comprising deputations nominated by the Docks Committee, the Merchant Venturers' Society, and the Chamber of Commerce, held a meeting at the dock office, the mayor (Mr. I. A. Cooke) in the chair, with the view of considering the question of improved dock accommodation. After a long discussion on the advisability of constructing a large dock at the mouth of the river, it was resolved, by a majority of 12 votes to 4, that the interests of the port would be best promoted by converting the Avon, throughout its tidal area, into a floating harbour. On the 14th September, in compliance with a requisition signed by upwards of 500 of the principal citizens, the mayor convened a public meeting in the Guildhall, which was densely crowded on the occasion. Mr. P. W. Miles having moved, and Mr. C. W. Finzel seconded, a resolution declaring that further accommodation was essential to the interests of the port; Mr. J. G. Shaw, representing the non-progressive party, brought forward a "rider" to the motion, declaring that it would be unjust and injurious to the owners of fixed property to raise additional funds by local taxation. The resolution having been adopted, Mr. E. S. Robinson moved that the rider should not be put, and this, after an excited discussion, was also carried. An influential committee was then appointed to co-operate with the Chamber of Commerce in devising means for carrying the resolution into effect. A special meeting of the Council was held on the 7th November to consider the course recommended by the citizens, when it was proposed to appoint a committee to further the object in view. Mr. J. G. Shaw, however, returned to the attack,* and by a majority of 25 against 24, an amendment was carried by the fixed property party, refusing to appoint a committee to meet any representatives of public bodies for promoting increased dock accommodation. The committee of citizens, bereft of the expected support, found it necessary to surrender all thoughts of an extensive scheme, and the construction of a pier at the mouth of the Avon was suggested as an advisable temporary expedient. It was soon afterwards intimated, however, that the Board of Admiralty, by the advice of its engineer, Mr. Walker, would not allow the erection of a pier encroaching upon the anchorage ground at Kingroad. The subject thus fell into abeyance for a time, but its urgency soon brought it again into prominent notice. At a meeting of the Council, on the 2nd August, 1859, two voluminous reports were laid on the table. One of these, by Mr. William Parkes, an eminent engineer, disapproved of the project for "dockising" the Avon, and also condemned the proposal for docks near Kingroad, but recommended the deepening and widening of the Avon, the cutting of a new channel to avoid the Horseshoe Point, and the closing of the old course of the river at Dunball. The other report, by Mr. Howard, engineer to the Docks Committee, proposed the damming up of the tidal river near its mouth, and the construction of an outer tidal harbour off the Somerset shore at Kingroad, to be enclosed by two piers, the entrance to be sufficiently deepened to permit steamers to enter at low water. The cost of the works was estimated at £800,000. At another meeting of the Council, in October, Mr. Shaw moved that it was inexpedient to expend money either for docks or dockisation; but an amendment was carried by 27 votes against 15, directing the whole question to be submitted to Sir William Cubitt (or, as it was afterwards determined, to Mr. John Hawkshaw) and Mr. Thomas Page. The only

* Mr. Shaw was an Irishman, and is said to have been not a little vain of his exuberance of speech. He was naturally unpopular amongst the advocates of improvement, and it appears from one of his own speeches that he earned for himself the nickname of "Jaw Jaw Jaw"—John George Shaw.

actual work undertaken by the Corporation at this time was the erection of a small stage, called a landing slip, near the Lighthouse, for the accommodation of passengers arriving by the Irish steamers. With an increasing foresight, however, the Docks Committee purchased, in January, 1860, the island of Dunball for £850. It had been bought two or three years previously, at the sale of Mr. J. A. Gordon's estates, for £100, by an eccentric publican named Hooper. The reports of Messrs. Hawkshaw and Page were laid before the Council in October, 1860. Mr. Hawkshaw, whilst strongly condemning the dockisation of the Avon (the cost of which he estimated at £1,200,000), and recommending that the bed should be deepened and improved, pointed out that, whatever was done to the river, there was no likelihood that ocean steamers, increasing as they were in size, would ever come up to Bristol. The construction of docks near Kingroad was deemed practicable, but as they would lead to a divided and competitive trade, Mr. Hawkshaw recommended that, after the river had been improved, the Corporation should be content with constructing a dock for steamers, connected by a railway with the city. The expense of his proposals was estimated at £1,213,000. Mr. Page, who also disapproved of dockisation, on the ground of its costliness and probable ill effects on Kingroad, considered that it was unnecessary that ships should come up to the city if their cargoes were brought to it, and advised the construction of a pier near the river mouth, with a railway to Bristol quays and to the through lines of communication. He further suggested that when trade had developed, a dock should be constructed in the channel of the Avon, between Dunball and the mainland, of which the pier would form one side, the estimated cost being £260,000. Finally he proposed extensive alterations at Cumberland Basin, and the "floating" of the new course of the Avon. The reports, of which that of Mr. Page found most supporters, gave rise to a debate in the Council extending over two days, Mr. E. S. Robinson having moved that steps should be taken for obtaining an Act to effect improvements on Mr. Page's plan, at a cost not exceeding £400,000. The party which obstinately resisted improvements, on the ground that no guarantee for the interest on the amount expended ought to be required from the ratepayers, were ultimately defeated by 33 votes against 22. The influence of the fixed property party was, however, so powerful that the discussion ended in the passing of an empty resolution approving of docks, and appointing a committee to frame a scheme which could be accomplished without imposing any charge on the ratepayers. Even this modest advance was succeeded by a retreat in February, 1861, when a resolution was proposed by Mr. R. P. King, another champion of vested interests, declaring that it was "not expedient to incur any further liability on the fixed property of the city for the purpose of making dock accommodation at the mouth of the river," and that the surplus revenue of the dock—on which the "progress party" relied for effecting improvements—would be best disposed of by improving the river and existing works, or by reducing the dues. An amendment to this motion was proposed by Ald. Abbott, to the effect that the cost of a well-considered scheme of dock extension, the interest upon which could be provided out of the surplus revenues of the harbour, might be beneficially raised upon the guarantee of the borough rate; but this was rejected by 31 votes against 24; and Mr. King's resolution was adopted. In pursuance of its instructions, the Docks Committee shortly afterwards presented a report, recommending a reduction of the dues to the extent of about £6,000 a year. The report, clearly devised to tie the hands of the Council as regarded the improvement of the port, was adopted, and the dock dues were reduced in May, 1861. How an indispensable work was at length accomplished by private citizens, and how the Council had in the long run to retrace a selfish and reactionary policy, and to buy off the competition its own shortsightedness had created, will have to be related in future pages.

St. James's Market, Union Street, was reopened on the 26th June, 1858, after undergoing a complete restoration. The front elevation of the new structure was deemed even below the usual poor taste of civic erections in Bristol, and was for some weeks the object of mingled ridicule and censure.

About the end of June, Messrs. Baillie, Cave & Co., of the Old Bank, in extending their subterranean strong-rooms, discovered a large vaulted cellar of good mediæval architecture. The place was supposed by some who visited it to be the old crypt of St. Leonard's Church; but that building, as has been already recorded, was found under Stuckey's banking premises in 1851 [see p. 324].

At a meeting of the Merchant Venturers' Society on the 18th September, it was determined—subject to the approval of the Charity Commissioners—to purchase the vacated bishop's palace at Stapleton, and to convert the building into a school-house for the boys of Colston's School. The removal of the institution from the city was opposed by many persons as a flagrant repudiation of the intentions of its founder, who distinctly prescribed that the school should be maintained "for ever" in the mansion which he had purchased for it; and suspicions were expressed that the ulterior object of those promoting the removal was to divert the benefits of the charity to individuals in a rank of life far above those for whom it was designed. Especial attention was excited by the remarks of one of the prime movers in the matter, Mr. A. Hilhouse, who declared that the sons of working men were sufficiently provided for in national schools, and that the great want of the day were "schools for the poor sons of decayed good livers, such as bankrupt merchants, bankers, traders, deceased clergy, and other professional men." Mr. Edward Colston, the representative of the family, together with six past masters of the Merchants' Society, took the lead in protesting against the projected removal, declaring it to be "an entire breach of trust;" the mayor (Mr. I. A. Cooke), Mr. Langton, M.P., and many of the magistrates, aldermen, and councillors also presented a memorial against the design. The Charity Commissioners were, however, favourable to the views of the majority of the Merchants' Society, and an application to the Master of the Rolls (Sir J. Romilly) to prevent the removal was unsuccessful. Stapleton house and grounds were then acquired for £12,000. The Merchants' Society paid half of this amount, taking the land not required for the school. A large dining room and master's house were added to the premises, which underwent the needful modifications to fit them for the reception of 140 boys (an addition of twenty to the previous number) at a cost of £3,000. The scholars were removed to their new abode on the 21st October, 1861. The net income of the charity at that time was £3,433, and the expenditure (before increasing the number of boys) £2,421. Mr. Hilhouse's suggestion for the misappropriation of the charity was subsequently defeated by the action of the Endowed School Commissioners, to be noticed under a later date.

At the annual dinner of the Anchor Society, on Colston's day, Mr. Berkeley, M.P., at a time when a number of French military officers and some Paris journals were using menacing language towards this country, drew the attention of his hearers to the neglected state of the national defences. He contended that England ought to be always free from the danger of foreign invasion, and strongly urged the economy and general desirability of training the youth of the country to arms, as had been the custom amongst their forefathers. Mr. Berkeley subsequently ventilated his proposal through the press; and in January, 1859, a movement was started in Bristol which speedily spread to other towns, and assumed a national character. On the 2nd February a preliminary meeting took place in the city with the view to establishing a rifle corps, and at another gathering, 18th May, the mayor (Mr. J. Poole) presiding, the project assumed a definite form, a series of resolutions being drawn up and forwarded to the Lord Lieutenant, the Earl of Ducie, who was asked, but declined, to accept the office of colonel. It was then resolved that the mayor for the time being should be honorary colonel; Major Robert Bush, a retired army officer, was recommended as lieutenant-colonel, and Major Savile, of the local militia, as major. The corps was the first embodied in the kingdom. The Ministry of Lord Derby—in deference, probably, to the authorities of the Horse Guards—refused a grant for expenses, and declined to supply the volunteers with arms and clothing, although, as Mr. Berkeley observed in the House of Commons, this policy necessarily deprived the country of its strongest defence—the working classes. An application of the volunteers to be allowed to choose their own officers was declared to be inadmissible, and an attempt was made to prevent the various corps from being formed into regiments, the Horse Guards wishing to restrict the organisation to unconnected companies. The cost of the equipment was £10 a head. Nevertheless, by the beginning of July, 275 Bristolians had commenced drill; dresses and rifles were ordered from private firms; and the motto of the old Bristol volunteers —"In Danger Ready"—was again adopted. A pleasing incident of the movement was the concession by the majority of merchants, professional men, and respectable tradesmen, of a weekly half-holiday on Saturdays to their employés, many of whom joined the corps. The first parade took place in Queen Square on the 24th September, 1859, when over 600 men had entered the corps. The officers, who had by that time received their commissions, were as follows:—

Honorary Colonel, The Mayor of Bristol for the time being.

Lieutenant-Colonel, Major Robert Bush.

Major, Captain Henry B. O. Savile (who resigned in December and was succeeded by John Selwyn Payne).

No. 1 Company. Captain, Samuel Edward Taylor; Lieutenant, Edward Poole; Ensign, Richard W. R. Hassall.

No. 2 Company. Captain, John Bates; Lieutenant, William Britton; Ensign, James Gibbs.

No. 3 Company. Captain, William Wright; Lieutenant, Frederick F. Fox; Ensign, Frederick Pinney.

No. 4 Company. Captain, Colston Lucas; Lieutenant, William Fuidge; Ensign, George Ley King.

No. 5 Company. Captain, Andrew Leighton; Lieutenant, Perigrine Hammonds; Ensign, Edward M. Harwood.

No. 6 Company. Captain, Charles Ringer; Lieutenant, Alfred R. Miller; Ensign, Mark Whitwill.

No. 7 Company. Captain, Henry Goodeve; Lieutenant, Charles H. Prichard; Ensign, John C. Aiken.

No. 8 Company. Captain, John E. Pattenson; Lieutenant, Philip D. Alexander; Ensign, Charles Bevan.

Staff. Adjutant, A. M. Jones; Surgeon, Henry A. Hore; Quarter-master, Daniel Burges, jun.

Two additional companies were added in the early months of 1860.

No. 9 Company. Captain, James Ford; Lieutenant Alfred Elton, Ensign, Charles F. Ivens.

No. 10 Company. Captain, Boddam Castle; Lieutenant, John P. Gilbert; Ensign, Thomas Barnes.

The first building used for drill and depôt purposes was a portion of the vacant Royal Western Hotel, College Street. The erection of the Drill Hall in Queen's Road will be recorded under 1861. The first volunteer review before the Queen took place in Hyde Park on the 23rd June, 1860, when, of the 20,000 citizen soldiers present, Bristol contributed nearly a thousand. A review of local corps was held for the first time on Durdham Down on the 19th June, 1861. The original shooting range of the Bristol rifles was temporarily formed in Sneyd Park. The more extended range at Avonmouth was opened in April, 1865, in which year Lieutenant Colonel Bush, who had displayed much energy in the command of the regiment, resigned. He had, in September, 1862, been presented by the volunteers with a handsome service of plate in recognition of his services, and a second testimonial was offered to him on his retirement. Colonel Bush was succeeded by Colonel P. W. Taylor, who died in March, 1881. The next commandant was Lieutenant-Colonel S. E. Taylor, who resigned in a few months, when Lieutenant-Colonel A. M. Jones, who had been adjutant for several years, received the appointment.

At a meeting of the Council in January, 1859, Mr. Robert Lang suggested the establishment of drinking fountains in the chief thoroughfares of the city, for the accommodation of pedestrians, offering a donation for that purpose of £100. The suggestion met with cordial approval, and the first two fountains were erected about the end of June, one at the south end of Prince's Street, and the other on the Welsh Back. A few days later Mr. T. P. Jose erected a chastely designed fountain in the wall of St. Augustine's churchyard, and Mr. R. Lang was the donor of another, opposite the Bishop's College. About twenty more were given by various citizens in the course of the year. In 1876 a large fountain was erected on the Downs at a cost of 100 guineas, contributed by the local committee in connection with the local meeting of the Bath and West of England Agricultural Society. The most artistic fountain, however, was that constructed by Alderman Proctor, in the spring of 1872, at the top of Bridge Valley Road, to commemorate the liberality of the Merchant Venturers' Society in connection with the transfer of the Downs to the Corporation.

On the 4th January, 1859, a fire occurred in a tavern in Cider-house Passage (anciently Beer Lane), Broad Street, which caused the destruction of a mediæval hall, standing over the passage, and then used as a concert room. An etching of this building is to be found in Skelton's "Antiquities of Bristol," where it is erroneously designated "part of a monastery." The roof was of wood, supported by handsome groined ribs in the style of the latter part of the fifteenth century. The square-headed windows were of about the same date.

In March, 1859, a number of the inhabitants of Clifton resolved upon the erection of a chapel of ease to Clifton Church, in commemoration of the Rev. J. Hensman's fifty years' labours amongst them. The chapel, which was dedicated to St. James, but is more commonly known as the Hensman Memorial Church, was consecrated by Bishop Thomson, during his brief episcopate, in December, 1862, when Mr. Hensman was still incumbent of the parish. The cost of the building was about £3,000.

During the spring of 1859 the local Charity Trustees entered into correspondence with the Charity Commissioners in reference to certain proposed alterations in the scheme under which the Grammar School was governed. Although the success of the school since its re-organisation exceeded all hopes, yet through the slenderness of the endowment the head-master and teaching staff had been inadequately remunerated for their labours. It was consequently suggested that the fees paid by the elder class of boys should be slightly raised, that admission should not be restricted to youths residing in the city and suburbs, and that the head and second masters should be allowed to take boarders. The last-mentioned proposal was strongly condemned by a minority of the trustees; and, though approved by the Charity Commissioners, the Master of the Rolls, on an appeal for his interference, refused to give it his sanction. Mr. C. T. Hudson, the head-master, in consequence resigned his post in May, 1860. He was succeeded by the Rev. J. W. Caldicott, M.A., tutor and mathematical lecturer at Oxford University, under whom the school attained an unexampled reputation, the successes of its pupils in competitive examinations being in some years proportionably greater than in any other public school. Dr. Caldicott resigned his post in 1883, on being appointed to the valuable college living of Shipston, Worcester. He was succeeded by Mr. R. Leighton Leighton, M.A., who had taken high classical honours at Oxford.

In the month of March an American merchant ship put into Cork harbour, having on board Baron Poerio and sixty-six other Neapolitan patriots, most of whom had suffered ten years' imprisonment, without trial, in dungeons the character of which had been exposed by Mr. Gladstone to the horror of Europe. The exiles had been liberated by "King Bomba" by virtue of what he called an act of grace, on condition that they would transport themselves to America for the rest of their lives. Whilst on the voyage they compelled the captain to alter his course to a British port. After a short stay at Cork, the patriots made their way to this country in detachments, the first of which landed at Bristol on the 19th March, and was greeted with extraordinary marks of sympathy by all ranks and parties in the city. Mr. Langton, M.P., and the mayor (Mr. J. Hare) personally welcomed the party, who were entertained at the Angel Inn. Two further contingents, which arrived during the following week, received a like hospitable reception. During their brief sojourn, the fugitives expressed their fervent thanks for the generous treatment they had received. The incident excited great interest in all parts of the island, and a subscription started for the relief of the patriots produced a sum of over £10,700.

At a meeting of the Bristol Board of Guardians on the 8th April, a controversy which had been long carried on in reference to the desirability of building a new workhouse was concluded by a vote in the affirmative, the site selected being Stapleton. The plans of a Gloucester firm, who estimated the cost at £12,000, were adopted. On obtaining tenders, however, it was found that the lowest was several thousand pounds above the expected sum, and the opposition to the scheme was renewed. Eventually, in March, 1860, it was resolved to let the contract for £15,895, and the foundation stone of the workhouse was laid in the following July by Mr. J. Perry, governor. Large additions were made to the plans, and the outlay on the building up to August 1864 was stated to have exceeded £22,500.

The *London Gazette* of the 12th April announced that a baronetcy had been conferred on Mr. William Miles, of Leigh Court, many years M.P. for West Somerset, and chairman of the Somerset quarter sessions. Mr. Miles, who was highly respected by all parties for the sterling honesty of his character and the conscientious performance of his public duties, was by birth a native of Bristol, where he was the chief partner of a large private banking company. The most striking incident in his parliamentary career was his unsuccessful attempt to impose a duty on foreign cattle and meat, for the "protection" of English farmers. An anecdote illustrative of his candour and sincerity was narrated in the House of Commons on the 4th July, 1879, by the Right Hon. John Bright, who stated that, some years after retiring from Parliament, Sir William Miles, who had been an indefatigable opponent of the repeal of the Corn Laws, came up to him in the lobby and said: "Well, now, I may as well make a confession. Your friend Cobden and you are the best friends that the landowners ever had." Mr. Bright replied that he could tell the baronet another thing just as good was the great measure of 1846 (meaning the reform of the land laws); but Sir William, looking serious for a moment, said, "No: I have no faith," and walked away.

The Parliament of 1857 having been dissolved on the advice of Lord Derby's Cabinet, the nominations for Bristol took place on the 28th April. The Liberal members, Messrs. Berkeley and Langton, were again proposed; while the Conservatives, who had again become united, brought forward Mr. (afterwards Sir) Frederick Wm. Slade.* The contest, which was of an exciting character, resulted as follows: Mr. Berkeley, 4,432; Mr. Langton, 4,285; Mr. Slade, 4,205. In pursuance of a new Act, the expenses of the candidates were published shortly afterwards. Those of the two successful candidates were returned at £1,488, and those of Mr. Slade at £2,276.

On the 30th April, whilst the ceremony of declaring the poll was proceeding at the Exchange, one of the most destructive fires recorded in the history of the city broke out in the extensive sugar refinery of Messrs. Fuidge & Fripp, near the Stone Bridge. The flames rapidly spread over the

* Mr. Slade, though an able lawyer, does not appear to have sacrificed to the Muses. In a libel case tried at Bristol, he cast much ridicule on one of the parties in the action, for having made "one Boston, a weaver, talk about roaring like a sucking dove." It was clear, said the matter-of-fact counsel, that a dove could not have roared.

building, and damage to the extent of £80,000 was done before they could be subdued. The refinery was not rebuilt, and 250 workmen were thrown out of employment. A local paper, in recording the disaster, said, "All the sugar refineries in Bristol have now been burnt down once."

A remarkable sale of wine took place at the Grove, Brislington, in June, consequent upon the death of Alderman Henry Ricketts, a member of an old Bristol family, and the last survivor of a firm once extensively engaged in the manufacture of flint glass. The chief competition was for the port wine, which included samples of all the celebrated vintages between 1793 and 1836. "Magnums" of 1820 brought the unprecedented price of £3 8*s.* each. One lot of the vintage of 1812 fetched £18 10*s.* per dozen ordinary bottles. The entire stock of 180 dozen of port averaged £8 a dozen, the purchasers being chiefly Lancashire manufacturers. The other wines also sold at high prices.

The foundations of the first houses in what was subsequently called the Royal Promenade, Queen's Road, were laid about the end of June.

Up to this time the internal arrangements of Bristol cathedral, adopted in the reign of Charles II., were such as to prevent more than a handful of persons from attending divine service. There being no nave, the appearance of one was produced by cutting off a large portion of the space originally included within the choir. The transepts and aisles were also shut off, and formed mere ambulatories for strollers. The area actually available was thus reduced to the proportions of a small college chapel, and was chiefly occupied by stalls and pews; the only accommodation offered to persons who did not purchase the favour of the beadles consisted of narrow, unfurnished, unbacked benches—to one of which, as has been noticed, the Prince of Wales was relegated on his visit to the building. Dissatisfied with this arrangement, the dean and chapter applied to Mr. (afterwards Sir) G. G. Scott, the celebrated architect, for his advice. Mr. Scott recommended the removal of the organ gallery, which blocked up the centre of the church, the erection of the organ in the north aisle, the construction of a light screen at the end of the choir, the throwing open of the entire space east of the transepts, and the introduction of chairs, by which the number of persons taking part in the services might be increased from 300 to 1,000. A considerable sum having been raised by subscription, the work of reconstruction, which involved a complete clearance of the stalls, screens, etc., was begun in

April, 1860. On the walls being stripped of the woodwork and partially freed from whitewash, so beautiful a structure was disclosed that the work of thoroughly cleansing and repairing the edifice seemed a necessary consequence, though it involved further appeals to the citizens for assistance. The expense of the restoration was £4,600, towards which the chapter subscribed £1,550. [Such at least were the amounts stated in an official report read to a meeting of citizens in March, 1861. In a letter to the Cathedral Commissioners, dated January, 1885, the Dean of Bristol alleged that the restoration cost the chapter £7,393, and the public £5,474, "giving a total of £12,867."] The sedilia, destroyed about 1603 to make room for a monument to Sir John Young and his wife, was successfully restored, enough of the original design remaining to guide the carvers in reproducing the work. The only early relic destroyed was the heraldic pavement in the Berkeley Chapel—an inexcusable vandalism which cast discredit on those concerned. It must be added that the monument of Sir J. Young, which was of enormous size, was removed in fragments, and that nothing has since been done for its preservation. The cathedral was reopened, June 27, 1861, when the Corporation attended in state. Bishop Baring had been expected to occupy the pulpit on the occasion; but his relations with the chapter were not cordial, and he declined to be present. His lordship, who was translated to Durham a few weeks later,* preached only once in the cathedral during his episcopate—probably through unwillingness to admit the contention that his use of the pulpit was conditional upon the good pleasure of the chapter. Soon after the completion of the works, the condition of the central tower began to excite apprehension; and the chapter having set apart a sum of £6,000 for its restoration, operations began in 1865 with the massive piers supporting the tower, which were completely renovated. The later history of the building will be found recorded under 1866.

A chapel was built this year in St. James's Parade by the Scotch Presbyterians of the city, who had not previously possessed a special place of worship. It was opened on the 7th September, 1859, by the Rev. Dr. Macfarlane, of Glasgow.

* Dr. Baring, who had a large private fortune, displayed an amount of hospitality towards his clergy which is said to have been unprecedented in the history of the see. He resigned the bishopric of Durham, one of the great prizes of the Church, in 1878, owing to impaired health, refusing to accept the large retiring allowance to which he was entitled. His successor in Gloucester and Bristol was the Rev. William Thomson, rector of Marylebone, London, who was soon afterwards translated to the Archbishopric of York.

The cost of the building, including the site, was upwards of £5,300.

The great popularity of the rifle volunteers led to various suggestions for an extension of the movement. At length, on the Palmerston Ministry having informed the Earl of Ducie, Lord Lieutenant, that "an artillery corps for the city would not only receive official sanction, but would be considered a valuable adjunct to the volunteer force already established," a meeting was held in the Guildhall, on the 8th November, the mayor (Mr. J. Poole) presiding, to take the matter into consideration. Resolutions approving of the creation of a corps, and appointing a committee for that purpose, were unanimously adopted. The formal approval of the Government having been obtained, about 200 men were forthwith enrolled, and the first parade took place on the 31st December. The motto adopted by the corps was "Fidus et Audax." Captain H. B. O. Savile, then major in the rifle regiment, transferred his services to the artillery, of which he was appointed major commandant. The captains originally appointed were J. B. Harford, W. M. Baillie, H. Grant, and Capt. F. P. Egerton, R.N.; a fifth, W. H. Barlow, was nominated afterwards. The lieutenants were F. Tothill, S. V. Hare, H. L. Bean, G. Garrard, F. W. Savage, H. S. Ames, E. G. Langton, and C. D. Cave. In despite of the professions of the authorities in London, their real feelings towards the citizen soldiers were strikingly exemplified by the material which was forwarded for training purposes—four enormous siege guns of the obsolete type of the reign of George III., and utterly unfit for field practice, being sent down from Woolwich in April, 1860. Notwithstanding the disrespect evidently implied in the gift, the cannon were cordially received, and their removal from the railway station to the enclosure in front of the Victoria Rooms was made the occasion of an imposing volunteer demonstration. In the following month, the Secretary for War informed the town-clerk that it was the intention of the Ministry to restore the old battery at Portishead Point, for the protection of Bristol. Some trifling repairs having been effected soon after, the battery was used for ball practice by the artillery corps, which had previously resorted to some earthworks thrown up near Avonmouth. Buildings were constructed for stores, etc., in Whiteladies road, at a cost of about £1,100, and a drill hall was added in 1865 at a further outlay of £1,200. In the meantime, Major Savile had applied to the ordnance authorities for lighter and more serviceable guns, but his appeal was peremptorily refused. But in April, 1864, Mr. Berkeley indignantly commented in the House of Commons on the stupid perversity which had dictated the armament of the artillery corps, and the Government thereupon undertook that the shortcoming should be remedied. Some field guns of modern construction were subsequently forwarded to Bristol.

A large tract of ground lying between Stokes Croft and Grosvenor Place, which up to this time had been let in garden allotments, was laid out during the autumn of 1859 for building sites. The principal street, City Road, was commenced soon afterwards. A chapel at the western end of this thoroughfare was built by the Baptist congregation previously worshipping in the Pithay, at an outlay of £4,800. It was opened in September, 1861, by the Rev. C. H. Spurgeon, of London, then the most popular of dissenting ministers. Whilst the city was rapidly extending in this eastern suburb, building operations were proceeding on an extensive scale in Clifton Wood, on an estate previously belonging to Mrs. Randall, the last tenant in tail under the will of a member of the Goldney family.

The Prince of Orange, heir apparent to the throne of Holland, and reputed at the time to be a suitor for the hand of the Princess Alice, paid a brief visit to the city in February, 1860, on his way to Badminton. The prince was received at the railway station by the mayor (Mr. J. Bates), and by the newly organised volunteer rifle and artillery corps. Prince Jerome Bonaparte, cousin of the French emperor, paid a visit to the city in the following September.

The death was announced, on the 27th February, of Mr. James Palmer, who had held from youth until nearly the close of a long life a confidential position in the Old Bank, where, being of pénurious habits, he accumulated a fortune of about £180,000. By his will he bequeathed £20,000 to ten charitable institutions in the city, the residue being divided between a relative, who had kept house for him, and two private friends, both wealthy men. His other kindred, including the needy children of an uncle who had been his surety upon entering the bank, were passed over unnoticed.

Although the construction of high level reservoirs by the Water Company had rendered fire engines practically unnecessary in the lower portion of the city, the principal insurance companies continued to maintain the old apparatus. In March, 1860, however, the Norwich Union office availed itself of a simple but efficient "hose reel," devised some years before by a working fireman at Newcastle-upon-Tyne, and the economical arrangement was soon generally adopted.

A movement was started about this time for increasing the income of the vicarage of St. John, Broad Street, the value of the living being only about £50 a year. About £1,500 having been contributed, an arrangement was made with the Ecclesiastical Commissioners, by which a further payment of £79 yearly was assured to the incumbent.

In March, the authorities of St. Stephen's parish set about the renovation of the beautiful tower of the church. The structure had suffered much from natural decay, but more from the hands of ignorant churchwardens, all the delicate lattice-work attached to the pinnacles, and resting upon gurgoyles at the corners of the tower, having been deliberately cut away with a mason's saw in 1822, with disastrous results to the effect of the building. Plans of the original work having been preserved, its faithful reproduction was resolved on, and appeals were made to the public for funds to restore the lower storeys of the tower. The response was not sufficiently liberal to carry out the design in its entirety, but the restoration of the pinnacles and of the upper storey was effected in a creditable manner, the work being completed in September, 1862. About fourteen years later the interior of the church was restored; the walls of the aisles—barbarous constructions of 1704—were rebuilt, and an unsightly altar screen in a debased Greek style, which blocked up the east window, gave place to an appropriate reredos.

At a meeting held in Clifton on the 16th May, the mayor (Mr. J. Bates) presiding, it was resolved to establish, by means of a company, a first class public school for the education of the sons of gentlemen, members of the Established Church, and a provisional committee was appointed to carry out the object in view. The result of this gathering was the establishment of Clifton College. The capital was fixed at £10,000, in £25 shares; and a large piece of ground (including a public house called the Gardeners' Arms) having been purchased for £14,000, the erection of the "big school," designed by Mr. C. Hansom, soon after commenced. The cost of the building was £5,038. In January, 1861, the Council elected as head master the Rev. C. Evans, M.A., one of the masters at Rugby. After appointing several undermasters, however, Mr. Evans sought for and obtained the head-mastership of a school at Birmingham. The Clifton authorities thereupon appointed the Rev. John Percival, M.A., Fellow of Queen's College, Oxford, whose university career had been of almost unsurpassed brilliancy; and the college was opened on the 30th September, 1862, with about sixty boys. In 1866 a chapel was added to the buildings by Mrs. Guthrie, at an outlay of £5,000, as a memorial of her husband, Canon Guthrie, a zealous promoter of the college. [The chapel was in 1881–2 considerably enlarged.] In 1866 a new wing was added to the buildings, and in the following year a physical science school and gymnasium were erected. In 1869 Mr. Percival undertook to provide a library for the institution at his own cost; swimming baths were also built, and a sanatorium provided. In 1874 the assistant masters, the boys, and their friends added a museum to the library, and a preparatory school was erected. Many other additions were made from time to time. It was originally intended to have a "modern" school equal in size to the "big" school, but this was afterwards found to be unnecessary. The quadrangle, which formed part of the architect's design, was also given up. In 1886 a further extensive addition was made by the completion of the east wing, and the erection of a drawing school, laboratories, etc. The progress of the college exceeded the utmost expectations of its promoters; and in December, 1877, with a view to its establishment on a more permanent and unsectarian basis, and to place it on a level with the other great public schools, it was resolved to wind up the company and to petition the Crown for a charter of incorporation. This document was obtained in March, 1878. In the following October, Dr. Percival, on being appointed President of Trinity College, Oxford, vacant by the resignation of the Rev. S. W. Wayte, relinquished the head-mastership of Clifton, and was succeeded by the Rev. J. M. Wilson, M.A. (senior wrangler in 1860), then first mathematical master at Rugby. In October, 1879, Dr. Percival was presented with a costly and beautiful service of plate in recognition of his eminent services to the college, and of his successful efforts for the advancement of education in Bristol. The presentation was made by the Earl of Ducie. Dr. Percival was nominated to a canonry in Bristol Cathedral in 1882, but relinquished it early in 1887, having been appointed head-master of Rugby.

At the midsummer quarter sessions for the city, in 1860, leave was granted for the diversion of an ancient footpath in Tyndall's Park leading into Cotham Road, near Hillside. The application was made with a view to the formation of what is now known as Woodfield Road. From the legal notice given of the intended deviation, it appeared that the portions of the park over which the footpath ran were formerly known as "Cantock's Closes, Long-leaze, Claypitts, High-meadow, and Traitor's-well." In June, 1861, a new street through Tyndall's Park, connecting Whiteladies Road with Cotham Road, near Highbury Chapel, was opened for foot passengers.

Although occasional attempts had been made from time to time to revive public interest in the proposed Suspension Bridge at Clifton, nothing had really been effected since the abandonment of operations in 1843, caused by lack of funds, down to the period now under review, and it would be tedious to record the various schemes which were ventilated only to be thrown aside. In the spring of 1860, when it became known that the Hungerford Suspension Bridge, in London, another of Brunel's works, and of nearly the same span as that proposed at Clifton, was about to be replaced by a railway bridge, two well-known engineers, Mr. [Sir John] Hawkshaw and Mr. Barlow, believing that the material set at liberty might be successfully applied to the completion of the unfinished structure, arranged for the purchase both of the chains, etc., in London, and of the piers at Clifton, and then laid their project before the public. The opportunity of constructing the bridge at a cheap rate proved attractive, not merely to many Bristolians but to distant capitalists, and the shares of the proposed new company, with a capital of £35,000, exclusive of borrowing powers, were soon absorbed. [The sum of £2,000, in paid-up £10 shares, was accepted by the old company for the piers and approaches, which cost £25,000.] Sir J. Greville Smyth soon afterwards offered to give £2,500 towards the undertaking, provided that the bridge were increased in width from twenty-four to thirty feet, and this condition was assented to. A Bill to authorise the construction of the bridge was brought into Parliament in 1861, and passed without opposition. The object which Mr. Vick had in view when he made his celebrated bequest [see p. 131] was not, however, forgotten by Lord Redesdale, the chairman of committees in the House of Lords. Vick contemplated a bridge free from toll, and a large part of the funds subscribed in 1830 was given on the same understanding. Lord Redesdale therefore insisted on the insertion of a clause providing a sinking fund of £50 a year; and the promoters, much against their will, were compelled to acquiesce. The design of Messrs. Hawkshaw and Barlow for the structure was somewhat different from that of Brunel. The main chains on each side were increased from two to three; the girders were all of iron, instead of a combination of iron and wood;

and the anchorage was brought nearer to the piers, thereby shortening the land chains. Against these improvements, however, was to be set the bald, unfinished aspect of the piers, which Brunel intended to have finished in the Egyptian style of architecture, in the spirit of the great remains at Thebes. The towers were to have been cased with iron, decorated with figures illustrating the whole work of constructing the bridge and the manufacture of the material. The execution of this design would have involved an outlay of several thousand pounds. The works were commenced in November, 1862, as soon as the chains at Hungerford were set at liberty. During the following summer wire ropes were carried across the river and over the east side of the piers on each side, and upon these a platform of planks was laid, forming an airy bridge for the use of the workmen. This was finished on the 4th July, 1863. Another rope, slung above this fabric, had attached to it a "traveller" capable of moving a body of considerable weight to any part of the chasm. The eastern main chains were thus gradually put together, link by link, upon the platform, and as soon as this was completed the framework was shifted to the western side of the piers, where the remaining chains were laid in a similar manner. The next operation was to suspend to the chains the girders for the permanent roadway, and as this task could be prosecuted from both sides, it was soon successfully accomplished. On the 2nd July, 1864, when the last of the cross girders was fixed in the centre of the bridge, a small party was allowed to pass over by Mr. Airey, the resident engineer. In the following September a number of members of the British Association (including the celebrated traveller, Dr. Livingstone), then holding their annual congress at Bath, also visited and passed over the bridge. The permanent roadway was then being laid down, and towards the close of November the bridge was tested, preparatory to the visit of the Board of Trade inspector, by placing about 500 tons of stone on the centre of the roadway. The deflection caused by this weight was only seven inches, and it at once disappeared when the burden was removed. The formal opening of the bridge took place on the 8th December, and was celebrated with much rejoicing. A procession of trades and friendly societies—more than a mile in length—marched through the principal streets of the city, and then directed its course to Clifton Down, where an immense crowd of spectators, thousands of whom had thronged in from the surrounding rural districts, occupied every spot commanding the new structure. The procession which first passed over was headed by the contractors, the resident engineer, and the artisans by whom the work had been accomplished. These were followed by the volunteer corps of the city, the Lords Lieutenant of Somerset and Bristol, the bishop and clergy, several members of Parliament, the chairman, directors and engineers of the company, the mayor, Council, and magistracy, the members of the Merchants' Society and boards of guardians, the local fraternity of Freemasons, and lastly the procession of trades, etc. On the return of the vast party to Clifton Down, prayer was offered up by the bishop of the diocese; and the two lords lieutenant, each for his own county, then declared the bridge open for traffic. A grand banquet at the Victoria Rooms brought the proceedings of a memorable day to a close. [The bridge seems to possess an irresistible attraction to persons afflicted with suicidal derangement. The first suicide from it took place in May, 1866; since that date the roll of fatalities has increased to upwards of twenty. The most surprising incident connected with this mania occurred on the 8th May, 1885, when a young woman threw herself off the bridge, but was picked up uninjured on the right bank of the river.]

During the cricket season of 1860, the attention of lovers of the game was drawn to the unusually large scores made by Mr. E. M. Grace, a native of Bristol, who in the course of a year or two acquired a national reputation for his skill. In 1860 he played in thirty-two matches, and scored 1,372 runs. In 1861, in thirty-seven matches, he made 1,747 runs. In 1862 he played in thirty-six matches and scored 2,190. And in 1863 he was engaged in fifty matches and made 3,074 runs. One of his scores in those years reached 241, and twenty-four others ranged between 100 and 208. In addition to his batting exploits, moreover, he took 1,347 wickets, an average of more than four per innings. Subsequently his younger brother, Mr. W. G. Grace, achieved still greater triumphs in the game. In 1865, when only seventeen years of age, his skill was already so widely known that he was selected to play in the premier match of the year—that of the gentlemen against the players of England. Passing over many remarkable seasons, in 1871 he made 3,696 runs for sixty-three innings; and in 1876 he made in three innings, 400, 344, and 318 runs, though in two of those matches he was playing against the Kent and the York county clubs, two of the strongest in the kingdom. Down to 1879, counting only first class games, his scores reached a total of 20,832.

His bowling, moreover, was equally formidable, he having between 1863 and 1879 taken 1,349 wickets in first class matches alone, while in secondary games the results were still more extraordinary. In July, 1879, upon his partial retirement from the cricket field in order to apply himself to his profession as a surgeon, Mr. W. G. Grace was presented by Lord Fitzhardinge, on behalf of the cricketers of England, headed by the Prince of Wales, with a purse of £1,400 (to which this district had contributed £770) and a handsome clock, in testimony of their admiration of his achievements—which, so far as batting was concerned, had never been approached. The youngest brother of the family, Mr. G. F. Grace, was also invited to take part in first class matches before he had attained his sixteenth year. In subsequent seasons he became almost as famous as his brothers, and assisted in raising the fame of Gloucestershire cricketers to an unexampled height. A leading London journal, recording his premature death in his 30th year, spoke of him as "hardly second as an all round cricketer to any man in England."

In October, 1860, the *Dœdalus*, an old twenty-gun frigate, was ordered by the Government to be fitted up and sent to Bristol, for use as a training ship by the recently established Royal Naval Reserve. The ship arrived in the Floating Harbour in June, 1861.

At the annual Colston festival, in November, a proposal was started by Mr. G. W. Franklyn, M.P. (mayor in 1841–2) for the erection in the city of a statue of the great philanthropist whose birth was then being celebrated. The expense was estimated at £500, towards which Mr. Franklyn and another citizen offered £50 each. The proposition fell stillborn. In 1870, during the restoration of St. Mary Redcliff, it was suggested that the great window in the north transept might be appropriately filled with stained glass in memory of Colston. The proposal was received with coldness, but a sufficient sum was eventually obtained to carry it into effect.

A singular distribution of property took place in the city in December. In explanation of the affair, it is necessary to state that five of the large family mansions standing on the east side of Brunswick Square were built by what was called a tontine, established in 1786. The sum expended was 5,000 guineas, divided into 100 shares of 50 guineas each, held by as many lives. Although the speculation was substantially a lottery, the subscribers embraced many prominent Quakers, as will be seen by the following names: John J. Harford, John P. Fry, George Eaton, Thomas Mills, Edward

Ash, John Cave, John Godwin, Edward Harwood, Abraham Ludlow, Joseph Were, and Matthew Wright. The number of surviving lives having been reduced to five in 1860, it was determined that a ballot should take place, when Mrs. S. P. Anderson, of Henlade, became the owner of the largest house, No. 7; Mr. R. Ash got No. 8; Miss F. Wright had No. 9; and Alderman R. H. Webb, representing two lives in one family, was allotted Nos. 10 and 11. Brunswick Square was originally planted with elms, in which a colony of rooks soon established themselves. The trees, becoming old and dangerous, were cut down in December, 1858, when the birds took flight to the woods near Redland Court. Many of the trees in which they took refuge were destroyed in the spring of 1886, when the grounds formerly belonging to that mansion were laid out for building purposes.

About the close of 1860, the ancient Deanery, in College Green, was abandoned as a residence by the Dean of Bristol, on the ground of its alleged insalubrity. The house was afterwards occupied by the Young Men's Christian Association; subsequently a large portion was removed during the construction of Deanery Road.

The Bristol Pleasure Gardens Company, with a capital of £10,000 in £1 shares, came into existence towards the close of this year. About a twelvemonth later, the directors bought from the Rev. H. Richards eight acres of agricultural land at Horfield for £2,000, and converted the fields into a garden for public recreation. The place was opened with a fête given by the Order of Foresters on the 25th August, 1862, when 14,000 persons were present. The enterprise, however, proved unprofitable, and in February, 1871, the site of the garden was sold for £2,950. In September, 1873, the estate was purchased by the Corporation for £3,875, with the intention of erecting upon it a new prison for the city. The gaol, as will afterwards be noticed, was eventually erected by the Government.

In January, 1861, an attempt was made by the Rev. Precentor Caley, and a few other gentlemen interested in the restoration of the cathedral, to recover for that edifice the brazen eagle which Dean Layard and his colleagues thought proper to sell in 1802 [see p. 18]. It appeared that the lectern had never been used since its removal to St. Mary-le-port, and that the Rev. S. A. Walker, the incumbent, had emphatically declared he should never read from it. The reverend gentleman, however, changed his mind on the subject; and as the inscription placed on the eagle by Mr.

Adey stated that it was to remain "for ever" in the church, the vestry refused to part with the ornament. Mr. Caley then appealed for subscriptions to obtain a new lectern for the cathedral, but died in November, 1861, before the needful amount had been promised. An eagle was, however, erected in the cathedral in August, 1862, as a memorial of his services as precentor for nearly twenty-five years.

The first general collection in churches and chapels for the benefit of the Infirmary and Hospital took place on the 20th January, 1861. In a great number of cases the clergy and ministers at first declined to respond to the movement for a "hospital Sunday," and the total amount acknowledged in the newspapers at the close of the week was only £637, a large portion of which was contributed by the rural parishes. The institution has since been generally recognised. In 1847 only one congregational collection was made in the city on behalf of the Infirmary.

St. Bartholomew's Church, Union Street, was consecrated on the 22nd January. The building, which accommodates about 450 persons, cost, including the site, £3,600. By an Order in Council of the following April, an ecclesiastical parish, consisting of the southern portion of St. James's to the Horsefair, was connected with the new church. St. Luke's Church, Bedminster, was consecrated on the 23rd January. It had cost about £7,000.

At a meeting held in the city in February, to support a Bill then before the House of Commons for the abolition of church rates, Mr. H. J. Mills produced some statistics from a Parliamentary return to show, as he contended, that the enforced contribution to the Church dried up the sources upon which the Establishment might safely rely if they were left uncontrolled. There were, he said, only three parishes in Bristol where church rates were levied. In St. Augustine's £1,160 had been obtained by compulsion in seven years, while the voluntary offerings were only £150. In St. George's, Brandon Hill, force had secured £1,007 in the same period, while nothing had been contributed voluntarily. In Clifton, £1,942 had been levied by the tax, and nothing had been given. On the other hand, taking the comparatively poor parishes, St. Andrew's had obtained voluntarily, £277; St. Barnabas', £280; St. Clement's, £280; St. Matthias' £196; St. Paul's, £454, St. Philip's, £479, and Trinity £474: "making a total of £2,500 given in the poor parishes, against the solitary sum of £150 offered in the rich parishes where there were church rates."

In the spring of 1861 the Charity Trustees purchased some quaint old houses on the east side of Steep Street for the purpose of enlarging the adjoining almshouse, founded by John Foster. Plans for the complete rebuilding of the institution were obtained; but as the funds in hand were insufficient to carry them out, the trustees contented themselves with removing the houses in Steep Street, and with erecting the western wing of the hospital on an enlarged scale. Some years later a piece of ground at the back of the almshouse was purchased, and laid out as a recreation ground for the inmates. It was not until the summer of 1883 that the trustees were in a position to commence the reconstruction of the south and east wings, and the renovation of the interesting little chapel of the Three Kings of Cologne, which works were effected at a cost of £5,000. The design, which was praiseworthy, in spite of some meretricious details of a continental character, included the construction, under the almshouses, of four shops fronting Christmas Steps.

At a meeting of the Council on the 26th March, the Dock Committee reported that they had negotiated with the Society of Merchant Venturers for the surrender by the latter of their interest in the lease of 1764, under which the wharfage dues were held of the city for 99 years, at a rent of £10 a year. The Society having offered to give up the lease on the payment of a sum equal to one third of the net receipts during the three previous years, the committee recommended that those terms be accepted, and their proposal was approved. The Merchants' Company at the same time made a donation of £2,000 towards the erection of goods sheds upon the quays. These buildings, much ridiculed for their tastelessness, were commenced on the Broad Quay; a column bearing a sundial, which had stood there for at least two centuries, being removed in March, 1862, to make way for them.

The seventh national census was taken on the 8th April, when the population of the "ancient city" was found to be 66,027—the highest number it ever attained, later returns denoting a tendency to migrate from the central districts. The population of the extended city was 154,093. For purposes of comparison it may be stated that Clifton was credited with 21,735; the district of St. James and St. Paul, 9,944; St. Philip's, out, 31,753; St. George's, 10,276; Bedminster, 22,346; Mangotsfield, 4,222; Stapleton, 5,355; and Stoke Bishop tything, 5,623. In this census Horfield began to assume the importance of a suburb: containing only 119 persons in 1801, and only 328 thirty years later, its inhabitants had now sprung to 1,746.

The *London Gazette* of April 16, 1861, contained an official announcement of the creation of the 2nd Gloucestershire Engineer Volunteer corps. Mr. W. Harwood was appointed commandant; Mr. J. Pierson, captain; Messrs. B. S. Cooper and G. P. Marten, first lieutenants; Messrs. P. S. Protheroe and W. P. Wall, second lieutenants. The privates were at that time almost exclusively workmen in the employment of the Bristol and Exeter railway; but from 1870 the corps has been recruited from the artisan class generally. The first parade took place on the 6th July, 1861. [About the same date Mr. Berkeley commented strongly in the House of Commons on the perversity of the military authorities, who asked for a vote of £90,000 for the yeomanry cavalry, which Mr. Berkeley termed worse than useless, while only £42,000 were granted in aid of the volunteer movement throughout the kingdom.] Drills at first took place in the Exchange, and subsequently in a large house in Avon Street, Temple. Later on, premises were rented in Trinity Street, where, in 1883, a large drill hall was erected, together with an armoury and other buildings required for engineering practice, the outlay being about £2,500. The corps, which from its importance has been granted the title of the Bristol Engineer corps, then consisted of 671 officers and men, exclusive of the Clifton College Cadet corps, attached to the regiment, and numbering 81.

Up to this time, no attempt having been made by the civic authorities to water the streets of the borough, the nuisance created by dust during the summer months was a source of loss to many tradesmen, and of much discomfort to all classes. In Clifton some of the roads had been watered by private subscription; but the refusal of mean-spirited people to contribute to a work of which they enjoyed the benefit caused discontent and failure. At length, upwards of thirty memorials were presented to the Council, praying for the establishment of a general system of watering; and in April, 1861, the Board of Health Committee proposed that the main thoroughfares of the city, comprising a length of nearly twenty-four miles, should be dealt with, the yearly expenditure being estimated at £2,500. This proposal, which received the approval of the Council, caused dissatisfaction amongst the ratepayers dwelling in the non-watered thoroughfares, who contended that it was unfair to tax all the city for the benefit of only a part. At the next meeting of the Council, petitions signed by several thousand citizens were presented against the scheme, the people of St. Philip's out-parish especially protesting against an arrangement by which only three miles of road in their extensive district were to be watered, against eight miles of road in Clifton. The Council, submitting to popular feeling, determined to relinquish the project. The dust nuisance remaining unabated, in February, 1867, the Health Committee presented another report, recommending that £2,500 a year, equivalent to a rate of little more than a penny in the pound, should be voted for watering thirty-two miles of streets, including all the leading thoroughfares. The report was adopted, and the plan came into operation during the summer. No concerted opposition was offered on this occasion by the residents in the unwatered streets, but they speedily began to press the authorities to be included in the favoured area, and it was at last found necessary to make the system practically universal.

In the course of the parliamentary session of 1861, an Act was passed by which Cardiff, Newport, and Gloucester were exempted from the provisions of the Bristol Pilotage Act of 1807, and the pilotage service in those ports, hitherto compulsory, became voluntary. The Corporation of Bristol stoutly fought for the retention of the compulsory system, but without success. The management of the Bristol pilotage service, which had been in the hands of the Merchants' Society for about 250 years, was transferred during the summer to the Docks Committee.

An exhibition of industrial and ornamental art was opened on the 7th August in the Fine Arts' Academy. Although the value of the articles exhibited was estimated at £150,000, while the admission was fixed at sixpence, the public manifested great apathy towards the collection, which, though open nearly three months, was visited by only 24,000 persons.

An amusing action for what was legally called an assault took place at Bristol assizes on the 19th August. For a quarter of a century previously a contest had been waged between certain persons at Clifton and Mr. William Mathias, an eccentric parishioner, in reference to an alleged right of way between Rodney Place and Ferney Close (now Victoria Square). Mr. Mathias, the owner of the adjacent houses in Boyce's Buildings, admitted that there was a footpath, but denied the right of carriages to pass; and a wall which he erected to prevent the alleged invasion on his property, was thrown down, rebuilt, and re-demolished on numberless occasions. Eventually he erected an arch over the path, and set up an iron gate, when the old struggle recommenced over the latter construction, which was frequently removed and replaced. Although Mr. Mathias was a singularly impracticable man, his complaints of persecution against the Corporation and the Merchants' Society met with considerable public sympathy, the repeated injuries to his property being invariably committed during the night-time, in order to prevent him from tracing out and prosecuting the perpetrators, who were undoubtedly hired by persons in the background. The charge on which the action was brought against him was of an insignificant character. A lady had, it appeared, gone down the disputed path with a perambulator, which she had lifted over the iron barrier, when Mr. Mathias slightly pushed her on the shoulder, and ordered her to go back. The action, nominally prosecuted in her name, was really brought by the Corporation. The chief witness for the prosecution, Mr. George Ashmead, surveyor, admitted that when he made a survey of the city, thirty-seven years previously, there was a gate across the roadway in question, and that no carriage could have passed there without being lifted over. The vehicle stopped by Mr. Mathias being a perambulator—then a novel invention—no precedents could be adduced, and there was much legal contention as to the right of such a carriage to pass along footpaths. The absurd female fashion of wearing crinoline, an article which had just swollen to extreme monstrosity, was also amusingly introduced. Mr. Mathias's counsel asked if a lady whose dress spread the entire width of the path was to be turned back by a perambulator, upon which Mr. Justice Byles thought that a baby's carriage would not be half so formidable an obstruction as the meeting of one lady with another. Eventually the jury disagreed, and were discharged. The Council next resolved upon raising another action, though a memorial signed by several thousand persons protested strongly against what was termed the vindictive oppression of Mr. Mathias, and alleged—not without reason—that far more serious encroachments on public roads and footpaths had been winked at by the civic authorities. The case was set down for trial at Bristol assizes in August, 1862; but a compromise was previously arranged, by which the defendant retained his right to set up a gate, and the record was withdrawn. For several years afterwards, Mr. Mathias's name came frequently before the public in connection with his conflicts with the authorities, and he became locally known as "the general," from his astute and obstinate tactics in conducting "the battle of Boyce's Buildings," and other wars of a similar character. At length, in 1873, he was committed to prison for contempt of the Court of Chancery, having disobeyed an order to restore a roadway near Manor House, with which he had interfered. Mr. Mathias, who was then in his 92nd year, and had been reduced from affluence to poverty, was not released until he had undergone six months' imprisonment. As he disposed of the wrecks of his property about the same time, "the battle of Boyce's Buildings" came to an end.

Reviving a suspended scheme [see p. 291], the Council, during the autumn of 1861, resolved upon widening Bristol Bridge to the extent of about twelve feet on the eastern side, by removing the heavy stone battlement, and laying a new footpath upon iron cantilevers outside the additional space thus obtained. Two of the stone edifices erected for toll-houses were removed during the alterations, the plan of which provoked much public dissatisfaction, and even a suit in Chancery against the Corporation, instituted by some of the neighbouring tradesmen. Instead of following the convex lines of the bridge, the new footway was constructed horizontally, on the level of the highest portion of the curve, so that each end was some feet above the carriage road, and could be reached only by steps. The arrangement was so universally condemned that the Corporation were forced to remedy the unsightly blunder. Although the cost of the improvement was £5,000, it was complained that the alterations had been carried out with a striking disregard of architectural proprieties, and with a reckless indifference to picturesqueness of effect. The work of widening the west side of the bridge was commenced in March, 1873, when the two remaining toll-houses were demolished. As the stone balustrade was also taken down, and replaced by cast metal railing in harmony with the eastern side, the "lopsidedness" of the structure disappeared, though many citizens continued to complain that the bridge, in an artistic point of view, had been ruined. The structure was completed in June, 1874.

A new Congregational chapel, erected in Redland Park, was opened on the 4th September, with sermons by the Rev. Dr. Raleigh and the Rev. Dr. Vaughan. The edifice cost £4,700, and was described as unusually ornate in the interior, but its slate-covered spire was characterised by some critics as more prominent than beautiful.

The first local Post-office Savings Bank was opened at the

Clifton office on the 16th September. Some delay occurred in providing a similar institution in the city, but on the 10th March, 1862, an office was opened at the money-order office, then located in a shop in Albion Chambers, Small Street.

The Council having definitively refused to undertake works near the mouth of the Avon for the accommodation of large vessels [see p. 362], a scheme was proposed in the autumn of 1861 for initiating so urgent an improvement by means of private enterprise. The project—the chief promoters of which were Messrs. P. W. S. Miles, Robert Bright, and C. J. Thomas—took the form of a Bristol Port Railway and Pier, the line to commence near the Hotwell, and to terminate at a pier, to be erected at the mouth of the river, opposite to Dunball island. An Act to authorise the undertaking having been obtained in 1862, a company was formed, with a capital of £125,000 in £10 shares, very few of which, however, were subscribed for by the public. The construction of the line was begun by the turning of the "first sod" on the 19th February, 1863, and the railway was opened for traffic on the 6th March, 1864. The pier at "Avonmouth"—the new name given to the place—was completed about three months later.* The development of this undertaking into an extensive dock will be recorded later on; but it may be stated here that the railway has never returned a dividend to its proprietors. In 1869 a holder of a debenture bond for £10,000 demanded payment of his loan, which the company were unable to meet, whereupon the line was placed by the Court of Chancery in the hands of a receiver, and the proprietors have never recovered possession.

The record of the above pier affords a convenient opportunity for noticing a geographical phenomenon which has taken place within the memory of many persons still young, namely, the removal, so to speak, of a portion of the county of Somerset from the south side of the Avon, and its junction with the county of Gloucester on the opposite bank of the stream. In the chart of the Severn and Avon published by G. Collins in 1693, a large promontory on the Somerset shore of the latter river, nearly opposite to where the Lighthouse now stands, forced the stream before joining the Severn to make a sharp bend towards the north. In Donn's beautiful map of the environs of Bristol, issued in 1770, the course of the Avon is depicted as by Collins, but a thin line is figured

* Avonmouth hotel and pleasure gardens were opened on the 10th April, 1865, but the attempt to make the place a popular summer resort resulted in heavy loss to the original projectors.

as cutting across the promontory, and marked "the Swash," by which line, as we learn from tradition, light boats at high water could make a straight course from the Severn to Pill. No further change took place for nearly a century. In 1852, when Mr. Howard, the Bristol docks engineer, made a survey, "the only available channel for shipping was the 'North Channel,'" though "the Swashway was gradually becoming more used by small craft." The Swash had indeed become so deep that the northern end of the promontory had practically become an island, and had obtained the name of the Dunball. The construction of the pier mentioned in the preceding paragraph shows that its promoters felt no fear of the permanence of the North Channel. In fact, Mr. Howard stated (British Association reports for 1875), "the depth of water was good up to 1865, when the Irish and other steamers used to land their passengers there. Even in October, 1867, Captain Bedford, R.N., who was surveying this channel, found forty-two feet of water in it." An extraordinary change was, however, then taking place. The Swash rapidly deepened, and large ships were able to pass over it safely. On the other hand, the North Channel silted up with marvellous celerity, and when Captain Bedford saw it again in 1871, "he found only eight feet of water, showing an accumulation of thirty-four feet" since his survey four years before. In 1875 the silting had risen to forty-one feet,* and soon afterwards the North Channel disappeared altogether, while "Dunball Island,"—the end of the old promontory—had become indissolubly joined to Gloucestershire. The piece of ground in question, about twenty-five acres in extent, was, and indeed is, part of the parish of St. George, or Easton-in-Gordano. In March, 1886, a Local Government Board inquiry took place at Bourton, under the Divided Parishes Act, the result of which will probably be the separation of the spot from its former county and parochial connections.

The prospectus of the Bristol and Clifton Railway Company was issued in the closing months of 1861, and was received by the citizens with a wide measure of approval. The object of the promoters was the extension of the trunk lines of railway from Temple Meads into the city and to Clifton, and the connection of the railway system with the quays and Floating Harbour by means of tramways. The passenger line was to have crossed over Temple and Redcliff Streets and the

* Mr. Howard estimated that a million cubic yards of silt had accumulated within ten years.

Float to Queen Square, which was to have been converted into a central terminus, and from which a new branch line was proposed to be carried to the lower slopes of Brandon Hill, near Clifton. The capital of the company was fixed at £250,000, and the Great Western board undertook to subscribe a moiety of the amount, and to guarantee a minimum dividend of 4 per cent. yearly on the remainder. At a meeting of merchants and leading citizens, the project was cordially welcomed by the mayor (Mr. J. Hare), the master of the Merchants' Society (Mr. F. W. Green), and the president of the Chamber of Commerce (Mr. P. W. Miles); an influential committee was appointed to further its success; and a petition in its favour, signed by upwards of 5,000 ratepayers, was presented to the Council. Its reception by the "fixed property party" in that body was nevertheless of the most hostile character. It was alleged that the scheme, in conjunction with that for the port railway and pier, was an insidious device to divert the commerce of Bristol from the city; and a resolution approving of the line was defeated by the customary manœuvre of a reference to a special committee—26 members voting for the amendment, and 25 for the original motion. (The obstructive nature of the opposition was indicated by the fact that the appointed committee never even pretended to undertake the duties conferred upon it.) Subsequently, the anti-progressive party found that those tactics would not serve their end, as the promoters were enabled to proceed unopposed with their Bill in Parliament. The measure itself was then referred to the Parliamentary Committee of the Council, which body, after suggesting certain modifications in details, recommended that the Bill should be allowed to pass. Their report excited the intense wrath of the opposition, Alderman Ford—an extensive owner of warehouse property—designating the supporters of the scheme as "traitors to their native city." Nevertheless, the report was confirmed by 34 votes against 23, some of the absentees at the previous meeting being now present and turning the scale. The opponents of improvement next began an agitation out of doors, excited appeals being made to the citizens to resist the appropriation of Brandon Hill and Queen Square, and the "destruction" of the Float. Alarming pictures were also drawn of the danger of fire to which shipping and house property would be exposed if locomotives were allowed to pass through the city, and various other arguments of a similar character—equally remote, it was alleged, from the true grounds of resistance—

were incessantly urged upon the ratepayers. A large majority of the intelligent classes remained uninfluenced by the clamour, but the opposition, changing the field of battle to Westminster, paraded before the committee of the House of Commons as the defenders of local interests, and a crowd of witnesses, including "three respectable washerwomen" from Jacob's Wells, were brought forward to testify against the scheme. After a prolonged inquiry, the committee refused to approve of the preamble of the Bill, and the triumph of the anti-improvement party, though costly, was complete. The Great Western board, which had offered the city a great boon, relinquished the idea of a central station, and a project which many persons regarded as the most advantageous for its purpose ever devised was irrecoverably lost. The parliamentary expenses incurred by the promoters of the scheme were stated to have amounted to £12,000.

Another railway project of this date was promoted by the London and South Western Railway Company, who proposed to connect their system with the city by the construction of a new line from Gillingham, Dorset, through Frome to Temple Meads, thus opening out a large district in Somerset. The threatened invasion of its domain by a narrow gauge undertaking was stoutly resisted by the Great Western Company, which carried the war into the enemy's country by proposing to construct a broad gauge line to Southampton. The board also revived a plan for a railway from Radstock to Keynsham, for which an Act had been obtained several years before, but the powers of which had expired through effluxion of time. After a lengthy and expensive struggle in Parliament, the Bills of both companies were rejected.

The want of a commodious hall for public meetings, entertainments, etc., had long been painfully felt, the only building suitable for such purposes in the commercial part of the city—the Broadmead Rooms—being too small in regard to the population, besides being inconvenient in its arrangements and difficult of access. Upon the removal of Colston's School from St. Augustine's Place, the vacated "great house" was purchased by a few public-spirited gentlemen for £3,000; and the Colston's Hall Company, with a capital of £12,000 in £10 shares, was formed in November, 1861, for the purpose of constructing an edifice worthy of the city. The demolition of the great house took place in May, 1863, and shortly afterwards the directors of the new company entered into a contract for the erection of the large hall for the sum of £17,000. The hall was opened on the 20th September, 1867. The cost greatly exceeded the estimates, and so completely exhausted the resources of the company that the directors were unable to proceed with the other portions of the building. In 1869 a further sum of £15,000 was raised through the zeal and liberality of some ten or twelve of the original promoters, and the structure, in the complete form designed by the architect, was completed in February, 1873, the aggregate outlay having been £40,000.

The Bishop's College at the top of Park Street [see p. 141] was purchased in December, 1861, for £5,400, by Mr. Wm. Wright and Mr. James Ford, officers in the volunteer rifle corps, with a view to converting it into a head-quarters and club house for the use of volunteers. The project was cordially approved by the riflemen and their friends, and further expenditure being necessary to provide a drill-hall, class rooms, racquet courts, etc., it was determined to form a company, and to raise £10,000 by means of shares. The concern was soon after registered as the Bristol Rifles' Head-quarters Company. The apartments for the club were "inaugurated" on the 27th September, 1862, and within a few months 440 members were enrolled. The drill-hall, which cost about £2,500, and was then the largest hall in the kingdom having no intermediate support, was opened in October, 1862. In aid of the fund for its erection, the ladies of the city contributed handsomely to a bazaar in the following month, and succeeded in raising £1,300, which were handed over to the company, "in consideration of which," said the first report of the directors, "the corps had the use of the drill-hall for five days in the week, an armoury, orderly room, sergeants' room, store room, etc., at a very low rent." The rent fixed for the drill-hall and appurtenances was in fact £150, including gas, taxes, etc. At the outset the Head-quarters Company was prosperous; but from various causes the club lost many subscribers, and at last ceased to pay its way. The board, in the meantime, raised the rent for the drill-hall, etc., first to £200, and then to £250. At a meeting of the company in March, 1872, the directors reported that as the expenditure was £400 in excess of the income, it was advisable to let the club premises to private persons for £280 a year, and to further increase the rent paid by the volunteers. The sum mentioned by the chairman, Major Bush, as fairly chargeable to the corps was £295, exclusive of repairs, gas, and taxes, or, in plain terms, over £400 a year. It transpired during the subsequent discussion that the chief officers of the corps, Colonel Taylor and Adjutant Jones, had resigned their seats at the board in consequence of the decision of the majority, and that they maintained that the £1,300 produced by the bazaar was still the property of the volunteers—a contention which, though denied by the directors, was apparently held by nearly all who had taken part in the movement. Mr. Josiah Thomas, city surveyor, advised the regimental committee that their claim to the £1,300 had been practically admitted in a previous report of the directors, and that, taking this fund into consideration, the fair rent of the hall and appurtenances was £210, or, if the hall were given up to the company for four months in each year, £115. A lengthy controversy ensued, in the course of which the company gave the corps notice to quit the premises, while the latter threatened legal proceedings for the recovery of the amount they held to be due to them. Eventually an arrangement was made in 1873, by which the officers of the regiment undertook to pay £195 for the use of the hall for six months yearly, and for the occupation of the offices, etc., for the entire year, the company to be responsible for repairs and taxes. It was mutually understood that the question at issue respecting the bazaar money should be left to arbitration; but the matter dropped, and was not revived. The club has been twice reorganised since it fell under private management.

The unprotected state of the Bristol Channel had been for some time previous to this date under the serious consideration of the Government. There was not a single effective fort between Gloucester and the Land's End, nor was there any harbour, accessible at all times of the tide, into which a vessel pursued by an enemy could run for shelter. It was announced, however, in January, 1862, that the Government had selected, as the base for the construction of a line of fortifications protecting the ports in the upper part of the Channel, the hill known as Brean Down, projecting into the sea near Weston-super-Mare, which was to be connected with the promontory called Lavernock Point, on the opposite coast, near Penarth, by means of double batteries on the two well-known islands, the Steep and Flat Holmes, thus securing a cross fire of a formidable character, and virtually closing the gates of the Severn and its tributaries. The works, for which votes were granted by the House of Commons from time to time, were not finished until 1872. In the spring of the following year a garrison of about sixty artillerymen occupied the fort upon Brean Down, which, like the others, was armed with seven-ton guns. In 1874 the Bristol Artillery Volunteers were attached to the service of the forts, and annual encampments for training have since taken place on Brean Down.

A new electric telegraph enterprise—the British and Irish Magnetic Telegraph Company—was started about this time in competition with the Electric and International Company, which had a monopoly of the railway lines. The telegraph wires of the new concern were carried along the turnpike roads, the first line in this district being commenced in March, 1862, between Bristol and Birmingham. Another undertaking, the United Kingdom Telegraph Company, also made its way to the city, and opened a station in Corn Street.

A public meeting was held in the Guildhall on the 20th March, to consider the propriety of erecting a suitable memorial to the late Prince Consort. The mayor (Mr. J. Hare) presided, and, after several influential citizens had advocated the movement, a committee of fifty representative inhabitants was constituted to secure the erection of a statue in front of the Victoria Rooms, at an estimated outlay of £3,000. The subscriptions offered, however, were so small that they were ultimately returned, the committee at the same time expressing regret that while Dublin, Edinburgh, Liverpool, Manchester, Birmingham, and other towns had succeeded in similar projects, Bristol should be wanting in a monument to adorn her streets, and to testify her admiration of an illustrious prince.

The passenger steamer *Mars*, plying between Bristol and Waterford, was wrecked on the 1st April, whilst returning to this city, by striking upon Linney Head, near Milford, during a heavy gale. Thirty of the passengers and twenty of the crew lost their lives by this disaster.

An arrangement was concluded in June, between the dean and chapter of Bristol, and the Ecclesiastical Commissioners, by which the former body transferred to the latter (with a few reservations) the whole of its estates, in consideration of the receipt of a yearly sum of £6,796. The commissioners further agreed to provide £6,000 for urgent repairs and alterations in the cathedral [see p. 370]. The property retained by the chapter consisted of the deanery and other dwellings adjoining the cathedral, four houses in Lower College Green, the Upper Green and one house therein, the spring at Jacob's Wells, with its pipes, etc., and a small piece of land at Wapley. The chapter has had reason for congratulation that the transfer was negotiated before the setting in of the agricultural depression of later years. From some cause, the lands of the Gloucester chapter were not taken over by the Commissioners, and a Bristol journal of November 6, 1886, stated that, owing to the reduced value of the estates, the income of the deanery of Gloucester did not exceed £200, and that of each canon had sunk to £100 per annum.

On the 17th June a very brilliant military spectacle took place on Durdham Down. The day had been chosen for a review of the volunteer corps of Bristol and the neighbouring counties, and 6,746 men partook in the manœuvres. Amongst the regiments which had agreed to be present were the Gloucestershire and North Somerset Yeomanry, the Bristol, Gloucester, Newnham, Clevedon, Weston, and Cardiff Artillery, the Bristol and Gloucester Engineers, and the Bristol, Gloucester, Stroud, Tewkesbury, Cirencester, Forest of Dean, Stow, Moreton, Cheltenham, Pershore, Malvern, Evesham, Ombersley, Droitwich, Upton, Bromsgrove, Birmingham, Saltley, Bath, Keynsham, Temple Cloud, Taunton, Bridgwater, Wellington, Williton, Stogursey, Wiveliscombe, Yeovil, Crewkerne, Langport, Wells, Burnham, Weston, Frome, Shepton Mallet, Glastonbury, Wincanton, Somerton, Baltonsborough, Wrington, Salisbury, Swindon, Trowbridge, Chippenham, Bradford, Warminster, Melksham, Wootton Basset, Old Swindon, Highworth, Hereford, Ledbury, Bromyard, Archinfield, Leominster, Kington, Monmouth, Chepstow, Cadoxton, Dorchester, Wareham, Poole, Weymouth, Wimborne, and Sherborne rifles. Owing to the well-ordered preparations, the volunteers reached the ground at the appointed time and in good order; and the review, which was held before Major-General Hutchinson, passed off satisfactorily. A stand which had been constructed, capable of seating 5,000 spectators, was well filled, and it was computed that at least 100,000 persons witnessed the manœuvres.

The prospectus of the Clifton Hotel Company was issued in August. The capital was fixed at £40,000, in £10 shares. The intention of the promoters was to build the hotel on a site opposite to the post-office; but in the autumn of the following year the Bath Hotel came into the market, and having been bought by the company, together with several adjoining houses, the existing building was constructed on the site. The new hotel was opened on the 24th July, 1865.

At a meeting held in the Guildhall on the 21st August, 1862, the mayor (Mr. J. Hare) presiding, a resolution was passed, earnestly inviting the railway companies to reconsider the determination they were understood to have arrived at in reference to an expensive enlargement of the Temple

Meads terminus, and to co-operate in the construction of a joint station in some central situation in the city. A committee of citizens was also appointed to select an appropriate site, and numerous designs were subsequently prepared and submitted for approval. Of these the committee selected two—one of which, favoured by the "fixed property" party, was for a station at the Stone Bridge, while the other suggested a terminus in Frogmore Street. At another public meeting, on the 25th September, the Stone Bridge scheme was approved, and a prospectus forthwith appeared of the Bristol Central Railway and Terminus Company, with a proposed capital of £300,000 in £10 shares. A Bill to authorise the project was laid before the House of Commons in the following session, and it was stated that notices had been delivered to no less than 6,000 owners and occupiers of property affected by the scheme. A competing proposal, promoted, like the Bristol and Clifton plan of the previous year, with the object of uniting the trunk railways with the intended line to the mouth of the Avon, by means of a tunnel at Clifton, and a bridge near Cumberland Basin, was opposed in Parliament by the Corporation, at the instance of the fixed property party. The Stone Bridge scheme was withdrawn, it being found that none of the railway boards would give it either support or countenance. The other proposal was also abandoned. In the session of 1864 rival Bills were again introduced into the House of Commons. The promoters of port extension proposed to cover over the Avon to Bristol Bridge, to lay a railway over the stream, and to carry the line by Castle Street, Union Street, and the Pithay to Christmas Street (where there was to be a station for the city), thence under Brandon Hill to near Trinity Church (where the Clifton station was fixed), and finally by a tunnel to a junction with the port railway. The rival projectors proposed to cover the Float from the Drawbridge to the Stone Bridge, and to build a grand terminus on the site. The Bill for the latter plan was rejected by the House of Commons. The other scheme received the royal assent, but in consequence of the great outlay required for its execution (estimated at £700,000), no steps were ever taken to carry it into effect.

The civil war in the United States of America having entirely cut off the supply of raw cotton from that country, the manufacturing towns of the North of England were at this time plunged in deep distress. This district was also affected by the "famine," the Great Western Cotton Factory having been forced to close in October through lack of raw material, when 600 operatives were thrown out of work. Energetic efforts were made by the public on behalf of the sufferers, and upwards of £12,000 were subscribed in a few weeks, all classes contributing liberally to the fund. The factory was not reopened until the spring of 1865.

At a meeting of the Council in October, the Docks Committee presented an important report, recommending extensive and costly improvements in the Avon and the Floating Harbour. The document was based on plans furnished by Mr. Howard, the engineer to the docks, whose chief recommendations were the deepening of the bed of the river to the extent of seven and a half feet for four and a half miles below Cumberland Basin, and the construction of a new basin for steamers at Rownham, the cost of the proposed works being £557,000. The committee estimated that the annual interest on this sum, which would become a charge on the dock estate, would be £22,300, being £16,300 in excess of the actual receipts. This deficiency they proposed to meet by imposing dock dues on corn and provisions, hitherto exempt, by reimposing half the dues taken off in 1861, and by charging a rent on vessels lying in the harbour, the three items being expected to yield £9,000. The wharfage dues about to fall in were estimated to produce £3,000, and £2,000 more were expected from increase of trade. The balance of £2,300 was to be provided by an increased tax on the ratepayers. The report caused a great sensation, for it was the production of a party which had hitherto opposed every scheme of port improvement on the ground that the dock dues should be kept down, and that the ratepayers should not be further taxed for the maintenance of the harbour. The Council, however, by a majority of 32 votes against 15, adopted the report, and resolved on applying to Parliament for the necessary powers. The excitement of the public, already considerable, was increased upon the discovery that in the Bill laid before the House of Commons the amount proposed to be spent had been increased by nearly a quarter of a million sterling, or to £800,000, on the plea that considerable improvements were needed in the Floating Harbour. Meetings of the ratepayers were held in each ward, at which the scheme was condemned by large majorities. The Chamber of Commerce also vigorously opposed the measure, and the minority in the Council renewed their protests. In the result, the promoters reduced the intended expenditure to £400,000, of which, £125,000 were to be spent in deepening the river. A motion to withdraw the Bill altogether was defeated in the Council by 36 votes against 24; another, to proceed with it, was carried by 33 votes against 26. The opponents of the scheme renewed their efforts before a committee of the House of Commons, where it was affirmed on their behalf that the project had been proposed simply to thwart the construction of docks at Kingroad. After a protracted inquiry, the committee rejected the Bill.

The church of Emmanuel, St. Philip's, was consecrated on the 9th December. It had cost about £3,000 in construction, exclusive of the site.

A Bill for authorising the construction of a dock near the mouth of the Avon was laid before Parliament in the session of 1863. The chief promoters of the intended "Bristol Port and Channel Dock Company" were Messrs. Robert Bright, Robert Bush, Philip W. S. Miles, Charles Nash, Henry A. Palmer, Christopher J. Thomas, and Thomas T. Taylor—all or nearly all of whom were promoters of the previous Port Railway and Pier scheme. The share capital was fixed at £295,000 in £20 shares, with power to borrow £98,000. When the advocates of port improvement had proposed that a Channel dock should be constructed by the Corporation, the fixed property party had constantly declared that their resistance was based on an unwillingness to impose fresh burdens on the ratepayers, and that if a private company would undertake the work it would meet with no opposition. But these assertions were now repudiated, and at a meeting of the Council on the 7th January a resolution to strenuously oppose the Bill, as an attempt "to deprive the citizens of their rights and privileges," was carried by the advocates of a stand-still policy, an amendment in a contrary sense being rejected by 28 votes against 25. After a lengthy struggle before a committee of the House of Commons, the Bill was rejected.

Before continuing the history of the Avonmouth project, it will be convenient to notice the early schemes in connexion with Portishead, and the incidents which led to the creation of a rival harbour at that place. Many years before Channel docks were thought of, engineers had suggested the construction of a pier at Portishead for the accommodation of shipping, Mr. Milne's plan of 1832 being followed in 1839 by that of Mr. (afterwards Sir) John Macneil, for which an Act of Parliament was obtained, at the instance of Mr. James A. Gordon, in July, 1841. The project having proved abortive through defects in the design, Mr. Brunel, in May, 1845, propounded another scheme, for a floating pier near Portbury, with a railway (on the atmospheric principle) to Bristol. The Portbury Pier and Railway Company, with a capital of £200,000 in £50 shares, was formed to carry out this proposal, for which an Act was obtained in 1846; but after the promoters had striven earnestly to obtain the necessary funds, they announced in February, 1852, that they had abandoned the enterprise, and the company was wound up during the following summer. In 1853 a Mr. Croome produced a scheme for two gigantic docks of fifty acres each, with a canal to the Avon, at Pill; a rival plan, for a dock in Portishead pill, was produced in the same year by a Mr. W. R. Neale. Although all these propositions were severally commended to the attention of Bristolians on the ground that the Portishead estate of the Corporation would be vastly increased in value by the creation of a new harbour, none of them met with much countenance from the advocates of port improvement, and the failure of each in succession appears to have excited no regret. When it was found, however, that the promoters of the Port Railway and Pier were preparing to develop their project into a dock, their leading opponents, including Aldermen Ford and Robinson, Mr. Mich. Castle and Mr. Rich. Fry, most of whom had contended that the creation of shipping accommodation at Kingroad would be absolutely destructive to the commerce of the city, set about the formation of the Bristol and Portishead Pier and Railway Company, with the view, as their critics mockingly maintained, of averting the doom of Bristol by duplicating the machinery which was to ruin her. The pier was proposed to be of about the same dimensions as that projected by Mr. Brunel in 1845. The Bill authorising the works met with little serious opposition, and received the royal assent in June 1863. The construction of the works began in the following year. Amongst the buildings removed during the laying out of the railway were two or three dwellings (called in the old directories "chocolate houses") on the shore of the Avon, nearly opposite to the Hotwell, which were amongst the most favourite summer resorts of working men and their families. Much apprehension was expressed by lovers of the picturesque that the construction of the railway would destroy the beauty of the Leigh Woods scenery; but Alderman Ford declared, at a meeting of the company, that those fears were wholly unfounded. "He believed that no better security could be taken for the preservation of the beauty of the woods than the construction of the railway, as it would put a stop to the quarrying and blasting which had so much damaged them" —an assertion which can be read only with a sigh by those who witness the wholesale havoc now being committed by the Corporation of Bristol and other tenants of the landowner. The Portishead railway was opened on the 18th April, 1867. The tidal section of the pier was opened in June, 1868, and the low-water extension—for which another Act had been obtained—in April, 1870. The total cost of the works up to that time had been about £290,000.

Although somewhat interfering with the chronological character of this volume, it may save the reader trouble to continue the narrative of the "battle of the docks" until the close of the struggle. In the session of 1864 the promoters of the Port and Channel Dock again applied for parliamentary authority to proceed with the undertaking. Since the conflict of the previous year, the annual municipal elections had significantly tested the feeling of the ratepayers, six or seven of the opponents of the Avonmouth Bill having been rejected on soliciting re-election as councillors. Conciliatory negotiations, moreover, had taken place between the cooler heads of the two parties in the civic body. The promoters of the Channel dock offered to surrender to the city a portion of the dues to be levied on goods and shipping, while the inability of the Floating Harbour to meet the growing requirements of commerce was acknowledged by some who had hitherto resisted improvement. The Parliamentary Bills Committee of the Council consequently changed its attitude, and now suggested that "dearly-bought experience ought to satisfy all parties of the folly of prolonging a fruitless contest." The advice was disregarded by the uncompromising section of the "fixed property" party, an amendment with dilatory objects being proposed in the Council, but the committee's report was approved by 33 votes against 18. The Bill was nevertheless obstinately resisted before a select committee of the House of Commons, the opponents professing to represent fixed property worth £20,000 a year (out of an aggregate annual rental of £600,000). After a long hearing, the preamble of the Bill was approved by the committee, and the measure soon after passed the Lower House. A closing effort in the Council was then made by the anti-progress minority, but they were again unsuccessful, and with a final protest by Alderman Ford, who declared that the proposed docks were "fraught with the greatest peril to the trade and prosperity of the city," the opposition sulkily quitted the field, and the Bill became law. The local controversy on the question had been raging with little intermission since the fierce debates of 1859 [see p. 360], and it is now difficult to realise the amount of ill-feeling excited during the contest. The *Bristol Times* of May 7, 1864, remarked that the question had been "like a sort of nightmare on the society of the city. Worse than politics, because more bitterly fought, more personally fought, it has cooled if it has not quite destroyed many friendships, and certainly broken up many associations. . . . [The struggle had been] of a character to break up old acquaintances, to chill conviviality, to make men look pale and spiteful at one another when it was introduced at table, and to feel a personal irritation in discussing it which perilled the preservation of good manners amongst a company." Owing to the financial collapse of 1866, the promoters of the dock were for a long time prevented from proceeding with the undertaking. In 1868, however, the Bristol Port and Channel Company was definitely constituted, Mr. P. W. Miles becoming chairman, and Mr. Charles Nash vice-chair of the board of directors, which embraced, in addition to the gentlemen mentioned in a previous page, Messrs. H. H. Goodeve, Wm. H. Wills, and Mark Whitwill. It was announced that the dock, with the surrounding quays and warehouses, would be seventy acres in extent, and that the land had been purchased at a reasonable price from the Corporation, Mr. P. W. Miles, Mr. G. Cox, and others. The first sod of the undertaking was cut on the 26th August, 1868, by the chairman of the company, and earnest appeals were addressed to the citizens to assist by their subscriptions in furthering the progress of the works. The attitude of the promoters of the Portishead scheme, however, was well calculated to deter cautious capitalists from taking such a course. After promulgating many warnings through a sympathetic newspaper, the directors of the Portishead Pier and Railway Company announced in November, 1870, that the time had arrived for providing a dock at Portishead for the accommodation of the largest class of ocean steamers. It was alleged in support of this decision that the advantages of the site were unequalled, and that as the pier works had been constructed with a view to their forming part of a complete scheme, the cost of the intended dock and its accessories would not exceed £160,000. The announcement of the board did not surprise those who had carefully watched its movements, for in despite of the vehement assertions of its leaders that Channel docks were unnecessary, and that Bristol would be ruined by their construction, it was plain that the pier was intended only as a stepping-stone to greater things. In the Bill laid before the House of Commons the promoters sought to confer power upon the Council to contribute £100,000 towards the construction of the dock, undertaking to give the Corporation as many directors on the board as were appointed by the shareholders. By this time it had become clear that the Avonmouth Dock, through lack of financial support, could not be finished within the period allowed by statute, and, concurrently with the Portishead measure, a Bill was prepared by the rival board, to obtain an extension of time for the completion of the work, and to empower the Council, if it thought fit, to contribute to the undertaking (the Docks Committee having already recommended a vote of £100,000). It appeared that the total amount subscribed up to that date was about £120,000, the chief subscribers being Mr. P. W. S. Miles, £10,000; Mr. Morley, M.P., £5,000; the Merchant Venturers' Society, £2,500, and Messrs. J. W. Miles, W. H. Wills, Francis Tagart, C. Norris, and Robert Bright, £1,000 each. Amongst the subscribers to the Portishead scheme were Sir J. Greville Smyth, bart., £15,000; Messrs. J. Ford, R. Fuidge, and G. R. Woodward, £6,000 each; Mr. Lewis Fry, £5,000; Mr. J. D. Weston, £2,500; Mr. T. Canning, £2,000; Mr. R. Fry, £1,500; and Messrs. J. C. Wall, S. Wills, Finzel & Sons, W. Fuidge, and James & Pierce, £1,000 each. "The battle of the docks" was waged vigorously before committees of both Houses, but neither party was successful in preventing the other from obtaining its Act. The conflict was next transferred to the Bristol Council Chamber, to which each company appealed for a subscription in aid of its funds. The remnants of the old fixed property party were soon defeated, their resolution declaring that any grant to either dock was inexpedient being rejected by 38 votes against 18. Thereupon, throwing aside their former arguments, the party went over to the Portishead camp, and secured it an easy victory. On the 1st July, 1872, Mr. E. S. Robinson moved the appointment of a committee with a view to the Corporation becoming interested, by purchase or otherwise, in the completion of the Avonmouth undertaking, affirming—with only too accurate foresight—that a divided jurisdiction would revive the evils created by the old Dock Company, and would be strongly disapproved by the citizens. His motion was rejected by 33 votes against 22. Alderman Hathway then proposed that £100,000 should be subscribed by the Council to the funds of the Portishead Company, and this was carried by 36 votes against 19. In order to soothe the susceptibilities of the ratepayers, the subscription was made a charge on the dock estate, which at that time showed a large yearly surplus; though, as will be shown hereafter, the burden (from which no profit was ever derived) was laid upon the backs of the inhabitants in 1880. In consequence of this decision, which caused much surprise and dissatisfaction amongst the citizens, the directors of the Avonmouth scheme were plunged in extreme embarrassment through lack of funds, and to the delight of their opponents the work of construction was practically suspended. In August, 1873, however, the directors announced that they had made arrangements with a contractor for completing the dock, and operations soon after vigorously recommenced. In August, 1876, when on the eve of completion, the dock was the scene of a disastrous landslip, caused by the treacherous bed of an old "pill" running under the east wall, about 400 feet of which collapsed, together with two large warehouses. The reparation of this disaster was not effected for some months. The progress of the Portishead project had been also arrested by an accident. After having been furnished with funds by the Corporation, the directors—promising the rapid completion of the dock—set about the preliminary works, the most important of which was a huge dam for excluding the waters of the Channel. On the 15th February, 1874, the dyke, then nearly finished, gave way under the pressure of a high tide, causing extensive havoc; and the task of damming back the Severn was not achieved until June, 1875. Through the delay thus occasioned, the Avonmouth scheme recovered its original lead in the competition; and the dock was formally opened on the 24th February, 1877. The directors obtained the use of a large steamer, the *Juno*, to convey the mayor (Mr. G. W. Edwards) the members of the Council and of other public bodies, and many of the leading citizens, to the mouth of the river, the party numbering about six hundred. A great concourse of spectators lined the banks of the Avon for nearly two miles, while about 15,000 persons assembled near the dock and greeted the *Juno* upon her arrival with repeated cheers. Having steamed around the basin, the vessel was brought up in front of one of the warehouses, when a short prayer was offered by the Archdeacon of Bristol (the Rev. Canon Norris). The mayor then declared the dock open, and complimented the directors on the successful termination of their arduous and public-spirited exertions. Owing to the proverbial exigencies of the tide, the ceremony was very brief, and the visitors returned immediately to Bristol. In the evening the mayor gave a grand banquet in the Merchants' Hall in honour of the occasion. Much rejoicing took place at Shirehampton and Pill in the course of the day. The first commercial vessel which entered the dock was the steamer *Evelyn,* which arrived on the 8th April, with 1,500 tons of barley. It was hoped by the Portishead board that their undertaking would be opened in the summer of 1878. On the 18th March of that year, however, another serious disaster took place, a large portion of the nearly completed dock wall falling over, while a further portion showed so many rents as to require reconstruction. This entailed great delay, and an additional outlay of about £30,000. By dint of energetic efforts, the undertaking was completed in the following year, and the passenger steamer *Lyn* entered the basin, amidst much local rejoicing, on the 28th June, 1879. The first foreign arrival, about a week later, was a steamship named the *Magdeburg,* with a cargo of 1,100 tons of barley. Both the Avonmouth and the Portishead companies undertook to pay to the Bristol Dock authorities 50 per cent. of their dues on all sailing vessels under 1,200 tons and on all steamers under 800 tons entering their docks. It will be seen under a later date that this attempt to safeguard the interests of the Floating Harbour proved ineffectual.

Another of the numerous schemes which absorbed local attention during the session of 1863 was the Bristol and North Somerset Railway, a project for opening out a large district of Somerset by means of a line from Radstock to Bristol, and also for facilitating commerce in the city by means of a tramway from the quays to the terminus. The Bill received the royal assent, and a company to carry its powers into execution was soon afterwards formed, with a capital of £275,000 in £20 shares. Only about £16,000 of this amount, however, was actually subscribed. The first rail of the tramway was laid by the mayoress (Mrs. S. V. Hare) on the 8th October, 1863. Pecuniary difficulties soon after arose, and flung the company into extreme embarrassment. The first contractors for the works quarrelled with the directors and withdrew; their successors became insolvent; and the financial crisis of 1866 for a third time caused a lengthy suspension of operations. The company made repeated but fruitless attempts in Parliament to connect their railway with the narrow gauge systems on the south coast. In 1866 the directors, abandoning hope in this direction, concluded an agreement with the Great Western board, by which the latter undertook to work the line when completed.

At an early period of the company's financial difficulties, some of the directors, in their zeal to further the undertaking, made themselves individually responsible for a sum of about £180,000—part of the liabilities of the concern—with the effect of completely ruining themselves. A report presented by a committee of investigation in May, 1867, was an astounding revelation of mismanagement, the conduct of the secretary, a parliamentary agent, named John Bingham, being especially censured. Amongst the items of the company's expenditure, a charge was discovered of £28,634 for legal and parliamentary expenses, and another very heavy bill of the same character remained unpaid. [Bingham, who sought to gain popularity by making "Church and Queen" orations at political dinners, and by delivering unctuous addresses at religious gatherings, pleaded guilty in June, 1870, to a charge of having forged an endorsement on a draft for £536, with intent to defraud Mr. Wm. M. Baillie, a Bristol banker, and was sentenced to twelve months' imprisonment with hard labour.] In 1869 an Act was obtained for relieving the company from its liabilities by paying off the creditors in shares, power being also obtained to complete the undertaking by the issue of debentures. The creditors assented to this arrangement, which enabled the directors to make a new contract for the completion of the railway. The tramway to Wapping was definitively abandoned in May, 1871, by an agreement with the Corporation. The railway was opened on the 3rd September, 1873, when it was worked by the Great Western staff. The receipts, however, were disappointing to the promoters, and fresh financial embarrassments arose. In 1881 a new board of directors was appointed, the chairman of which stated soon afterwards that the former board, which had refused to meet the shareholders, and finally deserted them, had left the concern in a "state of chaos," the books having disappeared. A creditor had brought an action against the company, and, as there were no effects, the Court of Chancery had appointed three of the new directors receivers and managers. There was not a sixpence in hand, the Great Western authorities retaining all the receipts. The old board had divided £900 a year amongst themselves. Shortly after those disclosures, attempts were made to sell the line to the Great Western Company, when the latter offered the ordinary shareholders a permanent dividend of 12*s*. per cent. per annum. The proposal was not accepted. At length, by an agreement arrived at in 1884, the line was purchased by the Great

Western board, the proprietors accepting 17 per cent. on the nominal value of their shares.

Dr. Wm. Thomson, Bishop of Gloucester and Bristol, having been translated to the archbishopric of York, Dr. Charles John Ellicott, Dean of Exeter, was in February, 1863, nominated as his successor.

A prospectus appeared in March of the Bristol City Hotel Company, with a capital of £30,000 in £10 shares, the intention of the promoters being to purchase the well-known White Lion establishment in Broad Street, and to build a new hotel on the site. In the following July the directors, being unable to obtain immediate possession of the property, purchased the adjoining White Hart Hotel, in which they commenced business. An ancient inn, known as the Plume of Feathers, near the White Hart, was also acquired about the same time. Two years later the lease of the White Lion fell in, and the house was demolished. The purchase of the three properties, and the cost of the cellars and foundations, however, had exhausted the original capital, and it was found that the completion of the extended design would require a further expenditure of £35,000. The directors in the first place proposed to create new shares to the value of £45,000, but as the public declined to subscribe, the board decided to issue debentures for £35,000. This form of investment meeting with little more favour than its forerunner, the company were compelled, in June, 1867, to fall back upon a less costly scheme, by which a row of shops was placed upon the ground floor, the cost of the structure in this form being estimated at £25,000. The hotel was opened in January, 1869, but the expense of the building had exceeded the estimates by several thousand pounds, and the concern narrowly escaped a compulsory liquidation. In 1874, when the business of the hotel had become prosperous, the Plume of Feathers inn was ordered to be rebuilt at a cost of £2,500. The name of the hotel was at the same time altered from the White Lion to the Grand Hotel.

The marriage of the Prince and Princess of Wales on the 10th March was celebrated in Bristol with universal manifestations of joy. A committee had been previously appointed, and liberally furnished with funds to provide recreation and amusement for all classes; a general holiday had been determined upon with one consent; and the entire community seemed to give itself up to merry-making. In the morning a parade of the volunteer riflemen, artillery, and engineers took place on Durdham Down, where the members of the Oddfellows and Foresters benefit societies also repaired in procession with numerous bands of music. It was computed that upwards of 30,000 persons were present. Rustic sports followed the military pageant. The children of nearly all the schools in the city were gathered in various suitable localities, and, after singing the national anthem, each scholar received some memento of the day. Dinners were given or provisions distributed to upwards of 10,000 poor persons, and the inmates of the almshouses were suitably entertained. The most attractive features of the rejoicings, however, were the firework displays and the illuminations in the evening. All the public buildings and most of the large places of business, as well as numbers of private houses, were brilliantly lighted up with designs and transparencies in almost infinite variety; and the central streets were one continuous blaze. Those thoroughfares were densely thronged until midnight, and the scene was one of extreme animation and gaiety. The displays of fireworks were numerous and effective, and the electric light—then in its infancy—added a new feature to such exhibitions. The evening concluded with a ball at the Assembly Rooms. The ladies of Bristol made a magnificent present on the occasion to the Princess of Wales. It consisted of a large sapphire pendant, set in diamonds, and valued at 800 guineas; and was placed in an elegantly carved casket of oak, taken from St. Mary Redcliff Church, ornamented with ivory and gold. Speaking of this casket, the *Times* observed that "as a work of art it was as noteworthy, and quite as beautiful, an offering as the jewel itself." The gift, accompanied by an appropriate address, was presented to the princess by the mayoress (Mrs. S. V. Hare), who was introduced by the Duchess of Beaufort. Her Royal Highness expressed great admiration of the present, for which she gracefully returned thanks.

At the annual Easter vestry of the parish of Clifton, a document produced by one of the churchwardens gave a noteworthy account of the financial difficulties of the authorities. Great objections, it was stated, were made to the payment of church rates, on the ground that the church was for the most part a proprietary building, and that many owners of the pews declined to contribute towards the maintenance of divine worship. An appeal had been made to them on the subject, but about eighty proprietors had either positively refused to subscribe, or had returned no reply. The largest pew owner, holding thirteen seats, declined to render any assistance, because his family had invested a large sum in building vaults in the crypt, which, under the recent Burials Act, could not be used. Another had become a Dissenter, and felt "conscientious scruples" against contributing towards the services of the church, though his conscience did not prevent him from collecting his pew rents. The majority of the pew owners lived beyond the parish boundary; some resided permanently abroad; others in various distant parts of the kingdom; and several had angrily rejected the appeal for help, practically contending that the residents in the parish—although unable for the most part to find accommodation in the church—were bound to keep it in repair for the benefit of those who farmed out pews. The vestry eventually resolved to fall back upon a voluntary church rate. In some comments on the subject, the *Bristol Times* stated that one of the pews had sold by auction for £190. In spite of the scandal excited by such traffic, no attempt at reform was made during the long incumbency of Bishop Anderson. At length, in 1884, in consequence of the efforts of a new vicar, the Rev. Talbot Greaves, several of the pews were given up to the parochial authorities; and the churchwardens were authorised by a vestry meeting to apply for a faculty to reseat the church. But the opposition of many of the pew owners could not be overcome except by purchasing their property, for which purpose upwards of £3,000 were raised by subscription, and quickly expended in buying up seats. About £2,000 more were spent in the reconstruction of the sittings, which was soon after accomplished, and the church was reopened in December, 1884. It is intended to purchase the remaining proprietary sittings as funds are provided, though some of the present owners demand prices which will not be given. Already, through Mr. Greaves' exertions, there are, he states, "about 700 good free seats out of the 2,000 sittings in the church."

At a meeting of the Council in May, 1863, a resolution was passed empowering the Improvement Committee to carry into effect a plan suggested by them for the widening of Nicholas Street, by removing the *Gazette* office and some old houses standing near St. Nicholas' Church. The estimated net cost of the alterations was £7,150, exclusive of Corporation property valued at £1,174. The improvement involved the removal, early in 1864, of a remarkably picturesque ancient house—the Angel Inn—which stood in High Street, near the corner of Nicholas Street. A portion of the site of this hostelry, having only 14 feet frontage in High Street, and 35 feet in Nicholas Street, was sold at a ground rent of £151 per annum. Owing to the removal of the Angel Inn, the house in High Street adjoining it on the north—a building of about the same age—became insecure, and finally collapsed in July, 1865.

In May, 1863, whilst workmen were preparing the foundations of the Royal Insurance Company's new building, at the end of Bank Court, Corn Street, they laid bare portions of an apparently extensive mediæval structure. The window and door quoins of the cellar walls showed remains of moulded and traceried window-heads and jambs, but the worked faces had been turned inwards and built into the walls. The new building was completed in June, 1864.

During the autumn of 1862 an advertisement appeared in the local press offering prizes for the best designs for laying out about 170 acres of Leigh Woods, including Nightingale Valley, for building sites. It was subsequently announced that prizes had been awarded to two firms which had responded to the invitation, and in the spring of 1863 it was understood that approval had been given to a design which mapped out the locality for 350 houses, with an extensive hotel, and a bridge over the valley. The prospect of the destruction of the sylvan scenery occasioned deep regret amongst the public, and evoked bitter comments in the newspapers. After an interval, however, the mayor (Mr. S. V. Hare) was informed that Sir John Greville Smyth, the owner of the estate, would spare the woods, provided the Corporation undertook to lease them for fourteen years at a rental of £500 per annum, and a ready-money payment of £300. The mayor, in reply, suggested an extension of the proposed term, or a sale of the freehold to the Corporation, but was informed that no alteration could be made in the terms. The Finance Committee having declined to approve of a short lease of unproductive land at a rental of £3 per acre, the matter came to an end. In September, 1864, it was stated that Sir Greville Smyth had sold the woods to a London speculator for £50,000, and that the purchaser had sent down a plan of his intended operations. "The plan showed," said the *Bristol Times*, "some 800 tenements—many of them of a poor character, several of them small shops—to be erected on the romantic site, thereby of course making it an eyesore to Clifton. . . . As might be expected, the mayor and other gentlemen who saw it were appalled at the threatened desecration, and a private meeting was called to consider the offer of the speculator, who required £10,000 for his bargain—that is, that the citizens should pay him

£60,000." Suspicions as to the *bonâ fide* character of the speculator's threats were, however, excited in many minds; in spite of the menaced devastation, it was soon clear that the city would not subscribe the exorbitant amount demanded; and the next tidings of the projector were, that he had failed to pay the first instalment of the purchase money, and had departed to speculate in parts unknown. It being apparent that the permanent preservation of the scenery depended solely upon the public spirit of the citizens, the Leigh Woods Land Company was formed by a few generous-minded persons, Mr. George Thomas being appointed chairman. The capital was fixed at £50,000 in £25 shares, and after some negotiation the purchase of the property was effected for £40,000. The extent of ground acquired was about 160 acres, of which sixty were set apart for ornamental purposes, and about twenty more for roads. This arrangement left an area of about eighty acres applicable to building, and it was anticipated that the ground rents would ultimately produce upwards of £3,000 per annum. It ought to be stated that Mr. H. A. Palmer suggested a subscription for purchasing the ground for the free use of the public, offering to head the list with a donation of £1,000; but his proposal met with insignificant support. Subsequently, when complaints were raised as to the appropriation of so large a portion of the woods for building purposes, Mr. George Thomas offered to give up his £500 worth of shares, and Mr. Slaughter made a similar proposal as to half that amount, on condition that the citizens would raise £10,000 for securing a further reservation of the land; but the liberal-hearted overtures met with no response. The last instalment of the purchase money due to Sir J. G. Smyth was paid in 1875. Previous to that date the company had been brought to the brink of collapse through an unfortunate building speculation, by which it lost nearly £3,600; but the amount was paid off by three or four of the leading proprietors, who were granted in return 147 unissued shares.

Victoria Chapel, Whiteladies Road, the most beautiful local structure hitherto erected by the Wesleyan Methodists, was opened in June, 1863, by the Rev. F. A. West. The building and site had cost nearly £6,000.

The prospectus of the College Green Hotel Company, with a capital of £40,000 in £10 shares, appeared in October. A block of property extending from College Green to Trinity Street was soon afterwards purchased, and the houses were demolished. One of the dwellings removed, No. 2, College

Green, containing a finely carved hall and staircase, was the residence in 1741 of Mr. Jarret Smith (afterwards Sir J. Smyth, bart.), who was visited there by Sir John Dinely Goodere, a few hours before the seizure and murder of the latter by his brother, Captain Goodere. The new hotel, styled the Royal, was opened in March, 1868.

About this time, a number of stables and coach-houses fronting Queen's Road, appertaining to the houses on the north side of Berkeley Square, began to be converted into shops. At a later period, some of these little places of business were let at a higher rent than was paid for the mansions to which the old outbuildings were attached.

The Red Lion Inn, Redcliff Street, an ancient hostelry, with a courtyard and galleries in the style of the fourteenth or fifteenth century, was removed in 1864, and warehouses were erected on the site.

In June, 1864, a lifeboat, named the *Albert Edward*, the cost of which had been raised by a local subscription, arrived in the city, and was taken through the streets in procession, escorted by the volunteer corps. At a gathering on Durdham Down, the mayor (Mr. Jose) handed over the boat to the officers of the National Lifeboat Institution. It was afterwards transported to Padstow, Cornwall, for service on that stormy coast. In October, 1866, another lifeboat, styled the *Bristol and Clifton*, the cost of which had been raised by the exertions of the Bristol Histrionic Club, was welcomed into the city with similar ceremony. The boat was conveyed to the Zoological Gardens, where it was presented to the Lifeboat Institution by Mr. Commissioner Hill. The boat was afterwards stationed at Lossiemouth, Scotland. In March, 1871, a third boat, named the *Jack-a-jack*, paid for by Bristol merchants and ship-captains trading to the West Coast of Africa, passed through the city with similar honours, on its way to Morte, North Devon. By the will of Lady Haberfield, another Bristol lifeboat was presented to the institution in 1875, and two others have been given by local philanthropists.

The first agricultural show held in Bristol by the Bath and West of England Association was opened on the 13th June, 1864, under the presidency of Earl Fortescue. The exhibition took place on Durdham Down, 25 acres of which, lying to the south-west of the Stoke Bishop road, had been enclosed, and proved the most successful ever organised by the society. The entries of stock on the ground reached 545. The number of visitors was 88,138, and the receipts from admissions amounted to £5,966. During the week, the mayor and the local committee gave a dinner to the council of the association at the Victoria Rooms. The society held another exhibition on the same site in 1874, when the development of the institution was indicated by the increased area of the show-ground, the inclosure measuring 38 acres. The entries of stock numbered 732, and those of machinery and implements marked a still greater advance over the previous meeting. The president for the year was Sir L. Massey Lopes, bart. The attendance of visitors exceeded anything recorded in the history of the association, the number of admissions being 110,105, and the amount received £8,378. The mayoress (Mrs. Barnes) was presented by the society with a beautiful screen in Honiton lace, in recognition of the courtesy and hospitality with which the executive had been received by the mayor and herself. The third visit of the society took place in June, 1886, under the presidency of Lord Carlingford. The show of animals showed a further advance in numbers, the aggregate reaching 969, and there was a still more notable increase in the exhibits in some other departments. Much interest was excited by specimens of ensilage from a store made at Long Ashton, under the supervision of a special committee. Although the number of persons entering the showyard—100,579—was less than in 1874, owing to the unfavourable weather, it was still greatly in excess of the attendances recorded at any other meeting held by the society. The total receipts amounted to £7,226. The leading members of the association were again sumptuously entertained by the mayor (Mr. Wathen) and the Society of Merchant Venturers.

A vessel named the *Royal Sovereign*, the largest iron sailing ship ever built at this port, was launched by Messrs. W. Patterson & Son during the summer. From this time the shipbuilding industry in Bristol, formerly very extensive, appears to have rapidly declined.

A reference to the extreme drought of the summer of 1864 has been made in narrating the progress of the Bristol Water Company [p. 283]. The Council took active measures to alleviate the suffering of the poor, many of whom depended upon private wells. Several of these becoming exhausted, 200 old wells were reopened and pumps erected in populous districts. An arrangement was also made by which the vestry of St. John's gave up to the city the parish conduit, upon the Corporation undertaking to maintain it for the future. A suggestion was started that the Council should purchase Mother Pugsley's well [see p. 249]; but it was ascertained that the expense would be great, and the supply very limited.

Representations were made to the Government about this time by Mr. Berkeley, M.P., of the claims of Bristol and the neighbouring ports to a visit of the Channel fleet—a compliment which had been already paid to other maritime towns. Although the suggestion could not be complied with, the Admiralty directed that the armour-clad frigate *Defence* should make a cruise in the Bristol Channel. Accordingly, in September, the *Defence* dropped anchor off Clevedon, and her commander, Captain Phillimore, forthwith received an invitation from the mayor (Mr. T. P. Jose) offering him the hospitalities of Bristol. Captain Phillimore thereupon paid a visit to the city, and invited the mayor and other leading residents to inspect his vessel. A small steamer having been engaged, a numerous party embarked for the excursion; but unfavourable weather greatly marred the anticipated pleasure of the trip, and on nearing the *Defence* the pitching of the two vessels rendered a transit from one to the other more amusing to the blue-jackets than to the guests. The visitors were provided with a luxurious repast on board the frigate, and were honoured with a salute of seven guns on their departure. The return journey was made under as unpleasant circumstances as was the trip down channel. One unlucky member of the Council fell into the Avon while attempting to land at Shirehampton, but fortunately sustained no injury.

At a meeting of the Council in September, the Docks Committee reported that Mr. Howard, their engineer, had prepared new plans for the improvement of the port, which they believed could be executed without adding to the existing charges. The principal features of the revised designs were: a new and more commodious entrance lock from the Avon into Cumberland Basin, the cost of which was estimated at £127,580; a new junction lock from the basin into the Floating Harbour, estimated at £72,450; and the removal of projecting obstructions on both sides of the Avon, including the Hotwell House, Suspension Bridge, Round, Tea and Coffee House, and Pheasant Quarry "Points," the outlay for which was set down at £95,470. To meet the interest on the expenditure—£300,000 in round numbers—the committee estimated that the annual surplus income of the dock estate would be £13,000, irrespective of prospective increases; while an accumulated surplus of £32,000 would be in hand before the works were commenced. The plan was approved by a unanimous vote of the Council. In November, 1866, a contract was entered into with Mr. Tredwell, of Birmingham, for the entrance lock at Cumberland Basin, the removal of the Round Point, and some minor improvements, for the sum of £184,023. The removal of the rock at Tea and Coffee House Point was then in progress.* According to Mr. Howard's design, the earth removed in forming the lock and in cutting off the "points" was to have been employed in filling up the "bight" in front of the Port Railway station and the opposite bay below Nightingale Valley, by which the course of the Avon would have assumed a more symmetrical form. But it was subsequently resolved to make use of the material to fill up three of the great quarries which disfigured the Downs. This necessitated the construction of a tramway along the river side, the cutting of an inclined plane to the Down, and the erection of an engine-house on the summit of the cliff. The improvement works were in full operation by the summer of 1867. In February, 1868, the Council resolved to proceed with the inner lock and remaining works, at an estimated cost of £157,000. It was stated during the discussion, that although the dues had been reduced by one half, the dock receipts had increased from £28,784 in 1847 to over £30,000 in 1867. The inner lock, seventeen feet wider than the old one, was completed and opened on the 16th October, 1871; the works at Round Point (which had involved the removal of a shoulder of St. Vincent's Rocks) were finished soon afterwards. The new entrance lock into Cumberland Basin, a noble work, was opened on the 19th July, 1873. In the following September, the tramway on the Down was removed, after having effected great improvements. The quarry near Upper Belgrave Road was not, however, completely filled up until 1880.

On the 11th October, 1864, the fourth annual Church Congress was opened in Bristol under the presidency of the bishop of the diocese. The city was filled with distinguished clergymen and lay-supporters of the Establishment, and the proceedings, which occupied three days, excited general interest. The visitors were the objects of much hospitable attention on the part of leading citizens.

Amongst the incidents of the above gathering was the somewhat startling appearance of a Mr. Lyne, a person in deacon's orders styling himself Brother Ignatius, who had

* A pleasant and innocent place of resort was destroyed by these operations, without much advantage to navigation, the rocky bank of the river below high-water mark being left practically undisturbed for nearly twenty years. The work of removing the rock was at length begun in 1885, and is still unfinished.

assumed the costume of a monk, and professed to have re-founded in the Church of England the monastic system of St. Benedict. Some of his admirers in Bristol had already set up an "Order of St. Benedict," composed chiefly, if not wholly, of youthful laymen, who hired a room in a house in Trinity Street; and three or four clergymen—visitors during the Congress—assisted at "Benedictine services" held there during the week. At a later date, the local brethren of the "order" removed to an unoccupied workshop in Trenchard Street, where their eccentric proceedings caused crowds to assemble, and led to several disturbances. On one occasion two of the brethren attempted to take part in the service when intoxicated, and as they declined to obey the "prior," a youth named Dundas, they were removed by the police. On being informed of the escapade, Brother Ignatius sent an order to the prior requiring the delinquents to perform penance in white sheets in the "oratory," but they proved refractory, and were "excommunicated," amidst great uproar. At the Romanist "feast of the Assumption," the brethren, bearing candles and banners, and chanting hymns, walked in procession through several streets, about two o'clock in the morning. Exhibitions of this kind were frequently repeated, and the police had much difficulty in maintaining order. After several unseemly incidents, Brother Ignatius fulminated a decree deposing the prior (who called himself Brother Cyprian); but the latter repudiated the authority of the inventor of the order, and excommunicated some of the refractory brothers and sisters on his own account. Subsequently the "order" removed to Montpelier, where Brother Cyprian, who had come into possession of a valuable estate, built a chapel, established a "home," and started a newspaper. The services at the chapel soon attracted a great number of profligate young people of both sexes, and, after many unedifying scenes, the building—an iron one—was presented by Mr. Dundas to the Vicar of Bedminster, who placed it at Ashton Gate, and opened it in March, 1873, as a chapel of ease. [In June, 1883, it was removed for the purpose of erecting on the site the permanent church of St. Francis.] In 1872, through pecuniary difficulties, Mr. Dundas's establishment at Montpelier was altogether broken up.

The foundation stone of a new church in Pembroke Road, Clifton, intended to be dedicated to All Saints, was laid on the 3rd November, 1864. The first portion erected was the chancel, to which was attached a large temporary nave, and in this form the building was consecrated in June, 1868.

Owing to the large proportions and costly details of the edifice, the permanent nave was not ready for consecration until August, 1872, when £27,000 had been expended. Upwards of £10,000 more have been since spent on the building. Sufficient funds are still lacking for the erection of the tower and spire, although, from the absence of those adornments, the church, viewed from a distance, presents the appearance of a gigantic barn.

To increase the accommodation for worshippers in St. James's Church, a new north aisle was added to the building during the autumn of 1864, at a cost of £4,000. The incongruity of its style of architecture with that of the original fabric provoked much criticism.

The foundation stone of a proposed harbour of refuge for the Bristol Channel was laid, or rather supposed to have been laid, off Brean Down, near Weston-super-Mare, on the 5th November, by the wife of Sir John Eardley Wilmot, bart., the originator of the company formed for the purpose. The stone was lowered into the sea from a steamer lying off the promontory, a buoy being attached to mark its whereabouts. Unfortunately the rope was of insufficient length, and as the buoy was capable of sustaining more than twice the weight of the stone, the latter never reached the bottom; and at the rise of the next tide both buoy and stone drifted away, and were lost. The incident appears to have had a depressing effect on the undertaking, which was eventually abandoned. The Bristol and Exeter Railway board obtained powers, in 1866, to connect their main line with the proposed works, but no steps in that direction were ever taken.

Oakfield Road Chapel, erected by the Unitarians of Clifton and the neighbourhood at a cost of £6,000, was opened in November by the Rev. James Martineau, of London.

Although the opening of the Bristol and South Wales Union Railway had much facilitated intercourse between Bristol and the other side of the Channel, it was confessed by its promoters that their hopes of its availability for heavy traffic had been disappointed. The double shifting of goods at the two piers was, in fact, an insuperable obstacle to the transit of coal and iron; and as the enormous mineral resources of South Wales were more largely developed every year, the urgent need of placing Bristol in closer connection with the Principality was ever more widely acknowledged. In November, 1864, notice was given of the intended prosecution of a Bill in the following session for diverting the traffic of South Wales into a new course. Mr. Fowler, engineer to the Great Western Company, designed a railway from Wootton Bassett to the Old Passage, with a bridge over the Severn—an immense structure two miles in length, estimated to cost £1,800,000. This project being obviously prejudicial to Bristol, notice was given of another Bill, for a tunnel under the Severn near the New Passage, the construction of which, according to the estimates of Mr. Richardson, C.E., might be effected for £750,000. A meeting of merchants and traders was held on the 6th January, 1865, to consider the question, when it was stated that the promoters of the tunnel scheme were Messrs. C. J. Thomas, George Wills, T. T. Taylor, E. S. Robinson, and M. Whitwill. Resolutions in its favour were adopted unanimously; but the construction of a tunnel four miles in length under an arm of the sea was not an enterprise likely to commend itself to any but robust-hearted investors. The parliamentary deposit was not forthcoming, and the Bill was dropped. The Bill authorising the bridge obtained the royal assent, but no steps were taken to carry out its powers. The whole subject, in fact, was expelled from the minds of capitalists by the disastrous panic of 1866, and nothing was heard of it for some years. In the session of 1872, a Bill reviving the tunnel project was introduced into Parliament by private persons; and it was soon afterwards announced that the Great Western Railway board—moved by the aggressive designs of the Midland Company in reference to South Wales—had resolved to adopt the measure, which received the royal assent. Another Severn bridge scheme—on this occasion at Sharpness—was promoted by an independent company under the patronage of the Midland board, and also received legislative sanction. The first sod of the tunnel works was cut on the 18th March, 1873, near Portskewet, the directors having resolved to make a preliminary investigation into the nature of the strata by cutting a six-feet driftway under the Channel. The sinking of a shaft for this purpose was greatly impeded by land springs, which poured into the works to such an extent that powerful pumping machinery was required to overcome the difficulty, and it was not until October, 1874, that tenders were invited for the first section of the "heading." The proposals received being much in excess of the estimates, the directors resolved to carry out the experiment by their own officers. Only 120 yards of the driftway remained to be excavated to unite the two ends when, in October, 1879, another prodigious flood of water, proceeding from land springs near Portskewet, burst into the southern headway, and welled up into the shaft. A contract was now entered into for the completion of the undertaking, and Sir John Hawkshaw was engaged as engineer in chief. Under his advice the line of the tunnel was lowered 15 feet, in order to maintain more "cover" under the Channel, and in consequence of this alteration it was subsequently found advisable to make a second driftway beneath the original one. Further additions were made as rapidly as possible to the already numerous steam pumps, but more than a twelvemonth passed away before the invading waters could be effectually walled out. In February, 1881, the directors, in announcing that the difficulty had been surmounted, stated that the nature of the strata (principally hard rock) had proved satisfactory, and that the construction of the permanent tunnel had been begun. The two ends of the driftway were united in the following September, when the centres were found to join within three inches. In April, 1881, an irruption of water took place on the Gloucestershire side of the Severn, which for a time exceeded the power of the pumping machinery. A more serious disaster occurred in October, 1883, when a third outburst of Monmouthshire land water, the volume of which was estimated at 25,000 gallons per minute, occurred near the site of the disaster of 1879. Although the effects of the irruption were circumscribed by the walls built for the purpose, the tunnel was flooded to the extent of a mile and a half, and a lengthy delay occurred before the water could be overcome by the help of four additional pumping engines. This was the last serious difficulty encountered, the flooding of a section by a huge tidal wave in October, 1883, being only a transient embarrassment. The works, on which 5,000 men were for some time employed, were so far completed that a passenger train containing Sir Daniel Gooch, chairman of the Great Western board, and several of his brother directors, passed through the tunnel—which is 7,664 yards in length—on the 5th September, 1885. It was stated that 75 millions of vitrified bricks had been used in the construction. Much, however, remained to be done before the undertaking could be made available for traffic. The doubling of the Bristol and South Wales Union line, involving the widening of the tunnel at Patchway was found indispensable, and this and other alterations required considerable time. An experimental train, laden with Welsh coal for Southampton, passed through the tunnel, however, on the 9th January, 1886. For the purpose of ventilation, a fan was afterwards erected on the Sudbrook side capable of discharging 240,000 feet of air per minute. The tunnel was opened for regular passenger traffic, without any ceremony, on the 1st December. The total cost of the undertaking was then estimated at about two millions sterling.

As the Severn Bridge scheme has been casually mentioned in the above narrative, it may be added that its promoters succeeded in erecting, near Purton Passage, the longest and perhaps the most remarkable structure of the kind in the kingdom, consisting of twenty-two large arches extending over a space of 1,387 yards. The cost of the bridge, including the railways connecting it with the Great Western system in the Forest of Dean and with the Midland line near Berkeley, was about £400,000. It was opened amidst much local rejoicing on the 17th October, 1879.

At a meeting of the Council in January, 1865, it was determined to appoint a committee, to be called the Sanitary Committee, for the purpose of exercising the powers of the Local Government Act, under which increased facilities were offered for effecting public improvements. The new body, which took the place of the Board of Health Committee, was itself superseded, under the provisions of the Public Health Act of 1872, by the "Sanitary Authority," consisting of all the members of the Council. Mr. Josiah Thomas, about the same date, became sole city surveyor.

Some amusement was created about this time by the lucubrations of a gentleman named John Hampden, who, having convinced himself of the impending destruction of the world, published a local periodical styled *The Armourer*, with a view of awakening a thoughtless and unconverted community to its approaching doom. Mr. Hampden proclaimed in January, 1865, that England had seen its last "merry Christmas;" and for several successive months his predictions of an imminent cataclysm became more positive and more gloomy. Eventually he admitted that the final catastrophe might possibly be reserved for 1866, but this was the extreme limit conceded to papacy and infidelity. Even in December of the latter year he stoutly repeated his prognostications; but as events were not precisely in accord with his fears—or rather, apparently, with his hopes—*The Armourer* ceased to appear, and its author removed to London. Mr. Hampden afterwards gained notoriety by first making a bet of £1,000 that an impartially conducted engineering experiment would prove the world to be a plane, and then—when the said experiment had proved the contrary—appealing to the law courts to debar the gentleman who had won the wager from recovering his money. In the course of the controversy he was amerced in £600 damages for libelling his antagonist, and was afterwards sentenced to two lengthy terms of imprisonment for repeating his annoyances.

In February, 1865, the Council entered into negotiations with the Ecclesiastical Commissioners for the purchase of Rownham Ferry, part of the ancient estate of the Abbey of St. Augustine's, and subsequently of the Dean and Chapter of Bristol. The ferry was transferred to the Corporation in August, 1866, for the sum of £10,000.

During the later years of the reign of George IV., Sir C. Wetherell, recorder of Bristol, held two criminal assizes annually for the city under the charter of Edward III. After the events of 1831, Sir Charles discontinued this custom; and in 1835 the Corporations Reform Act abolished the jurisdiction of the recorder in weighty criminal cases, prisoners charged with grave crimes being thenceforth remitted for trial to the Gloucestershire assizes, to the great inconvenience of prosecutors and witnesses. The Council, shortly after its institution, and several times afterwards, addressed urgent, but fruitless, appeals to the Government for the restoration of the criminal assizes. Early in 1865, it was intimated to the mayor that the desire of the city would at length be complied with; and the first commission was opened on the 31st March. Contrary to the custom of centuries, the name of the mayor was not on this occasion associated with that of the judges in the commission of oyer and terminer; but the Council protested against the withdrawal of an ancient privilege, and the Home Secretary promised that the omission should not be repeated. It now became necessary to provide a second assize court, the Guildhall furnishing only a court for civil cases, and the Finance Committee, to whom the matter was referred, were forthwith besieged by rival projectors. In addition to plans for the erection of additional buildings at the rear of the Guildhall, designs were sent in for entirely new law courts in Queen Square, upon the Float near the Stone Bridge, on the site of Colston Hall, on the site of the Upper Arcade, and other places. "The battle of the sites" was fought for a time with as much obstinacy as "the battle of the docks," and was marked by similar vicissitudes. The Council in the first instance approved of a costly proposal to build upon the Float; but the Dock Committee having protested vigorously against any diminution of the harbour, the vote was practically annulled. The Queen's Square site was next recommended for adoption by the Finance Committee, but an influentially attended meeting in the Guildhall adopted a memorial emphatically condemning the project. On the 1st January, 1866, when the report of the committee was discussed by the Council, an amendment in favour of the Guildhall site was negatived by 29 votes against 25. Another amendment, approving of the Stone Bridge site, was also rejected by 31 votes against 21. Proposals in favour of College Green, the Haymarket, and the Exchange were successively negatived without a division. Finally, the report recommending the Queen Square site was rejected by 37 votes against 13. Still another motion, affirming the expediency of petitioning the Government to revoke the grant of an assize, was defeated by a overwhelming majority. The Council is reported to have made merry over the negative results of the debate, but the comments of the ratepayers on the proceedings were the reverse of complimentary. It soon became impossible to ignore the preponderating opinion of the citizens, and at another Council meeting, in March, it was resolved to build the new court on property belonging to the Corporation, at the back of the existing hall, plans being asked for to carry out that determination. When the proffered designs were considered, however, it was found that a satisfactory result would be impracticable unless the site of a house belonging to Christ Church parish were made available. Much dissatisfaction was created by the bungling of the authorities, while the judges, who found most inconvenient provision made for the assizes, did not conceal their indignation at the discomfort of the arrangements and at the lethargy of the Corporation. In August, 1867, the Council at length adopted the plan which was eventually carried into effect. The architect succeeded in preserving two Romanesque chambers in the mansion in Small Street erroneously styled "Colston's." The new building cost £16,000. A portion of it was used by the judges for the first time at the August assizes in 1870, and the second court was opened at the spring assizes of the following year. The interesting ancient apartments were granted to the Incorporated Law Society, who fitted them up for their library.

The Council, at a meeting in February, 1865, resolved to enforce the provisions of a permissive Act by which public houses and refreshment rooms were required to be closed between the hours of one and four o'clock in the morning. The new regulation materially added to the tranquillity of the streets.

During the parliamentary session of 1865, a Bill was introduced on behalf of the Great Western, Midland, and Bristol and Exeter Railway Companies, empowering them to co-operate in the erection of a new joint station at Temple Meads. After the measure had become law, the companies disagreed amongst themselves as to the proportionate amounts which they should contribute towards the outlay, and nothing was done for several years. In August, 1870, it was asserted at a meeting of the Bristol and Exeter Company that their Bristol station—designed by Mr. Brunel—was "the most disgraceful, dangerous, difficult, and impracticable in Europe." At length, in February, 1871, the companies came to an understanding, and the construction of the new building commenced. The work was one of much difficulty, since the structure had to be reared without interfering with the traffic on the three lines. The "down" platform was opened for passengers on the 6th July, 1874, and the entire station—which cost nearly £300,000—was completed shortly afterwards.

The local newspapers of the 3rd June, 1865, contained an appeal for subscriptions on behalf of a proposed Hospital for Sick Children. [An institution for youthful sufferers, under a somewhat different name, had existed in St. James's Square since 1857, but treated only out-patients.] The promoters intended at the outset to fit up a suitable house for the reception of a few patients, and asked for only £300 a year to set the establishment on foot. The appeal was signed by Messrs. Mark Whitwill, W. K. Wait, W. Turner, A. Phillips, A. N. Herapath, T. Fry, and Dr. Carter. A dwelling in the Royal Fort was soon afterwards purchased for £750, and was opened on the 20th October, 1866. A bazaar held a few weeks later yielded a profit of over £1,600. The building having been found too contracted for the requirements of the charity, a meeting was held in April, 1882, to promote the erection of a large and commodious hospital, near the same spot, in a style worthy of the city. A design in the Tudor style having been selected, the foundation stone of the structure was laid on the 5th April, 1883, by the Duchess of Beaufort, who also opened the new hospital on the 1st August, 1885. The outlay for the new building was nearly £20,000.

In the course of the summer the directors of the Liverpool and London and Globe Insurance Company purchased extensive premises in Corn Street, for the purpose of building offices upon the site. One of the houses, some of the upper apartments of which had been occupied by the Law Library from its establishment in 1818, was of the sixteenth century, and contained a stately Elizabethan chimneypiece, with an elaborately ornamented ceiling and panelling. (These relics were purchased by Alderman Baker, who had them reconstructed in the dining-room of Broomfield House, near Brislington.) The new building—which surpasses all others in the city as regards the richness of its front—cost £11,500. The Law Library Society, as has been already recorded, found accommodation in the new Law Courts, Small Street.

On the dissolution of Parliament, in July, Mr. Berkeley again offered his services to the citizens. Mr. Langton retired into private life, and the candidate adopted as his successor by the Liberal party was Sir Samuel Morton Peto, bart., a member of a great firm of railway contractors. The Conservative aspirant was Mr. Thomas Francis Fremantle, son of Sir T. F. Fremantle (afterwards Lord Cottesloe), the former owner —through a Bristol ancestor—of Pugsley's field. The result of the poll on the 12th July was as follows: Mr. Berkeley, 5,296; Sir S. M. Peto, 5,228; Mr. Fremantle, 4,269. The Conservative press insinuated that the defeat of their party was due to bribery; and, although no proof was offered in support of the charge, it was undeniable that the expenditure of Sir Morton Peto was extremely profuse. According to the official return, the outlay on behalf of Berkeley and Peto was £4,500, against £1,614 spent by the Tory candidate.

An Industrial Exhibition was opened on the 19th September, the event being celebrated by a general holiday. The Prime Minister, Lord Palmerston, had undertaken to be present, but owing to severe illness, which proved fatal in the following month, he was unable to fulfil his promise. In the morning a procession of trades marched through the principal streets to the Council House, where it was joined by the mayor, sheriff, and corporate officials, and the gathering then proceeded to the Drill Hall, at which the bishop, Mr. Berkeley, M.P., the committee, and many leading citizens had already assembled. The inaugural ceremony passed off amidst general applause. The exhibition was highly successful, the number of visitors having been nearly 117,000, and the gross receipts £3,254. Out of the profits, £431 were awarded to exhibitors in the shape of prizes, which were presented by Mr. Berkeley, and £575 were distributed amongst the principal local charities. The chairman of the committee, Mr. J. M. Kempster, was presented with an elegant silver salver in recognition of his energetic services. In 1871 Mr. Kempster presented the salver to the Corporation, and it now forms part of the civic plate at the Mansion House.

The revival of local trade, which became marked during

the autumn of this year, induced the authorities to recognise the urgency of various street improvements which had been from time to time deferred. The first work undertaken was the opening of a new thoroughfare from College Green to Hotwell Road, the then existing route by Cow Street (now buried under Park Street viaduct) and Frog Lane being not merely inconvenient but dangerous. The dean and chapter co-operated in this undertaking, which included the lowering of the road in front of the cathedral—leaving the threshold of the original north doorway three feet above the new level —and the removal of a large portion of the deanery.* More important operations were ordered by the Council in September. A sub-committee recommended the adoption of a plan by Mr. R. S. Pope for improving the gradient of Park Street from the Mayor's Chapel to Great George Street. The design contemplated bridging over Unity Street as well as Frogmore Street, and the purchasing of about forty houses, at an estimated cost of £31,000. The Council limited the line of improvement to the space between the top of Unity Street and the (then) Philosophical Institute, the net outlay being estimated at £11,400. [The actual cost of the new street, opened on the 4th April, 1871, was £27,000.] The second scheme—for the construction of a new street from the northern end of Thomas Street to the railway terminus—was practically a revival of the design of 1845. Mr. S. C. Fripp, who laid out the later plan, estimated the net cost at £53,000. [It actually cost about £46,000.] Two proposals were made by Mr. Josiah Thomas, the first being for widening the roadways leading from Redcross Street and Old Market Street, while the second was for opening a thoroughfare from Old Market Street to Stoke's Croft, the net estimated expenditure being £8,700. Finally Mr. Pope proposed a new road from the western end of Maudlin Street to Upper Park Row, the expense being estimated at £9,200. [The outlay was actually £13,000.] All the schemes were approved. In November, 1867, another series of improvements, completing plans already partially executed, was ordered to be carried out. It included further alterations in and near Deanery Road, Park Row, Redcliff Street, Temple Street, Narrow Wine Street, Redcross Street, Baldwin Street, Corn Street, and Bedminster. In addition to these works it was resolved to make a new street (Colston Street) from Colston Hall to Maudlin Street, to extend

* In carrying out this improvement, the corporate officials wantonly destroyed a trefoiled Gothic parapet on each side of the steps leading into College Green, in front of the High Cross, and replaced it by an ugly iron handrail.

Jamaica Street, and to construct a road from Victoria Square to Carlton Place, another from Victoria Square to Clifton Park, and a third from Clifton Park into Pembroke Road. The net cost was estimated at £126,000. Parliamentary sanction having been obtained in due course, the whole of the improvements were completed in a few years.

During the autumn of 1865, two pigs of lead, each bearing a Roman inscription, were disinterred near Wade Street, on what anciently had been the bank of the Froom before the river was narrowed at that point. Both the pigs had been cast in a mould in which the name of the reigning emperor had been mutilated, but competent antiquaries believed the inscription to refer to Antoninus Pius. Being the only important Roman relics ever discovered in Bristol, the discovery excited some interest, and a paper on the subject appeared in the *Archæological Journal* for 1866.

In October, 1865, a large portion of the beautiful grove known as Lovers' Walk, Redland, was sold by auction by order of the executors of the late owner, Mr. James Evan Baillie. One lot, consisting of two closes of land and part of the avenue, altogether about 10 acres, sold for £4,620. Another lot, known as the Long-acre, and including the lower part of the grove, with an area of about 4¼ acres, was sold for £2,740 to Mr. G. O. Edwards, who had privately bought from the executors the mansion and grounds of Redland Court. The first-mentioned lot was forthwith mapped out for sale in building sites; but Mr. George Thomas and a few other public-spirited citizens, in order to prevent the entire destruction of an agreeable resort, made an agreement with the new owners by which one of the best parts of the avenue was preserved. In February, 1879, it was reported to the Council that Mr. Francis Fry and his brother, owners of that portion of the property extending from South Road to the end of Cotham Grove, had offered to convey an area of four acres to the Corporation for the use of the public. The offer was gratefully accepted. The land adjoining the walk was subsequently enclosed and laid out as a pleasure ground, at a cost of about £850. Finally, in September, 1884, it was reported to the Council that Mr. W. H. Edwards, son of Mr. G. O. Edwards, had executed a conveyance to the Corporation of that part of the avenue which extended from Redland Road to near the railway bridge, for the perpetual enjoyment of the public. A cordial vote of thanks was accorded to the donor. About the same date, Mr. Edwards disposed of Redland Court and its surrounding grounds for £12,250. The mansion was soon afterwards acquired for the Redland High School for girls.

The rinderpest, or cattle plague, reached this country during the autumn, and spread rapidly over the island, more than 200,000 animals being attacked within a few months. Of these over 120,000 died from the malady, while 40,000 more were killed. In some localities the recoveries did not exceed two or three per cent. of the animals affected. The parish of Bitton especially suffered in this district. It was literally swept by the pestilence, upwards of two hundred head of cattle falling victims in a few days. Stringent measures were taken by the local authorities to check the spread of the pest. The movement of stock, at first limited to fat animals ready for slaughtering, was eventually wholly prohibited. Butchers were consequently obliged to kill their purchases at the farms where they were fed. The Bristol cattle market was not re-opened for store cattle until June, 1867.

An iron church, erected in Tyndall's Park for the accommodation of the rapidly increasing residents in that locality, was opened on the 13th December. Funds having gradually accumulated for the construction of a permanent church, dedicated to St. Mary, building operations commenced about the close of 1870, and part of the choir was consecrated by Bishop Ellicott in June, 1874. [The iron building, become unnecessary, was removed to Woolcott Park in 1875, where it was again the forerunner of a permanent edifice, St. Saviour's.] The western portion of St. Mary's was finished about seven years later, when nearly £10,000 had been spent upon the building.

On the 15th December a disturbance occurred in Clare Street, the record of which will probably be regarded by later generations as denoting a curious survival of lower-class intolerance. A French merchant captain, whose vessel was lying at the Grove, was walking down the street in company with his wife, when the peculiar head-dress of the latter —who was probably a Breton woman—attracted the attention of a number of boys, and a crowd rapidly gathered around. A rumour then spread that the lady was a Mrs. Law, who had been lecturing during the week against Christianity, and the report so excited the rabble that they made a violent attack on the unfortunate foreigners, who had at last to beg for refuge in a neighbouring shop. After keeping out of sight for some time, the refugees made an attempt to return to their ship; but the populace again surrounded them, and the captain was so brutally ill-treated that he and his wife, whose life was also seriously menaced, were again driven to appeal for protection. A body of policemen, which at length arrived, had great difficulty in reaching the luckless couple, the mob surging around the place and refusing to disperse. After considerable delay, the pair were removed to their vessel in a cab, followed by a howling multitude.

At the close of this year, on the retirement of Mr. C. T. Eales, Stamp Distributor for the city, the office, which from its lucrativeness was one of the great prizes of party patronage in ante-Reform days, was abolished, the duties being afterwards performed by the Inland Revenue authorities.

The financial condition of the kindred societies at the two extremities of Park Street—the Bristol Library and the Institution—had for some time previous to 1866 caused much anxiety to their supporters. The Library Society had somewhat increased its roll of subscribers since its removal from King Street, but its funds were inadequate to maintain it in a state of efficiency. It now received notice from the Headquarters Company that it must pay a greatly increased rent, or remove elsewhere. The subscribers to the Park Street Institution had been diminishing for many years, and an energetic effort was evidently required to save it from dissolution. In the meantime the apartments devoted to the museum had become too contracted for the proper display of the contents, and no funds existed for their extension. In the face of these embarrassments, a proposal to unite the two institutions, and to place their treasures of literature, science, and art under a single roof, was received with much approval. A joint committee having been appointed, steps were taken for the purchase of a piece of ground adjoining the Drill Hall, and the plot was acquired for £2,500. Plans for the proposed building having been obtained in June, a design in the Venetian style was selected. Meetings for giving legal effect to the union were held early in 1867, and were practically unanimous. Financial resources, however, continuing to be painfully deficient, a meeting was held in January, 1868, the mayor (Mr. F. Adams) presiding, when the committee reported that the new building, even though certain portions would be postponed, could not be erected under a cost of £17,000, and an urgent appeal was made to the citizens to contribute £5,000 towards that sum. The report went on to promise that, if the amount in question were forthcoming, the museum should be opened free on certain days of the week, and students of limited means should be admitted to the library either gratuitously or at a reduced payment. The response of the city was, however, disappointing, only a few liberal contributions being received, and the committee were compelled to open the building in an unfinished condition. Early in 1871, when about £14,000 had been expended, the two institutions took possession, and started on their joint career under the style of the Bristol Museum and Library. About the same time, the old Institution at the bottom of Park Street became the property of the Freemasons of the district for £5,960. [After undergoing internal re-construction and decoration, the building was "dedicated" to the purposes of the craft by the Earl of Limerick, P.G.M., on the 2nd February, 1872.] In 1873–4 the committee made another appeal to the public to enable them to proceed further with the original design, by erecting a lecture room, a museum of antiquities and industrial products, and certain much-needed offices, but the subscriptions were far from adequate to meet the expenditure (£7,000); and the institution was saddled with a heavy debt, the interest on which has since crippled its executive and grievously impaired its efficiency and usefulness.

A Bill passed through Parliament in the session of 1866, authorising the construction of the Bristol Harbour Junction Railway and Wharf Depôt, a scheme promoted with the view of lessening the traffic in over-crowded thoroughfares by forwarding goods directly from the quays to the railway station. The cost was estimated at £165,000, which outlay was to be divided between the Great Western Company, the Bristol and Exeter Company, and the Corporation—the latter being required to lay out £50,000, for which it was guaranteed £2,000 per annum as interest. The construction of the railway necessitated the removal of the old vicarage of St. Mary Redcliff and nearly all one side of Guinea Street. As the line passed under the burial ground of the parish, the vestry received £2,500 in compensation, with which sum land was purchased and laid out for a parochial cemetery near Arno's Vale. The railway opened out a district little known to the citizens in general; and the *Bristol Times* of February 9, 1867, stated that in laying out the line the surveyors had lighted on a considerable withy bed, lying between Redcliff Church and the station. A few weeks later the local journals reported the (supposed) discovery of an extensive network of subterranean caves under Redcliff Hill. The largest of the caverns was octagonal in form, about forty-five feet in diameter and about seven feet high.

"The vaulted roof was supported on eight columns at equal distances, and a ninth in the centre of the place. A well, bored from above, had passed through the central column. A wide, lofty, and well-finished corridor led to the cavern on the other side, but this being walled at the end, the party could not explore further." Upon reading those statements, the owner of Redcliff Wharf, Mr. Henry Charles Harford, of Frenchay, addressed a letter to a Bristol newspaper, stating that the caverns were well known to him. They had, he said, formed part of the Redcliff Wharf property, and he had when a boy explored them to an immense distance, Redcliff Church standing on one of them. Mr. Harford hinted that they had, at an earlier period, been used for smuggling and even for worse purposes (kidnapping and slave dealing). He believed they had been originally dug for sandpits, and they had certainly proved valuable to the owners of Redcliff Wharf. In 1812, a gentleman (indicated as Mr. Thos. King, merchant,) had claimed that portion of the caverns which existed under his property, and this claim being substantiated, the wall found by the workmen was built to separate the estates.—In 1869, the railway companies, finding it desirable to increase their waterside accommodation, applied to Parliament for further powers, and obtained the assent of the Corporation to the extension of the wharf by the addition of 400 feet water frontage west of Prince's Street Bridge. The railway was opened in March, 1872. In a few months it was found that the wharves were insufficient to accommodate the trade, a largely increased number of steamers frequenting the port, and in 1873 parliamentary sanction was obtained for the further development of the works. The new Act provided that the two wharves on either side of Prince's Street Bridge road, already constructed, and a third towards Wapping—1,483 feet in length—were to be exclusively city property, while two contiguous wharves lower down, 1,208 feet long, with power of extension over 398 feet more, were to belong in fee simple to the companies. The rent-charge of £2,000 payable to the city was to be suspended until the completion of the new works. The wharves devolving on the Corporation by this Act were estimated to have cost £60,000.

At the annual meeting of the Bristol Turnpike trustees, in March, 1866, it was reported that the mortgage debt upon the entire trust—which embraced 163 miles of road, and was, with one exception, the most extensive in England—had been nearly paid off. The only charge remaining was one of £5,500 on two of the northern sections. As the surplus receipts for a further period of eighteen months would clear off this burden, it was resolved that the tolls should be abolished on the 1st November, 1867. The resolution was carried by the narrow majority of 26 votes against 22, many of the rural trustees being opposed to a step which threw the maintenance of the roads on the local ratepayers, whilst some of the Bristol trustees objected that the abolition of tolls would entail a burden of £2,000 a year upon the citizens for repairing the eighteen miles of turnpike within the borough. In accordance with the resolution, the district was included in the Turnpike Act of 1866, under the provisions of which the powers of the trustees expired on the 1st November, 1867, when all the turnpike gates were removed. Within the borough there were no less than fifteen of those obstacles to locomotion, namely: Whiteladies, St. Michael's, Clifton Down and Gallows Acre gates in the Aust district; Cutler's Mills and Redland Road gates in the Horfield district; St. John's Lane gate in the Whitchurch district; Lawford's and Baptist Mills gates in the Stapleton district; West Street gate, and bars at Packhorse and Barrow Lanes in the Toghill and Bitton district; Parson Street and Luckwell Lane gates in the Dundry district; and Coronation Road gate in the Ashton trust. The sites of the toll-houses were in most cases claimed by the owners of the adjoining property, and the buildings were demolished.* The surplus funds of the trust (£6,760) were divided amongst the local highway authorities.

In the spring of 1866, Mr. Thomas W. Hill, of Clifton Park, acquired from the Merchants' Society a piece of ground near Jacob's Wells. After clearing it of a number of cottages, he built upon the site an almshouse for the residence of twelve aged persons, for whom he provided a small weekly income. A few months later Mr. Hill presented the Infirmary with £3,000 for the erection of two additional wards, and subsequently, by gift and bequest, he distributed upwards of £10,000 amongst charitable and religious institutions. The residue of his estate, which was very large, was devoted to his almshouses, to the church and schools of St. Silas, Baptist Mills, to the schools of St. Luke, Bedminster, and to the Infirmary. In consequence of this bequest, the trustees of

* The Clifton toll-house at the top of Bridge Valley Road had a large rustic portico, under which the public were accustomed to take shelter during sudden showers of rain. A member of the Council proposed that the construction should be preserved for the sake of its utility; but his suggestion met with no support, and promenaders are worse off now than they were twenty years ago.

the almshouses added forty non-resident almswomen to the number receiving weekly pensions, and built a large room, intended for a chapel and library to the almshouse.

The local journals of July 21st contained an address to the public, signed by J. P. Norris, canon and sub-dean of Bristol cathedral, appealing for aid in the great work of reconstructing the nave of that edifice. The tower, it was stated, was undergoing restoration at the expense of the chapter [see p. 370], but it could not be effectually buttressed except by the completion of the cathedral in its original form. (During the previous year, whilst the road in front of the cathedral was being lowered by the Corporation, the workmen laid bare the foundations of a nave and north porch which had been commenced—probably by Abbot Knowle—but never completed, thus disposing of the foolish legend that they were destroyed during the civil war. Traces of the original Romanesque nave, which had been of small dimensions, were also found during the reconstruction.) In October, a committee of influential citizens was formed with a view to pressing the subject upon public attention; but it soon afterwards transpired that a majority of the chapter, consisting of the dean and canons Bankes and Girdlestone, believing that funds would not be forthcoming for a perfect reconstruction, were in favour of building a truncated nave of three bays. This proposal being universally condemned, the committee requested Mr. Street, the Gothic architect, to advise them on the subject. His report stated that Abbot Knowle's nave was intended to be of six bays, and that only such a structure would properly bring out the beauties of the choir. He also thought that the addition of western towers would greatly improve the appearance of the building. The entire reconstruction according to his designs was estimated to cost £52,800, but the completion of the nave and towers up to the level of the roof was set down at about £43,000. Subscriptions amounting to £13,000* having been already promised—some leading Dissenters offering handsome donations—it was resolved to undertake two bays, as suggested by Mr. Street, and a contract was signed in August, 1867, for £14,270. The foundation stone of the new work was laid on the 17th April, 1868, with masonic honours, by the Earl of Limerick, P.G.M. Early in 1870, when the two bays were completed, Mr. W. K. Wait, then mayor, offered to build the new north porch (esti-

* The first subscriptions—afterwards largely increased—of the five originators of the movement, Canon Norris, Sir Wm. Miles, and Messrs. Francis Adams, J. J. Mogg, and W. K. Wait, were £500 each.

mated to cost £1,200), provided a like sum was subscribed to raise the north wall of the nave for its reception. The required sum was soon forthcoming, and by a further effort, in 1872, subscriptions to a large amount were contributed for the purpose of completing the nave and the lower portion of the western towers. In the autumn of 1875 the state of the central tower was reported to be so critical that it was deemed advisable to remove the battlements,—greatly impairing the former stately appearance of the building,—in which denuded condition it still remains, the fund appropriated to its restoration by the chapter having proved inadequate. The singular incidents of the following year, and the completion of the nave, will be noticed hereafter.

At a meeting of the Council, in September, 1866, Mr. Christopher J. Thomas drew attention to the urgency of a redistribution of the seats allotted to the several municipal wards of the borough, the movement of population since the ill-advised arrangement of 1835 having rendered the existing system a mockery of the representative principle. Mr. Thomas succeeded in obtaining the appointment of a committee to consider the subject, but its deliberations led to no result. In December, 1869, Mr. Thomas reintroduced the subject, the anomalies of which had been in the meantime greatly increased by an Act conferring the municipal franchise on householders whose rates were paid by their landlords. Mr. Thomas moved that a petition should be addressed to the Crown praying for an equitable reform, reminding his opponents that the unfairness of the arrangement would become every year more glaring. The following was then the position of the seven principal wards. The figures are well worth contrasting with those given at page 209.

	Ratepayers.	Yearly Value.	Members.
St. Augustine	987	£40,956	6
St. Michael	1594	64,090	3
Clifton	2548	131,706	9
St. Philip	4818	86,687	3
Bristol	1751	93,925	9
Bedminster	2267	44,629	3
Redcliff	1781	61,856	6

The Conservatives, who predominated in the four favoured wards, met Mr. Thomas with an amendment, asserting that, as it was not established that public good would result from a change, it was inexpedient to make any alteration. The amendment was adopted by 31 votes (including 12 aldermen) against 22. The question was again brought before the Council in June, 1875, by Mr. H. J. Mills, when the relative state in the wards had become more anomalous than ever. The four favoured wards, shown in the above table as returning thirty councillors, had in 1875 only 7,565 burgesses, while the remaining wards in the city, returning only eighteen councillors put together, had an aggregate of 15,844 burgesses. The predominant party in the Council continued to defend the arrangement, on the ground that it worked well and that the grievance was a sentimental one. It was admitted, however, that the matter was deserving of further consideration, and a committee was appointed to report as to what should be done. The committee had the subject under discussion for nearly four years, the majority being very unwilling to disturb the existing arrangement. At length, in March, 1879, a report was presented recommending certain reforms. The large wards of Bedminster and St. Philip were each divided into two wards, having three members each, the additional representatives being obtained by taking three from Bristol ward and three from St. Augustine's. A third new ward was created out of the northern portions of Clifton and St. Michael's wards, and called Westbury ward, the three members for which were obtained by reducing the representatives for Clifton from nine to six. Finally, the portion of St. Philip's Marsh south of the Feeder was transferred to Redcliff ward, which was to retain its six members. Under this rearrangement, the wards stood as follows:—

	Councillors.	Burgesses.	Rated Value.
Bedminster, East ...	3	2076	£30,044
Bedminster, West ...	3	1825	30,562
Central	6	1873	110,578
Clifton	6	2222	135,288
Westbury	3	1307	62,015
District	3	2014	49,408
Redcliff	6	2289	87,903
St. Augustine	3	1030	48,619
St. James	3	1011	30,316
St. Michael	3	1210	48,670
St. Paul	3	1554	35,698
St. Philip, North ...	3	2902	43,108
St. Philip, South ...	3	2950	58,880

This plan was so distasteful to some of the Conservatives that the leader of the party, Alderman Ford, moved its postponement, to enable his friends to get "educated" on the question. A delay of a fortnight was carried after a warm discussion. At the adjourned meeting the report was adopted by a majority of 46 against 6—the latter number representing the "uneducated" Conservatives. A Bill to carry out the reform having been approved at a statutory meeting of the ratepayers, the measure was laid before Parliament in the session of 1880. It was opposed in the House of Commons by Mr. W. K. Wait (mayor 1869–70), a member of the Council then representing the city of Gloucester, who obtained the assistance of a number of Conservative members. His motion for the rejection of the Bill was, however, defeated by 163 votes against 98; and the measure received the royal assent on the 14th June. Shortly afterwards, three members from each of the reduced wards were transferred to St. Philip's, Bedminster, and Westbury—much against the wishes of some of the gentlemen thus "transparished," amongst whom there was much heart-burning.

At a meeting of the Bristol Board of Guardians, in October, statistics were produced showing the annual local taxation of the ancient city during the previous 26 years. During that period the average had been nearly 6*s*. 1*d*. in the pound. The rates had been about 1*s*. in the pound more during the later half of the term than they were in the previous moiety, owing to the large expenditure for sewers incurred by the Board of Health. The highest year was 1856, in which the total rates amounted to 7*s*. 6*d*. in the pound, divided as follows: poor rate, 3*s*. 4*d*.; borough rate, 1*s*. 7*d*.; harbour rate, 3*d*.; dock rate, 4*d*.; board of health rate, 2*s*. From a table kindly furnished by Mr. Alderman Naish, it appears that in 1886 the local burdens in the "ancient city" had fallen to 5*s*. 9*d*. in the pound; namely, poor rates, 1*s*. 6*d*.; borough rates, 11*d*.; dock rate, 4*d*.; harbour rate, 2*d*.; sanitary rates, 2*s*. 10*d*. In the city portion of Bedminster the local charges in 1886 amounted to 5*s*. 5*d*.; in Clifton and St. Philip's (out), 5*s*. 2*d*.; in Westbury (within the city), 5*s*., and in the District, 4*s*. 10*d*. in the pound. The rateable value of the entire city in October, 1886, was £932,496.

In October, Mr. J. H. Chute, the manager of the Theatre Royal, purchased of Mr. Rich. Fuidge a large house in Park Row, formerly the residence of Colonel Baillie [see p. 78]. Mr. Chute soon afterwards constructed a handsome theatre on the site, at a cost, including fittings, of nearly £18,000. The building was intended to accommodate 340 persons in the dress boxes, 100 in the orchestra stalls, 800 in the pit, 360 in the upper circle and amphitheatre, and 800 in the gallery.

It was opened on the 14th October, 1867, as the New Theatre Royal, but was afterwards styled the Prince's Theatre.

Pembroke Chapel, Oakfield Road, erected by the Congregationalists, was opened on the 31st October. It took the place of an iron chapel, which had been in use there for some years. On the following day, Trinity Chapel, the second place of worship built by the Wesleyan Methodists in Whiteladies Road, was opened by the Rev. W. Shaw and the Rev. W. M. Punshon.

Emmanuel Church, Clifton, was opened on the 18th December, its erection having occupied less than thirteen months. In 1868 the building was considerably enlarged; it was consecrated by the bishop of the diocese on the 7th January, 1869. A lofty tower was added subsequently—in which a peal of eight bells was placed in September, 1884, but funds have not yet been forthcoming for the construction of an intended spire.

A mysterious affair, under which no doubt lurked a villanous murder, caused great excitement towards the close of the year. On the afternoon of the 6th of December, a man named Charles Jones, about eighty years of age, who pursued the business of a money lender, was seen to enter the yard of a beerhouse called the North Somerset Railway Arms, in St. Philip's Marsh, kept by one Nathaniel Ramsden. Jones was never seen or heard of again. In the yard of Ramsden's house was a lime-kiln and furnaces, used by the occupier in his business of a lime dealer and tar distiller. Ramsden owed the deceased about £330, of which Jones had been endeavouring to obtain repayment for some time, and Ramsden was in difficulties and had just been made a bankrupt. On the 8th December Ramsden called on Jones's agent and man of business in the city, and produced a paper, purporting to be a receipt signed by the deceased for £340, alleging that he had paid £10 too much and was to receive it back again. Jones's agent, however, intimated his belief that the signature was not genuine, whereupon Ramsden went off, carrying the paper away with him. When questioned by the police, Ramsden asserted that he had paid the money to his creditor, but two of the persons said by him to have been present at the transaction deposed that they saw no money pass. A careful search was made of the premises, but no trace of the body could be discovered; and it was generally believed that it had been burnt in the lime-kiln. Ramsden left the country a few months later, and the affair has ever since been wrapped in impenetrable mystery.

The Duke of Buckingham, President of the Council, having paid a visit to Bristol in January, 1867, to distribute the prizes to the successful pupils in the Trade School, the opportunity was seized by the Merchant Venturers' Society to present him with the freedom of the incorporation. The Duke was a lineal descendant of Robert Nugent, Lord Clare, many years M.P. for Bristol, his grace's great-grandfather having married the only daughter and heiress of that nobleman.

A distinguished native of Bristol, and one of the most accomplished British sculptors of the present century, Edward Hodges Baily, R.A., F.R.S., died on the 22nd May, in his eightieth year. The artist was the eldest son of Mr. William Hillier Baily, of this city, and was born on the 10th March, 1788. He was for about two years a pupil at the Grammar School, where he is said to have been deft in carving portraits of his companions, but to have shown no capacity for ordinary work. Mr. Hillier Baily was a ship carver, in which avocation he displayed much ability, and his figures doubtless awakened a love of art in his son, who at the age of 16 abandoned the mercantile desk over which he had bent for a couple of years, and soon after gained admission to the studio of Flaxman, where he made rapid progress. At 19 he gained one of the prizes of the Society of Arts; at 21 he was awarded the first silver medal of the Royal Academy; and at 23 he carried off the gold medal and 50 guineas which were then the "blue ribbon" of the latter institution. In the year following this last success, he produced his grandest imaginative work—"Eve at the Fountain"—which won for its creator the prize of 100 guineas from the British Institution as the best specimen of British sculpture. The loveliness of the work at once established his reputation, and casts were eagerly purchased for the chief schools of art in France and Germany. In 1819 Baily was elected an Associate of the Royal Academy, and was raised to the rank of Academician in 1821, being the only sculptor who attained that honour during the presidency of his fellow Bristolian, Sir Thomas Lawrence. The mythological group sculptured in the frieze of the portico of the Institution (now the Freemasons' Hall), in Park Street, was presented by Baily as a token of affection for his native city. Amongst the best of the artist's very numerous works were: "Eve Listening," "The Graces," "Motherly Love," "The Sleeping Nymph," a statue of Fox at Westminster, and colossal statues of Sir Robert Peel at Manchester, and of Earl Grey at Newcastle. The statue of Nelson, on the column in Trafalgar Square, London, was also from his chisel. "Eve at the Fountain" was purchased by a local subscription for £600, and was placed in the Bristol Institution—now the Museum and Library. Though much profitable work was placed in his hands, Baily was, like Lawrence, unthrifty; and the later years of his long life were passed in painful embarrassment.

On the 17th June, during the progress of the Reform measure of 1867 through the House of Commons, a Liberal member moved that the six English provincial boroughs having a population of upwards of 100,000 (Bristol being one of the number), should return three representatives instead of two. The proposal was resisted by Mr. Disraeli on behalf of the Ministry, and on a division it was rejected by 247 votes against 239. Subsequently, the Cabinet conceded the claim for another member made on behalf of Liverpool, Manchester, Birmingham, and Leeds, whereupon Mr. Berkeley put in a similar demand for Bristol. He was, however, defeated by 235 votes against 136. In July, 1870, the Council unanimously resolved to petition Parliament for an additional member but the effort was without result.

At a meeting of the Docks Committee in June, it was determined to erect a new and improved Drawbridge at the end of Clare Street—the roadway of the bridge to be more on a line with that street than was the old structure. The improvement cost about £2,500.

A local newspaper of the 20th July stated that in consequence of the Governments of France and Belgium having granted a "drawback" on exportations to the sugar refiners of those countries, the loaf sugar trade in England had been so largely monopolised by the foreign manufacturers that some of the chief British refiners had been obliged to contract their operations and reduce the number of their hands. The making of loaf sugar appears to have been practically discontinued in Bristol before this date, the manufacturers having devoted themselves to the production of crystallised sugar, in which they excelled. The *Bristol Times* of September 28, 1872, stated that "last week, sales by Messrs. Finzel & Sons reached 1,800 tons, the value of which would probably be £70,000." In 1876 the same firm, whose premises were already amongst the largest in the country, purchased Counterslip Chapel and the adjacent schools for about £10,000, and converted them into warehouses. The step was not justified by the financial condition of the firm—which had sustained an irreparable loss by the death (21st

October, 1859) of Mr. Finzel, its founder and manager*—and the house went into liquidation in the spring of the following year. It was stated at an attempted sale of the premises and plant, that the outlay upon them had exceeded £400,000. The agitation in reference to the foreign sugar duties continued for several years, and was made an instrument for the promotion of the doctrines of a party calling themselves Fair Traders. In 1878 the Bristol Chamber of Commerce forwarded a memorial to the Government praying for the imposition of a duty on foreign refined sugar equal to the amount of the bounty on exports alleged to be paid by the French and other Governments. But Lord Beaconsfield's Ministry refused to take any legislative action which savoured of protection, and an attempt of certain professional agitators, styling themselves working men, to secure the support of the Trades Union Congress, during its gathering in Bristol in August, 1878, was emphatically defeated. In the autumn of 1878 a few public-spirited citizens formed a company, with a capital of £150,000, with the view of taking over Messrs. Finzel's works—offered at £71,500—and of reviving the business. The experiment unfortunately resulted in heavy loss to the promoters, and the manufactory was finally closed in April, 1881.

During the summer of 1867, building operations were carried on with unusual vigour in the suburban districts. In July a number of fields and nursery gardens near Redland and Hampton Roads were laid out for new streets. On one somewhat extensive estate, styled Woolcott Park, a great number of houses was subsequently built. For several years after this date, the only outlet westward from the estate was an old footpath, known as Nettle Lane; but the Corporation refused to lay out a street unless the landlords interested would contribute £500. This they refused to do, and the ground required for the street was allowed to be built over. In 1877 the Council—amidst much ridicule—admitted the necessity of a thoroughfare, and was compelled, at considerable cost, to buy and demolish the houses which stood in the way of the improvement. The "Goodhind estate," near Stapleton Road, was also sold in building lots during the autumn of 1867.

* Mr. Finzel, who was a German by birth, and began his career in England as a working sugar refiner, invented improvements in the apparatus for refining, the patent rights of which are said to have brought him in £10,000 a year. He was exceedingly generous, and for many years is said to have given between £5,000 and £10,000 per annum to Mr. Müller's Orphanages.

At the Wimbledon rifle competitions, in July, the great prize of the gathering—the Queen's gift of £250, with the gold medal of the Association—was won by Sergeant Henry Lane, of the Bristol volunteer rifle corps. His success was hailed with much satisfaction, and he met with an enthusiastic reception on his return. Mr. Lane was afterwards presented with a handsome testimonial, "in recognition of the honour he had gained for Bristol." At the meeting in the following year, Drum-major Hutchinson, of the same corps, won the silver medal, the silver badge, and £60, as the most successful shot in the first stage of the Queen's prize.

The church of St. Silas, St. Philip's Marsh, was consecrated on the 2nd October. Owing to the spongy nature of the subsoil, the church speedily began to show signs of subsidence, and its condition at length became so perilous that it was closed in March, 1872. The building was soon afterwards taken down, and the foundation stone of another edifice was laid on the 9th October. The new church, which cost about £2,100, was opened in August, 1873.

A small church in Maudlin Street, intended to serve as a chapel of ease to St. James's, and dedicated to St. James the Less, was consecrated on the 30th November.

On the 22nd January, 1868, several members of the Ministry of the Earl of Derby were entertained to a magnificent banquet by about 1,300 of the leading Conservatives of the district. The dinner took place in the Drill Hall, the standing order forbidding the use of that building for political purposes having been rescinded for the occasion. The Duke of Beaufort presided, and the chief speakers amongst the guests were Lord Stanley (now Earl of Derby), Mr. G. Hardy (Lord Cranbrook), and Sir John Pakington (afterwards Lord Hampton). The proceedings were marked with much enthusiasm.

The Royal Commission appointed for the purpose of re-adjusting the limits of counties and boroughs after the passing of the Reform Act of 1867, presented its report early in the following year. In dealing with Bristol, the commissioners recommended that Bishopston and St. George's parishes in Gloucestershire, and a further portion of the parish of Bedminster, in Somerset, should be included within the limits of the borough. The suggestion was condemned as unreasonable in view of the fact that the city had been refused the third member to which it was entitled by its population. A Committee of the House of Commons recommended the rejection of the report so far as Bristol and some other boroughs were concerned, and their advice was adopted.

In recording the removal, on the 25th March, 1868, of the Bristol Post Office from Corn Street to Small Street, an opportunity is afforded for a brief sketch of the progress of the institution during the present century. The onerous postal charges exacted down to 1839 have been already recorded [p. 244]. Their effect was to deter the entire community from making use of the office except for matters of urgency; and the postal revenue, in spite of the constant growth of population, made scarcely any advance for many years. The local office, when removed from Small Street to Corn Street, about 1748, required only the basement floor of the house on the west side of the Exchange. With the addition of a small apartment at the back, the accommodation remained sufficient until the days of penny postage. The staff, in 1820, consisted of 17 persons; it had risen only to 19 (6 clerks and 13 postmen) in 1837. The number of letters delivered at the latter date is unknown, but did not probably exceed 16,000 weekly, while, owing to the charge imposed on money orders (eightpence in the pound on small sums, and a higher rate on remittances above £2) the entire amount of the transactions in Bristol averaged only about £500 a year. A rapid development followed the reduction in charges, and besides an absorption of rooms on the upper floors, large extensions of the premises were made in the rear, a corner of the vegetable market being appropriated. But the work of the office expanded more rapidly than the space allotted to the staff, the number of which in 1855 had risen to 93 (42 clerks, 51 carriers). More elbow-room being then indispensable, a separate office for money orders was opened in September in a shop in Small Street. In February, 1856, the introduction of pillar letter-boxes led to a further growth of correspondence. Until nearly the close of the eighteenth century three mails a week from London were considered adequate. Thanks to the railways, the public were accommodated with three mails daily, and increased facilities were offered in various other directions, with satisfactory results. The time at length arrived when it was no longer practicable to conduct the work of the office in the old premises. In 1865 a site was purchased in Small Street, then occupied by Messrs. Freeman and the Brass and Copper Company; and a large building was erected at a cost of £10,000. [While the ground was being cleared, says the *Bristol Times* of November 18, 1865, the workmen came upon an old safe, falling to pieces, which, from some papers found in it, had belonged to the long extinct banking firm of Vaughan, Maxse & Co. An ancient mulberry tree, the last of several that once grew in the city, was destroyed about the same time.] When the new office was opened for business, the staff had augmented to 141; the weekly average of letters, etc., delivered in Bristol exceeded 157,000, and the transactions of the money order department represented upwards of £400,000 a year. The marvellous development effected under the new system, however, did not warn the authorities to make reasonable provision for future growth. Only the ground floor of the building was reserved for the postal officials,—the first and second flats being appropriated to the Inland Revenue staff, who removed there from Queen Square. The transfer of the telegraphs to the Government (see January, 1870,) hastened the breaking up of an arrangement which was from the outset injudicious. Before the close of 1871 the Inland Revenue officers returned to their old quarters, and the evacuated apartments were soon after occupied by the telegraphists. A few years later the money-order and savings-bank branch was again removed to a separate building, to make room for the growing needs of the postal service. Yet in spite of the relief afforded by successive migrations, the new office, before it was fifteen years old, was condemned as inadequate. The question of removing the institution to another site was brought before the Council in 1885, at the instance of the authorities in London, but the suggestion was not approved. In the autumn of 1886 the Government purchased a block of offices in Small Street, known as New Buildings, and some warehouses in the rear, with a view to an extensive enlargement, the cost of which was estimated at £15,000. The postal staff had then swollen to 356 persons (127 clerks and 229 carriers), to which were added 214 telegraphists and messengers. The average number of letters, etc., delivered weekly was 438,040; the yearly number of telegraphs transmitted and delivered was nearly 620,000; the transactions in postal orders and notes marked a total of nearly 300,000 annually, while the sum turned over in the savings bank reached nearly £100,000 a year.

In consequence of the failure of Messrs. Peto, Betts & Co., the great contractors, through the financial panic of 1866, Sir Morton Peto, M.P., in April, 1868, made use of the usual procedure for resigning his seat. His action having been foreseen, both political parties were prepared, and a smart contest ensued. The Conservative candidate was Mr. John William Miles, of Kingsweston, brother of a former member for the city. The Liberals were at first threatened with a division in their ranks, Mr. E. S. Robinson offering himself against the wishes of the leaders of the party, who brought forward a Mr. Bowring; but eventually both of the gentlemen withdrew, and a new selection was made in the person of Mr. Samuel Morley, a Nottingham manufacturer distinguished for munificent philanthropy. The polling took place on the 29th April, and the figures at the close were as follows: Mr. Miles, 5,173; Mr. Morley, 4,977. At the declaration of the poll on the 30th April, Mr. Morley affirmed that his defeat was due "to an undue use of money, beer, and intimidation," and a petition against the return was forthwith presented to the House of Commons. In the course of the subsequent investigation, evidence was given charging the Conservative committee with hiring a number of "roughs," with wholesale treating, with paying non-voters to personate electors, and with several cases of bribery. The petitioner's counsel also pointed out that the secretary to Mr. Miles's central committee and two other prominent agents had absented themselves from Bristol to avoid being summoned as witnesses. In the result, the committee, of whom a majority were Conservatives, declared that the election was void, and that Mr. Miles was, by his agents, guilty of bribery. Mr. P. W. S. Miles, brother of the unseated member, having immediately offered himself for the vacancy, repeated motions were made in the Commons for the issue of a new writ; but, as a general election was imminent, the House refused its assent. The election and its consequences excited considerable irritation in both political camps.

The death was announced, on the 14th June, of the Rev. Robert Vaughan, D.D., one of the most eminent Nonconformists of his time. Dr. Vaughan was born in Bristol in 1795, of poor parentage, and in early life worked as a carpenter. By dint of energy and ability he overcame the difficulties of his position, and ultimately became Professor of History in University College, London, and afterwards Principal of the Lancashire Independent College. His best known works are a biography of Wycliffe, a history of England under the Stewarts, "Revolutions of English History," and "The Age of Great Cities." He was also the founder and many years editor of the *British Quarterly Review*. In May, 1866, Dr. Vaughan was presented by Mr. S. Morley, as chairman of a meeting of prominent Dissenters, with a cheque for £3,000, in recognition of his distinguished services as a minister, a teacher, and a man of letters.

The new thoroughfare connecting Park Row with Maudlin

Street was formally opened by the mayor (Mr. F. Adams) on the 20th August, with some state, a civic procession wending its way from the Council House to the place fixed for the ceremony. The mayor, in a brief address, stated that the street would thenceforth be called "Perry Road," in honour of the chairman of the Streets Improvement Committee. In the construction of the new thoroughfare, which cost upwards of £13,300, or nearly 50 per cent. in excess of the estimates, a great number of crowded and ill-constructed dwellings were cleared away, one side of Lower St. Michael's Hill being entirely demolished. Amongst the old structures removed was an octangular tower, which was embedded in an old house nearly opposite to the southern front of the King David Inn. This tower was the only relic of the White Lodge, built in the sixteenth century upon the northern extremity of the garden of St. Bartholomew's Hospital, Christmas Street. Subsequently, at an expenditure of £37,600, Upper Park Row and Maudlin Street were widened, nearly the whole of the south side of the latter thoroughfare being rebuilt. Lower Maudlin Street was also improved, and the result was a spacious road from Clifton to St. James's Churchyard, and also to Stokes Croft. In September, 1872, the new street named after Colston, extending from St. Augustine's Place to Lower Maudlin Street, where it forms a junction with Perry Road, was completed, and offered an easy communication from the fashionable suburbs to the centre of the city.

The Baptist denomination erected this year a handsome place of worship in Whiteladies Road, which was opened by the Hon. and Rev. Baptist Noel on the 30th September, under the name of Tyndale Chapel. The original outlay, £7,500, was increased by upwards of £5,000 in 1880, through the addition of lecture rooms and schools.

A French Roman Catholic Sisterhood, styled the Little Sisters of the Poor, which about 1861 took up their residence in Bedminster, and subsequently removed to Trinity Street, and then to Park Row, having been compelled to leave their last-named dwelling by the improvements in progress there, purchased a house on Cotham Hill, to which they now removed. They afterwards built, in connexion with their convent, an asylum for the reception of about one hundred sick and aged poor, means for the maintenance of whom they obtained by soliciting alms from door to door. A chapel was added to the asylum in 1876, when about £7,000 had been expended on the institution.

A large boarding-house in Sion Row, once the pump-room

of the Sion spring, was purchased during the year by a joint stock company, and was opened in October under the name of the St. Vincent's Rocks Hotel.

At the general election in November, the political events which had occurred in the city a few months before added greatly to the excitement customary on such occasions. Mr. John William Miles was again nominated by the Conservatives, who expressed confidence in his triumph, owing to the gain of 579 votes on the new register claimed by their Association. The Liberal candidates were Mr. Berkeley and Mr. Samuel Morley. The poll, which took place on the 17th November, resulted as follows:—Mr. Berkeley, 8,759; Mr. Morley, 8,714; Mr. Miles, 6,694. The figures show a great increase over those recorded at the contest seven months before; and it is necessary to explain that the household suffrage conferred by the Reform Act of 1867 had added about 7,000 electors to the constituency, which was thus enlarged nearly 50 per cent. The election was marked by disorder to an extent unknown for many years. During the proceedings Mr. Morley was twice attacked in the streets with stones, and was painfully wounded in the face. Much destruction of property was committed on the nomination and polling days by "red" and "blue" mobs, which rivalled each other in brutality and violence. It was asserted in the Conservative organ that the city was "sacked and wrecked" by a rabble organised for the purpose by the Liberal committee. Major Bush further declared before a committee of the Commons, in 1869, that intimidation prevailed to a great extent, and that organised mobs, hired as he believed by the Reform League, were turned loose to prevent Conservatives from voting. He estimated that about 900 voters were deterred from going to the poll. Mr. Herbert Thomas, a leading Liberal, gave evidence of a flatly contradictory character. The Liberals, he deposed, hired no "roughs," though to his knowledge as many as 1,200 were paid in April, 1868, by the Conservatives, who opened 200 public-houses, and obtained a three days' holiday for the labourers employed on the river improvement works, in order that they might act against the Liberals at the nomination. With regard to the disturbances in November, Mr. Thomas added that out of the 17 ruffians punished for rioting by the magistrates, 15 were wearing blue colours when arrested. In consequence of the outrages, the Council petitioned Parliament, by a unanimous vote, to abolish the system of public nominations, which had everywhere degenerated into a disorderly and useless farce.

Clifton Down Chapel, erected by the Congregationalists who had long worshipped in Bridge Street Chapel, was opened on the 11th November by the Rev. S. Martin, of London. The new building, which is in the fourteenth century style, cost nearly £10,000. Funds were not available for raising a highly ornamental spire. The congregation traces its existence to 1682, when a licence from Charles II. (still exhibited in the vestry) was granted to John Weeks to preach in a room in St. James's Back. Subsequently the congregation removed to a building erected for a theatre in Tucker Street; and upon that place being demolished for the construction of Bath Street, a migration took place to Bridge Street, where the basement of the chapel was leased to a wine merchant for cellarage. The arrangement, of which there have been other local examples—one in fact still exists—gave rise to the following lines:—

"There's a spirit above and a spirit below,
A spirit of weal and a spirit of woe;
The spirit above is the Spirit Divine,
The spirit below is the spirit of wine."

During the year 1868 the two bells of Clifton Church were increased to a peal of eight, at the expense of Miss Clay, a resident in the parish.

During this year a novel and interesting movement was started by Dr. Percival, in co-operation with the teaching staff and the elder students of Clifton College. A ragged school was established in one of the poorest eastern districts of the city—on the borders of the parishes of St. Emmanuel and St. Silas—and in a short time about one hundred and twenty children were receiving instruction. After the passing of the Education Act of 1870, it was felt that the School Board might be safely left to provide secular teaching in the locality, and Dr. Percival addressed a communication to the commissioners for church extension purposes, appointed by Bishop Ellicott, offering to maintain a mission in any district they should select. The result was the establishment in 1875 of a mission in Newfoundland Road (St. Barnabas' parish), and an invitation to the boys of the College to co-operate in the movement met with a cordial response. A large workshop was converted into a mission room, and two adjoining houses were afterwards taken for the purposes of the work. The accommodation being found insufficient, about £2,000 were subscribed, and a new mission room, with class rooms, soup kitchen, etc., was opened in May, 1882. An additional building, used as a workmen's club and library, was added shortly afterwards. The institution proved of great service to the sufferers from the disastrous inundation of 1882, when the College, assisted by friends, raised an extra subscription of £618. In the following year the district undertaken by the mission was separated from St. Barnabas' parish, and constituted the ecclesiastical district of St. Agnes, and a new church was built at a cost of upwards of £5,000, of which the College and its friends provided one half. The building was consecrated on the 2nd March, 1886. It ought to be added that the example of the College stirred up some of the Clifton parishes to establish similar missions in the eastern districts.

Under the will of Miss Hannah Ludlow, a Quaker lady, who died in February, 1869, aged about ninety years, the Charity Trustees came into possession of about £20,000, the interest upon which was ordered by the testatrix to be divided into annuities of £30 each, for the benefit of women of respectable character and position, but impoverished by unavoidable circumstances. The wealth of Miss Ludlow, who was a native of the city, came to her from a brother, who was for many years an ironmonger in Old Market Street.

An influentially attended meeting was held on the 8th April, the mayor (Mr. F. Adams) presiding, for the purpose of promoting the establishment of a training ship for the reception of homeless and destitute boys. The subscriptions announced at the close of the proceedings amounted to nearly £1,500. In the following August, the Lords of the Admiralty granted the loan of an old man-of-war, the *Formidable*, pierced for eighty-four guns, which arrived at Kingroad in September, when Commander E. Poulden, R.N., was appointed captain-superintendent. About 1,200 homeless boys have since been rescued from misery, trained as sailors, and passed into active life, where the vast majority have conducted themselves worthily. In 1874 a tender, the *Polly*, intended to take about thirty of the elder lads on cruises for practical training, was purchased at a cost of about £1,000.

The merchants attending the corn market in the Exchange having presented a memorial praying for protection from the weather, the Council, at a meeting in June, resolved to expend £2,800 in covering the open quadrangle with glass. The proposal was opposed by many members, the most amusing objection being that of Alderman Webb, who contended that if the market were made "too comfortable, the farmers, a dilatory set of men, would keep the corn merchants there much longer." The resolution was carried by a majority of

20 votes against 18. Subsequently, the Council requested a committee to consult with an architect as to the propriety of the proposed design. As shrewd observers anticipated, the selected architect lost no time in producing a plan of his own, and although the estimated cost was increased to £4,000, his proposal was adopted. The new design entailed considerable alteration in the details of the interior, a number of offices being built upon the top of the colonnade, and much allegorical enrichment introduced. The actual cost of the improvement, which was completed in August, 1872, was little short of £7,000.

The Right Honourable Sir John Cam Hobhouse, Lord Broughton, G.C.B., F.R.S., died at his residence in London on the 3rd June, 1869. The son of a Bristolian—Sir Benjamin Hobhouse, bart.—he was born at Redland on the 27th June, 1786, and received his early education on St. Michael's Hill, at a school of great repute kept by the Rev. Dr. Estlin, minister of Lewin's Mead Chapel. Having formed a friendship with Lord Byron at Cambridge, he accompanied the poet in his travels in 1809, and on his return published an interesting narrative entitled "A Journey through Albania." He had previously produced a volume of poems and translations; and the fourth canto of "Childe Harold" was dedicated to him by the author. Mr. Hobhouse, who took advanced views as a politician, was one of the few who then advocated a reform of the House of Commons, and having published in 1819 a biting pamphlet, entitled "A Trifling Mistake," he was committed to Newgate for a breach of parliamentary privilege, but recovered his liberty a few weeks later, on the death of George III. He was immediately afterwards elected one of the members for Westminster, which he represented for several years. In 1832 he entered Lord Grey's Ministry as Secretary of War, which office he exchanged in 1833 for that of Irish Secretary; a twelvemonth later he became Chief Commissioner of Woods and Forests. His candidature and rejection for Bristol in 1835 have been already recorded [p. 203]. On the return of his party to power in the same year, he became President of the Board of Control, and filled the post for more than six years. In 1846 he was again nominated to that office, in which he continued until 1852. For his distinguished public services he was raised to the peerage in February, 1851. After retiring from public affairs, he occupied his leisure in composing "Recollections of a Long Life," privately printed in five octavo volumes, and stated by the *Edinburgh Review* (vol.

133) to be replete with interesting anecdotes relating to political, literary, and social life.

During the summer of 1869 a memorial was addressed to the Poor Law Board by a number of local magistrates, members of the Council, and guardians of the poor, pointing out the anomalies that had arisen in the constitution of the Bristol board in consequence of the changes effected by time in the ancient wards. Each of those districts was represented at the board by four members, but while All Saints', St. Ewen's, and St. Mary-le-port each contained less than 200 ratepayers, the assessments in St. Michael's numbered 2,586, and those in St. James's 4,152. The memorialists further complained that the guardians representing the ratepayers were generally outvoted on important questions by the nineteen churchwardens who were guardians ex-officio, and non-representative.* The memorial having been sent to the Board of Guardians, a motion was brought forward in November, recommending a reconstruction of the body. To this an amendment was moved, asserting that the ratepayers had a sufficient control over the board, and were generally satisfied with the old system. On a division the ratepayers' guardians were outvoted, and the amendment was adopted.

The branch railway from Yatton to Axbridge, Cheddar, and the neighbouring district was opened for traffic on the 3rd August. The new line, which was originally projected by the Somerset and Dorset Company, was extended to Wells in the following April.

On the 4th August, the Midland Railway Company offered the public an alternative route between Bristol and Bath, by opening a branch from Mangotsfield to the latter city. The line had been originally proposed by Hudson, "the Railway King," in January, 1846. For the accommodation of the passengers on this railway, the Company soon afterwards constructed an independent station near their goods depôt at Whipping-cat Hill, St. Philip's (erected in 1866), and it was opened early in 1870.

The National Association for the Promotion of Social Science opened its thirteenth annual congress in Bristol on the 29th September, under the presidency of Sir Stafford Northcote, bart. (Earl of Iddesleigh). The congress was very

* Speaking of these churchwarden guardians at a meeting of the Council, January 2, 1878, Mr. H. J. Mills said: "He remembered one ward where the churchwarden would call a vestry meeting—it was a close vestry—would be the only person present, would vote himself into the chair, elect himself guardian, pass the usual vote of thanks to the chairman, and vote himself out again."

'numerously attended by social reformers and philanthropists from all parts of the kingdom. In addition to an inaugural address, the president delivered a speech at a crowded meeting of working men in Colston Hall.

Under the provisions of an Act recently passed, conferring the municipal franchise upon women, the burgess roll for this year was considerably enlarged, the names of 2,465 female ratepayers appearing upon it. The addition was strikingly conspicuous in the Clifton list, in which were the names of 641 female and 1,907 male burgesses. A large majority of the new electors evincing Conservative sympathies, the three Liberal councillors for Clifton successively lost their seats.

During the autumn, to the regret of many residents in the neighbourhood, a number of the fine old elms which decorated Queen's Square were cut down, their partial decay awakening a dread of accidents in heavy gales. As in the case of Brunswick Square, whose deprivation of sylvan ornaments has been already noticed, a colony of rooks, an interesting feature of city life, was left homeless. Many of the Queen Square birds appear to have quitted the city, but a few betook themselves to the neighbourhood of Tyndall's Park and Cotham.

The Deanery Road, affording a new route from College Green to the Hotwells and Clifton, was opened on the 29th November by the mayor (Mr. W. K. Wait), accompanied by a large civic procession. The road had cost the Corporation about £20,000.

The death of Mr. George Thomas, which took place at his residence at Brislington, in December, excited general regret, and his funeral was the occasion of almost unexampled manifestations of respect. Upon the hearse entering the city on its way to the Friends' burial ground in Rosemary Street, the carriages of the mayor, sheriff, and other members of the Corporation joined the procession; and at the cemetery about five thousand citizens, including the Dean of Bristol, several clergymen and ministers, and members of every public body, were present to testify their sympathy. Mr. Thomas had during his life made many munificent gifts to public institutions. By his will about £13,000 were bequeathed to various charities and religious societies.

The most tragical accident recorded in the modern history of the city occurred at the New Theatre, Park Row, on the 26th December. Being "boxing day," a great crowd had assembled previous to the opening of the doors, to witness the Christmas pantomime. Unfortunately the avenue leading to the low-priced departments of the house sloped from the level of the street for about 50 feet, and the roadway outside being densely packed with people, there was a heavy pressure upon those below. After the doors were opened, the pressure became greater, and eventually it became so excessive that some of the weaker persons in the crowd, becoming exhausted, fell, and were trodden under foot. Their cries were drowned by the shouts of the stronger portion of the multitude; and it was a remarkable fact that their bodies were walked over by many persons who, forced on from behind, entered the house and enjoyed the performance in ignorance of what had occurred. Reports of the disaster, however, reached the ears of the police, who by great exertion forced back the crowd, and partially cleared the avenue. A fearful sight then presented itself. Upwards of forty victims were found upon the ground, some dead, others insensible from injuries. Fourteen dead bodies, mostly of women and youths, were soon after laid in the lower refreshment room of the theatre, where the performance was still going on, it being deemed perilous to make an announcement of the facts to the audience, which might have brought about a panic, and perhaps a still greater catastrophe. Four more of the sufferers expired after being rescued. The coroner's jury which inquired into the case returned a verdict of "accidental death," but recommended that separate entrances should be constructed for the pit and gallery, so as to divide the pressure in the avenues. The calamity had long a disastrous effect upon the fortunes of the New Theatre.

On the 1st January, 1870, the telegraphic business of the country was transferred from the private companies by whom it had been previously conducted to the Post Office. Some alterations were made in the new building in Small Street in order to accommodate a portion of the telegraph officials; but it was not until January, 1872, that room was found there for the entire staff, which then consisted of 90 clerks and 50 messengers. Soon after the new system came into force, the telegraphic system in the district was extended to all the small towns and rural villages.

On the 1st January, in accordance with a Bankruptcy Act passed in the previous year, imprisonment for debt ceased throughout England. The bankruptcy statute of 1861 had already reduced the number of debtors in prison to an insignificant number, and there was only one to be liberated from Bristol gaol when the later Act came into operation. A local journal, commenting upon the fact, stated that at a time within the experience of the then governor of the prison, the total liabilities of those detained had amounted to over £200,000. Various small bequests had been made from time to time for the benefit of destitute debtors. They were transferred, in 1875, to the endowments of the Grammar School.

The Court of Bankruptcy also ceased at the above date, the business being transferred to the County Court. Mr. M. D. Hill, who had been appointed commissioner on the death of Serjeant Ludlow in 1851, and who had gained a wide-spread reputation for his exertions on behalf of reformatory institutions and prison reform, retired into private life amidst many tokens of respect.

A vacancy in the representation of the city was caused on the 10th March by the death of Mr. Henry Berkeley, who had held his seat in no less than eight Parliaments. His friends expressed much regret that he was not spared to witness the success of a measure with which his name will be associated in history. The Ballot Bill received the royal assent during the session of 1872, and those who had poured ridicule upon Mr. Berkeley's advocacy of its principle were soon found practically admitting that they had miscalculated its effects. Mr. Berkeley's demise caused a division in the Liberal party, Mr. Kirkman D. Hodgson, a London merchant, being selected by the Liberal Association, while Mr. Elisha S. Robinson put forward his claims as a "local man," and a section of the working classes supported the pretensions of Mr. George Odger, of London, who had been a journeyman shoemaker. As none of the fractions showed a disposition to give way, it was suggested, and finally determined, that a "test ballot" of the constituency—excluding those known to be Conservatives—should be taken, and that the successful aspirant at that stage should have the united support of the party. This novel procedure accordingly took place on the 22nd and 23rd March, when 8,698 electors took part in the voting; the result showing that Mr. Robinson had 4,502 supporters, Mr. Hodgson 2,861, and Mr. Odger 1,335. Reckoning upon a certain amount of irritation amongst the friends of the defeated candidates, the Conservatives now entered the field, their champion being Alderman Sholto Vere Hare (mayor in 1862–3). The election took place on the 28th March, and the sheriff declared the poll as follows: Mr. Robinson, 7,832; Mr. Hare, 7,062. About a thousand Liberals declined to support Mr. Robinson. Shortly afterwards the Conservatives petitioned against the return; and on the 23rd May Mr. Baron Bramwell opened a court of inquiry at the Guildhall. The case turned out to be of an unprecedented character. Some cases of alleged corrupt practices at the election were adduced against Mr. Robinson, but the judge held them to be unfounded. It was proved, however, that before and during the test ballot a sum of between £8 and £10 had been spent in treating electors by two agents employed by Mr. Robinson, with the object of inducing voters to select him in preference to his competitors. The learned judge refused to decide whether those acts voided the election, and the case was remitted to the Court of Common Pleas, which was unanimously of opinion that the test ballot was one of the steps in the election, and that the treating was within the provisions of the Corrupt Practices Act. Mr. Baron Bramwell thereupon unseated Mr. Robinson, but refused to grant costs to the petitioners. Another writ having been issued, Mr. K. D. Hodgson was brought forward by the Liberals—Mr. Odger withdrawing in his favour—and Alderman S. V. Hare was again nominated by the opposite party. The nomination—the last of the many tumultuous scenes enacted in the Exchange previous to the passing of the Ballot Act—took place on the 24th June, and the polling followed on the 25th. The number of votes recorded was: for Mr. Hodgson, 7,816; for Mr. Hare, 7,238. This was the fourth parliamentary contest in the city within a period of twenty-six months.

The church of St. Gabriel, Upper Easton, erected at a cost of £4,400, was consecrated on the 14th March. An ecclesiastical parish, subtracted from Trinity, St. Philip's, was created for this church by an Order in Council.

An Act for reforming and reorganising the endowed schools of the kingdom having passed in 1869, the commissioners appointed under the statute sent Mr. Fitch, a sub-commissioner, to Bristol, to inquire into and report upon the schools of the city. Whilst the measure was passing through Parliament, the local authorities had appealed to the Government to exempt Bristol from its provisions, whereupon Mr. Forster, the minister who had charge of the scheme, in declining to comply with the request, assured the applicants that, as the Bristol endowments were admirably managed, the Bill was not intended to interfere with them. In spite of this assurance, Mr. Fitch speedily published suggestions the character of which excited much local indignation. Colston's School, Queen Elizabeth's Hospital, and the Red Maids' School, which had an aggregate income of about £16,300 a year, were practically to be swept away, in order to found, by means of their property, a series of first, second, and third class schools, in which education was to be offered to both sexes, though at rates which the working classes could not afford to pay. The intention of the founders of the three charities to assist poor and deserving parents was condemned by the sub-commissioner as the root of an immense mass of mischief and abuse that should be wholly cut away. To the objection, that the proposed changes would deprive the poor of institutions expressly founded for their benefit, and divert the funds to classes able to provide for themselves, Mr. Fitch retorted, that while the benefit of the charities was monopolised by about 400 families, and those perhaps not the most deserving, the entire population would reap the advantage of a system better fitted for the age; that in the primary schools "for twopence or threepence a week, every working man would have within his reach the most appropriate education he could desire for his children"; and that the endowments would be more beneficially spent in "creating a ladder to the universities," the approach to which would be an object of general emulation. The details of the draft scheme of the commissioners, issued in December, were in accordance with the principles formulated by Mr. Fitch, and evoked a general expression of disapproval, the only voice raised in favour of the plan being that of the Rev. J. Percival, the headmaster of Clifton College. The exception was not calculated to allay local dissatisfaction, for it further appeared that the commissioners had not merely adopted the sweeping proposals of their subordinate in reference to Colston's, Carr's, and Whitson's endowments for the poor, but had also sanctioned his scheme for crippling if not degrading the Grammar School, in order, as Mr. Fitch avowed, that it might not interfere with the development of Clifton College—at that time a denominational class school belonging to a joint stock company. The features of the commissioners' plan underwent great modifications. It will therefore suffice to say that Queen Elizabeth's School was to retain 200 boarders, whose parents were to pay from twenty-five to thirty guineas per head yearly; the Red Maids' School was to have 250 boarders, the annual fee for each being from eighteen to twenty-five guineas; whilst Colston's School, degraded to the third class, was to contain 300 boys, the charge for whom was also to range from eighteen to twenty-five guineas a head. Other children might attend the schools, but they were to be simply day pupils. Out of the endowments set free by this arrangement, the commissioners proposed to create an institution styled the Queen's School, for girls of the upper classes, together with some inferior schools. A few free scholarships were provided in each of the boarding schools as prizes for meritorious children drawn from the primary schools; but those gifts were to be open to competitors from all parts of the kingdom. In May, 1871, the Charity Trustees, on behalf of the two great schools under their charge, proposed alternative schemes, introducing important changes in the existing regulations, but maintaining the local and charitable objects of the endowments. In August the commissioners abandoned the features of Mr. Fitch's plan which had excited wide-spread objection, and made various other concessions to local opinion, the attack on the Grammar School being entirely defeated. They insisted, however, that forty free scholarships in Queen Elizabeth's Hospital and twenty in Whitson's School should be reserved for children selected by competition from the elementary schools of Gloucestershire and Somerset, and that two members of the governing body should be appointed by the members of Parliament for those counties. In March, 1872, the Merchants' Society proposed an alternative scheme on behalf of Colston's School, rejecting the commissioners' suggestion of day schools, and proposing to render liberal assistance to the Trades School. Under this arrangement the boys in Colston's School were to be reduced from 120 to 100; and the patronage as to nominations—which it was admitted had been sometimes exercised without reference to fitness or merit—was to be surrendered; on the other hand, the right of preferring a certain number of orphans was reserved. The Society added, that if its proposals were accepted it would endow the reorganised institutions with the sum of £10,000 (including certain debts due to it by Colston's Hospital). This scheme, with some modifications as to details, was agreed to in 1874 by the commissioners, who at the same time relinquished their attempt to open the City and Red Maids' Schools to children from the country districts. It was determined that the foundation boarders in the City School should not exceed 160, and that the surplus income should be applied to the endowment of day schools. The boarders were to be preferentially elected as follows: sixty poor orphans or children of incapacitated parents, residents of Bristol and Congresbury; fifty boys chosen by examination from the Bristol elementary schools, and fifty selected from the new day schools to be created under the scheme. The boarders in the Red Maids' School were fixed at eighty, as before, of whom fifty were to be orphans or children of incapacitated parents; fifteen to be chosen from the elementary schools in the city; and fifteen to be drawn from new day schools to be established and supported out of Whitson's endowment, aided by a sum of £5,000 drawn from Peloquin's charity. The boarding school in Denmark Street was to be eventually removed to a more appropriate site, and the old building converted into one of the day schools just referred to. As regarded the Grammar School, the scheme provided that the existing endowment, which was very limited, should be supplemented by £5,000, a further part of Mrs. Peloquin's bequest for doles to the poor, by £4,250 of the local Loan Money charity, and also by £355 left for the redemption or relief of poor debtors in prison. A new school was also to be erected in a suitable locality. Finally, the governing body of the three foundations was to comprise the existing Charity Trustees and six gentlemen elected by certain local constituent bodies, with an addition, in the case of the Red Maids' school, of four ladies, to be appointed by the other governors. The scheme received the approval of the Crown on May 13, 1875. By the scheme dealing with Colston's endowment the Merchants' Society and the Colston nominees lost their patronage as regarded the admission of boys, who were thereafter to be selected by order of merit, 80 from the elementary schools in Bristol, and 20 from those of Gloucestershire, Wilts, and Somerset. In addition to the foundation boys, the governors were to admit others, on payment of about £30 a year, to all the advantages of the school. Exhibitions to the value of £100 a year were to be created, to enable meritorious boys to finish their education at a grammar school. In accordance with the founder's injunctions, all the pupils were to be instructed in the doctrines of the English Church. The governors were to consist of the bishop of the diocese, the rector of Stapleton, eleven persons nominated by the Merchants' Society, two by the magistrates of Somerset and Gloucestershire, three by the Bristol School Board, and three by co-optation. The management of the Trades School was transferred to the governors of the school, who were also charged with the establishment of a school for girls when funds were available. The scheme received the Queen's approval on the 4th February, 1875.

In the Parliamentary session of 1870, a Bill was promoted for an extension of the Port and Pier railway from Sea-mills to the South Wales Union line, near Ashley Hill, by which the dock at Avonmouth would, when finished, be brought into communication with the great trunk railways. The Port and Pier Company had no funds to carry out the work, and upon the Great Western board discovering that a refusal to support the scheme would throw it exclusively into the hands of the Midland Company, the two directorates entered into negotiations. The result was an arrangement under which another Bill, for the construction of the extension line by the two companies jointly, was presented to Parliament, and received the royal assent in 1871. The works were commenced in the following August. The Clifton station was built upon a portion of the nursery grounds of Messrs. Garraway & Co., and the line from the Joint Station to that point was opened on the 1st October, 1874. The driving of the tunnel under the Downs, almost exactly a mile in length, was an arduous operation, but was completed in February, 1875. The cost of the line had been estimated at £225,000, but the actual outlay was £450,000. Its joint proprietors were at that time anxious to open the line for passenger traffic, but the Government inspector withheld the needful certificate, contending that a station should be constructed at the junction near Sneyd Park, and his objection was upheld by the Court of Appeal in January, 1877. Subsequently the companies became unwilling to carry passengers beyond Clifton station, and in spite of repeated remonstrances, the western section of the line remained closed to passengers for upwards of ten years, although the additional works required by the Board of Trade would not have cost more than about £600. It must be added that the debenture holders of the Port and Pier line, who had thrown it into the hands of a receiver [see p. 386], were equally obstinate in refusing to supply the deficiency. In 1884 the Midland board obtained parliamentary powers to provide the required signal station, etc., and to charge the expense on the receipts of the Port and Pier Company. The necessary works were soon after completed, but the receiver of the Port line then refused to provide one or two servants to work the signals. At last, in August, 1885, his resistance was overcome by a judgment of the High Court of Justice, and the railway was opened throughout on the 1st September following.

A meeting of the Council was convened in December, for the purpose of considering what steps should be taken in reference to the Elementary Education Act of the previous session. According to statistics prepared under the supervision of the town clerk, the number of elementary schools in the city was 236, but 38 of them had not sent in a return of their pupils. With regard to the remaining 198 schools,

70 were Church of England schools, with 10,628 scholars; 36 belonged to Nonconformists, and had 6,326 pupils; 7 were Roman Catholic, with 1,057 children; and 5 were endowed schools, having 421 inmates. There were also nine ragged schools, six industrial schools, and two orphanages, in which were altogether 3,265 children. The total number of scholars in attendance was nominally 23,286. Finally, 11 schools were being built, with accommodation for 3,252 children. This left a deficiency in the accommodation required by the Act of 6,591; but the insufficiency was in fact much greater, the central and Clifton districts being over-supplied with buildings, while there was a general lack of accommodation in the poorer parishes. The Council unanimously resolved to apply to the Government for the formation of a School Board. The request having been complied with immediately, the election of a board of fifteen members took place in January, 1871, and the proceedings, through their novelty, excited much interest. The Conservatives nominated seven churchmen, hoping, with the assistance of the Roman Catholics, who accumulated their fifteen votes upon a single candidate, to secure a majority in favour of denominational education. The Liberals nominated only five gentlemen, but counted upon the aid of candidates representing the chief dissenting bodies to maintain their principle of unsectarian teaching. Four additional Conservative candidates were brought forward by the Orangemen, the High Church party, and the Conservative Working Men's Association. The schoolmasters, the secularists, and some other interests also brought nominees into the field. The election, which was by ballot, occupied two days, and resulted in the return of three of the Conservative and of all the Liberal list. The entire board consisted of nine unsectarian and of six denominational members. The chairman, elected at the first meeting, was Mr. Lewis Fry. An educational census was next taken, from which it appeared that 5,300 children between 5 and 12 years of age—being nearly a fifth of that class in the city—were not attending any school. On further inquiry, it turned out that the estimate was too favourable, upwards of 4,000 children alleged by their parents to be at school being unknown at the respective institutions. The actual number not in attendance was thus 9,392, or one-third of the children of school age. A newspaper critic nevertheless continued to speak of the School Board as a "white elephant," and to censure the Council for having needlessly added to the taxation of the ratepayers. The compulsory clauses of the Act

were put in force; but, in spite of numerous prosecutions of careless parents, the daily absentees from school were for some time rarely under 7,000. The first building operations of the board were in the St. Philip's district, schools in Freestone Road for 650 children being opened in August, 1874, and at Barton Hill, for 750 children, in September, 1875. Six schools were transferred to the board about the same time. Subsequently, large school buildings were erected to accommodate the districts of Ashton Gate, the Hotwells, Redland, Baptist Mills, etc.; and within a few years the authorities were enabled to boast that the names of practically all the children of school age were upon the registers of efficient schools; though in point of regular attendance there was still much to be desired. A considerable addition to the educational machinery of the city has been made since 1870 through the efforts of voluntary bodies. Elections for the School Board have been held triennially, but the principle of unsectarian teaching which predominated at the first election, though often attacked, has not been overthrown.

During the year 1870 efforts were made by various philanthropic persons to enable working men to enjoy social intercourse during their hours of leisure in places where they might have the conveniences of the public house without its disadvantages. One of the first of those institutions in Bristol was the "British Workman," established in College Street; and although the class for which it was designed were somewhat slow in conferring their patronage, the new system steadily made way. The necessity of a reform in the licensing laws was at this period generally acknowledged. Beer licences being obtainable by almost any one at a trifling cost, beer shops sprang up in excessive numbers. As an illustration of the evil, it was stated at a Council meeting in February, 1871, that in Hotwell Road between Trinity and St. Peter's churches—a distance of about a quarter of a mile—there were thirty drinking establishments. (The number of inns, taverns, and beer-shops in the whole borough had increased from 400 in 1820, and 650 in 1840, to about 1,250.) The operation of the Licensing Act of 1872 gradually effected a reduction of the public houses in over supplied localities. Under this measure the time of closing on Sundays was fixed at ten o'clock, and one hour later on week days. In 1876, another temperance organization, called the Bristol Tavern and Club Company, was formed for carrying out the system of "public houses without the drink," and several such taverns were opened. The increasing enlightenment of the working classes has also greatly promoted temperance and thrift, the growth of which, to those who remember the social habits of the labourer half a century ago, is one of the most gratifying features of the age.

The decennial census of the kingdom was taken on the 3rd April, 1871. Owing to the demolition of dwellings for street improvements in the ancient city, there was a considerable decrease of population in some of the parishes, especially in St. James's, St. Nicholas', Redcliff, and Temple. The aggregate was 62,662. The population of the entire borough was 182,552. St. Philip's out-parish (42,287), Clifton (26,364), St. George's (16,209), and the District (13,841), showed a great advance. The other parishes stood as follows: Stoke Bishop tything (within the borough), 9,211; Bedminster, 32,488 (of which 23,522 were within the borough); Horfield, 2,985; Stapleton, 6,960; Mangotsfield, 4,533.

Greenbank Cemetery, an extensive burial place for the out-parish of St. Philip, laid out by the Burial Board of the district at a cost of about £11,500, was consecrated on the 14th April, 1871. Owing to the rapid growth of population, it was deemed advisable to extend the limits of the cemetery in 1880.

The story of the famous Bristol porcelain factory of Richard Champion does not come within the chronological limits of this work. Those desirous of information on the subject may be referred to Mr. Owen's beautiful and trustworthy "Two Centuries of Ceramic Art in Bristol." It may be stated, however, that at an auction in London, in April, 1871, some pieces of the magnificent service presented by Champion to Burke, soon after that statesman's election for the city, sold as follows: the teapot (the beautiful decorations of which were attributed to Henry Bone, R.A., one of Champion's apprentices), 190 guineas; cream-jug and cover, 115 guineas; a chocolate cup and saucer, 90 guineas; two teacups and saucers, 70 and 40 guineas; the cover of the sugar basin, 60 guineas. A fine Bristol vase was bought in at over £200. At another sale, in February, 1875, a cup and saucer of the Burke set brought £83, and a set of three jugs £120. In July, 1876, at the sale of Mr. W. R. Callendar's collection, the Burke teapot sold for £215 5*s*., and a chocolate cup and saucer of the same set brought £91. Another famous Bristol service was that ordered by Burke for presentation to his friend Mr. Joseph Smith, of Queen Square. The teapot of this set sold, in 1876, for £74 10*s*., and a teacup and saucer have brought £55. On the dispersion of the Edkins' collection, in 1874, a Bristol vase, with landscape, sold for £300; four figures emblematic of the quarters of the world brought £610; and a pair of compotiers £270.

In consequence of the complaints of some of the inhabitants, a Government order was issued in July for the closing of the three burial grounds connected with Clifton parish church, and of the cemetery attached to Dowry Chapel, subject to certain reservations as regarded surviving relatives of those already interred there.

The Odd-Fellows' Hall, Rupert Street, was commenced during the summer, and opened in the following January. The building cost about £2,000. In February, 1873, the local Foresters, with a similar purpose in view, purchased a house in Broadmead known as the Alhambra Music Hall. A portion of the building continued to be used for public entertainments, and in June, 1874, after an evening concert, it was destroyed by fire. The Foresters appear to have relinquished the property in 1880.

The foundation stone of Cotham Grove (Baptist) Chapel was laid on the 22nd June, and the building was opened for public worship in the following year.

After many years interruption, regular steam communication between Bristol and New York was revived this summer by Messrs. Mark Whitwill & Son. The first vessel of the new line, the iron screw-steamer *Arragon*, 1,500 tons register, sailed from Bristol on the 1st July, with forty-four passengers and a general cargo. The vessel returned to the Avon on the 11th August. In March, 1872, another steamship, the *Great Western*, was placed on the service, which took the name of the Great Western Steamship Line. Other vessels were added at intervals. The *Great Western* was wrecked near New York, through a collision, in March, 1876. In May, 1878, the first cargo of live American cattle arrived in this port, and an active trade in meat subsequently sprang up. In 1881 the Great Western Steamship Company was formed, with a capital of about £300,000, for purchasing the above line and extending the business. The development, however, was followed by a reaction; and the transatlantic trade became so unprofitable, except as regarded vessels of great burden, that several of the ships ceased to run. In February, 1886, it was announced that four vessels, the *Cornwall*, the *Somerset*, the *Devon*, and the *Gloucester*, which were too small for the American trade, had been sold to the Turkish Government for £39,000. The *Warwick* and the *Dorset*, each of about 4,000 tons, were then trading regularly between Avonmouth and New York; and the *Bristol*, the only remaining small boat, was laid up. At the annual meeting, a few weeks later, it was stated that a large part of the capital was lost; but the directors expressed confidence that if additional large vessels were purchased, and weekly sailings re-established, the concern would work through its difficulties. In 1879 another line of steamers, called, after the first vessel, the Bristol City Line, was started by Messrs. Charles Hill & Sons, and is still continued. The *Bristol City*, after leaving New York on the 28th December, 1880, with a crew of twenty-six men, was never heard of again. The *Bath City* was lost off the coast of Newfoundland in November, 1881. The crew suffered dreadfully from the frost, and the captain and several men perished. The *Gloucester City* foundered at sea on the 23rd February, 1883. The *Wells City*, of the same line, was sunk in New York harbour on the 10th February, 1887, through an accidental collision with another steamer. There was no loss of life in the last two disasters.

During the summer the ancient thoroughfare bearing the appropriate name of Steep Street, up and down which the Welsh mail once crawled on its to-and-fro journey, was entirely swept away by the Streets Improvement Committee. A fierce hand-to-hand struggle between the Royalists and the Parliamentarians is recorded to have taken place in this thoroughfare after the surrender by Fiennes to Prince Rupert. The street contained a notable seventeenth century house, long known as the Ship Inn.

A small wooden chapel of ease to Bedminster was erected at Knowle early in 1865. The attendance increasing, the chancel of a permanent church, in brick, dedicated to the Nativity, was erected, and the building was consecrated on 14th September, 1871. A large portion of the permanent nave was added in 1883; but Bishop Ellicott, before its consecration in June of that year, required the removal of a structure called a baldacchino, surmounting the Communion-table, and the incumbent, with much lamentation, complied with the demand. The church, which was soon after reported to be fitted up with "confessional boxes," had cost £6,000 up to that date.

The Jewish synagogue in Park Row, constructed upon a portion of the site evacuated by the Little Sisters of the Poor [see p. 441], was consecrated with much ceremony on the 7th September, 1871. The building cost about £4,000.

Upon the death, in 1871, of the Rev. John Hall, for many years rector of St. Werburgh's, the Council represented to the

Lord Chancellor, the patron of the living, the desirability of removing the church to one of the necessitous districts in the suburbs, by which a great public improvement would be effected in the city. It was shown that the number of parishioners was only eighteen—not one of whom was a ratepayer—and that the congregation attending divine service was extremely limited. The carriage way in front of part of the church—one of the most crowded thoroughfares in Bristol—was only 18 feet wide. Lord Hatherley consented to suspend his presentation, provided that a new church were built in a suitable position; and the Council thereupon resolved to apply for powers to remove the edifice, and to widen Corn and Small streets. Advantage was taken of the opportunity to apply for powers to make a new street from Lower Maudlin Street to Broadmead, to effect some improvements at Montpelier, and to improve a road from Regent Street to Victoria Square opened by the Merchants' Society, the total expenditure being estimated at £30,000. No measures, however, were taken for a considerable time to carry out the removal of St. Werburgh's, which in the meanwhile had been supplied with a new rector; and in the session of 1875 a Bill was privately promoted in Parliament for transferring the church and its revenues to another district. The lovers of ancient monuments warmly disapproved of the scheme, but finding that resistance to the improvement of Corn and Small streets had no prospect of success, they contented themselves by agitating for the preservation of the tower of the church, as a graceful ornament as well as an historical feature of the city. They were defeated in the Council, however, by a large majority. The Corporation subsequently resolved to acquire the site of the church and churchyard; but the promoters of the Bill, pleading the cost of carrying it to success, withdrew it from Parliament. In 1876, when a second Bill received the royal assent, the Council approved of an agreement with the parish authorities for the purchase of the site for the sum of £11,900, being £2,400 in excess of the price asked by the parish in 1872. Another agitation now sprang up for the maintenance of the tower, which the Council at one meeting resolved to preserve; afterwards reversed its decision; and again rescinded the latter vote on the antiquaries offering to contribute upwards of £1,000, the estimated value of the site. In consequence of these changes of policy, and of the necessity of ascertaining whether the ecclesiastical authorities would allow the tower to be separated from the church, the signature of a positive contract for the purchase of the ground was deferred from time to time. At length, in March, 1877, it was ascertained that the bishop and archdeacon would permit the tower to remain, provided the Corporation would hold itself responsible for accidents which might occur if the fabric fell when deprived of support. To this condition the Council demurred, and the matter threatened to be again indefinitely postponed, when the London and South Western Banking Company offered to buy of the Corporation as much of the site of the church as was not required for widening the streets, undertaking to retain the tower, to make a thoroughfare through its base for foot passengers, to keep the structure in repair, and to be responsible for accidents. As the Council had not completed the purchase, it could not have dealt immediately with the bank's proposal, even if it had felt a wish to do so. What it really did, was to again reverse its decision with respect to the tower, which was finally condemned by a great majority. It was further resolved to complete the long suspended contract. In the meantime, the churchwardens of the parish had received a direct application from the South Western Bank, and at a meeting of the vestry it was resolved that, as the Corporation had allowed more than a year to elapse without definitively accepting the proposal made by the parish, the negotiation should be considered at an end. The bank then purchased the site for £15,130, and gave £3,120 additional for the old parsonage on the north side of the passage leading from Small Street to the Commercial Rooms. The church, in which divine service was performed for the last time on the 12th August, 1877, was taken down in the spring of 1878,* when forty large chests of human remains, and about a hundred leaden coffins, were removed to Greenbank Cemetery at an outlay of about £700. The monuments in the church were placed in the new St. Werburgh's (erected in Mina Road, Baptist Mills), which was, or rather professed to be, a reproduction of the ancient edifice, and which was consecrated on the 30th September, 1879. The foundations of the new bank were carried down to an unusual depth, and bones were found at such a distance from the surface as to lead to a belief that the cemetery of the original church was fully twelve feet below the level of the fifteenth century edifice. The purchasers of the site adopted a design for a lofty building, occupying the whole of the

* With the removal of the tower the citizens also lost the notes of the curfew bell, which rang nightly at eight o'clock. The nine o'clock curfew of St. Nicholas is now the only one remaining in the city.

ground purchased, excepting that reserved for widening the streets, and extending over the passage leading to the Commercial Rooms. But the committee of the latter institution obtained injunctions restraining the company not only from covering the passage but from raising their new premises to a height which would obscure the lights of the reading room. After three years of costly litigation, the proprietors of the Commercial Rooms succeeded in maintaining their rights, and the great structure contemplated by the bank was left unfinished. The closing incident in this protracted affair occurred in the Council in August, 1881, when, as the result of an arbitration, the sum of £9,639 was ordered to be paid to the banking company for the value of two small slices of ground given up for the improvement of Corn and Small Streets, a further sum of £1,200 being paid in the shape of costs. As the Corporation had thus to give considerably more for an insignificant fraction of the site than was asked for the entire plot nine years before, its vacillating and dilatory conduct provoked much angry and derisive criticism.

During a heavy gale on the 20th December, 1871, the spire of the Church of St. Mary, Stoke Bishop, was entirely demolished by the wind. It was a wooden structure, 90 feet in height, and had just been completed. The spire was soon afterwards rebuilt in a more substantial manner.

A private company, unconnected with the city, having brought forward a scheme for furnishing Bristol with a series of street tramways for the accommodation of passengers, the subject engaged the attention of the Council for some time, there being much difference of opinion as to whether the new system of commmunication should be allowed to pass into the hands of private persons, or should be dealt with by the Corporation. A committee recommended the former course, but at a meeting in October, 1871, a resolution was carried desiring the Local Board of Health to obtain plans for a tramway from St. Augustine's Place to Redland, and also for another from Castle Street to Lawrence Hill. The necessary powers were obtained in due course, but owing to the inflated price to which iron soon after advanced, the lowest tender for constructing the lines amounted to £25,356, being more than double the estimate made by the civic surveyor. The Council at first resolved on a postponement of the undertaking, but subsequently determined to lay down the Redland line, reserving the other for a later period. In the meantime, preparations were made for the eastern route by the widening of West Street, which was effected at a cost of upwards of £7,500. Nothing was done towards the construction of the Redland line until July, 1873, when the term granted by law for the execution of the works was drawing to a close. Excavations were then made in Whiteladies Road, but the first rail was not laid until the 19th November, and as the needful supplies of iron were unobtainable, the road continued in a half blocked condition for upwards of six months, to the great wrath of those using the carriage way. When at length the work was finished, in the spring of 1874, at an outlay of £14,200, a new difficulty was encountered by the Corporation—the Tramways Committee could not obtain a reasonable offer for working the line. In July, a few responsible citizens suggested the formation of a company for the purpose, but they required in the first place certain concessions from the Corporation, amongst them being a claim for the use of the tramway free of charge for seven years. No better offer was forthcoming, but at a Council meeting in August a great majority refused to entertain the proposition. The promoters of the intended company thereupon abated their demands, and in October an arrangement was entered into, by which the Council granted a lease of the tramway for twenty-one years, the first three [afterwards extended to five] years free of charge, and the rent for the remainder of the term rising at intervals from £360 to a maximum of £600 per annum. The Council also sanctioned the construction by the company of a line from Old Market Street to St. George's, with a branch to Eastville, and of another line from Castle Street to Perry Road. Those schemes were resisted in Parliament by certain tradesmen in the suburbs, and also by the advocates of "Sabbath" observances, who strongly objected to Sunday travelling, while a few persons avowedly opposed the lines from a dread of the influx into the fashionable suburbs of working men and their families on holidays. The tramways were, however, sanctioned. The line from Perry Road to Redland was opened on the 9th August, 1875. The first three cars used on the occasion contained the mayor (Mr. C. J. Thomas), several members of the Council, the directors of the company, and a number of friends, the party subsequently dining together to celebrate the event. So great was the popularity of the line that upwards of 115,000 persons were carried during the first month, although only three cars were at work during part of the time. The dividend for the first half year was at the rate of 15 per cent. per annum. In September a prospectus was issued of the Bristol Tramways

Company, with a capital of £50,000 in £10 shares, with a view to the further development of the system. The tramway from St. Augustine's Place to Perry Road was opened on the 4th December, and a few weeks later the Council was asked to sanction the extension of the rails from the Victoria Rooms to Victoria Square, and from the Drawbridge to Bristol Bridge and Totterdown. The former of those projects was warmly opposed by influential residents in Clifton, and was rejected by a large majority of the Council. The other scheme having being referred to a committee, it was resolved, by 30 votes against 17, that no additional tramway should be sanctioned unless the company undertook to suspend traffic during the hours of worship on Sunday mornings and evenings. In February, 1876, a tramway from Bristol Bridge to Totterdown was sanctioned, subject to the condition just mentioned, to which the company objected. The line to Eastville was opened in June, that from Old Market Street to Perry Road in September, and a section of that to St. George's in October, 1876. The completion of the last-named line was prevented by the opposition of Messrs. Garton & Co., of Lawrence Hill, who contended that the thoroughfare was not wide enough to admit of the construction of a tramway in accordance with legal requirements. The obstruction was ultimately overcome by the Corporation giving Messrs. Garton £8,500 for setting back their premises, by which the width of the street was increased to forty feet. The Tramway Company (which during the year increased its capital to £150,000) subscribed £2,000 towards the improvement. In November, 1876, the Council approved of two new schemes—for a line from the Talbot Hotel to Totterdown, and from the Old Market to Victoria Street. A revulsion of opinion was observable on the Sunday question, for an attempt to prevent the cars running on these lines during the hours of service in the evening was defeated by 31 votes against 12. In October, 1878, the company applied for permission to make five new lines, namely, from the Victoria Rooms to Clifton Suspension Bridge; from the Drawbridge to the Port Railway station; from the Drawbridge, by way of New Baldwin Street, to the joint railway station; from Old Market Street to Victoria Street, and thence to Bedminster; and from St. James's Churchyard to a spot near Bishopston church. The directors subsequently proposed a sixth line—from St. Augustine's Place, by way of Park Street, to a junction with the existing tramway in Queen's Road; but this, as well as the Suspension Bridge line, was withdrawn. As the extensions were calculated to throw much additional traffic on the corporation tramway, and thus enhance the cost of its maintenance, borne by the ratepayers, it was agreed that the rental should be increased £100 a year. The Council thereupon sanctioned all the plans, save those withdrawn; and again rejected a motion requiring the suspension of traffic on Sunday evenings. Early in 1880 the Corporation assented to the construction of a line from St. James's Churchyard to the Drawbridge, bringing all the routes into communication with each other; but though it was soon after laid down, one or two punctilious persons in the neighbourhood raised legal objections against its being worked. The company also applied for powers to construct tramways on the quays in connection with the Harbour Railway; but the Council, after approving of the plan, subsequently reversed its decision. The tramway to the Hotwell was opened in June, 1880; and the Bedminster and Horfield lines came into operation in the following November. The last named was worked by steam; but the engines were neither economical to the company nor agreeable to passengers, and were removed after a year's trial. The Baldwin Street extension was opened in April, 1881, in which year powers were obtained, but never exercised, for extensions to Fishponds, Kingswood, and Horfield barracks. In January, 1882, the Council sold to the company, for £8,000, the original tramway of 1873, the construction and maintenance of which had cost the ratepayers at least double the money. In 1887 the company applied for parliamentary powers to make various improvements in their system, including the substitution of steam or other mechanical power instead of horses. The introduction of tramways has in no wise prejudiced previous modes of conveyance—omnibuses excepted. The report of the local inspector of public carriages for 1886 stated that the number of licensed vehicles was as follows: tram-cars, 60, four-wheel cabs, 214; hansom cabs, 99; breaks, 56; omnibuses, 9; wagonettes, 38; wheel-chairs, 50. The total, 526, was 129 in excess of the licences of the previous year.

On the 1st April, 1872, the second class railway carriages on all the Midland lines, except a few "through" vehicles running in connection with the trains of other companies, were withdrawn, and third class carriages were added to all the trains upon the system. The maximum fare for the latter class was fixed at a penny per mile. This bold measure, which gave deep offence to other great railway boards, was received with applause by the public, and proved profitable to the company, who, in the first three months, affected by the change, had, as compared with the same period in 1871, an increase of 38,000 first class and of 1,185,000 third class passengers, against a decrease of 266,000 in the second class. The augmented first class receipts were stated to have covered the loss on the second class, whilst there was an enhanced receipt of £70,000 from the third class. The action of the company forced the Great Western board to add third class carriages to some Bristol trains from which they had been excluded, with the effect of greatly increasing the number of travellers. At a meeting in February, 1873, the chairman, Sir Daniel Gooch, stated that during the previous half year they had carried 106,000 more first class and 3,594,000 more third class passengers, against a decrease of 1,109,000 in the second class—results which did not deter him from lamenting over the revolutionary policy of the Midland board. The latter company, on the 1st January, 1875, discontinued running second class carriages on all their trains. A sensible abatement was also announced in first class fares; but the Great Western board, under the provisions of an old agreement, placed an interdict upon any reduction in the districts in which the two companies had competitive lines. One of the consequences of this intervention was, that the Midland Company's first class fare from Bristol to Birmingham was maintained at 16*s*. 6*d*., whilst a similar ticket issued at Clifton Down station (opened after the agreement was signed) cost only 12*s*. 6*d*. The matter having been remitted to the Railway Commissioners, the agreement was abrogated as regarded most of the lines in this district. The liberal policy of the Midland directorate necessarily had an influence upon the directors of the Great Western, who made concessions from time to time. In June, 1878, third class carriages were added to the first morning express train from Bristol to London, thereby enabling Bristolians to transact business in the capital and return home on the same day. The citizens, however, still complained of the treatment they received from a company expressly formed to promote their interests. Before a committee of the House of Commons, in 1882, Mr. C. Wills, President of the Chamber of Commerce, stated that the company carried third class passengers from London to towns westward of Bristol by certain trains, but refused to extend this privilege to Bristolians. As to the first and second class fares, he added, they were from 43 to 50 per cent. higher between London and Bristol than they were between London and equally distant northern towns. A year or two later, the board, bending to public opinion, remitted the excess fares imposed on travellers by express trains, and added third class carriages to all the trains passing through Bristol, save one or two of unusual speed.

The foundation stone of St. Nathanael's Church, Redland Road, was laid on the 8th April, 1872. The edifice was consecrated by Bishop Ellicott in the following year.

At a meeting of the Council in June, it was resolved to convert the carcase market in Nicholas Street into a fish market, in order to remove the latter from its exposed situation on the Welsh Back. The alterations entailed an outlay of about £2,300. The market, which was opened on the 1st May, 1874, proved too large for its requirements, and became the resort of a worthless class who deterred respectable persons from entering the building. The Council at length gave orders for its reconstruction; and a smaller but more convenient market was opened on the 1st July, 1884.

Several pieces of land near Montpelier, on which were the field works thrown up by the Parliamentary army at the second siege of Bristol, and the farm house in which Cromwell is said to have slept on the eve of the assault, were purchased at this time for building purposes. The field works were subsequently levelled. A neighbouring mansion, Ashley Court, was demolished about 1876, and the site and adjoining land were converted into building plots, the demand for which was then very active.

The Midland Railway Company's branch line to Thornbury was opened on the 2nd September.

The latter half of the year 1872 was remarkable for an unusual activity of trade and industry, especially in connection with coal and iron works. The price of coal advanced with "leaps and bounds," owing in part to the unexampled demand, but still more to the conduct of the colliers, who not only insisted on repeated advances in wages, but refused to work more than a few hours a day for three or four days a week. Under the operation of this "stint,"—on which the masters, who were reaping unparalleled profits, were said to look with secret satisfaction,—a certain description of coal required for making gas, previously sold at about 5*s*. per ton, advanced to 25*s*. The Bristol Gas Company, in order to maintain their 10 per cent. dividend, twice advanced their prices to consumers. As an example of the speculative spirit excited by the inflation, the *Bristol Times* of May 3rd, 1873, stated that a suspended colliery within fifteen miles of the city, which had been offered before the "fever" for £1,000, had been bought by two mining agents, who forthwith started a company with £30,000 capital, to which they disposed of their purchase for £6,000 in debentures and £15,500 in paid-up shares. In October, 1874, some collieries at Nailsea, which had not been worked for sixty years, were re-opened; but the tide of prosperity was then fast ebbing, and the speculation was unsuccessful. In consequence of the inordinate prices of coal, the demand for iron at length fell off, while the opening of many new collieries brought fresh supplies into an already glutted market, thereby greatly depressing values and wages. For two winters, however, the dearth of fuel caused much suffering amongst the poor.

For several years previous to 1872 communications had been addressed from time to time to the Corporation by the Home Secretary, complaining that the condition of the gaol and of the house of correction was not in accordance with the requirements of the Prisons Act; to which the city authorities had repeatedly responded that the subject should receive earnest attention. In September, a more peremptory missive was received from the Home Office, declaring that the buildings in question were unfit for their purposes, and that immediate steps must be taken to comply with the law. A deputation was appointed to wait upon the Minister, to acquaint him with the heavy pecuniary burdens of the ratepayers, and to point out that the gaol, notwithstanding admitted shortcomings, was in a healthy condition and fairly adequate for its object. The mission proving fruitless, the Council, in June, 1873, determined to build a gaol upon a new site, it being anticipated that the sale of the ground occupied by the two prisons would go far to cover the expense of another building. In the following September, the Corporation gave £3,875 for Horfield Gardens [see p. 379], and in 1874 the Home Secretary approved of the Council's plans for the intended erection, the estimated cost of which was £65,000. A contract was entered into for the boundary walls, which were to cost about £4,000. But when tenders were invited for building the gaol, the lowest offer, owing to the abnormal rise in prices and wages, was £32,000 in excess of the estimate. It appearing probable that the engineering works, furnishing, etc., would raise the total cost to nearly £120,000, strong protests were made against such an outlay for the retention of criminals whose average number did not exceed 150. Whilst the subject was still under consideration, it transpired that the Ministry of Mr. Disraeli contemplated legislation for transferring the gaols of the kingdom from the local authorities to the Government; and the Corporation prudently kept the question in suspense until 1877, when an Act was passed to carry out the Ministerial policy. The last gaol delivery under the old system took place in April, 1878, in which month the Government entered upon the ownership and management of the prisons. Bridewell was closed in the following May, and the Home Secretary at that time intended to abolish the gaol also, and to remove Bristol prisoners to another district. This design was afterwards dropped. In the meantime, the Council was called upon to pay £17,161, as compensation for the certified cell accommodation which it had neglected to provide in the gaol, and a further sum of £4,320 on account of similar deficiencies in Bridewell. The latter building was thereupon reconveyed to the Corporation, which saved about £4,500 a year by being relieved of the management of the prisons. At a later date, the Government entered into an exchange of property with the Council, by which the latter again became possessed of the condemned gaol, upon surrendering the ground purchased at Horfield. The site of Bridewell, saving a portion required for the extension of Rupert Street, was granted on lease, at £600 a year, to Messrs. Budgett & Co., who built warehouses on part of the site. The prison at Horfield was sufficiently completed in April, 1883, to receive the prisoners detained in the old gaol, which was thenceforth deserted.

The curious statue of Neptune, said by some local writers to have been cast in 1588, and presented to the city by a resident in Temple parish to commemorate the defeat of the Spanish Armada, but which *Sarah Farley's Journal* of December 22, 1787, alleges to have been cast by one Randall and erected in 1723, was bronzed and burnished during the autumn, and "inaugurated" as a drinking fountain on the 26th November, by the chairman of the Sanitary Authority, Mr. F. Terrell. The site now occupied by the figure is the fourth which it has occupied in the locality; it having originally stood near the bottom of Temple Street, next near the site of Dr. White's almshouse, and thirdly near the parish church.

The rainfall of the year 1872 in this city was believed to have been the greatest that had occurred for upwards of half a century. The quantity collected at Clifton reached a total of 42·36 inches. The statistics of 1870 recorded a fall of less than 23½ inches. During the second half of the year rain fell in Bristol on twenty-five Saturdays in succession. Amongst many newspaper notices of the farming adversities of the season, was one stating that a field of clover grass, mown at Doynton in September, was not stacked until the following March.

From about the close of 1870 many citizens had been annoyed by the adoption, at a factory in St. Philip's, of an American invention called a "hooter," devised for the purpose of arousing operatives from their morning slumbers. The instrument created so violent a vibration of the atmosphere that the sound was sometimes heard at a distance of twelve miles, and its effect within the limits of the borough proved extremely distressing to invalids and nervous persons. The invention being popular amongst labourers, however, it was rapidly adopted in various parts of the kingdom, several being frequently set up in a single town. The nuisance at last became so intolerable that an Act of Parliament was passed in 1872, forbidding the use of the instrument except with the consent of the local authorities. In Bristol the Health Committee refused to sanction it; but upon the question being brought before the Council, in January, 1873, the decision was overruled by 21 votes to 18. The vote was significant of the increasing influence of the labouring classes on corporate affairs, for the majority made no attempt to answer the arguments advanced against the nuisance, but contented themselves with asserting that the comfort and convenience of a minority of the inhabitants should not be allowed to override the desire of the masses. In compliance with an order of the corporation, the noise made by the instrument was afterwards greatly diminished.

On the 18th January, 1873, a meeting was held in the Guildhall to consider the desirability of establishing a periodical series of musical festivals in Bristol. The mayor (Mr. Hathway) presided, and resolutions approving of the movement were carried unanimously. About 250 gentlemen, who had offered to guarantee £50 each in the event of a deficiency in the receipts of the first festival, were appointed a provisional committee. An executive committee was afterwards formed, of which Mr. Alderman Baker was elected chairman and Mr. William Smith vice-chairman. Mr. Alfred Stone was appointed chorus master, and a choir of 290 voices was soon in training. Mr. Charles Hallé was chosen to conduct the public performances. The first festival opened on the 21st October in Colston Hall, to which galleries had been added by the festival committee, and the building was filled with one of the most brilliant audiences ever assembled in the city. The first oratorio given was "The Creation," the leading parts being sustained by

Messrs. Sims Reeves and Santley, and Mesdames Sherrington, Alvsleben, etc. "Elijah" was performed on the 22nd, Rossini's "Stabat Mater" and Macfarren's "John the Baptist" were given on the 23rd, and "The Messiah," on the 24th, completed the series. Evening miscellaneous concerts also formed part of the programme. The total receipts amounted to £5784. The surplus after paying expenses was made up by the committee to £250, which sum was divided between the two great medical charities. The second festival was held in October, 1876, for which the oratorios selected were "Elijah," "Israel in Egypt," the "Fall of Babylon," "Engedi," and "The Messiah;" evening concerts being given as before. The chief vocalists were Messrs. E. Lloyd, W. H. Cummings, Kearton, Pope, Maybrick, and Behrens, Mdlles. Titiens and Albani, and Mesdames Wynne, Patey, and Trebelli. Though the receipts (£6473) showed an increase, the guarantors were called upon to pay a guinea each to cover the expenditure. Collections, amounting to £210, were divided as before. The third festival commenced on the 14th October, 1879, and extended over the three following days. The chief works given were "Samson," "Elijah," Mozart's "Requiem," Rossini's "Stabat Mater," and "The Messiah." The leading vocalists were Mesdames Albani, Trebelli, and Patey, Miss Emma Thursby, and Messrs. Santley, Lloyd, and McGuckin. The chorus had at this festival increased to 346. The receipts amounted to £6136, and the accounts showed a surplus of £402, exclusive of £208 collected at the doors. The Infirmary and Hospital received £250 each, the balance being reserved. The fourth festival was opened on the 17th October, 1882, and, being under the presidency of H.R.H. the Duke of Edinburgh, the proceedings excited more than usual public interest, though, singularly enough, the aggregate attendances showed a falling off. The oratorios performed were "Elijah," Gounod's "Redemption," Mackenzie's "Jason" (written for the festival), and "The Messiah." The leading vocalists at the morning and evening performances were Messrs. Lloyd, Santley, Maas, Kearton, and Warlock, Miss Williams, and Mesdames Albani, Patey, and Trebelli. The performance on the 19th was attended by the royal duke and duchess, who were welcomed into the city with great cordiality. Their Royal Highnesses were met at the railway station by the mayor (Mr. Weston) and members of the corporation; and the prince was presented with an address, for which he gracefully returned thanks. The streets were gaily decorated, and the volunteers supplied an efficient guard of honour. [A local reporter records that on the arrival of the distinguished visitors at Colston Hall, a prominent member of the Council, who was also a very active member of the festival committee, observing that the path from the carriage to the vestibule was somewhat dirty, pulled off his overcoat and placed it on the ground for the duchess to walk over, which she did.] The duke, before leaving, thanked the committee for their intention to devote the surplus of the receipts to a fund for establishing a Bristol scholarship in the new College of Music; and he also accepted the office of president of the Festival Society. The receipts of the week (£6,263) left a balance over expenditure of £148, which were forwarded to the College. The collections (£215) were divided in the usual manner. The festival of 1886 opened on the 20th October with Handel's "Belshazzar," the other oratorios of the week being "Elijah," Berlioz's "Faust," and "The Messiah." The chief singers were Mesdames Albani, Trebelli, and Patey, Miss Williams and Messrs. Santley, Lloyd, Hilton, and Maas. The chorus, numbering 360 voices, excelled all its previous performances. The attendances, however, were below the average, and the guarantors were called on for a guinea and a half each to supply the deficiency in the receipts. The collections for the hospitals produced £146.

The new church of St. Matthew's, Moorfields, was consecrated on the 28th January, 1873, by the Bishop of the diocese.

A report on the charities of Bristol was published in February by the Charity Commissioners. The following is a summary of the yearly value of the endowments then belonging to the city:—For education, £19,986 12*s*. 6*d*. Apprenticing and advancing the young, £803 10*s* 10*d*. Clergy, lectures, and sermons, £702 17*s*. 11*d*. Church purposes, £4,727 14*s*. 10*d*. Dissenting chapels and ministers, £983 19*s*. 3*d*. Education of Dissenters, £308 4*s*. 3*d*. Public uses, £143 8*s*. Almshouses and pensioners, £12,176 12*s*. 1*d*. Doles in money and goods, £3,336 11*s*. General uses of the poor, £4,998 6*s*. 6*d*. Total, £48,167 17*s*. 2*d*. In January, 1875, the Rev. J. Percival, head master of Clifton College, observed that many of the gifts to the poor, instead of alleviating poverty, perpetuated a spirit of dependence and improvidence, and suggested that £1,000 yearly of the doles should be employed to encourage the regular attendance of children at school, by the payment of the fees of orphans, providing clothes for the offspring of distressed parents, and establishing prizes. Mr. Percival offered, if his proposal were accepted, to guarantee £100 a year for similar purposes from the offertory of Clifton College. There was, however, no response.

A local journal of the 1st March stated that, in excavating for a Roman Catholic School adjoining Victoria Street, a discovery had been made of the foundations of an old religious house. Some old coins and a monastic token were said to have been found in the rubbish.

On the 19th March the opening of a new Bristol racecourse, at Knowle, took place under the patronage of the Prince of Wales. The ground had been laid out, and a grand stand, accommodating 3,000 persons, built by the Bristol and Western Counties Racecourse Company, which had been established in the previous year, with a capital of £8,000 in £100 shares. The first meeting was chiefly devoted to steeple-chasing, but there was some flat racing on a course of a mile and three quarters. The attractiveness of the gathering, which extended over three days, was much increased by the fact that the National Hunt Steeplechase Association had determined that its annual prize should be competed for on the ground. The Prince of Wales, who was a guest at Berkeley Castle, proceeded to the course each morning with a numerous party of friends. The attendance of the public on each of the first two days was estimated at 100,000. The money given in prizes during the meeting exceeded £2,000, the most notable gifts being the Bristol Grand Steeplechase prize of £500; the Association prize of £350; the City Hurdle Race of £200; the Ashton Court Steeplechase of £200; and the Clifton cup of £200. At the close of the last day's sport, the Prince of Wales was driven to the offices of Messrs. Miles Brothers & Co., Queen Square, where tea was provided. At the railway station, a great crowd assembled to cheer the departing visitor. In 1874, besides the spring steeplechase meeting of three days, there was a September meeting of the same duration for ordinary races, the prizes for which were also on a munificent scale. The company sustained a heavy loss on the two gatherings, and the autumn meeting was afterwards relinquished. The last spring races under the management of the company took place in 1878, in November of which year, owing to repeated heavy losses, it was resolved to wind up the concern. The races were continued by private enterprise in the spring and winter of 1879, and again in the spring of 1880; but the results were so unsatisfactory that the ground was given up. Subsequently the grand stand and other buildings were demolished, and the materials sold by auction.

In the spring of 1873 the faculty of the Medical School in Old Park were taking steps to remove to more convenient premises, when a proposal was started for founding a Technical College of Science, of which the school might form a department. An appeal was soon afterwards made to the public for pecuniary assistance towards carrying out the design. At this stage of the movement, a communication was received from the master of Balliol College, Oxford, stating that his College, and probably at least one other, would be disposed to co-operate in the work. This led to further negotiations, resulting in a definite offer from Balliol and New Colleges to contribute £300 a year each for three years under certain conditions, the chief of which were that the instruction given should be literary as well as scientific, that the requirements of adult education should be specially considered, and that the College (the medical classes excepted) should be open to women. This proposal having been assented to, the promoters of the movement again addressed themselves to the public, dwelling upon the importance of such an institution to the West of England, and the urgency of establishing it upon a creditable basis. On the 11th June, 1874, a meeting in aid of the project was held in the Victoria Rooms, the mayor (Ald. Barnes) presiding, when addresses in approval of the scheme were made by Professor Williamson, then president of the British Association, Professor Jowett, master of Balliol, the Bishop of Exeter (Dr. Temple), Mr. E. A. Freeman, the Rev. J. E. Sewell, warden of New College, the members of Parliament for the city, and others. It was estimated that £40,000 would be required to establish the College, and that £3,000 a year would be needed for its maintenance. In July, 1875, a meeting of peers and members of the House of Commons connected with the West of England and South Wales was held at Westminster, the Earl of Cork, Lord Lieutenant of Somerset, presiding, for the promotion of the Institution. A similar meeting was held in Bristol a few weeks later, during the sittings of the British Association, when the value of the proposed College was strongly urged by Sir John Hawkshaw, president of the Association, Sir William Thompson, Professor Jowett, and other eminent visitors. In December it was announced that £22,000 of the required capital had been promised (£19,000 by Bristolians); and steps were then taken for the incorporation of the College. Soon afterwards the Clothworkers' Company, of London, offered a subscription of £500 a year for five years to assist in the establishment of a department of textile industries. A staff of two professors and four lecturers having been selected (Professor Marshall* being subsequently appointed Principal), the work of the College commenced on the 10th October, 1876, a large house in Park Row, vacated by the Deaf and Dumb Institution, having been temporarily engaged. In 1880 the council, though inadequately supported by wealthy Bristolians, ventured upon building a portion of the north wing of the proposed quadrangle in Tyndall's Park, at a cost of £5,000. This was opened for certain classes at the beginning of the winter term of that year. About the same time, £800, the fruit of a subscription for a memorial to Miss Catherine Winkworth, of Clifton, an earnest advocate of female education, were invested as a fund for providing scholarships for women; while the Anchor Society offered £300 per annum for three years to found an additional professorship. The College continuing to progress, another wing of the building was erected, at a cost of about £6,000; and on its completion, in January, 1883, the house in Park Row was given up. The annual subscriptions then amounted to about £1,200, and the receipts from students to £2,200, while the yearly expenses were £4,600. The two Oxford colleges still continued to support the institution. A few words must be added with reference to the Medical School, whose needs originated the College movement. The opening of the winter session of 1879–80 took place in a plain but serviceable building situated near the College. The removal from Old Park was accompanied by an extension of the curriculum. The management of the school had shortly before been placed by the faculty in the hands of an independent governing body, elected by the council of University College, the leading officials of the Infirmary and Hospital, and the faculty of the school. The effect of those changes was to nearly treble the number of students.

On the 31st March, 1873, while some excavations were being made in an orchard at Little Sneyd, overlooking Sea Mills, the workmen found, a few inches below the surface, a gravestone of pentagonal form. It bore a rude representation of a head with rays, on one side of which was the figure of a dog, and on the other of a cock, while below was a deeply cut inscription in Roman letters, SPES C. SENTI. The discovery excited much interest, some antiquaries believing that the stone marked the resting-place of a Roman Christian; but the weight of authority was against this supposition.

* Professor Marshall resigned in the autumn of 1881, and was succeeded by Professor William Ramsay, Ph.D.

The success of wood pavements for carriage roads in London induced the Council, at a meeting in March, to order a trial of the system in some of the central thoroughfares in the city. A contract was soon afterwards entered into with the Improved Woodpaving Company for laying down the roadway in Wine Street, at a cost of £960. The experiment was deemed so satisfactory that the pavement was extended to Corn Street and part of Broad Street before the close of the year.

The old building known as Dowry Chapel having been removed in 1872, a new church, dedicated to St. Andrew the Less, was erected on the site, at a cost of about £2,700, and was consecrated on the 24th September, 1873.

During the autumn Narrow Wine Street, until then appropriately named, was widened by the demolition of several projecting houses at the western entrance.

At a meeting of the Council in November, it was announced that Alderman Proctor had expressed his willingness to plant trees along the riverside footpath in Coronation Road, from near Bath Bridge to Vauxhall Ferry. The expense was estimated at £500. A vote of thanks was passed to the alderman for his liberal gift. A foolish attempt has been made to style this parade a "boulevard," but the public have declined to adopt the misnomer.

The recovery by the city of its ancient library has been recorded under a previous year [see p. 333]. At a meeting of the Council on the 28th November, Mr. J. D. Weston moved that the corporation should take measures for the proper maintenance of the institution under the provisions of the Public Libraries Act. Only one councillor disapproved of the resolution. The question was laid before the ratepayers at a public meeting held in May, 1874, the mayor (Alderman Barnes) presiding, when Mr. Weston moved that the powers of the Act should be brought into operation; and he was as successful with the citizens as he had been with the Council, only three dissentient hands being raised against the proposal. Mr. Weston offered to give £1,000, provided £10,000 were raised by subscription, towards building a structure worthy of the end in view; and other donations, amounting altogether to £1,100, were promised at the meeting. Nothing further, however, was done in this direction. In May, 1875, the Council resolved on the purchase, for £400, of the building known as the St. Philip's Literary Institute, which had been founded by a few philanthropic inhabitants, but had proved unsuccessful. The place was opened as a branch library by the mayor (Ald. J. A. Jones) in July, 1876. A house in King Square, bought for £1,070, and fitted up as a branch for the northern parts of the city, was opened in March, 1877, by the mayor (Alderman Edwards). The Library Committee also purchased, for £1,550, the premises of a defunct Conservative Institute in Bedminster, and a well appointed branch library was opened there in the following September. In May, 1883, the Council sanctioned the creation of a new branch, in Whiteladies Road, for Redland and West Clifton. A plot of 666 square yards was bought for £650, and a building having been erected thereon at a cost of £2,400, and 10,000 volumes placed on the shelves, the building was opened by the mayor (Mr. Weston) in June, 1885. Two months later, the Council resolved on purchasing the abandoned Church of St. Peter, Jacob's Wells [see p. 345], and on converting it into a branch library for Hotwells and St. Augustine's. The building, with alterations, cost about £3,000.

In the course of the year 1873, the committee of the Children's Hospital appointed a female physician, Dr. Eliza Walker, to the office of house surgeon; but the lady was compelled to relinquish the post a few weeks later, in consequence of the hostile action of the rest of the medical staff, who succeeded in their object by resigning in a body. In referring to the subject in a letter read at a public meeting in Gloucester, Mr. Wait, M.P. (mayor 1869–70), said, he had become a convert to the agitation for female suffrage, "its necessity having been driven home by a trades' union combination among a section of the medical men at Bristol to prevent a woman earning her bread in their profession."

At the general election, which took place in February, 1874, the candidates nominated were Messrs. Morley and Hodgson, the Liberal Members in the previous Parliament, and Messrs. S. V. Hare and George Henry Chambers, who were brought forward by the Conservatives. The latter were sanguine of success, as Mr. Hare had been defeated by a small majority in 1870, and in the four registration courts which had subsequently been held the Conservative Association claimed an aggregate gain of 1,614 votes. This was the first Bristol election held under the Ballot Act; and the good order which reigned during the struggle offered a marked contrast to the disturbances which were almost chronic under the old system. The counting of the votes on the evening of the poll (February 2) occupied many hours, and the result could not be announced until nearly three hours after midnight; yet, though many thousand persons remained in the streets, there was no symptom of tumult. The return was as follows:—Mr. K. D. Hodgson, 8,888; Mr. S. Morley, 8,732; Mr. S. V. Hare, 8,552; Mr. G. H. Chambers, 7,626. The last mentioned gentleman, in the course of one of his electioneering addresses, made a singular avowal of his regret at the abolition of slavery in the West India colonies.

A fourth volunteer organisation was started in February, under the name of the Royal Navy Artillery Volunteers. The 22 persons first enrolled paid all the expenses attending the launching of the Corps. In August, Mr. Ward Hunt, first Lord of the Admiralty, visited Bristol with a view to promoting the movement, in which, Mr. Hunt stated, the Admiralty felt much interest. At a public meeting, held a few weeks later, the Corps was definitely constituted, Captain Dunn, R.N., being recommended to the Admiralty as the commanding officer.

During the spring the Cattle Market was reconstructed by the local railway companies [see p. 123], at a cost of nearly £10,000. The new market afforded accommodation for 9,700 animals.

The most serious disaster which had happened in the Avon since the stranding of the *Demerara* occurred on the 1st April to the *Kron Prinz*, a steamer which had arrived from the Danube with a cargo of 7,000 quarters of barley. In proceeding up the river at high water, the vessel struck on the right bank, near the Horseshoe Point, and became practically a wreck. Her removal was not effected until the 20th April, when the damage was estimated at £34,000. A somewhat similar disaster occurred in the beginning of May, 1878, to the *Gipsy* steamer, said to be worth £15,000, which struck on the right bank of the Avon, near Black-rock quarry, as she was proceeding to Waterford, and became a total wreck.

At a meeting of the Council on the 28th April, 1874, the town clerk stated that he was instructed by Alderman Proctor to offer as a free gift to the city the mansion in which he lived—Elmdale House, Clifton Down, to be dedicated to the use of the mayor for the time being. The house was charged with a ground rent of £50 per annum, but the donor had taken measures to redeem this burden. The value of the property was estimated at £16,000. It transpired that Mr. Proctor had had the object in view for several years, and had in fact constructed the house for this especial purpose. At the request of Mrs. Proctor the transfer of the property took place on the 1st May—the anniversary of the wedding of the estimable couple. The deed of gift was executed on the 20th

June, when Alderman Proctor presented the city with the fittings of the house, and a cheque for £500 for effecting decorations and repairs. Mr. Robert Lang presented the Corporation with a cabinet of Bristol china, valued at £750, for the drawing-room of the house. The mayor (Mr. Thomas) presented a picture by C. Branwhite, a local artist; and similar gifts have been made by many of his successors. Mr. T. Canning (mayor 1870–1) gave a portrait of the late Mr. R. H. Davis, M.P.; Mr. Cruger Miles forwarded two pictures by Danby, R.A., another Bristol artist; and other handsome presents were made by Alderman Edwards (mayor 1876–9) and Mr. Mundy. The furnishing of the Mansion House cost the Corporation £8,263, and the permanent charge for its maintenance was estimated at about £1,000 a year. It was hoped that the establishment would effect a saving in the yearly charge incurred for the entertainment of the judges of assize, for whom private lodgings had been provided since 1831. Their lordships, however, would not take up their quarters in the civic building. In June, 1875, Alderman Proctor added another to his various gifts to the city, in the shape of a recreation ground at Fishponds, which he fitted up for the entertainment of school children, some thousands of whom are taken there yearly on summer excursions.

The Council, in July, resolved upon another extensive series of street improvements. For many years the ever increasing flow of traffic through Corn and Clare Streets had been strengthening the arguments of those who urged the necessity of a new thoroughfare between the central districts and Clifton. Various plans had been proposed to supply the want, but the great expense involved in all of them had deterred the Council from taking action. The city surveyor, Mr. Josiah Thomas, now proposed a scheme for obtaining the desired relief at a comparatively limited outlay, namely the widening of Baldwin Street from Back Street to Baldwin Street Hall, and the continuance of the thoroughfare from the latter spot to the west end of Clare Street. The estimated net cost was £62,000. The plan was adopted by a large majority. The Streets Improvement Committee further recommended alterations in the following localities, at the estimated expenditure affixed to each :—Black-boy Hill, Redland, £16,000; Narrow Plain and Unity Street to the Old Market, £20,000; the widening of Redcliff Street, £45,000; two new thoroughfares near Kingsland Road, £6,500; Lower Ashley Road, Brigstock Road, and Montpelier, £8,550; Stratton Street to Lawson Street, £5,000; Back Street,

£13,500; West Street, Bedminster, £4,500; Granby Hill to Hotwell Road, £3,000. The whole of these schemes were approved with little or no opposition. The total expenditure voted during the sitting was £184,050. Mr. Spark, the chairman of the Committee, stated that between 1854 and 1864, before extensive improvements were effected, the rateable value of the city increased only from £455,000 to £503,000, while the advance in the ten subsequent years marked by improvements had been from £503,000 to £727,000. He added that the estimated cost of the properties taken under previous improvement schemes had been £280,300, but that the actual outlay had been only £226,000. The Baldwin Street scheme was afterwards warmly opposed by influential citizens possessing property in the locality; and the subject remained in suspense for some time. Early in 1877, however, the Council obtained power from Parliament to borrow £194,000 (afterwards increased to £214,000) for carrying out the schemes, and orders were given to proceed with the plans relating to Baldwin Street, Back Street, and Redcliff Street, the last-named thoroughfare being described by Mr. Spark as "a disgrace to the city." New Baldwin Street was opened with some ceremony on the 1st March, 1881, by the mayor (Mr. Weston). The gross cost of the improvement was £120,000. The surplus lands not having been disposed of, the net cost has not been ascertained.

The members of the British Archæological Association assembled in Bristol in August, to hold their thirty-first annual congress. Mr. K. D. Hodgson, M.P., was the president for the year. The proceedings extended over a week, visits being paid to all the important historical monuments of the district. A local committee, of which the mayor (Ald. Barnes) was chairman, was indefatigable in its attentions to the visitors, who were also hospitably entertained by the mayor, the Society of Merchants, the vestry of Redcliff, and other bodies. The Association's "Transactions" for 1874 contain a full record of the proceedings.

A scheme of the Endowed School Commissioners for reorganizing the Cathedral School received the assent of the dean and chapter in August. The school formed part of the cathedral corporation as established by Henry VIII.; but the chapter for many generations manifested indifference to the original purposes of the foundation. In the statutes of Henry the salary of the head-master was fixed at £8 8*s.* 8*d.*; of each prebend, £7 17*s.* 8*d.*; of each minor canon, £5 2*s.*; and of the dean, £27. In our own time, the dean has an income of £1,500, while the canons receive about £700 each. But the head-master's yearly share of the cathedral revenues in 1874 amounted to only £120. Under the scheme, the dividends on a sum of £12,000, furnished by the Ecclesiastical Commissioners, were devoted to the establishment of a training college and a grammar school. In the latter, eighteen choristers were to be instructed free of charge. The new system came into operation in January, 1876, but the college proved a complete failure. In May, 1882, the institution was again reorganised, the college being suppressed.

The first Cabmen's Rest in Bristol, constructed at the expense of Mr. Henry Taylor (mayor, 1879–80), was opened near the Drawbridge stand on the 7th November. Mr. Taylor's example was soon afterwards followed by Mr. Hodgson, M.P., and several citizens, and altogether fifteen Rests have been provided. Some "Chairmen's Rests" were set up in 1876.

A special meeting of the Council was convened on the 20th November, in consequence of the sudden death, ten days previously, of the town-clerk, Mr. Daniel Burges. Mr. William Brice was unanimously elected to the vacant office. The friends of Mr. Burges subsequently resolved on establishing a lasting memorial of that gentleman's services, and subscriptions amounting to upwards of £1,200 having been received, a scholarship called the Daniel Burges Scholarship, tenable at Oxford or Cambridge, was founded in connection with the Grammar School. The first holder of the scholarship was Mr. Cyril Travers Burges, then a student at St. John's College, Oxford. The Charity Trustees grant the income (about £53) for four years to a pupil educated at the Grammar School.—Mr. Brice having relinquished the town-clerkship after holding it nearly six years, the Council, on the 28th September, 1880, elected Mr. Daniel Travers Burges to the post, which had been successively held by his grandfather and father.

Upon the death, on the 5th December, of Lady Haberfield, widow of Sir John Kerle Haberfield, it became known that her ladyship, some time before her demise, had executed a deed by which she transferred a considerable real estate to trustees, who were charged with the erection and endowment of almshouses for twenty-four poor persons. The building was to be erected on ground at Jacob's Wells, which Lady Haberfield had bought for that purpose. The deceased also bequeathed £5,000 to the Infirmary, £500 to the Charity Trustees for establishing doles to poor women, and handsome sums to various charities. The trustees for the almshouse resolved to delay the erection of the building until the expiration of certain life interests in the estate, which exceeds £40,000. In the meanwhile, the piece of ground bought by Lady Haberfield has been acquired by the Corporation for street improvement purposes.

An extraordinary ecclesiastical case, said to be the first of the kind which had arisen since the Reformation, came on the 8th December before commissioners appointed by Bishop Ellicott, sitting in the Chapter House. It appeared that, a considerable time before this date, a gentleman named Henry Jenkins, of Vyvyan Terrace, Clifton, entertaining doubts as to the existence of demoniacal spirits, and deeming certain passages in the Bible concerning them unfit to be read in the presence of children, published a selection of passages from the Old and New Testaments for use in family devotion. Copies of the book were sent to various persons, amongst others to the incumbent of the parish, the Rev. Flavel S. Cook, Vicar of Christ Church, who took no notice of it. During the month of July, 1874, however, Mr. Cook preached a course of sermons against Ritualism, which Mr. Jenkins sharply criticised in a private letter; whereupon the irritated vicar, calling to mind that his correspondent had written a book, proceeded to its examination—probably with a view to returning his parishioner's compliment. To use the expression of his counsel, he then "discovered to his extreme sorrow that the volume was a systematic and wicked mutilation of the Bible." The reverend gentleman forthwith called upon Mr. Jenkins to expostulate upon his conduct. And as Mr. Jenkins declined to hold any communication with him, and even claimed the right of using his book in the devotions of his own family, Mr. Cook, professing profound grief, informed him by letter that so long as he refused to disavow his mutilation of the Scriptures he could not "be received at the Lord's Table in my church." Mr. Jenkins retorted that if the church was the minister's it was also the parishioners', and gave notice that on a certain day he should present himself at the Communion Table. He did accordingly attend, but Mr. Cook refused to let him communicate. An appeal was then made to the bishop, who issued the above commission of inquiry. Mr Cook's counsel contended that the promoter, having been guilty of slandering the Word of God, was properly rejected from the Table. The commissioners were of opinion that the matter ought to be decided in the ecclesiastical courts, and the case thereupon proceeded. In the course of the subsequent arguments before Sir R. Phillimore, Dean of Arches it transpired that the vicar, before repelling Mr. Jenkins from the Communion, had consulted the bishop of the diocese, Dr. Ellicott, who had dictated the letter addressed to the promoter of the suit. His Honour, in giving judgment, held that Mr. Cook was justified in practically excommunicating a person who held sceptical views as to the personality of the devil. An appeal having been lodged, the parties were heard before the Judicial Committee of the Privy Council, and Lord Chancellor Cairns gave definitive judgment in February, 1876, reversing the previous decision, admonishing Mr. Cook for his illegal act, and warning him against its repetition. The vicar then intimated that if Mr. Jenkins insisted on communicating at Christ Church he should resign the living, and as Mr. Jenkins replied that he should exercise a right which it had cost him a large sum to vindicate, Mr. Cook carried out his intention, and quitted the parish. The heavy law costs incurred by the reverend gentleman were defrayed by his admirers, who also presented him with testimonials to the value of upwards of £4,500.

Another remarkable instance of growth in the value of ancient charitable bequests was brought before the Charity Commissioners during 1874. One Abraham Birkin, by a will dated in 1668, bequeathed six acres of land in the hundred of Barton Regis, then worth £10 a year, to the feoffees of St. Mary-le-Port church lands, upon trust to distribute 40*s*. yearly amongst four poor people of that parish, and a similar amount amongst poor in St. Nicholas', St. James', and Temple parishes respectively. £1 was to be paid for a yearly sermon, 10*s*. for bread given to the poor after the sermon was preached, 9*s*. 6*d*. to the collector of the rents, and 6*d*. to the lord of the manor for chief rent. For upwards of a century and a half the estate brought in only sufficient to provide for the bequests; but about 1820 the ground was let on building leases, and, when the leases began to fall in, the yearly proceeds rose to £400, with the prospect of advancing to £600, or sixty times the original value. The testator having left no directions as to the appropriation of a surplus, an application was made to the Charity Commissioners, which resulted in the settlement of a scheme. After providing for the 40*s*. gifts, it was ordered that seven-twelfths of the surplus should be employed in promoting education amongst the children residing in the parishes of St. Mary-le-Port, St. Nicholas, St. James, Temple, St. Philip, and St. Paul, in the elementary schools of those parishes, and in granting bursaries at the same schools, or in assisting children of both sexes to obtain instruction in technical subjects. Out of the remaining five-twelfths, £50 were to be paid in augmentation of the living of St. Mary-le-Port, half of the residue to be applied to repairing the church, and the remainder to the purposes to which the seven-twelfths had been devoted, the poor of St. Mary's having a preferential claim to this portion. The scheme was ordered to come into operation on the 25th March, 1875. Some fifty bursaries have since been established for the benefit of meritorious poor children.

Early in the year 1875, the Right Honourable Stephen Cave, M.P., a member of an old Bristol family, purchased of a lady living at Cheltenham a curious goblet, called the Colston Cup, the history of which is unknown. It was elaborately carved, and bore figures of members of the Colston family, with representations of the arms of Bristol and of a ship entering the port.

At a meeting of the Council in March, the inconvenience and unwholesomeness of the police court [see p. 109] were strongly represented by the mayor (Mr. Thomas) on behalf of the magistrates. The Finance Committee shortly afterwards recommended the construction of a new court in Bridewell Street, extending into St. James's Back. Three houses in the former street were bought for £2,540; most of the tenements in the latter, inhabited by a dissolute class, belonged to the Corporation. The design was subsequently extended, accommodation being provided for the city fire brigade; and the total outlay amounted to £17,000. Through one of those unlucky freaks by which the Council is sometimes tempted to deal with ancient names [see p. 356, note], St. James's Back was ordered to be called Silver Street—the name of an old thoroughfare swept away by recent improvements. The new court was opened for magisterial business in March, 1880.

The tendency of a centralising system of government to be made ridiculous by routine and "red tape" was illustrated about this time by a dispute between the Local Government Board and the Bristol Board of Guardians. In 1701, Alderman Samuel Wallis bequeathed a sum of money to the Incorporation of the Poor, on condition that they should pay 20*s*. yearly to the incumbent of St. Peter's, for a sermon to be preached on the election of each governor. A year or two earlier than this bequest, the Incorporation had begun to pay 20*s*. to the incumbent and clerk of St. Stephen's (or of St. Nicholas) for an annual service, Dr. Edward Tyson having made the guardians a gift under that condition. The two payments were made for upwards of a hundred and seventy years as a simple matter of course. At the revision of the accounts in 1875, however, a punctilious auditor refused to allow the items; and the chairman, who had signed the cheques, was ordered to refund the amount. An appeal was made to the Local Government authorities, but they affirmed the decision of the auditor. After submitting to two years' surcharges, the guardians discontinued the payments in 1877, whereupon one of the clergymen interested in the gifts sued for his money, and obtained a verdict. The auditor, nevertheless, still refused to pass the items, and after the fees had been defrayed on two or three occasions by the chairman, the board again ordered the payments to be stopped. In February, 1882, as the result of another action, the bailiffs entered St. Peter's Hospital, and seized four antique chairs, which were put up by auction (they were purchased by the chairman), and produced sufficient to satisfy the clergyman's claim, with costs. Notwithstanding the scandal, the auditor again made a surcharge on his next visit. The guardians were by this time resolved on obtaining relief from petty official persecution, and being about to apply to Parliament for the abolition of the Harbour rate, they introduced clauses into their Bill to legalise the disputed payments. The clauses having become law in 1883, the unseemly controversy might have been expected to terminate; but the pedantic auditor, on discovering that a yearly payment had been made before the Act came into force, made another surcharge. His superiors at the Local Government Board were, however, tired of the controversy, and the item received their sanction in the following September.

Soon after the reorganisation of Colston's School, the new governing body resolved upon the abolition of the uncomely and irksome garb in which the boys had been hitherto arrayed. In lieu of a long gown, short breeches, and flat cap, each lad received a uniform of modern cut, the badge of the dolphin being placed on a peaked cap. The action of the governors was not lost upon the authorities of the City School, who also, for a time, clothed their boys in a costume consistent with modern ideas and with the requirements of youth. Finding, however, that jackets and trousers were slightly more expensive than gowns and breeches, the governors ordered the revival of the grotesque old habiliments.

At a meeting held in July, Dr. Beddoe, F.R.S., presiding, it was resolved to establish an association for promoting and antiquarian pursuits, under the title of the Bristol and Gloucestershire Archaeological Society. Many of the local nobility and gentry and other influential inhabitants had previously promised their support to the movement. The society was "inaugurated" at another gathering, in February, 1876, at which the Earl of Ducie, Lord Lieutenant, took the chair. The first general meeting was held at Gloucester, the president being Sir William V. Guise, bart. The third annual gathering took place at Bristol in July, 1878, Mr. C. J. Thomas being the president of that year. A winter meeting was also held here in January, 1880, under the presidency of Mr. T. G. Parry. The society has published an annual volume of "Transactions."

The forty fifth annual congress of the British Association was opened in this city on the 25th August, when the president for the year, Sir John Hawkshaw, delivered his inaugural address in the Victoria Rooms. The vice-presidents were the Earl of Ducie, Sir S. Northcote (late Earl of Iddesleigh), the mayor (Mr. C. J. Thomas), Sir Henry Rawlinson, Dr. W. B. Carpenter, and Mr. W. Sanders, F.R.S. Although the gathering did not kindle the enthusiasm which greeted the association on its former visit, the proceedings excited much interest, and a hospitable reception was offered to the guests. The work of the week was divided amongst seven sections. Mathematical and Physical Science (presided over by Professor Balfour Stewart) had its quarters in the Fine Arts Academy; Chemistry (Mr. A. G. V. Harcourt, F.R.S.) at the Freemasons' Hall; Geology (Dr. T. Wright) at the lecture room of the Museum; Biology, three departments (Dr. P. L. Sclater), at the Royal Hotel, the Grammar School and rooms in Park Street; Geography (General Strachey, C.B.), at the Blind Asylum; Economic Science (Mr. J. Heywood, F.R.S.) at Victoria Chapel schoolroom; Mechanical Science (Mr. W. Froude, F.R.S.) at the Fine Arts Academy. Lectures and conversaziones took place in the evenings at Colston Hall. With one exception, the meeting places of the previous congress were abandoned, and the list of new buildings made available illustrated the local progress that had been made in forty years. At the close of the proceedings, the courtesy and hospitality of the inhabitants, and the energetic services of the local secretaries, Mr. W. L. Carpenter and Mr. J. H. Clarke, were the themes of much eulogistic comment.

Owing to complaints as to the unhealthy condition of the Infirmary, the committee resolved, in September, upon closing the building with a view to extensive alterations. A range of warehouses in Colston Street was hired and fitted up for the accommodation of about seventy patients whose cases might be considered of an urgent nature. The alterations, which entailed a cost of nearly £15,000, were completed in about a twelvemonth, and the institution was reopened in October, 1876.

In October, 1875, a meeting was held under the presidency of the mayor (Mr. Thomas), with the object of promoting a movement, originated by Canon Norris, for the erection of a memorial in the city to Bishop Butler. It was suggested that the north-west tower of the cathedral should be raised in honour of the bishop, and a donation of £50 was announced from a gentleman at New York. The subscriptions promised at the meeting did not amount to £400, and the proposal met with a cheerless reception out of doors. A suggestion, made about the same time, that the companion tower of the cathedral should be erected as a memorial of Colston, fell still-born. In October, 1886, however, Mr. J. W. Dod, of Clifton, offered a donation of £5,000 towards the construction of the towers, under conditions which, it may be hoped, will be realised.

During the autumn a company was formed, under the title of the Bristol Industrial Dwellings Company, with a capital of £20,000 in £50 shares. A lease was obtained from the Merchant Venturers' Society of a plot of ground at Jacob's Wells, and, as a preliminary effort, the company erected, at a cost of £8,000, three blocks of buildings, containing altogether eighty tenements, provided with all appropriate sanitary arrangements. The experiment proving popular amongst the working classes, another large block, containing fifty-one tenements, was erected, and the company secured additional land adjoining, with a view to future extensions. The movement was started by Miss Susannah Winkworth, who for many years had taken a deep interest in solving the problem as to the better housing of the poor, and had begun the work by a practical experiment in Dowry Square, where she hired two or three large houses, and let them to poor families at low rentals. The results there were so satisfactory that Mr. George Wills, Mr. W. K. Wait, Mr. W. H. Budgett, Mr. L. Fry, and a few other philanthropic citizens assisted in the promotion of the more extensive project described above.

It was announced in October that an agreement had been entered into for the purchase of the Bristol and Exeter Railway by the Great Western Company. The terms agreed upon provided for a yearly dividend on the ordinary stock of the Bristol and Exeter Company at the rate of 6 per cent. for seven years, and thereafter at the rate of 6½ per cent. The amalgamation took effect on the 1st August, 1876. Four days before that date, an accident happened near Long Ashton to the express train known as "the Flying Dutchman," which left the rails whilst on its journey towards Bristol, the two men on the engine being killed and several of the passengers seriously injured. At the coroner's inquest, the jury declared that the fatality was attributable to the defective condition of the permanent way, as represented to them by the Government inspector, and "great blame" was passed on those officials who were responsible for the default. On winding up the accounts of the Bristol and Exeter undertaking, upwards of £14,000 were distributed amongst the old officers and servants of the company.

During the autumn and winter of 1875, which were marked by excessive rains, the eastern parishes of Bristol bordering on the Froom suffered severely from inundations. For some years the population had rapidly increased in that neighbourhood, and a number of houses were built on low-lying ground which had been at all times liable to be flooded. In many of these dwellings the floors of the lower rooms were occasionally from three to four feet under water; and the poor tenants were reduced to extreme misery. In February, 1876, the Council voted £10,500 for repairing the banks of the river from Ashley Road bridge to Wade Street, and for clearing the bed of the stream. A still more disastrous inundation occurred in October, 1882 [see p. 520].

An attempt to form a social centre for the mercantile classes in the city was started about the close of 1875, when a large new house in Quay Street was fitted up at a cost of £3,500, and opened as the Bristol and County Club. About 250 members, paying a yearly subscription of three guineas, were enrolled; but the expenditure largely exceeded the receipts, and repeated additional demands on the subscribers led to withdrawals, and, after a four years' trial, to the closing of the premises.

The excitement caused by the theological lawsuit of Jenkins *v.* Cook [see p. 482] had not wholly subsided when a new and more acrimonious controversy arose with respect to certain decorations erected in front of the cathedral. According to the architect's designs for the new north porch, statues of the four great doctors of the Western Church—Gregory, Jerome, Ambrose, and Augustine—were to adorn the portal.

The figures were in consequence executed, at a cost of about £450, and they were elevated to the niches constructed for them about the middle of February, 1876. For some days they occasioned as little remark as had similar statues of the same personages when erected, shortly before this date, at Gloucester and Salisbury cathedrals. At length, however, a vigilant Protestant, signing himself "No Pope and No Popery," published a letter in the newspapers, and his protest was forthwith re-echoed by still more vehement disputants of the same school. A few days later, the local journals were authorised by Canon Girdlestone to assert that the statues had been erected without the consent of the dean (who was in Italy) or of the chapter, whereupon Mr. Wait, M.P., at whose expense the porch had been built, retorted that the plans, including the figures, were submitted to, and approved by, the capitular body in 1867. [Mr. Wait subsequently admitted that this statement was "stronger than was warranted by the facts of the case."] At an excited meeting—"one of the absurdest meetings," said an influential London journal, "that British citizens ever attended"—after violent speeches by some Low Church clergymen, it was resolved that the images were insulting to English Protestantism and ought to be immediately removed, Dr. Percival and Mr. J. H. Mills, almost the only cool-headed persons present, being interrupted and insulted whilst deprecating the passionate proceedings. On the return of the dean, early in April, a chapter was held, at which it was resolved —Canons Norris and Wade protesting—that the dean should take measures for the rèmoval of the figures. The dean having been informed that the restoration committee would resist this step until the figures had been pronounced illegal by a judicial tribunal, a band of workmen was secretly engaged, who carried out their orders at an early hour. After the large statues had been torn from the niches, "a couple of masons," according to the *Bristol Times*, "went on with the work of demolition, splintering off the lesser saints that enriched the moulding of the doorway; so that the passer-by was for a moment beguiled by the fancy that he was back in old commonwealth times." The *Daily Press* stated that the figure of St. Gregory was injured, and that "the day's work concluded with the excision of the Virgin Mary, who was one of the two top figures on the outside of the arch." This figure was broken to pieces by the workmen. In defence of his action, the dean informed Mr. Wait that the chapter had not sanctioned the subjects of the figures, and had taken the sketches in the design to represent the Evangelists. It appeared that the restoration committee were not responsible for the artistic treatment of the statues, and did not approve of the papal tiara, cardinal's hat, and other insignia introduced by the sculptor (Mr. Redfern), which gave so much offence. It was also admitted that those decorations were as much in contradiction to historical truth as they were opposed to Protestant sentiments. The anachronisms might easily have been removed; but the dean, who became more unconciliatory and peremptory as the matter proceeded, at length objected to the erection of any figures save those of scriptural personages. For excluding the Virgin from this category he pleaded an iconoclastic Act of Edward VI. On the 18th April the restoration committee resolved that, as Dr. Elliott had "expressed no regret for the outrage, or for the discourtesy offered to the donor and architect of the porch," they felt that their only course was to discontinue their work. The committee also addressed a letter to the dean, in which they contrasted the indifference he had all along exhibited in reference to the restoration with the vigour he had shown in defacing "a very beautiful work of art." As they had no security, they added, that this conduct might not be followed by other mutilations, they repudiated further responsibility. The dean, rendered uneasy by this issue, appealed to Canon Norris, asking for his endeavours to influence the committee to acquiesce in the removal of the figures, and to accept scriptural subjects in their place; but the canon replied, that after the affronting resolution of the chapter, and the indecorous way in which effect had been given to it, the committee naturally expected some expression of regret for the steps which had been taken. Dr. Elliott, retorting that the only persons in the wrong were the committee, thereupon appealed to the public, stating that the chapter would accept the responsibility of completing the building, and asking for pecuniary help on behalf of a new committee, which would finish the works "under the presidency of the dean." If that dignitary anticipated that the response would be such as to prove that public opinion applauded his proceedings, the result must have been mortifying. The original committee had obtained about £43,000 from the public; but the appeal of the chapter for £1,500 to enable them to open the nave was somewhat coldly received, although the dean and his supporters in the capitular body (Canon Girdlestone and Canon Reeve) subscribed £200 of the amount. What was still more edifying, the entire sum contributed by those who had excited the "No Popery" agitation did not exceed £300. After considerable delay, and some further expenditure, the new nave was opened on the 23rd October, 1877, when the mayor (Ald. Edwards) and the members of the Council attended in state. The bishop of the diocese, the Bishop of Bath and Wells, and the Deans of Canterbury and Westminster took part in the opening services, which extended over two days. About £48,000 had been expended on the reconstruction at that date. In January, 1885, the dean, in a report addressed to the Cathedral Commissioners, stated that the sum disbursed in the renovation of the cathedral, between 1860 and 1884 inclusive, was £77,447, of which £14,508 had been contributed by the chapter. Figures of the four Evangelists, said to have cost fifty guineas each, but of slender artistic merit, were placed in the vacant niches during the summer of 1878. The rejected statues are now in the tower of East Heslerton Church, Yorkshire.

The most extensive fire which had occurred in the city for nearly half a century broke out during the night of the 24th May, in the premises of Messrs. Clutterbuck & Griffin, drysalters, Christmas Street. The flames rapidly spread to the warehouses of Messrs. Couzens & Co., clothiers; Messrs. Leonard & Co., drysalters; Messrs. Gardner & Thomas, wholesale grocers; and Mr. S. Hunt, provision merchant; as well as to an old-established inn, the Old Globe. The destruction in those buildings was in most cases complete, and the entire loss was estimated at upwards of £80,000.

A friendly suit in Chancery, between the governors of Colston's School and the trustees of Colston's Free Schools in the parish of Temple, was occasioned during the summer through a bequest of £5,000 having been made by a Mr. McGhie to "Colston's School, Bristol." A suggestion of the Master of the Rolls, that the money should be divided between the two institutions, being accepted by the parties, a formal judgment was given to that effect.

In consequence of the Government having introduced a Bill into Parliament for preventing the pollution of rivers—a measure which, when passed, turned out to be utterly valueless—the Council, at a meeting in August, determined upon the purchase, for £6,000, of Clift House, Coronation Road, with about seven acres of land adjoining, for the purpose of establishing works on the spot for deodorising part of the sewage of the city. The latter project excited so much opposition in Clifton that it was never carried into execution.

The passenger toll at Prince's Street Bridge having been

long regarded as a grievance, negotiations were opened during the autumn by the Corporation with the Great Western Railway Company, which had purchased the bridge when the Harbour Railway was constructed; and at a meeting of the Council, in November, it was agreed to give £15,000 for the property, to abolish the tolls, and to build a more convenient bridge. The tolls had previously been let for £1,100 a year. Parliamentary powers were obtained in the following session, and the new bridge, made to open and close by hydraulic machinery, came into use on the 27th January, 1879.

A scheme for the improvement of Jacob Street, Tower Hill, Ashley Road, Castle Mill Street, and Newfoundland Road, and for making a new street on the north side of the Froom, was recommended by the Streets Improvement Committee and sanctioned by the Council on the 9th November. The estimated outlay for carrying out the design was only £6,000.

Upon an announcement being made that the Ministry of Lord Beaconsfield were resolved upon recommending Parliament to create four additional English bishoprics, a movement was started in Bristol for obtaining a restoration of the privileges withdrawn some forty years before. At a meeting held in January, 1877, the mayor (Alderman Edwards) presiding, a memorial to the Home Secretary was adopted, pointing out that £1,500—half of the income proposed to be conferred on each of the new prelates—could be secured by uniting the office of dean with that of bishop. It was added that Dr. Ellicott was prepared to surrender £500 a year of his income if the united dioceses were separated, and that the remainder of the endowment would be speedily furnished by the public, provided the Government would aid in restoring the see. Several large subscriptions were promised at the meeting, and the contributions soon exceeded £8,000. The Ministry, however, refused to countenance the movement. During the autumn of 1883 some influential citizens, then promoting a scheme of church extension which will be noticed in a later page, placed themselves in communication with the Prime Minister, Mr. Gladstone, in reference to the question of the bishopric. It was soon after intimated that the Ministry would render assistance in carrying out the wishes of local Churchmen. The chief conditions imposed were that the old see of Gloucester should be left in its integrity, and that £1,500 a year should be provided by the public towards the income of the new bishop, in addition to the £500 offered by Dr. Ellicott. At a meeting in January, 1884, the mayor (Mr. Weston) in the chair, thanks were voted to Mr. Gladstone, and a subscription was started, Canon Norris, the Merchants' Society, Miles & Co., Sir J. G. Smyth, Mr. H. C. Miles, Mr. A. Gibbs, Alderman Edwards, Messrs. Daniel & Sons, and two anonymous donors contributing £1,000 each. In July, the £20,000 required by the Government preliminary to taking action having been subscribed, a Bill for the creation of a new diocese of Bristol (to consist of the deaneries of Bristol—with slight modifications to include the docks at the mouth of the Avon—and the three deaneries of North Wilts) was brought into the House of Lords by the Archbishop of Canterbury. Special facilities were granted by the Ministry for the progress of the measure in the Commons; and Mr. Gladstone, on the 9th August, upon the motion that the House should go into committee on the Bill, delivered a brilliant address in its favour, declaring that it would be "hardly compatible with the dignity of Parliament" to refuse the city what it was seeking to obtain. The Prime Minister's intervention practically put an end to opposition, and the Bill received the royal assent on the 14th August. Mr. Gladstone, on the day on which he addressed the Commons, forwarded to the Archdeacon of Bristol a donation of £50 in aid of the bishopric fund, being desirous, he said, "to render a tribute, however small, of gratitude as well as admiration to the illustrious memory of Bishop Butler, whose episcopal career was chiefly passed at Bristol." An anonymous friend has promised £10,000 towards the endowment fund, provided an equal sum (in addition to the subscriptions previously offered) be raised before June, 1888. The amount subscribed in March, 1887, was about £24,000.

The insurance offices, which up to this time had maintained fire engines in the city (the Imperial office excepted), having given notice of their intention to discontinue their establishments, the Council, in March, 1877, unanimously affirmed the desirability of founding a city fire brigade. The Watch Committee soon afterwards recommended that the brigade should form part of the police force, that the staff should consist of a superintendent and twelve additional policemen, and that a powerful fire-engine should be purchased, and stationed at the central police station. The report was adopted, and, as already recorded, offices for the brigade were built in St. James's Back.

For some years previous to this date, the reputation of Clifton as a watering-place had been injured by the quarterly returns of mortality issued by the Registrar-General, whose statistics were founded on the deaths reported in the entire Union of Clifton—a district embracing a large population residing in the poorest parishes of eastern Bristol. Repeated remonstrances having been made on the injustice of the arrangement, the Local Government Board at length ordered that, from the 14th March, 1877, the name of the Union should be changed to Barton Regis. The mortality in Clifton alone is now included in the Registrar's returns of watering-places, with the effect of proving the parish to be amongst the most salubrious in the kingdom.

The steam vessels and business of the Bristol Steam Navigation Company were sold during the spring to certain capitalists in Cork. The price given for the concern was £120,000, half of which amount was accepted in shares of a new company bearing the same name, which started in July with a capital of £150,000.

Arrangements were made during the spring for the amalgamation of the banking firms of Messrs. Baillie, Cave & Co. (the Old Bank) and of Sir William Miles, bart., & Co. The union took effect on the 1st May, the business of the new firm being carried on in the premises of the Old Bank. The partners were Messrs. Charles D. Cave, George O. Edwards, Hon. H. Baillie, and George Bright from the Old Bank, and Sir Wm. Miles and Messrs. John Miles, W. H. Harford, W. H. Miles, and Fenton Miles from the other concern. The latter thereupon ceased to issue bank notes, a step which had been adopted by the Old Bank some years before.

At a Council meeting in June, the desirability of obtaining a park for the eastern districts of the city was affirmed, and a committee was appointed to choose a site and to consider the best means of meeting the expense. The site suggested by Mr. L. Fry, the mover of the resolution, was certain fields, about sixty-five acres in extent, situated between Fishponds and Stapleton roads, and bounded by the Froom on the north. It was ascertained that the owner, Sir J. Greville Smyth, bart., required, as a condition of sale, that the land should be settled for all future time as a park, and that the Corporation should, under no contingency, sell any portion for building sites. As the price demanded for the ground (£25,000) was nearly double its value as agricultural land, the Council declined to pursue the negotiation.

At a meeting of the Council in September, it was resolved that the Black-rock quarry, which had been worked since 1868 for road material, should be closed, as the excavations were attended with danger to the surface of Durdham Down, and tended to destroy the beauty of the scenery. The Sanitary Committee, encountering difficulty in obtaining supplies of stone elsewhere, entered into negotiations with Sir Philip Miles, bart., for opening a quarry on the Somerset shore of the Avon; and in February, 1879, a lease was concluded, for twenty-one years, at a rent of £250 per annum, with a royalty of 6*d.* per ton on all rock quarried beyond 10,000 tons a year. Another hideous gash was consequently made in the sylvan prospect; and the destruction necessarily became more extensive from year to year. Towards the close of 1883, the Council passed a resolution for closing the great quarry at the top of Pembroke Road—the only one remaining open on Clifton Down. But in the February following the vote was rescinded, the Sanitary Committee having reported that if the 7,300 tons of stone obtained annually had to be purchased elsewhere, the additional cost would be £714 per annum.

Towards the close of the year considerable uneasiness began to be felt by many citizens respecting the future prospects of the port. The results predicted by Sir John Hawkshaw, and foreseen by thoughtful persons in the city, had, in fact, arrived; for the business of the city docks was seriously affected by the competition for trade arising from the opening of accommodation at the mouth of the river. The diminished arrivals in the Float led to various suggestions. The Chamber of Commerce expressed itself strongly in favour of the "dockisation" of the Avon; but while the vast estimated cost of the undertaking deterred most of the ratepayers from lending it their support, it was pointed out that, even if it were executed, the competition of the Channel docks would continue unabated. Another section of the citizens was of opinion that the Corporation should purchase the works at Avonmouth and Portishead, thus fulfilling the warnings of those who had prophesied that the Corporation's refusal to provide for indispensable wants would have a similar costly result to that which followed its supineness seventy years before. Eventually, at a meeting of the Council in January, 1878, a committee was appointed to consider as to the measures which should be adopted. In November of the same year, at the instance of Alderman Baker, the Council resolved that directors of the two Channel docks should be ineligible to sit on the Docks Committee, a motion which had the effect of expelling from the board four eminent members of the civic body—Messrs. C. J. Thomas, C. Nash, T. T. Taylor, and M. Whitwill—who were shareholders in the Avonmouth Company. In the summer of 1879, the Docks Committee reported to the Council that, with a view to obviate competition, it was expedient to purchase the Avonmouth undertaking on equitable terms. At a meeting on the 1st July, however, the Council unanimously resolved that the matter should be deferred until the Avonmouth Company made an offer to negotiate. The river dockisation scheme was discussed at the same meeting, Mr. Howard, the docks engineer, having produced two plans for carrying it out—one proposing locks at the mouth of the Avon, at an estimated cost of £850,000; the other for a dam below the Horseshoe Point, the outlay for which was set down at about £700,000. The expense of constructing quays and of diverting the sewage of the city was not included in either sum; but Mr. Ashmead reported in favour of carrying the sewage to Charlcombe Bay, near Clevedon, a distance of nearly ten miles, at an approximative cost of £280,000. The Council, dismayed by the costliness of the project, resolved that dockisation was, under existing circumstances, inexpedient. The competition of the rival docks, in the meantime, continued unabated, and the diminished receipts of the Floating Harbour caused much dissatisfaction in the Council. At a meeting in August, 1880, a resolution was passed, condemning the rivalry of the three concerns, and urging the directors representing the Corporation on the Portishead board to effect an arrangement by means of a sub-committee emanating from the three undertakings. The Avonmouth board, it appeared, had agreed to act in concert with the civic authorities; but the arrangement had broken down through the action taken at Portishead, which was spoken of as "a daughter seeking to cut the throat of her mother." At a subsequent meeting, the Docks Committee recommended, with the view of meeting the competition, that the town dues levied on grain in the Float should be reduced to a nominal sum, that the wharfage dues should be suspended, and that the expense of discharging grain cargoes should be defrayed out of the dock estate, so as to encourage corn merchants to bring vessels to Bristol. Alderman Baker, in moving the adoption of those recommendations, asserted that the grain trade had been diverted to the new docks by means of bribes, and that vigorous retaliatory measures could alone restore matters to a right footing. The resolution was condemned by other speakers as a further outcome of the huckstering and senile system which it was alleged had long characterised the management of the docks. The opposition pointed out that the timber and sugar arrivals had fallen off still more largely than those of grain, although there had been no competition in those trades; and they strongly censured a scheme by which poor ratepayers would be saddled with increased burdens in order that a few corn merchants might put £5,000 a year into their own pockets. The motion, however, was carried by an overwhelming majority, and similar bounties were afterwards conferred upon other importations. The dockisation party had by this time recovered courage. At a meeting of the Chamber of Commerce in September, a motion recommending that the three dock properties should be vested in a single governing body was met by an amendment in favour of dockising the river, and the latter was carried by a large majority. Similar resolutions having been passed at various ward meetings, the Council appointed a committee to make an inquiry into the practicability of the project. In October the Docks Committee reported that although the Avonmouth board were willing to agree to a non-competitive tariff, the Portishead authorities had again positively refused to enter into an arrangement. Much indignation was expressed at the policy of an undertaking which was deeply indebted to the liberality of the Corporation; but the representatives of the Council on the Portishead board contended that it was their duty to maintain the interests of the dock. The Council next proposed to apply the principle of arbitration to the purchase of the rival concerns; but the Portishead board, asserting that the interests of their railway were inseparably identified with the dock, advanced conditions which rendered negotiations impossible. This attitude—not a little irritating to many who had voted for the grant of £100,000 in 1872—strengthened the predominant party in the Council, which determined upon applying for parliamentary powers to reduce the charges on shipping and goods entering Bristol dock as the Corporation might see fit, to levy dues upon ships and goods entering within the port of Bristol (thus including the Channel docks), to impose dues and wharfage rates on goods conveyed from the rival docks to Bristol, to spend £48,000 in erecting free warehouses to be maintained out of the rates, and to provide free steam-tugs for vessels coming up the Avon. The injustice of levying taxes for the benefit of the city on shipping entering the Channel docks, thereby ruining the two companies, and enabling the Corporation to buy up the concerns at an insignificant fraction of their cost, which was the supposed object of the scheme, was denounced by Alderman Ford in the Council as "worse than the worst description of communism"; and the same argument was strongly urged before the select committee of the House of Commons by whom the Bill was considered. In the result, the latter body struck out the clause for levying dues in the Channel docks, as well as those permitting a system of rebates at Bristol and the establishment of free steam-tugs. Soon after the Bill, in its restricted form, had become law, the Council, with the view of crippling the competing docks, and in despite of the decision of the House of Commons, made further reductions in the town and wharfage dues on timber, sugar, and other imports, the increased charge thereby imposed on the ratepayers being estimated at £5,000 a year. This policy, by which, according to Alderman Ford's statement in the Council, over £20,000 per annum were taken out of the purses of the citizens for the benefit of particular trades, was disapproved in many quarters; and the position of its author and most vigorous advocate, Alderman Baker, the head of a firm which reaped large profits from the system, occasionally gave rise to insinuations which he indignantly repudiated. At length a citizen, Mr. Henry White, disputing the legality of the Council's proceedings, laid the facts before the Attorney General, who applied for an injunction against the Corporation in the High Court of Justice. The case was not heard till May, 1884, before Mr. Justice Field, who delivered judgment against the civic authorities. His lordship held that the Council, as trustees of the ancient town and wharfage dues, had acted illegally in practically abolishing those charges, the revenues of which ought to have been applied to the benefit of the ratepayers. The act complained of was, he added, as illegal as if the Corporation had given up the rents of the city property, or relieved certain inhabitants from the payment of rates; and the fact that an attempt had been made —unsuccessfully—to obtain parliamentary approval of the system, showed that the Council was aware that its action was unwarrantable. He did not doubt, however, that the members had intended to protect the interests of the city. Whilst these legal proceedings were in their infancy, eighty influential merchants and tradesmen proposed the formation of a Harbour Trust Association, with the object of uniting the docks into one property, under the supervision of a board. A Bill for effecting that object was introduced into Parliament in 1882; but although the Council was memorialised by upwards of six thousand ratepayers to co-operate in settling the details of a satisfactory scheme, the Chamber resolved, in February, 1882, to strenuously oppose the Bill. A motion declaring that the docks ought to be under one management was defeated by 23 votes against 19. The advocates of an uncompromising policy of "beggar my neighbour" began, however, to yield to the influence of public opinion, and, at a subsequent meeting, Alderman Fox, describing the competition between the three docks and the squandering of £25,000 a year as a scandal and reproach to all, moved that the mayor (Mr. Weston) be requested to communicate with the belligerents with a view to an equitable arrangement. The mayor having expressed his willingness to attempt a reconciliation, Alderman Fox's resolution was adopted unanimously. When the Harbour Bill was remitted to a committee of the House of Lords, it encountered a rival scheme of a similar character, ostensibly promoted by obscure persons in London; but their lordships summarily rejected both measures. The mayor's intervention put an end to a conflict which had never been creditable to the practical sagacity of those concerned in it, and which had become almost universally unpopular owing to the certainty that the reckless waste of money would have in the end to be borne by the public. At a Council meeting on the 9th May, 1882, the mayor was enabled to report a provisional arrangement for a year, which he had successfully effected. Its chief points were, that the dues on foreign arrivals were to be 2½*d*. per ton less at Bristol than at the Channel docks; that the town and wharfage dues, equal to 1½*d*. per quarter on grain, should be reimposed in the Float upon a due of a similar amount being levied at the other docks; and that the reductions in dues made to old lines of steamers should not exceed 25 per cent. until the same concession was made to new lines. His worship added that the Sharpness dock board —which had been compelled to reduce its rates through the competition—had promised that the dues of that undertaking should again be raised. The action of the mayor was unanimously confirmed. Shortly afterwards the Docks Committee reported that arrangements had been made with the Avonmouth and Portishead companies, under which a uniform tariff of charges would be established at the three docks. This was expected to increase the income of the Corporation by about £4,000 a year. The opportunity was taken to consolidate the Bristol charges, so that a single payment superseded the three imposts known as dock, town, and wharfage dues, whilst ships were in future to pay one due instead of five. The working of the new arrangement gave general satisfaction, but its temporary character caused uneasiness as to the future, and the desirability of consolidating the undertakings began to be acknowledged on all hands. As Mr.

Weston had been so successful in the last negotiation, it was suggested in November, 1883 (when he was again re-elected mayor), that he should undertake another, with a view to arriving at a definitive settlement. His worship accordingly addressed himself to the two boards, and after making a thorough investigation into the pecuniary position of the companies, he advised the Council to promote a Bill for powers to purchase the two undertakings. His suggestion was adopted by 47 votes against 3. The main difficulty encountered at this stage arose out of the attitude of the Portishead board, which refused to sell the dock without also disposing of the pier and railway. The mayor appealed to the Great Western Railway Company to assist the city in the emergency, and his application was successful, an arrangement being soon after made for the absorption of the railway and pier into the Great Western system. The issue of the whole negotiations was communicated by the mayor to the Council at a meeting on the 19th February, 1884. The amount of capital expended at Avonmouth on the dock, warehouses, and land was (nominally) £718,000, but the directors expressed their willingness to transfer the property for £550,000, of which £450,000 were to be paid on the 1st September, 1884, in Corporation bonds, bearing 3½ per cent. interest; £75,000 more were to be taken in deferred bonds, bearing no interest for five years, and the remaining £25,000 in bonds to bear interest in seven years. The nominal amount expended in constructing the dock and warehouses at Portishead was stated to have been £375,000, but the undertaking was offered for £250,000, of which £25,000 were to be accepted in deferred bonds, bearing no interest for the first five years. The mayor stated that the charge on the city incurred by the purchases would be £23,550 a year, while the income of the two companies was only about £18,000. But by raising certain small dues and rates to the amount charged previous to the competition, £4,710 yearly would be realised, so that the direct annual loss to the city would be only about £900; and as the citizens had been losing £16,000 a year during the rivalry, he thought there were good grounds for making the existing conditions permanent. [Some alterations having been subsequently made in the arrangements, Mr. Weston produced a revised estimate in July, showing that the loss to the city at the outset would be about £5,000 a year, exclusive of a sinking fund of £2,800 per annum, also to be provided for.] After a brief discussion, in which the mayor's exertions received unqualified eulogy, a resolution approving of the purchase was passed by a unanimous vote. Outside the Council the feeling in favour of the compact was equally cordial, and the statutory meeting of ratepayers convened to consider the Bill manifested enthusiasm in expressing its approval. The measure received the royal assent in due course, and the formal transfer of the two docks to the Corporation took place on the 1st September, 1884, when the sums above mentioned were paid over to the companies. A few weeks later a banquet was given to Mr. Weston by the leading citizens, when he was presented with a massive and elegant piece of plate, in recognition of his valuable public services in connection with the purchase of the docks. In the division of the sum paid for the Avonmouth property, certain classes of debenture holders received bonds for the full amount of their claims, while other categories received 60 and 80 per cent. of their respective (nominal) advances; and the shareholders in the warehouse company were paid £14 for each £20 share. The balance, about £35,000, remained for distribution amongst the ordinary shareholders. In respect to Portishead, the debentures were paid in full; the preference shareholders received about 62 per cent., and the ordinary shareholders, both in the dock and in the railway, obtained about 25 per cent. on their investments. The £100,000 advanced by the Corporation ranked in the last category, so that three-fourths of the money were lost. The Docks Act of 1884 abolished the fourpenny rate imposed in 1848. No real relief, however, was afforded by the abolition; on the contrary, the annual deficiency of the dock revenue to meet the expenditure was made a charge on the borough rate, and the burden on the inhabitants was increased. But against this was to be set the marked improvement which soon became visible in the trade of the port. In 1885 the tonnage of vessels entering the three docks from foreign and colonial ports was 653,594 tons against 566,100 in the previous year; while the coasting tonnage also increased from 642,198 to 684,494; and this in despite of a marked depression in the trade of the kingdom. The report of the Docks Committee for the year ending April 30th, 1886, stated that the revenue from all sources, including a borough rate of £14,500, amounted to £148,637, while the expenditure, inclusive of £5,559 devoted to a sinking fund for discharging the debt, had been £148,547. There had been a profit of £4,063 on the Floating Harbour, and a loss of £1,322 at Avonmouth, and of £2,651 at Portishead. For the year 1886–7, the committee anticipated that, owing to further outlay on the works, the receipts would be insufficient to meet the expenditure by £18,339, and, to avoid increased taxation on the citizens, they proposed that a small due should be levied on goods landed coastwise, which up to that time were exempt from dock charges, and a trifling addition made to the charge on certain foreign imports. The tax on the coasting trade excited so much opposition out of doors that the matter was deferred; but at a meeting in October the Council resolved that the dues on foreign goods, reduced in 1881 during the competition between the docks, should be raised to their former amount.

Although the scheme for dockising the Avon ceased to interest the public after the amalgamation of the docks, it is necessary to complete the story of the committee appointed in 1880. In June, 1882, that body presented a preliminary report, stating that, in order to prevent disasters from floods, it would be needful, before carrying out dockisation, to construct a culvert from the Froom at Stapleton to the Avon near Cook's Folly, at an estimated cost of £200,000. The outlay for the proposed dam at Avonmouth was put down at £790,000; and these sums, added to the expenses involved in Mr. Ashmead's sewer scheme, raised the estimated charge for dockisation to £1,270,000. The committee, which had spent £900 on the inquiry, asked for a further grant, and the Council voted £1,500 more. In May, 1883, the committee reported that the cost of the scheme would be about £1,750,000, the payment of interest on which would entail an additional borough rate of 2*s*. in the pound, unless the trade of the port should increase. A further grant of £3,000 was asked for, to make a new survey and further investigations. The Council, however, was almost unanimous in regarding dockisation as beyond the range of practical projects, and, by a majority of 34 votes against 8, it was declared to be inexpedient to pursue the inquiry further.

A prospectus was issued in June, 1878, of the North Clifton Hotel Company, with a capital of £20,000 in £10 shares. The directors purchased a portion of the nursery garden fronting Whiteladies Road, and erected an hotel, at a cost, including furniture, of about £18,000. The "Imperial Hotel" was opened in the following year.

The Royal Agricultural Society having undertaken to hold its annual exhibition in Bristol in 1878, and the Prince of Wales having intimated his intention to visit the city on the occasion, great preparations were made for the fitting reception of the expected guests. A subscription amounting to upwards of £4,000 was placed at the disposal of a local committee, to make additions to the prize list and meet the incidental expenses of the show. A further sum of £1,000 was contributed for the decoration of the streets through which the royal visitor was to be conducted. The show-yard on Durdham Down occupied nearly the entire space between the Stoke Bishop and the Westbury and Combe Dingle roads, the hoarding being nearly a mile and a half in length. The exhibition was one of the largest ever held by the society. The progress of scientific agriculture since the show held in 1842 was strikingly manifested by a comparison of the entries made on each occasion. In 1878 the number of horses entered was 350 against 60 in 1842; of cattle the figures were 443 against 213; of sheep, 397 against 134; and of pigs, 164 against 95. The development was still more remarkable in the mechanical department. In 1842 the number of implements shown was 455, whereas in 1878 the collection exceeded 6,000. In point of value the advance was still more considerable. The exhibits in 1878 of a single manufacturer—Mr. Fowler, of Leeds—were stated to be worth £60,000, and the whole of them were sold in the show-yard. Ample accommodation was afforded in 1842 by an enclosure of six acres, while the area required thirty-five years later was 67 acres. The president on the latter occasion was Colonel Kingscote, M.P. (one of whose short-horned calves was sold during the exhibition for a thousand guineas). The attendance was very large, the aggregate admissions to the yard numbering 121,851, and £10,825 were received at the gates.

The visit of the Prince of Wales took place on the 13th July, the fourth day of the meeting, his Royal Highness reaching the city by special train from London, accompanied by his suite and the chairman and vice-chairman of the Great Western railway. On his arrival he was received in state by the mayor (Ald. Edwards) and the members of the Council, in the presence of a large gathering of leading citizens. About a thousand of the local volunteers formed an imposing guard of honour. An address having been presented by the mayor, the Prince briefly returned thanks, expressing his regret that he could devote only a very brief period to the inspection of the objects of interest for which the city was so deservedly renowned. He was well aware, he added, of the highly favourable impression produced on other members of his family by the noble town, the splendour of its public and private buildings, and the good disposition of its inhabitants; and it would be his privilege to report to the Queen the loyal terms which had been used towards her Majesty in the address. The Prince was then conducted to an open carriage, in which he was accompanied by the mayor, Lord Skelmersdale, and Colonel Kingscote. Other carriages followed, containing the Prince's attendants, the sheriff (Mr. W. H. Wills), Mr. Morley, M.P., and others, two squadrons of Lancers forming the guard of the *cortége*. The streets through which the heir apparent passed had been decorated in a manner unprecedented in local annals. Victoria Street was lined throughout with Venetian masts, flags, trophies, and floral devices, the general effect of which was highly picturesque. At Bristol Bridge, an arch in the Tudor Gothic style had been erected, representing an old city gate, with side arches, battlements, towers, and portcullis, the centre being emblazoned with heraldic devices. About a hundred persons were accommodated in galleries over the fabric, which was one of the most effective designed for the occasion. High Street was plentifully decorated with cordons of flags stretched across the roadway. At the entrance into Corn Street was another triumphal arch, the effect of which was heightened by the decorations of the adjoining Council House. Corn Street and Clare Street were one long blaze of brilliant drapery; and at the approach to the Drawbridge ranges of Venetian masts, trophies, etc., imparted additional animation to the scene. The decorations reached their climax in College Green, which was "transfigured into a garden worthy of Aladdin's palace." Two Gothic arches were raised to the right and left of the restored High Cross, and through the co-operation of the principal tradesmen the roadway was densely hung with festoons of flowers, banners, and streamers, interspersed with richly coloured trophies. Park Street was also elaborately beautified by the concerted action of the inhabitants. The Prince's colours—red, white, and blue—artistically clothed the fronts of the houses, and at the top of the street was an arch of Saracenic type, with a dome and minarets, the colours of which harmonised with the surrounding objects. The general effect was much admired by the Prince as he ascended the hill. The Royal Promenade and the Triangle had also received artistic attention, and Whiteladies Road, though less copiously decorated, was set off by the brilliant dresses of the ladies assembled in balconies before nearly every house. Another triumphal arch, situated on Black-boy Hill (just cleared of its old hovels by the Council at an outlay of £11,000), was of large dimensions, the central span being 30 feet, and the two side arches 20 feet each in width. The spandrils were adorned with heraldic shields, and from the summit waved a gigantic royal standard. Redland was richly caparisoned, no less than 3,700 pennons and streamers being counted in that locality alone. The Prince of Wales, who was enthusiastically greeted along the route by an enormous crowd of spectators, expressed himself as equally surprised and gratified by the splendour of the display which his visit had evoked. His Royal Highness, who reached the show-yard in somewhat less than an hour, on his arrival was entertained to luncheon in a beautiful pavilion. He afterwards made a rapid survey of the chief features of the exhibition, accompanied by the Earl of Ducie, Lord Fitzhardinge, Colonel Kingscote, and the sheriff of Bristol. He then left the ground, and was driven slowly along the Downs to the Suspension Bridge, and thence to Clifton-bridge station. A special train being in readiness there, the Prince cordially bade farewell to the mayor and other officials.

A new iron bridge over the Froom, connecting Monk Street with Paul Street, Pennywell Road, was opened for traffic in September.

On the 9th September, great consternation was excited in the city and the adjoining counties by an announcement that the West of England and South Wales District Bank had suspended payments. This financial catastrophe was stated to be due to adverse rumours circulated for some weeks previously, causing so rapid a drain that the directors had not time to realise the assets; but it was added that the bank was still solvent as a going concern. On the books being handed over to official liquidators, however, it was discovered that the paid-up capital (£750,000), and the reserve fund (£156,000) had entirely disappeared, and that against the liabilities, about £3,500,000, there was a further estimated deficiency of assets exceeding £300,000. These calamitous results were found to be attributable to the imprudent advances made to two iron firms in South Wales, begun upwards of thirty years previously, and afterwards enormously increased from time to time in the vain hope of ultimately extricating the bank from the difficulty. The collapse of the concern was ruinous to the bulk of the shareholders, several of whom had invested their entire capital in the establishment. As these sufferers were unable to provide their share of the deficiency, the wealthier proprietors had to sustain a double burden, under which some of them succumbed. The calls of the liquidators amounted to £12 per share. A resolute effort was made to resuscitate the bank, with the view of preserving the profitable business which it possessed in Bristol and Somerset; and a new company, entitled the Bristol and West of England Bank, was formed on the limited liability principle, with a capital of £300,000 in £20 shares, of which £7 10*s*. were paid up. In August, 1879, the Home Secretary (Sir Richard Cross) ordered a prosecution to be instituted against the chairman (Mr. Jerom Murch) and five directors of the original company (Messrs. G. H. Leonard, J. Coates, A. Allen, C. Lucas, and the Rev. H. B. George), and also against the general manager (Mr. J. P. Gilbert), the defendants being charged with publishing fraudulent balance sheets with intent to deceive. The trial began in London in April, 1880, and resulted, after an eight days' hearing, in the acquittal of all the accused. The liquidation of the bank was not concluded until 1887, although repeated complaints as to its tardiness were made in the House of Commons. Dividends amounting to 16*s*. 6*d*. in the pound on the debts were, however, paid within eleven months of the failure. The creditors who consented to relinquish interest on their claims were satisfied in April, 1880; and the remaining liabilities were discharged in March, 1881. The sum of £2 10*s*. per share was afterwards returned to the proprietors who had paid the calls, and it was announced in January, 1887, that a final sum of 5*s*. or 6*s*. per share would shortly be distributed.

An election for the city was rendered necessary in December, 1878, by the retirement of Mr. K. D. Hodgson, owing to a severe illness (which soon after proved fatal). The candidates were Mr. Lewis Fry, a member of an old Liberal Bristol family, and Sir Ivor B. Guest, bart., a Conservative connected with the South Wales iron trade. On this occasion, for the first time, the Liberals made choice of their candidate by means of an organisation called the Four Hundred—or, as their opponents styled it, the Caucus—chosen by the voters at district meetings. Mr. Fry had a majority of nearly two-thirds in this body, and his competitor, Mr. E. S. Robinson, withdrew. The contest excited interest throughout the kingdom from its being the first of any moment after the signature of the peace of Berlin. Sir Ivor Guest strove, indeed, for local sympathies by recalling the fact that his maternal grandmother [a daughter of Dean Layard] lived in Bristol in her younger days. The polling took place on the 14th December; and the declaration, made by the sheriff shortly before midnight, was as follows: Mr. Fry, 9,342; Sir I. B. Guest, 7,795.

The parish church of St. George was totally destroyed by

fire on the morning of Sunday, the 22nd December. The disaster was attributed to the overheating of the stoves. The church was insured for £3,000, and no time was lost in setting about its reconstruction, which was completed at a cost of about £6,000. The new edifice, the tower of which is finished in a bizarre foreign style, was reopened in May, 1880.

Towards the close of 1878 a movement started in London for converting disused churchyards into ornamental gardens spread to this city. The authorities of Temple parish spent £800 in removing the unsightly walls of the extensive churchyard, and converting the dilapidated enclosure into a pleasant place of recreation, which was opened in July, 1880, by the mayor (Mr. H. Taylor). The burial ground of St. Nicholas' parish, on the Welsh Back, and also that adjacent to the church, were repaired and planted with shrubs. A most successful improvement of the same character was effected in 1881–2 by the authorities of St. James's, who laid out upwards of £600 in converting the parochial cemetery into an agreeable promenade and garden for the use of the crowded population of the locality. The ground was opened by the mayor (Mr. Weston) on the 30th June, 1882. In 1884 the churchyard of St. Philip—in a closely packed district still more destitute of open spaces—was similarly transformed at an outlay of £1,150, chiefly borne by a few philanthropic citizens connected with the parish. It was opened on the 5th of November by the mayor (Mr. Weston), who warmly congratulated the authorities on the results.

At a meeting of the Council in February, 1879, the town clerk produced a return of the indebtedness of the Corporation up to the 31st of December of the previous year. The bonds outstanding amounted to £123,263. The unredeemed debt of the Bristol Docks was £690,113. The sums owing by the Sanitary Authority, expended on public improvements, amounted in the aggregate to £461,481 (the gross cost of these works had been about £700,000). The total indebtedness of the civic body was upwards of a million and a quarter. The amount was increased to upwards of two millions by the subsequent purchase of the Channel Docks.

The Corporation, at a meeting in March, determined upon opening out a street at the back of the abandoned Bridewell, over the covered course of the Froom, with the view of facilitating traffic from the quays to the northern parts of the city. The improvement was completed soon afterwards. The Docks Committee, about the same time, ordered the construction of a shed on the quay at the bottom of Clare

Street—an erection which was strongly condemned as tasteless and unsightly, and as destroying the picturesque view previously obtainable from St. Augustine's. An extensive range of cattle sheds, erected at Cumberland Basin for the accommodation of foreign stock, was opened in May. The buildings entailed an outlay of £5,000. The Council in August, 1882, voted a further sum of £7,000 for the erection of sheds on the quays.

In accordance with the scheme of the Endowed School Commissioners for the future management of the Grammar School [see p. 453], the new governors took measures for the removal of the institution to a more convenient site. A piece of ground was purchased in Tyndall's Park, and an imposing building in the late Perpendicular style was erected for the school, adjoining which was placed a residence for the headmaster. The outlay for the land and buildings was about £20,000. Mr. W. H. Wills gave an organ, which cost about £1,000, and the same gentleman, with other members of his family, contributed a clock and chimes; while generous gifts were made by Mr. Herbert Thomas (chairman), and other governors for launching the school in a manner worthy of its high reputation. The new school buildings were first occupied by the boys on the 15th February; but the formal opening ceremony was deferred until the 17th May, when an address was delivered to an influential gathering of citizens by the Right Honourable W. E. Forster, who expressed himself as much struck by the magnificence of the schoolroom.*

At the Wimbledon Rifle competitions in July, Captain Sam Lang, of the local Engineer corps, won the prize for the highest aggregate score at the meeting, thereby enabling his corps to hold for the ensuing year the Dominion of Canada trophy—a splendid shield given by Canadian riflemen in 1877. Captain Lang's score was then the highest ever made at Wimbledon. The shield was deposited at the Mansion House.

During the summer, a well, which had once been in or adjacent to the keep of Bristol Castle, was discovered in Castle

* By a vexatious inadvertence, a paragraph recording the reorganisation of this school by the Charity Trustees was omitted under its proper date. It must now suffice to say that the trustees were for some years held at defiance by Dr. Goodenough [see p. 47], who persisted in regarding his post as a sinecure, and that he was not ejected until September, 1844. His claim for a pension was defeated, but his obstinate litigation cost the trustees £3,220 in law costs. A new scheme for the management of the school, sanctioned by the Lord Chancellor in 1847, gave the right of admission to boys resident within two miles of the Exchange, the maximum yearly fee being fixed at £6. Dr. Robert Evans having been appointed headmaster, the school was re-opened, January, 24, 1848, with about 200 boys.

Green. It had probably been closed when the castle was demolished, and contained several cannon balls of stone, including some cut for "cannon royal," the largest siege guns of the seventeenth century.

A Telephone Exchange was opened in the city in November. The value of the new invention was so little appreciated at the outset that only twenty subscribers to the Exchange were obtained during the first three months of its existence.

Although the Gloucestershire house of correction at Lawford's Gate had been disused as a prison some twenty years previous to this time, the justices had taken no steps for disposing of the site. Early in 1880 the subject was considered at quarter sessions, when it was resolved to sell the garden ground at the back of the building. But the Corporation of Bristol at once claimed to be the owners of the land, the rents of which, in fact, had been paid to the city treasurer. At the Michaelmas sessions at Gloucester, it was reported that the right of the county to the ground could not be established, there having been an adverse possession of more than twenty years. It was determined to confer with Mr. Fry, M.P., with the view of getting the land appropriated to the purposes of public recreation. No further reference to the subject has been found. It would appear that the city authorities denied the claim of the county to dictate conditions as to the future disposition of the property; but its ultimate appropriation to recreative purposes is highly probable.

Mr. Charles Branwhite, an eminent painter in water colours, died on the 15th February, 1880, aged 62 years. Mr. Branwhite, who was born in Bristol, and was the son of a portrait painter of some standing, gained wide repute for his pictures of winter scenery.

An exciting struggle took place at the general election in April. Owing to the defeat sustained by the Conservatives in 1878, they were unprepared with a candidate; and possibly, if the Liberal party had continued united, no opposition would have been offered to Messrs. Morley and Fry, who solicited re-election. But Mr. Elisha S. Robinson, who had taken umbrage at what he deemed the neglect of his pretensions, entered the field as an "independent" candidate, avowing himself a partisan of what was called the "Imperialist" policy of Lord Beaconsfield; and the Conservatives, inspirited by the incident, induced Sir Ivor B. Guest to re-enter the field. The polling, which took place on the 2nd April, resulted as follows: Mr. Morley, 10,704; Mr. Fry,

10,070; Sir I. Guest, 9,395; Mr. Robinson, 4,100. Nearly nine-tenths of Mr. Robinson's poll consisted of split votes given to him by Conservatives. This was Sir Ivor Guest's fourth unsuccessful attempt to win a seat. Lord Beaconsfield, a few months later, rewarded the baronet's zeal by conferring upon him the title of Baron Wimborne. The Bristol Conservatives subsequently presented his lordship with his portrait, which cost about £2,000.

The Council, at a meeting in April, gave its consent to the closing of the Guard House Passage, Wine Street, the owner of the adjoining property having offered to open a more convenient thoroughfare, and to set back his houses without demanding compensation. A beautiful Perpendicular archway at the entrance of the passage, of which a representation is given in Seyer's Bristol, was consequently removed. The arch was re-erected by Mr. Henry Stevens, at Cheltenham House, Bishopston. The guard house had disappeared several years previously.

Immediately after the election for the city of Gloucester, which resulted in the return of two Liberals, Alderman Thomas Robinson (brother of Mr. E. S. Robinson, of Bristol) and Mr. Monk, son of the late Bishop Monk, a petition to the House of Commons, asserting that the issue was due to bribery, was forwarded by a supporter of the defeated Conservative candidates, Mr. W. K. Wait (mayor of Bristol, 1869–70) and Mr. Ackers. The petition caused as much dismay in the political camp from which it proceeded as in the other; but the step taken was irrevocable, and a judicial inquiry was opened on the 9th June. The proceedings were significantly brief. The petitioner's counsel withdrew the charges against Mr. Monk; on the other hand, Mr. Robinson declined to defend his seat; and evidence having been adduced that a servant of the latter had bribed two or three voters, the election as regarded Mr. Robinson was forthwith declared void. It subsequently transpired that the proceedings before the judges were the outcome of an arrangement between the local leaders of the two parties, who had further agreed that Mr. Wait should fill the vacant seat without opposition. But the report of the judges stated that extensive corruption had prevailed, and a second investigation was ordered to be made by special commissioners. Before this tribunal, Mr. John Bernard, a magistrate of Gloucester, and a partner of Mr. Wait, deposed that, on learning that money would be required to secure the success of his friend, he wrote—unknown to Mr. Wait—to another partner in the firm, Mr. J. W. Dod, of Clifton, who forwarded him £1,500 in small notes, and that the money was handed over to the secret agents of corruption. A further sum of £500 was obtained from Mr. Wait, who, while admitting that Bernard had told him that the £1,500 would be wanted before it was sent for, declared that he did not know in what manner the two sums were expended. But he confessed to having paid between £600 and £700 after the election of 1874, knowing that the money had been spent in bribery. At the election under review, it was discovered that bribes to the amount of £1,300 had been distributed by the Liberals, that 2,756 burgesses out of the 4,904 who polled were paid for their votes (some of them by both parties), and that upwards of 200 citizens, including twenty men holding the offices of magistrate, alderman, or councillor, had acted as bribers. In the result the writ for the vacant seat was never issued, and the ratepayers were compelled to pay £4,400 for the expenses of the commission.

The centenary of the establishment of Sunday schools was celebrated in many of the parish churches on the 27th June, 1880, and a meeting of clergy, laity, teachers, and scholars took place on the following day in Colston Hall. On the 8th July about 16,000 children attending schools maintained by dissenting congregations walked in procession, accompanied by their 2,000 teachers, to the Zoological Gardens, where they spent an agreeable holiday.

At a meeting of the Council on the 20th July the Dock Committee reported that, in the existing state of the revenues under their control, they could no longer undertake to pay the interest on the sum of £100,000, borrowed for the purpose of subscribing towards the construction of Portishead Dock [see p. 400]. They therefore requested the Council to provide for the charge. The interest—£4,000—thereupon became a charge upon the borough rate.

A new religious denomination styled the Salvation Army, founded by a person styling himself "General" Booth, rose into notoriety during the summer, and gained many adherents amongst the poorer classes. An old circus near North Street was hired by the local leaders, and opened as a chapel on the 21st of August. The noisy parades of the "Army" in the streets provoked for some time antagonistic displays amongst the lower orders.

The Council, at a meeting in September, resolved to remove Bedminster Bridge, which had become insufficient for the traffic of that district, and to erect a more commodious structure. After a tedious delay, contracts were obtained in the spring of 1882, and about £16,000 were borrowed to carry out the works. The new bridge was opened by the mayor (Mr. Weston) on the 1st February, 1884, though it had been partially available for traffic from the previous November. A temporary foot-bridge, used during the reconstruction, was permanently erected in May, 1884, opposite St. Luke's Church, and was found very serviceable.

A large steamship called the *Ailsea*, trading between Bristol and Glasgow, was totally wrecked on the 16th November, 1880, near Milford Haven, while on her way to Scotland. The crew, twenty in number, and seven passengers, perished with the vessel.

Owing to the activity of speculative builders, the erection of new houses in the suburbs for some years previous to this date had been largely in excess of the demand. A collapse at length occurred, and during the winter of 1880 there was great distress amongst the families of workmen connected with the building trades. The extent to which speculation had been carried was shown by the fact that, in the spring of 1881, the unoccupied houses within the limits of the borough were officially reported to number 3,567, exclusive of 308 then in course of construction. If the uninhabited houses in the suburbs had been added, the aggregate would have exceeded 5,000.

An unusually intense frost, accompanied by a great fall of snow, commenced on the 13th January, 1881, and the low temperature continued for about a fortnight. During the snowstorm, a fast train, which left Bristol for London at half-past five in the evening, did not reach its destination until seven o'clock on the following evening, having been snowed up near Didcot. The chairman of the Great Western Railway Company, at the half-yearly meeting held soon afterwards, stated that 111 miles of their lines had been drifted up, and that 64 of their trains were buried in the drifts, exclusive of 141 temporary blocks sustained by others. The clearing away of the snow added many thousand pounds to the working expenses of the company. Postal communication in some parts of the country was suspended for three days.

Early in January, when proposals for substituting the electric light for gas were exciting national interest, the Council ordered an experiment on the subject to be made in the city; and seven lamps, constructed on the "Brush" system, were placed on the 17th January in the four great business thoroughfares converging at the Council House.

Owing to the defective apparatus by which electricity was generated, the experiment was not deemed satisfactory, and the lamps were withdrawn in a few weeks.* The chief objection to the new illuminant was the enhanced cost of electric motors as compared with gas. In November a novel proposal for surmounting the difficulty was laid before the Council by Mr. William Smith, who suggested that the ebb and flow of the tide might be made available for generating electricity, and expressed his belief that the adoption of the course proposed would effect a saving to the city of about £6,000 a year. According to calculations made for Mr. Smith by Professor Sylvanus Thompson, upon data supplied by Mr. Howard, the engineer of the docks, the available tidal power at Totterdown was over 6½ billions of foot pounds per annum; equal to 279,389 horse power per tide. At Rownham the power was estimated to be more than threefold greater; while at the mouth of the river it was 50 billions of foot pounds per annum, or considerably more than 2 million horse power per tide. The power required to light by electricity the 4,274 existing street lamps was, by Swan's system 4⅛ billions, by Edison's system 3½ billions, and by the arc light on the Brush system 2 billions of foot pounds yearly. A committee of inquiry was appointed, but the investigation led to no practical results.

On the 25th January, 1881, a dinner was given in the Victoria Rooms to Major-General Sir Frederick Roberts, G.C.B. (who passed his early boyhood and received part of his education in Bristol), in honour of his distinguished military services. The mayor (Mr. Weston) presided over a large party, and the health of the gallant guest was drunk with enthusiasm. On the following day Sir Frederick was presented by the mayor, on behalf of a number of leading citizens, with a service of plate, valued at £350. In the evening the Merchant Venturers' Society gave a grand ball in honour of the general, at which upwards of five hundred persons were present.

On the 30th March opening services were held in a new Congregational place of worship at Bishopston, styled the David Thomas Memorial Church, in memory of a distinguished minister of Highbury Chapel, Cotham. The cost of the building was about £6,300, and nearly the entire amount was contributed at or before the opening services.

---

* More than two years before this date—on the 28th November, 1878—the electric light had been tried in Bristol cathedral, the first ecclesiastical edifice in which its power was tested. The effect was exceedingly fine.

The census of 1881, taken on the 4th April, showed a further large decrease in the population of the "ancient city," whose numbers were returned at 56,964. The extended city, on the other hand, had largely increased, the aggregate for the borough being 206,874. The population of the suburban parishes was: Clifton, 28,695; the District, 19,114; St. Philip's out, 50,108; St. George's, 26,423; Bedminster, 44,759; Mangotsfield, 5,707; Stapleton, 10,833; Stoke Bishop tything, 13,347; and Horfield, 5,739.

The remains of the mansion of the Canynges' family, in Redcliff Street, occupied by Messrs. Jefferies & Sons, booksellers, were seriously damaged by a fire which occurred in the premises on the 9th October. The woodwork of the "oratory" was almost entirely destroyed, but the fine roof was preserved.

A religious census of the city was taken by the *Western Daily Press* on the 30th October. According to the published statistics, it appeared that out of a population of about 210,000, there were 48,596 persons present at the morning, and 60,856 at the evening services on the day in question.

The Council, in October, resolved upon redeeming the rent charge of £6,734 15*s*. 6*d*. payable under the provisions of the Docks Transfer Act of 1848. The sum required for this purpose was £168,381 5*s*. The Corporation had also borrowed £636,400 for dock purposes, including the subscription to Portishead Dock, and it was resolved to issue 3½ per cent. bonds in lieu of the old securities, whereby a saving of £4,000 per annum would be effected. In August, 1882, Alderman Baker informed the Council that bonds to the amount of £283,660 had been taken up, at an average price of £98 8*s*. 4*d*. per cent., which was considered satisfactory. Further conversions took place as the old bonds expired.

The Corporation gave notice in November of its intention to introduce a Bill into Parliament to strengthen the hands of the police in dealing with disorderly houses, gambling, street nuisances, and other matters. The more important clauses of the Bill were copied from the Police Acts of Manchester and other cities; but they were obnoxious to certain classes of tradesmen, and an agitation was excited on the pretext that the measure would be injurious to the liberty of the subject. At the statutory meeting of citizens convened to consider the proposal, it was almost unanimously condemned. After two years' delay, the Council resolved, in November, 1883, to make another effort of the same character. With the view of disarming the leading opponents of the previous Bill, the clause prohibiting overhanging signboards was omitted, and tramcars were exempted from the regulations for street traffic. Nevertheless, at the public meeting convoked to give assent to the scheme, an excited crowd refused to listen to the explanations of the mayor (Mr. Weston), and the Bill was condemned by a large majority. A poll was then demanded, the result being a definitive disapproval of the project by 15,409 votes against 6,798.

The Dolphin Society, which for about a century had attended morning service at the cathedral on the Colston anniversaries, suspended that custom in 1881, owing to the action of the dean. It appeared that Dr. Elliott, on receipt of the usual application, had consented to a sermon being preached on Colston's Day, and that the preacher should be the Rev. R. W. Randall, of All Saints', Clifton. But Canon Girdlestone, who was in residence, having protested against the admission into the cathedral pulpit of Mr. Randall, on account of his obstinate defiance of the orders of the bishop in reference to ritualistic practices at All Saints', the dean thereupon withdrew his permission. The society attended service at St. Mary Redcliff, where Mr. Randall preached.

Whilst some alterations were being made, during the autumn, in the premises No. 19, Maryleport Street, a handsome mantelpiece was exhumed from a thick covering of mortar. The mantelpiece was elaborately sculptured, and bore a shield of arms—on a chevron, between three pairs of garbs saltierwise, three barrels. These arms, which occur on the fronts of two houses in the same street and of a house in the Pithay, were borne by George Harrington, mayor in 1617. They were at all events placed on his monument. Being really the coat of the Brewers' Company of London, it is probable that the local brewers adopted the bearings, and that Harrington, who was a brewer, used them with some trifling "difference," just as his contemporary, Robert Aldworth, adopted the arms of the Merchants' Society. Curiously enough, the monuments of the two men—both too proud to claim heraldic devices to which they were not entitled—are to be found almost close together, in St. Peter's Church.

The Duke of Edinburgh visited Bristol in November, for the purpose of inspecting the Royal Naval Reserve and the local brigade of Naval Volunteers. The visit was purely of an official character, and at the duke's request there was no public reception.

An appalling catastrophe occurred on the 15th November in the steamship *Solway*, trading between Bristol, Belfast, and

Glasgow. During a storm in the Irish Channel, a barrel of naphtha broke loose and was burst by concussion, when by some means the contents became ignited. The result was the partial destruction of the ship, and the death of eighteen persons, most of whom perished in the flames.

About the close of 1881, when the carving of the west front of Bristol cathedral had just been completed, the dean and chapter ordered the removal of the chapter-office, a mean structure which had partially concealed that portion of the cathedral. An older and more interesting building near the abbey gateway—the minster-house—the roof and walls of which anciently formed part of the Prior's lodgings, was removed shortly afterwards. Its demolition evoked some protests, but certainly improved the appearance of the western front. Nothing now remained of the unsightly modern constructions between the cathedral and the grand gateway except the house partially incorporated with the latter, and occupied by the precentor. Fears were entertained that this excrescence could not be removed without endangering the gateway, some of the upper portions of which were in the last stage of decay. At a meeting in October, 1883, a committee was appointed to consider what steps should be taken; and after careful consideration of the remains, it was determined to restore the archway and the fifteenth-century building above it, to remove the precentor's house, and to rebuild the tower which had previously abutted upon the south-east corner of the gate; the estimated outlay being £3,100. The precentor's house was demolished in May, 1885, when some interesting relics of the old tower were brought to light.

About the beginning of 1882 Mr. [Sir] J. D. Weston, who had purchased Manilla Hall, Clifton (the mansion built by Sir William Draper and subsequently possessed by the Gordon and Miles families), detached from it a portion of the grounds for the purpose of converting them into building sites. In the following September the hall was bought by a French Roman Catholic sisterhood styled the "Dames de la Mère de Dieu," who established a school there. The nuns ordered the removal of the cenotaph erected by Sir Wm. Draper; but it was rescued from destruction by the exertions of Dr. Beddoe, F.R.S., and was, together with the obelisk to the elder Pitt, re-erected upon Clifton Down, not far distant from the original site, by means of a private subscription.

The dearth of religious agencies amongst the rapidly increasing suburban population having impressed itself upon the bishop of the diocese, his lordship entered into conferences with several prominent citizens, and eventually issued a commission to consider what remedies should be attempted. An investigation having been made, a public meeting was convened at the Guildhall in February, 1882, at which Bishop Ellicott stated the results of the inquiry. It was proposed to build and endow six new churches in the following parishes: St. Andrew's (which had a population of 8,340); St. Barnabas (10,232); Trinity, St. Philip's (13,450); St. Luke's, Barton Hill (9,851); St. Silas (6,700), and in Bedminster (20,847). The church of St. Matthew, Moorfields (6,989), was proposed to be enlarged, and it was recommended that sites should be secured in the districts of St. Mark's, Easton, Downside, and Windmill Hill, Bedminster, where the growth of population was considerable. The commissioners further advised the building of three mission chapels, and the provision of nine curates or missionaries. At a meeting in the Merchants' Hall, in March, resolutions approving of the scheme were adopted, and subscriptions amounting to over £19,000 were announced, the bishop contributing £1,000, Mr. A. Gibbs, £3,000, the Merchants' Society, £2,500, Messrs. Baker & Son, £1,000, and the Old Bank, £1,000. The foundation of Christ Church, Barton Hill, the first undertaken, was laid by the mayor (Mr. Weston) in July, 1883. During the course of that year four new parishes were constituted by Orders in Council, namely, St. Francis, Ashton Gate; Holy Nativity, Knowle; St. Agnes, Newfoundland Road; and St. Lawrence, Lawrence Hill. Within about two years, the commission received nearly £27,000 from the public, and building operations were prosecuted with great vigour. Christ Church, Barton Hill, was consecrated on the 12th November, 1885. On the 16th November, 1886, Bishop Ellicott consecrated a church dedicated to St. Michael, near Bedminster railway station. The only portion then finished was the chancel, but a temporary nave had been constructed of timber. Two mission chapels had been built in the same district, where the total outlay had been £3,645. Towards the church of St. Agnes [see p. 444] the commission contributed £2,500 and the site, besides giving £3,000 to the endowment fund.

During the early weeks of 1882 a temperance movement was started in Bristol by Mr. R. T. Booth, by whom great crowds were attracted to Colston Hall. The public were invited to assume "the blue ribbon," which Mr. Booth had selected as the badge of total abstinence, and 36,000 persons followed the example of Mr. Morley, M.P., in accepting this decoration, 21,000 of the recipients being, it was said, converts to teetotalism. The agitation materially affected the consumption of liquor in the city, and some publicans and beershop-keepers withdrew from the business.

In the parliamentary session of 1882 the Incorporation of the Poor promoted a Bill, the chief object of which was to secure the abolition of the Harbour rate imposed on the "ancient city" by the Dock Act of 1803 [see p. 14]. The charge of £2,400 per annum had at the outset involved the imposition of a rate of sixpence in the pound. Through the increased rateable value of the city, the burden had fallen to one-third of its original amount, but the guardians had long regarded as a grievance the immunity enjoyed by the suburban parishes, and now sought to include them within the rateable area. The Bill was opposed by the Corporation on the ground that property in the ancient parishes was largely enhanced in value by the construction of the Float. It was also contended that the rate was the result of what was considered, in 1803, a fair agreement between the city parishes and the dock promoters, and that it would be unjust to alter its incidence in the interest of one party only. The House of Lords approved of these arguments by rejecting that portion of the Bill. The remaining clauses received the royal assent.

St. Saviour's Church, Woolcott Park (which had been preceded by an iron construction removed from Tyndall's Park in 1875), was consecrated on the 30th May. The building cost upwards of £4,000.

For some time previous to this date, the members of the Bedminster board of guardians who represented rural parishes had repeatedly urged that the urban district of the union, where pauperism was always prevalent, should be separated from the country districts. Arguments of a like character had occasionally been advanced at the Bristol board, some members contending that the city ought to form a single union instead of being divided into three; but as the change would have involved the abolition of the Incorporation of the Poor and of the system of churchwarden guardians, it had been always deprecated by a majority. In consequence of the complaints of the Somerset guardians, the Local Government Board sent down an official inspector, who opened an inquiry at St. Peter's Hospital on the 19th June. The Barton Regis guardians being, most of them, opposed to an amalgamated board, refused to take part in the proceedings, which extended over two days, and elicited wide differences of opinion. In the following January another inquiry took place in the same building, the Board in London having in the meantime approved of the principle of a union conterminous with the municipal borough. The Council had discussed the subject previous to the inquiry, and had determined, though only by 25 votes against 23, that the proposal was inopportune. A similar diversity of views was manifested amongst those who attended the renewed investigation. In April a committee of the Bristol guardians, believing a consolidated union to be inevitable, drew up a scheme to carry it into effect, under which the churchwarden guardians were to be abolished. The plan was rejected by their colleagues. After lengthy deliberation, the Local Government Board announced in September, 1883, that "it was not prepared at the present time to proceed further in the matter."

At a meeting of the Council on the 15th June, the Sanitary Committee reported that, with a view to providing open spaces for public recreation, they had inspected a piece of land near Clift House, Bedminster, the property of Sir J. Greville Smyth, having an area of rather more than twenty-one acres; and they recommended that it should be purchased for a public park. The report having been adopted, the chairman of the committee, Mr. Low, read a letter from Sir J. G. Smyth's agent, stating that the owner of the land, having read the committee's report in the newspapers, would have great pleasure in presenting the ground to the city for the purpose of forming a pleasure ground, but expressed a hope that a portion would be reserved for the Bedminster Cricket Club. A vote of thanks to Sir Greville for his gift was passed by acclamation. In September, 1884, after the ground had become legally vested in the Corporation, a sum of £3,000 was voted by the Council for works to protect the park from inundations, to which it was liable in winter, and for entrance gates, etc. At the same meeting £1,500 were granted for laying out two pieces of ground near Newfoundland Road —for which the Corporation had given £2,358 to the feoffees of St. James's parish—one piece to be asphalted as a playground for children, and the other planted as a pleasure ground. A plot of land near Baptist Mills, adjoining Mina Road and Cowmead Walk, having been offered as a recreation ground by Mr. William Hunt, the Council voted £1,480 for laying it out. Another plot, left after making a new street from the Broadweir to Redcross Street, and valued at £2,700, was devoted to a similar purpose. For these improvements, and for alterations at Lovers' Walk and the Tabernacle burying ground, referred to elsewhere, the Council proposed to borrow £12,100 on mortgage of the rates; but the Local Government Board, being aware that the Redcross Street ground already belonged to the Streets Improvement Committee, reduced the amount to £9,400. In April, 1886, the Council resolved to purchase, for £1,800, two acres of ground belonging to the vestry of St. Mary Redcliff, for the purpose of adding the land to the Bedminster park. The price demanded was deemed extravagant by many ratepayers, and the Council soon afterwards rescinded the resolution. The Mina Road and Broadweir recreation grounds were opened by the mayor (Mr. Wathen) on the 30th June, 1886. In January, 1887, the Council resolved to purchase, for £450, a quarter of an acre of ground in St. Philip's Marsh, to be converted into a playground, and it was reported that negotiations were pending for the acquisition of plots of land, for a similar purpose, in the eastern district of Bedminster and at Barton Hill.

On the 10th July a meeting was held in the Council House to receive a deputation from the Royal College of Music, who attended to urge the claims of the institution on the cultivated classes. The mayor (Mr. Weston) presided. The deputation having advocated the interests of the college, it was resolved to raise £3,000, the amount required to found a Bristol scholarship. About £350 were subscribed in the room, but the movement met with slender support out of doors.

The sheriff of the city (Mr. W. E. George) having had an addition to his family during his term of office, was presented in August by the committee of the Grateful Society, of which he was then president, with an elegant piece of plate in the form of a silver cradle, as a memorial of the double functions which he had fulfilled during the year. The presentation was made by the mayor (Mr. Weston).

Owing to unusually heavy rains during the month of October, which attained their maximum on the 22nd and 23rd, when upwards of three inches of rainfall were measured within forty-eight hours, a large area of country around Bristol was deeply flooded, and much property was destroyed. The damage in the city was still more serious, thousands of houses being flooded at and near Baptist Mills, Stapleton Road, and Bedminster. On the evening of the 23rd a portion of Stapleton Road was about four feet under water, and as the Froom continued to rise during the night, the district near its banks presented an extraordinary aspect on the following morning, when traffic was entirely stopped. At the Black Swan Inn, Stapleton Road, the water mounted nearly to the signboard over the door of the premises. The only means of communicating with a great number of houses in the locality was by means of rafts and boats, by which provisions and necessaries were supplied to many of the imprisoned inhabitants. In the afternoon, the accumulated waters spread in an immense lake along Newfoundland Road and Newfoundland Street to Paul Street, Portland Square. All the low-lying streets in that district were submerged several feet. When the flood receded on the following day, a deplorable sight was presented in the neighbouring dwellings, the basement floors of which were thickly covered with mud. The disaster was attended with fatal results to a young baker, named Foot, who, while delivering bread in a cart in Mina Road, was swept away by the torrent, both man and horse being drowned. A brewer's dray was carried off near the same place, but the driver escaped. Two houses in that road were undermined by the water, and fell into ruins; but the inhabitants, about twenty in number, warned by some premonitory crumblings, had escaped on rafts. Some idea of the extent of the calamity may be formed from the fact that in the single district of St. Agnes 372 houses, inhabited by twice that number of families, suffered from the inundation, the furniture of many of the inmates being irreparably damaged. The low-lying districts of Bedminster were devastated in a similar manner. In Hereford Street, the flood was nearly eight feet in depth, and the dwellings in many other thoroughfares were submerged fully three feet. Altogether upwards of a thousand houses suffered in that locality, the effects being quite as deplorable as those recorded in the eastern suburbs. The clergy and other citizens made devoted efforts on behalf of the poor who were practically ruined by the disaster, and a large fund was raised; but many of the families nevertheless suffered from sickness during the winter owing to the soaked condition of their dwellings. Several houses became totally unfit for habitation, and their ruins still remain as memorials of the flood. At a meeting of the Council, in May, 1883, the town clerk stated that he had been served with 194 notices of claims for compensation for damages, by persons owning property in the Froom district, who alleged that the disaster was mainly due to the negligence of the authorities. The claims amounted to £44,890, but no attempt was made to prosecute them. It was notorious, indeed, that many of the houses ravaged by the flood had been erected by unscrupulous speculators on land which was more or less under water every winter. The Council, on the

28th September, 1886, with a view to mitigating the effects of future inundations, resolved to apply for parliamentary powers to construct a culvert from the Froom, near the Broadweir, to the Floating Harbour, near St. Philip's Bridge. The outlay was estimated at £13,000, but the Bill, as finally approved, sought for power to expend £52,500. The scheme was sanctioned by a practically unanimous vote of the ratepayers.

At a meeting of the Council on the 28th October, 1882, a report was read from the Sanitary Committee, explaining the provisions of the new Electric Lighting Act, and stating that ten companies had given notice of their intention to apply for powers to supply the new illuminating agent in the city. The Council was recommended to defeat attempts to create a private monopoly by claiming its right to put in operation the provisions of the Act. Application was accordingly made for a legislative order authorising the Council to supply electricity within the borough. The order, which was granted in the session of 1883, required the Council to light the main thoroughfares within two years. Motives of economy deterred the authorities from exercising the powers.

Much local interest was created in 1883 by the introduction into Parliament of a Bill for authorising the construction of a railway to connect the London and South Western line, near Andover, with the North Somerset line at Radstock, and thus to open out a new communication between Bristol and London. The capital of the proposed company was £1,866,000. The contemplated works in Bristol were of a gigantic character, the projected line being intended to run through a dense mass of property between St. Philip's Marsh and the Stone Bridge, while a site for the city terminus was to be obtained by covering over the Float from the Stone Bridge to the Drawbridge. The scheme met an amount of approval rarely accorded to local plans of improvement, the provisional committee formed for promoting the Bill comprising a majority of the Council and of the leading mercantile firms, while the Merchants' Society made a liberal grant towards the expenses; the Chamber of Commerce forwarded petitions in favour of the scheme, and meetings in its support were held in every ward. In fact, as was observed at the time, Bristolians presented the rare spectacle of being unanimous. The public satisfaction was visibly diminished by an announcement that the proposed station was to be indefinitely postponed. The junction with the North Somerset line was also abandoned through the opposition of the Midland Company, and the promoters had to fall back upon a proposed railway to join the Midland system at Bath, thus diverting Bristol traffic by way of Mangotsfield. After a long struggle with the Great Western Company before a committee of the House of Commons, the Bill was rejected. Shortly afterwards the Great Western and South Western boards entered into a compact, by which they mutually undertook to refrain for ten years from an aggressive policy towards each other. The agreement raised an insuperable bar against the revival of the above scheme.

Some years before this date, the Corporation, in obtaining powers for the construction of new streets, had "scheduled" a portion of the Redcross Street burial ground belonging to the Tabernacle congregation, with the intention of opening a thoroughfare from Redcross Street to the Weir. Negotiations for the purchase of the ground had subsequently taken place; but as the trustees insisted that the human remains should be removed to another cemetery, while the civic authorities believed that they could not legally spend money for that purpose, the matter remained in abeyance. About four o'clock one morning in June, 1883, however, a number of labourers, employed by no one knew whom, broke down the wall of the cemetery, fenced off a portion for the proposed road, and began to dig and cart away the mould, which was largely mingled with the relics of the dead, the tombstones being, it was said, buried. As soon as these proceedings became known, the trustees lost no time in applying for, and obtaining, an injunction from the High Court, restraining the Corporation from further proceedings until the case had been judicially heard. At a special meeting of the Council, a few days later, some members of the Streets Improvement Committee defended the measures that had been taken; but a resolution was adopted regretting the course pursued, and directing operations to be suspended until an arrangement was effected. The Corporation eventually purchased the cemetery for £300, and paid £187 for removing the remains. The portion not required for the street was laid out as an ornamental garden at a further cost of £600. The Council had also to defray the legal expenses arising out of the affair, which had excited great disapproval.

Much discussion arose during the spring in reference to the announced intention of the Docks Committee, which had purchased a property known as Green's dock, St. Augustine's, to close that place, in consequence of the expense incurred in maintaining a bridge which crossed the entrance. The Council, at a meeting in June, approved of the committee's decision, and resolved on purchasing, for £10,000, another property known as the Albert dock, which it was stated could be converted into a graving dock capable of accommodating the largest class of vessels entering the Float.

In response to an appeal made to the Government by the civic authorities, an Order in Council was issued in July, by which the practice in the Bristol Tolzey and Piepoudre courts was reorganised and amended, portions of 1 and 2 William IV., c. 58, and of the Common Law Procedure Act, 1860, relating to interpleader summonses, being applied to the ancient institutions.

The dilapidated old building known as Dr. White's almshouse, in Temple Street, was removed during the summer by order of the trustees, and a block of dwellings was constructed on the site for the accommodation of 32 inmates. The cost of the new buildings, which were opened by the mayor (Mr. Weston), on the 22nd December, was £3,250.

At a meeting of the Council in October, a number of minor improvement schemes, recommended by the Streets Improvement Committee, and estimated to cost about £50,000, were approved. They included alterations in Hotwell Road, near Dowry Square; at Blackboy Hill and Ellenborough Buildings, Redland; Highbury Place, Cotham; St. Michael's Park; Rupert Street; Lewin's Mead; Lower Maudlin Street; Richmond Road, Montpelier; East Street to Church Lane, Bedminster; Redcliff Mead Lane; Redcliff Street; Thunderbolt Street; and Leek Lane. Two schemes affecting Clifton were rejected, but a strong feeling was excited out of doors in reference to one of them—for opening a thoroughfare from Pembroke Road to Worcester Terrace—which was obnoxious to some members of the Council living in the vicinity. Public opinion was so strongly manifested that the original vote was reversed. The schemes received legislative sanction in the following year, but some of them still remain unexecuted.

About this time an interesting panel-fronted house in King Street, built by John Romsey, town clerk, in 1664, was demolished without any apparent reason. The site still remains unoccupied. It was in this house that Judge Jeffreys was entertained by Romsey, who furnished him with the facts on which he founded his famous invective against the mayor and aldermen for "kidnapping."

The Prince of Wales arrived in Bristol on the 28th January, 1884, on a visit to Sir Philip and Lady Miles, at Leigh Court. In accordance with his desire there was no public reception. On the evening of the following day, the Prince attended a concert in Colston Hall, given by his hosts in aid of the funds of the Infirmary and Hospital. The attendance was much below expectations, but £110 were handed over to the charities. The Prince left for London on the 31st.

At a meeting of the Council in February, the Docks Committee presented a report disapproving of a proposal for the construction of graving docks, which it was stated would involve an outlay of £60,000; while the construction of a gridiron, at a small fraction of that expense, would adequately supply the wants of the shipping interest. It was accordingly determined to construct a gridiron near Cumberland Basin, at an estimated cost of £6,000. A floating fire-engine was also ordered at an outlay of £2,500. The gridiron was completed in April, 1885.

The Whitsuntide of 1884 was fixed for the first parade of draught horses employed in the city, an experiment promoted by several influential residents. About 600 animals were brought together at the cattle market, and passed in procession through the principal streets to Clifton Down, where prizes were awarded. The exhibition met with so much approval that it was repeated a twelvemonth later, when nearly 750 horses (valued at over £40,000) entered into the competition, and a dinner was subsequently given to about 600 carters. In 1886 the number of horses exhibited was 775. The show has now become a local institution.

At the quarter sessions in July, the Corporation, acting as the local Sanitary Authority, and Mr. T. D. Sibly, a ratepayer, applied to the recorder to put in force the provisions of a clause in the Gasworks Act of 1847, by which the court was enabled, on the petition of two ratepayers, to appoint an accountant to examine into the accounts of the Gas Company, with a view to discover whether their financial condition did not admit of a reduction in the price of gas. The directors of the Gas Company contended that the Sanitary Authority, although immeasurably their largest customer, was not a ratepayer within the meaning of the Act; but the recorder at once made the order, and Mr. E. H. Carter, of Birmingham, was appointed as accountant. Mr. Carter presented his report early in the following year. He stated that in 1880 the company had applied upwards of £6,000 out of their reserve to erecting works, instead of charging the amount to capital. A somewhat similar error, and for about the same amount, was committed in 1875. The company had further maintained a contingency as well as a reserve fund, which they were not entitled to do, and the aggregate of these funds was about £9,200 above the legal maximum. Mr. Carter thought that the working expenses might be considerably reduced. He was also of opinion that the meter rents were excessive. The company had made a reduction in the price of gas since his appointment, and the state of the accounts did not warrant another. The capital account stood after his correction at £721,000. The company were ordered to pay the cost of the inquiry.

A new hall, attached to the premises of the Young Men's Christian Association in St. James's Square, was opened at the end of June. The building had cost about £4,000, the whole of which was provided by the friends of the institution.

A prospectus was issued in August of the Bristol Joint Stock Bank. The company commenced business in Corn Street in the following December.

An Industrial and Fine Arts Exhibition for Bristol and the adjoining counties—on a scale never before attempted in the city—was opened on the 2nd September in the Rifle Drill Hall. On the platform were the mayor (Mr. Weston), the Bishop of Bath and Wells, several members of Parliament, and the mayors of Gloucester, Bath, Wells, Taunton, Yeovil, Chard, Tewkesbury, and Glastonbury. In addition to the accommodation afforded by the Drill Hall and its appurtenances, the committee had erected extensive temporary buildings for the exhibition of machinery, working models, and manufactured products, the result being a satisfactory representation of the industries of the district. A valuable collection of works of art was an attractive feature of the affair, which was admirably organised throughout. Shortly after the close of the exhibition, at the end of November, it was announced that the admissions had reached 210,000, and that although the expenses had amounted to £7,889, there was a surplus of £1,520. The money was handed over to Bristol University College, for whose benefit the exhibition had been promoted.

In anticipation of the Redistribution of Seats Bill, introduced into Parliament in 1885, Mr. Gladstone's Ministry prepared plans for the extension of the parliamentary boundaries of the city by the abstraction from Gloucestershire of the local government district of Horfield and of the parishes of Stapleton and St. George, and by the appropriation from Somerset of the Knowle and Totterdown districts of the old parish of Bedminster. The representatives of the city were increased by the Bill from two to four, but the electors, instead of voting for the whole number according to ancient custom, were divided into four constituencies, named after the cardinal points, and having one member each. At a court of inquiry held at the Guildhall, on the 15th January, 1885, before Mr. J. J. Henley and General P. Carey, R.E., boundary commissioners, an application was made on behalf of the Council for the inclusion within the borough of the Sneyd Park district of Westbury parish; but this was energetically opposed by the inhabitants and disapproved by the commissioners. The following arrangement—which had the assent of the local leaders of both political parties—was approved.

Western Division. Population, 60,874; comprising the municipal wards of Clifton (22,915), Westbury (13,324), St. Michael (10,712), and St. Augustine (9,147), and the local district of Horfield (4,766).

Northern Division. Population, 64,713; comprising the municipal wards of the District (19,114), St. Paul (15,083), and St. James (8,420), so much of the ward of St. Philip North as is bounded by Wade Street on the west and Stapleton Road on the south (11,263), and the parish of Stapleton (10,833).

Eastern Division. Population, 61,986; comprising so much of the ward of St. Philip North as is bounded by Wade Street on the east and Stapleton Road on the north (13,202), the municipal ward of St. Philip South (22,351), and the parish of St. George (26,433).

Southern Division. Population, 65,633; including the municipal wards of Bristol (10,022), Redcliff (17,274), Bedminster East (13,014), and Bedminster West (20,737), and so much of the Somerset portion of Bedminster parish as extends from the municipal boundary to Redcatch and Knowle lanes (4,306).

These divisions were subsequently embodied in the Redistribution Bill, which was passed in the following session.

A steam vessel, called the *Bulldog*, designed for river improvement purposes by Mr. J. W. Girdlestone, recently appointed engineer to the Docks Committee, was brought into use in March, 1885. Amongst the apparatus belonging to the boat was a centrifugal pumping engine, capable of raising 6,000 gallons per minute from a depth of 30 feet, or 10,000 gallons per minute from a depth of 10 feet; a crane lifting 5 tons; a large dredger bucket, and an electric dynamo machine, generating a light of 6,000 candle power.

A public room, styled St. James's Hall, erected in Cumberland Street by the Bristol Public Hall Company, and capable of seating an audience of 1,200, was opened in April.

A meeting was held in the Council House on the 1st June, the mayor (Mr. Wathen) presiding, to consider the desirability of raising a memorial to Mr. Frederick John Fargus, a Bristolian whose premature death, on the 7th May, at the outset of what promised to be a brilliant literary career, had caused wide-spread regret. It was determined to erect a tablet and bust in the cathedral, and to found a literary scholarship at University College. Upwards of £750 were subscribed on behalf of those objects. The monument in the cathedral, executed by Mr. J. Havard Thomas, was erected in March, 1886.

On the evening of the first Sunday in June, a band of forty musicians, engaged by "a number of gentlemen interested in the welfare of the working classes," assembled on Durdham Down, and played a selection of pieces from the works of Handel and other eminent masters. There was a large attendance, and the newspapers estimated the numbers present on subsequent fine evenings at upwards of twenty thousand. The concerts excited great indignation in certain circles; and upon the supporters of the movement announcing that they would be continued throughout the summer, the Council passed a resolution declaring Sunday bands inexpedient, and instructing the town clerk to request their patrons to discontinue them. The promoters having declined to acquiesce, a special meeting of the Council was convened by their opponents, who intended to have a bye-law enacted, expressly prohibiting Sunday bands. On second thoughts, however, the leader of the anti-band party contented himself with moving an instruction to the Downs Committee to draft bye-laws for the regulation of the public property. By this time the action of the promoters of the concerts had been defended by Canon Percival and other clergymen; and, as the Downs Committee took no action, the programme of the band committee was successfully carried out. The performances were revived in the summer of 1886, when the attendances of the public were greater than ever. But the expectation of the promoters that the sale of programmes would go far to meet the expenses was disappointed, the public purchasing a very limited number. After the experiment had been continued for about two months, the committee found their funds exhausted, and discontinued their efforts.

The advisability of giving a more permanent character to the composition of the Barton Regis board of guardians having commended itself to many of the members, it was resolved to take a vote of the ratepayers in June, upon the question whether future elections should be annual or triennial. A majority declared in favour of the triennial system, and the alteration was approved by the Local Government Board. The first election under the new regulation took place in April, 1886.

Shortly after the death, on the 29th April, 1885, of Mr. Edward Phillips, who, previous to his retirement from business, had been a wine merchant in Broad Street, the Charity Trustees were informed that they had a large reversionary interest in his will. Mr. Phillips devised his personal estate, subject to the payment of certain legacies, and of a life annuity to his wife, to the trustees, "for the relief of deserving needy persons, either by gifts, apprenticing boys and girls to learn trades, or by granting annuities to widows, or for such other charitable purposes as may be consistent with the above directions." A sum of about £4,600 was received from the testator's solicitors, with an intimation that about £24,000 more would be available upon the death of Mrs. Phillips. The interest of the sum in hand is dispensed by the trustees in pensions to aged gentlewomen of good education, born in Bristol, or resident in the city for at least ten years.

At a meeting of the Council in July, a report was presented by the Docks Committee, urging the necessity of taking further measures for improving the accommodation of the port. One of the most pressing requirements, it was alleged, was the provision of facilities for the shipment of steam coal. The committee were of opinion that existing wants might be supplied by the erection of coal "tips" at Avonmouth, at an outlay of £60,000. They further recommended the construction of a new entrance lock to Avonmouth dock (estimated at £20,000), and of a new graving dock there (£45,000), the construction of a deep-water wharf at Canon's Marsh, on the site of Liverpool wharf, with storage accommodation on the city quays (£85,000), the reconstruction of buildings at Avonmouth to the extent of £100,000, and the purchase of a powerful dredger at an outlay of about £30,000; the total estimated expenditure being £340,000. The chairman, Mr. Low, in moving the adoption of this report, which would have taken away the breath of any previous generation of civic senators, congratulated his hearers upon the results of their recent dock policy. Future prospects, he added, had been improved by the starting of a fortnightly service of large steamers from the Avon to Montreal. There was practically no opposition to the motion. The meeting of the ratepayers to consider the Bill for obtaining the necessary powers sanctioned the scheme by a unanimous vote, and the measure received the royal assent on the 25th June, 1886.

The inclusion of the Trades School in the scheme for the future management of Colston's School has been already recorded [see p. 453]. On the 25th July, the former institution, under the name of the Merchant Venturers' School, was installed in a vast pile of buildings in Unity Street (on the site of the old Grammar School), erected and fitted up by the Merchants' Society at a cost of upwards of £40,000.* Amongst those who took part in the ceremony were the bishop of the diocese, Sir Frederick Bramwell, C.E., and Mr. S. Morley, M.P. The visitors, after inspecting the great hall, the engineering workshops, library, laboratories, lecture rooms, class rooms, etc., were entertained to a luncheon, provided by the master of the Company (Alderman Butterworth).

The death was announced on the 29th August of Mr. Elisha Smith Robinson, for many years an active member of the Council and of the Corporation of the Poor. Entering the city in humble circumstances, he succeeded by energy and skill in founding a highly prosperous business, whilst by his public spirit he won the approval of his fellow citizens, and filled the highest offices they could bestow with general satisfaction. His funeral was attended by the mayor, the members of the Council, and representatives of many religious and charitable institutions, the procession comprising upwards of fifty private carriages. A bust of Mr. Robinson was shortly afterwards placed in Colston Hall.

The dissolution of Parliament, consequent upon the concession of household suffrage to counties and a redistribution of seats, took place in November. The event having been long foreseen, both political parties were prepared for the struggle, and much curiosity was felt as to the result. Owing to the extension of the parliamentary borough, and to the increased facilities given to persons claiming the lodger franchise, the constituency had largely increased, the total number of electors being 36,549, of whom 33,233 were householders, 1,930 freeholders, 939 lodgers, and 447 freemen. The nomin-

---

* The profuse liberality of the Society was regarded with mingled feelings by many friends of education. Dr. Beddoe, F.R.S., in a letter published in the local journals in July, 1884, wrote: "It is the curse of Bristol and of Bristolians that, instead of helping on and developing whatever they possess that is good and capable of improvement, they think progress consists in the starting of several institutions. Thus, while we have a Grammar School and a University College, both admirably officered, and doing great good, but sadly hindered and hampered by want of funds, we see a gigantic Trade School arising to be a rival to them both. The result will be that all the three will be crippled in their usefulness for years; whereas half the money that is being expended on the new Trade School would have placed the success of the University College beyond question."

ations took place on the 23rd and the polling on the 25th November. It will be convenient to record the issue under separate heads:—

In Bristol West (with 7,657 electors) the Conservatives nominated Sir Michael Hicks-Beach, bart., then Chancellor of the Exchequer. The Liberal nominee was Mr. Brinsley de Coucy Nixon, of Westward Ho, Devon, banker. The poll was declared as follows: Sir M. H. Beach, 3,876; Mr. Nixon, 2,463.

In Bristol North (9,002 electors) the Liberals brought forward Mr. Lewis Fry, one of the former members for the city (his colleague, Mr. Morley, retired into private life). The Conservative candidate was Mr. Charles Edward H. A. Colston, of Roundway, Wilts. The numbers polled in this division were: Mr. Fry, 4,110; Mr. Colston, 3,046.

Bristol East (9,506 electors). Mr. James Broad Bissell, of Diptford, Devon, was the Conservative aspirant, and was opposed in the Liberal interest by Mr. Handel Cossham, of St. George's and Bath, an extensive colliery owner in the district. The deputy sheriff's declaration was as follows: Mr. Cossham, 4,647; Mr. Bissell, 2,383.

Bristol South (10,384 electors). This was the most exciting conflict of the day. The Liberals brought forward Mr. Joseph Dodge Weston, of Clifton, who had served the office of mayor for four successive years, and had gained universal applause for his solution of the docks difficulty. The Conservatives nominated Lieut.-Colonel Hill, C.B., of Cardiff and Bristol, shipowner. The polling resulted as follows: Mr. Weston, 4,217; Lieut.-Col. Hill, 4,121.

The total poll for the city credited the Liberals with 15,437, and the Conservatives with 13,426 votes. The polling booths, under the new law, remained open until eight o'clock in the evening. Although immense crowds thronged the streets until after midnight, awaiting the declarations, the proceedings passed off with perfect tranquillity.

The Council applied for parliamentary powers during the session of 1886 for the erection of a bridge from St. Philip's Marsh to Totterdown. The estimated cost of the structure was originally stated at £12,870, but it was subsequently deemed advisable to acquire additional ground at a further cost of £8,000, an expectation being held out that a re-sale of the surplus plots for building purposes would more than cover the extra outlay. The Act received the royal assent in April; and the Council, on the 1st June, authorised the Streets Improvement Committee to carry its provisions into effect.

It has been already recorded [see p. 496] that Mr. Ashmead, the city engineer, prepared a plan in 1879 for carrying the sewage of Bristol to the Channel, at a cost of £280,000. His proposal was referred to Sir Joseph Bazalgette, who, in January, 1886, reported favourably upon the project, but estimated the expenditure at £300,000. Sir Joseph was of opinion that the works might be deferred for several years, provided the sewer outlets were removed beyond the city boundaries, the locality indicated being Sea Mills, and the cost £85,000. At a meeting of the Council in May, it was resolved, by a majority of 24 to 20, that it was inexpedient at that time to proceed further in the matter.

In March, the Princess Beatrice was presented with an elaborately carved marriage chest and an embroidered coverlet by "the women of Bristol," in testimony of their affectionate interest in her recent marriage. The chest, which was chiefly made from ancient oak taken from Redcliff Church, was richly carved by Mr. C. Trapnell, the lid having a representation of Queen Elizabeth's visit to Bristol, while the front displayed Henry VII. presenting his sword to the mayor on confirming the city charters. The Princess expressed much admiration of the gift in acknowledging its reception.

An elaborately decorated suite of offices in Queen Square, erected for the use of the staff of the Bristol Docks, was opened on the 10th May. The cost of the site and buildings was £9,200, but, as portions of the premises were let to private persons, it was stated that the rent fairly chargeable to the dock estate would not exceed £150 per annum.

Another dissolution of Parliament took place in June, 1886, in consequence of the defeat of Mr. Gladstone's Ministry on the question of Irish Home Rule. The Bill introduced by the Premier had caused a disruption of the Liberal party in the House of Commons, Mr. Fry being one of several members who withdrew their support from the Cabinet. Much difference of opinion also prevailed amongst the Liberal electors in all parts of the kingdom. The nominations in Bristol were made on the 1st July, and the polling took place on the following day.

In Bristol West the Conservatives again nominated Sir M. Hicks-Beach, while the Liberals brought forward Mr. James Judd, of Upper Norwood, London, printer. The contest resulted as follows: Sir M. H. Beach, 3,819; Mr. Judd, 1,801. [Another election for this district took place in August, consequent upon the appointment of Sir M. Hicks-Beach as Secretary for Ireland. The right hon. gentleman was returned without opposition.]

In Bristol North, Mr. Lewis Fry again offered himself; and the Conservatives, instead of opposing his re-election, lent him their support. The Liberal Association nominated Dr. Alfred Carpenter, of Croydon, London. Mr. J. D. Marshall, a labour candidate, entered the field, but withdrew on the eve of the nomination. The polling was as follows: Mr. Fry, 3,587; Dr. Carpenter, 2,737.

In Bristol East, the re-election of Mr. Handel Cossham was opposed by Mr. James Inskip, a solicitor in the city, but without success, the voting being: Mr. Cossham, 3,672; Mr. Inskip, 1,936.

Bristol South. Mr. Weston, who had supported the Government Bill for Ireland, lost the support of several influential Liberals in this district, with the effect of reversing the decision of the previous November in favour of Lieut.-Col. Hill, the Conservative candidate. The declaration of the poll was as follows: Lieut.-Col. Hill, 4,447; Mr. Weston, 3,423. [The latter gentleman, on the 26th November following, received the honour of knighthood.]

The total poll for the city was 25,422, or 3,441 less than on the previous occasion upon the same register.

During the great Indian and Colonial Exhibition in London in the summer of this year, a local movement was started for inviting representatives of the various dependencies to pay a visit to Bristol. The invitation was accepted with much cordiality by the colonists, about 150 of whom arrived in the city on the 6th September, and were welcomed at the railway station by the mayor (Mr. Wathen), the members of the Corporation, and many leading citizens. The visitors inspected the chief local objects of interest, and various entertainments were provided in their honour, including a dinner at the Mansion House, luncheons by the Chamber of Commerce and Society of Merchants respectively, a concert by the Madrigal Society, and a grand ball and supper. The colonists departed on the 8th September, expressing themselves highly gratified with their hospitable reception.

Mr. Samuel Morley, who had represented the city in three Parliaments, expired on the 5th September, aged 77, to the general regret of charitable and religious circles, as well as of the political party of which he was an earnest supporter. In some of the notices of his career which appeared in the newspapers, it was stated that Mr. Morley had for many years dispensed between £20,000 and £30,000 of his large income annually in the support of pious and philanthropic objects. Some months before his decease, a movement had been started amongst the Liberals of Bristol with a view to erecting some permanent memorial of his connection with the city. Upon his demise, a feeling was evinced by many citizens of both political parties that the work of commemorating his memory was worthy of being assumed by the inhabitants generally; and a meeting held at the Guildhall on the 1st October, the mayor presiding, was attended by representatives of every school of religious and political opinion. Addresses were delivered by the bishop of the diocese, Mr. Fry, M.P., Mr. Cossham, M.P., the vicar of Temple, and several other gentlemen, and it was resolved to start a subscription for the purpose of securing the erection of a statue of the deceased, in testimony of his distinguished charity and public services. The commission was confided to Mr. J. Havard Thomas. The subscriptions in a few weeks exceeded £1,100.

At the triennial election of aldermen in November, Mr. Charles Nash, who had represented St. Augustine's ward for thirty-five years, was raised to the aldermanic dignity. Mr. Nash was the first councillor on whom this honour had been conferred during the existence of the reformed Corporation—a period of more than half a century.

A scheme for supplying the city with water from certain mines near Frampton Cotterell was noticed at page 285. Subsequently, a company styled the West Gloucestershire Water Company, with a capital of £100,000, obtained an Act enabling them to supply a district extending from Wotton-under-Edge to the suburbs of Bristol and Bath. The mains to Frenchay were completed in September.

A meeting was held in the Guildhall on the 29th September, the mayor (Ald. Edwards) presiding, for the purpose of considering the desirability of improving the water supply of the city. Many influential citizens took part in the proceedings. It was resolved that an increased supply of pure water was urgently required, and that such a supply could be best obtained by utilising the Severn tunnel springs [p. 416], which were stated to produce 14,000,000 gallons daily. It was further determined to support a Bill for this purpose promoted by a new undertaking styled the Bristol Consumers' Water Company, which had bound itself to transfer the works to the Corporation if required so to do; and the Council was requested to avail itself of this provision, and also to reopen negotiations with the existing company for the purchase of its property on equitable terms. At a meeting of the Council on the 7th January, 1887, a resolution approving of the Bill, and appointing a committee to consider the whole question in the interests of the Corporation, was adopted by a large majority. At another meeting, on the 1st March, a report was presented by the committee, stating that the existing company had declined to negotiate for a transfer of their property whilst the Bill for the new project was pending in Parliament. With respect to the Sudbrook springs, the committee had obtained a report from an eminent analyst, who stated that he had never met with a purer water, but that for household purposes it was of an undesirable "hardness." The above estimate as to the supply was deemed correct. The Council, on the motion of Mr. Charles Townsend, adopted the report, and resolved to petition the House of Lords in favour of the Bill promoted by the Consumers' Water Company; an amendment deprecating that step being defeated by 29 votes against 19.

On the invitation of the mayor (Ald. Edwards), a meeting of influential citizens took place in the Guildhall on the 20th December, to consider what steps should be taken to commemorate the approaching jubilee of the reign of Queen Victoria. A proposal for the erection of a statue of Her Majesty had been previously started by the mayor, who subscribed £100; and his suggestion to the meeting that this project should be carried out was generally approved. A proposition had also been made for the founding of a Maternity Hospital, but considerable diversity of opinion was evinced on this subject; and eventually a committee was appointed to consider the whole question. The committee, at a meeting on February 24th, 1887, adopted a resolution recommending that subscriptions should be invited for three purposes: the erection of a statue at a cost not exceeding £2,000, the contribution of not less than £2,000 towards the establishment of an Imperial Institute in London, and the celebration of the jubilee in the city by public rejoicings and entertainments to the poor. These suggestions were unanimously approved at a public meeting held in the following week.

CATHEDRAL AND CIVIC DIGNITARIES. 1801–1887.

BISHOPS.

1797 April, Folliot Herbert Walker Cornwall, translated to Hereford, 1802.
1803 February, Hon. George Pelham, translated to Exeter, 1807.
1807 August, John Luxmore, translated to Hereford, 1808.
1808 September, William Lort Mansel, died June 27, 1820.
1820 July, John Kaye, translated to Lincoln, 1827.
1827 February, Robert Gray, died September 28, 1834.
1834 October, Joseph Allen, translated to Ely, 1836.
1836 October, James Henry Monk, Bishop of Gloucester, died June 6, 1856.
1856 July, Charles Baring, translated to Durham, 1861.
1861 December, William Thomson, translated to York, 1863.
1863 March, Charles John Ellicott.

DEANS.

1800 February, Charles Peter Layard, died April 11, 1803.
1803 May, Bowyer Edward Sparke, appointed Bishop of Chester, 1809.
1810 February, John Parsons, appointed Bishop of Peterborough, 1813.
1814 January, Henry Beeke, died March 9, 1837.
1837 May, Thomas Musgrave, appointed Bishop of Hereford, 1837.
1837 October, John Lamb, died April 19, 1850.
1850 May, Gilbert Elliott.

MAYORS AND SHERIFFS.

The civic year, under the old charters, began and ended on the 29th September. The first election of mayors under the Municipal Reform Act took place in January, 1836, and all since that date on the 9th November.

	Mayors.	Sheriffs.
1800	William Gibbons . . .	Robert Castle, Samuel Birch.
1801	Joseph Edye	Samuel Span, Richard Vaughan, jun.
1802	Robert Castle,* David Evans	John Foy Edgar, Henry Protheroe.
1803	David Evans	Samuel Henderson, jun., John Haythorne.
1804	Edward Protheroe . .	Levi Ames, jun., Philip Protheroe.
1805	Daniel Wait. . . .	William Inman, John Hilhouse Wilcox.
1806	Richard Vaughan, jun. .	Henry Brooke, Edward Brice, jun.
1807	Henry Bright,* Samuel Birch	Sir Henry Protheroe, John Haythorne.
1808	John Haythorne . . .	Benjamin Bickley, Philip George.
1809	John Hilhouse Wilcox . .	Michael Castle, George King.
1810	Philip Protheroe . . .	William Inman, James Fowler.
1811	John Hilhouse Wilcox . .	Edward Brice, Benjamin Bickley.
1812	Michael Castle . . .	George Hilhouse, Abraham Hilhouse.
1813	James Fowler . . .	Benjamin Bickley, Philip George.
1814	William John Struth . .	William Fripp, jun., James George, jun.
1815	Sir William John Struth .	Benjamin Bickley, Philip George.
1816	John Haythorne . . .	Edward Daniel, John Barrow.
1817	John Haythorne . . .	George Hilhouse, Abraham Hilhouse.
1818	Henry Brooke . . .	Thomas Hassell, Nicholas Roch.
1819	William Fripp, jun. . .	James George, jun., John Gardiner.
1820	George Hilhouse . . .	Thomas Hassell, Robert Jenkins.
1821	Abraham Hilhouse . .	Nicholas Roch, Thomas Camplin.
1822	James George . . .	Gabriel Goldney, John Cave.
1823	John Barrow . . .	John Savage, Charles Pinney.
1824	Thomas Hassell . . .	John Gardiner, Charles Ludlow Walker.
1825	John Haythorne . . .	Gabriel Goldney, John Savage.
1826	Thomas Camplin . . .	Thomas Hassell, Daniel Stanton.
1827	Gabriel Goldney . . .	Charles Payne, Henry Wenman Newman.
1828	John Cave	Charles L. Walker, Thomas Hooper Riddle.

* See page 23.

	Mayors.	Sheriffs.
1829	John Savage	Hugh William Danson, John Evans Lunell.
1830	John Savage	George Protheroe, William Claxton.
1831	Charles Pinney . . .	George Bengough, Joseph Lax.
1832	Daniel Stanton . . .	Jas.NorrowayFranklyn,Mich.Hinton Castle.
1833	Charles Ludlow Walker .	James Lean, Peter Maze, jun.
1834	Charles Payne . . .	James N. Franklyn, William Killigrew Wait.

1836	January, William Fripp .	Daniel Cave.
1836	November, James George .	Thomas Kington.
1837	John Kerle Haberfield . .	Thomas Kington Baily.
1838	John Kerle Haberfield . .	Francis Savage.
1839	James Norroway Franklyn .	Richard Vaughan.
1840	Robert Phippen . . .	Hugh Vaughan.
1841	George Woodroffe Franklyn.	Thomas Jones.
1842	James Gibbs. . . .	Jeremiah Hill.
1843	William Lewton Clarke .	Thomas Wadham.
1844	Richard Poole King . .	John Harding.
1845	John Kerle Haberfield . .	Thomas Hill.
1846	William Goldney . . .	Abraham Gray Harford Battersby.
1847	John Decimus Pountney .	Edward Sampson, jun.
1848	John Kerle Haberfield . .	Peter Maze, jun.
1849	John Kerle Haberfield . .	John Jasper Leigh Baily.
1850	John Kerle Haberfield . .	Joseph Walters Daubeny.
1851	William Henry Gore Langton	John Battersby Harford.
1852	Robert Gay Barrow . .	Robert Bright.
1853	John George Shaw . .	Philip John William Miles.
1854	John George Shaw . .	Robert Phippen.
1855	John Vining. . . .	Albany Bourchier Savile.
1856	John Vining. . . .	George Oldham Edwards.
1857	Isaac Allan Cooke . .	J. H. G. Smyth (see p. 355).
1858	James Poole . . .	William Henry Harford.
1859	John Bates	William Montague Baillie.
1860	Odiarne Coates Lane . .	Joshua Saunders.
1861	John Hare	George Rocke Woodward.
1862	Sholto Vere Hare. . .	Charles Daniel Cave.
1863	Thomas Porter Jose . .	William Wright.
1864	William Naish . . .	Henry Cruger William Miles.
1865	Joseph Abraham . . .	Joseph Cooke Hurle.
1866	Elisha Smith Robinson .	William Henry Miles.
1867	Francis Adams . . .	William Gale Coles.
1868	Francis Adams . . .	Robert Phippen (died July, 1869).
1869	William Killigrew Wait .	Thomas Proctor.
1870	Thomas Canning . . .	John Fisher.
1871	William Proctor Baker. .	William Thomas Poole King.
1872	William Hathway . .	Thomas Todd Walton.
1873	Thomas Barnes . . .	Thomas Todd Walton.
1874	Christopher James Thomas .	Charles Hill.
1875	John Averay Jones . .	George Bright.
1876	George William Edwards .	William Smith.
1877	George William Edwards .	William Henry Wills.
1878	George William Edwards .	Charles Bowles Hare.
1879	Henry Taylor . . .	Robert Low Grant Vassall.
1880	Joseph Dodge Weston . .	Francis Frederick Fox.
1881	Joseph Dodge Weston . .	William Edwards George.
1882	Joseph Dodge Weston . .	John Lysaght.
1883	Joseph Dodge Weston . .	Henry Bourchier Osborne Savile.
1884	Charles Wathen . . .	John Harvey.
1885	Charles Wathen . . .	Reginald Wyndham Butterworth.
1886	George William Edwards .	Francis James Fry.

ERRATA.

Page 61, line 4th, for "*basso*" read "*alto*."
,, 109, ,, 17th from bottom, for "Bailey" read "Baily."
,, 223, ,, 5th, add "daily" after "train."
,, 228, ,, 4th from bottom, for "Commissioners" read "Dean and Chapter."
,, 287, ,, 12th, for "Nash" read "Sanders."
,, 288, ,, 17th from bottom, for "Stucky" read "Stuckey."
,, 421, ,, 3rd, for "Broomfield" read "Broomwell."

INDEX.

N N

Lightning Source UK Ltd.
Milton Keynes UK
UKHW03f0127160518
322624UK00005B/134/P